Theoretical Sociology

Theoretical Sociology
Perspectives and Developments

edited by
John C. McKinney and Edward A. Tiryakian
both of Duke University

 APPLETON-CENTURY-CROFTS
EDUCATIONAL DIVISION
New York MEREDITH CORPORATION

Preface

This volume represents the efforts and contributions of many people. The idea for it originated during the period when the senior editor was organizing the program for the San Francisco meetings of the Theoretical Sociology Section of the American Sociological Association. Preliminary and abbreviated versions of several of the chapters included were presented at those meetings on August 28, 1967. Eric Valentine of Appleton-Century-Crofts suggested that the content of that program be used as the base for the development of a comprehensive volume on theoretical sociology. He and Provost R. Taylor Cole of Duke University arranged for and provided funds for a symposium on the topic to be held at Duke University. As a result all the authors—except two, who were in Europe at the time and could not make the additional trip—met at Duke University on January 25–26, 1968. The symposium consisted of a discussion and critique of each of the papers, which had been circulated in advance to the collective authorship. This was followed by an extended period in which the authors revised and completed their chapters. Simultaneously Professor McKinney conducted a graduate seminar at Duke using preliminary drafts of the chapters as substance for the seminar. The following students presented to the authors their critical commentaries, which were of utility in the process of revision: R. Bruce W. Anderson, Monica Boyd, Stephen C. Bunker, Charles W. Camp, and Daniel F. Collins.

Frances C. Thomas organized and managed the symposium at Duke University and supervised the preparation of the manuscript in all phases. Marion Menapace was primarily responsible for the editorial work on the manuscript. Harriet Hodges provided the index for the volume. We are grateful for this invaluable assistance. Finally we are extremely grateful for the continuous interest, involvement, and cooperation of our distinguished array of authors in the entire project.

J. C. McK.

E. A. T.

Contents

Theoretical Sociology

Introduction

Our approach in this volume is toward a pluralism of sociological theory. In view of the fact that sociology is a highly pluralistic enterprise involving a great variety of approaches to the vast complexities of social phenomena it seems inevitable that sociological theory should reflect that pluralism. Different sociological problems call for different perspectives and formulations. We take as a given that all sociologists study the *social system*. In the practical conduct of inquiry, however, they concentrate on particular and limited aspects of the system and upon particular and limited problems with respect to the structure, functions, and processes of a system. As a consequence various *levels* and *sectors* of sociological theory have emerged and have been developed over time. These are not necessarily competitive or incompatible. Indeed, they can be complementary, although frequently they are only implicitly so.

Each contributor to this volume was chosen primarily on the basis of his ability to elucidate and develop a particular theoretical posture. Different levels and styles of theory that are worked with are presented by scholars noted for their contributions to those styles. Each contributor presents something of an appraisal of the capabilities and limitations of a theoretical stance on the contemporary scene. This in effect produces a statement of the general aspects and properties of the theoretical position and a forward look at it from the standpoint of its utility and potential. It is to be noted that several of the chapters emphasize sociological theory *per se,* several strongly emphasize methodological considerations, some focus on particular substantive applications, and some on the linkages to our related social scientific disciplines. In sum these contributions constitute an exposition and evaluation of many of the crucial sectors of contemporary sociological theory.

In the first chapter on "Some Problems of General Theory in Sociology," Talcott Parsons remarks that his primary object is to refine the grounding

1

of the four-function paradigm of adaptation, goal-attainment, integration, and pattern-maintenance. This, of course, is that part of the scheme of general theory in sociology with which he has been working and which has for some years served as perhaps the most central reference point for a wide range of more restricted theoretical enterprises. He attempts to make a more cogent case than in any previous discussion in print that the paradigm is deeply grounded in the intellectual exigencies of the analysis of living systems generally. Parsons expresses the view that this grounding seems to have been strengthened by theoretical developments in biology and general science during roughly the last generation. These developments have clarified the conceptions of the mechanisms of "control" of the processes of living systems in relation to their environments.

Parsons notes that the conceptions of homeostasis and cybernetic control pose problems in understanding the mechanisms of the integration of living systems. He thus believes it is significant that the four-function paradigm proved useful in integrating economic theory with that of the social system, in particular by analyzing money as a mechanism of integration—indeed a cybernetic mechanism at the symbolic cultural level— through ramified systems of market exchange. Even more important, in Parsons' view, has been the possibility thus suggested of using both the four-function analysis of the primary subsystems of societies and the mechanisms involved in their integration as the framework for developing a more sophisticated analysis of the total society as a system, including its integration through the interchange of generalized media of interchange and control among the different subsystems. The first step of generalization beyond the economy to the polity, and the attendant analysis of political power as a generalized symbolic medium, was decisive to Parsons in demonstrating the soundness of this extension.

The four-function paradigm had originally been grounded in the pattern variables. The demonstration that these were in turn grounded at the general action level, and not only at that of the social system, raised again the question of the relations between the social system and that of general action. Parsons has attempted to carry the analysis of this relation further than before by attempting to lay the groundwork for a paradigm of interchange mechanisms at the general action level. The main reference point has been the adaptive sector of the paradigm set forth in "Pattern Variables Revisited." A complete paradigm of interchanges has been worked out, but because of its highly tentative nature, he has presented it in the Appendix to this chapter, rather than in the main text.

Finally, this chapter has attempted to demonstrate the point, so central to its theoretical argument, that sociological theory with its concern for social systems as such needs to be systematically articulated with the general system of action. Parsons has therefore presented a condensed account of two major processes of development in modern societies, both

related to changes in the system of higher education. The first of these concerns the development of the matrices of solidary association in which modern individuals are socialized. The second context is the more familiar one of the development of achievement motivation as this issue was raised by Max Weber in his famous thesis about the implications of the Protestant ethic for occupational behavior. Both of these phenomena come to focus in very salient processes and problems of the social system. Yet, Parsons argues, they are not understandable without careful consideration of both the cultural and the psychological, or personality, components in their genesis. Parsons concludes by expressing the hope that even these sketchy discussions make clear that not only are these general action considerations programmatically essential, but the theoretical scheme involved makes possible going beyond programs to substantive explanations, however incomplete.

In the following chapter on "Toward a Macrosociology," Amitai Etzioni undertakes the development of a theory of "societal guidance." He starts with the premise that an act is in itself neither micro- nor macroscopic; the quality of the act is determined by its consequences. Macroscopic theory deals with the acts that have macroscopic consequences and with the relations of these consequences to each other. Those utilizing macro-theory tend to follow one of two major approaches. The *collectivistic* approach focuses upon ongoing processes and change while the *voluntaristic-cybernatorial* approach is largely concerned with guided processes and change. Etzioni in his analysis is seeking a synthesis of these two major approaches with the intention of providing for a more adequate and balanced theory of societal change. This synthesis balances the non-rational focus of the collectivistic approach, which tends to stress the study of societal ties of sentiments, values, and institutions, with the rationalistic perspective often exhibited by cybernetics. Etzioni devotes considerable attention to the element of "power" which is generally neglected by both approaches.

This societal cybernatorial model exhibits factors of control equivalent to the capacities of other similar systems. The input of knowledge, for example, into a societal unit follows the same basic patterns other inputs do. This is a part of the larger consideration of "information processing." The "overlayer" of the societal control unit is a decision-making élite—the socio-political equivalent of the electronic center. The élites choose between alternative policies, issue signals to the performing units, and respond to feedback information. Cybernatorial factors other than processing of information and decision-making include various attributes of societal goals. All of these are important to the control factor.

Etzioni links these cybernatorial elements to the second general factor involved in control—power. He indicates that societal structures are not

just patterns of interaction of actors, but in addition involve patterns of allocation of societal assets, the possessions of a societal unit. Assets can be used to generate more assets, be consumed or stored, *or* be used to overcome the resistance of other actors, which is what by definition societal power means. Each societal unit has a level of activation which is defined as the ratio of its assets that are available for collective action over its total assets. Each application of power, furthermore, produces some amount of alienation, the degree of alienation depending on the application of power.

The main difference between societal and electronic cybernetics is that in the former it is systematically taken into account that the controlled units have some of the controlling capacities themselves—thus making consensus possible. There is a trade-off curve between control and consensus; that is, for any given level of activation, the more congruence of preferences of the units concerned, the less need for control, and vice versa.

Using control (cybernatorial capacities and power) and consensus formation as two dimensions of a property space, Etzioni constructs a typology of societies. He characterizes them as: *active,* high on both consensus and control; *passive,* low on both consensus and control; *overmanaged,* high on control but low on consensus; and *drifting,* low on control but high on consensus. High control and high consensus, high activation and low alienation, are seen as being mutually reinforcing. Of these four types, the active society has the highest capacity for self-transformation. Etzioni suggests that the conditions under which such a society will be advanced is a major subject of macrosociology.

In Chapter 3, Marion J. Levy, Jr. writes on the topic of "Scientific Analysis Is a Subset of Comparative Analysis." The central argument of the analysis begins with the assumption that sociology *as a science* is the central concern. The major assertions of the argument are that: (1) Sociology aspires to being scientific; (2) Scientific theory consists of interrelated, generalized statements involving relationships among variables; (3) Generalized statements imply comparisons—and require comparison of empirical phenomena for verification—therefore there is no non-comparative sociological theory; (4) What most sociologists do does not involve comparison and therefore is nonscientific. Levy thus delivers a sweeping indictment of the present state and practice of sociology and then proceeds to suggest certain strategies for improving the present state of affairs.

Levy suggests that we must define a unit of central focus and apply *requisite* analysis to it—in effect, apply that special form of analysis which attempts to erect a minimum number of categories in terms of which any two or more instances of the phenomena referred to can be compared.

Such a framework of analysis, with its built-in assumption of stability, underlies any comparison. Levy contends that anyone who argues that we must have a special framework for each case because at some level no two systems are alike, argues against the assumptions basic to any scientific work.

Levy also suggests that we commonly ask help from other disciplines. He cites demography and economics as likely sources of major assistance, primarily because it is held that few things of interest to sociologists are likely to vary randomly with respect to demographic and economic variables.

His third suggestion is that we ought to seek those leads around which there seems to be great closure on extremely general levels. He then proceeds to describe six such leads for comparative investigation with potentially high payoff. They are: (1) The family, for which he lists nine characteristic features which obtain in some form or other in all known societies; (2) Asymmetry of income distribution—which he argues is nearly universal; (3) Bases of role differentiation—especially those of age, sex, and generation—which are present in all societies; (4) Integration to uncertainty (magic, faddism, etc.) and to too much certainty (boredom), which also appear to be very general phenomena; (5) Governmental decentralization or structural form; and (6) The instrumental role of the military. Levy views these as basic societal phenomena. Essentially, his argument is intended to prescribe a point of departure for the development of a parsimonious set of theoretical generalizations having high explanatory power. The task he suggests has two aspects. First, learn how intersocietal variability among them may be accounted for. This presumably moves sociological theory toward greater abstraction, fewer variables, and hence increased parsimony. Second, learn how these relate to inter- and intrasocietal variability with respect to other variables of interest. This would move us in the direction of greater specificity and greater explanatory power over empirical events.

The contribution by Edward Tiryakian, "Structural Sociology," gives major attention to social structures as the foundations of social systems, including large-scale societies. Social structures are not objective entities but rather phenomena of collective consciousness which have intrinsically a normative or moral component of meaning for social actors. Further, they are not static or atemporal but are subject to transformations in the historical process in which all social phenomena are grounded. These considerations lead Tiryakian to stress the interdependence of sociology with psychology and history.

In his conceptualization of the social order, he differentiates between "institutional" and "noninstitutional" phenomena. Every ongoing social system, including every ongoing society, is an actualization of a certain set

of courses of action which becomes endowed with moral legitimacy. Actions performed within this framework continuously validate it. However, this does not exhaust the range of possibilities, since other moral conceptions of social reality may be present *sub rosa*. Institutional phenomena are taken to be those which typify "public" or "institutional" life; they are understood to be aspects of the rationalization of conduct of everyday life. In contrast, noninstitutional phenomena derive from "radically different moral conceptions of social reality," but from a "common sense" point of view they are frequently dismissed as "irrational." Tiryakian suggests that noninstitutional phenomena are presentations of radically different conceptions of reality having a religious inspiration different from that of most members of the ongoing society; they deserve much more sociological attention than previously given as seedbeds of *societal change*. Societal change is understood as a change in the normative/moral structure of society, in contrast to social change which refers to sequential processes within a legitimated, institutionalized structure.

Tiryakian proposes that such a theoretical orientation leads sociology to a collaboration with social anthropology in the study of symbolic categorizations of the world. The cosmological categories such as "left-right," "up-down," to which many contemporary anthropologists, influenced by Durkheim and Mauss, have given attention in the study of non-Western societies may also be relevant to the study of large-scale Western societies. Social movements of a revolutionary nature make use of symbols which manifest their members' perception of reality, and the study and analysis of such symbols is essential for a sociological understanding of societal change.

Finally, the author suggests that sociological predictions concerning large-scale change are possible on a probabilistic basis, derived from a comparative analysis of present structural conditions with past historical settings. We may not be able to specify which particular course of events will emerge from present operative conditions, but we may be able to specify a finite number of such courses on the basis of comparative data. Tiryakian illustrates this in terms of the present American scene.

T. B. Bottomore follows with a chapter on "Sociological Theory and the Study of Social Conflict." He indicates the need for a search for the underlying properties, or structures, which may be common to all forms of conflict. He expresses the view, however, that there is no sociological theory of conflict and that such a theory would require a stance quite different from that of traditional "structural-functionalism." It is termed unfortunate that most of the work done on conflict has been of a descriptive nature. Bottomore then proceeds to indicate some of the insights into conflict which have been developed in the various inquiries.

Attempts have been made to explicate the diverse forms of conflict. One of the most simple distinctions has been that between international and internal conflict. While this distinction is important, Bottomore holds that it is also inadequate on various grounds. It does not, for example, convey the qualitative elements of conflict.

Bottomore suggests that after establishing some typology of conflict we move on to the search for regularities in the emergence, extent, and duration of social conflict. In seeking to investigate these dimensions of conflict we are necessarily faced with the problem of measurement. In many cases, of course, it will be necessary to use a variety of indirect measures, and to employ such imprecise quantitative terms as "more" and "less."

Establishing "causes" of conflict is cited as another major problematic area. Two approaches to this problem have been attempted previously. One of these is to look for the causes of conflict in human nature, and to posit a "fighting instinct." This is exemplified in the work of Simmel, Freud, and Lorenz. The second approach, based on a theory of interests, is essentially in the Marxist tradition. Bottomore describes difficulties with both of these approaches.

It is noted that to study the causes is considerably more difficult than to study the effects of conflict. One of the major effects of social conflict is seen in the context of social change, which needs to be examined much more closely than it has been. Conflict between and within groups may bring about change or create a propensity to change by unsettling established ways of life.

The renewed interest in the study of conflict is attributed primarily to practical concerns, and in particular to the desire to find some means of avoiding, or at least controlling and limiting, war in the nuclear age. This interest has given rise to a whole new field of inquiry, concerned on one side with those conditions and situations which seem likely to result in war, and on the other side with the outcomes or consequences of war. Bottomore calls attention to the use of game theory models as an aid to determining strategy in such studies. He accepts the fact that game theory offers a conceptual framework in which strategic analogues of conflict situations can be clearly formulated, but points out that there are also limitations to the theory of which we must be aware.

The studies of war, at present the most advanced of conflict studies, have begun to amass the kind of historical and statistical knowledge which is essential for any causal analysis. These studies have been instrumental in developing models of conflict situations which, for all their shortcomings, are a powerful aid to investigation. Bottomore contends that we shall have to pay increasing attention to conflicts if we are to explain events and provide the means by which men can make reasonable choices between alternative courses of social action.

In Chapter 6, Wilbert E. Moore develops an analysis under the rubric of "Toward a System of Sequences." As Moore notes, the fact that social events occur sequentially is not a new observation, but it makes possible here the exposition of an exploratory approach to social change. Change may be either unplanned or deliberate. The former is attributable to intrinsic sources of change—the view of society as a tension-management system. The latter has become a major part of contemporary collective activity—this is the case of modernization. In the study of this phenomenon, concern with political activity is necessary. Moore notes, however, that contemporary social theorists are characterized by a distinctly apolitical attitude. This is attributed, at least in part, to an incapacity to view a social system as a deliberate set of decisional processes. In Moore's view this is a serious theoretical error.

Moore contends that the most important source of social change in the modern world is in the planned decision-making of national states and decentralized units. The conceptual posture which prevails, and which Moore labels as the "comparative statics analysis of the social concomitants and consequences of attempts to modernize" is not cognizant of sequence. What is essential in the understanding of modernization, in Moore's view, is to set forth the necessary institutional antecedents of modernization (preconditions), specify those social and institutional changes inevitably associated with modernization, and then draw out secondary and tertiary consequences of the process. This requires, among other things, that "industrialization" not be taken as a static state.

If the study of the process of modernization of newly developing countries is to proceed beyond the commonplace comparative statics model, two major developments will be necessary. First, the process will have to be viewed in terms of a rather elaborate social change matrix, and second, a substantial input of quantities and trends needs to be produced and analyzed. Moore makes the point that both theory and methodology have been sadly atemporal, and feels that attention to the temporal order of structural changes is both minimal and long overdue. In brief, we must learn to think sequentially.

Sequential analysis is by no means totally missing from contemporary sociology, but it is sparse. Sociologists have typically been so immunized against the essential facts of man as an animal that the most elementary life-cycle (sequential) phenomena have received only cursory treatment. Moore points out, however, that "systems analysis," as an approach to problems, involves systemic interdependence, frequently seen as a chain including loops and feedbacks. It is held that systems analysis can be genuinely sequential in its approach. Within this model, Moore attempts to develop some testable subsets of theoretical sequences that might prove to be additive as additional information inputs can be obtained. Moore suggests that the practice of sequential analysis has implications for many

of the grave social problems we currently face. He illustrates with the case of the urban Negro revolution. The suggestion is that if attention had been paid decades ago to the signs clearly before us, action could have been taken which would have altered the sequence of events leading to such a revolt. Recognition of this does not lead us backwards to prime causes and the reversal of history, but it does, according to Moore, indicate the need for thinking sequentially in relation to a set of currently unstable conditions.

Robert A. Nisbet follows with a chapter on "Developmentalism: A Critical Analysis." This essay treats developmentalism as one of the master principles of the organization of Western thought and as a major position in the intellectual history of sociology. In addition to the intellectual look backward into the sociological tradition, the essay focuses on the developmentalist dimensions of contemporary theoretical treatments of social change. While admitting that nineteenth-century developmentalism is passé and that it is not adequate to tasks posed by contemporary sociology, Nisbet maintains that in its primary dimensions developmentalism has been absorbed into modern structural-functionalism. Indeed, it is the developmental features that in large part give structural-functionalism its capacity to deal with problems of social change. Nisbet shows that the salient points of developmentalism as a perspective lie in its emphasis on change as a process inherent to a structure, as originating from forces contained within the structure. He delineates six elements of developmentalism as a perspective that are relevant to current approaches to change: immanence, continuity, uniformitarianism, differentiation, time, and comparison.

Immanence is described as a quality of emergence from forces that lie within the structure of a system. This element led Marx to refer to laws of change ". . . working with iron necessity toward inevitable results." Nisbet refers to immanence as constituting one of the major problems or dilemmas of developmentalism as a perspective. He poses the dilemma in the questions: ". . . are major changes the product of smaller internal changes—with the micro-variations within the system becoming in time the macro-changes within the system?" or "Are the larger changes the product of external changes or conditions?" These questions are as relevant today as they have ever been.

Continuity is expressed in the Leibnizian principle "nothing happens all at once." Continuity, as a concept, may refer simply to persistence in time or space. But here it is used in the more classificatory sense, namely, as the notion of the "chain of being" in Western thought. Most properly developmental continuity is viewed as the conversion of the infinite gradations of the classificatory series into a time-series.

Uniformitarianism refers not to the notion of uniformity of stages of

development but to the idea of uniform causes or mechanisms of change within similar systems. "Like effects are produced by like causes" is the simplest way of stating the proposition; but it also implies that the causes to be seen operating today in the study of nature and society are the same as those which operated in the distant past.

Differentiation, like the other aspects of developmentalism, has its prototype in the mode of differentiation that is most evident in organic growth. What lies latent becomes progressively more complex and differentiated. This element, freed of some of its metaqualities, has of course become one of the cornerstones of contemporary sociological theory.

Time is another essential element of developmentalism. The developmentalist, abstracting from time, could put societies and cultures in a vast classificatory system in which varying stages of development could be seen, compared, and contrasted without respect to time. So while time is vital to change, the developmentalist can abstract beyond it.

The methodology of the developmentalist is essentially *comparative.* There are two aspects to this comparative method: (1) a comparison of different coexisting states and (2) a comparison of consecutive states.

Although Nisbet indicates the obsolescence of developmentalism as a historical phenomenon, he suggests that these major elements of its view still constitute a valuable perspective, particularly as they are incorporated in our contemporary view of the structure, function, and processes of social systems.

In their chapter, "Images of the Future: Theory and Research Strategies," Wendell Bell and James Mau investigate two distantly related areas: first, they discuss the concept of "images of the future" and propose a theory of social change incorporating this concept; secondly, they suggest a series of directives for research strategy and for the role of the social scientist.

Bell and Mau begin their paper with a brief discussion of two assumptions which underlie their theory. First they state that the past and future should not be viewed as separate entities, but as part of the present. This assumption is related to their theory of social change, in that images of the future exist in the present and are important factors in orienting individual and collective behavior. One of the basic hypotheses is that expectations about the future, whether short- or long-range, may enter into human behavior as a determining factor.

The second assumption on which their theory of social change is based is that a major trend of history has been an objective increase in the mastery of man over his natural and social environment, as well as a shift in his belief that this situation now exists. An implication of this assumption is that explanations of social change are only relevant to the events of the day

insofar as they accurately explain the amount of influence man himself may have in directing social change.

Bell and Mau state that new social theories and empirical inquiries are needed to take into account the fact that man is increasingly able to transcend the limitation of the present. The explanatory concept which they propose as a key variable in their modern theory of social change in that of "image of the future." In defining this concept, they draw an interesting analogy relating micro- and macro-theory:

Just as an individual's future is to some extent governed by his self-image of the kind of person *he has been, is, and hopes to be,* so also a nation's future course of development is, to some extent, controlled by the doctrines and dogmas of particular versions of the social and cultural history of that nation.

The future rests importantly on the nature of the images of future in the present, and the authors cite the work of Polak and Lasswell in support of their views.

Bell and Mau state that Polak's distinctive contribution perhaps is his effort to depict the social scientist *qua* scientist not only as an objective investigator, but also as a creator and disseminator of images of the future. In Polak's words, "The social scientist (and this is part of his specific responsibility both towards social sciences and society) may discover ways to rewrite the history of the future."

The authors then proceed to discuss their theory of social change and study of the future. Social change is explained within a cybernetic-decisional model, a feedback cycle, resulting in a progressive interaction between action and information, values, beliefs, and images of the future. Although the authors suggest that their model can be used on any size unit of analysis, from the individual to the supranational group, their primary intent in using the model is to analyze large-scale membership units. A number of hypotheses are enumerated by the authors in conjunction with their model. First, long-range images of the future will have possible sustained importance in directing behavior in contrast to the more limited effect of short-range images. Secondly, critical differences in human behavior are hypothesized to result from images that are basically pessimistic compared to those which are optimistic and from images that present man as a causal factor compared to those that do not. Thirdly, as part of the trend toward human mastery, Bell and Mau hypothesize that the long-term trends characteristic of modernization result in increases of rationality and consciousness, and therefore in deliberate planning of political, economic, social, and cultural change. To the extent to which such planning orientations become widespread—which they tend to do among people in modernized societies—they lead to the adoption of similar procedures at the microscopic level among ordinary individuals.

Bell and Mau assert that their model is an alternative to the structural-functional model, in that the study of society's structuration, destructuration, and restructuration, the role of man in these processes, and actions implementing planned change are included in their model. Finally, the authors suggest a set of directives which, if followed in the conduct of inquiry, would in their view increase the social relevance of social science. In aggregate the directives emphasize the constructive role of the sociologist in the shaping of the future.

The next chapter, written by John C. McKinney, is on "Sociological Theory and the Process of Typification." Typification, perceiving the world and structuring it by means of categorical types, is depicted as an essential and intrinsic aspect of the basic orientation of actors to their situation. It is important for structuring the "self," conceptualizing "roles," and as a necessary feature of institutionalization and the development of social structure. Two basic orders of types are distinguished: the *existential* type, "first order constructs" developed by participants in social systems, and the *constructed* type, "second order constructs" formulated by the social scientist for purposes of explicating those social systems. All typification is viewed as consisting in the pragmatic reduction and equalization of attributes relevant to the particular purpose at hand for which the type has been formed, and involves disregarding those individual differences of the typified objects that are not relevant to such a purpose.

It is asserted that types and typologies are ubiquitous, both in everyday social life and in the language of the social sciences. Everybody uses them, but almost no one pays any attention to the nature of their construction. McKinney holds that despite the omnipresence of typologizing in social inquiry it remains a relatively "underdeveloped" aspect of methodology generally. Historically typologies have served us well as we have expanded the range and depth of knowledge with respect to social phenomena. As we envisage the future, however, and contemplate the scope and magnitude of sociological problems yet to be explored, it would seem to be extremely unwise not to develop a vastly increased self-consciousness, as an aspect of both the common methodology and the common theoretical orientation, with respect to the construction and utilization of typologies. McKinney suggests that since typologies are used with great frequency in social inquiry, it would appear to be methodologically imperative that we develop and proliferate a greater understanding of their multiple roles in that inquiry.

McKinney delineates six major dimensions around which types are constructed. These are seen as a series of continua serving to delineate the structure of types. From these axes or dimensions six pairs of polar variables of type construction are derived thus presenting a "typology of types."

These are expressed as the contrasts between ideal–extracted, general–specific, scientific–historical, timeless–timebound, universal–local, and generalizing–individualizing. It is noted that a primary function of types and typologies is to identify, simplify, and order data so that they may be described in terms which make them comparable. Typification is viewed in the context of a pragmatic research methodology.

McKinney then proceeds with an exploration of selected theoretical and methodological issues with respect to the construction and utilization of typologies emphasizing problems of nominalism versus realism, ethnomethodology, social morphology, specification of the operations performed in the construction of types, and the relationship to general sociological theory, with particular reference to the social system as a construct. In the final section a description of selected substantive problems which are of crucial theoretical importance at this time, and for which typologies would be intellectually useful, is offered.

The next chapter, by Hubert M. Blalock, Jr., on "The Formalization of Sociological Theory" is also in the methodological-theoretical vein. Blalock discusses the advantages and the problems of formalization of sociological theory. Although advocating formalization and stressing the need to accelerate its practice, he emphasizes the fact that it leads to a simplification of theory and makes it less "realistic." Because it increases the specificity of theory, however, formalization is viewed as playing a crucial role in the verification of theory. The process of formalizing a theory is seen in terms of a series of decisions that one must make in order to specify the variables to be considered, to clarify how they are interrelated, to restrict the range of applicability of the theory, and to add sufficient auxiliary assumptions about measurement errors and disturbance terms to make the theory testable in a given research context.

Blalock indicates that one step in the process is to diagram a theory blocking off each major kind of variable from the others so that interrelations can be more easily examined. Each block will contain a number of particular variables, which must be explicitly identified and interrelated. Furthermore, the linkages between blocks must be specified more exactly. One way to begin the elaboration procedure is to attempt to specify the most important variable appearing in each of the separate blocks, and to indicate how they are expected to be interrelated. Once the interrelationship among variables within each block has been specified as well as possible, attention can be focused on a reexamination of the relationship between blocks.

Blalock suggests that if the theory is exceedingly complex and contains too many unknowns it may be inherently untestable, and that this is typically the case with most of our "verbal" theories. He also points out

the significance of the "identification problem." This term refers to the situation where it is impossible to assess the effects of any one variable on each of the others. Sociologists have often been accustomed to bypassing the identification problem by assuming that they can study a series of dependent variables one at a time, without worrying about why the various independent variables are intercorrelated, or about possible feedback effects from the "dependent" variable to the so-called "independent" variable.

It will be necessary, Blalock points out, to use at least some exogenous variables, to which there is no feedback, whenever there is reciprocal causation within or between theoretical blocks of variables. One possible resolution to the identification problem is to treat lagged values of some of the endogenous variables as though they were exogenous.

According to Blalock, if a theorist is actually interested in formulating a rejectable theory, he must pay careful attention to a set of auxiliary assumptions that will need to be combined with the original theory. He must first decide which variables can safely be ignored in his empirical research. Here it is essential to have an explicit theory that involves many more variables than will ultimately be selected. Another kind of assumption deals with the degree to which observations or replications are really independent statistically. Finally, the social scientist must be aware of the need to improve measurement procedures. Blalock expresses the view that measurement errors may be the most crucial single obstacle inhibiting the advance of sociology as a discipline. In sum, Blalock develops the thesis that there is much to be gained from the formalization of sociological theory—but at a cost. Specification of costs is in itself one of the major advantages of formalization.

In the next chapter, Paul F. Lazarsfeld writes on "The Place of Empirical Social Research in the Map of Contemporary Sociology." His main thesis is that methodological paradigms abstracted from empirical social research provide the basic bricks from which the home of general sociology can be built—not from their content but from their forms. Thus he maintains that the procedures, strategy, and logic—in short, the methodology of empirical social research—can be productively applied throughout the field of sociology, with theoretical consequences. He suggests the need for the whole gamut of sociological work, from purely "speculative" conceptualizations to "mere" careful fact-finding. He asserts, however, that the links between the different points in the spectrum are not very well known. This chapter, then, deals primarily with one of these points: the contributions of empirical social research to the clarification of basic intellectual procedures, which reoccur in every phase of sociological thinking. Lazarsfeld attempts no formal definition of "empirical social research" but does

equate it to "sociography" in the threefold classification of sociological work offered by Tönnies many years ago.

Lazarsfeld then proceeds with a discussion and a set of examples to delineate the basic components of empirical social research-variates and propositions. In a sense, variates are the individual "words" and propositions the "sentences" out of which empirical social research is constructed. Continuing with this analogy, the methodology of empirical social research, a methodology which Lazarsfeld feels is relevant to a broader range of sociological inquiry, may be seen as equivalent to the grammar of sentence construction. He indicates that the flow from concepts to variates generally proceeds in four steps. First, the sociologist has a vague image or construct. Second, the image is divided into components. Third, each component is linked to an empirical indicator. Fourth, these indicators are combined again—perhaps in an index—to form the variate, a more precise and usable version representing the original image or construct. This translation process implies theoretical antecedents for good empirical inquiry.

Lazarsfeld then expresses the view that the basic strategy of empirical social research methodology is the use of multivariate contingent cross-tabulations. He utilizes four extended examples to elaborate this fundamental proposition. First, he notes that the problem of positivism versus idealism is irrelevant to empirical social research because tentative expressions of *intentionality* (such as attitudes) can be converted into variates as easily as can any other type of data. Second, he shows how multivariate analysis can simulate *process* by introducing time as one of the variates under consideration. Third, he demonstrates that multivariate analysis can deal with *changes* in the behavior of social groups (for example, in the changing structure of the groups) in much the same way as it deals with simple process. Fourth, he shows that by taking as a variate the *context* (such as group, community, system) in which the individual finds himself, he can account for differences between the behavior of individual variates (or of one variate over time) when in different (or changing) contexts. Lazarsfeld does not imply that these examples represent all of the principles and strategies which guide empirical social research; he simply presents them as some of the many approaches to multivariate sociological reality.

Lazarsfeld concludes with brief treatments of the relation of empirical social research to qualitative analysis and to deviant case analysis. The meaning and scope of empirical research has been persistently alluded to throughout the chapter in terms of the methodology of theory construction.

In the chapter on "The Corpus of Knowledge as a Normative Order," Alan F. Blum describes various intellectual critiques of the social organi-

zation of knowledge and of the commonsense features of bodies of knowledge. Blum examines several variants of one method which has been used historically to characterize, criticize, and revise the authoritative bodies of knowledge of their disciplines. He points out that while bodies of knowledge have been found deficient on various grounds, the one method of criticizing knowledge which has been used persistently by a number of thinkers is that of depicting the producers of bodies of knowledge as commonsense actors. Blum selects Descartes, Hobbes, and Marx as practitioners of this method, and examines some of the implications of conceiving of producers of knowledge as commonsense actors.

Descartes, Hobbes, and Marx each came to the realization that existing bodies of knowledge are problematic. Descartes observed that the presence of varied and differing opinions as to the nature of things reflects a lack of certain knowledge. In Hobbes a somewhat different confrontation with the normative order of knowledge is noted. His observation, however, was the same. He depicted the traditional corpus of knowledge reflected in classical political thought as unrealistic, inapplicable, and conjectural. One of Marx's most important contributions was his argument that the construction of the corpus of knowledge is inextricably linked to the interests of those who produce it. All three saw the existing corpus of knowledge as being, in certain respects, deficient.

Since one of Hobbes's main concerns was the inapplicability of bodies of knowledge, he urged that the corpus be redefined in terms of examples rather than of general precepts. His proposal amounted to the assertion that a corpus of knowledge cannot be defined and warranted unless the objects of knowledge, societal members, are able to use such knowledge as a normative order in formulating routine courses of action.

Descartes' strategy for revision was his program of methodological doubt. Essentially this program was organized around the thinker's systematic and self-conscious distrust of commonsense knowledge. It specified the in-principle suspension of such knowledge for the purpose of "cleansing one's mind" in order to arrive at certainty. He proposed that the state of the world as it appeared to the thinker's senses be rendered as problematic, and offered instead a program based upon the discovery of simple, immediate, and certain truth.

Marx found both the historical corpus of knowledge and the body of philosophic knowledge deficient on two essential grounds: they are abstract and disconnected from empirical description, and they accept commonsense conceptions of events as "given" without treating them as problematic.

Descartes, Hobbes, and Marx could each argue that behind every corpus' conception of a factual, stable, real world there lies an unanalyzed, socially organized set of methods for producing such conceptions. Knowledge, they note, is organized and assembled methodologically by actors

acting under the auspices of some conception of an adequate corpus of knowledge as a maxim of conduct. Each of them seized upon some feature of knowledge which reflected the lack of "pure" objectivity, and used such a deficiency as grounds for their respective critiques.

Sociology can be seen in the same light—therefore we know that it is not an objectively discernible, purely existing external world which ac= counts for sociology. This means that sociologists must come to grips with the issue of the interaction between their investigative procedures and their "findings." Blum suggests that sociologists must begin to treat as problematic the unanalyzed features of their methods and procedures which become constitutive properties of the events-in-the-world as in themselves describable events-in-the-world. In this sense, Blum notes, sociological investigation is essentially a topic of sociological inquiry, or as he puts it, ". . . the methods and procedures of sociology are applicable to the empirical practices of sociology as an event-in-the-world."

The contribution of Harold Garfinkel and Harvey Sacks, "On Formal Structures of Practical Actions," has an affinity both with the preceding and with the following chapter. It is essentially an explication of ethnomethodology as conjointly analysis and theory, which the authors view as a major alternative to "constructive analysis" of professional sociologists (including the majority of the contributors of this volume). Since it is likely that most readers may find the frame of reference of this chapter quite different from their usual readings in sociology, we will make a few remarks relating this paper to its intellectual antecedents, rather than concentrating upon outlining its content.

Ethnomethodology considers as problematic what it regards that other sociological orientations take as given, namely, the practices of everyday life by means of which actors structure and construct their world and its reality. It was Alfred Schutz, influenced by Max Weber, who pointed out the significance of the phenomena of everyday life, including commonsense knowledge, as a vast accomplishment which we take for granted rather than question. In a sense, Garfinkel and Sacks take a *radical* approach to the fundamental problem of social order by investigating rigorously the structure of social action, which is disclosed in natural language. We can say that their chapter points to a sociological theory of language as social interaction. It relates and investigates the complex relationships between thinking and doing in conversing with others—what are the structures by means of which we express our feelings and by means of which we convey what we mean to others, given that we cannot directly express our subjective meanings? A person's fundamental endeavor is to converse with others and to *formulate* his conversations. The fact that this is achieved in an orderly manner yields observable and reportable phenomena, but laymen and sociologists alike do not put into question that such phe-

nomena are practical accomplishments nor do they place in brackets the structures of such accomplishments. Ethnomethodology, on the other hand, gives primary attention to analyzing how actors, unwittingly but nevertheless practically, achieve this formulation.

To be sure, the study of speech or conversing as social action is not new to social science. Much of Pareto's sociology uses as data speech reactions from which he sought to derive the variables and constants of social action (derivatives and residues). In a parallel fashion, Freud looked at the pathology of everyday life in terms of verbal slips of the tongue made in conversations, and Marxist analysis also takes into account how verbal statements (ideologies) are rationalizations of the class position of the speaker. But it may be said, in the terms of Garfinkel and Sacks, that all these approaches try to substitute objective for indexical expressions of natural language; that is, in a sense, they seek to remedy rather than to comprehend the practical activities of everyday life as the basic social reality. The authors find this tendency prevalent among contemporary social scientists, whose conceptualizations, formulas, models, or definitions, are also remedies for the nuisances of indexical expressions. Rather than remain at this second-order level of abstraction, Garfinkel goes back to the fundamentals. This methodological orientation derives from the founder of modern phenomenology, Edmund Husserl, who wished to redirect philosophical inquiry to "the things themselves," to the phenomena of consciousness. Ethnomethodology, then, is a re-direction to the fundamental structures of social action as disclosed in natural language. Garfinkel and Sacks argue that the formal structures of natural language practices are available to ethnomethodology but not to "constructive analysis," no matter which variety of the latter is considered (statistical analysis, structural-functional analysis, and so forth).

It might be suggested, though the authors do not discuss the question, that there is in their own orientation a methodological extension of Weber's *verstehende Soziologie,* which has a direct affinity with phenomenology. Weber himself did not offer a rigorous explication of the methodology of "comprehension," of how to go about *understanding* the subjective meaning of action. The focus of ethnomethodology on comprehending the "glossing practices" of speakers "whereby speakers in the situated particulars of speech mean differently than they can say in just so many words" —that is, the intricate and complex work each conversationalist does in conveying his meaning of action to others—would seem to us to be an important updating of Weber's methodology. And if we go along with the premise that the fundamental task of sociological theory is the rigorous description of social action, taking the notion of social action in the sense that Weber gave it, then it is plausible to argue that ethnomethodology sees itself for the first time explicitly "doing" sociology.

In the next chapter on "Deviance and Order in a Pluralistic Society" by Jack D. Douglas, we have an assessment of the relation of sociological theory to a specific substantive area. Douglas attempts to delineate a new and emerging perspective in the study of social deviance. He states that this developing perspective is an alternative to the dominant structural-functional viewpoint, as well as to that of the traditional conflict theorists Douglas views both of the latter positions as extremes; the one assumes that morals are the basic causes of patterned social actions, the other posits normative or moral behavior as "rhetorical" and as rationalizations of actions rather than causes.

Douglas considers the conflict theory of deviance to be a theory of minor importance and devotes the major effort in his chapter to describing and criticizing the posture of the structural-functionalists with respect to the study of social deviance. Twelve elements, or value-assumptions, are presented as the major dispositions of the structural-functionalist view of deviant behavior. Douglas discusses these orientations from the point of view of his alternative theory.

The theory advocated by Douglas takes the meaning of any action as basically problematic and proceeds to construct determinate situational meanings from the particular nature of the action. It conflicts sharply, Douglas says, with the structural-functional perspective. He attempts to specify how his theoretical perspective on social deviance conflicts with that of the structural-functionalists, and to show how his theory has greater adequacy as a perspective on social deviance.

Douglas states that "the traditional sociological perspective on deviance has assumed that deviance takes place in a social world that is unproblematically meaningful, based on moral consensus, homogeneous, stable, closed, and deterministic." Douglas challenges this perspective, and instead presents a view of the world as being pluralistic, ambiguous, conflictful, heterogeneous, and rife with problematic situations. In this world, abstract, homogeneous, and shared values do not determine the structure or patterns of social action. It is the very idea of value and the meaning such a value might have in defining a situation and in motivating or constraining an actor which is problematic.

Douglas does not deny that stability or order exists, or that there are generally shared moral meanings, but he does not feel that one can adequately explain deviant behavior in terms of majority values or social order. He develops three general areas in which structural-functionalists, proceeding from the belief in shared values, have misinterpreted the significance of these values.

Secondarily, Douglas takes issue with the validity of official statistics as indicators of social consensus. The interrelation and interdependence of official agencies means that "crime" or "deviance" rates must maintain a

certain stability so as not to disrupt the balance of the official system. The theorizing, hypothesizing, sampling, and testing techniques using official data more often than not reflect the systematic biases of official agencies rather than the action rates of deviance in a society. Douglas strongly favors the participant observation approach.

To view deviance in the hypothetical-statistical manner, Douglas states, is to view action from the bias of *a priori* categories of deviance. Such a perspective does not get at the crucial element in understanding the actions of men; that is, it does not get at the meaning of an action to the actor. On the basis of his arguments that society be viewed as pluralistic and at least privately undetermined by abstract shared values, Douglas views "deviance" as a ubiquitous phenomenon of actors in search of meaning for action. Such a perspective must alter radically any notion of social deviance. Douglas states that

One of the most apparent effects of the emerging perspective on deviance is to break down the conventional distinctions between deviant action and normal action. This primarily has the effect of redefining the field of deviance in terms of substantive problems rather than in terms of a conventional corpus of subject matter.

Alex Inkeles begins his chapter, "Sociological Theory in Relation to Social Psychological Variables," with a discussion of the analogues and differences in the study of personality and society. He presents the view that psychology is the study of the individual as a personality system, and sociology is the study of aggregates of people, large or small, constituting a social system. Inkeles asserts that the articulation of psychology and sociology comes largely through the study of personality, both the general theory of personality structure and functioning, and the assessment or measurement of discrete personality traits and syndromes.

Inkeles then proceeds to argue that sociological research has suffered from the failure to use psychological theory and established knowledge about personality as an element in sociological analysis. He holds that this is true in at least three major respects. First, an adequate general theory of the personality as a system is an important and at times crucial element in any analysis of a social system. Second, detailed knowledge about the distribution of particular qualities in the population is necessary to an understanding of the social system's functioning. He makes reference here to the degree and quality of the fit between the modal personality patterns prevalent in the population and the role demands characteristic of the social system. Third, some of the more specialized psychological fields, such as the study of learning, cognition, and perception, have great potential relevance for our understanding of major social processes. Inkeles concentrates on these three areas throughout the paper, concerning himself

exclusively with the ways in which psychology can be used as an aid in the solution of problems which are sociological in nature.

In his discussion of the role of general personality theory Inkeles admits that for large segments of standard sociology such a theory is probably not of crucial importance. He does, however, suggest the utility of explicit and adequate personality theory in several problem areas. He recommends, for instance, that such theory be incorporated into studies of rates (such as of suicide, homicide, fertility) which are the end products of uncoordinated individual decisions or actions producing relatively distinct stable rates. He contends that the use of general theory of personality should be utilized to deal with the individual who intervenes between the social condition and the resultant rate.

Inkeles states that the second major point of articulation between sociology and psychology lies in the effects on any social system which follow from the distinctive or modal personality characteristics of the system's population as status incumbents. He suggests that we consider the degree and kind of congruence between the role requirements typical of a given institution or social system and the personality patterns characteristic of those playing the roles which the system provides. The articulation of the individual's personality with the role demands of the social statuses he fills is relevant for an understanding of three central problems of sociological analysis: the adequacy of role performance, the integration of the diverse institutions which make up a society, and the problem of change in social systems.

Inkeles then comments on special psychological theories and their relevance to sociological theory and research. In contrast to the general theories of personality and to the approaches for assessing personality modes, the special theories and findings of psychology (such as those dealing with learning, cognition, or perception) cannot at this time be easily integrated with sociological theory and research. He suggests that students of learning should study the early learning of the child in the socialization process; that learning theory should deal more systematically with the principles which account for adult learning and for the failure of individuals and cultures to learn new ways; finally, that psychologists should also systematically relate variations in perceptual and cognitive patterns to factors in the individual's or group's sociocultural background.

In the final section of the chapter, Inkeles discusses the articulation of sociology and psychology, tensions between the two disciplines, methodological similarities and differences, and areas for further research.

Charles Tilly's contribution, "Clio and Minerva," examines various aspects of the relationship of sociology to history, including the fruitfulness and the limitations of historical materials for sociological analysis.

Tilly begins by noting a renewed sociological orientation towards his-

torical materials in North America, with a particular impetus being the testing of models of social change. At the same time, many contemporary historians have been drawing on the social sciences, including sociology and demography, for conceptual and methodological inspiration. This two-way interchange leads Tilly to raise as basic questions not only how historical research is affected by social science imports but also what changes will result in the practice of social science by the utilization of historical materials.

In his discussion of the utilization of historical materials, Tilly presents arguments in their favor. Some historical data, such as the American census materials of 1870 and 1880, contain more information than their contemporary counterparts, and some social processes (like occupational and residential mobility) may be studied better through such earlier materials. Second, Tilly points out that sociologists can often test a particular theory or hypothesis by turning to historical materials, since the latter extend the range of observations and variations of a phenomenon. This holds not only for relatively rare occurrences such as revolutions but also for phenomena of large-scale structures, formal organizations, urban spatial arrangements, and the like. Tilly states that the latter are difficult to obtain in conventional uses of survey research used by many sociologists in macrosocial phenomena, but that historical records are heavily weighted in favor of these very materials because "complex, formal organizations have continued to be the main producers of written records." Indeed, there is a bias in historical records in favor of large-scale institutionalized social relationships, but their relative abundance in the form of written documents should be cheerful news to sociologists.

Tilly notes that historical materials have been increasingly used by non-historians other than sociologists. On the other hand, historians have taken up with demography and social stratification more than with other fields in sociology, though stylistically they are most alien to the traditional work of historians. Tilly is of the opinion that historical materials will increasingly become the province of nonhistorians. One factor behind this development is the formulation of theories dealing with long-run processes like modernization and economic development; validating such theories requires going to historical materials since the present is too short.

This leads Tilly to discuss the confrontation between history and sociology in theories of social change, and particularly neo-evolutionary ones, many of which have been derived from or stimulated by recent writings of Talcott Parsons. A useful corrective which historical materials introduce in such theories of social change is to make sociologists aware of the complementary process of *devolution,* which involves as subtypes *dedifferentiation, disintegration,* and *particularization.* Devolution, which can be applied either to a whole society's development or to that of some of its elements, may occur when other elements of that society are en-

hancing its adaptative capacity (one form of evolution) or as a resultant of that change. In any case, Tilly suggests that any general theory of social change is incomplete if it overlooks how replete history is with devolutionary instances (such as agricultural involution or pastoralization) and countercurrents to evolutionary transformations.

As a final note, Tilly suggests that historians have been as neglectful of devolutionary processes as sociologists have, since they are the recipients of written records of large-scale organizations and bureaucracies. This introduces a note of caution to the uncritical use by sociologists of second-hand historical sources; Tilly advises that in analyzing large-scale processes of change, the sociologist tuned in on history keep in focus the development of small units, which may initially be autonomous, rather than begin with larger ones, since the latter will leave more tracks anyhow. In any case, working in the open fields of history rather than the cramped corral of the present, sociologists will strengthen comparative analysis and find useful correctives to their conceptions and assumptions of social change.

In his chapter "Complementary Approaches to Societal Analysis: The Economic Versus the Sociological," Joseph J. Spengler discusses general contrasts between the two disciplines of economics and sociology, the comparability of the units of analysis in the two disciplines, macro- and microanalysis in both economics and sociology, the economic and sociological universes, conceptions of static and dynamic states and concepts of causation in the two disciplines, and methodological and substantive similarities between economics and sociology.

Spengler introduces his chapter with a general discussion of contrasts between sociology and economics. He starts with the premise that economics approximates an explanatory science more closely than does sociology. He then comments on the assets of economics: economists have begun to study and apply the full methodology of the scientific enterprise; they have seen the need for careful, unambiguous, and reproducible rules of correspondence to effect the transition between reality and rational constructs or concepts; they have come to recognize exact mathematical theories and their confirmation; and they have translated crude facts into objective constructs by very specific operational definitions which make these facts objective, meaningful, quantifiable, and subject to logic and mathematics. He says that, as a consequence, "the theories which are blossoming forth take on increasing refinement and predictive power." Spengler also remarks that economics probably enjoys some advantage over sociology, inasmuch as its ideas are less likely to run counter to popular feelings and more likely to be considered applicable. Moreover, he feels that each is at a disadvantage compared with many natural sciences and hence less likely to progress rapidly.

Spengler then proceeds with a discussion of the comparability of the

units of analysis in the two disciplines. He states that microeconomics deals with one form of human behavior: the behavior of individuals acting as individuals or as members of small systems (households, firms, organizations, agencies of the state), who in effect are engaged in choosing among available alternatives. The units in both disciplines are always systems, and the economic theory of choice is considered applicable to noneconomic variables. Spengler asserts that often the group or system studied by the sociologist is engaged in choosing behavior also, and he believes that the sociologist tends to benefit from the incorporation of a choosing dimension into his analytical models.

In the next section of his chapter, Spengler discusses the sociological distinctions parallel to the distinction made in ecomonics between micro- and macroanalysis. Spengler begins by summarizing the past development of micro- and macroanalysis in the two disciplines. He asserts that in the early history of economics and sociology both, proto-macro-approaches were dominant, mainly because methods of analysis suited to lesser systems were slower to develop. According to Spengler, the macro-approach virtually enjoys parity with the micro-approach in economics today. In contrast, the macro-approach has continued ascendant in sociology both because useful small system models comparable to economic models of firms and industries have not flourished, and because functionalism has tended to assume a macro-form. Consequently, sociology has tended to stress the self-maintenance of large societal systems and to move from an understanding of the whole to an understanding of the parts. Spengler then develops a typification of macroanalytical approaches in economics and sociology. He notes that both focus excessively upon system-maintaining behavior and its significance for the behavior of subsystems; both exaggerate the role of structure and macrosystem; both neglect or underestimate the role and variability of behavior at subsystem and small-system levels, due to a lack of a solid psychological basis. He also suggests that sociological theory lacks an effective bridge between its macro- and micro-approaches.

Spengler then elaborates on the subject of the economic and sociological universes. In his words, ". . . the economist is dealing with an all-encompassing system consisting of many interacting lesser systems, whereas the sociologist is dealing with a discontinuous, Balkanized world smelling here and there of a clinic." The universe of the economist is comprised of units bound together by the price system or the market. Spengler finds, however, that the sociologist faces no such system. He goes on to state that economic theory is based on mechanistic theory, and notes that stable equilibrium is a special case of equilibrium in economics, that unstable and dynamic systems are also explored, unlike in sociology, and that the equilibrium systems in economics are more neutral with respect to goal-maintaining or integrating qualities of systems.

At this point, Spengler proposes a joint inquiry by sociologists, political scientists, and economists. He suggests a method, based on reciprocity and exchange, by which common areas of inquiry can be examined by members of these three disciplines from a common frame of reference. He discusses the concepts of reciprocity and exchange as used in these three disciplines, noting the commonalities and the difficulties that each discipline faces with these concepts, depending on the phenomena studied. Spengler concludes his chapter with a concise summary of the methodological and substantive similarities between economics and sociology, and suggests that joint undertakings by economists and sociologists may be facilitated through use of the socioeconomic system approach.

In the final chapter, Thomas O. Beidelman undertakes an analysis of "Some Sociological Implications of Culture." In his opening sentence he remarks that "the aim of this essay is to discuss what seem . . . to be some important aspects of current social anthropology which may be useful to sociologists." Throughout the chapter he then indicates a number of points where sociological theory and method might derive benefit from the experience of social anthropologists.

Beidelman indicates that one of the major current developments in social anthropology is the revival of interest in the notion of culture. The importance of this trend for sociologists, particularly those interested in large-scale social systems, is held to be considerable. There is a common historical base here since the main source of contemporary social anthropology is the French school which is primarily the achievement of Durkheim. The derivative model, which conceives of society as a moral community and gives central place to norms and sentiments in that community, is the one toward which much anthropological field work tends by its very nature. In connection with this the author notes that most social anthropologists have tended to lean upon latent psychological or cognitive factors as explanations of social phenomena.

Beidelman emphasizes the difficulty involved in maintaining "the view of a total society." Mauss's approach of seeing "total social phenomena" not only makes use of and integrates all the social institutions of a society, but also envisions the stuff with which society is fashioned, people and objects, as somehow also affecting and modifying social categories and processes, even as these act upon them. Levi-Strauss's arguments regarding different types of prescriptive marital alliance, with its concern for reciprocity and exchange, is clearly derived from notions originally advanced by Mauss. Like his predecessor, Levi-Strauss also employs a comparative frame of reference. His work stands as the major contemporary attempt to transcend the limiting divisions created by the formulation of social anthropology as the study of separate institutions.

The author calls attention to another of the major difficulties which

current anthropologists must continue to face, namely, that of achieving real understanding in situations in which a society's norms and values (the phenotype) are not actually closely related to their social meaning or cultural value (the genotype). Thus a type of behavior which appears comparable to some behavior within another society may not, in fact, be so. Implicit in this difficulty of comparability is the problem of understanding a foreign language. It is here that we find one of the most crucial differences in the approaches of the sociologist and the social anthropologist. The importance of translation in social anthropology has been emphasized by Evans-Pritchard, whose work has concentrated upon expounding the systematic normative aspects of ideological systems. The study of such belief systems, and concomitantly, of symbolic behavior, seems to be the major trend in social anthropology in the present age, being best characterized by the work of Leach, Middleton, Turner, and Levi-Strauss.

In his concluding section Beidelman suggests some reasons why he thinks the work and attitudes of most sociologists and most anthropologists, regardless of their theoretical orientations, are, and perhaps should remain, rather different and how these differences complement one another. Beidelman expresses the view that some of these differences cannot be resolved, and have led members of the two disciplines to possess two very different types of academic personalities. He holds that social anthropology is not simply the sociology of non-Western or preliterate peoples. It is a form of comparative sociology but of such a nature that, when practiced with the intensity required for excellence, it has a peculiar and diffuse impact upon the practitioner quite unlike that of field work by the vast majority of social scientists who work within their own societies.

The eighteen chapters briefly described in the preceding discourse present a panoramic, although certainly not exhaustive, view of the state and promise of contemporary sociological theory. In aggregate they constitute a pluralism of approaches to the analysis of social phenomena. Both divergences and convergences are visible in the varied approaches. Each, in its own way, constitutes evidence of the gradual enrichment of theoretical sociology.

1.

Some Problems of General Theory in Sociology

Talcott Parsons

Talcott Parsons was born in Colorado Springs, Colorado, on December 13, 1902. He received his B.A. from Amherst College and his Dr.Phil. in sociology and economics from Heidelberg. Since 1927, Professor Parsons has been on the faculty of Harvard University, and was chairman of the department of social relations from 1946 to 1956. He has contributed to many symposia and journals and is the author of Structure of Social Action, Essays in Sociological Theory, The Social System, Structure and Process in Modern Societies, *and* Societies: Evolutionary and Comparative Perspectives. *He coauthored* Toward a General Theory of Action, Working Papers in the Theory of Action, Economy and Society, *and coedited the* Theories of Society. *Professor Parsons is a past president of the American Sociological Association.*

My assignment as a participant in the symposium on the state of theory in sociology was to contribute something about *general* theory. The difficulty of the assignment lies nearly as much in its definition as in its execution. There is danger of being primarily programmatic, failing to confront genuinely substantive problems; and there is danger of being parochial, dealing with matters of more personal than general professional concern.

In this instance it seemed better to lean more in the latter than the former direction, dealing with a problem area which has been central to my own work for a good many years, but which has bearings of general concern. I am referring to the concept of function, which has been close to the center of the stage of general theoretical controversy for a long generation now. While much of the previous discussion—for example over the more naïve forms of functional teleology—is now only of historical interest, the general problem area is very much alive. An attempt to formulate the best statement of which I am capable in this general area should prove useful.

Furthermore, I have in previous work specified a paradigm of functional analysis considerably more circumstantially than has generally been the case, and claimed that this specified version has a high order of general theoretical significance. This, of course, refers to the four-function paradigm of adaptation, goal-attainment, integration, and pattern-maintenance which

has been used in a variety of contexts as a theoretical reference point. I should like then, first to consider the general status of the concept function in sociological theory, and then to discuss the justifications for the four-function scheme.

The focus of this paper is on problems of general theory in sociology, but this cannot reasonably be isolated from other branches of general theory. Within the province of the social system this must include economic and political theory, at the very least, and beyond that, in the sphere I have called *action,* it must include psychological and cultural theory, the latter in the anthropological rather than the humanistic sense. In the relevant sense action is, except for protophenomena, specifically human, and concerns those aspects of human *behavior* which are involved in and controlled by culturally structured *symbolic codes;* language is an obvious prototype. "Acts" in this sense are behaviors to which their authors and those who significantly interact with them attribute, in Weber's phrase, a "subjective," which is to say cultural or symbolic, meaning. This implies that the process of interaction takes place within a framework of *common* cultural codes: a conversation requires a common language.[1]

Action systems in this sense are a subclass of a broader set, which may be called *living* systems, as such a conception is used in the biological sciences. The subcultural behavior of organisms, their metabolic processes, and biological evolution are all important aspects of the latter category. For reasons of theoretical parsimony, I will not consider the extent to which other systems, for example physical-chemical ones, share the properties of living ones.

I wish to argue that the concept function is central to the understanding of all living systems. Indeed, it is simply the corollary of the concept living system, delineating certain features in the first instance of the system-environment relation, and in the second, of the internal differentiation of the system itself. This proposition is based upon a dual consideration. First, as has been clear at least since the great contributions of Bernard and Cannon,[2] a living system is one which maintains a pattern of organization and functioning which is both different from and in some respects *more stable* than its environment. Secondly, the maintenance of this specific and relatively stable pattern occurs not through total isolation or insulation from the environment but through continual processes of interchange with it. In this sense, all living systems are "open" systems. From this perspective, the functional problems of a living system concern the

1. See Talcott Parsons, "Interaction," in David L. Sills, ed., *International Encyclopedia of the Social Sciences* (New York: Macmillan, 1968).
2. Walter B. Cannon, *The Wisdom of the Body* (New York: Norton, 1932). Very little of Bernard's pioneering work in physiology has been translated into English, but some is available in Claude Bernard, *An Introduction to the Study of Experimental Medicine* (New York: Dover, 1957).

maintenance of its distinctive patterns in the face of the differences between internal and environmental states, the greater variability—in some respects —of the latter, and the system's own "openness."

Thus there would be a functional problem even if there were a single unified environmental condition of system-maintenance. In fact, however, there are always plural conditions which vary more or less independently of each other, but which often have complementary significance for the system. For example, in the animal world, in which oxidation is the basis of metabolism, the ingestion of oxidizable materials from the environment and the intake of oxygen are both necessary, and the two must be in proportion to each other. However, there is no reason to assume that the organically optimum combinations of these two in the environment will vary together. Furthermore, oxidation produces waste products, and their disposal without injury to the organism presents another partially independent functional problem. Hence the necessity of functional differentiation of different system–environment exchanges, which is fundamental to all living systems.

This differentiation of system–environment interchanges has implications for the internal state of the system. Insofar as the exchanges must be differentiated, so must different parts of the system be differentiated. Thus, to return to our example, alimentary and respiratory systems are structurally distinct in higher zoological organisms. Given internal differentiation, the relations among the parts within the system cannot be assumed to be stable on given bases, but must involve processes of mutual adjustment. There must be, in addition to processes which mobilize inputs and outputs across the system–environment boundary, different processes which mediate the combination of inputs within the system and the genesis of a differentiated plurality of outputs.

Thus, the kind of difference between system and environment which was postulated as basic to all living systems implies that within the living system itself there will be two distinctive types of mediation: mediation of external interchanges and mediation of internal combinations. This differentiation of the system along the axis of external relations to the environment and internal relations of the components to each other is one of the two primary axes on which the four-function paradigm is built.

The second axis is based upon the consideration that a living system not only is different from its environment in various respects at any given moment, but *maintains* its distinctive organization over periods of time (which need not be unlimited—witness the phenomenon of biological death [3]). In circumstantial detail, the processes which maintain this distinctiveness cannot be presumed to involve only instantaneous adjustment, but *take time*. If a postulated state of affairs is to be maintained in a vari-

3. The late Professor E. B. Wilson once remarked to me that the process of disappearance of the difference between the internal state of the organism and the environment was the best biological definition of death.

able environment, its underlying conditions must be involved in processes of complex sequence. To use our previous illustration, the intake of nutritional materials must precede the internal process of oxidation which produces organic energy. Output to the environment in the form of behavior which requires energy must therefore at some time have been preceded by both nutritional intake and oxidation.

There is a fundamental basis of differentiation along the range of temporal sequence which consists in the fact that there is not a simple one-to-one relation between conditions necessary for the attainment of a given goal-state and its attainment. The same conditional state of affairs (the establishment of which may itself constitute a goal) can often be a condition of the attainment of a plurality of different goal-states, some of which are alternatives to each other in that, given a set of conditions, only one of a pair of goal-states is realistically attainable. Therefore the processes involved with establishing conditions of future goal-states, and the more ultimate or "consummatory" processes of approaching such goal-states, tend to become differentiated in living systems. At the action level this is very much involved with the means–end relationship. Activities concerned with the procurement of means not only may be logically distinguishable from those concerned with goal-attainment, but are in many cases realistically different.[4]

This distinction has become increasingly prominent in the course of evolution because adaptive capacity has become increasingly generalized and goal-attainment capacity increasingly flexible. This is one of the bases of the "activism" which is far more prominent in the sphere of behavior than in that of metabolic or vegetative functions. Here it has become established usage—after much controversy—to speak of an organism as engaged in goal-seeking behavior. This may be defined as behavior which has the "meaning" (or possibly the intention) of altering the otherwise obtaining organism–environment relationship in a direction more favorable than otherwise to the maintenance of the pattern of the organism. This might be manifested, for example, in food-getting activities, where the procurement of food would constitute the attainment of a goal.

A similar distinction holds for the processes of internal mediation, namely between processes which preserve and protect the system's potential for actualization of its pattern, and those which "mortgage the future" in some kind of consummatory interest. We may thus take this axis of differentiation, of the establishment of general conditions for the attainment of system ends on the one hand, and action on the basis of such conditions on the other, as the second basic axis of differentiation of living systems, cross-cutting the first.

4. To take a familiar apposite case, the acquisition of a typewriter as a personal possession is clearly not the same as the use of it to write a particular letter or manuscript. A typewriter is a *generalized facility,* the properties of which do not determine the particular uses to which it may be put.

In a sense, both the system–environment and the temporal pattern maintenance–goal attainment axes are foci of continuous variation. The case for dichotomizing is more immediately clear in the former context. The differential between internal system states and those of the environment in general is not continuous but involves *boundaries.* In higher organisms, potential food in the environment is not the same as digested nutritional material in the blood stream; the former, among other things, is much more diverse. In the temporal axis, there is, however, a parallel in the "turn" from a system's "interest" in the "stock" of instrumentally utilizable facilities, and of their consummatory utilization for specific ends.[5] There are, then, boundaries of the meaning of temporal selection—on the action level "choice"—which in certain respects correspond to the boundary between system and environment. In both cases they constitute something akin to "watersheds." On one side of the boundary, processes work to produce one kind of result; on the other side, quite another kind. It is a qualitative distinction, not a question of position along an unbroken continuum. It should be made clear, however, that the distinctions being drawn do not imply that a structure in a living system cannot be involved in processes on both sides of either of the two "boundaries."

The logical outcome of dichotomizing on both of the two primary cross-cutting axes of differentiation is a four-fold classification of function. In terms of previously established usage, the four functions are referred to as pattern-maintenance (internal–means), integration (internal–ends), goal-attainment (external–ends), and adaptation (external–means).

Among the four, pattern-maintenance occupies a special place in that it is the focus of stability in *both* of the two main respects. It is internal rather than external, in the sense of being insulated from the more fluctuating processes of the environment, and it is associated with the long run and insulated from the continuing adjustments which the adaptive and goal-oriented processes on the part of plural units bring about in the internal subsystems. The distinctive features of this greater stability are formulated as constituting a pattern which is distinctive of this system or type of system, and which may be presumed to be, or to have a tendency to be, maintained in the face of fluctuations in the relevant environmental conditions and over time.[6]

This basic asymmetry is the main ground of the teleological character of living systems, and of the theory of living systems. It is reflected in the

5. In modern economic theory, which grounds in this general conceptual scheme, this is broadly the line of distinction between production and consumption.
6. This proposition, which has been stated in many variants, is perhaps the focus of the accusation of "functional teleology." The distinction between the teleological position and the functional one concerns the question of fact, whether indeed such a pattern exists for a certain class of systems. For example, Cannon begins his treatment of homeostasis in *The Wisdom of the Body* with the observation that certain higher organisms tend, *in fact,* to maintain a constant body temperature. The ques-

reversal of the direction of explanation characteristic of functional analysis. A functional explanation begins with a postulated state of affairs, and refers *back* to the necessary antecedent or underlying conditions. Such teleology must of course be conditional, couched in the form that *if* certain patterns are to be maintained, or certain goals achieved, certain conditions must be fulfilled.

It is a common experience in the history of science that the purely empirical assertion that a state of fact exists (for example, that certain species tend to maintain a constant body temperature) is later explained by understanding the processes at work. For a long time, biological science has stressed the importance of the distinction between the genetic factors in the functioning of organisms and the somatic or physiological factors, between genotype and phenotype, between germ plasm and somatoplasm. On the level of factual propositions in the action field, as well as in the organic field, there has long been a good case for singling out the function of pattern-maintenance as concerned with the mechanisms in the basic asymmetry of living systems. In relatively recent years, developments in both general and biological science have strengthened the basis on which it is reasonable to assert continuity in this respect across the class of living systems. These are the developments, first of cybernetic theory, and second, of the "new genetics" by virtue of which the genes are asserted to be a system of codes whose functions and operating processes are analogous to those of symbolic systems.

The general principles of cybernetics and its close relative, information theory, are now well known. A system, which may be mechanical or electronic and need not be living, is conceived as "programmed" to behave in a planned way within a range of developing contingencies, without the necessity of predicting the specific contingencies in advance. As the process of "behavior" of the system develops over time, there is a feedback of information about developments in the environment, including the consequences of the preceding operations by the system. This feedback information is evaluated in its relation to the program, and the outcome is the setting in motion of a new set of operations which are "adapted" to the new situation.[7]

---

tion then becomes *how* this pattern is maintained, which is not a teleological question. The answer includes delineation of the conditions under which it will *not* be maintained. The question of the functions of the pattern itself involves shift to a different level of theoretical system reference, in the body temperature case, that of evolutionary theory, not, as Cannon treated it, of physiology.

7. One of the simplest cybernetic mechanisms is the thermostat, a special type of thermometer which will turn on a heating apparatus when the temperature falls below a certain point, and turn it off above a certain point, thus keeping the relevant space at a relatively constant temperature. The "program" or "goal" of the system is the temperature range for which the thermostat is set. There *must* be a goal-attainment mechanism if the temperature of the relevant space is to be kept constant under fluctuating environmental conditions.

For the simplest cybernetic systems, such as the thermostat, there is only one goal-state and perhaps the possibility of positive and negative deviation from it, and hence a simple single either/or choice involved in operations to maintain the goal-state. In our terminology such a system has only pattern-maintenance and goal-attainment functions, performed respectively by the cybernetic mechanism (the thermostat) and the operative mechanism (the heating apparatus). For more complex systems, however, there may be many mechanisms which perform different kinds of operations, and there may be many linked cybernetic submechanisms. It is such complications which necessitate functions of generalized adaptation (such as the processing and integration of several sorts of feedback information) and of integration (the coordination of many different information processing systems and many "operative" mechanisms).

From our present point of view the great significance of the new genetics is two-fold. First of all it strengthens the evidence that living systems generally, in the sense of Cannon's homeostasis, maintain their stability through cybernetic control processes; and secondly it shows that the most far-reaching stabilities of all, those of species genotypes, are maintained by such mechanisms, the biochemical properties of which can now be understood in some detail. These turn out to have formal properties identical with those of symbolic codes, with their extraordinary combination of stability of pattern but with an indefinite variety of possible operative outputs and an indefinite capacity to make these outputs adaptive in the sense of maintaining the patterns—and perhaps, in a higher order of system reference, the functions—of the programmed system. Thus, given the functions of a language as communication among human users, the code elements of the language (its syntax, grammar, vocabulary) make possible an indefinite variety of specific utterances, which are adaptive in the sense that they are intelligible—they convey meanings which are or can be shared by both speakers and hearers. "Conversation" then carries such processes to a higher level in that there is mutual feedback among the speakers, who are also listeners.[8]

There is an important sense in which the above developments indicate that the properties of culturally ordered and controlled systems of human action, if properly interpreted, throw more light on the processes of sub-human organisms than, conversely, the properties of mechanical systems (in the sense of the older scientific materialism) throw on the operation of human societies. However important this may be, it does not follow that specific theory in the latter field is in some simple sense deducible from the continuities we have claimed. It does, however, suggest that there

8. The eminent biologist, Alfred Emerson, has spoken of the functional equivalence of gene and "symbol," by which he meant that for culture-level systems of behavior, which we here call action systems, symbolic systems have the same *order* of functional significance that genetic systems have at the organic level.

are sound scientific grounds for exploiting fully for our theoretical purposes the cybernetic, information processing, and communication aspects of human culture.

The central thrust of the argument then, is that the four-function scheme is grounded in the essential nature of living systems at all levels of organization and evolutionary development, from the unicellular organism to the highest human civilization. This holds true for the two basic axes of differentiation and for the significance of treating them, for analytic purposes, as dichotomous. The contributions of homeostatic physiology, the new genetics, and cybernetic and information theory lend strength to the view that in these basic respects there is strong continuity over the class of living systems, especially with regard to the central role of the processes we have characterized as pattern-maintenance.

A common complaint about such a scheme is that it is *too* simple, and thus cannot account for the complexity of the real world. In light of the history of science, this is not a very convincing criticism, since very generally simplification through abstraction has been a central feature of empirically fruitful theory. The fruitful path has not been to avoid simple schemes, but to use them to define elementary systems, and then to treat more complicated systems in terms of combinations of more elementary components on various different levels. For example, in mechanics, anything is a particle from a subatomic particle to the largest known celestial body, a simplification certainly as radical as any proposed here. Thus the issue turns on the usefulness of the abstractions proposed, and I hope to establish in the following discussion that the four-function paradigm is a powerful analytic tool.

Before we turn to the use of the paradigm, something needs to be said about the two essential categories of structure and process. For a considerable time it has been common to refer to structural-functional theory, even as constituting a "school." It has become my increasing conviction that this is not a proper designation. The concept *function* is not correlative with *structure,* but is the master concept of the framework for the relations between any living system and its environment. Functions are performed, or functional requirements met, by a combination of structures *and* processes.

The distinction and relation between the latter terms are essentially familiar. A structure is any describable arrangement of a system's elements which are distinguishable from each other, and the properties and relations of which can be presumed to remain constant for purposes of a particular analysis. A structure is not an ontological entity but is strictly relative to the investigatory purpose and prospective. It is continuous in the organic and the action sciences. Thus the anatomical structure of the organism is constant for purposes of most physiological investigations, but not over the life cycle, and not in the genesis of many pathological condi-

tions. Similarly the structure of a family may be treated as constant for purposes of the study of behavior of its members over short periods, but not through the phases of the family cycle.

Process, then, consists in the theoretically significant aspects of a system which undergo "change of state" within the time period of significance for a given investigatory purpose. It is structure and process which are correlative, not structure and function. *Both* structure and process are analyzed in functional terms.

It follows from our conception of action that the most important structural components of *any* action system are the symbolic codes by the use of which detailed adaptive activities take place.[9] Process, then, is of two orders. The more obvious is communication, the transmission of information or meaning from one acting unit to another in terms of a code, the rules of which are commonly understood and accepted. Communication is inherently *inter*unit and indeed, in action terms, a unit may be defined as a structural entity which functions as the sender or receiver, or both, of communicated meanings.[10] Where, as is prototypically the case, communication is not one-way but mutual between two or more acting units— the basic case of *interaction*—communications sent may be treated as outputs and those received as inputs.

Insofar as there is some kind of relationship between these inputs and outputs for a given unit, we must postulate a second order of process which occurs inside the "black box," the acting unit which relates antecedent inputs of communication to subsequent outputs. From the point of view of the process of determination of the relevant output or outputs, we may speak of this process as *decision*. This conception implies that only in limiting cases would the inputs completely determine the output. Something is conceived to be contributed by the deciding unit itself. Furthermore, it is only a limiting case where an output is related to only a single category of input. The general case is the occurrence of a set of combinations of input-contributions to bring about the output. The logic can easily be extended one step further to say that very frequently plural inputs are combined to produce not one but a plurality of outputs. In either case the acting unit is a node at which processes of sorting and combination take place, so that in a variety of respects what comes out is different from what went in.

9. It is probable that at least the most important components of the structure of the behavioral organism as an action system—not the total concrete organism—are given through organic hereditary processes. In the case of personality and of social and cultural systems, however, they are *learned* by the individual.

10. The unit does not need to be an individual. Intrapersonal communication is well established; the idea of James's plurality of selves implies this, as does Freud's personality theory. Social systems, as collectivities, communicate with each other, though through the agency of individuals who can "speak" for them. The same applies to cultural systems: I as an "agent" of sociology, am engaged in a "dialogue" with the discipline of biology.

Social Systems

Let us now consider the use of the four-function paradigm in the analysis of social systems. In the sense in which I have previously used the term, a social system is that aspect of a general action system organized about the patterns of interaction of the individual actors. In this sense it is an analytically abstracted subsystem of a general action system.

In the development of my work, a particularly strategic line of thought was a reconsideration of some of the main features of economic theory specifically in terms of its relations to the rest of the theory of social systems, but within the action frame of reference. The approach taken to this problem was that of the paradigm outlined above. Thus it assumed the relevance of the four-function scheme to any highly generalized theoretical task, and conceived of pattern-maintenance as having a special stabilizing and organizing significance. Furthermore, it assumed that action systems, like other living systems, tend to differentiate along functional lines. Interaction was conceived of as taking place at different levels between units, and taking the form of communication. Also important was the conviction that, although the significance of decision and communication in human action processes has long been recognized, there have been great difficulties in introducing a combination of true theoretical specificity and generality into the utilization of such knowledge, and the four-function paradigm might prove of value in this context.

On this basis, it made sense to treat the factors of production of economic theory as a classification of inputs, and the shares of income correspondingly as categories of output. But inputs from and outputs to what? If production in the economic sense could be treated as a differentiated function within social systems, then perhaps they could be treated as inputs from and outputs to *other* functionally differentiated subsystems of the same social system. A critical question here was whether it was the same *social* system or the same general action system. Thus it would be very easy, in the factor-of-production sense, to treat labor as an input from personalities of individuals, and land as an input from the physical environment. Any solution to questions such as this required highly generalized theoretical analysis.

I have elsewhere given in detail the justifications for treating the economy as the adaptive subsystem of a societal level social system, and will not repeat the arguments here.[11] However, it should be noted that the economy as conceptualized here is *functionally* defined. Thus it is not coterminous with the business sector, although there is a fit between the

11. See Talcott Parsons and Neil J. Smelser, *Economy and Society* (New York: Free Press, 1956).

two in that I would argue that the functional significance of the business sector for a society is primarily adaptive.

However this may be, a striking set of numerical relations emerged as soon as the problem was put in these terms. If the productive system, the "economy" in the technical sense of economic theory, could be treated as one primary functional subsystem of a society, it should, according to the paradigm, be one of four on a cognate level. Then there might well be input–output interchanges between it and the other three in a social system. Now modern economic theory, since Marshall and Schumpeter, has utilized a scheme of *four* factors of production—land, labor, capital, and organization—and four corresponding shares of income—rent, wages, interest, and profit. But interchange within a four-fold system called for three, not four, categories of each. In this dilemma a feature of economic analysis from the classical era came to mind, namely that land, and with it rent, constituted a special case. Its distinctiveness lay in the fact that the quantity of land in the system was, unlike the other three factors, not a function of its price. At the aggregate level of resources available to the system as a whole it could not be "bought" but was "given," and hence not involved in an interchange. This being the case, it made sense to assign each of the other three remaining categories to interchange with one of the three other primary functional subsystems of a society, which Smelser and I called the polity (or goal-attainment) system, the integrative system (or, recently, the societal community), and the pattern-maintenance system. The interchanges seemed to be, specifically, labor–wages between the economy and the pattern-maintenance system, capital–interest between the economy and the polity, and organization–profit between the economy and the integrative system.

At least to our satisfaction, this strategy seemed to work, as did the decision to treat all these interchanges as intrasocietal and not as between the social system and other primary subsystems of action. This left the problem of the status of the category "land," which traditionally had been treated as belonging to the physical environment. Our theoretical decision was to treat this physical aspect of land as derivative, and to redefine that category as the unconditional commitment of economically significant resources to the function of economic production, thereby withdrawing them from other potential uses. "Land," in this redefined sense, then became a primary case of the application of a set of societal value-commitments in social action. In its special function among the factors of production, land paralleled the pattern-maintenance function in action systems generally.

This line of theoretical codification implied that in the relevant respects, traditional economic theory could be regarded as a special case of the theory of social systems in the action sense, that is, the theory of the functioning of one primary, analytically defined subsystem of a highly

differentiated society. This in turn, however, raised the question of whether codification could be matched by generalization, so that, with appropriate modifications, the theoretical resources of economic theory could be utilized for the analysis of the other subsystems of societies. The first major attempt in this direction, to resolve some of the old problems of the political aspect of social systems, succeeded so well that I have made the task of generalized codification one of my main lines of work ever since. Indeed, one of its firstfruits was a departure from the view, stated in some length in *The Social System,*[12] that economic and political theory could not be treated as logically parallel.

The codification of the four-function scheme with economic theory seemed a major step in the development of general theory, especially insofar as the scheme is grounded in the general nature of living systems. To my knowledge, no economic theorist has contended that the four factors of production and corresponding shares of income had any generalized significance beyond the economic field.[13] Since economics is theoretically the most highly developed discipline in the action field—except perhaps, recently, linguistics—its conceptual fit with sociological theory and that of other disciplines seemed to be of high significance.

On this background, there developed leads into another aspect of action systems which had a grounding in economics but also linked up in exciting ways with the general field of symbolic codes and mechanisms. The main point of reference is the very simple consideration that with a high degree of division of labor, exchanges cannot be carried on simply on a barter basis, but must be mediated by some generalized mechanism. For the economic case, this medium is money. Thus in the classical case, labor is not remunerated in kind, by specific consumer goods, but by money, which in turn is used by household members to purchase needed goods. This line of reasoning raises two basic questions, namely, What is the nature of money as a medium of exchange, and Is it an isolated phenomenon or one of a "family" of such media?

The key to answering the first question lay in a distinction insisted on by the classical economists and taken for granted ever since, namely, the distinction between value in use and value in exchange. Money differs from commodities and services in possessing the latter and not the former— in the "pure" case, *only* value in exchange. It was not a very long step to the insight that money is not a "thing" in the usual sense, but is a mode of symbolic communication. An offer of money is literally a proposition:

12. Talcott Parsons (New York: Free Press, 1951), especially chap. 12.
13. There have been attempts to apply the economic perspective directly to non-economic domains, without the necessary prior generalization of economic theory. See, for example, Thomas N. Carver, *The Essential Factors of Social Evolution* (Cambridge: Harvard University Press, 1935); or, more recently, Anthony Downs, *An Economic Theory of Democracy* (New York: Harper, 1957). These attempts, it seems to me, have not succeeded—nor could they.

"If you will give me what I want—for example, possession of some physical good—I will give you a certain sum of money." The mood of the proposition is conditional. Money, then, not only resembles a language, but *is* a very specialized language through which intentions and conditional consequences of actions are communicated. If this is true, then a whole range of considerations about the nature and operation of symbolic media should apply to money. The working out of these connections has been a complicated task, but I can see no reasonable doubt about the fit.

The answer to the second question, about the uniqueness of money, was then strongly indicated. If money is a language, then it would not likely be a totally isolated case except for what are usually called general languages. It would, for example, be possible that certain specialized uses of "ordinary language" could be functional analogues of money. This turned out to be the case for the first major extension of this analysis outside the economic field, which was to the concept of political power and its field of application.[14] Power is defined as the capacity of a unit to mobilize obligations of the unit-members of a collective system in such a way as to make decisions binding on the collectivity and ensure their implementation through the performance of those obligations. The mobilization of such obligations, the promulgation of relevant decisions, and explication of their consequences for performance of obligations, all occur through ordinary processes of linguistic communication.

The distinctiveness of a power system, as analogous to a market, is the kinds of content communicated, and the conditions on which there will be, as Weber put it, a probability that they will be acted upon in certain ways. Here it is particularly important to make the distinction parallel to that between value in use and value in exchange. Many students think of power as capacity to exert an intrinsically effective sanction on the action of others, a line of thought which leads to special emphasis on coercion and ultimately to physical force. This would make power equivalent to a class of commodities, not to a medium of exchange. Hence working with the parallel to money entails a rather sharp break with much of the usage of political theorists. One must abide by the consequences of the assumption that the use of power, as a medium, asserts only expectations and claims, and is not intrinsically effective.

Besides definitional and categorical symmetries, what are the advantages of such a break with tradition? They must lie in the grounding of *theoretical propositions* which otherwise would not be "seen," or be passed

14. Talcott Parsons, "On the Concept of Political Power," *Proceedings of the American Philosophical Society,* vol. 107, no. 3 (June, 1963); reprinted in Talcott Parsons, *Sociological Theory and Modern Society* (New York: Free Press, 1967), chap. 10, and also in Reinhard Bendix and Seymour M. Lipset, eds., *Class Status and Power,* rev. ed. (New York: Free Press, 1966). A further discussion of this subject can be found in my article "The Political Aspect of Social Structure and Process," in David Easton, ed., *Varieties of Political Theory* (Englewood Cliffs: Prentice-Hall, 1966).

over as trivial, or might indeed be declared to be untrue. Let me illustrate with one case. Many of the most prominent users of the concept of political power have, explicitly or, more often, implicitly, used it in such a way as to build in the assumption that, in the language of the theory of games, power is a "zero-sum" phenomenon. This would mean that in a power system any gain in power by one unit or a class of possessing units would always have to be balanced by an equivalent loss on the part of other units. If this is correct, it is an exceedingly important property of power systems. We know, however, that it is not true for monetary systems. The phenomena of increase in amount of money through credit creation, and of inflation and deflation as processes of increase and decrease of this amount not strictly linked to distribution, are well established and well understood in economics. Parallel to this, I assert with some confidence that, under specifiable conditions, the power equivalent of the creation of credit by banks can and does occur, and that there are, in political systems, phenomena strictly parallel to—though of course not identical with—inflation and deflation in the economic sense. The scientific consequences of such a difference surely are not trivial.

Once an extension beyond the monetary case works out, as I think it has for the case of power, then the logic of the four-fold paradigm raises further questions. One concerns generalizing to all four subsystems the input–output pattern utilized in the case of the economy. This would entail identifying for each subsystem three mobile categories of resources which could be treated as inputs, one from each of the other three subsystems, and correspondingly, three categories of output, one destined for each of the other subsystems. A reasonable assumption here is that there is a complementary relation between the outputs or products from the point of view of one functional subsystem, and the transmission, in the opposite direction, of resources or factors from the point of view of its recipients. This clearly is the case for the exchange, fundamental to economics, between the aggregate of households and firms, namely, output by households of labor capacities, and by firms of commitments to provide consumer goods.

In working out this concept for the system as a whole, the considerations important to the nature and role of money become relevant. The proposition is that, in general, from the point of view of any given system unit, the sources of its most essential resource-inputs and the destinations of its product-outputs are not the same units. Exchange therefore cannot proceed on a barter basis but must be mediated in ways analogous to that in which money mediates economic exchanges. This means that, between any pair of functional subsystems, there should be not one but *two* primary types of interchange; namely, from the point of view of one unit, an interchange of resource for medium, and one of output for medium. For the pair of subsystems this would constitute a double interchange. If these

theoretical "expectations" can be realized, it should be possible to work out a system of four primary functional subsystems, adequately differentiated from each other, and linked by six double interchange systems involving four generalized media. The four media would be, in addition to money and power, one for the integrative subsystem, which we have called "influence" in a special technical sense, and one for the pattern-maintenance subsystem, which we have called value-commitments.[15] Each of the media should be involved in three of the six interchange sets, mediating interchanges from the subsystem in which it is "rooted" to the other three.

This theoretical program clearly involves many further complications, one of which we will mention. Each of the media apparently can be exchanged either for "intrinsic satisfiers" as in the prototypical case of money for the possession of concrete physical commodities, or for one of the other media, as when an employing unit through the contract of employment gains the specification of the employee's value-commitments to "work faithfully" for the employing organization within the terms of the contract. Since details of work obligations are not usually specified long in advance, what the employer acquires is an expectation of service of a certain kind and within certain limits, thereby transferring the interchange out of the market into one internal to the organization of requesting and performing the fulfillment of commitments.

After much revising over several years, I worked out a complete interchange paradigm for the social system, at the level of *media,* and published it as such,[16] leaving the systematization of the relations of the media to the control of intrinsic gratifiers to be worked out in more ad hoc fashion for more particular subsystems. The form of this media paradigm has proved, now, to be relatively stable over a considerable period.

What has been accomplished by working out such a paradigm? Given, as I think can reasonably be claimed, its embodiment of certain fundamentals of the theory of living systems generally, and the conjunction of these with the somewhat different theory of cybernetic control in its relation to symbolic systems, the paradigm is, *at a certain level,* a deductive propositional system. Furthermore, its empirical relevance has been strongly evidenced at a number of points, some of the most conspicuous of which have been reviewed, notably in general biological theory, including genetics; in linguistic theory and more generally in the theory of symbolic systems; and in economics. Considerations such as these make it virtually certain that it is neither purely speculative nor simply arbitrary.

15. Talcott Parsons, "On the Concept of Influence," *Public Opinion Quarterly,* vol. 27 (Spring, 1963); reprinted in Parsons, *Sociological Theory,* chap. 11; Talcott Parsons, "On the Concept of Value Commitments," *Sociological Inquiry,* vol. 38 (Summer, 1968).
16. Parsons, "On the Concept of Political Power." The interchange paradigm is in the Technical Note appended to the article.

If this is, however partial, a deductive system, it clearly is not a closed one. It is correct, as has often been said, that it is highly general and abstract, though this is by no means necessarily a fault. The fault lies rather in that at the many levels and in the many contexts where it is inherently relevant—if its general claims mean *anything*—the terms can-not be precisely defined, nor can they yet be adequately operationalized. It should not, however, be assumed that this is true across the board, but rather that the situation is spotty, in that in some areas, such as the economic, there is a great deal more precision than in others, such as in the "theory of social movements."

Action Systems

We have used the involvement with cultural level symbolic systems as the distinctive feature of the subclass we call *action* systems, within the larger category of living systems. The question now is how the general framework of functional analysis is to be applied and how its implications and uses are to be spelled out in this area. But this is a formidable task. It is necessary to designate correctly the lines of differentiation of the general system of action and the primary functional subsystems into which it comes to be differentiated.[17] Beyond that, it entails analyzing the input–output interchanges among these subsystems. Since, furthermore, they are both highly differentiated and their interchanges operate at the cultural-symbolic level, it is necessary to identify generalized symbolic media of interchange and to work out the principal contexts in which they operate as media.

For delineating the primary functional subsystems, the three-fold scheme of social system, personality (or more correctly, psychological) system, and cultural system was extremely helpful, but the scheme was rounded out only when it became clear that the "behavioral organism," as it has come to be called, should be included as a fourth primary subsystem. The significance of this addition is enhanced by the continuities between action theory and that of other types of living systems, which have made direct theoretical articulation with these others through specification of the significance of organisms even more important than before.

In this way it has proved possible to treat action systems at the most general level as differentiated on the basis of the four-fold scheme, with quite clear identifications of cultural systems as pattern-maintaining, social systems as integrative, psychological systems as goal-attaining, and behavioral-organic systems as adaptive in their primary functions for action

17. Others have been interested in the place of the social system in a more general framework. Cf. Pitirim Sorokin, *Society, Culture, and Personality* (New York: Cooper Square Publishers, 1962).

as general systems. Each of these primary action subsystems is defined on the basis of theoretical abstraction. Concretely, every empirical system is all of them at once; thus, there is no concrete human individual who is not an organism, a personality, a member of a social system, and a participant in a cultural system. The basis of the abstraction is function within a more broadly defined system. Similar considerations are involved in defining the boundaries vis-à-vis nonaction systems.

The total concrete organism is not an action system in our sense. On one level it can be identified with the "individual," but on another level (for example, with respect to the metabolic processes, which Murray has called visceral) it is not a system of action, because only very indirectly, if at all, is it controlled by symbolic mechanisms. A further very important consideration about the organism is that human relatedness to the physical environment exists *only* as mediated through it. For information, this involves the mechanisms of sense perception, while in the motor context it involves the processes of physical behavior. Even the most predominantly "cultural" activities such as speech are, in *one* primary aspect, organic.

Before considering the problem of generalized media of interchange at the action system level, we should note an important clarification of the four-function paradigm which resulted from systematizing its relationship to the pattern variables. Our point of departure is the conception that the structure of action systems consists in normative culture, internalized in organisms and personalities, institutionalized in societies and cultural systems. This proposition may be interpreted in terms of the code aspect of symbolic-cultural systems, which undoubtedly constitutes a structure (in the sense of "structural linguistics," for example). If this proposition be accepted, the pattern variable scheme should constitute a classification of the basic components of such code systems in the action area. These components would not comprise codes for understanding the physical world, or subaction types of living system, although there should be clear relations to the latter.

The pattern variable scheme was originally worked out as a way of categorizing the structure of social systems, mainly at the role level, but it eventually developed that this was a special case, and that the more general statement should be couched at the level of the general system of action.[18] Reconsideration of certain aspects of the pattern variable scheme should then throw considerable light on the problems of the present paper.

Here it is worthwhile to recall that I personally arrived at the four-function paradigm by establishing a new connection between the orientation and the object modality "sides" of the pattern variable scheme, and

18. Talcott Parsons and Edward Shils, eds., *Towards a General Theory of Action* (Cambridge: Harvard University Press, 1951), especially the essay by Parsons and Shils, "Values, Motives, and Systems of Action."

seeing that this converged with the functional analysis presented by Robert F. Bales in his *Interaction Process Analysis.*[19] Some years later, in "Pattern Variables Revisited," [20] I was able to show that this synthesis concerned the integrative standards of the general action system. In response to Dubin, I attempted to treat these as the principal components of the integrative subsystem of the general action system and to round out the other three in a set of logically determinate relations to this one.

The next step rested upon the assumption that the original distinction between the modality set and orientation set of the pattern variables could be formulated as the *L–G* [21] axis of the system, with the orientation variables in the pattern-maintenance position and the modality variables in the goal-attainment position, since *relations* to objects constituted the content of goal-striving.[22] Then the question arose as to whether sense could be made of an adaptive subsystem which was logically symmetrical to the integrative.

In the synthesis reported in *Working Papers in the Theory of Action,*[23] Bales and I had postulated a primary combination of two pattern variable components characterizing each functional cell, and a secondary combination which seemed related to the phase movements of system change, namely the phase out of which it came to enter the phase of reference, and the one into which it was tending to move. In "Pattern Variables Revisited" I suggested that the significance of these secondary combinations might be adaptive, and that they might therefore be put into the adaptive subsystem of the more general pattern variable paradigm. At that time, conceptualizing the adaptive subset in this way did not seem completely justifiable. Now, however, I think a good case can be made for using this formulation to characterize and distinguish the generalized media of interchange, both at the general action level and at that of the social system. I shall not take space here to spell out the fit for the much more fully

19. Cambridge: Addison Wesley, 1950.
20. Talcott Parsons, "Pattern Variables Revisited: A Response to Robert Dubin," *American Sociological Review,* vol. 25, no. 4 (August, 1960); reprinted in Parsons, *Sociological Theory,* chap. 7.
21. I am using here the established "short-hand" for the four functions, which is: *L* for pattern-maintenance, *I* for integration, *G* for goal-attainment, and *A* for adaptation.
22. This way of arranging the components almost certainly would not have occurred to me had it not been for a thorough reconsideration of Durkheim's theory of solidarity, and new understanding of the relationship between mechanical and organic solidarity, the former being interpreted in terms of the *L–G* axis, and the latter in terms of the *I–A* axis. See Parsons, "Durkheim's Contribution to the Theory of Integration of Social Systems" in Kurt Wolff, ed., *Emile Durkheim, 1858–1917* (Columbus: Ohio State University Press, 1960), reprinted in Parsons, *Sociological Theory,* chap. 1. This paper was written before "Pattern Variables Revisited."
23. Talcott Parsons, Robert F. Bales, and Edward Shils (New York: Free Press, 1953).

analyzed social system media reviewed above,[24] but I will use these criteria in setting forth a newly revised scheme of media for interchanges at the general action level.

Perhaps the best place to begin is with a famous concept-pair, namely two of W. I. Thomas's four wishes, for response and for recognition.[25] I have vacillated as to the placement of these two categories—though I have long assumed that they, or some semantic variant of each, can be characterized as generalized media at the action level. The connection with personality makes it plausible that the wish for response, or mutuality of affect, should be the medium focusing at the personality system (the G-subsystem of general action), and recognition at the social system level. Recent reconsideration, however, has convinced me that the reverse is the appropriate placing.

Affect, as the term was used in the later Freud and in subsequent psycho-analytic literature, seems to be the most appropriate term of which Thomas's response may be regarded as the alter-to-ego variant. According to the general pattern variable paradigm, the integrative medium should be affec-tive, as distinguished from neutral. The most obvious specific reference is to the motivational base of loyalty or collective solidarity. For the indi-vidual personality the reference is to the relation to positively cathected objects, not to the objects themselves.[26] The medium is, however, also defined by quality—as contrasted with performance—which is appropriate because a relation involving cathectic attachment is, once formed, a *given* one, involving mutual adaptation or adjustment.[27] The inclination to place affect at the personality level seems to me to have arisen largely from confusion between the general action and the social system levels. The impersonal normative order involving neutrality of attitude is part of the social system, not a general action grounding of it, unless it be at the level of moral authority rather than of societal norms.[28]

---

24. Thus, following a logic parallel to that used in defining the integrative standards, affective neutrality and performance should categorize money, which seems reason-able, since money is a way of "getting things." Particularism is relevant to power in that power operates to activate collective obligations; so is specificity, in that this is for specific goals, and is not an appeal to diffuse loyalty. Quality and affectivity categorize influence, in that it is directed to persons with common membership status, and in terms of their diffuse loyalty to the collectivity. Universalism and diffuseness characterize commitments, in that commitments invoke universalistically defined values on a diffuse basis not restricted to specific goals or interests.

25. William I. Thomas, *The Unadjusted Girl* (Boston: Little, 1923).

26. This focus on relationships to objects parallels the conception of values as used in the general scheme of action: values are not conceived of as aspects of *objects,* but as aspects of an actor's *relation* to objects.

27. This interpretation closely fits the excellent analysis of the code of the American kinship system as presented in David M. Schneider, *American Kinship: A Cultural Approach* (Englewood Cliffs: Prentice-Hall, 1968).

28. See Victor M. Lidz, "The Moral Legitimation of Party Systems," Ph.D. disserta-tion in preparation, Harvard University.

Thomas's category of recognition seems most relevant to the generalized medium of the personality system. For this medium the pattern variable components are specificity and particularism, and the medium is an analogy to power at the social system level. If recognition is taken as the way of rewarding socially valued achievements, then the pattern variable components would seem to underscore the fact that achievement involves specific actions toward particular goals. A further analogy to power is that recognition of achievement would seem to be subject to a kind of "bindingness" not connoted by affect, with its overtones of spontaneity. Probably the best term to designate the generalized medium is "performance capacity."

If we turn to the adaptive category, the starting point is the fact that the actor-type reference is to the behavioral organism. The pattern variable components are neutrality and performance. On the analogy of money we may say that, if the hereditary component is not too highly stressed, something like "intelligence" fits very well. Money should function as a generalized resource in action processes or, conversely, as a generalized medium for the mobilization of resources, of which knowledge and achievement motivation may be treated as the most significant.[29] Perhaps the other two of Thomas's famous categories, the wishes for new experience and for security, can be fitted in here. I suggest that they may be considered as the positive and negative references of the medium intelligence which, among other things, is involved in the balancing of innovation and its risks against preservation of secure statuses and its costs in lost opportunities.

The last of the four media operating at the general action level should be rooted in the cultural system. Its pattern variable markers are universalism and diffuseness. This suggests a generalized code through which action is oriented; Thomas's other famous concept of the "definition of the situation" seems appropriate here. One crucial property is that it is generated in the process of interaction itself—"a situation defined as real is real in its consequences." It is not specific to any particular goals of acting units—it is diffuse; and as cultural, it is not particular to any system of social inclusion or solidarity but is universalistic.[30]

---

29. For a considerable time, I tried to deal with erotic pleasure as the generalized medium of the behavioral organism in the general action paradigm, but abandoned it. Erotic pleasure, rather, is the "security base" of affect as a medium, in a sense analogous to that in which gold is a base for money, and coercion a base for power.
30. As components of a culturally structured code system, the pattern variables in this connection may be compared to the "distinctive features" which play such an important part in linguistic theory. Their "function" is to select, among a wide variety of plausibly significant bases of difference, those which have special *theoretical* significance. Thus Schneider, in *American Kinship,* suggests that the basis on which one of a spouse-pair does the cooking is sex role rather than marriage membership. A wife cooks because she is a woman, not because she is married, but she cooks for her husband rather than for other men because they are married to each other.

Perhaps the main thesis of the last few pages is that if the four-function paradigm is linked in systematic ways with the pattern variable scheme, it should be possible to systematize the relations, not only between the two, but also between the social system level, with which the present paper is primarily concerned, and that of the general system of action.

Given a formulation of the generalized media at the action level, it still remains to specify the input–output relationships among the different subsystems of action. Here it should be kept in mind that the ideal case is one involving six double interchanges among the four subsystems, with each medium involved in three of the six. After previous unpublished attempts I have essayed a new formulation in this direction. In an Appendix, I have made a very schematic and tentative statement of this formulation, which delineates the interchanges on the level of the general action system, as has already been done for the level of social system theory.[31] It should be clear that in order to develop a complete paradigm of the general action system even at this elementary level, it would be necessary to present three further interchange systems, namely for the behavioral organism, for the personality system, and for the cultural system—and to coordinate all five satisfactorily.

The Strategic Use of the Four-Function Paradigm

Since the present paper is concerned with general theory in sociology, I shall, in the space remaining, consider the advantages to social systems analysis that derive from systematizing both general action theory and sociological theory in terms of the four-function paradigm. The central problem here, of course, is to determine the best strategy for dealing theoretically with empirical complexity. Clearly the solution preferred here is the construction, at the general theoretical level, of a relatively simple system. From that starting point one deals with complexity beyond the capacities of a single empirical reference of the simple theoretical system by treating the empirical phenomena—with adequate empirical justification, of course—as resultants of the involvement of a plurality of systems which are variants of the generalized system. The theoretical scheme must therefore distinguish between primary categorizations, distinctions, and relationships on the one hand, and on the other, those which derive from involvement of multiple subsystem relationships as defined at this level.

However, the implementation of such a strategy is difficult. It requires specification of the proper level or levels for dealing with a given problem, and furthermore presumes a clear understanding of the level at which a given theoretical contribution is valid. For example, it is significant that

31. Parsons, "On the Concept of Political Power."

Thomas is generally categorized as a social psychologist. If it turns out that his influential scheme of categories can be fitted with the present one as characterizing the level of the general system of action, this confirms an impression I have long had, namely that the concept of psychology has not, frequently or even most generally, been used to designate, as I have generally used it the theory of personality (the *G*-subsystem of general action) or even the combination of the *G* and *A* systems, as in the common formula of psychology as the science of the behavior of organisms. I do not have a very strong feeling about which usage is correct, but it does seem to me important that in our usages we should be clear what our designative references are.[32]

From this perspective it is also important to note that perhaps the Achilles' heel of Bales's postulation of social psychology as the truly "fundamental" behavioral science lies in the implicit claim that the theory of cultural systems is a branch of "psychology." It is essentially for this reason that I prefer to use the term general action rather than psychology, because the latter usage runs a double risk, namely of neglecting the analytical independence of cultural levels, and of introducing a psychological type of reductionism into the treatment of the social system. Similarly, it is clear that the "psychological laws" of Homans's "elementary behavior" lie at the general action level.[33]

I should now like to discuss briefly two areas of interrelation of the theory of the social system with that of general action, the first having to do with the classical Durkheimian problem of solidarity in relation to the societal community, the second with the "achievement" complex in its relation to the occupational role system of modern societies, and in its relation to education as a component of capacity to achieve.

The societal community, conceived as the integrative subsystem of a society as social system [34] has long been understood to be the primary focus of articulation between a system of values and norms, deriving from the cultural system of general action, and the motivational attachments to social collectivities and to the normative system, relating to personality systems in particular. Durkheim was undoubtedly the classic theorist of the institutionalization of the normative component. A notable recent contribution has been T. H. Marshall's analysis of the three components of what he calls "citizenship" for modern societies: the legal (or civic), the po-

---

32. My colleague Bales has said that, to him, social psychology is the most fundamental discipline in the behavioral sciences, and is not interstitial between sociology and general psychology or correlative with sociology. It seems legitimate to interpret this view as locating social psychology as the theory of the general system of action in my terminology. On that interpretation, his assertion is correct.

33. George C. Homans, *Social Behavior: Its Elementary Forms* (New York: Harcourt, 1961).

34. See Talcott Parsons, *The System of Modern Societies* (Englewood Cliffs: Prentice-Hall, forthcoming), chap. 2.

litical, and the social.[35] The first of these components is central to the sociology of law, and a good deal has been learned in this area in the last generation.[36] The content of the political component has been elucidated by political sociologists, notably Lipset and Rokkan.[37] The third, the social component, belongs mainly to the area of economic sociology, and is quite well understood.

The relatively satisfactory state of theory with reference to the normative aspect of the integrative system is not, on the whole, matched on the motivational side. There has, of course, been a great deal of work done on deviant behavior, and on the alienation which underlies phenomena ranging from vague and diffuse discontent to violent protest and militant movements for change; but an adequate basis of generalization seems to be lacking.

As I have already suggested, I am increasingly convinced that part of the difficulty has lain in a confusion of "levels" of system reference, marked by vacillating tendencies to define the problem as sociological on the one hand, and social psychological on the other. My suggestion is that alienation and its opposite, motivational integration of the personality in the social system, should in the first instance be explained at the level of the general system of action rather than the social system, and only then should a careful theoretical articulation between them be worked out.

In my own previous thinking on this question, one factor which now appears to have been an obstacle to understanding was the inclination to consider *affect* as the generalized medium rooted in the personality subsystem of action. Reconsideration of the motivational bases of social solidarity has led me to the view that it is rooted in the social, or integrative, subsystem. This position seems defensible in light of the significance of affect for object relations, to use Freud's terms, and more specifically for the attachment of one person to one or more others and to the collectivity constituted (in part) by their mutual attachments. Mutuality of affect then may be considered to be a bond which unites two or more units of a social system, especially personalities, in a solidary or harmonious relationship—in the Confucian sense.[38]

Affect is obviously particularly relevant to what sociology calls "associational" relationships, based upon equalitarian value patterns. Such

35. T. H. Marshall, *Class, Citizenship, and Social Development* (Garden City: Doubleday, 1964).
36. This has been an area of special recent concern to me, reflected in a collaborative seminar given for two years with Professor Lon L. Fuller of the Harvard Law School. Fuller's recent book, *The Anatomy of the Law* (New York: Praeger, 1968), is an excellent introduction to the kind of sociologically relevant approach to law I have in mind.
37. Seymour M. Lipset and Stein Rokkan, eds., *Party Systems and Voter Alignments* (New York: Free Press, 1967), especially the editors' introduction.
38. The mutual solidarity of collectivities must be mediated by the affective orientations of individual persons.

relationships have become increasingly salient with the evolution of modern societies, and the citizenship complex, which seems central to the modern societal community, is one of them. This suggests that one fruitful approach to understanding the motivational integration of the personality in the social system could begin, for modern societies especially, with analysis of the development and generalization of affective associational ties.

The modern kinship pattern is an obvious departure point. Marriage is probably *the* prototypical associational relationship, especially by contrast with primordial ascription in terms of biological descent. It is true that in primitive and indeed in all nonmodern societies, the ascriptive element in marriage has been very prominent, but it is distinctive of modern societies that entry into it has become, very much in principle, *voluntary*. The modern pattern of marriage is not only voluntary, but in principle *affective*. The justification for establishing the tie is in the first instance that the partners are "in love." Among many other aspects of the definition of the situation, this legitimates their erotic relation to each other.[39]

From the perspective of the development of the individual's personality, involvement with and sensitivity to affect are rooted in the socialization experience in the family. The stage of "mother–child identity" is that in which no generalization, or differentiation as a medium, has occurred. However, the attitudinal foundations are here. As is generally said, a good mother loves her child and the child learns to love her. By the time the parent–child "love–dependency" stage is reached, affect has become generalized to the level of what Schneider calls "diffuse, enduring solidarity." It is then, and on this basis, that the child becomes a full member in his family. The crutch of erotic attachment to the parents has been discarded (during latency), and motivation to participation and fulfillment of expectations is grounded in the love relationship reciprocal among all members.

From the point of view of children, though not of parents to each other, this family membership is ascribed by "blood" ties, as Schneider calls them symbolically. The next major step of generalization of the affective medium for the child is to the context of *voluntary* association. The setting for this is in all modern societies provided by the relation of elementary formal education to residential community structures, and by the formation of peer or friendship groups among contemporaries. This new affective focus involves tension-laden reactive relations for the child. On the one hand, he begins to feel emancipated from the family, and attempts to escape its control. On the other hand, his peer group is an affective counterpoint to the pressures of school achievement and its competitive dimension. Since such groups are ascriptively composed of age-peers, and an-

39. The intricacies of this affective-erotic complex have, from a cultural perspective, been enormously elucidated by Schneider, *American Kinship*.

tagonism in both contexts is directed towards adult-controlled systems, it is not surprising that the autonomy linked to voluntary participation is colored by a generation conflict.

The voluntary peer association is in many ways analogous to a market, in that there is a considerable range within which the individual can exercise options of giving or withholding his participation in such relationships, and can regulate its intensity. The extent of the "market" is considerably enhanced when both sexes are included by virtue of coeducation, which in turn has many repercussions on the internal structure of the family.

Pursuing the market analogy further, we note that perhaps the most decisive step in the industrial revolution was to put the factors of production on the market to an unprecedented extent. Similarly in the family, and in much of premodern *Gemeinschaft,* the objects of cathexis have been prescribed: the child is *expected* to love his parents and siblings. Beginning with the modern peer group, however, there is a much broader choice of objects and of collectivities in which to participate and with which to identify. In a strict theoretical sense this shift parallels the differentiation between households and producing–employing units which made labor a marketable factor of production.

Analogous to the use of capital as a mobile factor of production, we find the development of what I shall call (in the Appendix to this chapter) the "moral sanction of association." This is to say that, within the framework of a highly generalized value pattern, there develops a greatly enhanced autonomy of unit choice with respect to associational participation and to moral sanction of such choices. Freedom of choice of a marriage partner is a first and prototypical instance, but a great many other associations belong in this category. In this respect, modern society has been moving in the direction of greatly increased associational pluralism, with the possibility of moral justification for increasingly broad ranges of acceptable choices.

This view casts serious doubt on the allegation that functional analysis of social systems implies an imperative of conformity. We must keep in mind that we are here speaking of the general action level, and that the term "moral" refers to any culturally grounded justifications of selection among alternatives for action, whether they be for sustaining a given social system, or for its revolutionary overturn, or for any of the wide variety of withdrawing or otherwise deviant modes of association. The essential point is that the affective exchange system is extended into the realm of moral questions and thus moral decisions come to be, in a new sense, contingent. From the societal point of view this means that legitimacy is not ascriptively given, but must be competed for. Among the bases of such legitimacy is the capacity to command, through moral assertion, *affective* response.

It should be clear by this point that the kinds of coordinative linking

of the motivational "investments" of individuals (somewhat in Freud's sense of cathexis) with the moral imperatives of a culture and society, and with the needs and expectations of human organisms, could not operate without the functioning of generalized media of interchange. Affect is the medium of most direct interest in the present analysis.

The extension of exchange relationships in which affect is involved to include the "factors of solidarity" clearly implies that the system of reference must become more differentiated; there is a plurality of more or less distinct "markets." It is noteworthy, in this connection, that adolescent peer groups in secondary school are generally segmented rather than differentiated, in that membership patterns are ascriptive by age and heavily influenced by the social class of the members' parents.

A major step in the process of differentiation occurs at the level of higher education, which by now is generally available to all. This does not eliminate ascriptive segmentation by social origin—which operates above all through the kinds of colleges attended—but it does considerably reduce it.[40] It seems reasonable to suggest that the system of higher education is particularly important in the development of mobile "markets" for the factors of solidarity. The paradigm of the Appendix calls attention to two particularly important processes, namely (1) the *I–G* interchange where affect is articulated with the performance capacity medium, one version of which is Thomas's recognition, and (2) the *I–L* interchange where the affective system articulates with the definition of the situation, particularly in its moral aspects.

The significance of higher education in these respects is enhanced by its relationship to the general pattern of solidarities and stratification in the society at large. In modern societies higher education has become the most important pathway to all higher occupational statuses and, for women, the road to the "best" marriage opportunities. It is also important to note in the present context that the company of educated men (and, of course, women) is rapidly becoming the most important prestige and leadership element of the societal community, and thus central to the system of stratification.

However, the affective bases of participation by students within the academic community itself is not unproblematic. The worldwide phenomenon of student unrest—in communist as well as noncommunist countries—in which affective factors seem to have such a salient role, is clear evidence of this. We might begin by noting that, from the point of view of the social system, higher education is a mechanism of socialization. In this respect, it is comparable to the family, although far more complex and differentiated. The two are also analogous in that the family is interstitial to the social and psychological systems, and higher education is interstitial

40. See Christopher Jencks and David Riesman, *The Academic Revolution* (Garden City: Doubleday, 1968).

to the social and cultural systems, most notably with regard to the complex focused on the values of cognitive rationality. In both cases there are certain roles which reflect this duality especially clearly: the father, who leaves the family to pursue his occupation; and the teacher, who is not only teacher but also researcher and author.[41] Structurally, then, the modern university "marries" agents of socialization and agents of socially important cultural functions, and students are in a position of partial and equivocal inclusion in some ways parallel to the status of children in the family.

Insofar as modern systems of education have become the center of a societal storm of sorts, affective factors have clearly been prominent. The attitudes of student activists are highly impassioned, and the symbolic themes prominent in the movements fit with the paradigm we have been discussing. Student power and oedipal aggression are similar in their implicit if not explicit claim to a right to "take over." [42] On the other hand, "student power" has strong overtones of moralism, manifest above all in the students' attempt at politization of the academic system and in their claim to the right, not only to condemn on moral grounds those exercising authority—the "fathers"—but to define for themselves the morally acceptable functions of the university. We can therefore see student discontent as a second oedipal crisis which could fully emerge only with the kind of development of higher education which modern societies have experienced, just as the full impact of the original oedipal problem could not have occurred before the industrial revolution.[43]

It should be clear that, for our purposes, the old Burgess formula that the family is a "set of interacting personalities," with the implication that its significance lies primarily in psychological factors, is inadequate for sociology. The family is part of the structure of society, with essential functions at the social system level, notably the socialization of children. Similarly the system of higher education is not simply a set of interacting personalities of students, faculty members, and administrators, to be understood psychologically. It is a particularly crucial part of the *structure* of modern societies, with very important functions at that system level: the appropriate part of the socialization function, the allocation of personnel in the occupational system, the "advancement of knowledge," and, most

41. See Talcott Parsons and Gerald Platt, "Some Considerations on the American Academic Profession," *Minerva,* 6, 4 (Summer, 1968), 497-523.
42. There may be an analogue of the incest taboo here. Students, while students, do not replace their teachers, nor achieve full equality with them with respect to the professional functions of the teacher role. They achieve the equivalent of adulthood in general, but in contexts *other* than that in which they have been students. They do not "marry" their *alma mater,* but by graduating they become eligible for a teacher or other fully adult role.
43. See Fred Weinstein and Gerald Platt, *The Wish to be Free* (Berkeley and Los Angeles: University of California Press, forthcoming).

important in the present context, the generalization of the factors underlying affective participation in modern social structures.

The preceding discussion originated in the general problem of understanding the modern type of societal community in terms of what we have called the citizenship complex. We were searching for an underpinning on a basis different from the role of law, democratic political organization, and social welfare; in particular, one which seemed more relevant to the motivational concerns of the individual. Given the natural inclination of a student of the sociology of higher education towards trying to understand the very salient phenomenon of student unrest,[44] certain aspects of the problem came to focus on the kind of community participation involved in the academic world and the peculiarities of the students' transitional status. This has proved to have implications for the more general problems of societal community.

It is our contention that the significance of these themes would not be understandable without reference to the general action level, and especially to the role of affect as a generalized symbolic medium and its articulation with the achievement and control system on the one hand, and with the moral aspects of the definition of the situation on the other. This relevance of general action, however, must be carefully articulated with analysis at the level of social systems as such. It would not be wise to treat these issues as wholly those of "social psychology" in the general action sense, or as sociological in the stricter sense of social system theory.

I should like to parallel this fragmentary analysis with a still briefer account of a closely related aspect of modern societies, that of the institutionalization of an achievement complex in the occupational system. This problem has become caught up in the nexus of socialization theory, extending with increasing intensity into the realm of higher education. It has become clear that, in this field also, puristic social system analysis is not adequate. Explicit concern for both motivational and cultural problems involving not only values, but also cognitive aspects of the definition of the situation, are indispensable.

This problem, of course, goes back to the implications of Weber's analysis in *The Protestant Ethic and the Spirit of Capitalism* and the difficulties this occasioned for the more naïve versions of the doctrine of the "rational pursuit of self-interest." One of the main difficulties in discussing Weber's analysis has been the tendency to assume that the religious orientations he was concerned with transformed themselves *directly* into motives for concrete action in concrete situations. This is tantamount to assuming that a cultural component, defined as such at the general action level, could be presumed to institutionalize itself without regard to the conditions of

44. See my forthcoming article on higher education, which will apear in a volume edited by Richard Simpson and Herman Turk on my work and that of George Homans, under the auspices of Alpha Kappa Delta.

institutionalization in the structure of the society—as well as the conditions of internalization in personality systems. Such an approach begs too many fundamental questions.

For Weber, the typical entrepreneur was still the selfmade man whose socialization took place mainly in the context of family and diffuse community setting, including, of course, a church. One important phase of the process of institutionalization of the achievement complex involved the phenomena with which Weber was primarily concerned, namely the rise of the bourgeois classes and their involvement with what he called "rational bourgeois capitalism."

Presently, however, the institutionalization of the achievement complex has been broadened and deepened all over that part of the world which is now building on the industrial revolution, and relatively independently of the current specification of ascetic Protestant values.[45] The relevant values have, by specification, come to be differentiated from their religious matrix and institutionalized in particular in the occupational system. Furthermore, the managerial stratum no longer consists primarily of selfmade men in the old sense, and the relevance of higher rational achievement has been immensely broadened, above all to include a proliferation of many types of professional roles.

The occupational system in turn has come to be integrated to an unprecedented degree with higher education and its accompanying institutions for the advancement of knowledge. From the point of view of the social system, the functional problem is, on the one hand, to anchor the individual in a sufficiently solidary community which, in the circumstances, centers on the age-peer group. On the other hand, it is the guiding of the motives of the achievement complex into meaningful channels which establish some kind and degree of coherent integration between the demands of society for labor force services and the choices of individuals within the manifold of opportunities offered by the educational system, in a sense of the word choice which includes commitment and not just preference. Assuming, as I do, that the American value pattern of instrumental activism (I deal here only with the American case) is in general intact, and further assuming a sufficient anchorage in socialization at the family level, then the educational system from elementary school on constitutes a far more effective mechanism for the socialization of *differentiated* achievement motivation than had been the case for an earlier period. Above all, its broad extension to the level of higher education has opened up an immense manifold of new opportunities for specific function, differentiated achievement, which in its rationality has a special affinity for this value syndrome.

45. This was the most salient "spearhead" of the development of a value system, but was by no means isolated. See my article "Christianity," *International Encyclopedia of the Social Sciences.*

Let us briefly examine the educational system from this perspective. If we approach the problem from the point of view of socialization, the most decisive development is entry into the system of formal education. This is now cushioned by kindergarten and, increasingly, nursery school, but its full impact comes with the standard elementary grades. It is crucial, as I have elsewhere argued [46] and many others have realized, that in a radical departure from the organization of the family, in the school class a group of age-peers who are presumptively equals are differentiated on the axis of personal achievement. There are, of course, two aspects of this differentiation. On the one hand, individual pupils fare unequally on the axis of valued performance. On the other hand, the class as a collectivity comes to be differentiated, and most obivously bifurcated, into groups of high achievers and low achievers. Furthermore, for our purposes, it is critical that the achievements with respect to which this differentiation is defined and legitimated are achievements of cognitive mastery, defined by standards of cognitive rationality.

It was an unexpected but very significant finding of a research project in which I was involved that the record of the elementary school period is— and I think this can be generalized—the primary basis of the expectation of going to college.[47] Though secondary education intervenes, it seems that —at least in New England circumstances—the winners of the elementary school competition, by being chosen for college preparatory programs, on the high average actually attend college. The relevance of these considerations to the preceding discussion of peer groups must be relatively obvious. The elementary school phase is one in which peer groups are in process of formation, stimulated partly by reaction against the pressures of school-performance competition. They are, however, particularly blocked by the imperative of sex segregation imposed by the social psychology (I use the term advisedly) of the latency period. With the emergence of adolescent cross-sex attractions, which we may assume are affective before they are erotic, an affective basis for comprehensive peer group structure can be attained. The suggestion is that for the individual the imperative at the secondary school level is to *maintain* his level of performance, established earlier, and of course its motivational underpinning.[48] It is thus in a sense a moratorium.

The college experience starts a new cycle. The emergence of mass higher education is of special importance in this context, as it was for the question

46. Talcott Parsons, "The School Class as a Social System" in *Social Structure and Personality* (New York: Free Press, 1963).
47. Ibid.; see also Talcott Parsons, "General Theory in Sociology" in Robert K. Merton, Leonard Broom, and Leonard Cottrell, Jr., eds., *Sociology Today* (New York: Basic Books, 1959).
48. As internalized in the personality, this motivation to perform seems to me to be essentially what McClelland has had in mind as need-achievement. See David C. McClelland, *The Achieving Society* (Princeton: Van Nostrand, 1961).

of solidarity discussed above. Well into the present century, higher education everywhere was reserved to a small élite of the age cohort, whose status
was for the most part ascribed by hereditary class status, though membership in this élite has been open to a minority of outsiders through channels
of mobility. Now, despite the retention of an élite component in the older
sense, the character of the system has been changed by its vastly extended
inclusiveness. One consequence is an intensification of the competitive
aspect which, in turn, is one cause of the emergence of intense affective
concerns.

The college experience seems to further the processes of internalizing
motivation to the higher levels of achievement which have come to be
institutionalized in modern societies. These motivations center about the
two primary areas of competence and responsibility, both of which are
linked to autonomy. Hence the college experience may be considered to
be, among other things, a major extension of the syndrome of "independence training" which has been such an important feature of the last
generation's views on pre-adolescent child training. Certainly a primary
focus of the restlessness of students is any restraint on their autonomy
which they feel to be unjustified, but which may often be at least partially
justified by the necessity of learning not only independence, but competence and discipline. Only the graduate ideally can be fully free from
the tutelage of his teachers, and there are many problems of defining the
nature and boundaries of justified tutelage, and they necessarily change
with changing circumstances.

By contrast, for the cohort *not* going to college, the socialization system
is and was in an important sense truncated. Termination of education with
graduation from high school, if even that is achieved, means the beginning
of adulthood, including entry into the labor force and eligibility to marry.
Thus, the processes of internalizing higher levels of achievement motivation do not go so far in developing competence and responsibility, nor,
indeed, so far as to produce certain additional strains.

The extent to which the occupational system has become linked to higher
education represents a major structural change in the society. College education has become almost a binding prerequisite for virtually all of the
higher occupational roles. Furthermore, the higher professional complex,
entry into which typically requires postgraduate training, has become much
more important in the total system. This development brings increased
pressure to bear on those who aspire to some kind of—to them—meaningful career, and at the same time provides them with a range of opportunities which, compared to earlier conditions, is immensely expanded.

The fact that the current phase of development centering on the occupational and educational systems is one of considerable alienation and unrest
does not by itself negate the soundness of the above analysis. My broad
interpretation is that this constitutes a phase of development of the total

system in which integrative problems have, for the time being, assumed primacy. This is a sequel to a preceding phase in which goal-attainment processes, at both societally collective and many other levels, have undergone an unprecedented development. It is particularly striking that the malaise of our time does not seem to have its internal focus in the structure of the industrial economy as such—it is not a period of major labor unrest —but in the generation structure with its close relation to the system of higher education, and in the status of those population groups who are, relative to the societal community, the most marginal.

Whatever the case may be, the essential *theoretical* point is that, here again, any adequate analysis in this field requires consideration of social system theory on the one hand, and of the general action level theory, including its nonsocial subsystems, on the other. Not only have we been discussing the institutionalization of a cultural value system, the primary analytic origins and anchorage of which must be extrasocial, but we have found that another cultural syndrome, concerned with cognitive rationality, is of paramount importance. Similarly it seems clear that neither institutionalization, which includes socialization in terms of these values, nor its opposite, alienation, can be adequately analyzed without consideration of the psychology of personality. It is as a demonstration of these analytical necessities that these two examples from the dynamics of modern society have been introduced.

Conclusion

In embarking on this paper my primary object was to refine the grounding of the four-function paradigm, that part of the scheme of general theory in sociology with which I have been working and which has for some years served as perhaps the most central reference point for a wide range of more restricted theoretical enterprises. I hope that I have made a more cogent case than in any previous discussion in print that it is deeply grounded in the intellectual exigencies of the analysis of living systems generally.

This grounding seems to have been strengthened by theoretical developments in biology and general science during roughly the last generation. These have clarified the conceptions of the mechanisms of "control" of the processes of living systems in relation to their environments. The earliest and more restricted of these conceptions was that of homeostatic mechanisms, associated above all with the name of W. B. Cannon. A more general and more radical conception then emerged in terms of cybernetic controls in relation to information theory, with its almost obvious relevance to culture. The relation of this theoretical complex to linguistics has also been notable. A particularly salient synthesis has been the emergence of the new genetics with its treatment of genetic mechanisms as "codes" carried by

very complex biochemical substances which are capable of reproducing their patterns in successive generations of concrete organisms and parts of them.

The conceptions of homeostasis and cybernetic control pose problems of understanding the mechanisms of the integration of living systems. It thus seemed significant that the four-function paradigm proved useful in integrating economic theory within that of the social system, and in particular by analyzing money as a mechanism of integration—indeed a cybernetic mechanism at the symbolic cultural level—through ramified systems of market exchange. Even more important has been the possibility thus suggested of using both the four-function analysis of the primary subsystems of societies and the mechanisms involved in their integration as the framework for developing a more sophisticated analysis of the total society as a system, including its integration through the interchange of generalized media of interchange and control among the different subsystems. The first step of generalization beyond the economy to the polity, and the attendant analysis of political power as a generalized symbolic medium, was decisive to me in showing the soundness of this extension.

The four-function paradigm had originally been grounded in the pattern variables. The demonstration that these were in turn grounded at the general action level, and not only at that of the social system, raised again the question of the relations between the social system and that of general action. In the third section of this chapter we carry the analysis of this relation further than before by attempting to lay the groundwork for a paradigm of interchange mechanisms at the general action level. The main reference point has been the adaptive sector of the paradigm set forth in "Pattern Variables Revisited." A complete paradigm of interchanges has been worked out, but because of its highly tentative nature, it has seemed best to present it in the Appendix to this article, rather than in the main text.

Finally, this paper has attempted to demonstrate the point, so central to its theoretical argument, that sociological theory with its concern for social systems as such needs to be systematically articulated with the general system of action. I have, therefore, in the final section presented a condensed account of two major processes of development in modern societies, both related to changes in the system of higher education. The first of these concerns the development of the matrices of solidary association in which modern individuals are socialized. It has seemed justified to interpret some of the phenomena of modern youth culture, and in particular the recent waves of student disturbances, at least partly in these terms. The second context is the more familiar one of the development of achievement motivation as this issue was raised by Max Weber in his famous thesis about the implications of the Protestant ethic for occupational behavior. Both of these phenomena come to focus in very salient processes and problems of

the social system. Yet, I have argued, they are not understandable without careful consideration of both the cultural and the psychological, or personality, components in their genesis. I hope that even these sketchy discussions make clear that not only are these general action considerations programmatically essential, but the theoretical scheme with which we have been working makes possible going beyond programs to substantive explanations, however incomplete.

Appendix

This Appendix [49] will follow the same format as the Technical Note to my paper "On the Concept of Political Power." The paradigms presented in the Technical Note applied to the social system, which is conceived to be *one* primary functional subsystem out of four of the general system of action. This Appendix is a very tentative delineation for the general action system of the categories of symbolic interchange, and the corresponding symbolic media and value and coordinative standards. The four-function scheme underlies the treatment of the general action system, as it did that of the social system.

The primary functional subsystems of action have been stably decided upon for some time. In order of descending position in the hierarchy of cybernetic control, they are: pattern-maintenance (L), the cultural system; integration (I), the social system; goal-attainment (G), the psychological (personality) system; and adaptation (A), the behavioral organism.

We follow the general principles used in the analysis of social systems which assert that, at a sufficiently high level of differentiation of the general action system and its respective primary subsystems, a *generalized symbolic medium* of interchange will be anchored in each of the four primary functional subsystems and involved in interchanges with each of the other three. Thus, if we include only the media and not the intrinsic valuables which they are able to command in exchange, at the level of differentiation of the whole system which is of theoretical interest here, there should be six double interchanges, as in the case of the social system paradigm. These will involve each of the four media in three interchanges. This will mean that each medium is involved in one double interchange with each of the other three.

49. In this whole enterprise I owe an immense debt, and to some degree an apology, to Victor M. Lidz. We have discussed these problems over a period of several years, and he first suggested that intelligence and the definition of the situation might be considered generalized media. We still differ over the latter: he would place it in the integrative system, and consider affect as the personality system medium. The apology I owe him is for rushing into print with this formulation before he has had an opportunity to mature his own views fully. My excuses are that the scheme belongs in the context of this paper, and that I have been responsible for holding up the publication of the volume for as long as my conscience will allow.

Since the media have above all integrative significance in the system as a whole, this is necessary if the integrative processes are to pervade the whole system.

Figure 1 simply presents the format of the four media and the six double interchange systems and, for convenience, gives a label to each of the latter. The most difficult and uncertain task has been to identify the four media and to place them correctly. Ever since first working on the problem I have thought that *affect* belonged in the list and that it was a variant, because of system-perspective, of W. I. Thomas's famous category of response, thereby linking a psychoanalytic type of theorizing with that of American social psychology. If response were to be included, it seemed logical that recog-

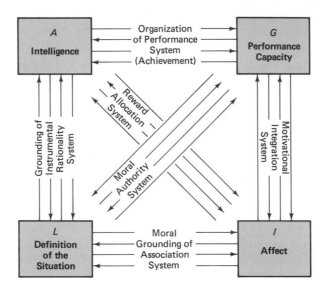

Figure 1. Format of the general action interchange system

nition also ought to be—here I differ from Victor Lidz. This left the problem of placing both categories and designating the proper more generalized term of which recognition is a variant. The best terminological solution I have come upon so far is *performance capacity*. The appropriateness of this term depends on placing affect in the integrative position and performance capacity in the psychological system. Here the analogue of performance capacity to power at the social system level works out well, since power has been defined as a capacity to implement *collective* goal interests, whereas performance capacity may be conceived to anchor in individual performance.

It was only with Lidz's introduction of definition of the situation into the discussion that it occurred to me that perhaps Thomas, in his famous paradigm, had gotten hold of the whole roster of the general action media,

though his terms were chosen from more particular and less theoretically generalized perspectives than the present one. In any case, definition of the situation seems to fit well as the culturally anchored medium.[50]

The pattern-maintenance system has a dual character which is related to its general stabilizing function in living systems. This has, in previous analyses, taken the form of distinguishing its lower and higher level references.[51] It seems to me that the concept of definition of the situation fits this theoretical requirement, and the clue to its interpretation lies in the relatively early Durkheim. This is to say that society, which most directly interacts with the cultural system, is for the participant individual at the same time an empirical entity which is to be cognitively known—in Durkheim's phrase, a *milieu social*—and a source of moral authority, the content of which is morally binding rather than situationally conditional. The relations between these two levels, and those of both of them to the other functional exigencies of action, can be stated in logical terms in the formula that the upper and lower levels of the pattern-maintenance system define the limits of the system of reference, in this case general action, with reference to its upper and lower environments respectively in the general cybernetic hierarchy. Thus, the lower limit concerns the subaction components of the organic world and the physical environment as its impact is mediated through the organism. The genetic constitution of the organism constitutes a set of givens from the point of view of action. At the upper limit it is some such category as "ultimate reality" [52] which is mediated through cultural symbolic systems, the kind of reality postulated in many if not all religious systems, but also metaphysical cognitive grounds such as the Kantian *Ding an sich*.

Finally, we suggest that *intelligence* is an appropriate designation for the adaptive medium at the level of general action. It has long been evident that there is a relation between economic resources at the societal level and cognitive resources at the general action level.[53] Intelligence, especially since we link it to the organism, may be presumed to have a centrally important hereditary component, but to be by no means only hereditary, as is indeed the prevailing psychological opinion today. Indeed, its *L* factor may be presumed to be hereditary. Intelligence seems to be particularly well suited to link the cognitive aspects of the cultural system with the ego-function, achievement-oriented aspects of the personality system.

Figure 2, as in the social system interchange paradigm, places the six

50. Thomas singled out the definition of the situation as a special case, set over against the "four wishes." If, as we suggest, two of the latter, the wishes for security and new experience, both refer to adaptation, we can regard the definition of the situation as the same kind of special case that all pattern-maintenance factors have within a fourfold scheme.
51. Cf. Parsons et al., *Theory of Action.*
52. Cf. Talcott Parsons, *Societies, Evolutionary and Comparative Perspectives* (Englewood Cliffs: Prentice-Hall, 1966), chap. 2.
53. See Parsons and Smelser, *Economy and Society.*

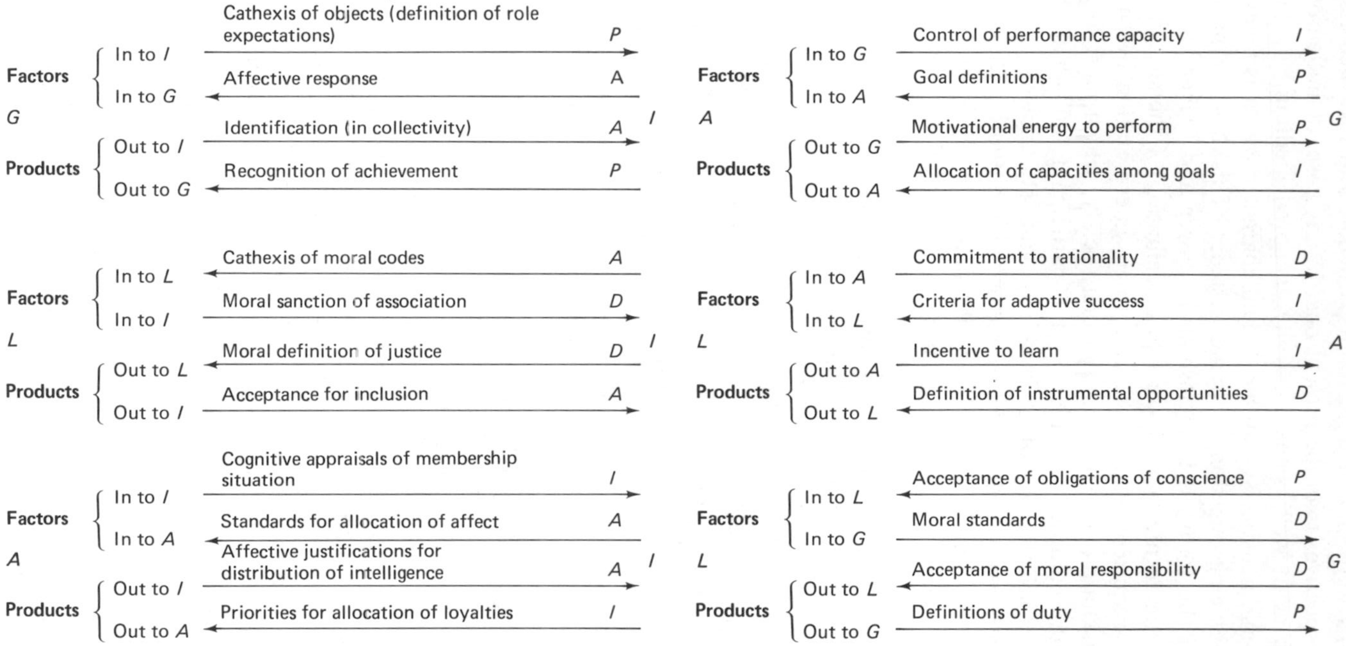
Factors
In to I
In to G
G
Products
Out to I
Out to G
Cathexis of objects (definition of role expectations) P
Affective response A
Identification (in collectivity) A
Recognition of achievement P
I
Factors
In to G
In to A
A
Products
Out to G
Out to A
Control of performance capacity I
Goal definitions P
Motivational energy to perform P
Allocation of capacities among goals I
G
Factors
In to L
In to I
L
Products
Out to L
Out to I
Cathexis of moral codes A
Moral sanction of association D
Moral definition of justice D
Acceptance for inclusion A
I
Factors
In to A
In to L
L
Products
Out to A
Out to L
Commitment to rationality D
Criteria for adaptive success I
Incentive to learn I
Definition of instrumental opportunities D
A
Factors
In to I
In to A
A
Products
Out to I
Out to A
Cognitive appraisals of membership situation I
Standards for allocation of affect A
Affective justifications for distribution of intelligence A
Priorities for allocation of loyalties I
I
Factors
In to L
In to G
L
Products
Out to L
Out to G
Acceptance of obligations of conscience P
Moral standards D
Acceptance of moral responsibility D
Definitions of duty P
G

Figure 2. General action system interchanges.
The medium exemplified by each category of input or output is indicated as follows:
D, definition of the situation; *A*, affect; *P*, performance capacity; *I*, intelligence

double interchange sets of the general action system on a horizontal axis for convenience of reading, though in the more generally used convention they should be placed in the format of Figure 1. Figure 2 gives names to each of the twenty-four input–output categories involved, specifies by directional arrows sources and destinations, identifies which medium each exemplifies, and designates whether, from the point of view of the function of the subsystems, the input or output is a factor or a product. Since it has been necessary to select twenty-four verbal designations, there is likely to be an even greater factor of arbitrariness than in the selection of terms for the four symbolic media, and the present formulations are tentative.

Since the primary interest of this article is in linkage with the social system, we may begin with the interchange systems most directly concerned with it, and with affect as a medium. The first of these, the *I–G* system, has been called the system of motivational integration. The first interchange category, a factor of solidarity, is the well-known Freudian category of *cathexis of objects,* which comes very close to the definition of role expectations. This is treated as an input of performance capacity rather than affect, whereas the other input from personality to social system, called *identification,* is designated as involving the medium of affect, thus endowing it with a *collective* reference, along the lines of my earlier analysis of the object relations syndrome.[54] The primary output from the social system to the personality, then, is *recognition of achievement,* again a form of performance capacity, whereas the related affective category is the place for Thomas's *response.*

In the *L–I* interchanges, which we have called the *moral grounding of association system,* the primary input of a factor of solidarity concerns the moral *sanction of association,* which was discussed on p. 52 of this paper, and the primary product output of the integrative system is the *moral definition of justice* (perhaps similar to Homans's category of distributive justice). Both of these are forms of the definition of the situation as a medium. They are balanced in the two interchanges by another form of cathexis, this time *cathexis of moral codes,* and the *acceptance for inclusion,* both of which are forms of affect.

Because of their special status I shall leave the two "diagonal" interchange systems to the last. Turning to the *A–G* interchange, the *organization of performance* system, we consider the factor input to *G* to be the *control of performance capacity,* of which perhaps the most important intrinsically valuable items controlled are knowledge and skill. This we interpret to be an input of intelligence, which is balanced by the output of intelligence from personality to organism of *allocation of capacities among goals.* The corresponding transfers of performance capacity are *definitions of goals* and *control of motivational energy to perform.* The latter is a

54. Cf. Talcott Parsons, *Social Structure and Personality* (New York: Free Press, 1964), chap. 4.

particularly important category in that it corresponds to the category of service as an output of the economy at the social system level. It seems close to the need-achievement which McClelland and his associates have studied so intensively.

The last schematically peripheral interchange system is that of the *grounding of instrumental rationality,* between *L* and *A*. We consider *commitment to rationality* as a factor output from cultural to organic system— for example, controls over emotions. The reciprocal input to the culture, corresponding to goods in the social system paradigm is the *definition of instrumental opportunities,* with their clear dependence on capacities of the organism. The intelligence interchanges, then, corresponding to the monetary interchanges in the societal labor-consumption system, are *criteria for adaptive success* (corresponding to wages) and *definitions of incentives to learn* (corresponding to consumer spending).

We have held that the diagonal interchange systems should be placed at the *code* level in the analysis of symbolic systems, rather than, to use a term from linguistics, that of message. In this sense they are integrative in significance. The *L–G* case seems to be the easier to define in terms of the appropriateness of the categories. The higher-level, "internal" pair we interpret as cases of definition of the situation, on the one hand *moral standards,* from *L* to *G,* and on the other, *acceptance of moral responsibility,* from *G* to *L*. The lower-level, "controlled" categories are *acceptance of obligations of conscience* and *definitions of duty*. These last two, which involve performance capacity, define more particular duties and obligations.

We generalize from the social system paradigm that the *I–A* interchange system has primarily allocative functions. Since the integrative medium is affect, we suggest that the output of this medium to *A* consists in *standards for the allocation of affect,* and the input of affect to *I* is *affective justifications for distribution of intelligence*. The corresponding transfers of intelligence consist in *cognitive appraisals of membership situation* and the setting of *priorities for allocation of loyalties*.

Figure 3 presents the generalized media in terms of the relations between the code and message components, and the significance of the latter as sanctions controlling both factors essential to the various functional subsystems and product outputs from these subsystems. The rows are arranged from top to bottom according to the hierarchy of control, each row designating one of the four media. The columns designate components into which each medium needs to be broken down if some of the basic conditions of its mediating interaction are to be understood. As in the social system case, it is necessary to distinguish two components of the code aspect of each medium, namely the relevant value principle, which is the pattern-maintenance component not directly involved in interchange processes, and the coordinative standard, which regulates the diagonal interchanges (as represented in Figure 1).

Components of Media and Interchange Reciprocals / Media in ... of Control	Codes		Messages	
	Value Principle	Coordination Standard	Factors Controlled (Source)	Products Controlled (Destination)
L — Definition of the Situation	*univ diff* — *Wertrationalität* "Constitutive Rationality"	*qual neut* — Moral Authority	Criteria for Adaptive Success *A* / Cathexis of Moral Codes *I*	Incentive to Learn *A* / Acceptance for Inclusion *I*
I — Affect	*qual aff* — Institutionalization (Moral Rationality)	*diff part* — Harmony (Confucian Sense) or "Love" (Christian Sense)	Moral Sanction of Association *L* / Cathexis of Objects *G*	Moral Definition of Justice *L* / Recognition of Achievement *G*
G — Performance Capacity	*part spec* — *Zweckrationalität* "Practicality"	*perf aff* — Success	Affective Response *I* / Control of Performance Capacity *A*	Identification in Collectivity *I* / Allocation of Capacities *A*
A — Intelligence	*perf neut* — Cognitive Rationality	*univ spec* — Cognitive Validity	Goal Definitions *G* / Commitment to Rationality *L*	Motivational Energy to Perform *G* / Definition of Instrumental Opportunities *L*

Figure 3. The media as sanctions. The pattern variable components, designated by abbreviations in the code columns, are: universalism—particularism, specificity—diffuseness, performance—quality, and affectivity—affective neutrality

The value principles for the different media are differentiated variants of the general pattern of rationality. It seems to me that Weber's famous concept pair *Wertrationalität* (translated as "constitutive rationality") and *Zweckrationalität* (translated as "practicality") should be placed in the L and G boxes respectively of the left-hand column. (It may be said that Weber was in some respects primarily a theorist of the L–G relationship, whereas Durkheim concentrated on the I–A relationship.) *Cognitive rationality* in relation to intelligence as a medium seems to fit the A cell of this column. For the I cell it was tempting to move the concept solidarity from the social system paradigm, but Lidz's suggestion of *institutionalization* (moral rationality) is more appropriate. This is a form of rationality in the sense that consistency between value commitments and beliefs on the one hand, and practice in going social systems on the other, is a central value.

The integrative column, labeled "coordination standard," is clearly related to the value principles. In the *L* cell the obvious entry is *moral authority* in Durkheim's sense, as grounding in social solidarity. In the integrative cell, perhaps the concept of *harmony* somewhat in the Confucian sense is appropriate, though some usages of the term *love* would fit. For the *G* cell, I have taken the concept *success* from the social system paradigm. I have not felt easy with its usage there and the individual performance emphasis of general action fits it better. Finally, the standard spelling out the value of cognitive rationality is *cognitive validity*.

The pattern variable components of the two code columns are taken from the paradigm presented in my article, "Pattern Variables Revisited." Briefly, the pattern variable components for the value principle column represent the adaptive subset of that paradigm, and those of the coordination standard column represent the integrative subset.

The other two columns are virtually self-explanatory. They arrange the input and output categories from Figure 2, except those of the diagonal interchanges, as factors and products of the functional processes of the subsystems of reference, indicating also their sources and destinations.

The reader who wishes to secure a clear understanding of this Appendix will undoubtedly find it helpful to compare it carefully with the Technical Note of my article on power.

2.
Toward a Macrosociology

Amitai Etzioni

Amitai Etzioni was born in Köln, West Germany, in 1929 and was educated at Hebrew University (B.A., M.A.) and the University of California at Berkeley (Ph.D.). He is chairman of the department of sociology at Columbia University, and a member of its Institute of War and Peace Studies. His major books are A Comparative Analysis of Complex Organizations *(1961),* Political Unification *(1965), and* The Active Society: A Theory of Societal and Political Processes *(1968). Professor Etzioni is the director of the Center for Policy Research and an associate director of the Bureau of Applied Social Research.*

A macrosociology is needed both on theoretical and on pragmatic grounds. I suggest that, theoretically, societies and polities have emergent properties, which it is fruitful to treat as the subject of a distinct subtheory, macrosociology. Such a theory is not to replace general theory, which deals with the universal properties of all social units, from the dyad to the world community, e.g. the level of integration. Both macro- and microsociology are additional tiers sharing this base, one dealing with the particular properties of macrounits (such as nations, classes), the other with properties of microunits (such as family, work teams, friendship groups). While sociological theory holds general, micro- and macrosubtheories, history is a macroscopic process.[1]

From a pragmatic viewpoint, a disciplined study of the substantive problems of society—such as modernization, democratization, change of status

For additional discussion, see Amitai Etzioni, *The Active Society: A Theory of Societal and Political Processes* (New York: Free Press, 1968). This article was written during my fellowship at the Center for Advanced Study in the Behavioral Sciences. I am indebted to Sarajane Heidt, Fred Dubow, and Miriam Gallaher for comments on earlier drafts. In conducting this work, I also benefited from a grant from the National Science Foundation, No. GS-1475. A different version of the second part of this article was published in *The American Journal of Sociology*, vol. 73 (September, 1967).
1. We usually do not refer to the history of microunits. There is a distinct term for the genetic study of persons or families (genealogies); sometimes this is referred to as life history or family history, but when the term "history" is used without additional characterization, it evokes a macrodynamic perspective.

relations among collectivities, societal reallocation of wealth, and political integration of previously autonomous units—cannot be much advanced without a systematic analysis of macroscopic factors.

The most basic distinction here, for reasons that will become evident below, is between guided and ongoing change. The higher the ratio of guided change over ongoing change, the greater the danger that instrumentality might rebel against the primacy of societal goals, and that collectivities whose vested interests rest in the realm of instruments might divert societal guidance to serve their goals. Hence, as has often been pointed out but has never been made the cornerstone of a sociological theory, the key problem of guided change is the development of more effective methods of societal guidance that will at the same time ensure the primacy of societal goals.

A Macrosociological Perspective

Macrosociology Defined

We can support the suggestion that macroscopic (social) units have emergent properties, above and beyond those of microscopic (social) units and beyond universal (social) properties, on tentative pragmatic grounds: Let us test this conception and see if it will enable us to gain some insight into substantive societal problems. We can further support the suggestion on empirical logical grounds, namely that macroscopic emergent properties account for a significant part of the variance of sociological data: explanation of those data cannot be reduced without a significant residue (that is, without unaccounted variance) to propositions drawing only on microscopic or universal properties. Finally, we can support the suggestion on mere logical grounds: a three-level referent structure—of units, subunits, and supraunits—can be applied at any level of analysis (such as roles, families, neighborhoods). There is in principle no reason why we cannot apply the same structure to societies, subsocieties, and suprasocieties. Thus, this differentiation is a private case of a universe of formal, hierarchical relations.

Whatever track we follow, the units of analysis must be substantively designated. In doing so we adhere to a functional approach in that acts are viewed as macroscopic if their consequences are macroscopic, that is, if they affect the properties of macroscopic units. These units are societies, their combinations, and their subunits. An act, let us say a peasant uprising, is in itself neither micro- nor macroscopic; its consequences might be both microscopic (a few families were destroyed) and macroscopic (a change of political institutions and stratification was forced). The same act might thus be studied from both viewpoints. However, because of the hierarchical

nature of the concepts, while acts that have macroscopic consequences always also have microscopic ones, those with microscopic consequences may or may not have macroscopic ones. (Some cutoff point in time is always to be specified because in the long run there might be consequences to consequences that would move from the microscopic to the macroscopic level.) Macroscopic theory deals with the acts that have macroscopic consequences and with the relations of these consequences to each other, not exploring their microscopic effects as long as they, in turn, do not have macroconsequences within the period specified.

Two Kinds of Reductionism

Two kinds of reductionism are prevalent in the social sciences. One reduces social or political analysis to the level of a universal theory of action or to psychology. This reductionism in effect denies both sociology and political science as distinct theoretical disciplines. It is widely embraced by philosophers and psychologists. Sociologists and political scientists naturally tend to profess to realize that their disciplines require a distinct theory, but their actual analyses are often psychological. This is particularly common in studies that use survey data about attitudes of individuals, such as studies of political sociology that deal only with aggregate data about various categories of voters, explaining their voting by attitudes they hold (for example, on a conservatism-liberalism scale) or personality variables (such as degree of authoritarianism). The explanatory processes are clearly intrapersonal. For instance, an individual who holds one attitude will tend to hold others that are consonant because dissonant attitudes cause a psychic cost or pain; or, aggressive attitudes toward foreigners fulfill a superego need. While various procedures for transition from such data to social analysis and suggestions for combination of such data with global data about the social units themselves have been advanced,[2] most studies of this particular tradition do not carry out such analysis.

The second kind of reductionism is to microsociology, on the ground that micro- and macrosociological theories are isometric, and therefore that studying small groups will provide all the theoretical statements needed to understand relations among macroscopic variables (thus, studies of cohesion of small groups are used to explain class solidarity), or else the existence of macroscopic emergent properties is *a priori* denied. The reductionism from macrosociology to microsociology, which has already been forcefully called to our attention,[3] is much less widely recognized by the

2. Paul F. Lazarsfeld and Herbert Menzel, "On the Relation Between Individual and Collective Properties," in Amitai Etzioni, ed., *Complex Organizations: A Sociological Reader* (New York: Holt, 1969), pp. 499-516.
3. C. Wright Mills, *The Sociological Imagination* (New York: Grove Press, 1959). Barrington Moore, Jr., *Political Power and Social Theory* (Cambridge: Harvard University Press, 1958), pp. 111-159. Sheldon Wolin, *Politics and Vision* (Boston: Little, 1960), pp. 429-434.

majority of sociologists and political scientists who work with empirical data than is psychological reductionism. Here, it is not only a matter of a threshold that is disregarded in actual research, but one whose very claim is questioned.[4]

Substantive Assumptions

Those who are engaged in macrotheory tend to follow one of two major approaches as to what substantive assumptions are to be made about the nature of macroscopic units, their properties, and their dynamics. We suggest a combination of the two approaches, and add a third ingredient. Before exploring these approaches, we briefly note the criteria used for differentiation among them.

We are interested in developing a theory for macroscopic social change, which is a formal concept for sociopolitical (or societal) history. Societal change, obviously, is affected both by factors which the participants control and by those beyond their control, a mix of guided and ongoing change. The approaches under discussion differ in the assumptions they make about the ratio of one kind of change as against the other. The collectivistic theories see chiefly ongoing changes; voluntaristic ones focus on guided changes. The collectivistic view of society—as an actor oriented toward himself—is rather passive; the voluntaristic is hyperactive. A third approach, which we favor, balances these two approaches.

We are dealing here with analytic languages (or metatheories), each one of which is used to formulate several theories. As we are concerned only with exposing their most basic assumptions, no attempt is made to do justice to any specific theory or to assumptions concerning dimensions other than the one explored: their position toward societal change.

Sociologists are most familiar with collectivistic theories. Social system theories, functionalist models, anthropological-cultural theories of configuration as well as phenomenological ones are collectivistic and basically passive. They do not recognize systematically a seat of action on the macroscopic, societal level. Scanning major theoretical writings of these traditions shows that concepts such as goals, knowledge, decision-making, and strategies—all typical concepts needed to characterize an actor who guides a change process—are absent or appear only infrequently and mainly in relation to microscopic units and not macroscopic ones. The typical society under study is treated as though it had no government, and political processes are described as ongoing.

The propositions associated with the concept of differentiation are representative of many other theorems that could be utilized as an example. The concept is increasingly used over recent years by Parsons, Smelser, Eisen-

4. Raymond W. Mack and Richard C. Snyder, "Approaches to the Study of Conflict: Introduction by the Editors," *Journal of Conflict Resolution*, 1 (1957), 107-108.

stadt, and others [5] to relate societal change to functional-structural analysis. The core image, which is typical of the collectivistic approach, is taken from biology, where we find simple units that split into two or more, each one more specialized than the previous. All the functions carried out by the simple unit are also carried out by the differentiated ones, except that now each of the functions has a substructure of its own, a differentiated unit. Most biological studies do not ask what propels the transition, or to what degree the transition may be guided by a unit other than units which are being differentiated. Those who did raise these questions in biology dealt with the function of codes in guiding the transition from a simple to a differentiated unit. The code, which is found in the undifferentiated unit, holds in an abstract form (as an information pattern or model) a full differentiated design of the future unit toward which the simple unit is to evolve. Research focuses on what the code specifically contains and how its messages are transmitted to the evolving unit.[6] In sociology so far, by and large the question which the conception of a code answers for biology— that is, what guides differentiation—has not been raised. The patterns of societal differentiation and its consequences are studied, but not its guidance mechanism.[7] In other words, the process is viewed as ongoing and the unit merely as subject to it, as passive.

The voluntaristic approach is almost unknown in contemporary sociology. On the other hand, voluntarism was quite influential in political science until recently, especially in the study of international relations between the two world wars and in studies of administration or formal organizations.[8] It is at the heart of general system theories, cybernetics, and

5. Talcott Parsons, "Some Consideration on the Theory of Social Change," *Rural Sociology,* 26 (1961), pp. 219-239. Talcott Parsons and Robert Bales, eds., *Family, Socialization, and Interaction Process* (New York: Free Press, 1953), p. 134ff. Neil Smelser, *Social Change in the Industrial Revolution* (Chicago: University of Chicago Press, 1959), chaps. 8-10. Morris Zelditch, Jr., "Role Differentiation in the Nuclear Family: A Comparative Study," in Parsons and Bales, pp. 307-351. Studies of favorable environmental conditions are not to be confused with those of guidance mechanisms. These are inputs and not system qualities by which the reaction of the system is explained. Most of these are ad hoc, for example those which see an explanatory factor in the contact of whites with a non-white civilization.

6. F. S. Grodius, *Control, Theory, and Biological Mysteries* (New York: Columbia University Press, 1963). For results of experiments with animals in which the brain was dissociated from the embryo and the effects of such dissociation on the embryo's development, see Heinz-Joachim Pohley, *Roux'Archiv für Entwicklungsmechanik,* 153 (1961), 443-458.

7. For an attempt to analyze differentiation from this viewpoint, see Amitai Etzioni, "The Function Differentiations of Elites in the Kibbutz," *American Journal of Sociology,* 64 (1959), 476-487, and "The Epigenesis of Political Communities at the International Level," *American Journal of Sociology,* 68 (1963), 407-421. Both are included in the author's *Studies in Social Change* (New York: Holt, 1966).

8. Among the contemporary writers along this line are those who believe that changes in the United Nations charter, especially weighted voting, would significantly enhance world government, and that direct election to a European Parliament would lead to the United States of Europe. See Leland M. Goodrich, *United Nations* (New

communication theories. The basic assumption of this approach, often implicit, is that there is a central unit that is able to guide the other member units of the particular system and more or less control them in accordance with its will. The voluntaristic theories divide sharply according to their assumptions about the nature of this will, or central unity, and its links to the other units. Some assume a rationalistic model (the subject units are reasonable), others an irrational one (the subject units are emotionally committed), but all share a view of a highly active guiding mechanism.

For our purposes, one rationalistic-voluntaristic model is of particular interest for reasons that will become evident below, namely the cybernetic model. The source of the model, it is important to realize, is the mechanical direction of machines, that is, the development of machines that take over control functions the way lower-order supervised machines took over earlier performance ("work") functions. The cybernetic model includes decision-making centers, and a communication network that carries the messages from the center to the units under supervision and feedback messages from the units to the center. The underlying assumption of the model, similar to that of the functionalistic full-integration model, is that in principle the center can guide the system. Disturbances such as overloading of the decision-making center are recognized; various solutions are worked out assessing priorities to messages. Similarly, gaps in the communication networks might appear, let us say, due to poor relay, and correction can be provided (for example, by including redundant lines).

When this model is applied to societal analysis, the government is viewed as the cybernatorial overlayer of society which provides it with a decision-making center, a communication network to member units, and feedback mechanisms. One of the most distinguished and influential political scientists of this generation, Karl W. Deutsch, has developed this application of the cybernatorial model.[9]

The irrational-voluntaristic model is held mainly by psychoanalysts who write about societies, some psychologists, and a few anthropologists.[10] The tendency is to view society as man writ large, each society interacting with other societies basically the way one individual interacts with others. For instance, the United States and the Soviet Union misunderstand each other,

York: Crowell, 1959). Eric Stein, "The European Parliamentary Assembly," *International Organization,* 13 (1959), 233-254. J. B. Scott, *Law, the State, and the International Community* (New York: Columbia University Press, 1939). For a more sophisticated approach, see Elmore Jackson, *Meeting of Minds* (New York: McGraw, 1952). Most writings in the "conflict resolution" and "problem solving" traditions are voluntaristic, often to a high degree.

9. *The Nerves of Government* (New York: Free Press, 1963).

10. Nathan Leites, "Psycho-Cultural Hypotheses about Political Acts," *World Politics,* 10 (1958), 102-119. Kenneth N. Waltz, *Man, the State, and War* (New York: Columbia University Press, 1959). For a discussion of a suggestion to consider the state as a person, see James M. Buchanan, "The Pure Theory of Government Finance," *Journal of Political Economy,* 57 (1949), 496-505.

which leads to frustration, which generates aggression, and so forth. Improved communication between the sides is expected to increase their reality-testing and cooperation. Charles E. Osgood, a former president of the American Psychological Association, is one of the best known representatives of this approach.[11] While this conception is diametrically opposed to the rationalistic approach in terms of its substantive assumptions about the mechanisms at work, which here are subconscious and emotional, the parallelism exists in that this voluntarism, too, views society as acting basically as a monolithic unit, being able to change, for instance, from a hostile to a cooperative mood as if it had one will.[12]

All the voluntaristic approaches see one main seat of action, and in principle recognize no limitations to "man's"—that is, society's—capacity to change. In that sense all these theories are hyperactive, because they do not include as an integral part variables that can account for the forces that resist change, that block or distort implementation of the will.

Toward a Synthetic Approach

We suggest that a synthesis of the collectivistic approach, which in effect focuses upon *ongoing* processes and change, and a voluntaristic-cybernatorial approach, largely concerned with *guided* processes and change, would provide for a more balanced theory of societal change, especially of modern societies in which both kinds of change are prevalent. It also balances the nonrational focus of the collectivistic approach, which tends to stress the study of societal ties of sentiments, values, and institutions with the rationalistic perspective cybernetics often exhibits, which pays more attention to knowledge and organizations. A third major element that both approaches tend to neglect needs to be added, namely a conception and theory of power. By power we mean a relational attribute which indicates the capacity of one unit to overcome the resistance of the other(s).[13]

The central position of power for our theory is manifest in our seeing in each society (and in each societal unit) an internal struggle between the guidance mechanisms and the passive elements, and not just an external, interunit struggle. The outcome of this struggle significantly determines the capacity of a societal unit to act upon itself (to effect its own change) as

11. *An Alternative to War or Surrender* (Urbana: University of Illinois Press, 1962). For additional discussion, see Amitai Etzioni, "The Kennedy Experiment," *The Western Political Quarterly,* 20 (June, 1967), 361-380.
12. Voluntarists, who face the question of the nature of the actor of the differing units of analysis, maintain their monolithic assumption by assuming a close relationship among the units, for instance between the president (or power élite) and public opinion. See, for instance, Osgood, *War or Surrender.*
13. Much has been written about the difficulties of defining power. To go into all the objections here would require more space than this entire article. We present our reasons for holding that the above definition is operational in detail in *The Active Society,* pp. 314-317.

well as to act externally and hence also to influence the patterns of the supraunit of which it is a part. Societies as supraunits, it is assumed, are composed of units having at least some cybernatorial capacities and power, as well as having, in principle, some such capacities and power of their own, on the supraunit level.

The collectivistic approach sees the members of the collectivity, configuration, or system as closely tied to each other. While some leeway or play is recognized, units cannot, basically, be moved around or changed unless other units change more or less simultaneously. If they do not, various pathologies are expected, described in such concepts as social lag and imbalance. And, as no guidance center is assumed—a center whose assumption would entail also assuming moveable and changeable, less "tied" units —the question of the source of the capacity to transform the units or the ties does not arise. Power has at best a marginal theoretical status. As a matter of fact, most collectivistic theories do not include the concept of power at all, while in others it is tacked on post hoc.

The voluntaristic-cybernatorial model stresses the importance of communication and information and the manipulation of symbols; largely excludes power other than that involved in manipulation of symbols; and does not, in principle, expect resistance of the units. It focuses on the problems of generating well-calculated messages, of relaying the messages from the center to the units, and of providing reliable feedbacks, but once the messages reach the performing units, no power is assumed necessary to overcome their resistance to the message. If the feedback indicates that the message did not trigger the expected action, the assumption is that the message was inappropriate (and the effective center is expected to revise it) or was distorted on its way because of communication difficulties, not that the message was appropriate and was "read" loudly and clearly, but was not backed up by enough power. Symbols, changes in patterns of information or meaning are transmitted, not power; [14] it is a matter of the nerves, not the muscles, of government.[15]

Rather than characterizing our approach as one of the collectivistic-voluntaristic power analysis, we shall refer to it as a theory of societal guidance ("sociobernetics" would be more colorful but less accurate, and linguistically impure).[16]

While the study of societal guidance draws on both the collectivistic and the voluntaristic approaches, it differs significantly on one major dimension from both: it does not assume that the societal unit it deals with is a monolithic or highly integrated unit. Authors of both traditions have argued that this assumption is just a heuristic device, a standard against which reality

14. Symbols are viewed as cognitive, not expressive, and hence have no motivational power.
15. Deutsch, *Nerves of Government,* p. ix.
16. For the main presentation, see *The Active Society.*

can be measured, and not an assumption about the nature of reality itself. However, even for those who remember that they are dealing only with a heuristic device, these models introduce the mistaken perspective that deviations from the standard are pathological, limited, and correctable; and they provide no model for the study of low integration or low compliance situations, which are abundant. We assume no particular relationship between the societal actors under study. The actors might relate to each other completely externally without any shared bonds, a situation approximated by nations in a state of all-out war. Or the actors might be related by complementary or shared interests, which bind them with ties that are limited to the transactions themselves and which are inherently unstable, because changes in the environment or in the actors that will change the interests concerned will lead to an abandonment of the relationship. Finally, the actors might be bound by shared values and institutionalized norms, which bind in a more generalized and stable way because commitments are non-rational and may have a moral force.

Relations might be classified accordingly as coercive, utilitarian, or normative. It should be stressed that while there are symbolic elements in all three kinds of relationships (for example, threats to use force play an important role in coercion), and one, the normative, is a relationship where the primary link is symbolic, the core of the other two relationships is non-symbolic. Utilitarian relationships draw heavily on interests and material objects, and besides the symbolic relation to the object (as has been stressed in the discussion of the institution of property), the nature and the distribution of the objects themselves are of much importance. The same holds for means of violence as the basis of coercive relations; too much has been made by contemporary sociologists of the symbolic element of legitimation in the concept of authority and too little of the other component, the actual capacity to use force.

We have argued elsewhere that these three kinds of relationships are analytically exhaustive, that every concrete relationship can be analytically classified in terms of various combinations of these three basic ones. The threefold conception of bases of societal order seems to answer the criticism raised by Dahrendorf and others on the symbolistic and non-conflict nature of prevailing sociological theory.[17] It should be noted that each of these relationships can be either horizontal or hierarchical—that is, a relationship either of actors having similar values, interests, or force, or of actors that are subject to an actor who has power of one kind or another over them. All the members of a cohesive group are committed to each other, but the commitments of leaders and followers are asymmetric. Exchange between roughly equal units, and between those which are not, is basically different. This difference between hierarchical and horizontal interactions, neglected

---

17. Ralf Dahrendorf, "Out of Utopia," *American Journal of Sociology*, 64 (1958), 115-127; Lewis Coser, *The Functions of Social Conflict* (New York: Free Press, 1964), pp. 20-26.

in many traditional as well as more recent writings, is central to the present approach.

System, Structure, and Transformability

Over the last decades the term *system* has been applied increasingly loosely, to such a degree that it has lost an essential quality of a concept, the ability to differentiate one referent from another. There is no relationship which has not been at one point or another directly or by implication characterized as a social system, including the relationships between the drivers of cars on the freeway. The essence of the concept as used in sociology, it seems, is collectivistic; no relationship makes a system unless there are nontrivial feedback effects among the members. If half of the American housewives were to have a cup of change-of-pace tea instead of another cup of coffee, the Brazilian economy would be damaged. This does not make these distinguished ladies and the Brazilian coffee plantations one system, however, because what happens to the Brazilian economy will not have significant feedback effects on the American housewives.

We see three kinds of relations: *situations* in which there are interunit relations but not linked by feedback loops; *systems* which assume nontrivial interdependence among the member units; and *communities* which assume a significant integrative supraunit capacity. Each of these three concepts covers a sector of a closeness-of-interaction continuum, and hence within each sector one might refer to more or less "tight" relationships (such as more versus less integrated units).

A system might be a relatively concrete concept referring to relations among units of action—tribes, nations, organized classes—or a relatively abstract one referring to relations among variables. Systems of either kind have boundaries which should not be confused with their structures. Boundaries determine which unit or variable is a member and which is not; structures characterize the specific pattern of relationship among the members. Boundaries change much less frequently than structures; the same system may have, over time, many structures.

Societal units whose structure includes an overlayer can partially guide the change of their nonsocietal situation, their relations to other actors, and their own internal structure. Relatively passive actors are those who react to environmental changes more than they introduce changes in their environment; they adapt by changing their internal makeup but the nature of their adaptation is itself often affected by external factors, including more active societal units. More active units are more able to initiate change both in themselves and in their environments, in accordance with their preferences.

Second, relatively passive units tend to be ultra stable, in the sense that when challenged they tend to introduce variants of the existing structure, attempting to maintain the same basic institutional "solution." More active

units have a self-transforming capacity: they can create on the cybernatorial level a map of a not yet existing future-system, and guide their self-change toward the realization of a new structure, which is not a variation of the existing one but a basically new pattern. This capacity allows them (a) to adapt successfully to a much larger variety of environmental changes, (b) to participate much more actively in changing the environment, and (c) to actualize more of their own values. The study of the conditions under which the capacity for self-transformation increases and of the elements involved is an integral part of any theory of societal guidance; it systematically ties the study of encompassing societal changes, planned and unplanned, to structural-functional analysis.

The tension between ongoing processes and guided ones is central to the study of societal guidance. To realize his values, an actor seeks to guide processes; but in doing so he faces the constraining effects of other actors in the situation, his system or community ties to others, and the institutionalized consequences of both his and their earlier actions. He faces other factors, too, such as conditions of the nonsocial environment, but these are not the focus of the present study.

The degree to which an actor is active depends on his cybernatorial capacities, his power, and his consensus formation capacity. Each of these factors has both an internal and an external dimension: how much he knows about himself and about others, how much he can mobilize power over members *and* over nonmembers, and to what degree he can gain the support of subunits and of external units. Since for many purposes it is useful to refer to both cybernatorial and power capacities together, we shall refer to them jointly as the actor's ability to control. When his skill in building consensus is also taken into account, we refer to his ability to guide. As we grant to the subunits and other units in principle the same capacities as to the actor under study, his capacity to be active is obviously not optimized by maximizing his control capacities but by optimizing the combination of control and consensus formation—that is, by maximizing the capacity of his guidance mechanisms.

We turn now to exploring these factors in some detail. Our approach is at first analytic, in that each factor is explored as if all the others were held constant; in the following section we shall take a more synthesizing and historical view of actors that are becoming more active generally, on all major dimensions. In the analytic section we briefly compare societies and subsocieties. (Suprasocieties will not be discussed here.) The societies we focus on are political—that is, encapsulated in a state which serves as their organizational tool for both control and consensus formation. Similarly, the subsocietal actors are collectivities that have organizational arms, such as working classes with their labor parties and unions. Nonorganized collectivities are treated mainly for comparative purposes.

The purpose of the following discussion is merely to illustrate the kind

of factors our theory focuses on, and not to provide here a set of propositions (not to mention data) in support of the theory. The statements, however, have the basic structure of propositions; each proposes that if all other conditions were equal, a change of the specific variable discussed would correlate in the way specified with the active capacity of the unit under study.

Control Factors

Cybernatorial Capacities

Knowledge input. Societal units differ in their capacity to collect, process, and use information. This holds not only for corporations that compete over a market, but also for political parties (Kennedy is believed to have used social sciences more effectively than Nixon in the 1960 campaign), federal agencies (the Air Force is thought to be superior in this respect to the Navy and the Army), and civic organizations (the NAACP's capacity to use information increased between 1955 and 1965).

We suggest that the input of knowledge into a societal unit follows the same basic patterns other inputs do; that is, it might be blocked (and hence partially or completely lost for action purposes) at each stage of the process. Societal units have varying facilities for collecting information (raw material input). This capacity seems to be associated with economic affluence but not in a one-to-one relationship. If we were to order countries (or other societal units) by their per capita income and then score their information collection capacity, say in terms of expenditure on research, we would expect the most affluent units to have much higher capacity than the next affluent ones, and all the other units would have few such capacities. Three powerful federal agencies in the United States spent more of the federal research and development (R & D) funds than the other 34 agencies together. Three affluent states out of 50 gain more than 50 percent of these R & D funds.[18] Societal units that spend highly on information spent more in the last generation than in all previous generations combined. In short, patterns of interunit distribution of information seem significantly more inegalitarian than are those of distribution of economic assets.

The ratio of investment in collecting over processing information is an indicator of the sophistication of the cybernatorial overlayer and the knowledge-strategy to which the particular unit subscribes. The United States and Great Britain, it seems, tend to invest relatively highly in collection; France,

18. Based on the preliminary figure for 1962–1963. U.S. Bureau of the Census, *Statistical Abstracts of the U.S.,* 1965, *New York Times,* October 25, 1964, p. 49; and *Christian Science Monitor* (Boston), December 12, 1964.

at least until recently, has stressed relatively more processing.[19] A societal unit that emphasizes disproportionally the collection of information will, we expect, have a fragmented view of itself and its environment; it will have many bits but no picture, like a survey study before tabulation. Such processing will tend to be associated with drifting (or passivity) as information that is not sufficiently processed is in effect not available for active societal guidance.

On the other hand, a unit that overemphasizes processing is expected to have an unempirical view of itself and its environment, because it will tend to draw more conclusions from the available information than are warranted; it is similar to acting on the basis of a poorly validated theory. Thus, overprocessing is expected to be associated with hyperactivity, as the actor assumes he knows more than he does. Master plans used to guide economic development are typically hyperactive in their assumptions. Finally, societal units whose collection and processing are relatively balanced (not in absolute amounts but in terms of intrinsic needs of the guidance mechanisms) are expected to have comparatively more effective controlling overlayers, all other things being equal, and to be active without being hyperactive.

Information that has been processed might still be wasted as far as the societal unit is concerned if it is not systematically introduced into the unit's decision-making and implementation overlayer [20] where the main societal consumption of information takes place. Two major variables seem useful for characterizing the different arrangements societal units have for interaction between the knowledge-producing and the decision-making units; one concerns the relative degree of autonomy of production, the other, the effectiveness of communications of the product. It is widely believed that structural differentiation between the producers and consumers of information is necessary; fusion of the two kinds of units—for instance, in the management of a corporation—is viewed as dysfunctional both for production of knowledge and for decision-making. For societal units whose knowledge and decision-making units are differentiated, various modes and forms of articulation and communication exist whose relative effectiveness remains to be explored. Here we can touch on only one aspect of this intricate subject.

The controlling overlayer itself has layers upon layers; processing is superimposed on the collecting of information, both in the logical sense that the one presupposes the other, and in the structural sense that those engaged in processing have higher ranks and more power to mold the societal input

19. This is one meaning that is implied when the Anglo-Saxon tradition is characterized as pragmatic and the French as rationalistic. For some evidence, related to differences in economic planning, see Andrew Shonfield, *Modern Capitalism: The Changing Balance of Public and Private Power* (New York: Oxford University Press, 1965), pp. 151-175.

20. George C. Homans, *The Human Group* (New York: Harcourt, 1950), pp. 369-414.

of knowledge than those who collect information.[21] Differences in the internal *structure* of the control overlayer affect the total action capacity of societal units. The division between those who work within a given knowledge framework and those who seek to transform it, and the structural relations between them, seem to be of much cybernatorial importance. Consumption and, to a degree, processing of knowledge are inevitably in part political processes. That is, which part of the available knowledge is used and what conclusions are reached on the basis of the knowledge is in part determined by political factors. These include considerations of the knowledge-producers in terms of the internal politics of the organizations in which knowledge is processed, their affiliations with political groupings in the society at large, and the differential absorption by various political actors of the knowledge produced, according to its political rather than its intrinsic value. The core of the politicization of knowledge lies not in deliberate or subconscious slanting of facts but in the interpretive and judgmental elements most items of knowledge include. It is not, as some students of administration would have it, that knowledge-units produce information and the political decision-making elites add the judgment. The producers of knowledge play an active role in formulating the judgments.

Within this context, one issue is of special significance for the study of societal guidance: the effect of the relative investments in two sections of the cybernatorial overlayer, namely, transforming versus stable knowledge production. Transforming knowledge rechecks and potentially challenges the basic assumptions of a system. Stable knowledge elaborates and respecifies, even revises, secondary assumptions within the framework of a basic set which is taken for granted. Most decision-making élites most of the time seem to prefer stable over transforming knowledge production, to seek closure on basic knowledge assumptions precisely because they cannot be selected and reviewed on wholly empirical grounds. Hence, once consensus has been reached on the basic assumptions of a worldview, a self-view, a view of others, strategic doctrine, and the like, it is expensive politically, economically, and psychologically for the élites to transform these assumptions. Therefore they tend to become tabooed assumptions, and knowledge production tends to become limited to specifics within the limits of the assumptions. At the same time, the ability to transform basic perspectives is sharply reduced and with it the capacity for societal self-transformation. The societal units survive as long as the range of tolerance of their knowledge and societal pattern allows for sufficient adaptation to environmental changes, but such adaptation tends to become increasingly costly.

More active units have supralayers that can be activated to review and transform tabooed assumptions. A comparison of corporations that have

21. Roger Hilsman, *Strategic Intelligence and National Decisions* (New York: Free Press, 1956).

shifted to a new line of products, restructured their internal organization, and found new markets when their old markets were gradually lost, with those whose sales and profits declined or "died" because of lack of innovations, suggests that transforming corporations maintained R & D units which were not only exempt from the tabooed assumptions but were also, among other things, expected sporadically to review these assumptions. That is, part of their institutionalized role was to engage in search behavior precisely where the decision-making élites would otherwise settle for satisfying solutions.[22]

The societal parallel of this cybernatorial arrangement is not difficult to see. The intellectual community acts as one major societal R & D unit, as a critical examiner of tabooed assumptions. Under what economic, political, and sociological conditions it can fulfill this function and what, if any, functional alternatives exist, are questions social scientists have much feeling about—but there is surprisingly little systematic research.[23]

These questions can be studied for any society and any societal units. As the input of knowledge becomes a major *guided* societal activity (more than 75 percent of expenditure of the R & D funds is federal), as the ratio of this input as compared to other societal inputs is increasing, both in relative expenditure and in sociopolitical importance, the macrosociology of knowledge becomes an unavoidable part of studies of societal change. Typically, earlier studies of a society stressed the size of its population, territory, and GNP; the present approach adds the number of Ph.D.'s a society turns out, the size of its professional manpower, and its investment in research and development as indicators of a major societal variable. Sociology of knowledge traditionally focused on the social conditions under which true statements are made;[24] macrosociology of knowledge focuses on the societal conditions under which knowledge for societal purposes is produced and consumed, opening a whole new field of inquiry for the study of societies.[25]

Societal Decision-Making

The head of the societal control overlayer are decision-making élites—the sociopolitical equivalent of the electronic center. The élites choose between alternative policies, issue signals to the performing units (guide the underlayer), and respond to feedback information. (The body of the overlayer

---

22. Herbert A. Simon, "A Behavioral Model of Rational Choice," *Quarterly Journal of Economics,* 69, 104-114.
23. For one of the few sociological studies, see Lewis Coser, *Men of Ideas* (New York: Free Press, 1965).
24. For an overview of this sociology of knowledge, see Robert K. Merton, *Social Theory and Social Structure,* rev. ed. (New York: Free Press, 1957), pp. 456-488.
25. For studies in this field so far conducted almost exclusively by nonsociologists, see Viscount Hailsham, Q.C., *Science and Politics* (London: Faber and Faber, 1963) and Don K. Price, *The Scientific Estate* (Cambridge, Mass.: Belknap, 1965).

is made up of communication networks which tie the élites to other member units and a power hierarchy.) Sociologists have studied élites by asking how closed or how open they are to members of various societal units, how dispersed control is among them, and how they relate to each other. But these are not cybernatorial considerations. They belong under the heading of consensus-formation (for example, closed and completely open élites are believed less effective for consensus formation than relatively open ones) and the study of power relations (for example, hierarchy plus decentralization is believed more effective than monopolization of control by one élite or its fragmentation among several). Cybernatorial aspects of élites have been studied largely by nonsociologists and have not been systematically related to analysis.[26] The cybernatorial study of élites concerns the procedures used by the decision-making élites, the strategies employed, and the communication networks that lead from the élites to the performing units and back.

When élites engage in decision-making, they draw on an implicit or explicit societal theory as to what the relations among the units under control are like, and as to how much and by what means these can be guided by the élites.[27] The validity of these theories varies from élite to élite; the greater the validity, the more effective one would expect the decision-making to be, which in turn is positively associated with the degree to which a social unit is active. This proposition is not earthshaking, nor are many other ones concerning the conditions under which decision-making is effective. However, the inclusion in or omission from a societal theory of a set of propositions about effective decision-making is of much importance. It is indicative of a central position regarding the nature of society and of societal change.

In seeking to explain the action or change of a societal unit, most sociologists are more inclined to explore background conditions, from the level of economic resources the unit commands to the educational opportunities of élite members, than to study the decision-making procedures the élites follow. There is a widely held assumption that such background factors constitute the basic substructure which not only sets the main limits of variability of societal action and change (poor countries lack the capital needed to develop) but also specifies the main factors which determine what decisions will be made among whatever options are left open (because of the revolution of rising expectations, democratic élites cannot defer increase in consumption). Differences in decision-making procedures are considered either dependent variables or trivial. In comparison, societal guidance views the societal actors as having more autonomy. Background

26. Deutsch, *Nerves of Government;* Alfred Kuhn, *The Study of Society: A Unified Approach* (Homewood, Ill.: Irwin, 1963).
27. See seven essays in part one of Herbert C. Kelman, ed., *International Behavior: A Social-Psychological Analysis* (New York: Holt, 1965), pp. 43-334.

factors are viewed as setting a broad frame; the course followed within its limits is affected by cybernatorial factors, of which decision-making procedures are significant elements. For instance, an effective élite might defer consumption increase in a poor country, and thereby lead toward a stable development.

Actually many of the underdeveloped nations are not poor in resources nor overpopulated, but are poor in cybernatorial capacities: their élites are highly impotent. For instance, in 1930 Canada and Argentina had similar economic indicators.[28] Since then Canada has continued to develop, while Argentina remains underdeveloped. A typical background conditions approach would stress the presence of the Protestant element in the one country and its absence in the other, as well as the differences in the Catholic stock in the two countries (in Argentina it is more that of Southern Spain and Italy, in Canada that of the French). These differences are expected, à la Weber, to correlate with attitudes favorable to capitalism.

An élite study would add the difference between the responsive democratic government of Canada and the authoritarian leadership of Argentina. True, this difference in leadership is in part due to differences in societal structure; thus, for example, Canada would not "tolerate" a Perón. But unless one assumes a one-to-one relationship between background factors and élite conduct and assumes that élite conduct has no significant independent effect on background factors, the analysis of the nature of the élites has to be included as an integral part of a theory of societal processes. To highlight the importance of systematically including the study of élites, it suffices to contrast the development of each country under different governments (such as Argentina under Perón and Illia) following different decision-making procedures.

One typical decision which societal élites in charge of guided change often have to make, at what are relatively critical turning points, is between acceleration and deceleration of the processes of change they guide. When a societal change is initiated—whether it be collectivization of farms, federation, or desegregation—resistance tends to accumulate because existing patterns are backed up by vested interests which are often threatened by the changes. As a change advances, there is often at least one critical turning point at which resistance rises to a point where it endangers the control of the élites. The president thinks he might not be reelected, the government believes it might be overthrown, or a part of the country might secede. The decision the élites then face is between acceleration, in hope of overpowering the opposition and reaching a stage at which the support of those that will benefit from the new pattern will rise, or slowing down to give more time for the opposition to be worked out, circumvented, educated, or otherwise dealt with.

28. See El Desarrollo Economico de la Argentina, E-CN. 12-429-Add. 4 (1958), pp. 3-5.

Obviously the question is not which one procedure or strategy is in the abstract the more effective; the question is under what societal conditions one is more effective than the other *and* under what conditions an élite chooses the suitable as against the unsuitable strategy. In a comparative study of four cases we found two élites that accelerated and two that decelerated in face of a premature situation, where opposition was high and forces in support of the change weak. The accelerating élites lost control (in the United Arab Republic, Syria rebelled and seceded; the West Indian Federation was disbanded). The decelerating élites are still in control, though in one of the two cases (the Scandinavian system) the élite had to decelerate so much that the process of change (unification) came to a standstill, while only in the fourth case (the European Economic Community) was continuation of the process assured by deceleration.[29]

Other societal decisions, often debated ideologically but rarely studied analytically and systematically, concern the conditions of militancy versus moderation, or confrontation versus coalition politics, and the holistic versus the gradualist approach. These and similar strategic decisions draw on explicit or implicit theories about the nature of societal linkages and control factors, such as how far a government can be relied upon as an agent of transformation, what the result of mass activation of apathetic publics will be, or to what extent "spillover" in one societal sector will generate change in others. Here lies the main link between the study of societal decision-making and of societal input of knowledge.

The quality of decision-making gains in importance the more active a societal unit is by other criteria. Obviously the more activated a unit is and the more assets it has, the more advantages it can gain by effective use of them, and the more it can waste them if it uses them ineffectively. For passive units, which barely guide their own processes, background factors are of much importance; for units that react more creatively to their environmental as well as to internal challenges, it is the quality of decision-making that is of much importance. Under what structural conditions—all other conditions being equal—élites make more effective decisions, is a question that has barely been explored sociologically.

Cybernatorial factors other than processing of information and decision-making include various attributes of societal goals, such as the clarity of their formulation, and the degree of compatibility of the various goals a unit pursues. Also important is the quality of the communication networks that lead from the decision-making élites to the performance units and back, including number and intensity of gaps, "noise" on the line, and so forth. As our purpose here is not to list all these factors, but to illustrate the main categories, we turn now from cybernatorial factors to the second element of control: power.

29. Amitai Etzioni, *Political Unification* (New York: Holt, 1965), *passim.*

Control: Power, its Sources and its Mobilization

Societal assets and power. Societal structures are not just patterns of interaction of actors, patterns of expectations and symbols, but also patterns of
allocation of societal assets, the possessions of a societal unit. These can
be classified analytically as coercive, utilitarian, and normative, concerning
respectively the distribution of means of violence, material objects and
services, and symbols. A measure of the assets a societal unit or subunit
possesses is not in itself an indication of its actual power, but only of its
potential. Assets might be used to generate more assets, be consumed or
stored, or used to overcome the resistance of other actors, which is what
by definition societal power means. (This does not mean necessarily to force
other actors; their resistance might be overcome, for instance, by offering
a payoff.) In exploring the relations between assets and power, it is essential
not to shift the frame of reference in midanalysis. Conversion of assets into
power in time one might lead to more assets in time two; in time one, however, the generation of power entails a loss of assets.

A central predisposition of societal guidance is that the relationship
between assets and power is a loose one—that is, the amount of assets
allocated to a societal unit in a given structure is a poor predictor of how
much societal power the unit will have. The amount of power generated
depends significantly on the intraunit allocation of the assets among alternative usages. A unit poor in assets can in principle command more power
than a much more affluent one, if the poor unit assigns more of its assets to
power "production." (With half the GNP the Soviet Union maintains a
defense budget similar to that of the United States.)

What fraction of the assets a unit possesses is converted into power is
itself influenced by the societal context and not freely set by the societal
actor (for example, the fact that Negro-Americans are politically less active
than Jewish-Americans is in part due to differences in educational opportunities). However, we suggest, the degree of intraunit assignment of assets
to power is a relatively more malleable attribute than the amount of assets
the unit possesses (at any given point in time). It is here that an important
element of voluntarism enters the societal structure. A comparison of
colonial societies in the years immediately preceding the takeoff of national
independence movements with those immediately after they won their independence seems to show that the takeoff involved more change in the
relative *use* of assets for power than in the assets base. Similarly, the American civil rights movement, which between 1953 and 1965 transformed important segments of the American Negro from a passive to an active grouping, entailed much more of a change in mobilization of power than in
amount of assets.[30]

30. See James Q. Wilson, *Negro Politics, the Search for Leadership* (New York:
Free Press, 1965), esp. pp. 3-7.

Mobilization. Each societal unit has at any given point in time a level of activation which we define as the ratio of its assets that are available for collective action over its total assets. The percent of the GNP spent by the government, the percent of the labor force employed by it, and the percent of knowledge producers that work for it are crude indicators of national activation level. Mobilization refers to an upward change in the level of activation, to an increase in the fraction of the total assets possessed by a unit that are made available for collective action by that unit. (Demobilization refers to a reduction in that level.)

The level of activation of most societal units most of the time is very low; if all their assets are taken into account, usually less than ten percent are available for unit action. Hence relatively small percentage changes in the level of mobilization may largely increase the action capacity of a unit. For example, an increase of ten percent in the assets of a unit that are mobilized might more than double its action capacity. Major societal transformations, such as revolutions and the gaining of national independence, usually involve relatively high mobilization. The secret of the power of social movements lies in part in the relatively high mobilization which their asceticism and the intense commitment of their members allows for.

Aside from the asset base a collectivity possesses and the amount of power it is mobilizing, the *kind* of power mobilized also affects the action capacity of the unit. To employ power is, by definition, to overcome resistance, but in society as in nature each application of power generates a counterpower, a resistance of its own (the result of the alienation of those who were made to suspend their preferences in favor of those of the power wielders). While all power applications have this effect, some generate more alienation than others.

In estimating the effect of the use of a particular kind of power on the relationships between the power wielder and the subjects, it is essential to take into account that this is as a rule a generalized relationship. That is, while a particular instance of exercise of power may generate little alienation, repeated use may generate much. Even when no alienation is manifest, it might accumulate covertly and express itself indirectly.

We suggest that when the power relationship is explored (and not just described), if the power used is coercive, all other things being equal, resistance will tend to be high; if utilitarian, lower; and if normative, lower still. Most power wielders may prefer to use the less alienating kinds, but there are limitations on their capacity to mobilize these kinds as well as on their understanding of the dynamics involved, with the consequence that they may opt to use the more alienating kinds of power,[31] even where this is not otherwise necessary.

A study of control thus adds to the exploration of the asset base of a

31. Amitai Etzioni, *A Comparative Analysis of Complex Organizations* (New York: Free Press, 1961), pp. 3-22.

unit, the degree to which it is mobilized for collective action, and which kinds of power are mobilized. These added factors in turn determine to a considerable degree how alienating control will be, and whether relations between the élites and the other units will be ones of open conflict, encapsulated conflict, or cooperation.

Consensus Formation

Consensus Defined

So far, guidance of change has been explored from a downward view, from the controlling overlayer to the controlled underlayer; even the discussion of communication feedback and subject resistance has been from the viewpoint of a controlling center. The main difference, though, between societal and electronic cybernetics is that in the societal we take into account systematically that the controlled units have some of the controlling capacities themselves: they input knowledge, make decisions, pursue goals, and exercise power. Hence the capacity of any one unit to act is determined only in part by its ability to control the others; it is similarly affected by the degree of consensus, that is, the degree to which the goals it has chosen to pursue and the means it employs are compatible or in conflict with those preferred by other units.

Consensus, the congruence of preferences of the units concerned, is viewed by typical collectivistic theories as largely given (or changing under the impact of ongoing processes); voluntaristic theories tend to view it as open to manipulation by charismatic leadership and/or mass media. From the viewpoint of the societal guidance theory, consensus is the result of a process in which given preferences *and* guided efforts affect the outcome, which is a changing consensus. Many studies have applied such a perspective; in societal guidance it finds a theoretical home. How much consensus is actually achieved changes with a variety of sociopolitical factors and cannot be explored here.

Control and Consensus

There is a trade-off curve between control and consensus; that is, for any given level of activation, the greater consensus, the less need for control, and the less consensus gained the more need for control. Which mix is used is, of course, not without consequences; it affects the level of alienation and of resistance, and hence the future capacity to act. It is important to realize that when both consensus *and* control are higher, more change can be guided than when both are lower, without an increase in alienation. (The additional consensus absorbs the additional alienation which the additional control would generate.)

Consensus Formation Structures

To illustrate a societal guidance study of consensus formation, we briefly compare *built-in* to *segregated* consensus formation structures. In a built-in structure, consensus formation is by and large the output of ongoing interactions among the societal units. Consensus formation in smaller and less complex preliterate tribes seems to rely largely on ongoing interaction between the member families. In the Soviet society, consensus is to a degree produced in the process of interaction between factory managements, union leaders, and party officials, though the prime function of these interactions is not consensus formation but is economic and administrative in nature (in the downward guidance sense of the term).[32] In a segregated structure, political units (such as parties and legislatures) exist as distinct from societal ones, and societal differences are translated into political ones before consensus concerning collectivization is worked out. Segregated structures seem more effective for consensus formation than built-in ones, though they can produce only enough to back up comparatively low levels of activation. They are like a sophisticated machine that cannot be used for heavy duty.

In the search for a structure that would allow for more guided change and higher consensus, a search that is far from completed, voluntary planning as developed in France in the postwar years and by the European Economic Community has gained much attention. There is less segregation of political and societal units than in the segregated structure (typical of traditional democracies) but more than in built-in structures (typical of totalitarian regimes). Above all, the knowledge input units are not related only to the decision-making units but are tied also into the consensus-forming process, thus informing the controlled and not just the controlling units, and remodeling the judgments that information units produce—on the basis of interaction with *both* groupings.

Comparative studies of consensus formation ought to supplement, and in part replace, the comparative study of constitutions and formal studies of governments. To supplement, because we need studies both of the political institutions and of consensus formation which will relate these institutions to societal groups and relations among them. To replace in part, because the studies of political shells have proved too rigid and simplistic for many purposes. The study of democracy might illustrate this point.

As democracy was traditionally defined—the rule of the majority—the concept was unable even to distinguish between totalitarian and democratic regimes. The more subtle definition—provision for the institutionalized change of the party in office—still disregarded less formal democratic

---

32. Joseph Berliner, *Factory and Manager in the U.S.S.R.* (Cambridge: Harvard University Press, 1957). Samuel P. Huntington, *Political Power: U.S.A.: U.S.S.R.* (New York: Viking, 1965), pp. 129-190.

mechanisms, such as changes in the coalition partners and the factions represented inside the ruling party in response to changes in societal power, and defines countries such as West Germany and Israel as non-democratic. Neither the Christian Democratic Union nor Mapai has been voted out of office since the establishment of the two states, and whether or not these parties can be voted out is an open question. Also, the formal study focuses on parliaments and parties as the consensus formation agents, but these are rapidly losing their effectiveness as the power of the executive rises. Thus, a polity that meets all the criteria of formal democracy might still not generate enough consensus for the prevailing level of activation, not to mention increased levels which are both needed and occurring, thus leaving the society with substandard consensus leading either to accumulative alienation or curtailment of activity.

Similarly, important differences among the consensus formation of various totalitarian societies and of authoritarian ones, a mode of government which prevails among the new nations and in Latin America, as well as their changes over time, can scarcely be studied in formal terms (which characterization of regimes as totalitarian or authoritarian are) or by the classification of regimes as one-, two-, or multi-party states. In comparison, a societal guidance study of consensus formation provides a less institutional and more total approach.

A Synthesizing View: The Active Society

We shall now illustrate the synthesizing perspective on societal change that can be attained once our understanding of the various components of societal guidance is more advanced, although here little more than a brief illustration can be provided. Using control (cybernatorial capacities and power) and consensus formation as two dimensions of a property space, we characterize, in an ideal-typical manner, a society which is high on both dimensions as comparatively active; low on both as passive; high on control but low on consensus as overmanaged; and low on control but high on consensus as drifting.

The *passive* society is approximated by highly primitive societies. Their low level of societal self-control is obvious. Their consensus is collectivistic and static, but it is largely not mobilized around societal goals and there is little machinery to form consensus when additional consensus is needed. Hence while background consensus might be high, the consensus *formation* capacity is low. One indicator of this low capacity is that when primitive societies do act, coercion often plays a rather central role in overcoming resistance.[33]

33. For a case study, see Donald R. Maurice, *The Washing of the Spears* (New York: Simon & Schuster, 1965).

The *active* society maintains a level of activation that is not lower, and is possibly even higher, than that of overmanaged societies, and it forms at least as much consensus as drifting societies. This is possible because the active society commands more effective control and consensus formation mechanisms; it can rely more on the less alienating kinds of power, especially on the normative. Also, high consensus requires a high level of activation and realization of some of the variety of goals the various subsocieties and the society as a unit are committed to. Effective control, in turn, requires support of those subject to the control; hence raising the level of control without at the same time raising alienation requires a high capacity to form consensus. Thus, high control and high consensus, high activation and low alienation, are mutually reinforcing. Finally, the active society has the highest capacity of the four ideal-types for self-transformation, which is the ultimate safeguard against widespread alienation as it makes possible that the rise of radically different goals and subsocieties may still be accommodated within the same system.

The active society is largely a utopia which does not exist, although it is not a utopia in the sense that no society might become one, for its functional requirements do not appear to violate any sociological law. Social-movement societies, such as Israel in 1948, approximate such an active society. A main difference between a social-movement society and the active one is that the latter stabilizes some social-movement features such as high consensus formation and intense commitment, rather than merely passing through such a phase. The mechanisms for stabilization cannot be discussed in the present limits of space.

The *overmanaged,* high control, low consensus type is approximated by the totalitarian societies. Typically these have inadequate consensus formation structures, and those they have are mainly of the built-in type. Societal action is oriented to hyperactive goals, which later are scaled down, as consensus mechanisms here do not allow discovery beforehand of where and how much resistance will be encountered in the various subsocieties as various societal changes are introduced. Typically, too, use of alienating kinds of power is high.

Whether overmanaged societies are transformable and what kind of societies they will become if they are, are two widely debated questions. The argument is between those who see democratization as taking place and those who argue that the totalitarian societies are ultra stable.[34] This dichotomy seems not to exhaust the possibilities. Democratization seems unlikely because democracies are themselves no longer well adapted, as their present control and consensus mechanisms are insufficient for the

34. The transformation view is presented by Gabriel Almond, *The American People and Foreign Policy* (New York: Praeger, 1960), p. xvi; the opposite one by Philip E. Mosely, "Soviet Foreign Policy since the 22nd Party Congress," *Modern Age,* vol. 6 (Fall, 1962).

higher level of activation needed, and because there is no legitimation of democracy or democratic experience in the history of most contemporary totalitarian societies. On the other hand, in view of the far-reaching changes of the Soviet Union since 1917, it is hard to maintain that totalitarian societies are not transformable.

The direction of any such change might be toward an active society whose level of control is relatively closer to that of totalitarian societies than of the democratic ones, whose less segregated consensus formation structure is closer to the totalitarian built-in one than to the democratic segregated one, and whose social-movement character can draw on legitimation of the most charismatic period of totalitarian societies. The sharpest transition needed would be from reliance on force and propaganda as central means of compliance to a focus on education and normative power; such a transformation, as drastic as it is, may be easier than a shift to a utilitarian focus characteristic of capitalistic democracies. In fact, this is the direction of change already evidenced by the Soviet Union.

Drifting societies are approximated by capitalist democracies. Their most important relevant feature is that they act as societies to introduce significant structural changes only when the need to act is "overdue," [35] in a "crisis," when broad consensus can be mobilized. Second, the action taken often does not remove the lag, as the changes introduced are the fruit of compromise between the more conservative and the more change-oriented subsocieties. The second major reason why capitalist democracies are drifting societies is that the more powerful subsocieties draw societal assets for their own consumption and power, either by neutralizing the societal controls or by slanting them to serve their subsocietal interests. In either case, as far as the society at large is concerned, it is not guiding its processes and change.

Consensus, Equality, and Activation

Here a conceptual addition must be introduced to tie the idea of consensus formation to those of asset analysis and alienation, an addition found in the concept of equality. Equality is more nearly approached the closer the distribution curve of assets approximates a straight line; in other words, groupings of the population that are equal in size possess equal amounts of assets. No society is completely egalitarian, but there are obviously significant differences in the degree of inequality. These in turn are associated, though of course not on a one-to-one basis, with differences in power. Now when consensus is formed it reflects the power relations among the members; the policy agreed upon tends to be closer to that preferred by the more powerful subsocieties. It is as if the weaker members say to themselves that

35. Etzioni, *Political Unification,* pp. 81-82, 95.

they had better go along with a suggested policy, in which their concurrence is traded for some concessions—for fear that otherwise the powerful would impose a policy even more removed from their preferences. The amount of alienation that remains in the weaker units, however, is clearly related to the measure of inequality. Consensus which leaves little or no alienation can be formed only under conditions of comparatively high equality.

While this cannot be demonstrated here, we suggest that there is a secular historical trend toward a reduction in inequality among the subsocieties making up the capitalistic democracies although so far this reduction has been limited. (The trend is fairly obvious as far as political rights and status symbols are concerned; it is less clear with regard to economic well-being.) Continuation and acceleration of such a trend, if it were to take place, would move democratic societies toward a high level of activation by allowing the formation of more consensus with less alienating undertones, and more facing of societal problems before they are overdue. A major force which propels the transition from a drifting to an active society is the mobilization of the weaker collectivities; this is triggered by the spread of education, by changes in employment opportunities, and other factors that generate imbalanced status sets, as well as by the priming effect of élites, especially intellectual ones. As this statement is rather central to our conception of societal change as far as the transition of Western societies into the postmodern (see below for definition) period is concerned, the assumptions implied should be briefly outlined.

As we see it, transformation of capitalist democracies is not propelled by conflict among classes, but by interaction among organized collectivities. Thus, the societal units may be an ethnic group, a race, a national community, and not just a class; the relationship might be of coalition, limited adversary, or the like, rather than all-out conflict; and, above all, the unit of action is not the collectivity *per se,* but that part of it which has been mobilized into organizational structures. Thus, history is not affected by the working class as such, which is a passive unit, but by labor unions, labor parties, social protest movements that mobilize a segment of the working class. (The same could be said about the civil rights movement and the Negro-Americans or of national independence movements and colonial people.)

Collectivities are bases of *potential* power, but generally only a small fraction of these potentialities are actualized for purposes of societal action and change. The capacity of any societal actor to influence the pattern of societal change (his actual societal power) depends as much on his capacity to mobilize—that is, *on the outcome of the internal struggle between mobilizers and the apathetics*—as on the actor's potential power base.

It might be said that the capacity to mobilize is itself determined by the distribution of assets among the collectivities; that the more powerful units hold down the capacity of the weaker societal units to mobilize. While this

is a valid observation, it is also true that the mobilization of any collectivity reduces the capacity of other collectivities to hold it down. For each point in time, hence, it is necessary to study not only the power potential of a societal actor but also his mobilization capacity, which affects his actual power at this point in time. The dynamic analysis then proceeds by comparing changes in potential and actual power over time and the effects of changes in the power of some actors over that of the others. A study of societal change which focuses largely on the stratificational relations among collectivities (as Marx did and in which he was corrected to a degree by Lenin),[36] not to mention theories which exclude power analysis altogether, provides at best a fragmentary view of societal change.

What does all this imply for the change of capitalistic democracies? In these societies, too, most members of most collectivities have a formal right to participate in the political process; they have an egalitarian political institutional status unmatched in their societal positions. An increasing number are also gaining an education, which has a mobilizing effect.[37] For historical reasons which need not be explored here, campus groups, professionals, clergy, middle-class members of ethnic minorities, all of which command political skills, are allowed to act as mobilizers, though under various constraints. And, we suggest, with weaker collectivities becoming increasingly mobilizable, and with an increase in the number of mobilizers, the total effect is increased societal power of the heretofore weaker and underprivileged collectivities. The effect of the mobilization of weaker collectivities, which is only in part neutralized by countermobilization of more powerful collectivities, is to transform the society in the direction of a relatively more egalitarian and active one. Whether such transformation will sooner or later lead to a showdown between the powerful and the mobilizing collectivities, or whether the mobilization will run out of steam on its own, or whether the scales will be tipped for an active society—that is, whether a structural transformation will take place—are questions which our study of societal guidance points to but cannot at present answer.

Overmanaged and drifting societies both seem to be tending in the direction of an active society (rather than either of the less active types becoming the prevalent type). The new means of communications and of knowledge technology may be working in this direction in both kinds of societies; continued mobilization of the weaker collectivities in capitalist societies and increased pluralism in totalitarian societies may also be supportive of such a transformation. Under what conditions an active society will be advanced is a major subject of macrosociology. The new cybernatorial capacities that have been increasingly available since 1945 offer a

36. Wolin, *Politics and Vision,* pp. 421-424.
37. For a review of several studies which show correlations between education and political activation, see Lester W. Milbarth, *Political Participation* (Chicago: Rand, 1965), pp. 42-54.

new range of societal options and hence mark a period that might be referred to as the postmodern one. The year 1945 marks also the opening of the atomic age and hence suggests that a major issue for macrosociology, not touched upon here, is that of changing not the structures but the boundaries of the systems. The question as to which conditions favor and which block the rise of active societies and the transformation of an anarchic world into a communal one, we suggest, is regained for systematic sociological study by such approaches as that of societal guidance.

3.

Scientific Analysis Is a Subset
of Comparative Analysis

Marion J. Levy, Jr.

Marion J. Levy, Jr. was born in Galveston, Texas, in 1918, educated at Schreiner Institute, the University of Texas, and Harvard University in economics and sociology. He is professor of sociology and international affairs in the department of sociology and the Woodrow Wilson School of Public and International Affairs, both of Princeton University. His books include The Family Revolution in Modern China, The Structure of Society, Modernization and the Structure of Societies, *and* Levy's Six Laws of Disillusionment of the True Liberal.

*I*t is something of an amusing scandal that among the contributions to a volume on theoretical sociology there should be a special paper on the subject of comparative analysis. It is my assumption that this conference has to do with sociology considered as a science—not as one of the humanistic, theological, or otherwise designated disciplines. If that assumption is correct, then there is no noncomparative sociological theory. All scientific analysis is a subset of the general set entitled comparative analysis. Extreme positivists might maintain that scientific analysis is the only subset of that general set, but that is an epistemological issue which need not detain the argument here. What people do in other houses is not our concern here; our concern is what we do in our house, if it is a house of science. If it is a house of science, we are primarily concerned with the search for sets of highly generalized propositions involving variables, constants (perhaps), and the relationships among them. It is to be hoped that eventually we will come up with sets which have powerful deductive interdependencies among the propositions. It is primer philosophy of science to point out that any generalized statement involving variables implies a comparison.

There is another sense which is perhaps an even greater cause for concern. Whatever the vagaries of definition of the field may be, sociologists as a lot pride themselves on generalizing about any and all social phenomena.

The most general concern of the field would therefore seem to lie with propositions that treat of any social action, any social system, and/or any society. When the term *comparative* is used for a meeting like this, its loose or lay application is generally to comparisons of two or more societies, or some other designation of large-scale membership units such as nations or countries. If you wish to discount my opening statement as once again illustrating my grim preference for argument rather than new enlightenment, consider matters on this level. It is not new enlightenment, but rather a close attention to the debris under the rug that I ask. The bulk of all of the material in our field has been written and is being written about isolated aspects—with no real attempt to hook one up to another—of one example of a single type of society in world history. That one example is of course modern United States society. Some years ago in an entirely loose way, some graduate students and I made a quick sweep through the two most prominent United States journals in our field and two in a closely allied one in a search for articles which were comparative in this sense. We were prepared to regard an article as comparative if it were about the French family, without requiring that it compare that with a family in some other setting—in other words, we were prepared to consider it comparative if it were about anything *but* an aspect of the United States considered in isolation. By that standard the number of articles in our major journals which can be described as comparative is small in absolute numbers and embarrassing when considered as a ratio. All of man may be our land, but we are prepared to leave most of our land virgin land.

Just as a matter of historical interest, particularly given a recent revival of interest in work of this sort, probably as a function of interest in underdeveloped areas, I would observe it was not ever thus. Herbert Spencer himself left his fortune to a Spencer trust for just such comparative studies. The elephant folio volumes of that work gather dust on the shelves of the better libraries of our universities and now rise only to haunt students who do not know of their existence. Alas, like most sociologists today, Herbert Spencer and his heirs seem never to have heard of the principle of parsimony, and the scheme of analysis they used has very little to say to us. But they did try to rack up studies done on a holistic basis with an explicit system of analysis with a view eventually to comparing them, one with another. This exists today in an active form, the Human Relations Area Files. Again one may not care for the system of analysis used to set up these materials. The whole idea behind the HRAF may have its greatest comparative advantage in racking up relatively small-scale societies, but again, like the characters in the musical about Southeast Asia, here are some men who try.

These historical antecedents and remnants do not tell the full extent of our neglect of these matters. For all of the work done on modern United States society there does not, as far as I know, exist a single serious effort to sketch out a general structural picture; or indeed, a general picture of any

other sort if one wishes to quibble about the word *structure,* of the United States society, unless one feels that that has been accomplished by Williams's book or that of Lerner.[1] There is no such study for any current country of Europe, of Asia, of Africa, of Australia itself or of South America. The probability of there being any studies worthy of recognition by modern scientific standards of the historical backgrounds of any of these current societies is even smaller. We seek knowledge of these worlds almost entirely from historians who have understandably, when at their best, generally used a frame of reference which consisted primarily of political leadership and chronology with an occasional dash of economic interest for spice and variety.

In ignoring this material, we leave unmined the enormously respectable scholarly endeavors of some of the ablest people concerned with social phenomena—the scholars who toiled on Greece and Rome, on the Byzantine Empire, on those fabulous records and encyclopedias of the Chinese. Current and past and with no view to the future, we continue to neglect studies save those of the most current fashionable areas in which an interest is more easily explicable on meretricious than on intellectual grounds.

In these rich soils which we make waste by neglect, there are giant nuggets and the wild man's view of future crops. All the world's materials on bureaucracies before we got drowned in those materials are here in such studies. One has only to look at the works of a popularizer like Harold Lamb to realize that some special fate led him to specialize on those very rare societies which were overwhelmingly centralized well in advance of what we consider to be high levels of modernization. Mr. Lamb wrote on Suleiman, Tamerlane, Genghis Khan, Alexander the Great, and the like. All conquered vastly, and all after them saw those empires disintegrate rapidly indeed upon those leaders' deaths. We talk a great deal about democracy and about possible combinations of high and moderate levels of modernization, and yet we have no holistic studies, let alone comparative analyses, of the set of societies like those of the Dutch, the Danes, the Norwegians, the Swedes, and the Finns, who combine varying levels of modernization internal to their countries with very high rates of conformity and very low rates of coercion—very low rates even of negative coercion in the form of crimes of violence. We have no holistic studies, let alone comparative ones, of those rare cases which may have been examples of relatively nonmodernized societies without an overwhelming agrarian base— the Hanseatic League cases and the Venetian city-states. We have no comparative analyses of the one overwhelmingly feudal social structure with a pedigree of stability extending for more than 50 years—Tokugawa Japan, history's great case of absentee administration in terms of which no ruler

---

1. See Robin M. Williams, Jr., *American Society: A Sociological Interpretation* (New York: Knopf, 1951), and Max Lerner, *America as a Civilization,* 2 vols. (New York: Simon and Schuster, 1957).

administered and no administrator ruled—with any of the ordinary forms of feudalism.

One could go on, and the matter is becoming more urgent, on intellectual as well as practical grounds. As the universal social solvent of modernization operates, as more of the patterns abroad in the world disintegrate and start moves, however doomed, in the direction of modernized societies, a trend toward uniformity in the world, despite all talk of a second, third, or fourth world, is heavily upon us. The violence which accompanies the trend not only saps the desire to learn from the past, but literally threatens the records from which we or future generations might learn something, if we are ever so inclined. The practical relevance, with or without the disguise of words like heuristic or propaedeutic, I leave to one side, or subsume under the assumption that, if current trends continue, it is the records about all those other now extinct cases which will contain the overwhelming majority of the variance we have to study on any given level of generality.

It must be clear that I do not think our major difficulty is that all of us have really been interested in doing science, but have labored in the face of great difficulties. It seems to me clear that most of us have not been interested in science at all. The interest in highly generalized propositions in terms of parsimonious variables would have taken care of the neglects, of the silliness to which I point. The big question is how to get on with the game—assuming that we or any after us are interested in getting on with the game. I have written a paper which must appear elsewhere about a sister field which states my views on science and the major errors committed in its name.[2] I wish I could attach it as an appendix because it applies equally well here, needing only the change of a few labels and names to excite tempers more accurately for this field. With so arrogant a come-on, however, it would be craven for me not to state explicitly some of the things which I feel must be done, some of the strategies which I feel should be followed. I have tried to do so briefly in what follows.

I

It is really quite necessary that one be prepared to define a unit as a central focus for this sort of work. I think that unit is most appropriately what we have generally referred to as a society, but I do not doubt that others can come up with different ones. What is essential is that it be a unit rather large in scale as far as the number of members and probably the territory occupied by them are concerned. I think a society as I have defined it elsewhere in my work is useful because one can maintain a hypothesis about it

2. See "'Does it matter if he's naked?' Bawled the Child," in Knorr and Rosenau, eds., *Contending Approaches to International Politics* (Princeton: Princeton University Press, 1969), pp. 87-109.

to the following effect: all social systems other than societies are either subsystems of a given society or the result of interdependencies among two or
more societies. This makes possible certain leverage on systems other than
societies. Given such a unit, I think requisite analysis much as I have
described it elsewhere and most recently in the current *International Encyclopedia of the Social Sciences,*[3] underlies other forms of analysis. In arguing for this, I assume that structural-functional analysis combed free of
nonsense is synonymous with analysis in general and not a special form of
it. A requisite analysis is, so correspondingly, a special form of analysis in
general. It is that special form of analysis which attempts to erect a minimum number of categories in terms of which any two or more instances of
the phenomena referred to can be compared. Implicitly or explicitly, we
never do otherwise. I prefer to do it as explicitly as possible. It is not static
as opposed to dynamic analysis; its propositions can easily be converted
into ones in which time is a relevant variable; and indeed, no propositions
in which time is a relevant variable are ever derived without first finding out
something about two different points in time, about two different states of a
unit presumed to be the same in some respects.

Requisite analysis, of course, involves some sort of a stability assumption.
Is it necessary to take the time here to argue that the use of a stability assumption in no way implies that the units analyzed in terms of such an
approach are in fact stable? Is it necessary once again to point to the conceptual regression in *defining* social systems as equilibrium systems? Is it
really necessary here to point out that the argument that the use of a stability
assumption of any sort invalidates all analysis of nonstable systems is tantamount to saying that no assumptions which give closure of any sort can
be used in any science?

Such a framework of analysis underlies any comparison whether across
time or across other lines of variation. Anyone who argues that we must
have a special framework for each case because at some level, presumably
the descriptive if no other, no two systems are alike, argues against the
assumptions that underlie any scientific work. If the hypothesis used here
about any society is correct, then failure to discover material in terms of a
given requisite implies one of three possibilities or some combination of the
three: either (1) the theory that a given thing is a requisite is incorrect, or
(2) one has misobserved, or (3) the unit referred to is not in fact a society
however much it may seem to have been. But if the hypothesis about other
social systems applies, by analyzing any given social system in terms of the
requisites of a society, one will have learned as a minimum what that system
is like by contrast with societies and what minimal interdependencies the
members of such a system must have with the members of other systems.

Implicit in this is even an interesting way to by-pass the old question of

3. See the article "Functional Analysis: Structural-Functional Analysis" (New York:
Macmillan, 1969), vol. 6, pp. 21-29.

applied analyses, namely, the problem that if you know what your policy interest is you are likely to bias your research in an especially relevant way,[4] and if you do not know what it is you are likely to do irrelevant research. With regard to any given system one could set up, say, three independent research teams. One would examine the system as it is planned to be; another would examine it as it actually is in terms of the requisites of any society; and a third team or individual would analyze it in terms of what it would have to be in order to achieve a given policy end. The third individual or team would, of course, develop a new set of requisites for that kind of unit. Since the first two sets of requisites would be the same, any point which appeared in the work of any of the three teams would have one of the following five policy implications:

(1) The planned is equal to the required; the required is equal to the actual. The situation is perfect just as it is. The policy implication is that one do nothing.

(2) The planned is equal to the actual, but the planned is not equal to the required, and the actual is not equal to the required. The policy implication is that one is executing properly, but that one is planning poorly and needs better planners.

(3) The planned is equal to the required, but the planned is not equal to the actual, and the actual is not equal to the required. In this case one is planning well, but is not executing properly.

(4) The planned is not equal to the actual; the actual is equal to the required, and the planned is not equal to the required. In this case one is not executing properly, and one is also not planning well.

(5) The planned is not equal to the actual; the planned is not equal to the required, and the required is not equal to the actual. This is the human condition.

After developing general criteria for requisite analysis, it would be useful to move on to some effective taxonomy of different types of society, or whatever unit one has chosen. I happen to feel that the distinction between relatively modernized and relatively nonmodernized societies is the distinction of the most general relevance for the construction of general theory. There is nothing hard and fast about that, however, and that taxonomy has certainly not been developed at lower levels of generality. The one caveat that should be kept in mind here is, of course, that no development of requisites and no development of taxonomy will be any substitute for really good theoretical ideas. All such efforts can do is facilitate analysis; they do not create it.

4. Not the worst of all charges since unbiased research is inexplicable research, and since no charge of bias, however well-founded, is anything more than an argumentum ad hominem if taken only on its merits. No charge of bias constitutes disproof of a proposition! No proved charge does either.

II

If the establishment of the type of analysis one intends to do of a given unit is the first step, the second can surely be to look to other disciplines for help. I think it is very useful indeed to look to more highly developed disciplines than our own. The fields of demography and economics come most obviously to mind. There are certain things to recommend at least consultation with experts in these fields. First, while many of the things in which we are interested may not vary as dependent variables of the density of peoples, of their mortality rates, of their fertility rates, of their age distributions, of their allocations of goods and services, there are very few things in which we are interested which vary at random to these matters. Second, the demographers and the economists have much more highly developed theoretical tools at their disposal than we in general do. On the whole, their empirical work is more firmly grounded than ours. Third, in going across difficult language barriers, the probability of our making serious errors in trying to get at questions of the sort asked by demographers, and to a certain extent economists as well, is less than in trying to get directly at the kind of attitudinal matters with which we are likely to be more directly concerned. Therefore, even though we may know that the matters in which we are interested are not in fact dependent variables of demographic and economic considerations in the strict senses of those terms, it might be a very useful strategy to act as though they were—to set up façade hypotheses which hold in essence that if this thing which we believe to be the case were true, these would be its implications for demographic factors and economic allocations. That may give us a better check than most of our current forms of data do.

III

One thing which can be done to press the suit of comparative analysis in this restricted sense is to raise exactly one of those questions which the general strategy of science would indicate. We ought to seek those leads around which there seems to be great closure on extremely general levels. I would like to mention a few in the remainder of this paper.

A. The most general lead into discussions of social phenomena in terms of organization is to be found via the family. Some of these closures about the family may be listed as follows:

1. There are no known societies lacking in family structures.
2. What is generally conceded to be the steepest part of the learning curve for all individuals takes place for virtually all known individuals past,

present, and presumably in the future in a family context. Incidentally, it can probably be maintained that the very first thing infants everywhere learn is to cry efficiently in order to attract the attention of others who are, most likely, family members.

3. Initial placement is in terms of family considerations.

4. Until relatively modernized societies developed, the vast majority of all people in history spent the majority of their time and had the majority of their interrelations in a family context. Ideally and/or actually—even if not ideally—the family context was the major focus of organizational behavior. It still is for a large proportion of the people of this earth.

5. Ideally and/or actually what happens to one in terms of the family affects the way in which one behaves in all other organizational contexts.

6. At all stages of the life cycle the overwhelming majority of all individuals have been (and are) considered to have some family membership.

7. Until quite high levels of modernization were reached, from birth to roughly age three or four, all children were reared predominantly in terms of feminine influence in the family context. After that age the females continued to be reared largely in that context, but the males—the vast majority of all males for any given society—were reared primarily under the supervision of men, even though that continued in the family context. This ceases to be the case when societies are highly modernized and, indeed on the impact of modernization this effect runs well ahead of others. Whether males can be stably reared under such intensities of female tending is by no means clear.

8. Despite enormous variations in the ideal structures of family organization for the majority of all people in history, the actual organizational context of the family varied little. Its maximum variation was in the average number of people per family, but even that did not exceed 75 percent. The number of generations represented, the number of marital spouse pairs involved, the age distribution, sex distribution, and so forth varied by very much less than 75 percent for all peoples.

9. Closely related to the matter of family structure is the hypothesis that the relationship between father and son is overwhelmingly likely to have been the major focus of solidarity for all family contexts, unless the family unit consisted of only husband and wife. Not until one gets into relatively modernized contexts does the husband and wife relationship take precedence over that of father and son, even after children are born, and other alternatives are not feasible.[5]

5. Uncle–son relationships can be substituted for father–son relationships in the case of matrilineal situations, but mother–son relationships probably cannot, because mothers never were family heads, ideally speaking. Brother–brother relationships are not likely to take precedence because under the kind of mortality conditions characteristic of these family structures, the probability is roughly that there be 25 percent of the families with two surviving sons, 25 percent with two daughters, and 50 percent with one daughter and one son. For the brother–brother relationship to take

Thus, despite the enormous variance in ideal family structures, the actual closure in the implications for family influence of numbers of people who are members of the family, their age distribution, sex distribution, generational distribution, marital distribution, etc., has been very restricted indeed. Again, a caution. I would not maintain that most of the things we are interested in are dependent variables of these factors, but I would maintain that very few of the things in which we are likely to be interested are likely to vary at random relative to these factors.

B. The vast majority of all societies in world history have exhibited a remarkably similar asymmetry in income distribution. The vast majority of all people in all societies, regardless of the ideologies of their members, have had very low incomes, very close to the margin of subsistence; very few people have had middle incomes relative to that particular society; and a small number of people have had relative to that particular situation high incomes. Apart from probably legendary Pacific Islands, no approaches to situations in which the median, mode, and mean of income fall very close together have been possible until relatively modernized societies have been achieved. Furthermore, a considerable part of capital formation, special education, and so forth, which are responsible for keeping as many people above the margin of subsistence as in fact are maintained there, is a function —regardless of how much wickedness is involved—of what goes on in that small set of relatively well-to-do people. Any change in the direction of greater unimodality prior to considerable improvements in productivity will push those people below the margin of subsistence. I would not take the position of economic determinism which maintains that man lives by bread alone, but he certainly does not live totally without regard to it either. If this overwhelming uniformity of relatively nonmodernized societies with regard to the distribution of income is correct, then one would also expect a radically asymmetrical distribution of everything relative to which income has any particular relevance. That is the case, and there are very few things for which the distribution of income is in fact irrelevant. The question is not whether the distribution of income causes the other things or not. The fruitful way to look at the matter is to ask what sorts of things could vary at random to the distribution of income.

C. There are an indefinitely large number of bases on which one can distinguish role differentiation. In my own attempt at requisite analysis I have distinguished nine such bases which I maintain are requisites for any society. Among those are role differentiations on the basis of age, generation,

---

precedence over the father–son relationship, if questions of succession to and preparation for family headship are at all involved, the age gap between those brothers must be roughly of the order of magnitude that one would expect between father and son. The probability of that obtaining in more than 50 percent of the 25 percent of cases mentioned is exceedingly slight.

and sex. I think no one would care to leave those out of consideration, regardless of whether he cares to agree with me on the other six. A special hypothesis can be maintained about these first three. In all known societies role differentiations on the basis of age, generation, and sex underlie all the others, and, I might add, are generally first inculcated on the individual in a family context. This of course raises the question of the general biological bases of human conduct in general and human social conduct in particular. Nothing seems to me less likely than that age role differentiation be unrelated to the physiology of aging of the organism. The case with regard to generational distinction is a bit harder to make out, but again nothing seems more probable than that role differentiation on the basis of sex has critical biological or psychobiological elements. We fought so hard against naïve forms of premature biological reductionism that we still today in general proceed as though biology had nothing whatsoever to do with the case. It is, however, a fact, or at least a hypothesis about the facts, that women everywhere are regarded as weak because they are women and not as women because they are weak. It is interesting that the modern anthropologists seem to insist—it may be the one thing on which they are in agreement —that there are no true matriarchies, ideally and/or actually. I feel that in order to pursue the kind of comparative analysis to which we are devoted we ought to go back systematically to biology and psychology and ask how many of the commonalities of human conduct we can account for more parsimoniously in biological or psychobiological terms rather than in others. After that, I think we should ask the much more difficult question of how much of the general variance can be so accounted for. The details of specific variance will forever elude us, I assume. The special comparative advantages of a genetically determined sixth finger in a social setting in terms of which pickpockets are prized is going to continue to be extremely difficult to predict, but the general form of the Homans–Parsons debate over psychological versus social variables seems to me as absurd as one over heredity versus environment.

D. It is a commonplace of modern analysis—we certainly have sufficient stimulus for such a commonplace—that there are problems of integration to uncertainty characteristic of every social study. Magic as such an integration, and faddism as one more readily combinable with rationality, are too obvious to be pled for. On the other hand, most of the people most of the time have been beset by high levels of certainty of certain types. The problem of the integration to boredom—it is interesting that faddism operates equally well here—is on the whole neglected by scholars who have not detected what one might have thought would be an equally great stimulus in this direction. The universality of gambling practices is another one of the closure elements which cuts across all social cases.

This sort of question may be elaborated in other ways. The majority of

all peoples who have ever lived have had rather long-range views of the future—that is to say, they have in general expected things to continue roughly as they were for their parents and grandparents—even though they have had relatively short-range futures for themselves. Only quite recently in history have people generally come to have quite long-range futures in terms of life expectancy at birth, and yet most of those people have a short-range view of the future. They expect change—great change and fast.[6]

E. Despite all talk of despotism, the vast majority of peoples who have existed with any considerable stability have been characterized by governments that were overwhelmingly decentralized, and at the local level the last element of decentralization has almost universally been the family unit. Only in the cases of the great world conquerors—the Tamerlanes, the Suleimans, the Genghis Khans, the Alexander the Greats—only these have been overwhelmingly centralized under relatively nonmodernized conditions, and these are empires which never long survived the death of their founders. The cement of large-scale, highly centralized governments for a relatively nonmodernized people has been the personality of the leader. High levels of modernization have changed this, but only a very small number of societies are so far highly modernized.

F. All societies of any scale as reckoned by the numbers of their members and the territories occupied by them have been characterized by some form of armed forces whether these are viewed primarily as having external foci for defense or offense or internal foci for the general maintenance of order. Whether one likes to think so or not, these armed forces have been a stronghold of emphasis on rationality, on learning, on predominantly universalistic criteria, on functionally specific relationships, on social mobility, and on change. Control over the members of armed forces has nearly always been primarily a question of outthinking palace revolutions, rather than of coping with mass mutinies. There have never been any peoples who failed to take an instrumental view of armed forces.

The preceding, briefly stated, are presented in an ad hoc set of examples of closure with quite general implications at the level of any society with only slight modifications for less general levels. Any sociologist who wishes to take the time to think can expand this list importantly. No sociologist has so far troubled to think in a way that enables us to present such a list in terms of one or a small number of highly general propositions and a set of deductively interdependent, less general ones. It is toward this task yet unaccomplished—to the hope for a Newton in the field, and I would point out that a Newton in the field would be very different from a Marx or a Freud —that all of our papers are in some sense directed.

6. There is in this a special lesson for those who would counsel us to trust no one over 30. Those have, in general, a fast-approaching 40 years of untrustworthiness to look forward to as their universal lot.

4.

Structural Sociology

Edward A. Tiryakian

Edward A. Tiryakian was born in Bronxville, New York, in 1929. He received his B.A., summa cum laude, *from Princeton in 1952 and his Ph.D. from Harvard in 1956. He has taught at Princeton and Harvard, and is now professor of sociology at Duke University. The author of* Sociologism and Existentialism, *he has also published many articles in the fields of sociological theory, methodology, social change, sociology of religion, and African studies. His major professional interest is in the historical transformations of large-scale social systems.*

As a distinguished contributor to this volume has pointed out elsewhere,[1] a fundamental question running through the development of general sociological theory has been the question of social order. What accounts for social order rather than social chaos, which in its asymptotic Hobbesian formulation would be the war of all-against-all? This basic sociological question is, parenthetically, of the same nature as the ontological question raised by the philosopher Heidegger: Why is there Being rather than non-Being? Indeed, directly or indirectly, this general sociological problem underlies the vast spectrum of sociological investigations involving the operations of social organizations and social institutions; it also underlies a great deal of sociological theory, including much of contemporary structural-functional analysis.

The question of how society is ordered has had several general answers, with two contrasting models being salient. The first is epitomized by (but not peculiar to) the Marxist perspective that the social order is contingent upon the *coercion* of the majority by a ruling minority's utilization of power facilities; an alternative variant of the coercion model is the *conflict* model which sees the foundation of social order in the conflict between groups becoming ritualized. The contrasting perspective is one receiving a socio-

1. Talcott Parsons, *The Structure of Social Action* (Glencoe: Free Press, 1949), *passim*.

logical formulation by Comte's focus on the primacy of *consensus,* a theme refined by Durkheim in his analysis of the virtual tendencies of social organization (with the substitution of solidarity for consensus). The latter perspective is reflected in the United States by the microsociological theory of George H. Mead and, in Parsons' sense, by the voluntaristic model of action. Until quite recently, the latter perspective had been generally accepted in America, or perhaps we should say had been taken for granted; the upsurgence of Marxist-inspired thought in sociological circles in recent years is now weakening the consensus with the consensus model—but that is not our preoccupation in this paper.

What has threatened to become lost from view is that the question of the nature of social order as a prime theoretical question was from the first a response to ongoing social upheavals of vast magnitude occurring with as great rapidity as intensity, as Nisbet has so well pointed out.[2] Sociological consciousness (that is, explicit, systematic awareness of the reality of society as a manifold totality) begins with Saint-Simon as a response to a societal crisis. This sweeping departure from a state of order was for him not solely a political matter, nor an economic one, but rather a "total social phenomenon," to use the famous expression of Mauss. From Saint-Simon to Comte, Le Play, and Marx, on to Durkheim and Weber, and down to at least Sorokin and Mannheim, sociological preoccupation with the precarious foundation of social order stems from an empirical background of large-scale social crises. In other words, I am suggesting that if continuing theoretical attention has been given to the problem of social order in our discipline, this may have been due at least in part to actual severe deviations from a state of order produced by recurring acute dislocations in the social fabric of western society.[3]

Perhaps as a reflection of the vast quantitative and qualitative changes going on in the world, ranging just in the last decade from the impact of computers to the impact of the civil rights movement, from the liquidation of overseas empires to the advent of the European Common Market, there has been in this brief period a resurgence of professional sociological interest in the area of social change, with Moore's *Social Change* [4] providing a useful codification of much of the literature. Indeed, not only do many of the papers in the present volume partake of this renewed sociological concern, but also it may well be that in a few years at most introductory textbooks in sociology will have "social change" featured as the first rather than as the now familiar residual last chapter.

2. Robert A. Nisbet, *The Sociological Tradition* (New York: Basic Books, 1966), pp. 21-44.
3. More recently, Georges Balandier has broadened the sociological horizon by extending the notion of crisis to the consequences of colonialism in Africa. See his seminal study, *Sociologie Actuelle de l'Afrique Noire,* 2nd ed. (Paris: Presses Universitaires de France, 1963).
4. Wilbert E. Moore, *Social Change* (Englewood Cliffs: Prentice-Hall, 1963).

In at least one major respect, social change and social order are not even analytically distinct. Only if the notion of social order is based upon some purely static model, wherein order is equated with immobility or a social analogue of physical constants, can such a distinction be made. We opt for the perspective that order and change are concretely part of any social process which takes place within and as a function of existing *structures*, and in doing so, latently validate the sanctity of these structures. We shall use the term "institutional life" to refer to the totality of social actions occurring within social institutions which implicitly if not explicitly are structured by a publicly legitimated normative framework.

It is our contention that social reality is not exhausted by institutional behavior, which tends to be orderly, that is, normatively patterned, legitimated, and rational. Such behavior constitutes what is publicly visible or at the social surface, although the question remains as to *how* it is constituted, how the society of everyday life is constituted and validated. This is the sort of investigation which is made to order for a structural approach in sociology, particularly one deriving from phenomenology, and it is well exemplified by Schutz and by Garfinkel.[5] The focus of this essay, however, is on a seemingly different topic, one which may appear out of keeping with a structuralist perspective, namely the question of societal change. We shall address ourselves to understanding how change may be distinguished conceptually from process, and to outlining a model of social reality fruitful for such an understanding.

Drawing upon a variety of intellectual sources, mainly from within the sociological tradition and from existential phenomenology, we shall draw attention to the nature of social reality as a historical, phenomenal reality. Second, we shall stress the need for general sociological theory to concern itself with social structures as the foundations of systems of social action. Such a concern involves a rethinking of the notion of structure which, we propose, has been given a rather residual consideration in contemporary sociological theory in marked contrast to recent anthropological theory. It is because of the centrality of structures as the background existential cadres of social life that we choose to term this essay in general sociological theory an exploratory essay in structural sociology.

One may wonder about the emphasis on "structure," given the well-established structural-functional theoretical perspective in sociology. As I have suggested, "structure" has received in sociology little rigorous attention. Even one of the most rigorous explications of structural-functional analysis, Levy's *The Structure of Society,* gives more weight to "structural differentiation" and to "function" than to "structure" itself; the latter, for him,

5. Alfred Schutz, *Collected Papers,* 3 vols. (The Hague: Martinus Nijhoff, 1962–1964), and *The Phenomenology of the Social World* (Evanston: Northwestern University Press, 1967); Harold Garfinkel, *Studies in Ethnomethodology* (Englewood Cliffs: Prentice-Hall, 1967).

. . . refers to an aspect of empirical phenomena divorced from time. The patterns of action, *qua* patterns, do not exist as concrete objects in the same sense that sticks and stones do. . . .[6]

Levy's use of structure seems to parallel, in some respects, Lévi-Strauss's notion of "social structure," but less extensively.[7] Both seem to be opting for a static, ahistorical notion of structure, quite different from Gurvitch's notion of social structure as multiple and dynamic.[8] For Gurvitch, social structures are neither static entities nor reducible to institutions, and our own approach owes much to Gurvitch.

In any case, the notion of structure is one which has little clearcut agreement as to its use, though its fundamental importance for a variety of disciplines has been widely recognized.[9] Anthropology has given much more attention to it than has sociology, which has been more interested in function. "Structural anthropology" has come to be associated with the works of Lévi-Strauss, who has given extensive treatment to this notion in several writings, linking it with the notion of model, which perhaps parallels the sociological concept of system. Frankly, I must admit to being perplexed as to whether Lévi-Strauss intends by the notion of model a construction the observer makes or constructs, or whether he refers to the implicit but real model held by the actors he is observing, or both (which might not be equivalent). In any case, I accept without reservation Lévi-Strauss's proposition that social structures are not of the same order as physical structures:

. . . social structure deals exclusively with those "spaces" the determinations of which are of a purely sociological nature, that is, not affected by natural determinants, such as geology, climatology, physiography, and the like.[10]

In this vein, we treat social structures as normative phenomena of intersubjective consciousness which frame social actions in social space. It might be suggested that Durkheim apprehended this with great insight to be the cardinal facet of human society, and it is these phenomena which he intended by the concept of *représentations collectives,* which derive

6. Marion J. Levy, Jr., *The Structure of Society* (Princeton: Princeton University Press, 1952), p. 58.
7. Claude Lévi-Strauss, *Les Structures élémentaires de la parenté* (Paris: Presses Universitaires de France, 1949); "Social Structure" in A. L. Kroeber, ed., *Anthropology Today, An Encyclopedic Inventory* (Chicago: University of Chicago Press, 1953), pp. 524-558; "Les limites de la notion de structure en ethnologie," in Roger Bastide, ed., *Sens et usages du terme structure dans les sciences humaines et sociales (Janua Linguarum,* 16 [The Hague: Mouton and Co., 1962]), 40-45.
8. Georges Gurvitch, "Les Structures Sociales," in his *Traité de Sociologie,* vol. 1 (Paris: Presses Universitaires de France, 1958), pp. 205-215; for a recent exposition of Gurvitch see Phillip Bosserman, *Dialectical Sociology, An Analysis of the Sociology of Georges Gurvitch* (Boston: Porter Sargent, 1968), esp. chap. 6.
9. See Bastide, ed., *Sens et usages.*
10. "Social Structure," in Kroeber, *Anthropology Today,* p. 533.

from a more undifferentiated structure, the *conscience collective*. Viewing social structures as (moral) phenomena of social consciousness, rather than as physical entities, will enable us to treat the problem of social change in terms of transformations in consciousness rather than in terms of transformations in physical reality. Since consciousness is not fixed or static, a focus upon social structure must make room for the correlative notions of structuration, destructuration, and restructuration being involved in the patterning of institutional life. Finally, as Lévi-Strauss has suggested in another context,[11] the kind of analysis underlying the structural approach partakes more of a qualitative than of a quantitative analysis; this is reflected in our viewing societal change as primarily a qualitative rather than a quantitative transformation of social reality.

Time and Society as Phenomena

In an earlier paper I have argued that in the established corpus of sociology the major themes and standpoints concerning social reality are congruent with the philosophical perspective termed existential phenomenology.[12] These themes not only are salient in the recognized phenomenological school of sociology (Vierkandt, Scheler, Mannheim) but also are cardinal presuppositions of a much broader and influential spectrum of theorists (Weber, Durkheim, Cooley, Thomas, Mead, Parsons, and Sorokin).

A common denominator to the sociological tradition in question is the presupposition that social reality is not reducible to physical reality, that the reality of social being includes a "cultural" or "superorganic" realm with distinct nonmaterial properties. In terms of human actors, their orientation to objects—both material and nonmaterial—is grounded in a cultural setting so that the *meaning* of their actions simply cannot be deduced from the biological, chemical, or physical properties of their situational objects. Concrete social action is a function of how the actor constitutes what is "out there" as an object-for-him in terms of the meaning which the object manifests to him. The meaning of the social object to the social subject *is* a cardinal element, a relational element, in the structuring of their relationship. The process of constituting objects from things, that is, essentially, of making the world relevant and meaningful, is not an ad hoc process save in rare instances. The process of socialization (which we could term *acculturation* had it not been preempted by another usage) functions so as to impart to a given collectivity of actors a world of pretty much commonly meaningful objects.

11. Ibid., p. 528.
12. "Existential Phenomenology and the Sociological Tradition," *American Sociological Review,* 30 (October, 1965), 674-688.

An intrinsic part of the perspective of existential phenomenology is that an object presupposes a subject; that is, objects do not have an existence apart from their relationship to subjects. Hence, reality is in its most elementary aspect a *relational* state of being. This is, after all, at the heart of the sociological image, as illustrated, for example, in the cardinal notion of role, which is fundamentally a relational category. Thus, common sense to the contrary, there is no such concrete thing as a "father" or an "employee"; each is an existential condition which becomes manifest in a social situation, hence contingent upon social interaction.

Further, implicit if not explicit in the sociological tradition is the idea that the description of social phenomena, if it is to be comprehensive, must include the elucidation of the social actor's horizon, which includes the components of meaning and intentionality in his comportment toward his situation. This is at the heart of W. I. Thomas's seminal notion of the "definition of the situation," [13] but also underlies Weber's approach in seeking to link the ethical meaning of modern economic activity to the religious consciousness of ascetic Protestantism, as well as Durkheim's investigation into the social nature of acts of suicide.[14]

It is on the basis of this preliminary discussion that we posit as a major convergence in the development of general sociological theory the notion that social reality is essentially a global phenomenon of intersubjective consciousness; that is, a social psychological reality. This, as I have previously suggested, underlies Durkheim's great discovery of social facts as verifiable manifestations of collective representations which are constituent elements of a more amorphous collective consciousness. Before we can relate this to a conceptualization of societal change, we need entertain some phenomenological considerations regarding history and society.

A phenomenon is that which appears or manifests itself to consciousness, that which emerges into view from a ground to become what it is here and now for a subject. In other words, for a phenomenon to emerge from a background which structures its appearance, it has to be *perceived*. The act of perception cannot be reduced to neurological or physiological elements operative in the perceiver, nor can it be reduced to properties in the object perceived; this has been ably pointed out by Merleau-Ponty in two seminal works of modern phenomenology.[15] Perception, as the

13. See Edmund H. Volkart, ed., *Social Behavior and Personality, Contributions of W. I. Thomas to Theory and Social Research* (New York: Social Science Research Council, 1951), *passim*.
14. For a recent work which uses Durkheim's study as a point of departure, see Jack D. Douglas, *The Social Meanings of Suicide* (Princeton: Princeton University Press, 1967). Another vein of sociological research, "reference group theory," should also be seen as part of this tradition: the concepts of "relative deprivation" and "relative gratification" would indicate that the objective or material status of men is not a necessary and sufficient condition for the consciousness of their social being.
15. Maurice Merleau-Ponty, *The Structure of Behavior* (Boston: Beacon Press, 1963); *Phenomenology of Perception* (London: Routledge and Kegan Paul, 1962).

general activity of human consciousness, is tri-modal: sensory, cognitive (that is, broadly speaking, factual), and normative or morally evaluative. The latter point is particularly salient in the perception of social phenomena: we do not perceive social objects ranging from "birth rates in Latin America" to "student activism" to "presidential campaigns" simply in factual terms but also in their moral aspects. Put in somewhat different terms, the meaning of a phenomenon always contains a moral significance for the perceiver, albeit in many instances this moral component may be latent in the subject's consciousness. Durkheim's term *conscience collective* has given translators many bad moments, but the ambiguity contained in the French term *conscience* is profoundly suggestive that "consciousness" and "conscience" are intrinsically wed.

I am not saying that all actors perceive a phenomenon from the same moral standpoint, to be sure; but I am saying that all social phenomena are in part perceived morally by actors. Thus, a high divorce rate may be seen as a good thing by some, as a social evil by others; though both groups would readily agree as to the facts, the situation is perceived differently in terms of its moral evaluation. The same thing can be said about any social condition, such as race riots or the use of drugs. And though we cannot treat this save in passing, moral differentials in the perception of social phenomena are conveyed by the use of language. For example, it makes quite a difference whether we label the Mau Mau movement as a "terrorist" activity or as a "national liberation" movement, or whether we label pop art as "decadent" or as "bold and exciting." Changes in descriptive language can give an entirely new coloring to the same phenomenon and radically alter its presentation.

These remarks lead us to observe that social phenomena *qua* phenomena have a *becoming* aspect; they are not frozen or static entities. Rather, they are actualizations or manifestations from an existential ground of possibilities, and it is this ground which we refer to as social structure. It may also be suggested that this latent but real ground which underlies social actualities, this ontological ground of social behavior, is nothing other than culture.

The actualization or "surfacing" of social phenomena from the ground of possibilities is, in one sense, a process wherein social existence takes on increasing configuration or form. That is, the increasing actualization of social phenomena within the structural framework of a certain mode of social being enables the form of the activity to become visible.[16] This process of formalization is, it seems to me, what underlies the concept of institutionalization. Form and structure are interrelated but not identical: structure is an inner condition regulating interchanges between elements;

---

16. For related materials on individual perception, see Jerome S. Bruner, "Social Psychology and Perception," in E. E. Maccoby, T. M. Newcomb, and E. L. Hartley, eds., *Readings in Social Psychology,* 3rd ed. (New York: Holt, 1958), pp. 85-94.

form is the external appearance of this configuration which derives from the underlying structure.

Actualization is necessarily a temporalizing process, which means that social phenomena have their existence unfolding in time. This, however, is not to be understood in terms of mathematical or physical time constructed in reference to some absolute or geometric space. The latter, as Durkheim so brilliantly suggested in *The Elementary Forms of the Religious Life* is an intellectual construct derivative of a more primordial or existential experience of time and space grounded in social life. It is only in the artificial or constructed realm of mathematics and physics that one unit in time-space has the same quality as any other unit, with each separated by equal intervals. As we shall indicate shortly, such is not the case for sociohistorical time.

Heidegger's magistral study, *Being and Time,* underscores not only the temporality of existence but also the *ec-stasy* of time; human existence stretches out into the future and into the past. The past and the future are not, for the subject, entities separated by an unbridgeable hiatus but rather very much part of the present in the subject's situation.[17] The past, existentially viewed, is a having-been present while the future is a will-be present, and both are grounded in the phenomenal emergence of the here and now. This has an important implication in terms of our previous remarks concerning perception, namely that perception is also a temporal phenomenon: human perception involves perceiving a present situation in the light of the past and in the expectation of the future.

It seems apposite at this point to introduce some remarks on the complementarity of history and sociology, postponing for later remarks on the complementarity of anthropology and sociology. Historians and sociologists engage in a basic act of perception, but their fundamental horizon which grounds their observations is seemingly different. Historians implicitly orient their perception to the past as such, whereas sociologists focus upon the societal structure. In each case historians and sociologists may be prey to a false reification of their horizon, leading to what Whitehead termed the "fallacy of misplaced concreteness," the mistaking of the analytical

17. Heidegger's stress that an understanding of the subject's *present* situation involves an existential understanding of the past and the future as elements of the here-and-now situation has implications for the methodology of structural-functional analysis; namely, a comprehensive analysis of the functions of social structures must not only take into account the interdependence and interrelationships of social institutions and their structures here and now but also must ask the questions of the historical ground from which the present social phenomenon under investigation has emerged, as well as what future consequences and states of affair may emerge from the present. Only when the past and the future are interrelated and seen as constitutive elements of the present can structural-functional analysis attain a "global" meaning of the situation. Both Durkheim and Weber in seeking to interpret sociologically the essential meaning of modern society implicitly worked in terms of the dynamic structural-functional analysis we have in mind.

part for the concrete whole, or in existential terms, the reducing of the ontological to the ontic.

There is a certain justification for viewing history as the objective past whose being is not contingent upon our perception. It is a historical datum that the Battle of Waterloo took place in 1815, that the fall of the Bastille occurred in the eighteenth century, and so forth. The present and the future cannot alter the facts of history. The past is, in this sense, full of historical events which have happened at a certain point in historical time and not at another point. The is-ness of the past, that which makes it historical, is the present-that-has-been, that has become historical.

But this does not mean that the past is a fixed object, like entities such as the Rock of Gibraltar or the Eiffel Tower or a chair. For one thing, the past is not a closed entity but rather continuously growing; and it will continue to grow as historical time unfolds, as the indefinite future becomes actualized in the happenings of the present. Moreover, the past also grows as historians seek to unveil the present-that-has-been. Historicizing, or the fundamental activity of historians, is to perceive and shed light on that present which once was visible but which tends to become invisible and covered over by time. The historian, thus, may be properly called the dis- coverer of the past. Paradoxically, even though historical research is always concerned with the past, nothing ever occurs in the past but only in the present. The meaning of the past is a meaning for a subject in the present; the historical past is meaningful only to those on the scene of the historical present. The present itself is always emergent against a back- ground of the future as a set of possibilities. As a corollary, the historical future, which is as much part of the totality of history as the historical past, only emerges from the background of the historical past. The implication of this is that history as the temporal structure of our being- in-the-world is a global phenomenon which escapes objectification. Since the historical past is always part of the reality of the present, the past is always to an important extent a perceived phenomenon (whether it be the colonization of Latin America, the Reformation, or the American Civil War); that is, it will always have emergent aspects as long as history con- tinues to be written. For the past to be exhausted as an object would necessarily imply that the future is exhausted, that is, that historical time would no longer have any possibilities of becoming. The ultimate mean- ing (or "meaning of meanings") of historical events, therefore, can only be *transhistorical;* a global perception of history can be undertaken only after all historical possibilities have been actualized, and that can be only after there is no more history.

Historical time is not an abstract thing nor a constant object but rather is intrinsically related to social existence. Historical time is as much a part of society as social phenomena are grounded in history. Following

the lead of Sorokin and Merton, but particularly that of Gurvitch,[18] we can point out that historical time is not homogeneous or undifferentiated. Different social groupings—social classes, age sets, religious groups, political parties, and so forth—have different temporal horizons and, to use the term of Halbwachs, different "collective memories," which are basic structural aspects of their experience of reality, and within which they orient their actions[19] Furthermore, global historical societies (which encompass concrete social groupings) experience discontinuous rhythms of events, so that it is necessary to bear in mind that the structure of historical time is elastic. To illustrate, the accelerated rhythm of events in France between 1780 and 1800 presents a qualitatively different time structure from that in a similar objective twenty-year period, say between 1700 and 1720; the same holds true for the temporal horizon of colonial Africa in the period 1945–1960 in contrast to the temporal horizon 1920–1935. This points to the phenomenon of societal change being involved in changes in the rates of flow of social events, and this is closely related to changes in the temporal structure of society.

If the reification of the past is a methodological pitfall of historical research, so are sociologists prey to reifying society or social structure. The fabric of society, including its cultural ground, is a dynamic "total societal phenomenon." Every human society, and particularly those with a heterogeneous population, contains a multiplicity of social structures which are, in a sense, potentialities for social action that some may seek to actualize; and in becoming, these often clash with other potentialities that have become and have already crystallized as publicly legitimated social institutions. Or the same structural condition may give rise to incompatible actualizations which nevertheless have the same ground. For example, the framework of the Constitution may, depending on how it is interpreted, provide either for increasing centralization of power or for its obverse. At another level, society as an ongoing phenomenon is in a state of dynamic tension between institutional phenomena which characterize "public life," and noninstitutional ones which fall outside the pale of publicly legitimated and rewarded activity. Institutional phenomena are by and large the visible layer of society. Noninstitutional phenomena which fall outside of and even go counter to the rationalization of conduct are not all of the same order nor do they spring from the same depth level of societal structure

18. Pitirim A. Sorokin and Robert K. Merton, "Social Time: Methodological and Functional Analysis," *American Journal of Sociology*, 42 (March, 1937), 615-629; Georges Gurvitch, "Social Structure and the Multiplicity of Times," in Edward A. Tiryakian, ed., *Sociological Theory, Values, and Sociocultural Change: Essays in Honor of Pitirim A. Sorokin* (New York: Free Press, 1963); also, Gurvitch, *The Spectrum of Social Time* (Dordrecht, Holland: D. Reidel, 1964).
19. Maurice Halbwachs, *La Mémoire Collective* (Paris: Presses Universitaires de France, 1950).

but tend to be concealed from public view, in part because they are "un-pleasant" and in opposition to the value-orientations embodied in the ongoing institutional system. Noninstitutional phenomena are manifesta-tions of radical conceptions of reality (for example, sexual, political, or economic conceptions) from those held by members subscribing to insti-tutional life. In other words, noninstitutional phenomena stem from radi-cally different moral perceptions of social reality; they obey quite different rules of action from those underlying the existing social order. It is be-cause of this that from the perspective of those operating within the normative framework of institutional life, noninstitutional phenomena fre-quently are dismissed as irrational. What is not realized always, though, is that what appears as irrational, if not as immoral, from the point of view of institutional "common sense" will be considered rational and moral by those operating from a different set of normative rules of conduct. Con-versely, institutional, morally approved behavior is held as irrational, if not immoral, within the radical frame of reference.[20]

In any event, it is in the depth dimensions of historical social structures, what is covert or latent (and this corresponds to an important degree with Parsons's conceptualization of the latent dimensions—or *L*-cell—of social systems) that we find the irrational, which, precisely because it is not rationalized conduct, has a high energy level that under certain cir-cumstances can break through institutional barriers and produce dramatic transformations in history. The rise of capitalism, Mahdism, the Boxer Rebellion, the colonization of Africa in the nineteenth century, the origins of modern scientific consciousness in the seventeenth century, the Red Guards' "cultural revolution"—these are but a very few of all historical phenomena having profound irrational (and noninstitutional) dimensions which partake of some form of religious inspiration.

Rather than viewing societies metaphorically as icebergs, it might be more appropriate to view them as volcanoes which for the most part are inactive. The reification of society and social structure may make us focus upon what is above the ground, with the volcano appearing as solidified lava—this being the stolid, overt aspects of public, institutional life. But the covert and depth dimensions of social existence have their being in the magma of the human volcano, the realm of the *sacred*,[21] which stands

---

20. Irrationality and immorality are intrinsic aspects of overt behavior but are in an important sense socially defined. From the perspective of the ongoing society, "hippies" throwing money away on the floor of the New York Stock Exchange are seen as behaving irrationally but not necessarily immorally; terroristic activity, on the other hand, is more likely to be perceived as immoral and possibly irrational. It may be that upon closer scrutiny, irrationality is always fused with immorality in the perception of a concrete action, but this lies outside the scope of these remarks.
21. We assume familiarity on the reader's part with Durkheim's *The Elementary Forms of the Religious Life*. It should be noted, though, that Durkheim gives residual attention to the sacred as such ("things set apart and forbidden") since he is more concerned with the social manifestations of the sacred (the organization of religious

in a dialectic relation to the major institutional spheres of public society, the *secular,* which is predominantly manifest in the spheres of economic and political activity (or, in the well-known paradigm of Parsons, in the "adaptive" and the "goal-directed" subsystems [22]). By the sacred I do not mean organized, institutionalized religion; the latter emerges from but does not exhaust the content of the sacred which transcends any particular sociohistorical reality. The sacred, to follow in the train of Durkheim, contains antithetical divine and demonic forces (this parallels Goffman's use of the terms "good-sacredness" and "bad-sacredness" [23]). The social order, in a sense, represents an ordering of these forces into some sort of equilibrium, or an equilibration of these forces. But these forces also surface in time within the historical setting in the form of such sociohistorical phenomena as philanthropism, the Enlightenment, Pietism, nationalism, or communism, all of which over time develop rational features of institutionalization which make us overlook their origins in the irrational.

It is from the fundamental antinomy within the sacred itself, that is, within ultimate being itself (whether we take it to be contained in social existence or transcending it is an issue which need not concern us here) that the social order emerges as the regulation of the irrational, of the sacred. The regulation of the sacred, the converting of irrational moral forces into rational means–ends activity, is the process of social structuration. It is, we might say, a process of moralization. Here we might note the congruence between this formulation and Goffman's observation that "to describe the rules regulating a social interaction is to describe its structure." [24] But we must go beyond this and note the obverse, the process of destructuration or deregulation of the institutional life; this demoralization of the social order is precisely what Durkheim intended by the term *anomie* (which he also referred to as *dérèglement*).

Structuration involves structural differentiation (an aspect of societal change treated at considerable length by Parsons [25]) and the rationalization of conduct in specific spheres; it is at the heart of what Weber termed the "routinization of charisma." [26] Structuration is orderly change and a prerequisite for social order, but destructuration, at least analytically, is a

---

beliefs and practices). For classic phenomenological approaches to the sacred, see Rudolf Otto, *The Idea of the Holy* (New York: Oxford University Press, 1958), and G. van der Leeuw, *Religion in Essence and Manifestation,* 2 vols. (New York: Harper, 1963).

22. Edward A. Tiryakian, "A Model of Societal Change and its Lead Indicators," in Samuel Klausner, ed., *The Study of Total Societies* (Garden City: Doubleday, 1967), p. 79.

23. Erving Goffman, *Interaction Ritual* (Garden City: Doubleday, 1967), p. 70 fn.

24. Ibid., p. 144.

25. See, for example, his "Some Considerations on the Theory of Social Change," *Rural Sociology,* 26 (September, 1961), 219-239.

26. In Hans Gerth and C. Wright Mills, eds., *From Max Weber: Essays in Sociology* (New York: Oxford University Press, 1958), *passim.*

very different phenomenon of change: the deformation of structures or structural dedifferentiation (which seems to me very closely tied in with Tilly's discussion elsewhere in this volume of "devolutionary processes"). An advanced phase of destructuration (or deregulation) of institutional life is commonly called social *disorder*.

Since social structures as the intersubjective cadres of social action are latent or covert (in the same sense as is the "ground" in Gestalt psychology), it is for the most part rarely that these "tacit dimensions" of social activity are questioned, that is, that perceptual awareness is directed to them. They are homologous to the "presuppositions" of a scientific theory. In general, sociological observations are hardly different from those of the layman; they focus on what is manifest without seeking to relate it systematically to the latent ground from which they emerge and placing the latter itself under closest scrutiny.[27] By way of analogy, the typical orientation is like that of a spectator at a movie taking as exhaustive of what is there, what is seen on the screen, or even mistaking the contents of the film as a rendition of reality. Not only do we not look back and notice the physical structures which make this reality possible (the projector, the screen), but also—and more important—we do not even think of considering other structures such as the fact that what is acted out is a function of what the director, the producer, and the playwright have wanted to depict on the screen. Who does the staging for institutional life, and with what intentionality, is seldom thought about, since attention is typically addressed only to what is staged.

What we have been saying thus far implies that sociological theory insofar as it seeks to be general—that is, to provide a comprehensive understanding of social reality—must relate institutional life to its latent structures. To do so properly it must take the latter not simply as given but as profoundly problematic. This is exactly, as I see it, the kind of truly rigorous empiricism which Garfinkel has been engaging in at the microlevel of analysis, and for which his paper in this volume seeks to provide a kind of codification. But we are nowhere even near this preliminary stage at the macrolevel of social structures, and to think properly about such an undertaking—that is, to think about making sociology a rigorously comparative social science—we must realize that sociology must become in a crucial aspect historical in its orientation. We are again reiterating our contention that, for sociology at least, a structural approach should never be thought of as divorced from considerations of social time or history.

The focus of structural sociology upon the emergence of social phe-

---

27. To consider the latent functions of manifest institutions is a step in the right direction but only a step, for we also have to treat the latent but existing structures operative in a given societal setting, only some of which have an institutional legitimacy.

nomena in social time or history leads us to other considerations which need to be discussed.

Culture and Societal Structure

If, on the one hand, the sociological horizon has to be expanded so as to incorporate the historical dimension into sociological analysis, so also, on the other hand, must sociological theory make room for a direct consideration of culture as the ground of society.[28] By this I mean that we cannot simply pay lip service to society and culture as analytically interrelated in a formal conceptual sense, but rather must rethink the nature of the cultural matrix. To think of it in a caricature version of introductory sociology textbooks as "the man-made part of the environment" or "all that is transmitted by learning" or some such summary statement is absurdly simplistic. To view culture as a manifold set of symbols which are expressions of value orientations is a closer approximation, provided we keep in mind that these symbols are at various depth levels of intersubjective consciousness and that they do not constitute a closed system. The deeper the levels, the more psychical and symbolic the cultural reality, which corresponds to the depth levels of personality structure. Cultural symbols, in this vein, may be seen as being at intermediate levels between the surface aspects of culture and the deepest, most tenebrous levels which are states of divergent and often conflicting moral ideals and antithetical religious forces. It is from these depths that charisma, for example, arises.

The idea that culture in its fundamental aspect is of a religious sort is suggested in the etymological connection of *culture* and *cult,* and in terms of the sociological tradition, Durkheim's magnum opus points to the structural forms of social life as being of a religious nature. As we have stated earlier, however, religious forces are not exhausted or contained in institutionalized religions and their intellectual expressions (creeds and theologies). Institutionalized religions, those which are publicly recognized and legitimated (churches and denominations, in the Western context) have a high degree of rationalization of religious forces, even though, in some instances, their names (such as the Quakers or the Shakers) indicate their early inspiration in a more turbulent encounter with religious reality. The latter also finds expression in more irrational groupings and esoteric orientations which constitute a sort of religious underground, and this underground (of which heresies and heretical movements are notable instances)

28. This is at the heart of Durkheim's statement, "Les principaux phénomènes sociaux, religion, morale, droit, économie, esthétique, ne sont autre chose que des systèmes de valeurs, partant, des idéaux. La sociologie se place donc d'emblée dans l'idéal," *Sociologie et Philosophie* (Paris: Presses Universitaires de France, 1951), pp. 140-141. Culture was for Durkheim the realm of moral ideas as the ground of social reality.

may be found in all the major world religions, including Christianity and Judaism (for example, the theosophic tradition on the pale of Christianity, or the Kabbala and the Zohar in Judaism).

The sociological significance of the religious underground lies precisely in the area of societal change. If societal change is to be a distinct phenomenon for sociological analysis, it cannot be mere change in the content of institutional life but rather a change in the societal structure within which institutions are organized. This general societal structure (which structures and orders the more differentiated structures of institutions) is a moral/religious frame of reference which for the social actors that operate in its framework is only tacitly experienced. In other words, it is not a situational "object" for them since it is part of their own subjectivity (in Durkheimian terms, the *conscience collective* is equivalent to this intersubjective general structure).

Innovations of societal structure, therefore, can only come from actors or collectivities who are consciously outside this broad normative frame of reference which we identify as societal structure. Societal change, as we have been using the term, thus stems from those who are religious radicals, alien to or alienated from the normative order of the ongoing society. From this I wish to suggest that the ground of any genuine social revolution is an attempted overturning and radical rotation (etymologically, revolution = rotation) of the normative axis which frames and orders institutional life. To localize revolution in the political or even the economic sector is to mistake the part for the whole, in the sense that a social revolution is a "total social phenomenon," of which political or economic transformations are only parts. We are thus advancing the hypothesis for a comparative analysis of societal change, and of revolution in particular,[29] that innovative political and economic structural changes represent not only transformations in the consciousness of political and economic structures and how these may be reordered, but also—and more significantly—that such transformations in consciousness may be traced to a religious inspiration which views reality in a radically different way from the majority of the members of the ongoing social order. Stated differently, some aspect of religious radicalism (heterodoxy or heresy in some form or other) is a prerequisite of political and economic radicalism.

The implication of this hypothesis is that a sociological analysis of structural change manifested in political and economic departures from established institutional channels must consider more rigorously than hitherto their background cultural setting in religious movements and groupings outside the pale of the visible social establishment. Furthermore, the cultural underground is not confined to strictly religious groupings as such but may also include quasi-religious groups whose manifest functions would seem

29. See our paper, "A Model of Societal Change and Its Lead Indicators."

unimportant for the analysis of political, economic, and cultural change. I would include here the vast array of domestic and fraternal associations, workingmen associations, recreational associations, as well as more occult and esoteric cults, such as theosophic societies of the kind that are secretive and/or initiatory in key aspects of their organization and structure. Aside from Simmel,[30] the realm of the secret in society has not been given much sociological weight, but for an understanding of the dynamics of structural change I would argue that quasi-religious groups which are organizationally secretive (even in some aspect to their own rank-and-file members) may be inspirational sources of the change in question.[31] Thus, "Liberty, Equality, Fraternity" as the rallying slogan of the political consciousness of the French Revolution was first formulated as the symbol of a quasi-religious fraternal lodge.

Treating the societal structure of an ongoing social order as a normative framework suggests an important base of collaboration between sociology and the kind of contemporary social anthropology which draws upon the influence of Durkheim and Mauss in particular. As Beidelman implies in his contribution to this volume, the renewed interest in cosmological systems which stems from the French sociological tradition is "where the action is" in the new generation of anthropology. This recent structural approach in social anthropology, in a vein parallel to our orientation (and which draws from the same source in Durkheim) finds as the key ingress to the analysis of social systems of primitive societies the system of symbolic categorizations of the world which underlies social organization. It is in particular the dualistic nature of these broad cosmological categories which is of note, among which the following are of particular importance: left–right, up–down, odd–even, pure–impure, dark–light, masculine–feminine, and color polarities, such as white–black and red–white. If sociologists think of these categories of being of interest only to anthropologists studying non-Western, nonmodern "folk societies," we may be overlooking a very fruitful entry into consideration of the structure of cultural reality as a general aspect of *all* societies, including large-scale "modern" societies. In other words, I am suggesting that these categories should be seen as socially universal representations of the moral forces which we have taken to be in this essay the substratum of social reality.

The fact that the categories are representations of antithetical moral forces implies that the antinomies are not of a logical but of an existential nature, which further implies that each of the antithetical forces seeks to

30. See his "The Secret and the Secret Society," in Kurt H. Wolff, ed., *The Sociology of Georg Simmel* (Glencoe: Free Press, 1950), pp. 307-376. For a different translation of the same work, see the earlier version of Albion Small, "The Sociology of Secrecy and of Secret Societies," *American Journal of Sociology,* 11 (January, 1906), 441-498.
31. For comparative descriptive materials, see Thomas Frost, *The Secret Societies of the European Revolution, 1776–1876,* 2 vols. (London: Tinsley Brothers, 1876).

become—that is, to express its dominance over its counterpart.[32] In other words, these forces are of a dynamic rather than a static sort. If these representations are further seen as being manifest in sociocultural reality as well as being fundamental frames of societal structure, then this opens a vast area of exploration for sociological theory, namely a systematic relating of the categories uncovered by structural anthropology to their manifestations in modern society. For example, as basic moral structures of social space, up–down and left–right seem of crucial importance. The antinomy of up–down underlies the movement of social mobility on a vertical axis, characteristically an economic movement, be it of individuals or of aggregates which is met by resistance on the part of those "higher up." The antinomy of left–right embodies another attempted kind of social mobility, characteristically a political movement along a horizontal continuum (this suggests, among other things, that polity and economy are orthogonal vectors, implying further that economic and political development cannot be simultaneously maximized in a given society). However, before this sort of structural analysis can be undertaken rigorously, we must set up a large-scale codification of ethnological research on the meaning of these categories in the cultural context in which they have been observed, establish their general properties, and then go on to the task of translating their relevance for the sociological understanding of the kind of large-scale, Western-type societies with which we customarily deal. Nevertheless, it is suggestive to think, for example, that in African societies *red* is associated with *left,* and *white* with *right,* and that the same color symbolism crops up in Western antithetical political movements.

We may also assert that this structural approach is germane to the study of large-scale societal change. An orderly society, one which is normatively integrated to a fairly high degree, may be seen as one whose categories—which underlie the patterns or forms of institutional life—are in a state of dynamic equilibrium. This means that institutional life occurs in a medial area (metaphorically, in an area within two standard deviations of the mean); oscillations within this may be thought of as zero-sum changes of the social order. Real or non-zero-sum changes in cultural patternings would be changes in the inversion of the moral interpretation of these categories, in their becoming ambiguous particularly as these apply to social groups and institutional life. This is another way of looking at societal change in terms of moral transformations of consciousness, or in the apt phrase of Nietzsche, the "transvaluation of values." As an illustration from the contemporary cultural scene in the West, or at least in the United States, the effeminization of men (symbolized in hair style, clothing, and so forth) and the corresponding masculinization of women represent an inversion of

32. Our earlier statement concerning the dualistic nature of the sacred in terms of the antithesis of the "divine" and the "demonic" should be considered as a possible ground for the dichotomous aspect of the cosmological categories.

masculine–feminine which should not be lightly dismissed as just a new cultural fad but rather as surface manifestations of cultural destructuration.

I have been suggesting in the course of this paper that for an adequate sociological approach to societal change we must embark upon the closest collaboration with history and anthropology. From the former we require comparative materials on the historical transformations of societies; from the latter comparative materials on levels and meanings of cultural symbols. Since cultural symbols are corporate representations of reality—that is, symbols of group identity (which implies how the group identifies itself religiously with reality)—the surfacing of new collective symbols onto the ongoing social fabric should be given much more importance in understanding the directionality of societal change, both in terms of locating the sources of change and also in terms of where it might be heading. Thus, for a comparative sociological analysis of rapid political changes of major scale, we might find it fruitful to probe into the historical origin of the swastika in the case of the structural upheavals of Nazi Germany: who in the Nazi movement suggested it, what sacred imagery it signified, when it was adopted and under what circumstance, and finally, what comparisons in meaning there are between the Nazi identification with the swastika and the latter's earlier manifestations in other cultures. We might make the same inquiry for the gnostic symbols on the great seal of the United States (appearing innocuously on the American dollar bill), or for the adoption of the code name *Spartacus* by the head figure of the Bavarian Illuminati in the eighteenth century, or its adoption as the code name of the head of an underground political organization in twentieth-century Germany.

At this juncture we might make explicit a further set of assumptions which underlie this essay. We assume that, taking the totality of human societies in social time and social space, the dimensions of culture are finite and the forms of structuration and destructuration are also finite. This implies that we can go behind the specificities of given historical-cultural situations and find essentially comparable structural conditions operative in different sociohistorical settings. That is, we assume that the range of variations in historical societal structures and in the channels of transformation of these structures is relatively small. We also assume that a society is a "total cultural phenomenon" by which we mean that some levels of it are irrational, not subject to rational manipulation and consideration or institutionalization. We would use the term "cultural reality principle" to refer to the fact that intended or planned social change, which is addressed to just the institutional life of society by its planners, will always be attended in a short time (one or two generations) by aspects from cultural reality which are not incorporated in the intentionality but which have sufficient force to divert the planned change from its course.

Yet, paradoxically, our theoretical considerations lead us to assert that the course of societal change is predictable, that the future may be soci-

ologically foreseen. Since the historical future emerges in the present from a ground of the historical past—we treat the future as an immanent condition of the structural possibilities and the channels of their actualization —prediction *on a probability basis* is possible. The all-important proviso is that we can relate with sufficient accuracy present structural conditions to those which in past historical settings have been anterior to a course of historical events. Suppose that we can specify that in present American society we have operative structural conditions $C_1, C_2, C_3 \ldots , C_n$ (where n is a finite number). Also suppose that in checking with the socio-historical past (treating all of recorded human history as one differentiated action space of societies) we find that C_1 and C_2 were operative in a historical setting where the significant course of change took the form of H_1, and suppose that we find that C_2 and C_3 were operants in another historical setting where the course of events took the form of H_2, and so on. Assuming that the forms of historical transformations in societal structures are not infinite, such a comparative sociohistorical analysis might yield a set, $H_1, H_2, \ldots , H_k$ (where k is a finite, small number). This would make it possible to foresee the future in terms of probability statements of the following sort. Given present manifest conditions, there is a probability of .4 that H_1 will be the course of events which will emerge as the future-becoming-present, a probability of .2 that H_2 will emerge, a probability of .1 that H_3 will emerge, and so forth. Ideally, or as a limiting case, in terms of knowledge of past courses of events and knowledge of present fundamental operative conditions, we should be able to specify with given probabilities all that can emerge (that is to say, the sum of the probabilities $= 1$). Included in the states of the emergent future are large-scale societal discontinuities which represent breakdowns in the organization of institutional life and which take place in a short time period, such as political and economic revolutions. The assigning of probability value to a likely course of events is not a fixed matter, a once-for-all affair, for as new observations are taken in, it should be possible to discern with greater clarity in which of major possible channels of development the society is progressing; in other words, from a given set of structural possibilities, concrete actualizations progressively diminish the degrees of freedom available. This, I think, fairly approximates what Smelser has discussed in terms of the "value-added process." [33] However, I would add that in terms of the present, there are always some degrees of freedom operative rather than one outcome being a necessary condition. To illustrate: in the eighteenth century, France and England had evolved remarkably similar conditions of societal destructuration, of sociocultural normlessness or anomie, yet while France went into a channel of large-scale political transformations, England went into a channel of economic and cultural transformations. If England was able to avoid in the nick of time

33. Neil J. Smelser, *Theory of Collective Behavior* (New York: Free Press, 1963), esp. pp. 13-19.

the violent French outcome it was, I suggest, mainly due to the coming into power, at least at the cultural level, of a new social class which drew its inspiration from the religious revival of the preceding generation (particularly spearheaded by Methodism), whereas in France the politically oriented Jacobins were able to redirect the course of events into political channels.

Conclusions

I have suggested in the course of this paper that structural sociology is a theoretical approach which is a macrodynamic analysis of societal systems, having as its starting point the analysis of the fundamental essences of a total society, located in its cultural framework, and which proceeds to consider the actualizations of these possibilities.[34] These actualizations are always historical channels or sequences, so that the past and the future may be seen as immanent aspects or conditions of the present.

We see our approach as a renovation of structural-functional analysis. Structural-functional analysis is not in itself a theory of the major parameters of social reality but it is a methodological prerequisite for any such theory; it is implicitly oriented to sociocultural reality as a global or total social phenomenon, irreducible to any concrete sector as a "prime mover" of the totality. An adequate structural-functional analysis of the present must at one level examine the historical past; at another level, the emergent future. In this context, Jules Michelet, the famous French historian, once stated what is in fact an admirable counsel for structural-functional analysts: *Celui qui voudra s'en tenir au présent, à l'actuel, ne comprendra pas l'actuel* ("He who would limit himself to the present, the actual, will not understand the actual"). This thought is echoed in a more recent statement by Werner Stark: "There is no greater laboratory of social experimentation than the past, and it is a pity that sociologists, fascinated by other kinds of laboratory, have not learnt more from it." [35] And as a complement we should remind ourselves of the dictum of Auguste Comte, the grandfather, if not the father, of structural-functional analysis, that the sociological endeavor is geared to *voir pour prévoir* (that is, our analysis of the seen must be geared to the foreseeable).

34. This, we might suggest, is a radical approach to social systems, provided we understand "radical" in its etymological sense of "going to the roots." This sociological approach may be thought of as a special case of Husserl's statement: "The old ontological doctrine, that the knowledge of 'possibilities' must precede that of actualities (*Wirklichkeiten*) is . . . in so far as it is rightly understood and properly utilized, a really great truth." Edmund Husserl, *Ideas, General Introduction to Pure Phenomenology* (New York: Crowell, 1962), p. 213.
35. Werner Stark, *The Fundamental Forms of Social Thought* (London: Routledge and Kegan Paul, 1962), p. 222.

What we must look for in the present must be in part the conditions of institutional life and the extrapolations we can make from these as projections of the future. But we must also, if we are to remain true to the sociological tradition, elevate ourselves from social consciousness to sociological consciousness or, in Husserlian terms, "bracket" our perspective from that of the natural standpoint,[36] or place in doubt the institutional life. By means of the phenomenological *épochè,* sociological awareness becomes an awareness of the noninstitutional infrastructures of the socially visible, that is, in a sense, of the nonrational and even irrational conditions and forces beneath the rationalized activities of the visible social world. To become "musically attuned" to the cultural underground is to follow in the footsteps of Weber, Durkheim, Pareto, and Scheler, each of whom was highly sensitized to the nonrational forces of modern society, each of whom treated the course of modern society as problematic rather than accepting bland assumptions that social progress was insured by technological progress.

A view of the present in terms of technology and economic development as the crucial determinants of society is bound to show the emergent future as a continuous and progressive development, a continuous betterment and progressive control of the physical environment. However, it may sober our analysis if we perceive the present in terms of broader cultural conditions which, structurally speaking, have been manifest in other sociocultural settings on the eve of large-scale societal transformations and discontinuities.

There are a number of features present in the American scene which parallel structural aspects found in England and France in the generation preceding the events of 1789. On the one hand, the so-called enlightenment viewed world history as having embarked on a course of unalterable continuous progress, propped by the new economics which would guarantee the march into the New Jerusalem. Then and now this surface optimism camouflaged conditions of sociocultural ferment and destructuration of normative cohesion; structurally speaking, we have today a similar cultural constellation of enlightened "liberal" monarchs estranged from the masses, a rival Phillippe Egalité, Jacobin clubs, widespread libertinage, profound splits within religious organizations as to what their orientation to society should be, political agitation on behalf of and by a *sans-culottes* class (the Negroes in our instance), rapid scientific and industrial developments (space explorations via rockets being analogous to space exploration via balloons), concern over the mentally ill, the effeminization of men and a more general ambiguity of sex roles, increased street violence, tensions between young and old (that is, an increasing social distance between generations), and a general ferment concerning the urgency to overhaul existing social and political institutions.

36. Husserl, *Ideas,* pp. 95-100.

From this perspective of structural comparability with the eighteenth century, the emergent future as a structural aspect of the present may well be another French Revolution, albeit there is also a smaller likelihood of an English nonviolent but equally significant alternative. But there are also present features found in historical situations which produced manifestly different if equally discontinuous outcomes. Thus, still in terms of present structural conditions, there are parallels with the preindustrial European setting on the eve of World War I: expanding economic affluence in consumer goods and the internationalization of economic growth, changes in clothing style from Victorian simplicity to Edwardian splendor, rapid technological progress including means of transportation and communication. It would have been hard in 1910 to foresee World War I as a logical outcome of political discontinuity—but it did occur, and we treat it not as an unfortunate accident but rather as a direct outcome of internal crises of European society (a tragic validation of Durkheim's notion of *anomie*.) On the eve of World War I, France and Germany, for example, experienced profound internal political conflicts between radicals and conservatives, a polarization of political life which structurally is that of our own internal situation. The crisis, as a general state of cultural destructuration, had multiple phenomenal manifestations not limited to the political and economic sectors. Thus, the crisis in the arts' depiction of reality reflected the underlying global destructuration, for the avant-garde trends in painting, music, and literature (reflected in the post-impressionists, expressionists, cubists, and by Schönberg, Ezra Pound, and others) all manifested the destructuration of a stable social world; and science, whose innovative impetus is a form of artistic creativity, also participated in the subjacent destructuration of reality (for example, through the theory of relativity or the psychoanalytic theory of the unconscious). The same sort of crises may be found in art and science today, reflecting a broader breakdown in the ordering of reality. Fragmentary as this discussion must necessarily be, I trust it suggests that a global war is another possible outcome of internal societal destructuration camouflaged by material opulence.

Let me in cursory fashion suggest structural similarities in the present cultural setting with other historical situations marked by discontinuities: the Weimar Republic of the 1920's on the one hand, and the sixteenth century on the other. The appearance on the American cultural scene today of swastikas and iron crosses, the craze of monsters, the hippie movement, the forms of demonic morbidity on the stage and other media of entertainment which not only have a pathological fascination with the Nazis (including a morbid fascination with sadism) but with other themes of decadence—all these should not be lightly dismissed. The Nazi movement which emerged on the political left of Germany in the Weimar period was not seriously taken as a threat by liberals in power, who were more worried by the Communists and by reactionaries, but the Nazis capitalized on the irrational

forces (which they themselves helped to accentuate) unloosened by the cultural destructuration of Germany. As to the structural similarity between the present and the sixteenth century, which certainly was an age of large-scale upheavals, the death-of-God cult in theological circles is a playback of the negative theology of that period, just as much as the new left youth movement as a political orientation is structurally similar to Thomas Münzer's Anabaptist movement. The very upheaval of the Catholic church today involved in its protestantization within one generation is one of the most far-reaching cultural events of world history, structurally identical to the Protestant Reformation of the sixteenth century. The breakdown of the hegemony of Catholic authority may be seen positively as having made possible the rise of industrial and scientific Western civilization since the net consequence of the Protestant revolution was to redirect spiritual energy to this-worldly activities, but we must also bear in mind that insofar as it also represented a climactic breakdown in the normative integration of Europe, this cultural destructuration was also attended by a century of "religious" wars—in a sense, the *first* world war in the West.

What I have been suggesting so far is that physical upheavals, or large-scale political disorders are short-term manifestations of underlying cultural disorder; or, to put it differently, large-scale physical violence, which dots the panorama of history, is a surfacing of irrational but real forces when the normative framework of the sociocultural milieu becomes inoperative. Going a step further, I consider all large-scale political upheavals to be of the same social genus as different species: revolutions, civil wars, world wars are functionally equivalent. From this point of view, the American Civil War is not only structurally similar to, say, the French civil war of 1870, but is also a resultant of internal strains and tensions which in Europe in 1914 culminated in World War I—and the strains involved should be shown by sociological analysis to have been found within the North, not just on an interregional level. (The parallels between the riots in New York over conscription in the 1860's and similar riots today concerning conscription for the Vietnam War should give food for thought.) If large-scale political upheavals partake of a deeper cultural destructuration, and if indeed they are of the same genus, we should consider it sociologically naïve that we can at the international level legislate against war as a solution to international tensions. Short of a totalitarian world government, the resolution of internal tensions is the only satisfactory prerequisite to world peace. And the resolution of internal tensions, which is a most critical problem today, has to be thought out in terms of cultural restructuration for which no economic or even purely political planning can be adequate.

Put in crudest terms, political planning can only bring about a mechanical integration of society, and economic solutions to societal ills are psychologically simplistic in their diagnosis. Economic affluence is no panacea for cultural disruptions; if anything, it accentuates the breakdown of social

solidarity by fostering a spirit of hedonism which has a logical linkage to nihilism.

I do not wish to impart the impression that the "spirit" of this essay leads to pessimism about the emergent future. The spirit of the structural approach I have touched upon is one of realism, not of pessimism. I think it is possible that a concerted effort by sociologists, historians, and ethnologists in a common social science enterprise might make it possible to uncover the fuller dimensions of the cultural matrix of social reality. In turn, this knowledge of culture may make possible its relatively adequate control, so that progressive (that is, orderly) sociocultural change can be insured. At present, the direction of sociocultural change which seems to me on the scene is more regressive than progressive; the surface cultural scene of Western society—perhaps of international society if we can begin to think on such grandiose terms—has more manifestations of regression or what I would term paganization than of progression or civilization. The eruption of archaic themes from the depths of the irrational—astrology, witchcraft, black masses, ritual murders (such as recent cases of Hell's Angels' crucifixion of the woman who performed an Aztec-like heart-plucking of her child)—may seem to be trivial considerations for sociological theory in terms of orthodox notions of social reality. But from a broader perspective of the sociological tradition, these are cultural data we simply cannot afford to ignore, not only in order to understand more fully the dynamics of sociocultural change, but also to do something about it, to give it a constructive direction if this is at all possible in an age where everything is possible. After all, Comte's dictum, as good a motto as sociology has ever found, is in full *voir pour prévoir pour pourvoir*. To assist in purveying society is, in the last analysis, a fuller justification of sociology.

5.

Sociological Theory
and the Study of Social Conflict

T. B. Bottomore

T. B. Bottomore was born in Nottingham, England, in 1920 and was educated at the Nottingham Boys' High School and the University of London (London School of Economics and Political Science). Mr. Bottomore is now professor of sociology at the University of Sussex, Brighton, England. He was head of the department of political science, sociology, and anthropology at Simon Fraser University, Vancouver, Canada, from 1965 to 1967, and before that reader in sociology at the London School of Economics. His published writings deal with social theory, especially Marxism, social stratification, and the sociology of development. His most recent book, Critics of Society, *examines radical thought and radical social movements in North America. He was Secretary of the International Sociological Association from 1953 to 1959, and is one of the editors of the* Archives Européennes de Sociologie.

We are very far from possessing a sociological theory of conflict at the present time. A number of writers indeed have pointed to a marked decline of interest in the subject from the beginning of this century until the last decade or so. Lewis Coser, for example, in his introduction to *The Functions of Social Conflict* [1] observes that while the early American sociologists (particularly Small and Cooley) recognized the importance of social conflict, and even assigned a positive value to it, the sociologists of the 1950's showed little concern with the subject, and when they treated it at all it was to dismiss it briefly as a purely disruptive phenomenon. This was in line with the prevailing functionalist conception of the nature of human societies. Another writer, Alastair Buchan, has remarked, with reference to international conflicts, that ". . . until very recently . . . the study of war and peace attracted nothing like the degree of intellectual attention that has been devoted for three or four generations to economic analysis . . . and, whatever the reasons, there is no generally acknowledged corpus of theory . . . ." [2]

This is not to say, of course, that there was no interest at all in the phenomena of social conflict after the period in which the founders of sociology and the classical nineteenth-century writers made their studies. Marxism,

1. Glencoe: Free Press, 1956.
2. *War in Modern Society: An Introduction* (London: Watts, 1966), p. xii.

which has been the preeminent social theory of the last hundred years, treats conflict, especially class conflict, as a fundamental characteristic of society. Even in this case, however, it is true to say that the underlying interest in social conflict did not produce much in the way of new reflection upon, or empirical investigation of, the class struggles and the international Wuit uf ihi iwentieth century It is chiefly since the mid-1950's that social scientists have rediscovered the significance of conflict- u velau il ii alien ing to the character of this century, with its two world wars, its ideological confrontations, its dictatorships, its revolutionary movements and wars of national liberation, and finally its possession of the means of mass destruction through nuclear war. From a somewhat unreal view of societies as harmoniously integrated wholes, disturbed only by minor and transitory "deviations," we seem now to have moved toward a conception of the co-existence of integrating and disruptive forces in the actual historical life of particular societies and in the system of relations between societies, a conception close to that which was set forth more than half a century ago by Simmel: ". . . there probably exists no social unit in which convergent and divergent currents among its members are not inseparably interwoven. An absolutely centripetal and harmonious group, a pure 'unification,' not only is unreal, it could show no real life process. . . . Society, too, in order to attain a determinate shape, needs some quantitative ratio of harmony and disharmony, of association and competition, of favourable and unfavourable tendencies." [3]

Yet this recognition of the social significance of conflict is scarcely even the beginning of wisdom. Any man, let alone a social scientist, living in the world of the 1960's, must be remarkably insensitive if the daily experience —either direct or through the mass media—of armed struggles in Asia, Africa, and Latin America, of Negro revolts in American cities, of student rebellions in many countries, does not awaken in his mind some notion of the ubiquity of conflict and of its importance in shaping human affairs. From the social scientist, however, we expect more than this simple acknowledgment of a fact. What is it that the sociologist, in particular, may be expected to provide? The list is long, and encompasses the main problems of a sociological theory of conflict. The diverse forms of conflict should be enumerated; the incidence and extent of conflict more precisely stated and their fluctuations noted; the varying balance between division and conflict on one side, integration and harmony on the other, more carefully described; the causes of conflict investigated (and so far as is necessary, or

3. From Georg Simmel's essay *Der Streit,* first published as chap. 4 of his *Soziologie* (Leipzig: Duncker and Humblot, 1908). I quote here and in subsequent references from the English translation by Kurt H. Wolff published under the title *Conflict* (Glencoe: Free Press, 1955). There was an earlier translation by Albion Small of a different version of the essay in the *American Journal of Sociology,* vol. 9 (1904). Small was profoundly interested in the problem of conflict and drew for his own theories upon Marx, Gumplowicz, and Simmel.

possible, traced from the social to the psychological and biological spheres);
the effects of conflict examined.

Types of Conflict

Many of these questions were considered by sociologists in the nineteenth
century, and have been taken up again in recent years. Let us see, first of
all, what the earlier writers contributed toward a body of useable theory.
Not all of them attempted to distinguish in a formal way between types of
conflict; nevertheless, a simple distinction was made implicitly between
international conflict (wars between nations, or empires, or tribal groups),
and internal conflict (revolutionary struggles, civil war). The relative importance of these two types of conflict was variously estimated. Comte and
Spencer were chiefly concerned with international conflict (and with a
historical contrast between militant and industrial types of society); so,
later on, were Gumplowicz and Oppenheimer. Marx, on the other hand, regarded internal conflict (the struggle between classes) as the most significant form, and his social theory has little to say about international conflict.
Later, there were attempts to develop, within Marxism, a theory of imperialism and war (by Lenin, Hilferding and Rosa Luxemburg among
others) but this still assumed as its starting point the fundamental conflict
between classes.

This simple distinction between internal and international conflict,
though important,[4] is clearly not adequate. There are variations in the intensity of conflict, and in the extent to which the use or threat of force is
involved; there may also be qualitative distinctions to be made. Simmel, for
instance, distinguished between conflict and competition, treating the latter
as an indirect form of conflict: "linguistic usage reserves the term only for
conflicts which consist in parallel efforts by both parties concerning the
same prize." [5] He went on to examine some specific features of competition,
namely, that its outcome itself does not constitute the goal, that each com-
petitor aims at the goal without using his strength on the adversary, and
that it does not begin from hostility. Within the forms of direct conflict, both
internal and international, there is a range of means employed, from intellectual persuasion, the influence of prestige or propaganda, economic or
political pressure, up to the use of overt violence. One of the characteristic
forms of conflict in modern societies, industrial conflict, displays several
of these features. In the early stages of industrialization in the Western
countries, industrial conflict was sporadic and often violent (notably so in

4. It can be generalized to refer to all social groups; and we may then refer to
internal and external conflict, or intragroup and intergroup conflict. The latter terms
are employed by Coser, *Social Conflict.*
5. In the second chapter of *Conflict,* pp. 57-86.

the United States); in the advanced industrial societies today such conflict is continuous, regulated, and generally nonviolent. Yet it is still not confined entirely or permanently to purely industrial issues or to the sole use of argument, influence, and economic pressure in disputes. Marx's theory envisaged an extension of industrial conflict into the political sphere and the eventual formation of a revolutionary working class; and although the actual course of events has not conformed in detail with these predictions (particularly in respect to the growth of a revolutionary movement), it has been close enough to leave open the question as to the scope and character which industrial conflict may assume. It is evident, in any case, that even in the most peaceful times the threat of force is never far distant from any major industrial dispute.

Such attempts to classify the forms of social conflict have been intended to make the problem more amenable to investigation. They do not presuppose the absence of more general characteristics which are perhaps to be found in all the diverse forms of conflict, or which link these forms together. Conflict may have its source in some universal element of human nature, as Simmel suggested when he wrote that "it seems impossible to deny an *a priori* fighting instinct," [6] and as a number of recent writers, whose work I shall review later, have indicated. Or it may be that there are universal features of social structure which necessarily generate conflict. These are questions to which I shall return.

Measurement of Conflict

The rudimentary classification discussed so far at least makes it easier to move on to a further stage of theoretical construction, namely, the search for regularities in the emergence, extent, and duration of social conflicts. This requires an accumulation of quantitative historical information concerning different types of conflict; and the work in this field, which in any case presents great difficulty, has so far been fragmentary. The two kinds of conflict which have been most fully examined from this point of view are war and industrial conflict. Among the early sociologists, Comte and Spencer both discussed the prevalence of warfare, but their conclusions on the tendency of warfare to diminish in an industrial state of society were not based upon any quantitative comparisons. Similar objections may be raised against most of the sociological discussions of war until quite recently. The earliest attempt to deal comprehensively with the incidence and scale of warfare in different periods was probably that of Pitirim Sorokin in the third volume of *Social and Cultural Dynamics*,[7] but the measures which he used were fairly crude and some of the inferences drawn from the material

6. Simmel, *Conflict*, p. 29.
7. Cincinnati: American Book, 1937.

are invalid. A few years later an exhaustive historical examination of warfare was published by Quincy Wright under the title *A Study of War*,[8] and this too assembled much quantitative information. The most thorough and reliable quantitative inquiry to date is that of L. F. Richardson in his *Statistics of Deadly Quarrels*,[9] which brings together a large volume of data—though covering a relatively short period (roughly from 1820 to 1949)—and attempts to discover the correlates of war, that is, other social events which are associated with the occurrence of war. Richardson's study did not yield any very significant positive correlations, but it did dispose of some facile generalizations about the causes of war and the conditions of peace, while at the same time suggesting that there had been a tendency for the incidence of warfare to decline in relation to population size in the twentieth century. There remains the possibility that an extension of such investigations to other historical periods would reveal long-term fluctuations in warlike activity.

The studies of industrial conflict have also been somewhat disappointing from the point of view of rigorous quantitative comparisons, even though many countries now publish statistics of some kind on the incidence, extent, and duration of industrial disputes. The most thorough statistical study is K. G. J. C. Knowles's *Strikes: A Study in Industrial Conflict*[10] which deals with the United Kingdom in the period 1911–1945 and attempts to correlate strike activity with other social phenomena. There is no work of similar scope on other industrial countries, and there have been few attempts to make comparisons between countries or between historical periods. Two short studies in this field—Clark Kerr and Abraham Siegel, "The Interindustry Propensity to Strike: An International Comparison,"[11] and Arthur M. Ross and Paul T. Hartman, *Changing Patterns of Industrial Conflict*[12]—do bring together data for international comparisons. The first suggests reasons for a greater strike-proneness in certain industries, which Knowles also discussed, while the second distinguishes varying patterns of strike activity as between different groups of countries, and also examines long-term trends. The authors discern a decline in strike activity—a "withering away" of the strike, as they call it—and also a change in the character of strikes, from major instruments of bargaining to sporadic protests; but it is possible that these are actually short-term fluctuations.

When we consider the difficulties which arise in measuring with any precision such phenomena as wars and strikes (although they appear to be relatively easy to isolate and define), and note how little work has yet been

8. Chicago: University of Chicago Press, 1942; 2nd ed., 1965.
9. Pittsburgh: Boxwood Press, 1960.
10. New York: Philosophical Library, 1952.
11. In Arthur Kornhauser, Robert Dubin, and Arthur M. Ross, *Industrial Conflict* (New York: McGraw, 1954), pp. 189-212.
12. New York: Wiley, 1960.

devoted to these problems, it is not surprising that other types of social conflict should have presented seemingly unmanageable difficulties for sociological analysis. How are we to measure the extent of class conflict in a society? How are we to determine the degree of competition, or its fluctuations over time? How then can we determine the balance between the forces of harmony and conflict, integration and division, within given societies; how can we make comparisons between societies in this respect, and how can we relate the phenomena to other social events? There is no obvious answer to these questions, except to say that in many cases it will be necessary to use a variety of indirect measures, and to employ such imprecise numerical terms as "more" and "less." For example, in the study of class conflict it is relevant to consider the formation of trade unions and employers' associations, the occurrence of conflict in various forms and especially the incidence of violence, the expression of attitudes in manifestos, journals, and other media, the emergence of political movements, and the elaboration of conflicting social doctrines. Some of these phenomena can be measured fairly precisely, while in other cases the magnitude has to be estimated very roughly in a mainly descriptive account. Notwithstanding these difficulties, which are additional to the conceptual difficulties encountered in dealing with such social entities as class or ideology, I think that some tentative historical and intersocietal comparisons could be formulated, when all the relevant criteria are brought together. If not, we should be obliged to conclude that conflict theories are as untestable as are functionalist (or, if you like, organismic) theories.

Causes of Conflict

The inability as yet to demonstrate any significant patterns in the occurrence of major forms of social conflict has not prevented the appearance of theories which claim to provide causal explanations of conflict, and especially of war, by correlating it with other phenomena; in the case of war, for example, with imperialism, with overpopulation, or with national characteristics. These claims must be regarded, for the present, as vain. This does not mean that any kind of causal explanation is ruled out. Leaving aside, for the moment, a more systematic inquiry into possible regularities and fluctuations in conflict, there are two other approaches, mentioned earlier, which may be considered.

One of these is to look for the causes of conflict in human nature, and to posit, as did Simmel, a "fighting instinct." In an exchange of letters with Einstein on the prevention of war, Freud asserted the existence of a destructive or aggressive instinct in human beings which cannot be suppressed, though it is always countered by another instinct, of sympathy or

love.[13] Recent biological and anthropological studies have generally supported the notion that there is an aggressive instinct, resulting from natural selection, which is widely distributed among the vertebrates and is to be found among the primates, including man. Washburn suggests that men "inherit the biology of aggression that was adaptive in the past," and that it is nurtured by many customs, although it is no longer adaptive: "for the modern, crowded, scientific world, the human actor, particularly the male, is too dominance-seeking and too aggressive." [14] Similarly, Konrad Lorenz in his book *On Aggression* [15] examines aggression as "the fighting instinct in beast and man which is directed *against* members of the same species," and which has as its chief positive functions the apportionment of territory, sexual selection, defense of the young, and the establishment of social ranking.

It is clear, however, that an explanation of actual conflicts along these lines cannot be complete. Neither individuals nor groups are perpetually engaged in conflict, and a theory which depends upon a permanent and constant aggressive instinct cannot explain the cycle of conflict and absence of conflict. What it does do is to draw attention to an underlying propensity to engage in aggressive behavior, and to show the biological basis of such a propensity. In order to explain actual conflicts we have to determine, in addition to this general condition, more specific causes. This may be done by adopting a theory of *interests*. Conflict occurs when territory is invaded, when young are threatened, when social ranking is disturbed or challenged. (This last case fits quite closely the Marxist theory of class conflict.) In human societies, biologically determined interests become culturally elaborated, and Lorenz recognizes this by the use of the term "militant enthusiasm" to describe the human version of biological aggressiveness in relation to interests.

These considerations lead back to the sociological aspects of the problem. Assuming the existence of an aggressive instinct, can we explain actual conflicts by means of a theory of interests and of the clash of interests, somewhat along Marxist lines? Marx's theory is, in a formal sense, genuinely explanatory. His conception of the universality of class conflict provides only a general model; the important part of the theory is that which deals with classes in capitalist society, and which asserts that the increasing

---

13. Freud's letter was originally published in 1933 by the League of Nations International Institute of Intellectual Cooperation. It is reprinted in Sigmund Freud, *Collected Papers,* vol. 5 (New York: Basic Books, 1959), and also in *War: Studies from Psychology, Sociology, Anthropology,* Leon Bramson and George W. Goethals, eds. (New York: Basic Books, 1964). This latter book very usefully assembles some of the major writings on war by de Tocqueville, William James, Sumner, Park, Spencer, Malinowski, Freud, and Raymond Aron, among others.
14. S. L. Washburn, "Conflict in Primate Society," in Anthony de Reuck and Julie Knight, eds., *Conflict in Society* (London: Churchill [A Ciba Foundation volume], 1966), pp. 11-12.
15. Vienna: G. Borotha-Schoeler, 1963; translation, New York: Harcourt, 1966.

divergence of interests between bourgeoisie and proletariat (together with a growing awareness of the divergence) will result in increasing conflict. Let us suppose that Marx's assertions have been falsified, that class conflict has in fact diminished in the advanced industrial societies—a view which many sociologists appear to hold strongly, even in the absence of rigorous measures of the extent of class conflict. If this is so, then we have now to explain the diminution of class conflict, by arguing that divergence of interests is not so closely correlated with conflict, or that the divergence of interests between the classes has decreased, or that some other factor has affected the degree of conflict. For example, we may refer, as I myself have done in a descriptive way, to the influence of nationalism in moderating internal conflict.[16] Another argument against the Marxist theory has been presented by Ralf Dahrendorf,[17] who suggests that the intensity of class conflict in the nineteenth-century capitalist societies was due to the superimposition of political conflict upon industrial conflict: "The opponents of industry—capital and labour—met again, as *bourgeoisie* and proletariat, in the political arena . . . ." [18] Dahrendorf argues that industrial and political conflicts have been dissociated in what he calls "postcapitalist societies"; there are now crisscrossing lines of conflict in place of a fundamental cleavage in society.[19] From this criticism of Marx, Dahrendorf proceeds to outline a more general theory of conflict, which is, very briefly summarized, that conflict is a necessary element in all imperatively coordinated associations.[20] If then it can be shown that imperatively coordinated associations are a universally necessary feature of human society, it follows that conflict is also universally necessary. This theoretical model, which does not of course encompass intersocietal conflict, resembles the biological theory of aggression in accounting for the occurrence of internal conflict in general, while not explaining the periodicity, scale, or intensity of conflict. To deal with the latter questions we need not only the kind of sociographic and statistical studies which I have mentioned in the previous section, but also an investigation of possible variations in the structure of social groups (and in a wider context, of the international system of relations between total societies) which favor or discourage conflict.

Some reflections upon these structural differences are to be found in

16. In *Classes in Modern Society* (New York: Pantheon, 1966; and London: Allen and Unwin, 1965). This argument itself follows Simmel's analysis of the effects of external conflict upon the internal cohesion of a social group.
17. See *Class and Class Conflict in Industrial Societies* (Stanford: Stanford University Press, 1959).
18. Ibid., p. 268.
19. This applies, in a particular context, an observation of Simmel's which has been elaborated by Coser in *The Functions of Social Conflict;* namely, that the crisscrossing of conflicts prevents the disintegration of a social group along one primary line of cleavage.
20. ". . . the distribution of authority in associations is the ultimate 'cause' of the formation of conflict groups." Dahrendorf, *Class and Class Conflict,* p. 172.

Simmel's essay, and they have been extended and systematized by a number of recent writers, among them Coser and van Doorn.[21] Simmel observed that conflict might become particularly bitter in groups based upon very intimate relations (such as kin groups or sects), or between groups which represented causes rather than interests (for example, classes since the time of Marx); but his remarks provide clues rather than conclusions. Coser sets out in a more formal way the propositions implicit in Simmel's essay, but his treatment is analytical, not empirical, and does not attempt to establish generalizations about the actual occurrence of conflict under varying conditions of group structure and goals. Similarly van Doorn, following Simmel, distinguishes between a coalition type of organization and a sect type of organization, and he suggests that tensions in the latter tend to produce extremely radical and ruthless internal conflict. The empirical evidence to support such assertions is admittedly slight. Do we know, in fact, that the intensity of conflict varies significantly with the structural difference between coalition and sect, between groups based upon intimate or impersonal bonds, between interest groups and ideological groups? Is it possible to establish that variations in conflict are correlated with the degree to which organizations are imperatively coordinated (or is there no sense in speaking of *degrees* of imperative coordination)? These questions can hardly be resolved, perhaps not even properly formulated, without a much more satisfactory natural history of conflict than we yet possess.

The Effects of Conflict

It has proved easier to study the effects of social conflict than its causes, although similar difficulties and inadequacies appear in both lines of inquiry. Lewis Coser's summary of his work on the functions of social conflict probably represents well the main direction of sociological interest: ". . . we have examined a series of propositions which call attention to various conditions under which social conflict may contribute to the maintenance, adjustment or adaptation of social relationships and social structures." [22] These "positive" functions of conflict, which were initially set out by Simmel, may be described as follows: intragroup conflict, if it is kept within limits, may help to maintain the unity of the group by providing a safety valve, or it may serve to reestablish unity; intergroup conflict sets the boundaries of groups, it may maintain a whole social system by upholding a balance of power between various groups, and it may enhance the internal unity of the groups which are engaged in conflict. Simmel refers particularly

21. Coser, *Social Conflict;* J. A. A. van Doorn, "Conflict in Formal Organizations" in *Conflict in Society,* pp. 111-132.
22. Coser, *Social Conflict,* p. 151.

to the way in which the modern centralized states were formed as a result of warfare, and he notes that estates and classes were also created by conflict. Marx had earlier expressed the same idea: classes engage in conflict, but they are also its product, as fully constituted and conscious groups. In these examples Simmel suggests the influence which conflict may have in promoting social change, and he also argues more generally that without conflict a social group could maintain its real life process." The recent studies of conflict have not emphasized to the same extent the connection between conflict and social change, in part perhaps because such an association is a prominent feature of Marxist theory. The point becomes clear if we consider how little attention sociologists have devoted to the study of revolutionary movements in the twentieth century, except occasionally as advisers on counterinsurgency. Revolution, like war, and perhaps even more than war, brings to the forefront those moral considerations which are interwoven with any kind of reflection upon the social meaning of conflict, the implications and influence of which are not always candidly avowed. However, the impact which revolutionary movements are beginning to have upon social thought may be seen in the recent appearance of new reflections upon the phenomenon of revolution,[23] and in the attention now given to the theoretical writings of revolutionaries, from Mao Tse-tung to Che Guevara, Frantz Fanon, and Regis Debray.

But before we turn to this theme, there are some other aspects of the connection between conflict and the maintenance or transformation of a form of social life which need to be discussed. Simmel, and most of the later writers, have been concerned with clarifying concepts and indicating possible relationships, rather than with asserting correlations. For example, Simmel observed that intergroup conflict would be likely to increase the internal cohesion of the groups involved in it, but he also observed that it did not always do so. To take a current example: the American war in Vietnam is quite obviously not increasing the unity of American society; in fact, it is dividing the society in an extremely bitter conflict. A more general case is that in which defeat, or the likelihood of defeat, in an external conflict produces serious divisions within the group concerned. In the twentieth century, revolutions have often followed military defeat. Yet the association is not constant; there have been defeats without any accompanying revolutionary struggles, and there have been revolutions without defeat in an external conflict. The Chinese revolution took place after victory. Thus it is far from sufficient to indicate possible connections between the existence and outcome of external conflict and the degree of internal cohesion. Some more elaborate theoretical model has to be constructed

23. Ralf Dahrendorf, "Über einige Probleme der soziologischen Theorie der Revolution," *European Journal of Sociology,* vol. 2 (1961); Hannah Arendt, *On Revolution* (New York: Viking Press, 1963); Carl J. Friedrich, ed., "Revolution," *NOMOS,* vol. 8 (1967).

which would allow us to make precise empirical statements about the effect of various types of external conflict upon various types of social groups.

The general relationship between conflict and social change also needs to be investigated much more closely. Conflict between groups and within groups may evidently bring about change, or create a propensity to change by unsettling established ways of life. Simmel observed that ". . . in the early stages of culture, war is almost the only form in which contact with alien groups is brought about at all," [24] and many sociologists have attributed to warfare the extension of the scale of early societies, and in more recent times, the creation of nation states. Warfare has been held by some writers to have a major influence upon the development of technology, and thus to contribute to more profound changes in society; while modern war, which affects the whole population of a society and which may be taken to date from World War I, has been credited with important political consequences, from the enfranchisement of women to the extension of social welfare legislation. Equally, internal conflict may bring about important social changes. Marx adopted, as he said, the view of bourgeois historians that modern Europe was the product of class struggles, and he expected new class struggles to result in still more fundamental changes in society; in fact, Marxist political movements in many countries have radically transformed the structure of their societies. Less dramatically, it may be argued that the conflict between organized political parties in the industrial countries, and in some developing nations, has been a major influence in establishing the rights of the individual, and notably the rights of dissent, criticism, and opposition.

One form of conflict which Simmel examined, but which has received little attention subsequently, is competition. Simmel disagreed with the view of the socialists, and of such liberals as J. S. Mill, that the effects of competition were generally harmful, and he emphasized what he termed the "socializing and civilizing function of competition." "Modern competition," he wrote, "is described as the fight of all against all, but at the same time it is the fight of all *for* all"; this in the sense that economic competition is directed toward maximum output at minimum cost. Furthermore, "given the breadth and individualization of society, many kinds of interest, which eventually hold the group together throughout its members, seem to come alive and stay alive only when the urgency and requirements of the competitive struggle force them upon the individual." [25] Competition, and the whole *laissez-faire* economy of nineteenth-century capitalism, may have been important in promoting economic growth; moreover, the exceptionally rapid development of the American economy may be attributable to the greater scope of competition in the United States. But still we can produce no exact correlations between the extent

24. Simmel, *Conflict*, p. 33.
25. Ibid., pp. 63-64.

of competition, or the intensity of the competitive spirit, and the rate of economic growth in different societies. And on the other hand, there are grounds for supposing that competition has other less welcome effects; its civilizing influence, which Simmel sees in the manner of Durkheim as the creation of a network of mutual obligations and dependencies, may be counteracted by its effect upon the rate of mental illness and of crime. Again, however, the demonstration of an exact correspondence is wanting.

Simmel, and following him Coser and others, have devoted much of their attention to the positive functions (meaning the *beneficial effects*) of conflict. One of these positive aspects is, as we have seen, that conflict engenders changes which are themselves judged to be on the whole beneficial. But aside from the fact that conflict may also produce changes which are judged to be harmful (a possibility of which we are uncomfortably aware in the nuclear age), there are other aspects of the relation between conflict and change to be considered. It cannot be demonstrated that all change results from conflict, although Hegel's philosophy of history and (with some qualifications) Marx's social theory, and the many theoretical schemes derived from them, assert or insinuate that it does. There may be changes which occur without conflict—the accumulation of scientific knowledge, for example—and which themselves then provoke conflict, as did modern science in the "battle of the books," in the conflict between science and religion, and more remotely in the struggles among interest groups and classes which were incited by the rise of a new technology. On the other side, there is no warrant for asserting that all conflict produces change. Some kinds of conflict, as Simmel suggested, help to maintain or strengthen an established form of social life; in some tribal societies ritualized conflicts seem intended to enhance social solidarity and to reinforce existing institutions.[26] Moreover, it is not difficult to conceive or to suggest instances of a sufficiently protracted and intense conflict within a social group which might produce a stalemate, and impede or halt changes which had already begun.

Prospect

The renewed interest in the study of conflict has been determined very largely by practical concerns, and in particular by the desire to find some means of avoiding, or at the least controlling and limiting, war in the nuclear age. This has given rise to a whole new field of inquiry, under the name of "strategic studies," which is concerned on one side with those conditions and situations which seem likely to result in war, and on the other

26. On this see Max Gluckman, *Custom and Conflict in Africa* (Oxford: Blackwell, 1955; New York: Barnes and Noble, 1964) and subsequently *Politics, Law and Ritual in Tribal Societies* (Chicago: Aldine, 1965).

side with the outcome or consequences of war. A work which reflects better than any other these new interests, and which is illuminating also in the variety of methods which it employs, is Raymond Aron's *Peace and War: A Theory of International Relations*.[27] After discussing those concepts and classifications which are needed in any study of war and peace—power, force, the international system of states, types of war, and types of peace—and considering the determinants of war, Aron turns, in the third and fourth parts of his book, to a historical examination of the global system of states in the nuclear age, and to a consideration of some moral evaluations of war and their political and strategic implications. Several of the subjects treated in the latter part of the book have been widely discussed. One of these is the question of the influence of the level of armaments (or more generally, military preparedness) and especially of an arms race, upon the probability of war. Richardson, whose work on the causes of war was mentioned previously, also constructed mathematical models of arms races,[28] one of which (the runaway arms race) he applied to the periods preceding the two world wars; at the time of his death he was studying the third arms race, which began in 1948, but he had not yet reached any conclusions about its outcome. It may not be possible to make any strict inferences from such work as to the probability of an arms race ending in war; but it is reasonable to argue that a stabilization or reduction of armaments is likely to diminish the chances of war, first because it represents already a measure of agreement between the conflicting nations, and secondly, because it will probably affect the mood of the nations involved—a factor which Richardson considered of great importance.

Another question discussed by Aron is that of an alternative to war as a means of regulating the relations between states, each of which is pursuing its own national interest. He examines two possibilities: peace through law, and peace through empire. Either course would involve a greater or lesser sacrifice of national sovereignty. Peace through law may be conceived, up to a point, as an extension of present international agreements, but its full realization would seem to require the creation in some form of a supranational legislature, executive body, and administration. Peace through empire would quite plainly involve the loss of independence for the nations incorporated in it; it is also quite unrealizable at the present time, since neither the United States nor the Soviet Union is capable of establishing a universal empire. There is also a third possibility: peace through the balance of power, as it now exists. Here the question is whether, and under what conditions, a stable and enduring balance of power is achievable.[29]

27. New York: Doubleday, 1966. Originally published in French as *Paix et Guerre entre les nations* (Paris: Calmann-Lévy, 1962).
28. L. F. Richardson, *Arms and Insecurity* (Pittsburgh: Boxwood Press, 1960).
29. The principal doubts concern the effects of rapid technological advance and of the spread of nuclear weapons.

The last of the themes raised in recent studies which I propose to consider here is that concerning the role of war in national policy. Is war any longer a rational instrument of policy, in Clausewitz's sense? Here we are obliged to distinguish between different kinds of wars. Wars of national liberation, counterrevolutionary wars, and some others, fought on a limited scale with what are now called "conventional weapons," may be rational in the sense that the gains may clearly outweigh the losses for one side, and that the common ruin of the contenders, though possible, is not necessary. But what of thermonuclear war between major powers? Majority opinion throughout the world would probably now consider that such a war would not be rational, that it would entail a common ruin, and even perhaps the extinction of mankind. There are, however, dissenters from this view, one of the best known being Herman Kahn, who has argued in his book *On Thermonuclear War,*[30] and in later writings, that the cost of such a war in casualties and destruction would not be prohibitive. One new element in these studies is the use of game-theory models as an aid to determining strategy; a use which, in the extraordinary fascination which it has for some social scientists and policy makers, has attracted much criticism. Aron concludes his study of peace and war with a criticism of the spurious realism of these models, and he advocates paying more attention to "reasonable policy" than to "rational strategy." [31] Anatol Rapoport in his *Fights, Games and Debates,*[32] and in a more recent article,[33] while acknowledging that game theory offers a conceptual framework in which strategic analogues of conflict situations can be clearly formulated,[34] points to the limitations of the theory, especially in non-zero-sum games (which are the analogues of many real conflict situations) in which a rational choice cannot be prescribed.

One circumstance which accounts for the rapid growth of strategic studies is the widespread desire to control war in the nuclear age, both on rational and on moral grounds.[35] The same degree of concern, and of moral agreement, does not exist in respect of other forms of social conflict. Hence the reluctance to see revolutions, industrial conflict, and until fairly recently, ethnic conflict, as subjects which might engage the attention of any substantial number of sociologists, or figure prominently in the theoretical models or descriptive accounts of a social system. Hence, too, the un-

---

30. Princeton: Princeton University Press, 1960.
31. Aron, *Peace and War*, Final Note.
32. Ann Arbor: University of Michigan Press, 1960.
33. "Models of Conflict: Cataclysmic and Strategic," in *Conflict in Society*, pp. 259-287.
34. Ibid., p. 277.
35. There are perhaps minor exceptions. The satirical *Report from Iron Mountain*, L. Lewin, ed. (New York: Dial, 1967), suggests that in some "think-tanks" and in other circles in the United States there may be greater concern about the horrors of peace; that is, about the difficulty of finding adequate substitutes for what are claimed to be the vital functions of war in the economic, political, sociological, demographic, and cultural spheres.

easiness which becomes apparent when the attempt to investigate such conflicts is made. Revolutions do not fit very comfortably into a conceptual scheme which regards the positive functions of conflict as being to maintain, with minor adaptations, a given social system. Only if a revolution is defeated is the social order maintained; if it succeeds, society is transformed. And whereas sociologists, like other men, are generally *against* war and can without any qualms see their studies of war as having the practical objective of limiting or avoiding it, they may be either for or against revolution (and other kinds of internal conflict) and suddenly become aware of the intrusion of moral attitudes and commitments into their inquiry. They may, and do, approach the study of revolutions with sympathy or aversion; they may become advisers to revolutionary leaders, or more frequently to counterinsurgency agencies. This should not deter them from such delicate inquiries, nor should it prevent them from expressing as clearly as possible the point of view which guides their research and writing, and which makes their studies humanly significant.[36] I see little to criticize in the expression "positive functions of conflict," if it can be taken to cover revolutionary transformations, as well as more gradual changes, or the maintenance of an existing order; and if the contrasting negative functions are defined and given their due importance. What is open to criticism is the view which seems often to prevail that a sympathy with movements of rebellion is somehow more ideological, and a greater threat to sociological objectivity, than is an attachment to the status quo; or more generally, that a preoccupation with social conflict is less scientifically pure than is a concern with social order. For such notions there is no justification whatsoever.

I began this essay by saying that we do not have a sociological theory of conflict. Yet the recent studies of conflict have made an important contribution, not least to sociological theory in a broader sense. The studies of war, at present the most advanced, have begun to amass the kind of historical and statistical knowledge which is essential for any causal analysis, and they have been fruitful in developing models of conflict situations which, for all their shortcomings, are a powerful aid to investigation. If these studies have not yet produced any general theory of war, they have at least made clearer the complexity of the phenomenon, they have identified some of the proximate causes, and they hold out the prospect of an eventual rational control of this form of conflict. The same degree of intel-

---

36. The ill-fated "Project Camelot" illustrates well some of these issues, and its implications have been lucidly examined by Irving L. Horowitz in "The Life and Death of Project Camelot," *Trans-action*, vol. 3 (1965), and by Ralf Dahrendorf, *Essays in the Theory of Society* (Stanford: Stanford University Press, 1968), chap. 10. It would perhaps illuminate one critical aspect of the project if we were to suppose that there had been another project, officially sponsored and financed by the Cuban government, to study sympathetically, and with a view to aiding them, the Negro rebellions in American cities.

lectual effort has still to be applied in the study of other types of conflict—
class conflict and revolutionary movements, industrial conflict and ethnic
conflict—and these phenomena present in some respects greater difficulties
because both the practical end in view and the extent to which rational
control of them is desired are more ambiguous. Nevertheless, it seems
likely that the methods which have been used in studying conflict in an
international system could be applied with profit in studying the relations
among groups within a society, or within segments of a society, so long as
we keep in mind the difficulties of judging what is positive and what is
negative in different forms of social conflict.

Perhaps the clearest gain from recent studies of conflict is the change
which they have initiated in our general conceptions of the nature of a
social system. It is no longer possible to place such great emphasis upon
social harmony, integration, and equilibrium, or to adopt such a static
view of social structure, as has been done in the last thirty years under the
influence of structural-functionalism. *Deviance* (one of the sloppiest terms
in the sociological vocabulary) no longer seems an adequate category to
embrace the varieties of dissent, conflict, rebellion, and repression which
occur in all societies and which have assumed such vast dimensions in the
rapidly changing societies of the twentieth century. Conflict is an intrinsic
part of social life, sustaining, modifying, or destroying the social groups
in which it takes place. It cannot be treated satisfactorily as a minor and
exceptional form of social relationship, in a brief apologetic appendix to
a theory of social solidarity, as has so often been done. Whether we like
it or not, we shall have to pay increasing attention to conflicts of interest
and doctrine, and to the role of violence in upholding or overthrowing a
social system, if we are to explain events and provide the means by which
men can make reasonable choices between alternative courses of social
action. And on the other side we shall need to eliminate from sociological
thought the vestiges of the melting-pot ideology, which assumes that vast
inequalities of wealth, power, and enjoyment can and should be harmoniously accommodated without any fundamental changes in the structure of society.

6.

Toward a System of Sequences

Wilbert E. Moore

Wilbert E. Moore was born in Elma, Washington, in 1914 and was educated at Linfield College, the University of Oregon, and Harvard University (Ph.D.). Mr. Moore is now sociologist, Russell Sage Foundation, and visiting lecturer with the rank of professor at Princeton University, where he has spent twenty-three years, fifteen as professor. Among his extensive list of published essays and books, the greater number deal with relations between economy and society, including demographic studies, industrial sociology, and social aspects of economic development. Two of his most recent books are on more theoretical themes: Man, Time, and Society *and* Social Change. *He is past president of the Eastern Sociological Society and past president of the American Sociological Association.*

$\mathcal{T}$he perception of a sequential order in social events is scarcely novel in sociological thought. The grand theories of history, whether assuming invariance in direction or recurrent cycles, attempted to place observed changes in an order and make them understandable rather than merely accidental. The failure of such grand theories to gain stature through evidential confirmation provides some basis for caution in new attempts to formulate and demonstrate sequential orders. The appropriate caution, however, may be directed toward excessive claims to generality rather than doubting the existence of linked chains at all.

After some preliminary polemical orientations, the principal message of this discussion will be the exposition of an approach to social change, with some hypothetical illustrations. As a tactical stance, potential testability will when necessary be preferred over level of generality, discretion being seen once more as the better part of valor.

Because this essay is frankly exploratory, the derogatory designation of what follows as "notes" may be a mildly benign description. However, I have also felt it allowable to be somewhat cryptic, since many of the preliminary points of view have been fairly extensively discussed in recent literature.

The Atemporal System and its Methodology

For several years I have contemplated the irony that just as most of the leading American graduate sociological training centers had come to the

point of insisting on a degree of competence by students in handling quantitative data, the kinds of methodological sophistication achieved were scarcely appropriate for at least part of upcoming sociological concerns. Specifically, it strikes me that if much of recent sociological theory has been static—and I think that allegation is correct—so have most of the progressive refinements in data analysis. "Theorists and methodologists, despite their manifest differences in other respects, have been remarkably atemporal, and thus seem to deserve each other." [1]

It seems to me unnecessary to argue that dealing with social action as caught up in social systems is intrinsically static; certainly it is not. Nor have systems analysts assumed a perfectly integrated system, at least when the analysts paid any attention to observed social phenomena. Yet it does appear to me that deviance has gotten more notice than discovery, and adaptation to accidental or external change more attention that creation of change for old or new goals. Merton, for example, in his famous discussion of "Social Structure and Anomie," [2] uses the term "innovation" to characterize behavior that accepts culturally approved goals but relies on deviant means. But this surely exaggerates the prescience of actors' predecessors in rulemaking and understates the potential ingenuity of actors in discovering "evasive innovations." For some actions there are simply no contravening rules; but there will be. And it is precisely the potentiality of this discovery that leads to a very general principle of social change: that enduring social structures will be characterized by normative accumulation.[3]

Intrinsic Sources of Change

The view of society as a tension-management system, making order problematical along with disorder and uncertainty, has at least that virtue as a heuristic approach. And such a stance permits a number of observations about societies in general: the universality of gaps between ideal values norms and practical ones, giving rise to the probability of attempts at successive approximations; the closely related universal absence of ideal adjustments to the nonhuman environment, giving rise to the probability of acceptable technical innovation.[4] The pervasive failure of human societies to achieve consensual ideals produces a tension that is consistent with social evolutionary theory, which would view long-term change in

1. Wilbert E. Moore, *Order and Change: Essays in Comparative Sociology* (New York: Wiley, 1967), p. 294.
2. Robert K. Merton, in *Social Theory and Social Structure,* rev. ed. (Glencoe: Free Press, 1957).
3. See Wilbert E. Moore, *Social Change* (Englewood Cliffs: Prentice-Hall, 1963), pp. 26-27.
4. Ibid., pp. 18-21.

terms of successive adaptations. I find evolutionary theory, however, as more retrospective than predictive, and ". . . the evolutionary model is poorly designed to include purpose." [5]

Deliberate Change: The Case of Modernization

Purpose, in effect, is a major lacuna in functionalist conceptions of collectivities, though precisely written into the behavior of actors in "social action theory." [6] Social theory deriving from the assumption of mindless and mechanical collectivities is analogous to pre-Keynesian economics, in which private vices add up to public virtues. We know better than that, and I shall not belabor the silliness of the position. But in case anyone could miss the message: real political leaders (not to mention their opponents) state goals and try to mobilize resources for the accomplishment of explicit goals attributed to the collectivity. In societies even faintly pluralistic, various private leaders do the same—in universities, corporations, religious organizations, foundations, and even family trusts. Planning and deliberate change have become a major part of contemporary collective activity. (Of course, deliberate change is rather old, at least in major nations with military establishments, and it would be needlessly patronizing to assume that the elders 'round the campfire did not engage in such calculated activity.) The apolitical stance of contemporary social theorists—and here I add my *mea culpa*—stems in part, I believe, from an incapacity to view a social system as a deliberate set of decisional processes, and therefore has deep roots in theoretical error and not just the casual incapacity to understand a neighboring discipline that should, of course, be a part of our own.

By all odds the most important source of social change in the modern world is the decision-making, according to plan, of national states and of various permissive, decentralized units. (Let no one raise the specter of technological change as a kind of autonomous variable. It is not autonomous, and is indeed on the whole planned. In the modern era, that has been rather uniformly true; and I grow weary of mindless prime movers.[7])

Fortunately, since the original draft of this paper was set down, a major theoretical work relating to deliberate social change has been published. Amitai Etzioni explores collective decision-making, and the sequential (sometimes optional) courses of deliberate undertakings.[8] It appears to me, now, as the most important work that treats both interdependence and se-

5. See Wilbert E. Moore, *Order and Change*, p. 295.
6. See Talcott Parsons, *The Structure of Social Action* (New York: McGraw, 1937).
7. See Wilbert E. Moore, *Order and Change*, p. 88.
8. Amitai Etzioni, *The Active Society: A Theory of Societal and Political Processes* (New York: Free Press, 1968).

quence with a sure grasp. Etzioni sees, correctly, that contemporary societies cannot totally overcome various mindlessly mechanical elements, but that political leaders do attempt to mold a consensus around stated values and mobilize constituents in the attempt to achieve them.

I cannot here adequately summarize what we know about the social con-Ⅰ ⅠⅠⅠⅠⅠⅠⅠⅠⅠ ⅠⅠ and ⅠⅠⅠⅠⅠⅠⅠⅠⅠⅠ ⅠⅠ attempts at modernization. That subject has, for example, enticed out of Marion J. Levy, Jr., a two-volume work,[9] and out of me, a rather more succinct 125-page extended essay.[10] Such snide asides aside, I have been most critical (and that includes self-critical) of the kind of conceptual posture that has been most productive, and most unfortunate: a kind of before-and-after, comparative statics analysis of "what must happen" in the end-result of modernization. That argument also has been well set out in the extant literature,[11] and I shall not replicate it here. What is essential is to search for scales and sequences of modernization, to set forth the necessary institutional antecedents of modernization (preconditions), those social and institutional changes inevitably associated with modernization—this is the historic heartland of functional analysis—and then to draw out secondary and tertiary consequences of the process. This means, among other things, that we do not take industrialization as a static state.

The distinction among preconditions, concomitants, and consequences is a relatively crude and flimsy conceptual stance, justified, if at all, by an extremely poor observational base for detecting genuine sequences.

Now let us dismiss, rather quickly, one alternative conception of the course, or at least the causes, of modernization. Hagen's sociopsychological theory posits the necessity of an increase in innovational personality types, which will be produced in segments of the population that suffer from withdrawal of status respect in the traditional social order.[12] The transformation of retreatism into creative innovation requires several generations as well as, admittedly, other propitious conditions. This thesis suffers from several serious defects: (a) it assumes a kind of "up-from-the-bottom" source of innovation, as though national leaders were irrelevant and in splendid isolation from the rest of the world; (b) it pretends that adult socialization is irrelevant (and that, too, is a silly assumption); (c) it falls heir to a long tradition in economic theory to the effect that entrepreneurship is a kind of *deus ex machina* for economic growth. It is a psychopathology of economists to think that private solutions are preferable to public ones. On the

---

9. Marion J. Levy, Jr., *Modernization and the Structure of Societies*, 2 vols. (Princeton: Princeton University Press, 1966).
10. Wilbert E. Moore, *The Impact of Industry* (Englewood Cliffs: Prentice-Hall, 1965).
11. Ibid.; see also *Social Change*.
12. Everett E. Hagen, *On the Theory of Social Change: How Economic Growth Begins* (Homewood, Ill.: Dorsey Press, 1962).

whole, in the modern world, that is ideologically-determined nonsense. Hagen's was a sequential system. It just happens to have little validity.

If the process of modernization of newly developing countries is now to proceed beyond the comparative statics model—or its amendment through attention to conditions, concomitants, and consequences—two major developments will be necessary: the process will have to be viewed in terms of a rather elaborate social change matrix; and if any more refined (and possibly useful) propositions are to be observationally based and not merely empty or speculative, a substantial input of quantities and trends would need to be produced and analyzed. Since the statistical systems of developing areas are likely to be as defective as their economic systems, crude approximations are likely to be necessary. Nevertheless, attention to the temporal order of structural changes does appear minimal and overdue.

Note that the world *matrix* above was used advisedly, for I could scarcely disagree with Parsons that the theoretical problem is dealing with changes in *social systems,* with what that implies for interplay, repercussions, and reverberations.[13] Yet a further cautionary note is in order, for contemporary societies are scarcely to be viewed as in autonomous isolation.[14] This means that neither rates nor precise sequences of change can be readily inferred from historic precedent, for that precedent now provides a cumulative and diversified set of available options. Nevertheless, the options are presumably not infinite, in view of systemic implications, and those implications presumably would not be equal in relative costs and benefits, even if those cannot be added into a single net sum.

The difficulties are indeed very great, even if we broaden our observational horizon to include modernized societies. Sheldon and I [15] are exploring a tactic of attempting to establish temporal trends in one statistical system, that of the United States, for major functional areas of the society, as a prelude to examining leads and lags in rates of change as well as regression equations expressing their relationships quantitatively. Some more particular examples of testable sequences will be examined shortly.

Thinking Sequentially

A major but relatively new approach to problem-solving uses the general term *systems analysis* in a substantially different sense from that common in the social sciences. Comprising such subcategories as operations research,

13. Talcott Parsons, *The Social System* (Glencoe: Free Press, 1951), chap. 11, "The Processes of Change of Social Systems."
14. See Wilbert E. Moore, "Global Sociology: The World as a Singular System," reprinted in *Order and Change.*
15. Eleanor Bernert Sheldon and Wilbert E. Moore, "Toward the Measurement of Social Change: Implications for Progress," in Leonard H. Goodman, ed., *Economic Progress and Social Welfare* (New York: Columbia University Press, 1966), chap. 7.

linear programming, cost-benefit analysis (or program planning and budgeting) and queuing theory, systems analysis contains both a technical and a theoretical lesson. The technical lesson is that in the attempt to solve some practical problem—commonly an optimizing situation—if a factor is considered to be relevant but no good measure is available, an arbitrary value is preferable to leaving it out of account. The theoretical lesson can be summarized aphoristically as "consequences have consequences." In some instances this represents no more than conventional notions of systemic interdependence. More often, however, a chain is involved, including loops and possible feedbacks, and thus a genuinely sequential system.

Contemporary sociology is of course not totally lacking in sequential analysis. The most conspicuous examples are afforded by demography. Demographers project the future size and compositional characteristics of a population implicit in current (or recent trends in) fertility and mortality rates. Attention to the demographic behavior of age cohorts takes account of life-cycle phenomena, which are clearly sequential.[16] This approach permits a distinction between current aggregative rates and the behavior of successive cohorts moving through a changing social environment. Sociologists other than sociological demographers have been so immunized against the essential facts of man as an animal species—let us have no biological determinism—that the most elementary life-cycle phenomena get rather casual treatment at their hands.

Some of the analysis of modernization has dealt with sequence and interplay, although less than ideally. Thus, Feldman and I suggested the concept of "cumulative, retroactive evolution," using as an example the necessity of sufficient agricultural modernization to permit the diversion of human and other resources to other production; that means of production (especially machines, fertilizers, and so forth) in turn make possible further agricultural growth.[17] I had earlier suggested (following in part Colin Clark [18]) what I called stages and would now simply call a sequence in the most rapid *rate of growth* by different sectors of an industrializing economy.[19] Incidentally, that tentative generalization was based on the economic history of Western industrial countries. It would require modification in newly developing countries of Asia, Africa, and Latin America, where urban service occupations are expanding at a far faster rate than the rate of industrialization, narrowly speaking. That circumstance confirms our earlier caution,

16. See Wilbert E. Moore, "Aging and the Social System," reprinted in *Order and Change.*
17. Arnold S. Feldman and Wilbert E. Moore, "Moot Points in the Theory," in Moore and Feldman, eds., *Labor Commitment and Social Change in Developing Areas* (New York: Social Science Research Council, 1960), pp. 365-366.
18. Colin Clark, *The Conditions of Economic Progress,* 2nd ed. (London: Macmillan, 1951), pp. 395-439.
19. Wilbert E. Moore, *Economy and Society* (New York: Random House, 1955), pp. 41-42.

which can now be rephrased: history may often prevent its own replication, for its consequences (including the so-called revolution of rising expectations) have altered the circumstances for latecomers.

Large-Scale Change: Some Further Illustrations

Failing the all-purpose grand matrix of social change, in which everything is related to everything, both by measurable cross-sectional regressions and by stipulated probability values in a stochastic (sequential) system—and that is the grand design—and rejecting the ridiculous neoscholasticism of some contemporary model-builders in economics where limiting assumptions are made that are patently absurd, my aim has been to develop some testable subsets of theoretical sequences that might prove to be additive (or more properly, accumulative) as additional informational inputs can be adduced.

My first illustration will be the most fully worked out, though still only partially, by way of clarifying the evidence and skirting some methodological pitfalls. I shall start with a set of assertions that ought to be testable, on the basis of American statistics.

1. There have been changes in the rate of change in the "participation rates" of females in higher education.

2. There have been radical reductions (a rate of change) in the age of mothers bearing their last child (making child-bearing over the age of 30 rare); and the leaders (with cross-sectional and temporal evidence) in that trend have been mothers with some college education.

3. There has been a rise (again a change in rate of change) in the entry or reentry of women over the age of 45 into the labor force.

The rationale of this argument scarcely needs extended explication, nor do I propose to give any here. The "intervening variables" can be readily inserted and explicated by the sociologically sophisticated. The illustration, however, is a rather good one in that some theoretical-methodological issues can be readily clarified. First, given adequate statistical data, it should be possible to test the multiple-correlation or factor-analysis relationship among separate bodies of statistical distributions. Second, since college education (if any) will normally precede child-bearing, which will (it is alleged) mostly precede middle-age female labor force entry or reentry, the sequence could be tested in terms of real cohorts. Third, the additional assertion here is that the changes of rates of change were in the order predicted in actual historical sequence. If this should prove to be true, then steps two and three have moved us from a formal, cross-sectional predictive model (in which the dependent variable is typically a matter of arbitrary convenience) into a genuine *causal* system, in which first things are first, and later ones follow sequentially.

Note that this is a selected segment of a causal chain, and not as such a quest for first causes: for example, *why* did a growing body of eligible women go to college?

Note also that the most difficult allegation to test, with available data, is the middle one, and that is an intervening or operational variable. There would be no point in pressing the awkward issue of establishing the middle term if the first and last parts of the sequence had no demonstrated relationship. Yet the correlation between college attendance of women and labor force reentry can be readily established, in a noncausal way. A cross-sectional set of data may establish something: which females, with what characteristics, are those that enter or reenter the labor force in mature years? But we too often reason from such inadequate data, without trying to see things sequentially. The sorting process is a long one, not a quick computer run.

If this kind of approach makes sense, the analytical system may be extended in both directions sequentially: the antecedents of female college participation, and its consequences (for example, for divorce rates of mature married couples, budgetary behavior of families with two incomes, social participation rates of employed mature women). They may also be extended by looking at other changes in rates of change: proportions of male breadwinners with reasonable expectations of rising real incomes during active employment, the increase in the demand for services as compared with physical (and often muscular) production, increases in the proportion of family budgets allocated to discretionary expenditures.

Note that what was illustrated here was not a mutually exclusive confrontation between "interdependence" and "sequence." Rather, one attempts to make each feed on the other. It has been true all along, of course, that in a formal sense any statement of static relation can be turned into a dynamic one, although the transformation is sometimes either definitional or trivial. (Clearly, the classic propositional form of "If A [under conditions X, Y, Z] then B," can be transformed to the statement that if A disappears then B *will* disappear, presumably with a measurable lapse of time, unless A was in fact the definitional equivalent of B and the statement therefore tautologous.) I am concerned with real sequences, and not with trivial transformations, and I confess a slight weariness with those who hide behind formalities in order to avoid hard theoretical and methodological issues.

Let me suggest some other measurable sequences, the testing of which would have less-than-trivial significance for our capacity to make genuinely predictive statements about the course of social processes.

1. We know that research and development expenditures represent a major source of capital input into the American economy. Could one not examine the changing rates of such expenditures, a measurable rate of patentable inventions, and a measurable rate of within-career occupational mobility (parcelling out mere bureaucratic advancement)?

2. We know (or could know) the rate of urbanization of "captive" minorities. We could also know the expenditure rate (and possibly the absolute number) of welfare measures. Could we not establish, first cross-sectionally and then sequentially, the relation of these two inputs to some index of civil disorder?

3. We know changing rates of educational participation rates for appropriate age-groups, and also changing years-of-school-completed data. Could we not test, again first cross-sectionally and then sequentially, the relation of these trends to the rate of participation in voluntary associations, and of rates of political participation?

Theory and Practice: A Final Cautionary Note

We witness today—and if we are alert, how could we fail to observe?—a sporadic revolt of a submerged minority of Americans, the Negroes, particularly in the residentially restrictive areas of American slums. An adequate historical and contemporary diagnosis of that problem would require a volume, or perhaps several—which the problem has, in fact, elicited. As a long-time student of that problem, I believe I could state the sequence in a dozen or so pages, but even that could prove tendentious for present purposes.[20] What we now experience is a sequential development (starting from changes in both the technology and the importance of agriculture in the South) that has put relatively unskilled Negro males in central cities, along with their "families." Several persuasive alternative explanations of black domestic arrangements are available: (a) the matrifocal Negro family is of African origin; (b) it is a product of forcible separation of biological parents and children under slavery; (c) it is a product of lack of jobs for unskilled Negro males in cities (abetted by ridiculous administrative rules that forbid federally financed aid to dependent children if a male is present in the mother's household by a midnight bed-check). These alternatives contain questions for verifiable research under carefully controlled design. Meanwhile, the questions remain moot.

Yet some sequences are clear: displacement from unskilled farm labor in the South to the quest for better opportunities in (especially) northern cities, and the resulting vicious circle (which could be expanded readily)—the poor, fatherless, excessively many, illegitimate, and largely untended children of the working mother or relief-supported family, the certainty of "cultural deprivation," lack of access to achievement motivation, lack of realistic and honorable opportunities for achievement, off-grade educational facilities, and (let us be honest) the possibility of genetic intellectual deficits also.

20. My Harvard doctoral thesis in 1940 was *Slavery, Abolition, and the Ethical Valuation of the Individual.*

Now what do sequences do for us here? A good deal in terms of reconstructing historic paths, but some of those paths are irreversible, short of inhumane measures simply inconsistent with American values. (We could, for example, simply exterminate American Negroes, require passes to move about and especially to get into cities, and so forth.) Current public policy clearly requires starting with "givens" (read data), and then asking where, with maximum effect—note that the short run and the long run may be radically different—one can deliberately break into what has apparently become a very coherent, if vicious, set of interdependencies. Whatever the cause of the matrifocal Negro family (it is *not* uniquely Negro), the cure is likely to be the assurance of stable Negro male employment. Whatever the cause of Negro educational deficits, some portion of the problem may be solved by genuine equality of educational opportunity for Negro children.

This did not start as, and will not finish as, a treatise on current American race relations. The theoretical point that ought to have emerged from these paragraphs was this: It may not be possible to go back to prime causes and change them. This does not mean that one is discharged from the responsibility of thinking sequentially. Under current circumstances unequally amenable to intervention, where can one enter the system, and what will be the consequences, in what order? One should now attend, not to reversing the probably irreversible or to regretting that the clear signs that were before us for some fifty years were not acted on, but to ask what are the sequences (preventable and unpreventable) from a set of unstable current conditions.

It is a manner of thinking, involving analytic techniques possibly not yet invented, but the answering of some partial questions might give us some basis for asking the grand ones—and for answering them.

A Methodological Note

The approach adopted here has been informed by several sources. I think I approximately understand those who write in English, and can confidently state that I do not follow any mathematical formulation, however simple. Yet I have tried to be informed by the essentially sequential approach displayed by Neil J. Smelser in his *Theory of Collective Behavior* (London: Routledge and Kegan Paul, 1962). For the self-searching and somewhat tortuous reasoning by Talcott Parsons in Chapter 11 of *The Social System* (cited in note 13), I have a considerable sympathy, but I feel that his insistence on the interdependent qualities of social systems blinded him to sequences of social orders (other than the institutionalization of rationality —which he does not state so neatly, but with which I essentially agree), and I am particularly perturbed by his neglect of self-evident demographic, economic, and social trends.

Despite relatively acerb comments within the text concerning the tendentious theory of Everett Hagen (cited in note 12) about the source of modernizing social change, I should commend his Appendix I, "Analytical Models in the Study of Social Systems," where he pins down and politely demolishes the pretensions of some anthropological and sociological "systems" theorists. Walter Buckley in *Sociology and Modern Systems Theory* (Englewood Cliffs, N.J.: Prentice-Hall, 1967) is also critical of approaches that rely solely on self-subsistent systems, to the neglect of tensions, feedback, and trends.

I have also attempted to follow the arguments of several people with mathematical sophistication, of which I have none. These include Hubert M. Blalock, Jr., *Causal Inferences in Nonexperimental Research* (Chapel Hill: University of North Carolina Press, 1964); James M. Beshers, "Mathematical Models of Social Change," in George K. Zollschan and Walter Hirsh, eds., *Explorations in Social Change* (Boston: Houghton, 1964), chap. 11; James S. Coleman, "Race Relations and Social Change," Occasional Paper, Johns Hopkins University Center for the Study of Social Organization of Schools, 1967.

7.

Developmentalism: A Critical Analysis

Robert A. Nisbet

Robert A. Nisbet was born in Los Angeles, California, in 1913. He received his B.A., M.A., and Ph.D. degrees from the University of California, Berkeley, the latter in 1939. Until 1952 he was a member of the sociology faculty at Berkeley. Since 1952 he has been professor of sociology on the Riverside campus of the University of California where, from 1953 until 1963, he was additionally dean of the College of Letters and Science. He has been visiting professor at Columbia University and the University of Bologna, Italy; in 1963–64 he was Guggenheim Visiting Fellow at Princeton University. He is past president of the Pacific Sociological Association. Most of his publications have been in the area of social theory and social history. His two most recent books are The Sociological Tradition *(1967) and* Social Change and History *(1969).*

The idea of development in the social sciences has more often been dealt with as a broad, panoramic view of social origins and stages than as the complex and subtle theory of the source and mechanism of change that it is in substance. We are familiar enough with the former: Comte's law of three stages, Hegel's tracking of the idea of freedom in time, Marx's iron sequence of epochs from primitive communism through slavery, feudalism, and capitalism to socialism, Lewis Morgan's evolution of kinship types; Tylor's, Gomme's, and Frazer's vistas of religious origins and sequences, Spencer's encompassment of human society in space and time into inexorable progress from the homogeneous to the heterogeneous, Durkheim's stages of mechanical and organic solidarity, and so on. All of this is indeed developmentalism, and the sheer size of the canvas in each instance is doubtless sufficient to make this aspect the most memorable in our overview of the idea.

But developmentalism is nevertheless much more than this—much more

The essential argument of this chapter may be found in modified and greatly enlarged form in my book *Social Change and History: Aspects of the Western Ideas of Development* (New York: Oxford University Press, 1969). Both this chapter and the book owe much to the work of the late Frederick J. Teggart of the University of California, Berkeley. It is a pleasure to thank two graduate students in sociology at Duke, Daniel Collins and Monica Boyd, for their important criticisms of an early draft of this chapter.

than origins and stages, whether unilinear or multilinear—and it is a serious mistake to suppose that because developmentalism in this macro-sense fell into disrepute it is absent from the scene today. All that has happened is that the focus has changed. Like modern biology, the social sciences have simply turned attention from the longer vistas of change and succession that captured the minds of nineteenth-century thinkers to the shorter-run mechanisms of change that the evolutionary process reveals; so, I think it may fairly be concluded, has sociology. Although there are interesting signs at the present time of a revival of interest in the larger patterns of the changes through which civilizations go (I think of some of the recent work of Eisenstadt and Parsons as examples), the bulk of work done in sociology during the past several decades on the problem of change has been directed to aspects of the problem not unlike those which have elicited the attention of molecular biologists and geneticists. It is—or has been—not so much the larger forms of change as the possible internal mechanisms of change in social groups and social systems that dominate. Functionalism, which has been erroneously charged with insensitivity to the problem of change, can in fact be seen as a post-developmentalist effort to combine both the statics and dynamics of social behavior in a single theory. I say "post-developmentalist" rather than non- or anti-developmentalist, for it is in light of the continuation of certain vital assumptions of developmentalism, but without the superstructure that these assumptions carried in the nineteenth century, that the functionalist treatment of change can best be understood. I will return to this point toward the end of the chapter.

Before analyzing the perspective of developmentalism, a few general background observations will be useful. First, I should stress that throughout the chapter, the words *develop* and *development* are used in their intransitive construction rather than in the transitive sense that is today, especially in the wide literature of the new nations, more common. Admittedly there is close relation between the two. When we speak of developing something—a plant-type, a human voice, or the civil service of a new nation—we presumably are seeking to make actual or vigorous what is potential, and not supplanting the old by something totally new as one does in replacing a piece of furniture. We may not go so far as did some of our nineteenth-century predecessors—Marx, for example—in assuming that what we are developing (trans.) *would* develop (intrans.) if we just left it alone and allowed indefinite time. But we nevertheless assume some kind of potentiality, some kind of process operating autonomously, however faintly, when we propose to develop a system or thing. Still, there are differences between them, and hence I stress that what I am concerned with is the first and oldest, the intransitive, use of development.

Second, I shall use *develop* and *development* as synonymous with *evolve* and *evolution*. There may be differences in the context of modern biology, and even of the social sciences, that are significant for certain purposes, but

not here. It is worth noting that throughout the nineteenth century, *development, evolution,* and also *progress* were used almost interchangeably. This was as true in biology as in sociology. Darwin, for example, made little use of the word *evolution;* much more of *development* and especially of *progress.* It was characteristic that Darwin wrote, toward the end of *The Origin of Species,* the following summation: "And as natural selection works solely by and for the good of each being, all corporeal and mental endowments will tend to progress towards perfection." [1] The word *progress* is here used in part evaluatively but in large part in the neutral sense of step-by-step advancement that is contained in the Latin *progredior* and that we find throughout the eighteenth and nineteenth centuries. That is, progress refers to a slow, gradual, and cumulative type of change, akin to what the physician has in mind when he speaks of the natural progress of a fatal disease. All three words, development, evolution, and progress come historically, as I shall indicate in a moment, from the Greek doctrine or concept of *physis.*

Third, it is important to stress that the idea of *social* development owes little or nothing to the currents of thought which flowed in the nineteenth-century study of organic evolution. Least of all does the idea of social development owe anything substantive to Darwin's great work, *The Origin of Species,* published in 1859. No doubt some of the prestige of that work was reflected in one way or another in nineteenth-century studies of social development, of social evolution, and it is true that Darwin's phrase, "survival of the fittest," was directly transferred by some social scientists to the industrial scene as added justification of the competition that had been, since the eighteenth century, assumed to be a natural and proper part of the economy. But all of this notwithstanding, it is important to remind ourselves that the major expressions of developmentalism in the social sciences— those of Comte, Marx, Spencer, among others—had appeared before Darwin's work. More to the point, these expressions proceeded, not from the study of biological evolution found in the pre-Darwinian works of Lamarck, Erasmus Darwin, and others, but from a line of interest that goes a long way back in Western social thought and includes the seminal eighteenth-century works of Rousseau (such as his *Discourse on the Origin of Inequality,* a remarkable piece of social evolutionism), of Adam Smith (I am thinking particularly of his essay on language here), and of Condorcet, to mention but three. What the eighteenth century called "hypothetical" or "conjectural" or "natural" history was not history at all as this word was understood by historians like Gibbon, Robertson, and Voltaire, but rather *development,* as this word was to be understood in the century following.

It is interesting to note that the idea of development was better understood indeed, and more widely accepted, in the nineteenth century with respect to the "social species" of kinship, community, or state, than with

1. Charles Darwin, *The Origin of Species* (New York: Modern Library, 1936), p. 373.

respect to the biological species. By this I mean simply that a genetic, filiative relation among these and other social types or species, with such
processes as conflict and competition posited as the dynamic means of fili-
ation, was widely understood in social thought, and had been ever since
Aristotle's famous developmental treatment of family, community, and
state. What was not so widely accepted—or, if accepted, understood—was
the matter of biological speculation, that is, of the filiative or genetic relation
among the species. Aristotle's pithy observation, "It takes a man to beget
a man," had tended to clothe this view of the species in a form that, with
rarest and most hazy exceptions, it was to keep until the nineteenth century.

What we observe in Darwin's great work is the utilization of a number
of ideas that had attained major significance in the study of society long
before Darwin's age. Everyone knows of Darwin's (acknowledged) indebtedness to Malthus for having suggested, metaphorically at least, the
type of mechanism responsible for the selective process by which some
variations are preserved and others lost in nature. But the matter does not
stop here, at least not for the intellectual historian. Of equal importance in
Darwin's work are still other great interpretative ideas—progressivism,
gradualism, continuity, uniformitarianism, differentiation, among others—
that had been for a very long time staples in the interpretation of social
change but that were only now, and chiefly by Darwin, given maximum
utilization in the study of biological change. It would be easier to defend
the proposition that social developmentalism precedes biological than the
contrary, although neither proposition, stated so starkly, is entirely correct.

Next it is useful to say something about the historical relation between
Christianity and the idea of development. Ever since Thomas Huxley skill-
fully created the impression in his valiant defense of Darwin's work that any
opposition to Darwinism was, and could only be, based on a literalist view
of the Old Testament, the rather widespread impression has persisted of a
conflict between developmentalism and the "creationist" view necessarily
involved, in one degree or other, in the Christian scheme. Such conflict,
however, would be the case only if *creationism* and *developmentalism* were
indeed antonyms. But they are not, and cannot be, for the words refer to
quite different orders of fact.

The opposite of creationism is a strictly naturalist theory of origins. This
theory is perfectly intelligible and is, clearly, incompatible with a Christian
or any other theistic view. But developmentalism is a process, and a process
moreover quite compatible with a world view in which the beginning of
things is a consequence of some single creative act, divine or other. The true
opposite of a developmental view of reality would be one in which everything *as we find it* in the world is held to have been created originally, with
nothing but persistence since. Or, more sophisticatedly, a nondevelop-
mentalist view would be one in which, irrespective of what was actually
created in the beginning, nothing has happened or changed since except

through a succession of external acts or events, either divine in inception or random and natural.

That there were, in Huxley's (as in our) day, religious literalists who declared either or both of these views is unquestioned. Because of them it was only too easy for Huxley to indict all opposition to Darwinism as being Christian in inspiration (which, of course, was by no means the case), with the implication that Christianity and developmentalism are opposites. But, of course, they are not.

When St. Augustine wrote *The City of God* at the beginning of the fifth century—primarily to refute pagan charges that the advent of Christianity was the doleful event that had started the breakdown of Roman polity—he placed the Christian view of mankind squarely in a developmental framework. Admittedly, God created it all and God remains sovereign throughout, always able to interfere, should he so choose, in the Augustinian-Christian perspective. But what distinguishes Augustine's view of man's past from the Hebrew sacred writ that forms the content of Augustine's philosophy of history is that, unlike the Hebrews who saw everything that had happened as a kind of genealogy of God's interventions or successive creations, Augustine placed the whole of mankind's past, present, and future in a pattern of unfolding or realization of what had in the beginning lain merely latent or potential. God, for Augustine, created the whole, but —and this is the Greek element in Augustine and the subsequent Christian tradition—he created potentialities that required time for their actualization. For Augustine, irrespective of the sovereignty that he places in God, the entire process, extending in his time-view several thousand years, has proceeded with a necessity, a continuity, and a cumulative character that is the result of internal, immanent forces.

This developmental emphasis never left Christianity. It is, as I say, a heritage of the Greek philosophy in which Augustine had steeped himself. In modern Western thought it is Leibniz, with his doctrine of the monads and his profound insistence upon what he called the Law of Continuity, along with the special form that the idea of plenitude takes in his thought, who is responsible for the pattern that Christian developmentalism has taken. If there is ineradicable tension within Christianity between its Hebrew stress upon event and crisis and its Greek stress upon continuity and emergence, the fault lies with the elements, not with the philosophers themselves.

In 1845, fourteen years before the publication of *The Origin of Species,* John Henry Newman published his momentous *Essay on the Development of Christian Doctrine.* It would be hard to find any nineteenth-century work that more deftly employs what I here call the developmental perspective. The challenge that had been thrown at Newman by critics was the stark contrast between apostolic Christianity, with its simplicity and freedom from the toils of both doctrine and hierarchy, and the powerful, complex, wealthy, and ecclesiastical reality that was Christianity in Newman's day.

How, the critics asked, is this difference to be explained? By development, Newman answered; by the emergence into actuality of what had been but latent in apostolic times; by slow, gradual, and continuous differentiation of what had first been homogeneous; by innovation, itself the product of internal, irresistible causes that are a part of the Christian essence.

We are perpetually brought back, however, by those who insist upon ~~full of subtle distinction, developmentalism~~ and religion to the matter of first cause. As I have said, the real antithesis is between religion and naturalism, and I can do no better than to leave the matter with Darwin himself. What he actually believed with respect to the existence or nonexistence of God I do not know. But he saw no conflict between the developmental view of the "chain of being" that the species form or have formed, and a view of original theistic creation. "There is grandeur," he writes in the concluding sentence of *The Origin of Species,* "in this view of life, with its several powers, having been originally breathed by the Creator into a few forms or into one; and that, whilst this planet has gone cycling on according to the fixed law of gravity, from so simple a beginning endless forms most beautiful and most wonderful have been, and are being evolved." [2]

The final prefatory point that I want to emphasize is the contrast that lies between the developmental perspective and the historical method.[3] By a good many in the nineteenth century, and still today, the two are made synonymous. Just as it has been claimed by one set of intellectual historians that the idea of social development is an offshoot of biological evolutionism, so is it claimed by another set that the developmental study of institutions in the nineteenth century was a consequence of the application of the "method of history" to what had been previously thought static or universal. But if, by the "method of history" we have reference to the kind of envisagement of the past that exists in historiography from Thucydides through Livy and Tacitus down to the Gibbons, Rankes, Mommsens, and Motleys of the eighteenth and nineteenth centuries, something very different indeed is involved. The developmental and historiographic perspectives have in common the premise that only by study of the past can the present be understood. But down at least through the nineteenth century, their ways of conceiving this past were very different. It is a difference that involves the nature of time and of the relative importance of event and process.

Comte made frequent use of the term "historical method" in his writings to describe his procedure, but the kind of exclusion of "exceptional events and minute details" that he called for, and his objective of "history without the names of men or even of nations" would hardly have appealed to historians in the tradition of Thucydides. And it was precisely against Comte's type of reconstruction of the past (Hegel's treatment of history was the immediate incitement, but the general point is the same) that the great von

2. Ibid., p. 374.
3. See Frederick J. Teggart, *Theory of History* (New Haven: Yale University Press, 1925), *passim.*

Ranke voiced his now celebrated prescription, *wie es eigentlich gewesen.* The past must be brought to light in terms of *exactly* (*eigentlich* has, I believe, the further quality of "uniquely") *how it happened.* All of the words in the prescription are crucial, including the final one. For the gulf that existed for so long between historians and social developmentalists was created by their contrasting envisagements of the past, quite as by their contrasting attitudes toward fact.

For the historian the past is to be seen most significantly as a kind of genealogy of events, happenings, occurrences—whether wars, invasions, treaties, foundings of dynasties, births of personages, great acts and deeds, promulgations of laws, and so on. Each event is held to produce its successor just as it is held to have been produced by its predecessor. The framework represented by the events and "begats" of the Old Testament is precisely the historiographic envisagement of the past, for no more history-oriented people ever lived than the ancient Jews. From the time God created the heavens and earth, and then man, each event followed the preceding one in the same way that individual followed individual. Whether conceived mythically, naïvely, or, as the nineteenth century fancied, "scientifically" (that is, objectively), history as understood by historians has been primarily a genealogy of events.[4]

But the developmental tradition, while not oblivious to events, was more interested in the past conceived as *change,* as a set of conditions altered, modified, occasionally transformed, by *process* (which I define, following MacIver, as continuous change taking place in a definite manner through the operation of forces present from the first within the situation). The developmentalist was interested in *things*—species, institutions, structures, and conditions rather than specific, datable happenings. And he was overridingly interested in them as undergoing change, change which, as I shall emphasize, was conceived in terms of immanent, even autonomous, process, and not as the fortuitous consequence of external happenings.

There is also the matter of time. I shall say more about this presently, for abstraction from time is one of the identifying attributes of developmentalism, but for the moment it suffices to emphasize the crucial role of time to the historian. The ideal of the historian is to date everything, but even when this is not possible by reason of paucity of records, he is still constrained by the "when-ness" of human history. History is the chronicle of annals writ large, and time is of the essence. As much as anything else it was the developmentalist's insensitivity to time, as well as to precise place, that made his studies of institutions conceived as "natural systems" seem to the historian so often to be but exercises in a timeless never-never land of the uniform and universal. The historian must always hear "time's wingèd chariot hurrying near," but this was not true of the social developmentalist who, like his biologist counterpart, could take sufficient satisfaction in before-and-after relationships, abstracted from historical time.

4. Ibid., chap. 2.

The Roots of Developmentalism

Although this chapter is an analysis rather than a history of the idea of development, something should be said about the antiquity and universality of developmentalism in Western thought. Greek thought was saturated with ideas of development, growth, and progress. To say, as many have, that these notions are modern in inception is nonsense. Fundamental to Greek science was the concept of *physis,* and in all Greek thought there is no single concept more directive than this. Unhappily, through Roman translation or mistranslation, we know this concept as *natura* or "nature." I say unhappily, for it was the Romans who, by making the word *natura* refer primarily to the merely physical or biological, established a dualism that has plagued Western thought ever since and makes possible the absurd distinction between the "natural sciences" and the "social sciences."

But dualism of this type is not Greek. To the Greeks *physis* meant quite literally "the way things grow." [5] The metaphoric product of Greek fascination with organic—particularly botanical—life around them, the concept of *physis,* from the Eleatics onward, was applied as often to social and cultural entities as it was to physical. The *physis* of anything—dog, tree, kinship system, *polis*—was simply the pattern of growth and change that was held to be inherent in it, natural to its very structure or being. Given the overwhelming vitalism, the organicism, of the Greek mind, it was inevitable that everything, from the sun even to the smallest being on earth, was endowed with life and therefore with a pattern of change that was natural to it, that is, that arose from its very structure or nature. Everything, Aristotle wrote, is either coming-into-being or going-out-of-being; nothing is fixed. Given this assumption, the task of science for any Greek was clear-cut: it was to identify the *physis* of whatever he was studying—tree, fish, or state.

More specifically, this task was fourfold. It involved (1) investigation of the origin or original condition, for in it lay, *ex hypothesi,* the essential elements of the thing in their pristine state, their state of nature, as Romans and subsequent philosophers were to regard it. But as I have said, for the Greek, "nature" was by no means limited to raw elements or to an aboriginal state; *physis* covered the entirety of the life-cycle of anything. Hence it was necessary (2) to identify the cycle or pattern of change, from origin to end, that was uniquely characteristic of the thing and its type. And it is here, of course, that "stages" are brought into light, for everything has, just as does any organism, a sequence of stages natural to it. But it was also held necessary (3) to identify the end, the goal, or *telos* of the process,

5. On this see especially F. M. Cornford, *Principium Sapientiae: The Origins of Greek Philosophical Thought* (Cambridge: Cambridge University Press, 1952), pp. 179-181 and *passim.*

for in growth, all changes are, by definition, relative to a specific end or result. Hence the teleological character of much Greek, and subsequent Western, concern with change. But the above three questions raise still another (4), which concerns the mechanism or efficient source of the whole process, for this, too, is an aspect of the *physis* of a thing. Specifically, what is the force or factor that through continuous operation gives dynamism to the whole pattern of development? Conflict, as Heraclitus and others had argued; cooperation, as Aristotle thought? One can classify a great deal of Western thought on development in terms of the factors variously held responsible for continuous operation of the developmental process in a given type, biological or social. In the nineteenth century, as we know, Darwin answered the question with his "natural selection," Marx with class conflict, and so on.

How the developmental perspective could be used sociologically by the Greeks is nowhere better illustrated than by Aristotle in his famous treatment of the nature (*physis*) of the state, which we find at the very beginning of his *Politics*. He begins with the family, for, he says, "He who considers things in their first growth and origin, whether the state or anything else, will obtain the clearest view of them." Aristotle then passes to the state's developmental pattern which is, he tells us, in three stages: *family, community, polis*. Everywhere, he implies strongly, this is the fixed pattern of growth. The end of the pattern is, of course, the state itself. "And therefore if the earlier forms of society are natural so is the state, for it is the end of them, and the completed nature is the end. For what each thing is when fully developed, we call its nature, whether we are speaking of a man, a horse, or a family." For Aristotle, thus, it would be wrong to limit the "state of nature," as did so many philosophers down through the eighteenth century, to the original state alone. The fully developed state—or economy or culture—is as "natural" as is the first and simplest condition. Aristotle, in this section at least, is less satisfactory on the matter of the efficient cause or the continuously operating source of the development. This source would appear to be war, necessitating ever more complete forms of security, but a case can be made out for something else, chiefly the human desire for sociability and with it cooperation.

Here, then, is the essential perspective of developmentalism, built deeply into Greek thought and into all subsequent ages in the West, including the Augustinian-Christian, as I have suggested above. Development, far from being a contribution of the nineteenth century, is in fact a master principle of Western philosophy. The perspective, with its four steps of inquiry (closely related, it might be noted, to Aristotle's so-called four causes), has had, of course, varying emphases in the two millennia since Aristotle. It cannot be said that the seventeenth century, for instance, was as developmentally minded, in the full sense of the term, as were the two centuries which followed. But, for all that, the Hobbesian and Lockean interest in

origins—and in the comparative data of existing prepolitical, savage people—is nonetheless related to a setting up of the problem that is, at bottom, on developmental foundations.

The Nature of Developmentalism

With these prefatory observations made, let us turn now to the nature of developmentalism considered as a theory to account for the facts of change in time. Change is, of course, a matter of observation; it is something experienced, something that we are justified in referring to as empirical. We become aware of change through our perception of differences in time within a persisting identity. All three of these elements are necessary: differences, time, and persisting identity. A mere array of differences does not betoken change, only differences. Unless the perceived differences are aspects of a persisting identity—tree, political state, individual human being—change cannot be said to exist, for apart from the persisting identity there would be nothing for which change could be predicated.[6] The dimension of time is equally important, for the succession of differences within an identity necessarily involves an earlier and later point of reference. Mere mobility, motion, or activity is not change even though each is in some degree involved in change. To say with the ancient philosopher "All is flux" is perhaps obvious. But to say "All is change" is far from obvious. There are, on the surface at least, too many clear evidences of fixity and persistence.

Change, then, involves the crucial characteristics of succession of differences in time but within a persisting identity. When we speak of a *process* of change, we are referring to the additional idea of a presumed causal connection of the various differences noted in time. That is, there is the implication that each of the differences is causally related to the others, with the terminal difference the outcome of a series commenced by the original condition of what it is we are observing in change.

Development is a more radical idea. It is change, of course, but development, where it exists, is change that proceeds directly from the structure, the substance or nature, of the thing that is undergoing change. Whereas change alone may be the consequence of external, intrusive factors, of random events or catastrophes, development is a process that proceeds from the thing itself. To understand the thing's structure is, if there is genuine development, to possess the key to the succession of its states of differentness in time, to be able to understand, moreover, the principle on which each gives way to its successor.

6. See the penetrating discussion in A. E. Taylor, *Elements of Metaphysics* (London: Methuen, 1921), pp. 159ff. See also Wilbert Moore's valuable *Social Change* (Englewood Cliffs: Prentice-Hall, 1963) and Kenneth E. Bock's profound *The Acceptance of Histories* (Berkeley: University of California Press, 1956).

Development, as I have suggested, is not only an old idea in Western thought, it is one of the master ideas of the West, to be found in virtually every major system since the time of the Eleatic philosophers. In the pages immediately following, I want to analyze or dissect this idea into the concepts which seem to me to compose it. My illustrations and citations are deliberately farflung, for it is important to see the developmental perspective in the widest possible compass.

Immanence

What gives development its distinctiveness above all else is its essential immanence; that is, its emergence or manifestation from forces that lie *within* the system that we are concerned with. If, as could be argued, no system ever changes except when external forces impact upon it, that apart from these external forces it lies fixed and inert, then, plainly, development as a concept would be irrelevant to this system no matter how often it might in fact be modified or transformed as the result of external impacts. Admittedly, development does not have to be, and is not in practice, insulated from things external to it. External events and processes can and do affect development: decelerate it, accelerate it, distort it, even obliterate it. This is not in question. What is in question is whether or not any given social system or social type does contain within it an identifiable process of change that bears relation to a point of departure and to a subsequent end. It does not matter how large or small the social system is. It may be the totality of human society, past, present, and future, as it was for Hegel and for Comte; it may be a single type of economic system, capitalism, as it was for Marx (though, as we know, capitalism is for Marx but a stage in the development of something much larger); or it may be the patriarchal family. Whatever the system or persisting identity, development, if it exists, is a function of the system itself, even as is growth in an organism.

"When I speak of the force and action of created beings," wrote Leibniz at the beginning of the eighteenth century, "I mean that each created being is pregnant with its future state, and that it naturally follows a certain course, *if nothing hinders it* . . . ." [7] It is in the last that we see the confrontation, so to speak, of the two types of change I referred to above *and also* of the developmental and historiographic perspectives that I dealt with in an earlier section. I will come back to this later. For the moment it suffices merely to stress the importance of this Leibnizian principle of immanence in the theories of development that mark the eighteenth and nineteenth centuries. Such theories were immanent in that, one and all, they were based upon the certainty—if nothing interfered in the short run—of

7. "New Essays on the Human Understanding," in Bertrand Russell, *A Critical Exposition of the Philosophy of Leibniz* (Cambridge: Cambridge University Press, 1900), p. 222. Italics added.

movement in time according to a pattern that the developmentalist had himself, so he thought, discovered. (Each of the great developmentalists— Condorcet, Comte, Hegel, Marx, Spencer, et al.—was convinced that *he* had discovered the law of motion or development that would thenceforth render obsolete prior opinions on fixity and change in society.)

Thus, for Comte the so-called law of three stages *was* a law because, in his confident belief, no more fluctuating parts in of changes in the bound up with forces internal to society as a whole, or to any specific society, and not the chance product of unforeseeable events (least of all divine decrees) which lay outside the realm of ongoing, indwelling, process. And for Marx the whole point of what he and Engels liked to think was scientific—in contrast to romantic, charitable, or utopian—socialism was that its coming would be the culmination of persisting, ineradicable forces within the system around them, namely capitalism. Only in terms of immanence, of actualization through the continuous operation of forces bound up with the structure of capitalism, was it possible for Marx to refer to laws of change "working with iron necessity toward inevitable results." That the process could usefully stand acceleration through the efforts of a revolutionary vanguard of the proletariat was clear enough. Marx had a large activist component in his makeup. But Marx's activism was closely related, nevertheless, to what he called the law of motion of capitalism.

Darwin's theory of evolution was, of course, an immanent one, immanent in the sense that the entire organic panorama of change could be interpreted, not in terms of adventitious (and hence unpredictable) forces, divine or secular, but in terms of natural selection that was immanent to the forms and types and also in terms of what Darwin called "an innate tendency towards progressive development."

Herbert Spencer has often been smiled at for his resounding statement: "Progress is not an accident . . . but a beneficient necessity." Yet he was, in context, merely saying what Marx, Comte, and Darwin, among many, were saying: that positivism, or socialism, or higher corporeal and mental endowment, was necessary because each was the result of processes internal to and constitutive of the system.

Continuity

Because each was the result of processes of change that were continuous, each exemplified the sanctified Leibnizian principle. "Nothing happens all at once," wrote Leibniz, "and it is one of my great maxims, and among the most completely verified, that nature never makes leaps *(natura non facit saltum):* which I call the Law of Continuity. . . . Everything goes by degrees in nature, and nothing by leaps, and this rule as regards change is part of my law of continuity." [8]

8. Ibid., p. 222.

It would be difficult to exaggerate the role played in developmentalist theory by Leibnizian assumptions of continuity. Darwin, who could find no exemplification of it in observations of biological types extant, nor in the geological record, nevertheless followed the principle of continuity religiously. It *must* be true, he argued—quoting the Leibnizian phrase in its Latin—and it was on the basis, at least in part, of faith in the principle of continuity that he declared the geological record, with its numerous breaks, to be imperfect, stating: "I do not pretend that I should ever have suspected how poor was the record in the best preserved geological sections, had not the absence of innumerable transitional links between the species which lived at the commencement and close of each formation, *pressed so hardly on my theory.*" [9] Elsewhere in the *Origin* Darwin wrote: "As natural selection acts solely by accumulating slight, successive, favourable variations, it can produce no great or sudden modifications; it can act only by short and slow steps. Hence, the canon of *Natura non facit saltum, which every fresh addition to our knowledge tends to confirm,* is on this theory intelligible." [10]

Marx, too, was an apostle of the precept of continuity. That there is indeed the call to revolution in Marx does not for a moment imply that such revolution would be discontinuity. Whatever there may be in the way of Marxian *obiter dicta,* the systematic Marx sees revolution as the product of a line of development quite as continuous as the line of embryonic growth leading up to birth. Even, wrote Marx, "when a society has got on the right track for the discovery of the natural laws of its movement—and it is the ultimate aim of this work to lay bare the economic law of motion of modern society—*it can neither clear by bold leaps nor remove by legal enactments the obstacles offered by the successive phases of its normal development.* But it can shorten the birth pangs." [11]

Darwin would have approved, and so would Leibniz—and also Aristotle, for the proposition that change in any social system, that is, *natural* change, is continuous is among the most deeply seated axioms of Western thought, and has been ever since the Greeks made the momentous analogy between change in society and the growth of the organism. That every institution or social system has a *normal* development—for Marx it was the development from slavery to feudalism to capitalism to socialism; for Aristotle from family through community to *polis* and then, within the political state itself, from monarchy through fixed, intervening stages to democracy and back to one-man rule—seemed as plausible, given the initial assumption of self-resident tendencies toward development in a living thing, as that it had a structure.

9. Darwin, p. 249. Italics added.
10. Ibid., p. 361. Italics added.
11. "Capital: A Critique of Political Economy," in Lewis Feuer, ed., *Marx and Engels: Basic Writings on Politics and Philosophy* (New York: Doubleday, 1959), p. 136. Italics added.

Continuity as a concept may of course refer simply to persistence in time or space. Thus, we speak of the continuity of a river bed as well as of the flowing river itself. There is also the purely classificatory sense of continuity, as in the whole notion of the "chain of being" in Western thought, from Aristotle to Linnaeus. Aristotle the biologist could write that "nature proceeds little by little from things lifeless to animal life in such a way that it ⲓⲩ ⲓⲓⲓⲓⲡⲓⲩⲓⲓⲓⲓⲓⲓⲓ ⲓⲓⲓ ⲓⲓⲓⲓⲓⲓⲓ ⲓⲓⲓⲓⲓⲓ ⲓⲓⲓⲙ ⲙⲓ ⲓ ⲓ ⲓⲓⲓⲙ ⲓⲓⲫ ⲓⲓⲓ ⲓⲓⲓⲙⲓⲓ ⲓⲓⲓⲓⲙⲓ, ⲓⲓⲓ ⲓⲓⲓ ⲙⲓⲓⲓ ⲓⲓ ⲓⲓⲓⲓ thereof an intermediate form should lie." This is continuity, but of a purely classificatory type. Developmental continuity is, in a sense, the conversion of the infinite gradations of the classificatory series into a time-series. I will come back to this point again when I deal briefly with the so-called Comparative Method.

For Marx it was as inconceivable that what he called the "normal development" of society should proceed in any area from capitalism to feudalism, or from socialism to capitalism, as that the maturity of an organism should precede adolescence, that puberty should follow adulthood. Merely to suggest it is to suggest nonsense—given, that is, the reality of change in an entity that is immanent and continuous.

Auguste Comte wrote: "The true general spirit of social dynamics then consists in conceiving of each of these consecutive social states as the necessary result of the preceding, and the indispensable mover of the following, according to the axiom of Leibniz,—*the present is big with the future.* In this view, the object of science is to discover *the laws which govern this continuity,* and the aggregate of which determines the course of human development." [12] It is in these terms that Comte offered his own proposition with respect to the path that continuity normally follows in a society: from the theological to the metaphysical to the positive.

It would be false to imply here that the developmentalists uniformly believed in the existential reality of continuity; that is, that a society or social system invariably and universally followed its line of normal continuity. For, as there are monsters in nature, along with aberrant lines of development, so must there be, from time to time, in society. Comte was too shrewd a mind, too knowledgeable an intellect, to suppose that pathologies do not occur. What is true in biology, he suggests, is even more true in sociological analysis. Here, pathological analysis consists in study of those cases in which the natural laws, either of harmony or succession, are disturbed by any causes, special or general, accidental or transient, such as in times of revolution and crisis. These disturbances are, in society, exactly analogous, Comte tells us, to diseases in the individual organism.

It will be recalled that I distinguished above between the two perspectives of developmentalism and historiography, suggesting that whereas the former is concerned with discovery of patterns of normal change in a system, the

12. *The Positive Philosophy,* trans. Harriet Martineau (*Bohn's Philosophical Library,* 3 vols. [London: Bell, 1896]), bk. 6, chap. 3. Second italics added.

latter has been occupied primarily with events in time, and that such ex-
emplary historiographers as Ranke and Mommsen could only shake their
heads in disbelief at the patterns of social evolution yielded by the works of
Hegel, Comte, Marx, and others. For the historian who was concerned, in
Ranke's words, with "exactly how it happened," it was scarcely credible
that laws of social development could be respectfully entertained in the
teeth of the manifest facts of *dis*continuity occasioned by events—by happenings and occurrences that did not emerge from the system under consideration but from the outside altogether—as in the cases of invasions,
catastrophes, and other events which all too plainly left their impress upon
the social system. How, it was asked, first by the historiographers, then by
such philosophers as Windelband and Rickert—and also Dilthey, though in
different key—could there be a science of society founded upon the principle of normality and continuity of change when the imperishable uniqueness of each and every event rendered propositions of normality and continuity invalid?

Comte had an answer before the philosophers named had even asked the
question. "In our search for the laws of society, we shall find that exceptional events and minute details must be discarded as essentially insignifi-
cant, while science lays hold of the most general phenomena which everybody is familiar with, as constituting the basis of ordinary social life." [13]
It is precisely in these terms that Comte then goes on to speak of the "abstract history" (to which I have previously referred) which would be, in
effect, history without the monstrous, the exceptional, the manifestly accidental; concerned with that which is natural or normal, and no more concerned with the accidental and unnatural than is, say, physiology or botany.

It was, then, in these terms that the perspective of developmentalism
flourished in the nineteenth century. "Historical" we may call such scholars
as Marx, Tocqueville, and Maine. But the word is applicable only in the
very general sense that they were concerned with the past and the relation
of past to present. These men were not historical in the sense in which
historians like Ranke, Mommsen, Stubbs, and Motley used that word; the
sense of telling "exactly how it happened" in a particular place within a
particular span of time. In this latter, historiographic, sense, any account of
the past that did *not* describe, to the best of the historian's ability, the major
events and personages, in an era all given specificity in time and place,
would have been laughed out of court. Hence the historian's necessarily
meticulous concern with documents and records; hence also his somewhat
less than respectful view of what the social evolutionists seemed to be doing.

It may be interjected here that Marx, to name one major developmentalist, gave intensive attention to England and to English capitalism. Think
only of the content of the first volume alone of *Capital,* of the many years

13. Ibid., bk. 6, chap. 7.

Marx spent in the British Museum studying records and documents of English economic history. True, Marx knew a great deal about English history, and *Capital* is studded with references to English experiences. But this does not affect the main point, which is that Marx's overriding interest was not in England, but in what he himself called "the economic law of motion of modern society" and "the natural laws of its movement." His concern was with the laws of development of capitalism, considered as a more or less contained system, as an entity, within which forces operated that would in time destroy its being and bring into existence, at one and the same time, the first stage of socialism. It was, in short, not England or English capitalism that was of primary interest to Marx, but capitalism wherever it could properly be said to exist. "The country that is more developed industrially only shows, to the less developed, the image of its own future." This was Marx's reply, in the preface to the second edition of *Capital,* to those who discounted the applicability to other countries of what Marx was illustrating about capitalism with English materials.

The same can be said of Tocqueville on the development of democracy. "I confess," Tocqueville wrote in his introduction to *Democracy in America,* "that in America I saw more than America; I sought there the image of democracy itself, with its inclinations, its character, its prejudices, and its passions, in order to learn what we have to fear or to hope from its progress." [14] And it has to be admitted by even the most ardent admirers of Tocqueville that what is weakest in that great book on democracy is what he has to say on the specific matter of *American* democracy in the age of Jackson. One could fill a book with what Tocqueville failed to note in the American political structure and behavior of that age. The reason for this is clear and follows directly from the statement I have quoted. Tocqueville was not, in fact, the student of American politics, nor did he aspire to be, any more than Marx was with respect to English economic behavior. In the strictly historiographic terms of "exactly how it happened," politically in America and economically in England, neither Tocqueville nor Marx can be, or is, taken very seriously. If, however, what we are looking for is analysis of a more or less universal social type—democracy, capitalism—complete with its structural characteristics, its endemic processes, its internal dynamics, its course of change in time—then we have, of course, in Tocqueville's and Marx's works classics of lasting relevance. What Tocqueville wrote about democracy in the passage quoted above, Marx could have written (indeed came very close to writing) about capitalism. So too could other developmentalists in the nineteenth century have written: Comte, Maine, Tylor, Spencer, and Morgan. One and all, these men were interested in the change and development of *systems*—intellectual, legal, kinship, religious —considered as universal and hence more or less autonomous types with,

14. Alexis de Tocqueville, *Democracy in America,* vol. 1, ed. Phillips Bradley (New York: Knopf, 1945), p. 14.

supposedly, their own intrinsic, self-sustaining principles of development. When specific countries, areas, and time-periods were brought into treatment, it was for the purpose of illustrating specific aspects of a pattern of development that was held to be universal and, as I say, to inhere in the system itself.

Uniformitarianism

Here I am referring not to the notion of the uniformity of stages of development from area to area, but to the idea of uniform causes or mechanisms of change within similar or identical systems; that is, the idea that capitalism —or kinship or caste or the community—proceeds in its normal development through mechanisms that are the same everywhere and at all times. Ever since Cartesianism had lighted up the European scene, the uniformity of the laws of nature had been, of course, one of the cardinal axioms of social as well as physical philosophy. "Like effects are produced by like causes" is the simplest way of stating the proposition in pure logic, but for the burgeoning sciences (social and physical both) of the eighteenth century, the Cartesian principle of uniformity carried with it a much more exciting and useful corollary: that the causes to be seen operating today in the study of nature and society are the same as those which operated in distant past. Such a corollary marvelously simplified the problem of time in the study of development.

Thus Kant—and I am selecting almost at random—in searching for the process that had activated society's evolution in all ages, settled on what he called the "unsocial sociability" of men: "their tendency to enter into society, conjoined, however, with an accompanying resistance which continually threatens to dissolve this society." The process, Kant declares, is timeless and universal, for "the disposition lies manifestly in human nature." Here, in a single principle, Kant presents us (as he thought) with the means of reducing multiplicity of effect to unity of cause; a uniform cause working through all ages, as instrumental in ancient Nineveh as in modern Germany. Hegel, as we know, found uniform process in his famous principle of dialectical opposition—of thesis and antithesis, to be followed by resolution of conflict in synthesis that then becomes fresh thesis, followed by antithesis, but at a higher level.

For Comte, the entire developmental process in human society is caused by the innate desire in man for making his condition better, and this infinitely small gradation of improvement in a single generation is, when multiplied into the whole long succession of generations that has been the evolution of the human race, the essence of human progress in the large.

Marx, too, dealt with the problem in terms of uniform process. That Marx thought he had discovered the master process, or had at least taken it

down from the heavens and placed it in material conditions, is of less importance to us than that, irrespective of context, he was doing precisely what Kant—and Hegel and Comte—had done, and that was to assign a single causative principle, working uniformly in all ages and areas, to human development. And this single, uniform process was, of course, the struggle among classes that, for Marx, was unremitting and directive in all human history, and would be until social classes had been once for all removed from human society. Unpleasant in the short run, class conflict was nonetheless the process that in the long run made for progress in human development. And it would work everywhere. Hence Marx's aside in *Capital:* "If . . . the German reader shrugs his shoulders at the condition of the English industrial and agricultural laborers, or in optimist fashion comforts himself with the thought that in Germany things are not nearly so bad, I must plainly tell him, *De te fabula narratur.*" [15] In this aside, it is uniformity of steps of development as well as of process that is stressed.

Tocqueville—not usually thought of when the word developmentalism comes to mind—saw the entirety of Western history, from the early Middle Ages on, as falling within a single pattern of development, and saw it all as being caused by a single, uniform process, the leveling of classes. What Marx was to assign to conflict among classes, Tocqueville assigned to egalitarianism. "The gradual development of the principle of equality," Tocqueville wrote, "is universal, it is lasting, it constantly eludes all human interferences, and all events as well as all men contribute to its progress." [16] Tocqueville thought this mechanism to be operative in democracy anywhere and everywhere, for as I have noted, *Democracy in America,* despite all its vivid insight into the United States, is no more about American society specifically than Marx's *Capital* is about England.

When Darwin, some time before the publication of the *Origin* in 1859, made explicit in letters to friends his preference for uniformitarianism over catastrophism, he was, in effect, doing exactly what Kant, Hegel, Comte, Marx, and others had already done in the realm of social phenomena: taking an ongoing, universal, and essentially timeless process—in his case, natural selection—and making it equally decisive in the long vistas of the past as in the present. The immediate source of Darwin's uniformitarianism was, of course, geology—or, rather, the school of geology so brilliantly represented by Sir Charles Lyell and, before him, the great James Hutton. It was Hutton, a contemporary of Kant, who, as a biographer has put it, saw "with the intuition of genius . . . that the only solid basis from which to explore what has taken place in bygone time is a knowledge of what is taking place today. He felt assured that Nature must be consistent and uniform in her working, and that only in proportion as her operations at the

15. *Capital,* p. 135.
16. *Democracy in America,* p. 6.

present time are watched and understood will the ancient history of the earth become intelligible." [17]

Hutton's, and then Lyell's, stress upon uniform mechanism of change was in sharp opposition to the so-called catastrophists (by no means limited to Christian creationists) who argued that uniform, timeless process was insufficient to account for the configuration of the earth's surface; that there must also be taken into account the effects of great "catastrophes" in the past, that is, discrete, unrepeated, geological events which had, at various times, profoundly disrupted this or that area of the earth's surface: great volcanic and seismic episodes.

In Darwin's day the conflict between catastrophism and uniformitarianism was often bitter, and when Darwin opted for the latter, he did so with a fervor that not even his geologist master Lyell had possessed. For, as Lyell well knew, the geological record did not itself support the thesis of exclusive action of uniform process; it revealed great gaps and discontinuities. But Darwin, single-mindedly pressing the claims of natural selection as the uniform process by which organic evolution had operated, was operating, and would always operate, referred, in a famous chapter on the geological record, to "the imperfections of the geological record." What he says is that the stratigraphic evidence of biological continuity and uniformity of change would be present in the geological record if certain untoward and biologically irrelevant obliterations or distortions of that record had not taken place. "But I do not pretend," Darwin wrote in charming artlessness, "that I should ever have suspected how poor was the record in the best preserved geological sections, had not the absence of innumerable transitional links between the species which lived at the commencement and close of each formation *pressed so hardly on my theory.*" [18]

The status of uniformitarianism in either nineteenth century or contemporary biology is outside my competence and real interest. I am only concerned with making clear that the heart of uniformitarianism lies in the asserted *mechanism* of change rather than in sequences of supposedly identical stages, and that uniformitarianism as a principle in social developmentalism, no more derives from its biological counterpart in the nineteenth century than do any of the other key elements in the perspective. In purely theoretical terms, Darwin was drawing from a tradition of thought in Western history that others, such as Comte and Marx, had independently drawn from, and that other sociologists down even to the present would continue to draw from.

But there is a related aspect that is of even greater significance. I wrote above of the conflict between uniformitarianism and catastrophism in

17. Cited by Teggart, *Theory of History,* p. 127.
18. Darwin, p. 249. Italics added.

geology (in post-Darwinian biology this would have its offshoot for a generation or so in the conflict between continuous variation and supposedly discontinuous mutation), and it is useful to mention briefly the counterpart of this conflict in the study of human society. Here we must go back to the contrast I mentioned earlier between the developmental and the historiographic perspectives, the first centering upon process, the second upon event. In the social perspective of the evolutionists, random events ("1066 and all that") have much the same significance that, for Darwinian evolution, was possessed by "catastrophes" or "mutations." They are, so to speak, excludable—excludable on the ground that the objective of a science of change, in contrast to a mere narration of happenings, is to uncover the dynamics of development that inheres in the system itself. It was in these terms that Comte, as we noted in our treatment of continuity, more or less expunged "exceptional events" along with other unnecessary "details" including the patently monstrous. It was precisely in these terms also that nineteenth-century historians found the Comtean (and Hegelian and Spencerian) type of reconstruction of the past unacceptable. For how, they asked, can one understand what actually happened in time to an institution—English law, for example—without reference to the discrete and unique events (great monarchs, lawyers, revolutions) of which it is composed? Hence the famous observation of Maitland that "by and by anthropology (read sociology as well) will have the choice of being history or being nothing." To the author of *Domesday Book and Beyond* it was inconceivable that law or any other institution could be understood in time in terms of uniform processes of continuous change that were to be found in the works of the developmentalists.

Differentiation

Like the other aspects of developmentalism I have referred to, this too has its prototype in the kind of differentiation that is most evident in organic growth, in the transition from the seed or embryo to the fully developed organism. What lies latent or rudimentary in the embryo, what is homogeneous, becomes progressively more complex and differentiated. Differentiation, along with the other elements we have examined, is shared in the nineteenth century by biological and social developmentalism, and what Darwin wrote on the subject would have been generally acceptable: "If we take as the standard of high organization, the amount of differentiation and specialization of the several organs in each being when adult (and this will include the advancement of the brain for intellectual purposes), natural selection clearly leads towards this standard: for all physiologists admit that the specialization of the organs, inasmuch as in this state they perform their functions better, is an advantage to each being;

and hence the accumulation of variations tending towards specialization is within the scope of natural selection." [19]

Such accumulation, within the scope of Herbert Spencer's law of progress or his principle of development, was also applied to social systems as well as to Comte's, Marx's, Hegel's, Kant's, Rousseau's, and others' theories of development, for it was axiomatic, and had been since the early Greeks had begun comparing various instances of social type encountered in their travels—comparing them, that is, within the framework of *physis*—that the more highly differentiated a given system is, the later in time it must be. The time-series is, under the principle of differentiation, made coterminous with the logical order of increasing complexity.

Time

Here it is necessary to pick up again the vital, if elusive, matter of time as a dimension of things. Earlier I suggested that one of the major differences between the historiographic and developmental perspectives in the nineteenth century was the contrasting use of time. For the historian, as I noted, time was vital. Any effort to deal with things save in terms of their specific when-ness would be as absurd as to deal with them without respect to precise location. It was not the neglect of "detail, document, and dust" in the works of the social evolutionists that offended academic historians so much as it was their neglect of precise place and time. For them, historicity meant both.

But in a very real sense time is expendable for the developmentalist. The kind of thing that Comte, Marx, Spencer, and the other developmentalists were chiefly concerned with in the relation of past to present and future did not really require an emphasis on "1066 and all that." Time for them was time more nearly in the sense of what we call geological time; I am thinking not so much of immensity here as of time in the before-and-after sense of, say, Pliocene preceding (rather than following) Pleistocene. The geologist or biological evolutionist may, for lay purposes, occasionally give us great blocks of time—one hundred million or five hundred million years ago—but time is really of no interest to him, for as long as before-and-after relationships are meticulously preserved in proper order, he has discharged his responsibility. What he does is abstract from time, that is, from time as the historian or annalist is consumed by it.

If we look at the process of development as here described, it can no more be chopped up into discrete, datable instants than can growth in an organism. When Comte divided the past and the present into the three great divisions of theological, metaphysical, and positive, he was not, of course, utterly oblivious to the dimension of time, and, as we know, he illustrated copiously from Egyptians, Greeks, and others. But it cannot be

19. Ibid., p. 94.

said that time, in the sense of datable time, was of crucial significance in Comte's division, for he was concerned, as we have noted, *not* with a genealogy of discrete events (events were to be subordinated, even omitted, in the timeless, dateless history of Comte's abstract fancy) but with processes of change that were contained, as growth is within the organism, within the great entity society—or knowledge or culture, as the case might be. Abstract history" meant timeless history, as it meant also placeless his tory, at least so far as specific locale was concerned.

This can be put in still another way. For the historian in the nineteenth century, time was unilinear, monistic, and encompassed all things and events within its single framework. But the developmentalist, abstracting from time, could put societies and cultures in a vast classificatory system in which varying stages of development could be seen, compared, and contrasted without respect to any iron framework of time. Time in the abstract sense, yes; but time in this mode of conception was as varied and differentiated as were the numberless peoples on earth. The notion of "contemporaneity" that Oswald Spengler made so much of in his comparison of cycles of civilization is a notion he derived, or could have derived, from the nineteenth-century evolutionists. Contemporaneity of forms, whether biological or social, had more to do with structural similarities and analogous place in a developmental cycle or pattern than it had to do with the monistic sense of time that is involved in the calendar.

The Comparative Method

It was the developmentalist combination of interest in process and abstraction from unilinear time that made possible the method, celebrated alike by social and biological evolutionists, that was known in the nineteenth century as the Comparative Method. This method, as employed by sociologists and ethnologists, was inseparable from the perspective of developmentalism.

This is not to say, of course, that the method of comparison is inseparable from the idea of development. No one used comparison of periods and structures more advantageously—and, as I would say, scientifically—than did Max Weber in his great study of religion, and specifically in his effort to establish the conditions involved in the rise of capitalism. This was comparison of instances within a class for the purpose of identifying causal conditions or functional relationships. It is comparison as found in the physical and social sciences today.

But the method that Comte and Spencer designated in uppercase, the Comparative Method, was something very different indeed from simple comparison. It was comparison, but comparison within the strict tenets of developmentalism. It is a synchronization of three distinguishable orders of fact: (1) the relationships of a coexisting logico-spatial series, (2) the

relationships of a selected temporal series with emphasis on before-and-after in time, and (3) an evolutionary or developmental series that is held to mark "normal" or "true" development of a type.

At its crudest, the Comparative Method was no more than a superimposition of the first, the classificatory or spatial series, on the third (or, rather, a derivation of the third directly from the first), and, it has to be noted, there are many examples of this kind of use of the method in the writings of both biological and social developmentalists. In his autobiographical account of the Comparative Method, Spencer leaves the impression that it is scarcely more than this: a note for each trait, a separate file for related traits, a chapter for the file when it is completed, then a book. Never, Spencer tells us, did he know a moment's perplexity or anguish when it came to organizing his material for writing. But even in Spencer's work, at its best in any event, there is more to the matter than this. For behind the scissors-and-paste work lay some rather subtle and profound judgments on the nature of change in time. Between the nineteenth-century Comparative Method and the idea of development there are close ties of conceptual relationship.

Comte has given us one of the most perspicuous accounts. He has made specific and explicit what is general and implicit in the works of others.[20] He begins with the method of comparison generally, common to all the sciences, but passes quickly to sociological uses. There is, first, comparison of human and animal society. This, Comte tells us, is useful in the studies of social statics; such comparison teaches us how deeply implanted is the social character of human existence. "In all that relates to the first germs of the social relations, and the first institutions which were founded by the unity of the family or the tribe, there is not only great scientific advantage, but real philosophical necessity for employing the rational comparison of human with other animal societies."

But what Comte calls the Comparative Method is no mere static comparison; its very essence is the continuous, progressive, uniform, and immanent development that is exhibited in all social systems. There are two aspects to the Comparative Method. The first aspect is a comparison of the different *coexisting states* of human society on the various parts of the earth's surface, those states being completely independent of one another. "By this method the different stages of evolution may all be observed at once . . . From the wretched inhabitants of Tierra del Fuego to the most advanced nations of western Europe, there is no social grade which is not clearly extant in some points of the globe, and usually in localities which are clearly apart . . . ." All possible degrees of social evolution are exhibited by existing societies. Why, given the fact of a universal tendency toward change and development, are some peoples to be found in the same

20. *The Positive Philosophy,* bk. 6, chap. 3. All of the quotations from Comte that follow on the Comparative Method are from this section of his work.

condition which once characterized even the most advanced? Comte has no answer for this, referring only to the fact that, through little understood forces, there have been "extremely unequal degrees of development, so that the former states of the most civilized nations are now to be seen, amidst some partial differences, among contemporary populations inhabiting different parts of the globe."

The second aspect of the Comparative Method is what Comte calls comparison of consecutive states. Here the matter becomes more complex. For it is not the "consecutive states" of any given, concrete area—say, Madagascar, England, or Russia—that is the object of attention here, but rather the consecutive states that are to be found in the development of humanity as a whole. Comte uses the phrase "historical method" to describe this type of comparison, but, as we have already seen, it is abstract history alone that interests Comte, that is, history from which exceptions and purely transient and local details have been expunged. "Where," Comte asks, "is the use of any exclusive history of any one science or art, unless meaning is given to it by first connecting it with the study of human progress generally?"

How do we acquire, however, a clear sense of the nature and direction of human progress, of mankind's development, or of a single institution of worldwide scope, such as kinship, economy, or polity? We do this in either or both of two ways. We may acquire it by our study of the coexisting types of culture that the earth's surface reveals, arranging these, as we have seen, in the order of the most primitive to the most advanced. "By this method," Comte told us, "the different stages of evolution may be observed all at once." Or—and here we come to the time-series—we may acquire our notion of the general course of development by restricting attention to "the development of the most advanced nations, not allowing our attention to be drawn off to other centres of any independent civilization which has, from any cause whatever, been arrested, and left in an imperfect state. It is the selectest part, the vanguard of the human race, that we have to study; the greater part of the white race, or the European nations,—even restricting ourselves, at least in regard to modern times, to the nations of Western Europe. When we ascend into the remoter past, it will be in search of the political ancestors of these peoples, whatever their country may be."

In short, the Comparative Method involved a synchronization of the time-series evidenced by what Comte called the most advanced nations—a time-series that could be extracted from the records of Western European civilization, going back to the Egyptians and Greeks and Romans—and the logico-spatial series evidenced as one looked over the distribution of cultures on the earth, in which series there fell cultures and civilizations of every degree of complexity. *But,* giving substance and direction to this synchronization, is the notion of a developmental series, that is, the series

of types that has been true for the human race as a whole over time and that in the future will tend to be true for all peoples who may now be still in simpler, less advanced, stages.

In sum, the so-called Comparative Method, as we find it in Comte, is far more than comparison (and substantially the same holds for Marx, Spencer, Maine, and the numberless others of the nineteenth century who were interested in the problem of development). It is comparison, but of a sort that is indistinguishable from developmentalism and its component ideas of continuity, uniformity, differentiation. There is indeed a curious type of circular reasoning involved in it. The method was designed to prove or demonstrate the reality of social development, but, as we have seen, its underlying, crucial premise is the very development that it is designed to prove.

It was nevertheless in these terms that man's age-old passion for prediction of the future was henceforth put. "In every science," Comte wrote shrewdly, "we must have learned to predict the past, so to speak, before we can predict the future." In tracing out developmental sequences of the past —drawn from Australia, from Ceylon, from China, from India, from all parts of the earth—such men as Comte and Marx were, so to speak, predicting: predicting the passage of different peoples from the theological to the metaphysical (Comte), from primitive communism to slavery or to feudalism or capitalism (Marx), and in this way alone making it possible confidently to predict an ultimate transition to Comte's positivism or Marx's socialism; or—reducing the canvas to a single institution—from the patriarchal family to the conjugal.

The Comparative Method could be put to ingenious uses. Wherever an entity or structure could be denoted—be it the ballad, the dance, religion, or law—the historical time-series could be depended upon to take the investigator back a certain distance, say, to the Homeric Greeks. Then one could turn, as did such men as Morgan, Engels, Gomme, and Frazer, to the evidence contributed by the spatial series, supplementing by judicious use of "survivals," to go back even further in time; all the way indeed to the very beginnings. What gave the Comparative Method such wide appeal in all areas of thought that were seeking recovery of cultural origins and the earliest stages of development was its implicit contention that contemporary preliterate peoples could be regarded as primitive in the temporal as well as the logical sense of this word. Through intensive study of these peoples, ranging from the aborigines of Australia (whom the majority of ethnologists in the late nineteenth century regarded as the most primitive) to the remaining tribes of the Iroquois Confederation in North America, detailed pictures could be provided of the earlier stages of mankind's development in time. All that remained was to fuse these with the documentary and archaeological data of Western history, and the full panorama of human development could be seen—or so it was believed. Truly, the Comparative Method was golden.

Neo-Developmentalism

Developmentalism, far from being dead in contemporary sociology, has merely altered its focus. Instead of concerning itself with the evolutionary panorama that interested the nineteenth century, it has turned its attention to what might be called the mechanisms of development as these may be found in social groups and systems. It is in this sense that I speak of much contemporary sociological interest in change as falling under neo-developmentalism. All of the essential attributes of developmentalism remain— continuity, immanence, derivation of dynamic processes from structural attributes, uniformitarianism—but the size of the canvas has been reduced.

It is in the work of Durkheim that we can best observe the transition from classic developmentalism to contemporary neo-developmentalism. Durkheim's first major writing was, as we know, *The Division of Labor.* This seminal work, although it contains much else (the elements indeed of all his subsequent work), is primarily a study in the classic mold of social developmentalism, replete with the recovery of origins, intervening stages, directionality, telic end, and so on. In it appeared Durkheim's distinction between mechanical and organic solidarity, a distinction that he intended— quite as Maine, Tylor, Morgan, Spencer had with their differentiations of social organization—as a developmental distinction.

As we know, Durkheim abandoned his distinction; never again, to my knowledge, did he employ it in his work, and he turned utterly away from the classic outlines of developmentalism. This does not mean, however, that Durkheim turned from developmentalism as such. What we find, first in his *The Rules of Sociological Method* and then in his great *The Elementary Forms of Religious Life,* is a shift of interest from his early evolutionary vistas to the more internal and microscopic aspects of development. We see this in his effort to place the origins of all processes of change in the social milieu, in the social group or system, an effort that becomes extended to the study of religion as a social system where, within the detailed confines of intensive examination of one primitive religion, all the molecular or genetic properties of religion are identified. To describe this book as simply an essay in statics is profoundly wrong. As a host of references in *The Elementary Forms* make evident, Durkheim had not ceased being a developmentalist, had not jettisoned interest in social change; he had merely altered the focus.

Within the past several decades, especially in America and England, neo-developmentalism has had its principal embodiment in functionalism. The relationship between this body of theory and the work of Durkheim need not, of course, be stressed here. To say, as so many have, that functionalism lacks a theory of change is false. In the writings of all major functionalists—Parsons, Merton, Davis, Levy, Firth, Murdock, and others—

there is a perfectly clear and consistent theory of change: like Durkheim's it is neo-developmentalist in its concern with the mechanisms of change within the social system rather than with classic evolutionary vistas. In its essentials the functionalist theory of change falls, moreover, in the main current of modern thought on change, a current that contains such anti-functionalist ideas as those identified with the name of Marx. For, just as Marx saw the sources of change *within* the system of capitalism, sources indistinguishable indeed from the elements that he regarded as central to the structure of capitalism, so does functionalism find the sources of change in the selfsame elements—role, status, function—that go to make up the social system. No one has stated this more lucidly than Robert K. Merton:

> Though functional analysis has often focused on the *statics* of social structure rather than the *dynamics* of social change, this is not intrinsic to that system of analysis. By focusing on *dysfunctions* as well as functions, this approach can assess not only the bases of social stability but the *potential sources of change.* . . . The stresses and strains in a social structure which accumulate as dysfunctional consequences of existing elements . . . will in due course lead to institutional breakdown and basic social change. When this change has passed beyond a given and not easily identifiable point, it is customary to say that a new social system has emerged.[21]

Although there are implications of this passage that, for reasons to be set forth below, I am unable to accept, it is nonetheless a splendid statement of the theory of neo-developmentalism. It is clearly an effort to derive, in systematic fashion, the elements of change in social structure from the elements which form the social structure. Its relevance to the modern theory of biological evolution is plain, for it seeks to relate the small, additive changes *within* a system to the larger changes *of* the system, just as the microbiologist seeks to connect the larger changes that are speciative in character to the succession of infinitesimal variations that, through natural selection, go on constantly within the species. As a theoretical statement, Merton's words would summarize, it seems clear, virtually all of the work being done in contemporary functionalist anthropology and sociology. And to seek, as some have done, to tag it with the label "conservative" is absurd on the face of it, for in its essentials it is as free of ideological overtones as any proposition in theory could be. But of its relation to the core of the theory of developmentalism there can be, surely, no question.

How a functionalist or neo-developmentalist theory of change can express itself in empirical terms is exemplified in Marion Levy's classic study of the Chinese family system. In this work, following exhaustive analysis of the structure of the Chinese traditional family, Levy seeks to show that the essential forces leading to the great change in these systems that the

21. *Social Theory and Social Structure* (Glencoe: Free Press, 1949), p. 42. Italics added.

twentieth century has witnessed—change manifest in structure, in function, in authority, and in component roles—are forces that have been operating *within* Chinese kinship for many centuries. Levy is certainly not unaware of the impact on China and on its kinship systems of Western technology, values, and power in the nineteenth and twentieth centuries. He recognizes that the study of Chinese culture is impossible without recognition of this impact. He is not, however, willing to assign to these external causative primacy in leading to the changes in kinship that he accurately describes in the final part of his book. On the contrary, he concludes that "the motivation for change in China lay primarily in *the stresses and strains created by, but contained within the 'traditional' structure. The contact with the industrialized West increased those stresses and strains." [22] This too is quintessential developmentalism as I have described it in the main body of this paper.

Talcott Parsons has given us, in his *The Social System,* and also in shorter, empirical studies, a comparable picture of endogenous change, change arising from role-elements *within* the social system. Parsons, it must be admitted, emphasizes two points that are not always found in contemporary neo-developmentalism: (1) the power of "integrative mechanisms" within a social system which manifest themselves in equilibrium or stability, and (2) what he calls "exogenous changes," changes emanating outside the system. For Parsons, "endogenous changes" are those which originate within the strict limits of what he calls the social system, within the specific context of the roles and values that form a system. Normally these changes are kept within the boundary limits of the system through the operation of the integrative mechanisms of the system.

How strictly Parsons defines the social system and, within it, endogenous changes, can be gathered from the fact that he specifically regards as exogenous those changes "originating in the personalities of the members of the social system, the behavioral organisms 'underlying' these, or the cultural system." I would hazard the guess that most developmentalists of the past, and indeed most neo-developmentalist functionalists of the present, would be inclined to regard as endogenous some of the impulses to change that Parsons, operating from strict adherence to his social system, terms exogenous. The important point here, however, is that Parsons gives no hint in his treatment of exogenous changes that they might be the product of forces not only outside his strictly defined social system, but even outside the personalities, behavioral organisms, and cultural system that he offers as originating contexts of these exogenous changes. Despite his distinction between the two types of change, one can scarcely refrain from concluding that endogenous changes are Parsons' most cherished (from the point of view

22. Marion J. Levy, Jr., *The Family Revolution in China* (Cambridge: Harvard University Press, 1949), p. 86. Italics added.

of his general theory), and that even his exogenous changes have, at least in non-Parsonian terms, a strongly endogenous character.[23]

I have mentioned three prominent American sociologists. But neo-developmentalism, as I use the term here, is a major characteristic of anthropology as well, English and American. The immense impact of Durkheim on English social anthropology—most notably evident in the works of Radcliffe-Brown—carried with it the same implications to the study of change that I have just noted for sociology. Neither Radcliffe-Brown nor any other anthropologist of Durkheimian persuasion abandoned the study of change. All that was abandoned was the type of study embodied in nineteenth-century evolutionary ethnology.

Thus Raymond Firth, in his study of the elements of the social system, refers to "autonomous change" which he regards as a process in unfilled needs *within* the social system. "The essence of the dynamic process lies in the continuous operation of the individual psyche, with its potential of unsatisfied desires—for more security, more knowledge, more status, more power, more approval—within the universe of its social system." [24] Plainly we are dealing here with the very essence of the developmentalist position, the derivation of causes of change from within the structure quite as we found it in Merton, Parsons, and Levy.

It is along exactly the same line that George Murdock, in his valuable *Social Structure,* declares that the "search for the sources of change must be shifted from the external factors to the social structure itself," and, further, that any "social organization is a semi-independent system comparable in many respects to language, and similarly characterized by an internal dynamics of its own." [25]

Critique of Developmentalism

Murdock's final words form an excellent takeoff point for an assessment of the value of the tenets or premises of developmentalism in the study of social change. As I have stressed throughout this chapter, development is *not* in itself a fact so far as social life is concerned; it is an inference, an interpretation, drawn from the facts of change in time. Its quintessence, as we have seen, is its stress upon immanent or endogenous sources of change and upon genetic continuity. In this final section I want to indicate what seem to me the conspicuous weaknesses of developmentalism considered in these terms.

The first point—and it follows directly from Murdock's concluding words

23. See Talcott Parsons, "A Functional Theory of Change," in Amitai Etzioni and Eva Etzioni, eds., *Social Change* (New York: Basic Books, 1964), chap. 12.
24. *Elements of Social Organization* (London: Watts, 1951), p. 86.
25. New York: Macmillan, 1949, pp. 199-200.

above—is that we *cannot* deal with social organization or any social system as an independent or semi-independent system; not, at least, for purposes of the study of the dynamics of change. Consider the prime example that Murdock gives: language. Admittedly the whole discipline of philology, or linguistics, is founded upon the premise that in the comparative study of linguistic forms there may be found also linguistic processes of change—modifications, shifts, transformations of an exceedingly complex nature in the popular mind still perhaps best illustrated by the famous Grimm's Law which covers the stops, or mute consonants, and their change from primitive form in the Indo-European languages to their later form in the various Teutonic derivations of these early languages. That such changes have taken place, and at different times in different places, that they are comprehended within a single law, and that they have been discerned through study of languages conceived as more or less independent systems —none of this is to be denied. The contemporary work of Chomsky among others is evidence of the reality and importance of all this.

But the sociologist who is interested foremost in the study of human behavior in specifiable areas must ask himself a question at this point. Admitting the reality of the internal dynamics of language, its more or less autonomous, endogenous shifts and modifications, could we ever explain through *these* the kinds of difference that are represented, say, by the language of contemporary England and England of the tenth century? Would *all* the internal, autonomous, and uniformitarian processes that might be discovered in the English language (or the larger group of languages of which it is a part) ever provide sufficient explanation of the difference between the language spoken in England at the time of, say, the *Beowulf* and the language spoken in England today? Certainly not. Nor would any philologist claim for a moment that such processes do or could. For, along with whatever have been the endogenous and autonomous processes operating in the language, there is the ineffaceable record of events and changes in *other systems* that have, over the centuries, taken place and left concretely denotable effects upon the English language. Think only of the Norman conquest.

Admittedly, two different questions are involved in the foregoing. One would pertain to the "English language" which, both in terms of its own structure and in terms of its spread to other parts of the world, is a distinctive entity that came into existence, as we know it, approximately in the Age of Chaucer. The other and very different question pertains not to the "English language" but to the "language(s) spoken in England" during the past ten centuries. In reply to the first question it is easy enough, and also of interest, to deal with the kinds of change that Firth and Murdock describe as autonomous and internal. And, it will be noted, we are in the presence of the selfsame processes that are involved in development properly so called. By looking at language conceived as an independent system,

all the familiar attributes of continuity, genetic emergence, universalism, and immanence are present. In such terms we can encourage ourselves in the belief that some day we shall arrive at a *theory* of change, one that will do for social structures what the modern theory of evolution does for biological forms, a theory in which the essential factors of change will be drawn from the elements which form the structure and its relation to environment.

But we will not! The differences between the types of data used by the modern biologist in his "population thinking" and the types of data that the social scientist is obliged to work with—the data of social groups, structures, and institutions—are vast. Some of these I have dealt with elsewhere, and will not repeat here.[26] It suffices to say that they are the insuperable differences that arise from the historicity of social data—that is, their ineffaceable location in fixed, measured, and finite time, their inextricability from the normative, purposive character of human behavior, and, finally, their incessant interaction with the events, whether small or large—that by their very nature, their ineradicable exteriority, and their necessarily fortuitous character, are not amenable to systems analysis. To pretend that these three powerful dimensions of the problem of social change can by any reach of the imagination be effaced or be subordinated to analysis, however microscopic, of roles, status, tensions, functions or dysfunctions, and conflicts *within* any given social system or structure (smaller than society or civilization as a whole) is to delude ourselves. There is not now, and there cannot be, a *theory* of change that will encompass at one and the same time the conditions to be found in any given present and the conditions to be found in that same entity in any given future. To suppose that there is or can be such a theory is to fly in the face of the powerful and utterly unpredictable *event*-nature of human history and the manifest impact of such events upon human social types and norms.[27]

In retrospect, the major difficulty with the theory of developmentalism as we find it both in classical and contemporary statements is this: as a theory of change it is inextricably related to universals and wholes: to civilization in its entirety, to capitalism or democracy or kinship, each conceived as a more or less autonomous and universal system. The premises of developmentalism—immanence, continuity, uniformitarianism, genetic cumulation—can easily be adapted to any of these universals. For, once we set up in our minds something called "capitalism" or "kinship" or "social system," attributes for these entities have to be found, and among them—

26. See "The Irreducibility of Social Change," *The Pacific Sociological Review,* vol. 8 (Spring, 1965), reprinted in Wilbert E. Moore and Robert Cook, eds., *Readings on Social Change* (Englewood Cliffs: Prentice-Hall, 1967), pp. 234-240.
27. This is the principal argument of Teggart, *Theory of History,* particularly chap. 12.

given a Western orientation ever since the pre-Socratics—is change, growth, development, however we choose to call it.

But the fact is these "things" do not "do" at all. They are metaphoric constructs, indispensable to conversation, to writing; even, I have no doubt, to thought itself. But to confuse them with what it is we are really concerned with in the study of change is delusive and dangerous.

What we are given in clear empirical fact is simply the behavior of human beings in their varied procreative, wealth-getting, comfort-seeking, status-aspiring, order-making activities. Second, we are given this behavior, not in the never-never land of universal systems, but in concrete, finite locales and areas. There may indeed be—as St. Augustine was the first to insist, on the premise of the fatherhood of God—something called "mankind," or, as Marx insisted, "capitalism." All well and good. But the fact remains that when we are trying to account for the processes of change we have to come up with something more than fine gradations of difference in a classification of types. We have to come up with inferences that are drawn from how human beings actually behave within finite space and time.

Sociologists, economists, anthropologists, and others are doing this. There is a great abundance of useful study of the mechanics and the incidence of social change: in East Africa, in the British Midlands in the nineteenth century, in Colonial America, in Detroit, in one or another of the innumerable "frontiers" that the history of mankind reveals, and elsewhere. There is no dearth of analytical, monographic material on how change in a given place and time has come about: its source, its transmission, its impact on human lives and life-styles. There is a vast amount of knowledge about change to be gleaned from these studies.

But such studies do not and cannot support the premises of developmentalism for, as I have said, these premises have to do with materials of an altogether different kind: with wholes and universals, not with human behavior in any clear and finite sense. What such studies *do* point to in the way of knowledge of change may be briefly summarized, I believe, in terms of the following propositions:

1. Social persistence. If one were of a Newtonian frame of mind, one could say, with respect to social phenomena, that a thing is at a state of rest until it is disturbed. Nothing is more sadly neglected in modern social science (and, for that matter, in a great deal of Western thought) than the simple, obvious, and unblinkable fact of fixity, persistence, and inertia. We see it, but we do not believe it. We assume that what we see is only appearance, not reality; that apparent lack of change in an institution is but a surface manifestation; that beneath the surface, processes of change are in fact germinating or otherwise taking place comparable to those known to the physiologist or the geneticist in the biological world. Activity and motion

are, to be sure, omnipresent, they are indeed ineffaceable qualities of all life and nature. But activity and motion do not in themselves have anything to do with actual change, much less with development. Persistent activity and motion are precisely that, nothing more.

The first major error of the developmentalist perspective is its neglect of, or rather its distortion of, the phenomena of persistence and fixity. Developmentalism assumes that what is normal is change and that the problem therefore becomes one simply of identifying it, classifying its manifestations, measuring it, and assessing it. Where the phenomena of fixity are so monumental, so inescapable, that they cannot be hidden within the recess of the theory of development, the developmentalist says that there has been "interference," the result of adventitious circumstances, and that such fixity is "pathological."

But persistence, fixity, and inertia are, despite the official canon of ubiquitous and incessant change, real. More important they are, and must be, the point of departure in any study of change in determinable, finite human behavior. To say this is not—I hope this is so evident it requires no emphasis—to deny the reality of change. I am not proposing any latter-day Pythagoreanism or Platonic theory of unchanging forms. Change there is in abundance in human history. And we are plainly living in an era of extraordinary change, though even so, as I have suggested, we overlook, in our sweeping characterization of the contemporary scene as one of change, immense amounts of mere motion and activity that add up only to persistence of type. The important point, however, is not descriptive; it is methodological. It is that, irrespective of how much incidence of genuine change there may be at a given time in a given area, it is still necessary, if we are to understand the dynamics of this change, to begin with the simple assumption that human behavior tends to be fixed in type until specifiable conditions *generate* change.

2. This leads to the second proposition, equally antagonistic to the perspective of developmentalism: *The source of change—major change—is rarely from within a unit or entity* (unless, I again have to say for clarity's sake, our entity is civilization as a whole). I am tempted to say that it is never from within; but I refrain for obvious reasons. Suffice it to say that examples, if they exist, are few and far between. Overwhelmingly, major change is the consequence of impact from outside the entity or system of behavior that is the subject of our attention. Everything we know about the character of human behavior suggests, as I have said, its strong tendency toward consistency, boundary maintenance, and adaptiveness. To suppose that the processes of major structural change emanate from within social systems is to suppose something that historical evidence over significant periods of time fails to support. It is useful to recall here Max Weber's famous essay on that major change in the European economy that we call

the rise of capitalism. Weber opposed what he called "emanationism," the view that major change is something that emanates from within a type of social behavior. What gives his essay on the rise of capitalism distinction that goes beyond even his ingenious proof of the impact of noneconomic forms of thought upon economic behavior is his demonstration that this major change in the European economy proceeded not from factors within the economy, but from factors—changes in religious evaluations of work outside the economy. We may think of Weber's work as primarily a refutation of Marxism's insistence upon the primacy of economic factors in economic change, and, of course, it is this. But Weber's argument goes beyond Marx alone in its implications, and takes in the whole of that developmentalist and neo-developmentalist perspective which seeks to find the crucial causes of change of a system *within* the system.

3. *Social change does not manifest genetic continuity.* Genetic continuity is a construct that we arrive at retrospectively as we survey the vistas of the past. It is not a reality that we can actually perceive in the present or, for that matter, demonstrate in analysis of changes in the past. In the biological world, whether in the evolutionist's concern with the differential fertility of infinitesimal variations within type, or in the biologist's concern with processes of growth within an organism, something resembling genetic continuity is manifest. Little changes do grow into big changes—continuously and sequentially. But in the world of social behavior what we actually have —and then confuse with cumulative continuity of change—is a combination of sheer persistence of types in time and alterations of these types, the consequence of *discontinuous* variations and changes.

I think the major error of reasoning to be found in functionalist and also social systems theory at the present time, so far as the study of change is concerned, is the monumental assumption that changes *within* a given social structure or pattern (the day-to-day tensions, conflicts, and adaptations which are inseparable from social behavior anywhere, anytime) necessarily become in time changes *of* that structure or pattern. The clear evidence of history is, however, that no such genetic continuity in time is discoverable.

It is important to cite here some of the most important words Durkheim ever wrote, words that, to my knowledge, have been overlooked entirely in sociological theory. I will not pretend that Durkheim was not at least a *neo*-developmentalist. Nevertheless, toward the end of his *The Rules of Sociological Method* we find a brilliant critique of genetic continuity. It is impossible, he declares, "to conceive how the stage which a civilization has reached at a given moment could be the determining cause of the subsequent stage. The stages that humanity successively traverses *do not engender one another."* What Durkheim is saying, and his argument comes close to Weber's argument against emanationism, is that *emergent* evolution is not a reality in social life. He carries this point further by stating

explicitly: "All that we can observe experimentally . . . is a series of changes *among which a causal bond does not exist. The antecedent state does not produce the subsequent one, but the relation between them is exclusively chronological."* [28]

Under these circumstances, Durkheim continues, all scientific *causal* prevision is impossible. We can indeed say that certain conditions have succeeded one another up to the present, but we can no more attribute this succession to any inherent genetic continuity of change—that is, emergent growth—than we can properly suppose that such succession must continue into the future.

The significance of these words to current theory in sociology is immense. For whereas we widely assume today that sufficiently painstaking and microscopic study of the present condition of any social system will yield us all necessary information regarding the future change of that system, Durkheim's words make us realize that study of the present condition yields us but one thing alone: knowledge of the present condition. Genetic continuity is a fiction in social behavior over time, one that allows us to impose a kind of intellectual order upon the past—quite as the historian assumes characteristically that events marry and have little events—but it is no more than that.

4. There is no autonomous change. By this I mean simply that despite the overwhelming weight of modern social anthropology in its theoretical aspects, and of sociological functionalism, there is no process of autonomous change inherent within given social systems. If there were, cultures in isolation—those in the remote parts of the world, or those in rural fastnesses within modern societies, or folk and peasant cultures—would surely evince somewhere, sometime, clear manifestations of significant change. But they do not. Not, at least, until they come under the impact of alien intrusions or of external events, or suffer the consequences of enforced migration. Even then, as is well known, the processes of conservatism, of strain toward persistence of type, are powerful. To say, as Levy has said in his study of the Chinese family, that the claimed fixity or conservatism of the traditional kinship system in China has been proved to be mere appearance *because* of the manifest structural changes in the nineteenth and twentieth centuries, misses the point, it would seem to me. The Chinese family system *was* stable and persistent (role tensions, status-conflicts, dysfunctions, and all) for a period of many centuries. It *did* change in the late nineteenth and early twentieth centuries, and *not* as the result of autonomous processes of change within the system but as the consequence of external impacts which are the substance of what we call Westernization.

I repeat, change in any significant degree—that is, change of major

28. Emile Durkheim, *The Rules of Sociological Method*, ed. G. E. G. Catlin (Glencoe: Free Press, 1950), p. 117. Italics added.

values, structures, and life-styles—rarely if ever is to be found in circumstances of isolation where presumably autonomous processes of change would be free to operate, but only in circumstances of social and cultural collision, impact, and intrusion.

5. *The study of social change is inseparable from historical events.* This thought is, I believe, the single most distinctive and important contribution of the late Frederick J. Teggart to the whole problem of social change. In several places in this chapter I have suggested that from early times in Western thought there has been a clear distinction between the historiographic tradition: the tradition of Thucydides, Livy, Gibbon, Ranke, the developmental tradition, and the tradition of Aristotle, Lucretius, Leibniz, Comte, Marx; the first concerned primarily with a genealogy of events, happenings, and persons; the second concerned primarily with change of conditions in time. But, as Teggart made powerfully evident in his *Theory of History,* the separateness of the two traditions has militated against the concrete, empirical, and scientific understanding of change.

Although, as I suggested above, it is possible to deal with "change"—in actual fact it is not so much change as it is successive differences, variable types in space and time—as an autonomous process in systems, as, for example, in language, we cannot deal with change in these terms when what we have before us is the behavior of human beings in a specifiable area and period of time. While there may well be a type of autonomous change in social caste, for instance, with caste conceived as a universal system, and attention focused on the small modifications and adaptations within caste behavior, the kinds of change in caste that we find in India in the twentieth century, or in the Negro–White relationship in the South in the United States, has far less to do with such types of change than it does with types specifically and identifiably associated with the impact of *events* upon the areas in question—events that by their very nature could never be deduced either in advance or retrospectively from study of the caste system itself.

Of course, the sociological theorist of neo-developmentalist inclination knows that events affect social life; he knows too that events "cannot be predicted," to use the popular phrase. However, what he is saying, in effect, is that he is concerned with those types of change in social structures that are generated more or less independently of external impacts and intrusions of change from other systems. But the net effect of all that we know about the incidence of major change in history is that there is no such change; or, putting it more modestly and accurately, that such change is confined to minor modifications and variations.

6. *The sociological fallacy.* I use this phrase by way of summary to describe a pattern of thought that is as old as Aristotle's *Politics* and as recent as the latest work in functionalist or social systems theory. The sociological fallacy

consists in the belief that the causes and essential forces of social change may be derived from the elements of social structure. Stated differently, the sociological fallacy declares that a single "unified" theory can account both for the processes involved in social cohesion or social equilibrium on the one hand, and, on the other, for those processes involved in change. Any such belief, however, manifestly flies in the face of history, of empirical observation, and—frankly—of common sense.

8.

Images of the Future:
Theory and Research Strategies

Wendell Bell & James A. Mau

Wendell Bell was born in Chicago, Illinois, in 1924 and was educated at Fresno State College and the University of California, Los Angeles (Ph.D.). He was a member of the faculty of Stanford University, Northwestern University, and U.C.L.A. before joining the faculty of Yale University in 1963 where he is professor and chairman of the department of sociology. His research has been in the fields of urban sociology, social change, and political sociology. In addition to his contributions to professional journals, he has authored or coauthored Social Area Analysis, Public Leadership, Decisions of Nationhood, Jamaican Leaders, *and* The Democratic Revolution in the West Indies. *He has been a Social Science Research Council Fellow and spent a year at the Center for Advanced Study in the Behavioral Sciences.*

James A. Mau was born in San Francisco, California, in 1935. He received his B.A. from the University of California at Santa Barbara in 1957, and his Ph.D. from U.C.L.A. in 1964. He is the author of Social Change and Images of the Future *and articles on social change and political sociology. His major professional interests are in political sociology, social change, and race relations.*

*I*n his presidential address to the American Sociological Association, Wilbert E. Moore raised the following questions:

Have we, in short, any obligation as social scientists to start taking account not only of the changeful quality of social life but also of the fact that some portion of that change is deliberate? And do we, still as social scientists, have anything positive to add to the fulfillment of human hopes for the future, or are we always fated to counsel the eager traveler that "you can't get there from here"? [1]

We agree with Moore's answers that social scientists do have such an obligation and do have something positive to add to such fulfillment. In this essay we explain our stand, and we elaborate some of the implications of our views for both social theory and the conduct of social research.

Revised version of a paper read at the annual meetings of the American Sociological Association, Miami, Florida, August 30, 1966. We thank the Russell Sage Foundation, New York, for a grant under which this paper was written and related work was done. Helpful comments on an earlier draft were made by Professors Rodolfo Alvarez, George Huaco, and Harold D. Lasswell, Miss Bettina Huber, and other members of the Yale Collegium on the Future.
1. Wilbert E. Moore, "The Utility of Utopias," *American Sociological Review,* 31 (December, 1966), 765. Also see Moore's *Order and Change: Essays in Comparative Sociology* (New York: Wiley, 1967).

Specifically, we (1) discuss the concept of "images of the future," (2) propose a theory of social change based upon it, and (3) suggest a series of related directives for research strategy and for the role of the social scientist. Our purpose is to bring the volitional aspects of social systems into the sociological net more fully and explicitly than is currently done under conventional social theory, and to take account of the social scientist himself *qua* scientist, as an agent of social change. First, however, we discuss two assumptions that are basic to our endeavor. One assumption involves the sense in which the future can be thought of as real, the other deals with the increase in human mastery throughout history.

The Reality of the Future

Time perspectives have varied considerably during the course of human history, and the immeasurable increase in the scale of modern man's conceptions of time has given new importance to the future and added meaning to the past and present. For modern man the past is not simply shrugged off as mere history but is viewed more and more in terms of its meaning for the present and future. This is not to suggest such aphorisms as "we learn from history" or "history repeats itself in different places for different people"; it is to emphasize that, through the interpretations and evaluations currently attached to it, the past has significance and reality in the present and in the future. "Since historical past is always part of the reality of the present, the past . . . will always have emergent aspects as long as history continues to be written." [2]

So, also, does the emergent future have present meaning or, in a sense, "reality" with consequences shaped by man's thoughts and expectations about alternative futures. Following Heidegger, Tiryakian recently stated:

. . . human existence stretches out into the future and into the past. The subject, understood phenomenologically, is not an entity contained in an absolute space but rather an existent whose being is a set of possibilities that became actualized in the present. The past and the future are therefore not separate entities, but are very much part of the present: the past is, existentially viewed, a *having-been* present, while the future is a *will-be* present, both being grounded in the phenomenal emergence of the here-and-now.[3]

The significance of this temporal interplay lies in mankind's ability intentionally to deflect the direction of sociohistorical change. Modern man

2. Edward A. Tiryakian, "Sociohistorical Phenomena: The Seen, The Unseen, The Foreseeable," paper prepared for a joint session of the American Studies Association and the American Historical Association (December, 1966), p. 9.
3. *Ibid.*, p. 7.

can alter his past as well as his future, although in somewhat different ways.[4] In nearly every generation of literate peoples there is the desire to shape the world to suit themselves by rewriting their history so they appear as they wish they had been, are, or hope to be. Intentional falsification may slip in but, even if it does not, facts themselves can be mustered to support different interpretations. No one would deny this who has read Edmund Wilson or Alfred Cobban on the historians of the French Revolution and the conflicting versions of that drama, who is aware of American historiography and the different scenarios that portray American history, or who has talked with twentieth-century, new, national élites as they decide what their nations' histories should be.

This is not to say that there is no historical truth or that some versions of history are not better or more accurate than others. Rather, histories are relative to the different frames of reference, selective perceptions, assumptions, concepts, and theories that are used to organize them. By recognizing this relativity, rather than denying it, and by making as much of the thought that went into the recreation of the past as explicit as possible, the conflicting versions of historical truth can be viewed with some hope of discerning which seems most credible.

The sociologist can see that this is true of history, but he may have difficulty accepting the fact that it is true also of sociology. The ways in which sociologists portray the present with their sample surveys, questionnaires, interview schedules, data, and statistical analyses are also relative and result in different versions of social reality. In recent years, sociological "truths" have come, in turn, to influence the way people see themselves and their societies and, thus, have been consequential for the behavior that emerges from such conceptions. Sociologists, who have long recognized the relativity of values, are now confronting as well the relativity of their findings and interpretations. Although we cannot go beyond this point here, we believe trends can be detected in current thinking that may lead modern social scientists full circle, from value relativism to the belief that it is the good that is absolute and the truth that is relative.[5]

4. Here and elsewhere in this essay there are similarities to some of the views of George Herbert Mead. For example, see Anselm Strauss, ed., *The Social Psychology of George Herbert Mead* (Chicago: University of Chicago Press, 1956).
5. That "truth" is relative seems simple to demonstrate compared to the difficulty of showing that the "good" is absolute. We do not wish to press the latter point here, nor are we convinced that it is defensible, but we have in mind certain universal values that derive from the survival, health, and dignity of man. For example, Moore in his presidential address cautiously suggests some common values and says that we have ". . . exaggerated the significance of cultural differences in human values, for many of these differences simply do not survive the extension of communication that makes the world a single system in important respects." "The Utility of Utopia," *American Sociological Review,* 31 (December 1966), 771. Also see Wilbert E. Moore, "Global Sociology: The World as a Singular System," *American Journal of Sociology,* 71 (March, 1966), 475-482. For three potential universal values, compare Hadley Cantril, "A Study of Aspirations," *Scientific American,* 208 (February, 1963), 42ff.

The future in important respects is as real as the past, since we know both in much the same way: through our conceptions of them. The future is as real as the present too, except for the momentary experience of the present in ways that transcend the organization of sense data into articulate and meaningful units for a given actor at a given time and place. We must remember that we will never know most of what goes on in the present at other places and what we do presume to learn of the present in other places we learn through reconstruction of it by others, even if such reconstructions are on-the-spot radio or television reports, since such reports are necessarily selected and edited, if by no more than a choice of the eyewitness interviewed or the camera angle. Comment on the reality of the future was recently made at a meeting of the American Physical Society by Harvard philosophy professor Hilary W. Putnam. He contended that if one takes relativity seriously then what ". . . appears in the future to one observer is in the past for another. The future to us seems unreal . . . because we cannot remember it. But in the context of combined space and time the past and future are just as real as up and down." [6]

The chief point to be made here is that the future is real in the sense that images of the future exist in the present. Not only are such images real in that they exist in the minds and in verbal and pictorial representations of men, but they are also, hypothetically, important factors in orienting individual and collective behavior. Thus, one of our basic hypotheses is that expectations about the future, whether short- or long-range, may enter as a determining factor into most human behavior.

The Rise of Human Mastery

Most theories of human behavior, quite apart from the terms in which they are stated and their criteria of application, are composed of at least two different, though related, parts. One consists of explanatory concepts and notions of causation. Here we introduce the concept of "image of the future," which we discuss in detail below, as a key variable in a theory of social change. Another is the "what-happened-in-history" part, which in historical research might include broad sweeps of time and space and grandiose attempts to unify, under a given interpretation, the entire history of all mankind. In sociological circles this might refer simply to the results of last month's sample survey in Ashtabula, Ohio, or last week's laboratory experiment in Ann Arbor, Michigan. It involves a story or version of what in fact did happen or what people thought or did at some time and in some place.

The theory of social change discussed in this paper rests, in part, upon

6. As reported in *The New York Times*, January 30, 1966, p. 10E.

the assumption that a major trend of history has been an increase in the mastery of man over his natural and social environment as well as a shift in his beliefs that this is so.[7] An implication of this is that explanations of social change are only more or less relevant to the events of particular epochs, depending upon how accurate the explanation is in assessing and taking into account the amount of influence man himself may have, and thinks he has, in directing social change. For example, traditional ecological explanations may be of considerable relevance to the behavior of primitive man, since his chief struggle was against nature and since his life was shaped by that struggle. Primitive man may have been influenced by images of the future, but the content of his images did not allow him much freedom of choice among alternatives. Ends were seldom questioned and means were often invested with ritualistic significance. Possibly the gods could be persuaded to bring about a desired future event, but fatalism was widespread. Likewise, explanations based on notions of economic determinism or technology, rather than ecology, had considerable relevance for industrializing men and societies of the seventeenth, eighteenth, and nineteenth centuries. Ends or goals were still largely unquestioned and defined fairly clearly, but means were increasingly free from religious dogma to be chosen according to criteria of efficiency and economy. Thus, current images of the future incorporated notions that permitted choice of means, although the criteria were generally agreed upon, but little choice of ends.

Today, traditional ecological and technological explanations are not sufficient to account for the behavior of an increasing number of people in advanced societies, because in such societies more and more men find that their chief struggle is with themselves and other men, not with nature or the lack of technology, because both the ends and the means of life have been increasingly freed for conscious choice. This freedom has been made possible for many people in advanced societies by their securing the essentials and amenities of life and by advances in philosophy and science, including sociology, that have reduced people's dependence upon superstition and fatalistic conceptions of the future. Of course, this freedom to select both goals and ways of achieving them, which permits some individuals and groups to establish new norms and values for entire societies, occurs in a context of certain limiting, agreed-upon principles of group survival which are seldom extensively violated. Nonetheless, the latitude of decision is quite large—large enough, for example, to bring new burdens of responsibility to modern man, especially the burden of knowing that his life and environment may become, in important respects, what he will make of them, and

---

7. Our discussion of the rise of human mastery converges with the view of Lester F. Ward. Increase in human mastery or as Ward defines it, civilization, is an increase in "the utilization of the materials and forces of nature" by man as the directive agent. See Lester F. Ward, *Pure Sociology: A Treatise on the Origin and Spontaneous Development of Society* (London: Macmillan, 1914), p. 468.

of knowing also that he is not always certain just what he wants, or should want, to make of them. Thus, in the most advanced societies, traditional explanations of social phenomena must be supplemented with moral explanations. But the latter represent a new, secular morality which is pragmatic and open to social choice and universal considerations.

John C. McKinney states a point of view similar to our own within the specific content of the difference between *Gemeinschaft* and *Gesellschaft* types of societies. His statement further clarifies the idea that theories of social change are relative to particular times and places:

It is now a standard view in the sociology of knowledge that different types of knowledge, as well as the techniques and motivations for extending knowledge, are bound up with particular forms of groups. *Gemeinschaft* types of society have a traditionally defined fund of knowledge handed down as conclusive and final; they are not concerned with discovering new ideas or extending their spheres of knowledge. Any effort to test the traditional knowledge, insofar as it implies doubt, is ruled out on moral grounds. In such a group the prevailing methods are ontological and dogmatic; its mode of thought is that of conceptual realism. In contrast, *Gesellschaft* types of organization institutionalize techniques for the attainment and codification of knowledge. In such a group the methods are primarily epistemological and critical; the mode of thought is nominalistic.

Given such difference in structural types and modes of orientation, it is clear that the problem of instigating change, of whatever purpose or form, must be perceived of in very different ways for the two contrasting types of systems. Moreover, there appears to be ample justification for saying that the instigation of any change will necessarily have to follow different procedures, adapted to two distinctly different social structures. The success of planning and execution of such change will in large part be determined by the extent to which it is appropriate to the system for which it is intended.[8]

From the above, McKinney draws an implication for the conduct of social research in the modern world: "If sociology is to play a key role in contemporary social research, then the major inquiries must be made in a world where the patterns of the past are under increased pressure from a dynamic future." [9] A reorientation of social research is in order, because the rise of human mastery is ushering in new dynamics of change under which man is increasingly liberated from the bonds of the past and increasingly able to transcend the limitations of the present. What is needed are new social theories and empirical inquiries that take this fact into account.

Most people of today's world do not yet live under the liberating conditions that technologically advanced society makes possible. The poor and

8. John C. McKinney, *Constructive Typology and Social Theory* (New York: Appleton-Century-Crofts, 1966), pp. 170-171.
9. Ibid., p. 171.

underdeveloped nations of the world, despite the positive future orientation of many of their people—especially of their modernizing leaders—contain masses of people who are at the mercy of natural forces or technological necessities, and some of them fatalistically perceive their destiny as being beyond their control. Even in advanced societies, some sections of the population do not have the liberating opportunities enjoyed by the majority, and many people are victims as well as beneficiaries of modern technology. The pollution of air and water and the disfigurement of land are unintended products of the application of technology, as are many of the economically marginal groups in societies with advanced technical capacity. Yet the long-term trends are clear: human mastery over nature and the power of technology have increased in the past and can be expected to increase further in the future.

The Concept of "Images of the Future"

The explanatory concept that we put forward as a key variable in a theory of social change is that of "images of the future." Here we rely on the prior work of Frederik L. Polak and Harold D. Lasswell.[10] In an effort aimed at "enlightening the past, orientating the present, and forecasting the future," Polak, in a recent book analyzing the intellectual history of Europe, lays the foundation for a theory of social change based on images of the future.[11] Polak says that man lives simultaneously in three worlds with respect to time: past, present, and future. (Of course, with respect to space, there are other worlds as well.) Actual past experiences of individuals and groups, perceptions and knowledge about the past of one's particular society and of the human past in general, both history and prehistory, shape what men and societies are in the present. They shape present forms, limitations, and possibilities; they shape fundamental fears and desires as well as conceptions of the good life; they influence the way people think about the future and what they are willing and able to do to alter or prepare for the actualities of the emerging future. In turn, the present conditions of everyday life, to which people adapt and which people more or less shape, affect perceptions and formulations of the past and can result in new and different

10. Although we cite Polak and Lasswell extensively in this section and wish to acknowledge our debt to them, we have tried to state the concept of image of the future in a way that represents our use of it. We are less interested in exegesis than in creative synthesis.
11. Frederik L. Polak, *The Image of the Future: Enlightening the Past, Orientating the Present, Forecasting the Future,* vols. 1 and 2 (New York: Oceana Publications, 1961). It is perhaps inevitable that errors would crop up, as they do, in such a sweeping review as Polak undertakes. Some readers may be put off by this as well as by the fact that Polak occasionally becomes a bit mystical. It would be a shame, in our judgment, if these debilities were permitted to interfere with the useful message that Polak has for the modern sociologist.

meanings being attached to historical development. As one copes with present realities as well as with attitudes and beliefs about them, one's images of the future can change. Thus the present helps mold the future as well as the past. Furthermore, the emerging future itself shapes the past— the meanings that are attached to it as well as the facts of history themselves —and it affects the realities of the present as well as our perceptions and evaluations of it. New hopes and fears concerning the future can lead to new historical research as well as to the formulation of new interpretations of old realities. In fact, debates about which interpretations of history are correct are often debates arising from conflicting images of what is desired in the future. Just as an individual's future behavior is to some extent governed by his self-image of the kind of person he has been, is, and hopes to be, so also a nation's future course of development is, to some extent, controlled by the doctrines and dogmas of particular versions of the social and cultural history of that nation.

In the modern world, man is deliberately bent on "making himself" according to his own choosing, although, as Polak states, the liberation that comes with this orientation is matched by new responsibilities and uncertainties:

In setting himself purposefully to control and alter the course of events man has been forced to deal with the concepts of value, means and ends, ideals and ideologies, as he has attempted to blueprint his own future. As long as the prophet-propitiator was acting only as a divine transmitter of messages from on high, man felt that he was accepting his ethics ready-made, with no alterations allowed. *In a latter stage man staggers under the double load of not only having to construct his own future but having to create the values which will determine its design.*[12]

The rise and fall of images of the future precede or accompany the rise and fall of cultures. History has been made what it is largely as a result of the ideas and ideals of man that have been congealed in the form of images of the future. The time that is yet to come rests importantly on the nature of the present images of the future. Thus, the vigor and potentialities of the society of tomorrow can be detected in the society of today.

Although Polak sees the transformation of man's orientation through history as involving a shift from fatalism to self-determination, he sees also that modern Western man, at least, partly as a result of new burdens, is overcome by apathy and is increasingly likely to view life as a meaningless existence. In Polak's view, the images of the future of Western culture are disintegrating and the result may be that there is no future for Western culture.[13] Polak sees a "fatal movement" in this direction, but he is opti-

12. Ibid., pp. 36-37. Italics added.
13. Ibid., p. 43.

mistic about man's ability to intervene and to reverse the undesirable trend, if only he will take the necessary steps. Throughout his book, Polak is clearly dedicated to positive idealism, constructive images, and optimism, yet his own image of the future ironically contains an overriding negative and pessimistic element with respect to developments in the recent past and future projections. This combination of pessimistic prediction and an optimistic view of man's potential to intervene for the better is often phrased, as in Polak's book, as a veiled threat to act now or suffer the consequences. It is, of course, a call to arms to intellectuals, intended to deflect an undesirable course of events.

Today's images of the future need elaboration, refinement, and revision; the actual future is rolling over people and whole societies before they are prepared; the possibilities of a better life are not being fulfilled as adequately as they could be. Polak's distinctive contribution to this viewpoint is his effort to depict the social scientist *qua* scientist not only as an objective investigator but also as a creator and disseminator of images of the future.

The concept *image of the future* is used in a double sense; as an object of research and as a statement of the problem. The social scientist is answerable for the future, in that he is both the carrier and the creator of an image of the future, consciously or unconsciously. In this time of culture-crisis he ought to be made aware of his role in the creation of the future. In order to achieve this awareness he must also consider the image of the future as an object for research. . . . The process of writing the history of the future through the study of the images of the future has its unique aspect in that the *writing* of history merges imperceptibly into the responsible act of *creating* history. One is reminded here of the concept of the personal equation—the influence of the observer on that which he observes. The formulation, as well as the act of describing the image of the future, may influence the future itself. *The social scientist (and this is part of his specific responsibility both towards social sciences and society) may discover ways to rewrite the history of the future.*[14]

Our purpose in citing Polak's work at some length is twofold: first, to call attention to the importance of images of the future in understanding social change, and second, to emphasize the active role of social science in the process of social change.

The American political scientist and pioneering advocate of the scientific approach to the study of political behavior, Harold D. Lasswell, has

14. Ibid., p. 57. Italics added. Bertrand de Jouvenel, in his introduction to the first volume of *Futuribles,* makes similar comments. He states that he and the group of authors in the *Futuribles* venture ". . . quite definitely take the view that what shall be depends upon our choices: it is precisely because the future depends upon our decisions and action, and these in turn upon our opinions regarding the future, that the latter so much need to be stated, weighed, and tested." See Bertrand de Jouvenel, ed., *Futuribles: Studies in Conjecture,* vol. 1 (Geneva: Droz, 1963), p. xi.

in many of his works been saying much the same thing as Polak. Although Lasswell has been more cautious than Polak in stating that the scientist influences the future less as a scientist than as a citizen, he has gone well beyond Polak in working out some of the details of the methods of creating images of the future, which are similar to what Lasswell calls "developmental constructs," and in specifying the direction of particular trends of modern society.

Many features of Lasswell's developmental analysis, the major tool of which is the developmental construct, are similar to Polak's concept of image of the future.[15] A developmental construct expresses expectations about the future, contains explicit anticipations of the shape of things to come, and is related to the facts of past trends. Society is viewed as an interval on some continuum of social change, and the developmental construct delineates the end points of that continuum, "the from what and toward what of developmental sequences." Lasswell stresses the possibility of a shift in social science from description and prediction to control and the introduction of the manipulative standpoint into the contemplative. In formulating scientific questions as a search for courses of action leading to some goal or maximizing some value, he shows how scientists may self-consciously enlarge their role of influencing society in some desired direction, a role which, in our opinion, the scientist plays consciously or not. Furthermore, Lasswell deals with the problems created for scientific analysis by the confounding nature of self-fulfilling or self-denying prophecies through which scientific predictions, as they become known, may themselves affect the very future predicted. In his developmental analysis, Lasswell attempts to make "a virtue of the fact—which gives social science in general a great deal of trouble—that a prediction, by becoming itself a factor in the definition of the situation, guarantees or prevents the emergence of anticipated results." [16]

Although Lasswell phrases his conceptions of the part to be played by social scientists in different terms than Polak, nonetheless he clearly urges the social scientist to make his work relevant to basic values and to the emerging future, particularly by using developmental constructs. These constructs serve the purpose of sensitizing the investigator to the relevance of his work for the future and especially for the conservation of values that he would desire to protect. Lasswell suggests that social science should

15. Harold D. Lasswell, "The Garrison State and Specialists on Violence," in H. D. Lasswell, ed., *The Analysis of Political Behavior: An Empirical Approach* (London: Routledge and Kegan Paul, 1948). Also see *The American Journal of Sociology* (January, 1941). An excellent summary of developmental analysis can be found in Heinz Eulau, "H. D. Lasswell's Developmental Analysis," *Western Political Quarterly*, 11 (June, 1958), 229-242.
16. Eulau, p. 240. For an analysis of the self-fulfilling prophecy, see Cecil Miller, "The Self-Fulfilling Prophecy: A Reappraisal," *Ethics*, 72 (October, 1961), 46-51.

include studies of "all factors that condition the survival of selected values." [17]

Certainly, neither developmental constructs nor images of the future are dogmatic predictions, yet we see no reason why they cannot be used scientifically. The idea that the study of the future can be scientific is not a new one. H. G. Wells proposed it over fifty years ago, in a lecture given at the Royal Institution in England.

All applied mathematics resolves into computation to foretell things which otherwise can only be determined by trial. Even in so unscientific a field as economics there have been forecasts. And if I am right in saying that science aims at prophecy, and if the specialist in each science is in fact doing his best now to prophesy within the limits of his field, what is there to stand in the way of our building up this growing body of forecast into an ordered picture of the future that will be just as certain, just as strictly science, and perhaps just as detailed a picture that has been built up with the last hundred years of the geological past? Well, so far and until we bring the prophecy down to the affairs of man and his children, it is just as possible to carry induction forward as back; it is just as simple and sure to work out the changing orbit of the earth in the future until the tidal drag hauls one unchanging face at last toward the sun as it is to work back to its blazing and molten past.[18]

Wells believed that the future could be studied by induction, just as the geological past could, and he included the future of human affairs although he thought that individual futures were beyond the scope of such investigation. With the explosive development of the social sciences since Wells made these remarks, can we not reasonably expect an equal increase in capabilities to study personal and social futures?

Extrapolation of trends, such as in the demographic projection of time series, for example, is perhaps the most obvious scientific method for studying alternative futures. Others include the specification of dynamic processes of cause and effect which may affect the future and go well beyond simple projection of time series. "If, then" statements can be made based upon knowledge of causal relationships, the implications of which are carried into the future. Quite directly, individual and collective images of the future can be measured just as other beliefs and attitudes are, and these can be tested against subsequent developments as they occur. The researcher may himself construct images of the future—for example, of some social group, an institution, or an entire nation—by any number of logical devices from the negation of selected aspects of the present to the hypothetical occurrence of alternative syntheses of different existing social forms. He could then test the probability of such images being fulfilled,

17. Lasswell, p. 157.
18. H. G. Wells, *The Discovery of the Future* (New York: B. W. Huebsch, 1913), pp. 36-37.

against whatever evidence his ingenuity would lead him to specify, and evaluate the desirability of such images against sample surveys of the values of relevant populations. Finally, to the extent to which the study of images of the future could be linked to social engineering, which seems increasingly feasible, quasi-experiments could be performed to test various hypotheses about the future and especially the role of deliberate action in shaping it. In our opinion, the scientific study of the future not only is possible but also offers a promising challenge to sociological research.

The relation of images of the future to action that is designed to bring about a particular future is the most significant fact in relation to the theory of social change to be proposed. Trying to look at the world through the eyes of new national leaders as they set about making the decisions of nationhood, we arrived in our earlier studies at the importance of images of the future. Thus, we have tried to incorporate the study of the future into our own empirical research.[19] Lasswell also apparently arrived at his notion of the developmental construct through his concern with decision-makers, and he connects a future orientation with decision-making, as the following comments on his work by Heinz Eulau make clear.

. . . a decision is an act, or a series of acts, involving the simultaneous manipulation of facts, values, and above all, expectations. The decision-maker cannot do without expectations about the future—expectations relating, for instance, to the probability of a long or short war, rising or falling national income, the stability or instability of foreign governments. Being explicit about one's expectations necessitates their assessment in terms of values, goals, or objectives, on the one hand, and in terms of whatever factual knowledge may be available, on the other hand.

. . . decision-making is predominantly future-oriented. It is, Lasswell points out, "forward-looking, formulating alternative courses of action extending into the future, and selecting among the alternatives by expectations of how things will turn out."

. . . a theory of the political process or, at least, a conceptual schema that has decision-making behavior as its empirical referent is predicated on the

19. Wendell Bell, *Jamaican Leaders: Political Attitudes in a New Nation* (Berkeley and Los Angeles: University of California Press, 1946); Wendell Bell and Ivar Oxaal, *Decisions of Nationhood: Political and Social Development in the British Caribbean* (Denver: University of Denver Press, 1964); Wendell Bell, ed., *The Democratic Revolution in the West Indies: Studies in Nationalism, Leadership, and the Belief in Progress* (Cambridge, Mass.: Schenkman, 1967); and James A. Mau, *Social Change and Images of the Future: A Study of the Pursuit of Progress in Jamaica* (Cambridge, Mass.: Schenkman, 1968). Also, the same orientation is more or less present in the recent work of two of our colleagues who participated with us in the Caribbean research; see Charles C. Moskos, Jr., *The Sociology of Political Independence: A Study of Nationalist Attitudes Among West Indian Leaders* (Cambridge, Mass.: Schenkman, 1968); and Ivar Oxaal, *Black Intellectuals Come to Power: The Rise of Creole Nationalism in Trinidad and Tobago* (Cambridge, Mass.: Schenkman, 1968).

availability of constructs which are descriptive of the emerging future. Such constructs presumably make possible "the planned observation of the emerging future [which] is one of the tasks of science." [20]

A Theory of Social Change

The outlines of a theory of social change based on the assumptions we have put forward are compressed in the diagram given below. Social change is explained within what we have called a cybernetic-decisional model that treats the entire process as a feedback cycle resulting in a spiral of progressive interaction between information and action.[21] Motivated individuals, acting as individuals or members of groups, with images of the future and resultant behaviors, are viewed as the key elements that keep the system moving and produce the actual future. The behavior is viewed as largely the result of decisions (or in some cases "decisions" not to decide) which are essentially choices among alternative futures; hence the use of "decisional" in the caption. Images of the future are of critical importance in influencing which of the alternative futures is chosen.

The unit of analysis to which the model may be applied can be a single individual choosing a career, a family selecting a neighborhood in which to live, a business firm selecting an office site, a nation formulating its foreign alliances, or a supranational group deciding who should next be admitted to membership. Thus, in applying the model, the analyst must first specify the relevant unit and identify the appropriate context that should be identified with the other elements in the system. Of course, one may use the model simultaneously on different levels of abstraction with the added analysis of critical intersections, such as in the case of a university selecting its new students for admission and a number of individual applicants seeking admission to the university.

Since we have already discussed indirectly most of what is in the diagram and why it is there, we will here explain only briefly its contents. We must, however, define our terms. Crucial to this theory of social change is the concept of belief, which we define as any ". . . given proposition about any aspect of the universe which is accepted as true . . . ." [22]

---

20. Eulau, pp. 230-231. On this specific point, cf. Bertrand de Jouvenel, "Political Science and Prevision," *The American Political Science Review,* 59 (March, 1965), 29-38, esp. 30ff. In general, the idea of images of the future has been elaborated by Kenneth E. Boulding. We regret that, because of lack of space, we have been unable to discuss his work here. We refer the reader in particular to his *The Image: Knowledge in Life and Society* (Ann Arbor: University of Michigan Press, 1956), and *The Meaning of the Twentieth Century: The Great Transition* (New York: Harper, 1965).
21. See also Amitai Etzioni's discussion of a cybernetic theory of "societal guidance," pp. 70-97, this volume.
22. McKinney, p. 181.

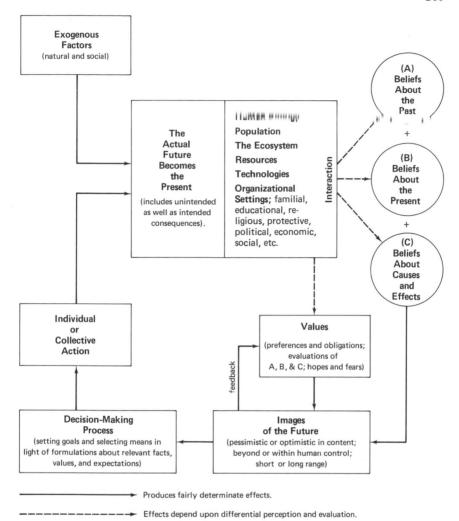

The significance of beliefs is not dependent upon the intrinsic, objective truth of the particular proposition. Of course, beliefs vary in accordance with the norms of standards against which they are tested. There are false beliefs (contrary to demonstrable evidence), true beliefs (in accord with empirical evidence), and beliefs that are methodologically untestable (unverifiable in form). A particular belief may be based on accumulated factual evidence or upon prejudice, intuition, superficial appearances, or faith. Accordingly, there can be empirical beliefs and nonempirical beliefs. The nature of its derivation need not affect the potency of the belief itself. People may act just as energetically and determinedly on the basis of unverified or unverifiable beliefs as upon the basis of empirically sound beliefs. . . . In brief, beliefs are formulations of what we think about the universe, its objects, and their relations. A belief system is a kind of cognitive mapping of the situation.[23]

23. Ibid.

We distinguish three kinds of beliefs in the cybernetic-decisional theory of social change: beliefs about the past, the present, and causation.

Beliefs about the past. Every individual and group has a history. Beliefs about that history limit the range of alternative images of the future and make it more probable that a particular one rather than others will be dominant.

Beliefs about the present. Individuals and groups have not only histories but also present existences. It is elementary to say that what individuals and groups think of themselves and what significant others believe to be true of them are important determinants of images of the future. Furthermore, formulations about the "facts" of the present define the maps of social reality that people use to make their way in the world. We include here not only beliefs about specific details of the present as perceived and understood by the actors but also definitions of the situation and, at the highest level of abstraction, basic views about the nature of man and the world.

Beliefs about causes and effects. The construction of an image of the future depends in part on the formulations about causes and effects held by the person or shared by the group doing the constructing. At one level, what people believe about the way the world works can contribute to making it work that way (for example, a widespread belief that bribes are offered and accepted by government officials may promote both offers and acceptances), and at another level it contributes, no matter how inaccurate the belief, toward directing human energies in one particular direction rather than in another. At the most general level, what people believe about social causation can lead them to adopt images of the future that are more or less fatalistic.

Values. Combined with beliefs about the past, the present, and causation in shaping images of the future are the values that are held by individuals either for themselves, for someone else, or for some social group. We include here basic values, whether they be primarily preferred choices or felt obligations. These provide a frame of reference for evaluating the past, the present, and presumed causes and effects and, in conjunction with such beliefs, for defining hopes and fears. Values also constitute a set of criteria for defining desirable and undesirable images of the future, and provide a basis for the evaluation of the costs and complex interactions between alternative images of the future in different spheres of activity.

When one deals with individual persons as the units of analysis, then the empirical problem is to determine the beliefs and values of particular

individuals and how these beliefs and values enter into each individual's images of the future and into his decisions and actions. When one deals with collectivities as the units of analysis, then there are the additional empirical problems of the distribution of beliefs and values within the collectivity, the degree and intensity of conflict involved, and the relative influence and power of persons holding particular beliefs and values. These factors, of course, would influence the various outcomes. Each element in the diagram, then, may take on a complex structure that in its own right invites investigation.

The fact that beliefs and values are shaped by various constraining and socializing factors is shown in the diagram by the arrows leading from the present (or the actual future) to the various beliefs and values. Since Durkheim, sociologists generally have taken society as prior in time to the individual, and in the Western world—especially in the United States—most sociological effort in the last five decades has been devoted to the study of the shaping of individuals and their behaviors by the natural (such as studies in human ecology) and especially social environments. Recent sociological inquiry has tended to focus on the structural determinants of social man and his behavior. We do not suggest that such studies be discontinued in favor of what we propose here. That would not correct a fault but simply lead to another. Rather, we suggest that the other side of the coin has been neglected in recent times. The study of society as becoming—its structuration, destructuration, and restructuration and specifically the role of man in the process—is no less a sociological question than studies of society's direction or constraint of man or of the change that takes place as a result of impersonal forces. Thus, although in our model we take account of the influence of society on man, we emphasize in the cybernetic-decisional theory of social change that man, individually and collectively, comes to take some action that results in altering natural, and especially social, arrangements.[24]

Images of the future. The definition of images of the future should be as bare and lean as possible, other things one might say about them being taken not as intrinsic aspects of the definition itself but as extrinsic to it. We propose this as a working definition: An image of the future is an expectation about the state of things to come at some future time. We may think most usefully of such expectations as a range of differentially probable possibilities rather than as a single point on a continuum.

Images of the future may vary in many ways. For example, they are specific to different aspects of reality and pertinent to different levels of abstraction. They may be about one's personal monetary success, a na-

24. Cf. Reinhard Bendix and Bennett Berger, "Images of Society and Problems of Concept Formation in Sociology," in Llewellyn Gross, ed., *Symposium on Sociological Theory* (Evanston: Row, Peterson, 1959), pp. 92-118.

tional military crisis, changing relations between different races, or the future of mankind as a whole. They may concern the immediate future or some time far into the future, and they may be about some particular location or some other place on this earth or elsewhere. They may be widely shared by many social groups or differentially held by different groups, considered desirable or undesirable, and promote either apathy or hyperactivity. They may be simple or complex, more or less achievable, more or less believable and persuasive, more or less different from the past and present, consciously or unconsciously created, more or less intentionally manipulated, and more or less influential in orienting behavior. They may be either sacred or secular and may vary according to the conditions under which they arise. In understanding behavior, the proximity of the images is of great significance—whether they are long-range, and therefore of possible sustained importance in directing behavior, or short-range.

Following Polak, we suggest two additional aspects of images of the future: (1) the pessimism or optimism of its content—that is, whether the future state of affairs according to the image is evaluated as worse or better than the present, and (2) the assumption contained in the image concerning the factors that will influence the actual future, whether they are beyond human control, or directly (man himself) or indirectly (prayer to the gods) within it. Critical differences in human behavior are hypothesized to result from images which are basically pessimistic compared to those which are optimistic, and from images which put man in the image as a causal factor compared to those which do not.

Decision-making process. It is beyond the scope of this paper to discuss the details of the decision-making process itself, nor is there need to do so since it has been the subject of considerable social inquiry in its own right.

We assume that, before action takes place, some decision occurs which results in a choice among alternative futures. This involves the specification of particular goals and the selection of means in the light of beliefs about the past, the present, and causation, and about values as they have become congealed in images of the future. This process varies in its deliberateness, consciousness, and rationality. The model may be applied even when the decision-making process is truncated, since the contents of the relevant beliefs, values, and images of the future explain in part how much conscious decision-making is likely to take place. However, the model, as an attempt to explain the liberated role of man as an agent of social change, is most efficacious when decision-making is most explicit. As part of the trend toward human mastery, we hypothesize that the long-term trends characteristic of modernization result in increases of rationality and consciousness and, therefore, in deliberate planning of political, economic, social, and cultural change. For, by definition, planning ". . . is essentially the attempt to resolve the problems of the future by assess-

ment of future consequences, as implicated in the activities and events of the present and our experience of the past." [25] To the extent to which such planning orientations become widespread, as they tend to do among people in advanced societies, they lead to the adoption of similar procedures at the microscopic level as ordinary individuals make their ways through time and space in their own daily lives.

Individual or collective action. As a result of the decision-making process, some action takes place; it may be individual or collective, depending on the unit under consideration and on the relevant context of applicability. Inaction is considered one alternative of possible actions with its own consequences for the future. Individual behavior or collective action of organizations or whole societies is consequential for the future. The ways in which images of the future cause social action are, of course, complex. An individual actor or social group may be trying to prevent something from coming about as well as trying to bring something about. An unstated image of the future that is the basis of action may be intended to negate stated images of the future. Meanings attached to behavior by the actors involved are of great importance in finding the link between images of the future, decision-making, and action.

The actual future. Finally, there is the actual future as it emerges from individual and collective actions. Certainly, there may be variations between the images of the future and the actual future, with considerable discrepancy and many unintended consequences. This is not to say that one necessarily needs to search for causal factors outside the system we have described. Rather, the struggle to control the future with the negotiations, compromises, wins, and losses that it entails may introduce—in fact it almost certainly does introduce—variations between the image and the actual future that occurs. The variety of images of the future, governing any one aspect of life, may be in conflict but, even with unanimity about images of the future, beliefs about the past, the present, and social causation may lead to action that is only more or less effective in achieving the intended results. For such beliefs may be inaccurate in ways that debilitate or misdirect social action.

Additional allowances must be made for various factors exogenous to the model that can and do help shape the actual future. Thus, such natural phenomena as earthquakes or tidal waves may unpredictably alter the actual future location or shape of a city quite apart from the collective action taken to locate it at a particular place and with a given internal structure. An outbreak of hoof-and-mouth disease may make a shambles

25. McKinney, p. 176.

of the future envisioned for the end of a five-year agricultural development plan. Social factors also may be exogenous, depending on the specification of the units of analysis. For example, in studying the move of a Jewish family in the United States from the central city to the suburbs, one may discover that the family's efforts to escape the Jewish ghetto for a primarily gentile neighborhood are thwarted by the simultaneous decisions of other Jews to move to the same neighborhood. The residential choices of all but the Jewish family being studied are exogenous to the explanatory system as applied to that family, although they can be studied in their own right by redefining the criteria of application of the model. To cite another example, the efforts of the emergent leaders of a new state to create national unity, expressed in new national symbols, may be undermined by the leaders of primordial groups within the country who cling to power by asserting the authority of tradition.

As the actual future emerges, more or less as planned but usually with unexpected features, it becomes the present and then the past. In our diagram we show specifically, as aspects of the actual future (or present), human biology, population, the ecosystem, resources, technologies, and organizational settings or institutions including familial, educational, religious, protective, political, economic, and social. In addition to these major institutions others, of course, could be listed. These structures, if we can subsume them together under this term, are shaped within certain constraints by the relevant expectation structures of the actors and groups as they behave.

With the discovery that growth and heredity are controlled by deoxyribonucleic acid, human biology may soon be more subject to manipulation than it is now. Population has been affected less by wars than by the reduction of famine and by international control of disease. These developments involved technologies to be sure, but they also involved revolutionary alterations in belief systems (including scientific knowledge) and implementation of the universal value of human life and survival. They involved, too, other actions of men such as those that result from the decisions of individuals to achieve their ideals of a particular number of children and a certain style of family life.[26]

Man is the chief disturber of ecological balance in the world, often as an unintended consequence of actions to achieve images of the future that are not related to ecology, but increasingly as a result of planned intervention in the ecological system (usually to correct past damage by human action). Obviously, resources are used up by man, and deliberate conservation may be increasingly necessary, but the relations between resources, beliefs, and images of the future are more subtle. In developed countries it is no longer resources that limit decisions, but in a fundamental

26. For a theory of population processes based upon decision theory, see James M. Beshers, *Population Processes in Social Systems* (New York: Free Press, 1967).

sense it is the decisions that make the resources, at least if any appreciable length of time is included in one's conception beyond the immediate present. David M. Potter comments on the relativity of resources as follows.

. . . it is, perhaps, necessary only to remember that the American Indians possessed, but benefited little from, the fertile soil which formed an unprecedented source of wealth for the colonists, that the colonists gained little more than the grinding of their grain from the water power which made magnates of the early industrialists; that the early industrialists set little store by the deposits of petroleum and ore which served as a basis for the fortunes of the post-Civil War period; that the industrial captains of the late nineteenth century had no conception of the values that lay latent in water power for generating electricity, which would be developed by the enterprisers of the twentieth century; and that these early twentieth-century enterprisers were as little able to capitalize the values of uranium as the Indians had been five centuries earlier. The social value of natural resources depends entirely upon the aptitude of society for using them.[27]

The fact that technologies and organizational settings or social institutions are created by man is too obvious to belabor here. Yet it is a major premise of this chapter that modern sociologists have so reified each that they have neglected the study of the processes involved in social development and change resulting from the actions of men themselves, especially actions which are directed toward planned change. Such reification has been the result of several factors, not the least of which is the fact that sociologists often deal with such overprocessed reality in the form of census statistics, IBM cards, computer printouts, and mathematical models, that it is understandable if man himself somehow slips through their fingers. Also, while most sociologists are socially distant from the centers of power where the role of decision-making is most obvious, they are, at the same time, remote from the intimate details of the daily lives of average persons and fail to see how a model of change based upon images of the future may be applied on the little stage as well.

As the actual future emerges, an opportunity occurs to assess the adequacy of beliefs about the past, the present, and social causation, and the desirability of goals and their relevance to basic values. Thus, old images of the future and beliefs may be revised. In this way a cycle is closed, but an element of feedback is introduced that keeps the system dynamic. At every stage in the process, between every element in the model, it is assumed that there is room for innovation and creativity.

The arrows in the diagram indicate both a time sequence and a flow of causality that results in maintaining or changing the various elements in

27. David M. Potter, *People of Plenty: Economic Abundance and the American Character* (Chicago: University of Chicago Press, 1965), p. 85.

the model. Present structures (human biology, population, and so forth) shape beliefs about the past, the present, and social causation, and the nature of social values, although how they do it depends in part on the different meanings attached to the present as a result of different definitions of the situation. Beliefs and values shape images of the future which, in turn, lead to certain decisional outcomes and social action. Such action, along with exogenous factors, produces change by helping to shape the actual future in particular ways. The emerging future becomes the present and the cycle begins again, an unending spiral of the creation of society— sometimes in its old forms, but in the modern world usually in changed forms.

The entire model is a feedback loop. We have indicated additionally in the diagram one feedback subloop, since we hypothesize that the reciprocal effects between values and images of the future are of particular importance. However, although we could have shown additional feedback subloops, we have not done so since we intend the arrows which are presumed to produce fairly determinate results not only to show direction of causality but also to indicate neglected questions for sociological research. For example, how do beliefs and values shape images of the future? How do images of the future enter into the decision-making process?

Some Directives for the Scientific Study of the Future

It seems clear that the use of scientific research for socially important purposes is increasing, regardless of the "pure" or "applied" intentions of the researcher. To the extent that this is true, what are the implications for the conduct of social research and for professional responsibilities? Must the social scientist be concerned with the action implications of his work? Should he be explicitly action oriented? Some find the idea of playing such a role, consciously or not, totally disagreeable. Most of us have been educated to believe, if not in the naïve notion of a value-free social science, at least in detachment, objectivity, and unbiased remoteness, as scientists, from the political and social controversies of the day. Some social scientists have seen the myth of scientific purity as a protective cover under which social science could be developed and free inquiry maintained without interference from powerful political and economic interests in the society. Most social scientists believe in it as devoutly as in any religious dogma, but if the assumptions and hypotheses we have presented here are correct, then some effort should be made to elucidate the contribution of social science to the shape of the future, and to restudy the professional responsibilities of the social scientist as maker of the future.

Because decision-making requires thinking about the future, there has

been less research on the future by conventional academic researchers than by agencies of decision-making bodies serving both public and private groups and, thereby, oriented toward the future through a concern with policy. Although many of the former have talked about the future or tried to predict it like oracles, they have not usually tried to study it.[28] It is our view that social scientific images of the future surely will promote *[one line illegible]* social scientists are willing to accept what may be intolerable consequences, the creation and dissemination of such images should not be left to the paid agents of special interests (whether of governmental organizations or private corporations); nor should they be left to the scientific "purists" among the social scientific fraternity who mistakenly claim that they are only after the facts, and who deny that through their research and teaching they are playing any role in shaping the future beyond discovering and spreading the "truth."

What may be needed is a reorganization of the focus of the discipline of sociology itself so that the future becomes a standard concern for at least some group of sociologists. Even the lone academic investigator might responsibly make his work a significant contribution to the emerging future. Our contention is that it is more or less of a contribution whether the researcher believes it or not, but its relevance to the future can be enhanced and can be made explicit. There may have been a few sociologists who made similar observations in the past, and there may be some sociologists who agree with this view. What has been neglected is strategy. How can those social scientists who wish to make their work as scientists more relevant to the future do so?

As answers to this question, we have formulated a set of directives which, if followed in the conduct of social inquiry, may increase the relevance of social science to the future. We regard these directives as hypotheses and, therefore, as tentative and subject to revision and elaboration. Their sources are to be found in our own studies of new national decision-makers, in the literature on the study of the future, and in the cybernetic-decisional theory of social change.

28. Most attempts to study the future appear to be confined to rather narrow technical projections such as those made in economics or demography. Others interested in the future have largely relied upon predictions of the shape of the future based upon conjecture. There have been exceptions, however; Hadley Cantril in *The Pattern of Human Concerns* (New Brunswick: Rutgers University Press, 1965) has compared studies of "hopes and fears for self and nation" in a number of different countries; and Nathan Israeli, who apparently was ahead of his time since his work was never followed up, carried out in the early 1930's some prophetic studies in the social psychology of the future. Current work includes Daniel Bell's *Commission on the Year 2000* and the Russell Sage Foundation project on social indicators which is under the direction of Wilbert E. Moore and Eleanor Bernert Sheldon. Bettina Huber has prepared an annotated bibliography of such works which will soon appear in Wendell Bell and James A. Mau, *The Study of the Future: Explorations in the Sociology of Knowledge,* forthcoming.

1. The directive of dynamic orientation. To increase a study's relevance for the future, the study should have a dynamic orientation. Society should not be viewed as a static system existing only in the present. Rather, past, present, and future should be seen as interpenetrating each other, and society should be viewed as moving *from* something *to* something else. A dynamic orientation leads the researcher to think in terms of what Lasswell calls "developmental constructs" where the time dimension is "built in" and "trend-thinking" is required.[29] Although longitudinal data are not necessary, they are helpful; but it is the point of view and interpretation of the researcher that are critical.

2. The directive of uncertainty. To increase a study's relevance for the future, the assumptions on which the study is based should include the notion that social reality is more or less uncertain. Reality should be viewed as problematic in at least two ways: first, it is problematic in the sheer knowing of it; second—and most relevant in the present context—, it is problematic in that it is contingent upon the actions men take. Although the emphasis should be on the probabilities of different outcomes for the emergent future, consideration should also be given to the problematics of the present and past, both of which are merely complexes of sense data organized with respect to some prior frame of reference.

Since our methods of attaching exact probabilities to different versions of social truth are so imprecise, the researcher may, at the conclusion of his work, report only one version of the past, present, and future, perhaps the most probable or the most significant; but as he carries out his investigation he may find it useful to be creating different versions, including (perhaps especially) unlikely or even currently outlandish ones, and examining their credibility. In this way, the scientist plays a role in creating new and different images of the future as well as in testing or finding means for implementing current images. In so doing, he himself, through the images he creates and clarifies, may become a causal factor in determining individual or collective action and, as such, the results of his work are among the contingencies upon which the emerging future depends.[30]

3. The directive of self-awareness. In order to increase a study's relevance for the future, the social scientist should recognize that his efforts are somehow, and to some degree, affecting the future. Researchers should be aware of the possible effects of their results in changing images of the future, and this awareness should be an explicit part of the inquiry. This

29. Lasswell, *Political Behavior.* Gardner Murphy advocates a similar future orientation and, to some extent, illustrates this and other directives; see his *Human Potentialities* (New York: Basic Books, 1961).
30. Several illustrations of the latter point are to be found in Jacques Freymond, "Introduction—Forecasting and Europe," in Bertrand de Jouvenel, ed., *Studies in Conjecture,* vol. 2 (Geneva: Droz, 1965), pp. xiii-xxx.

requires that thought be given to the question of just what effect given results may have, and it requires such thought whether or not the inquiry was *intended* to have any effect or to be relevant to the future.

4. The directive of value relevance. This issue has long been the subject of debate, and there still exist hard lines of disagreement that are sure to interfere with communication. Nonetheless, we suggest that to increase a study's relevance for the future the study should be oriented toward some basic values within a society. Special attention should be given to the possible existence of universal or common human values. The more value-relevant a study, the greater the chance that it will bear on the future, since the direction and tempo of change are geared to the basic values that are discovered, clarified, distributed, and created. Through social scientific research the sociologist can contribute to the discovery, clarification, and distribution of values. By combining different values on higher levels of abstraction he may even create new ones.

5. The directive of value-structure inconsistency. The study of those phenomena constituting areas of inconsistency or discrepancy between values (which define how society and people *should be* with respect to some particular social relationship) and social structure (which reveals how society and people *actually are*) should be of particular relevance to the emerging future. Assuming that there is tension in such situations that invites resolution through alteration of either the value or the structure, one may expect some change. Examples of such studies may be found in Myrdal's *An American Dilemma* and in the Kinsey Report. In the former, the value of equality was set against the structure of inequality of the Negro American; in the latter, values in the form of moral codes of sexual behavior were set against actual sexual behavior. The two authors differed in their suggested resolutions of the inconsistencies, and subsequent social change seems to have taken different courses. In the case of the Negro American, the structure is being altered to conform more closely to the value. In the case of sexual behavior, the moral codes appear to be eroding and conforming more to actual sexual practices. Wilbert E. Moore states this general point as follows.

Usually the inconsistency between the ideal and the actual is tension-producing and hospitable to change. Overt violation of prevalent practices must somehow be dealt with, for evil genuinely challenges the persistence of morally supported standards. Widespread recognition that human performance falls short of perfection may lead to the acceptance of more "realistic" standards, but this development is itself a significant change. Generally, however, ideals are somewhat more likely to be exalted than downgraded, and endure as a perennial challenge to imperfections.[31]

31. Wilbert E. Moore, *Social Change* (Englewood Cliffs: Prentice-Hall, 1963), p. 20.

6. *The directive of the pull of the future.* To increase a study's relevance for the future, the researcher should be explicitly aware of the assumption that the future is in some sense real and is pulling the present toward it. The pull of the future is primarily manifested in the present by images of the future. Thus, images of the future relevant to any social inquiry invite investigation. The actual future is to some extent a consequence of the images of the future that are present within a society, although not necessarily the most popular images. Among the questions that can be asked under this directive are the following. What images of the future are most commonly held? Do different socioeconomic, racial or ethnic, and age groups hold different images of the future? How do the élite differ from the masses in their images? How do images of the future function for the individual? What factors account for the strengths of some images of the future and the weaknesses of others in affecting the actual future? Who are the creators of the significant images of the future and what explains the varied content of the images they create? What explains the rise and fall of dominant images of the future?

Arthur L. Stinchcombe in *Rebellion in a High School* found that differential images of the future among high school students helped to explain whether or not the students became rebels. He says that the ". . . future, not the past, explains adolescent rebellion, contrary to the hypothesis that deviant attitudes are the result of distinctively rebel biographies . . . we hold that deviant values or crippling of the ego are traceable to differences in the futures of adolescents."[32] His argument is that adolescents whose images of their own occupational future are such that they expect to become members of the manual working class in the next labor market cohort see no clear relation between what they are doing in school and their future status. Thus, their current performance loses meaning, and current self-restraint is perceived as irrelevant to the achievement of long-run goals. The student ". . . reacts negatively to a conformity that offers nothing concrete. He claims autonomy from adults because their authority does not promise him a satisfactory future."[33]

Stinchcombe's study is an excellent illustration of how the future may cause the present, of some of the questions that may be asked about the pull of the future, and of the way conventional sociological explanations may be revised as a result of investigating the effects of the pull of the future.

7. *The directive of the substitution of space for time.* This directive is intended to alert the researcher to the possibility that the past or present of some particular place at one time may serve as a model of the future

32. Arthur L. Stinchcombe, *Rebellion in a High School* (Chicago: Quadrangle Books, 1964), p. 6.
33. Ibid.

of some other place. Thus, differentiation in space may serve as a heuristic device for differentiation in time. If one can determine that the flow of diffusion is from place *x* to place *y,* then one may be able to study the future of place *y* by studying the past and present of place *x.* In the same way that one might predict the weather in Chicago tomorrow by knowing the weather in Omaha today, one might predict the future internal struc- ture of metropolitan Omaha by knowing how metropolitan Dallas or Los Angeles has grown and differentiated in the last decade. As another ex- ample, we might ask if we can learn anything about the future of Vietnam by studying the past and present of Korea. Clearly, no simple equating of one place with another will reveal any exact prophecy, but as a technique of analysis and projection, the substitution of space for time offers many unexplored possibilities for the researcher of the future. Of course, as- sumptions and inferences will have to be made and borne out, as is always the case, if knowledge is going to be the result. If this directive is followed, comparative studies may take on a new significance in that they may acquire developmental and futuristic implications.

8. The directive of manipulative priority. To increase a study's relevance for the future, explanatory theories should be formulated to maximize the use of concepts that are within—or that are likely to be brought within— the power of men to control. Inevitable, natural, or impersonal forces as causes should be eschewed in favor of human behavioral or ideational variables. Explanations presented only in terms of broad processes, such as urbanization and industrialization, should be specified to include the actions, and ideas and ideals behind them, that men and groups have taken or might take to control their own individual and collective destinies. This may mean that the easy and handy explanation may have to be bypassed in the search for the manipulable variables that explain at least as much of the variance. One example of how the search for manipulative variables can be facilitated has been suggested by Robin M. Williams, Jr., in a dis- cussion of the contribution of action-experience in intergroup relations to social research.

Above all, observation of social action aimed at alteration or stabilization of intergroup relations can increase our sensitivity to the degree and kind of *accessibility to manipulation* characterizing the major causal factors in the situation, and can provide preliminary indications as to the magnitude of effects that may be anticipated.[34]

Williams suggests further that analysis of ". . . attempts to induce or retard social change can direct research attention to factors that are crucial, from the standpoint of social importance, but not seen in that

34. Robin M. Williams, Jr., "Application of Research to Practice in Intergroup Relations," *American Sociological Review,* 18 (February, 1953), 81.

perspective so long as a purely detached research orientation prevails." [35]
We would agree with him that good theory should serve this purpose, but
also that it frequently has not.

One implication of this directive is that effective control should be the
prime criterion of knowledge, rather than accurate prediction or precise
description, since each of the latter can exist without the former. Thus,
knowledge will be created that invites use for the purpose of shaping the
social realities of the emerging future. Social scientists can then forecast
the future not so much by projecting factors beyond man's control but
rather by participating in the process of deciding what the future should be
and finding the means for making it come about that way.

Some Directives for the Social Scientist as Maker of the Future

Implicit in this discussion are two directives that define the role of the
social scientist as maker of the future. The first is the directive of social
responsibility. In the course of his scientific investigation the social scientist, as maker of the future, should take responsible action about the effects
his results may have. There is perhaps little that we can add here to this
much-discussed and long-debated issue. On the one hand, there are the
well-known relations to social values of the processes of selection of a
problem for study, dissemination of results, and recommendations for
policy. On the other hand, there is the equally well-known conflict between
being simply a "tool" of some client, or even of "truth" in the abstract,
and being an active judge of the purposes for which knowledge should or
should not be used. Despite all that has been written about it, the latter
course remains largely uncharted, but we know of the experience of the
atomic scientists and of the impersonal bureaucratic behavior of the Nazi
functionaries: sticking one's head in the sand is not a satisfactory solution.

We suggest four neglected directions for future concern that involve
the directive of social responsibility. First, the effects of social science
knowledge on policy formation and action should receive greater attention
as a subject of investigation itself.[36] A sociology of social science could
tell us to what degree and in what way social science does in fact affect the
future. Without knowing this and without testing our hypotheses about it in
some rigorous way, there is nothing to judge about the effects of social
science on the future.

Second, there are few guidelines leading to the specification of common

35. Ibid.
36. An example of one approach to evaluation of the effectiveness of policy-rele-
vant social science findings is Rainwater and Yancey's social science and public
policy report on Daniel Patrick Moynihan's book, *The Negro Family: The Case
for National Action*. See Lee Rainwater and William L. Yancey, *The Moynihan
Report and the Politics of Controversy* (Cambridge: M.I.T. Press, 1967).

or universal values. Most people can now agree upon such values as human life, health, security, affection, and level of living. Other candidates for inclusion are emergent and generally derive from the values of human dignity and individual self-fulfillment. Given the fact that ends as well as means are increasingly open to choice and manipulation, then one must acknowledge that they are open also to be influenced by, among other things, social science. What are the dimensions of the good life? Is there an emergent set of universal or common values? What is the dynamic mechanism that tends to make certain values universal? Are there neglected social goals that should be pursued in the place of those that are actually being pursued? If so, in what way are their implications for social life superior to the goals they might replace? What might be accepted as convincing evidence that some values are better than others? In trying to answer such questions, the social scientist not only studies values in the usual way, but also consciously enters into the creation and appraisal of values.

Third, one strategy that may face the social science community as it becomes increasingly responsible for the future is the choice between monopoly and sharing of enlightenment. The level of control or the timing of release of certain information may itself importantly affect the future. The present tendency among sociologists to avoid facing this question squarely by repeating the litany of a free and open dissemination of information is understandable. It is a difficult question. One can envisage a situation in which the sociologist might behave just as public health officials do today when, fearing to cause panic and widespread disorganization, they decide to withhold certain information about the spread of a dread disease in a city. Our concern here is this: Should the individual social researcher of the future be left to confront such choices without guidance and institutional support from his professional group?

Fourth, the recruitment of social scientists may have significant effects on the nature of social scientific findings. Most of us would agree that the social backgrounds and social contexts within which social scientists work affect their selection of problems, style of research, and interpretation of findings. What strategies should be followed in recruiting social scientists so that their numbers contain a representative sampling of world experience? Persons of different nationalities, social classes, races, and religions, for example, should be represented in the profession. Such persons, we assume, would carry into their professional careers many of their previous experiences and identifications with consequences for the direction and form of new formulations about social reality. Whom do we select to become social scientists in order to decrease the probability that the parochialism of any one section of world experience will dominate the process of the production of new social scientific knowledge?

A second directive may be stated as follows: The researcher should

strive to give as much consideration to the formulation of positive idealistic images of the future as to negative and cynical ones. The construction of desirable self-fulfilling propositions should be as much the strategy of the scientific architect of the future as the picturing of deleterious trends combined with the faint, and usually unanalyzed, hope that somebody may intervene and prevent them from continuing. We raise the question: Until we know more about the effects of images of the future, is it not dangerous to create negative, pessimistic, or cynical images? Counter-utopias may, as Moore says, ". . . dampen and redirect trends of change." [37] But might they not sometimes become self-fulfilling? We are neither calling for the sort of optimism that Mills termed "sunshine moralism," [38] nor are we suggesting that the researcher should not be skeptical and realistic; rather, we suggest that the social scientist should search reality to the point where he can reveal some solutions for the problems he sees and can counter negativism with positive solutions equally founded upon social facts. The stubborn researcher who refuses to accept lightly an emergent conclusion of his research because it contains a pessimistic image of the future should perhaps drive himself on to additional data, other frames of reference, or new concepts that reveal reality more completely than before while also creating not complacency but rational hope and purposive action.

Social scientists should follow this directive without giving up their critical function as intellectuals and without becoming toadies to the establishment. We are simply saying that hypercritical negativism can become as much of an obstacle to progress as can unwarranted optimism. The tough combination of realistic observation with idealistic creativity that transcends the boundaries of the present into the real possibilities for the future may help us tell the "eager traveler" how he can get there from here. Thus can sociologists combat those who would condemn the future to the limitations of the present and, like the *philosophes* of the Enlightenment, help to change the world through their reinterpretations of it.

In conclusion, we stress that we do not intend to say anything anti-scientific in this paper. Quite the contrary, the theory of change and the directives should be put to work within the scientific framework. The canons of science with respect to data specification, collection, analysis, and interpretation must be met. Falsification must be avoided. The facts, such as they are, must be faced; the truth, relative though it may be, is itself to be valued. However, we wish to stress what every scientist worthy of the name knows: science includes speculation, and the scientific method is based to an important degree on the use of creative imagination. In the study of the future there is a need to cultivate both speculation and creative imagination.

37. Moore, "Utility of Utopias," p. 772.
38. C. Wright Mills, *The Sociological Imagination* (New York: Grove Press, 1961), p. 78.

9.

Sociological Theory and
the Process of Typification

John C. McKinney

John C. McKinney was born in Velasco, Texas, in 1920 and educated at Colorado State College and Michigan State University (Ph.D.). He was a member of the faculty at Michigan State University from 1947 to 1957. Since 1957 he has been professor of sociology at Duke University. He was chairman of the department of sociology and anthropology until 1969 when he became vice-provost and dean of the graduate school at Duke. During 1968-1969 he was president of the Southern Sociological Society. Dr. McKinney has contributed to many professional journals and symposia, and is author of Constructive Typology and Social Theory, *coauthor of* Introduction to Social Research, *coeditor of* The South in Continuity and Change, Social Aspects of Aging, *and* Aging and Social Policy.

The primary assumption of the following analysis is that the process of typification is a natural aspect of the social process. The program of this analysis will involve: (1) an examination of the context within which typification takes place, the delineation of existential types as first-order constructs; (2) an examination of the methodological and theoretical aspects of typification as practiced by sociologists, the delineation of constructed types as second-order constructs; (3) an assessment of the structure and function of typologies by means of an explication of a "typology of types"; (4) an exploration of selected theoretical and methodological issues with respect to the construction and utilization of typologies emphasizing problems of nominalism versus realism, ethnomethodology, social morphology, specification of the operations performed in the construction of types, and the relationship to general sociological theory, with particular reference to the social system as a construct; and (5) a description of selected substantive sociological problems which are of crucial theoretical importance at this time, and for which typologies would be intellectually useful.

The Context and Development of Typification: Existential Types

Symbolic interaction is the fundamental datum in the approach of sociology to human conduct. It is the process from which all sociocultural behavior

patterns emerge, therefore it is the bench mark or—at least implicit—point of departure for all sociological analysis. The individual as a personality inevitably is implicated in a social order. The individual biologic organism attains a state of selfhood by participation in the social process of inter-action. The individual, then, is an integral part of a social system, and it is only through interaction with other members of the system that he rises above the organism level and assumes the roles characteristic of a personality.

From a sociological viewpoint, interaction is a complex organic process, a dynamic and continuing whole, sustained, but not constituted wholly, by the stimuli and responses involved in it. The act of an individual is a unit act, comprehensible in terms of interaction, and best viewed as being a part of a complex social behavior pattern. Interaction is cooperatively sustained and hence has meaning at its own level rather than merely at the level of the unit acts involved.

Seen from this perspective, the self is not primarily a content but an activity which is a part of the social process. The self is a development; it is not initially present, but arises as a result of the experiential relations of the individual to the social process as a continuity, and to the other individuals involved in that process. Mead contends that the social process pre-exists, both temporally and logically, the self-conscious individual who is emergent in it.[1] Selves, then, are not psychical, but belong to an objective phase of experience.

In this view, the self is generated in interaction, and language is the mechanism that is essential to its development. The characteristic that primarily distinguishes the self from the body and from other objects is that it is an object to itself. Possession of this capacity and ability to become an object to one's self is one of the fundamental elements of difference between human behavior and that of other animals. The reflexive character of the self is of primary significance, and it is this characteristic that makes the self sociologically relevant. As seen in this fashion, the self has no significance unless it can turn back upon itself as an object and thereby distinguish itself in a plurality of other selves.[2]

The individual becomes an object to himself, and thus a self, only by taking the attitudes of other individuals toward himself, assuming the roles of others, and regarding himself from their perspective. He becomes aware of himself as others are. This is accomplished through utilization of the mechanism of communication which is essential to the emergence and maintenance of social organization. The individual does not at first experience himself directly as subject, but only indirectly from the particular

1. G. H. Mead, *Mind, Self and Society* (Chicago: University of Chicago Press, 1934), p. 186.
2. G. H. Mead, *Movements of Thought in the Nineteenth Century* (Chicago: University of Chicago Press, 1934), pp. 138-139.

standpoints of individual members of the social system, and later from the generalized standpoint of the social system(s) to which he belongs. He then can only develop a sense of selfhood within the context of social relations and the experience they involve. The importance of communication here is paramount in that it provides the form of behavior that enables the individual to become an object to himself in a social environment. The self, then, is firmly fixed in experience. Evidence of this is the achievement of the reflexive form in languages, the form that recognizes the self as both subject and object.[3] Communication is not something that can go on by itself, but rather must always involve something that can be communicated. It is a medium for such basic cooperative activities as exchange and assistance and therefore always serves the social function of enabling what is communicated to be socially utilized.

Viewed in this tradition of thought, the self is really a plurality of selves. An individual carries on a whole series of different relationships to different people. We are one thing to one person and another thing to someone else. A variety of selves exists for a variety of consociates in typically differentiated situations. There are different sorts of selves answering to different sorts of reactions. There are typical responses to typical stimuli in social interaction. What determines the amount or sort of self that will get into communication is the social experience itself. The self cannot appear apart from experience. In effect this means that the various elementary or component selves which are organized into a composite, or unitary, self answer to various aspects of the social structure. This in turn means that the self appears as the assumption of various specific and general roles. In brief, the individual can never grasp the individual uniqueness of his fellowman in his completely unique biographical situation. In the context of social interaction, the other appears at best as a partial self, and he enters even the most diffuse, in contrast to the most functionally specific, relationship with only a part of his personality. Schutz makes the point as follows.

The world of everyday life is from the outset also a social and cultural world in which I am interrelated in manifold ways of interaction with fellow-men known to me in varying degrees of intimacy and anonymity. . . . Yet only in particular situations, and then only fragmentarily, can I experience the Other's motives, goals, etc.—briefly, the subjective meanings they bestow upon their actions, in their uniqueness. I can, however, experience them in their typicality. In order to do so, I construct typical patterns of the actor's motives and ends, even of their attitudes and personalities, of which their actual conduct is just an instance or example. These typified patterns of the Other's behavior become in turn motives for my own action, and this leads to the phenomenon of self-typification.[4]

3. Ibid., p. 34.
4. Alfred Schutz, *Collected Papers, Vol. I: The Problem of Social Reality* (The Hague: Martinus Nijhoff, 1962), p. 60.

External activity is made meaningful by bringing social interaction *into* the individual. As Mead has put it, "It is the internalization within the individual of the social process of communication in which meaning emerges." [5] Through role-taking, first of the specific and then of the general other, and the development of significant gestures and symbols, the individual develops the ability to indicate to himself the same response that his gestures have brought out in others, and to control the response in terms of it. Thinking is thus a process within the individual, but it has its basis and origin, and experiences its sustenance, external to the individual. The mechanism used is the vocal gesture which is a part of the social process. The symbol one uses belongs to others as it belongs to him; it is always a common symbol, possessing a meaning that is typical for the social system. Mead has maintained that only by taking the attitude of the generalized other can the process of thinking take place. Only through taking the attitude of the generalized other is a universe of discourse established as a system of common or social meanings, which thinking presupposes as its context.[6]

In this view our so-called laws of thought are abstractions from social intercourse. It is social interaction that functions as the universal, and an internalizing of it makes it no less social, but on the contrary leaves as social our whole process of abstract thought, technique, and method. The general thesis of reciprocal perspectives inherent in symbolic interactionism implies that there may be differences in individual perspectives that have to be accommodated if the interaction is to proceed. Schutz has suggested that commonsense thinking overcomes these differences by means of two basic idealizations.

i) The idealization of the interchangeability of the standpoints: I take it for granted—and assume my fellow-man does the same—that if I change places with him so that his "here" becomes mine, I shall be at the same distance from things and see them with the same typicality as he actually does; moreover, the same things will be in my reach which are actually in his. (The reverse is also true.)

ii) The idealization of the congruency of the system of relevances: Until counterevidence I take it for granted—and assume my fellow-man does the same —that the differences in perspectives originating in our unique biographical situations are irrelevant for the purpose at hand of either of us and he and I, that "We" assume that both of us have selected and interpreted the actually or potentially common objects and their features in an identical manner or at least an "empirically identical" manner, i.e., one sufficient for all practical purposes.[7]

The mechanism of language brings the social interaction, with its reciprocity

5. Mead, *Mind, Self and Society,* p. 22.
6. Ibid., p. 156.
7. Schutz, *Collected Papers,* pp. 11-12.

of perspectives, into the individual as himself involved in the interaction, and thus makes predictability or "rationality" possible.

Although the process of reason, the manifestation of rational conduct, must be carried on in terms of language, it does not follow that it is constituted by language. Rational conduct involves the ability to indicate to one's self what the stimuli are that will call out a complex response, and by the order of the stimuli determine what the whole response will be. It involves an ability to articulate a relevant set of typifications in a "working" order. Rational action within the social process is merely action within an unquestioned and undetermined frame of typifications of the situation, including the relevant elements such as motives, means, ends, and courses-of-action. The successful articulation of these typifications, with the consequent achievement of the predicted results, warrants the imputation of the label "rational." In brief, it appears in behavior as essentially the ability to solve the problems of the present in terms of future consequences as implicated on the basis of past experience. It resides primarily in the socialization of knowledge. Only a very small part of any individual's knowledge of the world originates within his personal experience. The great bulk of it is socially derived and communicated to him by his family, peers, teachers, and others. The individual, in the continuing socialization process, is taught how to define the environment, the typical features of the world as perceived in the generalized view prevailing in the social system. Moreover, he is taught how typical constructs have to be formed within the system of relevances taken for granted within the social system. This includes prescriptions and proscriptions regarding ways of life, modes of coming to terms with the exigencies of the environment—in brief, typical methods for bringing about typical ends in typical situations.

It is clear that within this context, meaning is neither individualistic nor arbitrary, but is, on the contrary, a function of social interaction. The field within which meaning exists is constituted by a relationship within social interaction. The relationship is one between a given stimulus, as a gesture, and the later phases of the act of which it is an early phase. Meaning is not a psychical addition to an act, it is a development of something objectively present as a relation between phases of the ongoing interaction. Mead has delineated a threefold relationship as being constitutive of the matrix of meaning: a gesture by one organism, the resultant of the social act of which the gesture is a phase, and the response of another organism to the gesture. The triple relationship is of gesture to the first organism, of gesture to the second organism, and of gesture to subsequent phases of the social act.[8] Meaning is stated in terms of response, for the gesture stands for a certain resultant of the social act to which there is a definite response on the part of the individuals implicated in the act. Significance does not exist for the

8. Mead, *Mind, Self and Society,* p. 72.

individuals within the act unless the same tendency to respond is called out in the individual making the gesture as is called out in the individual affected by the gesture, who then puts himself in the attitude of the other.

The mechanism of meaning is therefore present in social interaction before awareness of meaning arises on the part of the participants.[9] The basis of meaning is thus objectively present in conduct. Meaning is a property of an object which is dependent upon the *relation* of an individual or collectivity to it. It is not primarily a psychical content, for it need not be conscious at all; in fact, it is not conscious until significant symbols are present. The symbol is theoretically distinguishable from the meaning it refers to; meaning is a forerunner of symbolization. Significant symbols are a later by-product of the meaning emergent in the interactive process. Meaning is described, or accounted for, in terms of symbols or language, but language merely lifts out of the social process, in less than complete and in inevitably imperfect fashion, a situation that is already implicitly there. Language, in a sense, is a *typifying* medium for transmitting socially derived knowledge. The vernacular of everyday life is primarily a language of labeled or named objects (things or events). Any label or name delineating an object implies a typification and generalization referring to the relevance system prevailing within the social system, which found the named object significant enough to provide a specific symbol for it. In this sense the everyday language of the members of a social system includes a veritable treasure-trove of typifications or types symbolically representing their relations to their object world. Relations to the object world vary considerably for individuals, however, with respect to the roles they enact within the social system(s).

Society and the individual are bound together by virtue of the fact that they are a part of one another. The essential principle of organization is interhuman communication. In taking the attitude of the other, especially the generalized other, the individual incorporates into his own roles attitudes that are common to, or typical of, society. By taking over specific attitudes that people typically assume under typical conditions, the individual preserves the structure of society. The content of this "preservation" and the nature of the relationship will vary widely, however, since societies are inevitably differentiated systems.

Parsons has defined the social system as essentially consisting of "a plurality of actors interacting with each other in a situation which has at least a physical or environment aspect, actors who are motivated in terms of a tendency to the 'optimization of gratification' and whose relation to their situations, including each other, is defined and mediated in terms of a system of culturally structural and shared symbols." [10]

For most purposes, at least those of microsociology, the most significant unit of the social system is the role, of which role expectations are the pri-

9. Ibid., pp. 77-78.
10. Talcott Parsons, *The Social System* (Glencoe: Free Press, 1961), pp. 5-6.

mary ingredient. Historically, role has been defined in various ways; one definition has delineated it as "that sector of an actor's orientation which constitutes and defines his participation in an interactive process." [11] Social roles have also been defined as "typifications of the attitudes and patterns of action ascribed to a category of social actors on the basis of a given trait which they have—or are believed to have—in common." [12] In this definition, role is seen as a category of constructs or typifications by which men orient themselves in their environment. In any case each individual is involved as a participant in a plurality of patterned interactive relationships. This participation revolves around the two reciprocal perspectives inherent in interaction.

Roles, of course, among other variations, vary in their degree of institutionalization and the degree to which they are common to members of the society at large. A pattern governing action in a social system may be considered institutionalized insofar as it defines the main modes of the legitimately expected behavior of the persons acting in the relevant social roles, and insofar as conformity with these expectations is of structural significance to the social system. Clearly one necessary feature of the institutionalization process is the establishment of the "typical." Expectations with regard to performance and sanctions are expressions of typical responses to typical situations as defined within a broader framework of typifications.

Parsons conceives of institutions as constituting the main link between the social system and the actor, in that they are related at the same time to the functional needs of actors and to those of the system.[13] The link evolves around the normative-voluntaristic aspect of the structure of action. The roles that individuals play in a social system are defined in terms of goals and standards; stated differently, in terms of typical objects of action and typical modes of conducting the action. From the viewpoint of the actor, then, his roles are defined by the normative expectations of the members of the group as they are formulated in the cultural tradition. Although the phenomenon of typification probably cannot account for the moral aspect of this normative order, it nevertheless is present as a necessary condition for the development of the "legitimate" or "moral" aspect of expectations.

Expectations are always an aspect of any social situation within which an actor is acting. "The expectancies that make up the attitude of everyday life are constitutive of the institutionalized common understandings of the practical everyday organization and workings of society as it is seen 'from within.' Modification of these expectancies must thereby modify the real

11. Ibid., pp. 38-39.
12. D. I. Offenbacher, "Norms, Roles and Typifications in Contemporary American Society," paper presented at the annual meetings of the American Sociological Association, August, 1967, p. 5.
13. Talcott Parsons, *Essays in Sociological Theory* (Glencoe: Free Press, 1949), pp. 34-36.

environments of the societies' members. Such modifications transform one perceived environment of real objects into another environment of real objects." [14] Expectancies, in their typical forms, are real to actions in that they have real consequences for them. Conformity or deviation brings consequences in the form of approval and reward or condemnation and punishment. These expectations are not only aspects of culture as shared typifications; they are internalized as aspects of the actor's personality. In the process of socialization the actor internalizes, to varying degrees, the standards of the social system so that they become motivating forces in his own conduct independent of external sanctions. The relation between role-expectations and sanctions is a reciprocal one. To the actor, sanctions are role-expectations to alter, and vice versa. Their institutionalization is always a matter of degree based upon the factors affecting the actual degree of sharing values and standards, and those determining the motivational commitment to the fulfillment of expectations. Institutional behavior cannot be conceived of in terms of a purely rational model or in self-interest terms, but it can be said that any individual can seek his own self-interest only by conforming to some degree to the institutionalized expectations.

In social structure, then, one has a system of patterned expectations defining the *proper* behavior of actors in specified roles: typical behavior to be enacted under typical circumstances as typically perceived within a social system. This system is positively enforced both by the individuals' own motives for conformity and by the sanctions of others. These typical and well-established patterns of expectations in the perspective of a social system are our institutions. These institutions constitute the structurally stable element of social systems, and their prime function is the preservation of role definitions of the constituent individuals. Viewed functionally, institutionalized roles constitute the mechanisms by which varied human tendencies become integrated into a system capable of dealing with the problems of society and its members. Moreover, this social structure has been *constructed* by actors in interaction over time. This construction activity is a natural aspect of the social process and in part is a process of typification. Typification as a central feature of cognition is the development of a selective and persistent attitude of an actor toward his environment. Typification is a process in conduct that so organizes the field of action that interaction can proceed on an orderly basis. Typification, perceiving the world and structuring it by means of categorical types, is evidently an essential and intrinsic aspect of the basic orientation of actors to their situation. The social world of the individual, largely through taking over in the socialization process the typifications people habitually assume under given conditions, is structured by a multitude of types: types of people, types of activity, types of relationship, and the like. These are what Schutz has termed "first

14. Harold Garfinkel, "Studies of the Routine Grounds of Everyday Activities," *Social Problems,* 11, 3 (Winter, 1964), 249.

order constructs." In this paper, we are calling them *existential types:* [15] typifications or types constructed by participants in social systems. They are fundamental data for the social scientist and stand in contrast to, and yet in continuity with, the second order constructs or *constructed types* he develops and utilizes.

The Methodological and Theoretical Aspects of Typification: Constructed Types

This examination of the process of typification leads inexorably to the conclusion that all concepts are constructs which have been *developed* out of experience. "The world as has been shown by Husserl, is from the outset experienced in pre-scientific thinking of everyday life in the mode of typicality. The unique objects and events given to us in a unique aspect are unique within a horizon of typical familiarity and pre-acquaintanceship." [16] Clearly, raw experience is never really raw even at the moment of perception. As a consequence of the socialization process, of having become personalities through symbolic interaction, human beings naturally and necessarily categorize their experience in terms of concepts. "Neither common sense nor science can proceed without departing from the strict consideration of what is actual in experience." [17] The everyday activity of people, their behavior within the vast complex of social interaction, results in the residue of a vast number of "folk typifications" or existential types which in effect structure society, and hence also the observational field of the social scientist.

It has long been recognized, although sometimes there has been denial that it matters, that the observational fields of the natural and social scientists are different. The object world that the natural scientist explores and explicates doesn't "mean" anything to his units of analysis: molecules, atoms, electrons. In contrast, the object world investigated by the social scientist has been constructed by actors living, believing, valuing, aspiring, expressing, thinking. The social systems constructed by actors have a meaning relevant to them, and their activities within that domain of relevance relate to the maintenance and change of those systems. Actors have preselected and preinterpreted—in brief, preconstructed—the world for the social scientist. This suggests that there is a continuity between the typifying and concept-formation activity of actors in social systems and that of social scientists treating social systems as phenomena for observation and explication. Although all of science is a social enterprise, social science is social

---

15. This label was suggested by Edward A. Tiryakian. See his "Typological Classification," *International Encyclopedia of the Social Sciences* (New York: Macmillan, 1968), pp. 177-186.
16. Schutz, *Collected Papers,* p. 59.
17. A. N. Whitehead as quoted in Schutz, p. 3.

in a double sense. It is social both in its conduct and in its object, by contrast to the rest of science which is social merely in its conduct. This establishes one aspect of continuity between the practices of everyday life and the conceptualization of the social sciences that is not present in the other sciences. Continuity, however, does not imply that the social scientist must settle for the same conceptual equipment that people in everyday social life utilize; on the contrary, it merely means that it is incumbent upon him to take cognizance of that equipment as data symbolically representative of the "social reality" he is exploring. Moreover, recognition of this continuity serves to remind us of the fact that all of our knowledge of the world, that provided by actors in the everyday or workaday world as well as that provided by science, involves constructs, which in turn involve abstraction, generalization, formalization, and idealization specific to the scope and mode of thought organization involved. The distinction made here between conceptualization by actors in the social process within social systems, and social scientists observing and exploring the social process and systems, is the basis for our distinction between the peoples' *existential* types and the social scientists' *constructed* types. The origins of the latter are clearly in the former, and the distinction has to do with levels. The former corresponds to what Schutz has called "first order constructs" and the latter to "second order constructs." [18] In this sense the constructed types are "typifications of typifications" which, in effect, constitute further reductions of the multiplex world in the interest and service of science.

The pragmatically inclined have been impressed by the fact that the scientist has no generalized problem of knowledge, despite the fact that it is his particular business to know. Knowing is not a matter of proceeding from the uncertain effects in the individual to the world beyond which is supposed to cause those effects, for scientific research always posits an unquestioned world of existence within which its problems appear and are tested. Any part of this world may become problematic and therefore an object of the knowing process. Knowledge in a scientific sense is not contemplation, but discovery through hypotheses tested in action by "things" which are for the moment unquestionably real, although in other situations they can be a part of the problematic area.

All phenomena are unique in their occurrence in space and time; therefore, no phenomena actually recur in their concrete wholeness. In order to make these phenomena intelligible and explicable they must be *reduced* through conceptualization. The reduction to existential types by people in everyday life is for the purpose of "living" and hence is only a start in the reduction process essential to the social scientist for "knowing" in a more theoretical sense. When science begins to classify and analyze its data, it is taking a definite and formal step away from reality at the level of folk classi-

18. Schutz, *Collected Papers,* p. 6.

fications and existential typologies. To comprehend is to introduce order into our experiencing of phenomena. This requires that phenomena be treated as though they were identical, recurrent, and general. The meaning of identity, however, is always "identical for the purpose at hand." The construction of classes, categories, or types is a necessary aspect of the process of inquiry by means of which we reduce the complex to the simple, the unique to the general, and the occurrent to the recurrent. To introduce order with its various scientific implications (including prediction), the scientist necessarily rises above or ignores the unique, the extraneous, and the non-recurring, and thereby departs from perceptual experience. This departure is prerequisite to the achievement of abstract generality, which, in turn, constitutes the basis of our ability to comprehend the world of concrete experience. To conceptualize means to generalize to some degree. To generalize means to reduce the number and variety of objects by conceiving of some of them as being identical in certain ways or for certain purposes. The reduction of the object world reduces the number and variety of relations to be examined and explained. It is on the specification of these relations that our comprehension of the world of phenomena is based. Structurally this process is the same in social interaction generally as it is in scientific endeavor; the latter differs in its extension, purpose, rules, and conventions.

Scientific concepts never exhaust perceptual experience, for they always involve selection. Concepts do not reflect the totality of raw experience in all its diversity and complexity and are therefore in a sense unreal. In brief, all concepts are generalizations and all generalization implies abstraction and reduction, and one aspect of this is the process of typification. Within the realm of formal inquiry this process is manifest in the explicit construction of types and typologies.[19]

19. See the following for recent important sources of theoretical work with respect to typology: Allen Barton, "The Concept of Property-Space in Social Research," in P. F. Lazarsfeld and Morris Rosenberg, eds., *The Language of Social Research* (Glencoe: Free Press, 1955), pp. 40-53; Howard Becker, *Through Values to Social Interpretation* (Durham: Duke University Press, 1950); Reinhard Bendix, "Concepts and Generalizations in Comparative Sociological Studies," *American Sociological Review*, 28 (August, 1963), 532-538; Reinhard Bendix and Bennett Berger, "Images of Society and Concept Formation in Sociology," in Llewellyn Gross, ed., *Symposium on Sociological Theory* (Evanston: Row, Peterson, 1959), pp. 92-118; Milton Bloombaum, "A Contribution to the Theory of Typology Construction," *Sociological Quarterly*, 5 (Spring, 1964), 157-162; A. D. Grimshaw, "Specification of Boundaries of Constructed Types Through Use of the Pattern Variables," *The Sociological Quarterly*, 3 (July, 1962), 179-195; C. G. Hempel, "Typological Methods in the Natural and Social Sciences," *Proceedings*, American Philosophical Association: Eastern Division, vol. 1 (1952), pp. 65-86; P. F. Lazarsfeld, "Some Remarks on Typological Procedure in Social Research," *Zeitschrift für Sozialforschung*, 6 (1937), 119-139; P. F. Lazarsfeld and A. H. Barton, "Qualitative Measurement in the Social Sciences," in Daniel Lerner and H. D. Lasswell, eds., *The Policy Sciences* (Stanford: Stanford University Press, 1951), pp. 155-192; C. P.

All typification consists in the pragmatic reduction and equalization of attributes relevant to the particular purpose at hand for which the type has been formed, and involves disregarding those individual differences of the typified objects that are not relevant to such purpose. This purpose resides in the theoretical problem (as in the case of constructed types) or practical problem (as in the case of existential types) which, as a result of our selective interest, has emerged as questionable from the unquestioned world in the background. In formal inquiry, typologies are subordinate to the aims of research, namely, the establishment of uniformities of explanatory value. Typologies are instrumental in the research process; they are functional in the sense that they have been constructed to be useful in the research process. The reference of the type to the problem for whose solution it has been constructed, its problem relevance, constitutes the meaning of the typification. Thus typologies should be constructed to aid in the analysis of specific bodies of data. The extension of the area of applicability of the type simultaneously involves the extension of problem relevance and the analysis of relevant data. Typologies must be understood as representative of a pragmatic research methodology and thus subject to evaluation in terms of the accuracy of predictions which result from their utilization. An empirical error criterion is as fundamental in typological procedure as it is in research methodology generally. It is clear that some particular typology can be used in the study of several different social systems or processes. This requires, however, that the goodness of fit of the typology to each set of data must be evaluated. Typologies, by the very nature of their construction, and by the very nature of concept formation generally, cannot have a perfect fit to any set of data. The better the fit, however, the greater the probability that the typology will be useful in the subsequent analysis.

For a long time, controversy has swirled around the concept of type and the problem of type formation and utilization. Considerable ambiguity remains with respect to the proper function of types in the chain of inquiry. Whatever else a constructed type may be, it is clearly a conceptual tool. Despite its varied use over the years, it is possible to discern an underlying consensus which has enabled us to define the constructed type as a purposive, planned selection, abstraction, combination, and (sometimes) accentuation of a set of criteria with empirical referents that serve as a basis

Loomis, "The Nature of Rural Social Systems: A Typological Analysis," *Rural Sociology,* 15 (June, 1950), 156-174; Arnold Rose, "A Deductive Ideal-Type Method," *American Journal of Sociology,* 56 (July, 1950), 35-42; Alfred Schutz, "Concept and Theory Formation in the Social Sciences," *Journal of Philosophy,* 51 (April, 1954), 257-273; R. F. Winch, "Heuristic and Empirical Typologies," *American Sociological Review,* 12 (February, 1947), 68-75; Vittorio Capecci, "Typologies in Relation to Mathematical Models," *Ikon,* 19 (1966), 63-124; and J. C. McKinney, *Constructive Typology and Social Theory* (New York: Appleton-Century-Crofts, 1966).

for comparison of empirical cases.[20] The elements and relations observed in historical contemporary social life supply the materials out of which the conceptual tool is constituted. These are identified, selected, articulated, and simplified into the constructed type on the basis of the social scientist's idea of the nature of social reality and on the basis of the purposes of his inquiry. Considerable ambiguity surrounds the question as to *how* this is done. A great many varieties of types have been described in the literature of the social sciences. Reference is frequently made to ideal, pure, extreme, heuristic, polar, empirical, real, classificatory, and constructed types. As descriptive labels, some of the above reflect purpose (the heuristic type), serial order (the polar type), character of attributes (the pure type), function (the classificatory type), or developmental procedure (the constructed type). Such contrasting bases for labeling have tended to obscure the fundamental qualities shared by all types. From a methodological point of view these qualities center around how types are conceptually developed. When one looks closely at the variety of types extant in any substantive field, it is impossible to avoid the central fact that the development of each of them involved a task of construction. This is not to assert that all types are alike in their construction; it is merely a way of saying that all types are constructed around certain persistent variables. In surveying a broad range of major typologies it would appear that the major variables are (1) the relation of type to perceptual experience, (2) the degree of abstraction involved in the types, (3) the purpose of the type, (4) the temporal scope of the type, (5) the spatial scope of the type, and (6) the function required of the type.

When these variables, which are either explicitly or implicitly present in any type, are viewed as the axes around which types are constructed, they appear as the main dimensions of types in general. They are seen as a series of continua which serve to delineate the structure of types. For purposes of

---

20. With this definition as our bench mark, it is possible to assert that *all* types are constructed, and that moreover the social scientist typically constructs the units with which he operates. The sociologist is dependent upon such notions as competition, conflict, accommodation, assimilation, socialization, superordination, subordination, institutionalization, community, society, caste and class, sacred and secular, rural and urban, democracy-autocracy, bureaucracy, the deviant, solidarity, primary group; these and many more may be constructed types. Economics is deeply indebted to its "economic man" from which the classical economic theory was derived. The essential concepts of perfect competition, the perfectly mobile factors of supply and demand, the perfect monopoly, or such classificatory labels as capitalist and socialist systems, money, credit, or barter economies are all constructed types. Even the ideographic historian, whose aim is different from that of the social scientist and who is legitimately concerned with the unique and individual, constantly utilizes constructed types. When he talks of epochs, eras, and periods, he has constructed them. When the historian speaks of the Greek city-society, the feudal system, the manorial system, early Protestantism, the medieval papacy, the Calvinistic ethic, the estates within the state, and countless other things, he is utilizing, usually without awareness, the procedure of constructive typology in his own particular way.

analytic convenience and description we have labeled the polar points of these continua and have treated them as the polar variables of type construction. We then have the following six variables: ideal–extracted, general–specific, scientific–historical, timeless–timebound, universal–local, and generalizing–individualizing.

It is possible to analyze any given type in terms of its tendency to conform to the requirements of one pole or another on each of the above continua. It is important to note, however, that these continua are not mutually exclusive and do not reflect the same level of abstraction. On the contrary, they are mutually implicated, overlap to a certain unavoidable extent, and reflect methodological relevance rather than logical purity. In other words, they represent the empirically persistent points of methodological concern in the development of substantive types. We have used them as the basis for the construction of a "typology of types." The primary purpose was to indicate the attribute sphere within which types are developed and the bases on which they vary in terms of their construction. A very brief résumé of the typology follows.[21]

Ideal–Extracted. Weber conceived of the ideal type as being both abstract and general. In his view, his types did not describe or directly represent concrete courses of action, but instead represented objectively possible modes of action. This would be a course of conduct assuming certain ends and means to be in consistent usage by the individuals involved. Further, this would be a typical course of action not necessarily duplicated in concrete situations by individual modes of behavior, but it would be normative in character. The ideal type would logically contain within its structure all the essential properties or elements of a concrete course of action, but not necessarily in the proportion or relationship pattern of any given empirical occurrence. These properties or elements constituted the variables within this type and were held in fixed relationship with each other for theoretical purposes.

As abstractions, Weber's ideal types were conscious deviations from concrete experience. They were structured in such a way as to accentuate some attribute or group of attributes relevant to his research purpose or interest. In a sense, they were a distortion of the concrete, in that all empirical occurrences appeared as deviations from the theoretically conceived ideal type. Weber conceived of ideal types as merely being necessary heuristic expedients. They were not in themselves empirically valid, and they merely served as consciously devised and delimited conceptual tools in the analysis of the empirical world.

At the opposite end of the continuum and from the pole represented by the ideal type, we have the extracted types. These types are definitely not exclusive of one another; on the contrary, they grade gradually into each

---

21. See McKinney, pp. 20-34 for a fuller development of this typology.

other. It must be pointed out that even though the ideal type is theoretically derived, it must still have empirical referents, for it is based upon the particularities of actual occurrence. Weber made this very clear in terms of what he did rather than in terms of what he said about the ideal type. Conversely, the extracted type, no matter how empirical its base, involves a certain amount of problem- or theory-oriented selection and hence construction. Both types serve the purpose of simplifying and identifying the object world. Their differences lie primarily in their formulation and the way in which they represent the object world; this, of course, has implications for what they can "do" in research.

Extracted types throw the average and common traits into bold relief; these are not necessarily the crucial or significant ones. The ideal type involves comparison from the ideal limits of the case, whereas the extracted type involves comparison from central tendencies. The extracted type is based upon the notions of average, common, and concrete rather than of accentuation and abstractness. Nevertheless, a certain amount of essential ideation is involved in the establishment of extracted types, as, for instance, in the delineation of the traits involved (a case of abstraction) and the treatment of a combination of traits as a composite whole (a case of simplification based upon elimination of the seemingly irrelevant and, hence, again a matter of abstraction). As one views the various typologies extant, it is easily recognized that none of them is either ideally or empirically pure; in actuality they are representative of tendencies to emphasize one pole or the other.

General–Specific. Types also can be distinguished by their relative generality or specificity. Cognizance must be taken of the levels of abstraction involved in the formulation of types. The more general a type is, the greater the simplification of the empirical attributes; and the more specific a type is, the greater the number of general characteristics obscured by the mass of ideographic detail. Generalization means omission and simplification of particularities. Consequently, as a type effects wide coverage, its adequacy in accounting for specific variations is lessened. This is not to say that general types are not useful; it is merely to take account of the fact that more specific types must be used in conjunction with them for many explanatory purposes.

Scientific–Historical. Construction of types may proceed in terms of the purposes of the social scientist or in terms of the purposes of the historian. It must be recognized that they can and do use the same data, for all data are in a sense historical. The social scientist, however, is in search of the general and recurrent, and the historian is primarily interested in the actual sequence of unique events. The field of the historian is the whole range of human activities. The social sciences in their division of labor cover the same range. But whereas the historian is concerned with processes and structures that are singular in their space–time occurrence, and does not

conceive of them as being repeatable, the social scientist adopts the opposite perspective. The social scientist is concerned with the repetitive and constant factors, or tendencies to regularity of human society. For example, a sociologist may try to determine and state the recurrent aspects involved in the process of urbanization; the historian, on the other hand, will try to state the specific course which urbanization has taken in a given place over a given period of time. Constructed types of historical value tend to be highly complex, time-bound, and localized, whereas those of scientific value tend to be *relatively* timeless and universal, relatively simple, contain a limited number of criteria, and include so limited a content that they are applicable in many diverse historical situations. The historical construct is general in the sense that it does not depict the full concrete reality in all of its concrete manifestation, and the scientific construct is historical in the sense that the behavior it symbolizes necessarily bears a resemblance to that which has historically occurred. The differences in the constructs answer to the purposes for which they are formulated.

Timeless–Time-bound. This axis is very closely related to the one just treated, in that the scientific universal is the closest approximation to the timeless pole of the continuum and the historical construct is the closest approximation to the time-bound pole. It must be recognized that scientifically useful contructs vary enormously in the extent to which they are timeless. They stand in different relative positions on the timeless–time-bound continuum. For example, the concept of superordination–subordination appears to be quite timeless in view of the fact that some type of hierarchical relationship can be found even in the most primitive of contemporary societies. It is not necessarily entirely timeless, for if there were ever such things as hordes or conditions of completely mechanical solidarity, it would not have been applicable. As a principle, however, it seems to be a close approximation to the timeless pole. In contrast, the sociologically significant concept of class appears closer to the time-bound pole of the continuum than the concept of superordination–subordination does. Most of recorded history is immune to analysis by many types which are quite useful within a limited temporal span. It is important to note that scientifically useful constructs are only *relatively* timeless. Time will still leave discernible markings on even the most general social scientific types.

Universal–Local. The spatial counterpart of the timeless–time-bound continuum is that which we call universal–local. Just as the former deals with the temporal scope of the type, the latter is concerned with its spatial scope, and together the two axes determine the area of applicability of any given type. Constructs vary as to where they fall on the spatial continuum. When a type is applicable *anywhere* the particular class of phenomena it deals with are available, then it may be said to be universal. If a type is applicable only to a very limited and specific locale, and is not approximated anywhere else, it may be called localized. As an aspect of his scientific

orientation, the sociologist is driven to search for universal types. In actual practice and as a function of the research process, however, most of his types tend to be localized, for spatial markings are difficult to remove from sociocultural types. Indeed, for purposes of most research, it is not even desirable to extend the applicability of the type beyond a given area. In the long run, however, our normative orientation toward science and comparative study demands that we universalize as many types as possible.

Generalizing–Individualizing. Constructed types may be conceived of as being primarily either generalizing or individualizing. They are not unrelated. Indeed, numerous generalizing constructs are usually required to support an individualizing construct and, conversely, through modification an individualizing construct frequently can be adapted to more general use.

Max Weber used the individualizing construct as a means of delineating what he called the "historical individual," the thing to be explained. The impossibility of handling all the data and determining its relevance made it necessary to construct the individual unit to be examined. For instance, the construct of "modern capitalism" was woven out of the particularities of a historical epoch; but it was obviously simplified, selective, and limited. It contained what appeared to be the crucial characteristics of the capitalistic form that distinguished it from other economic configurations. To describe this complex historical individual, however, it was necessary for Weber to imply numerous *generalizing* constructs such as "rationality" and "bureaucracy" which have a range of applicability far beyond the particular case of modern capitalism. It is only through the use of such explanatory generalizing constructs that the historical individual is made comparable in any respect. The construction of the historical individual has the function of preparing and organizing the mass of concrete data for analysis in terms of general constructs and ultimate predictive statements of relationships.

In the preceding analysis, we have emphasized the point that all types are constructed and that there are recognizable dimensions of the basis of construction. It should be made quite clear that we have made no attempt here to create an exhaustive taxonomy of types, but have confined our endeavor to pointing out the features of substantive typing that have been empirically persistent. All the variables are found to be analytically applicable to all substantive types; hence any formal system of classification of the construction of types would have to provide categories that would account for the phenomena dealt with here under our essentially empirical rubrics. In brief, we have constructed a typology of types. Our primary object has been to indicate the attribute sphere within which types are developed and the bases on which they vary in terms of their construction. The principal assumption is that the function of a type or typology is dependent upon its structure. The structure of any particular type or typology is made visible by locating it in the attribute sphere of the general process of typification. Our typology of types is presented as a rough, cognitive map

of that attribute sphere and hence is designed to differentiate between primary modes of type construction. However crude or limited this particular typology may be demonstrated to be in the future, it is clear that construction in typological procedure varies with respect to at least six different dimensions. Consequently, types can vary greatly in terms of their structure, depending upon where they fall on the series of continua which we here consider to be the major dimensions. It follows, then, that they function differentially in the process of inquiry.

Selected Methodological and Theoretical Problems

In the light of the preceding analysis it can be asserted that types and typologies are ubiquitous, both in everyday social life and in the language of the social sciences. Everybody uses them, but almost no one pays any attention to the nature of their construction. Despite the omnipresence of typologizing in social inquiry it remains a relatively underdeveloped aspect of methodology generally. Historically, typologies have served us well as we have expanded the range and depth of knowledge with respect to social phenomena.[22] As we envisage the future, however, and contemplate the scope and magnitude of sociological problems yet to be explored, it would seem to be extremely unwise not to develop a vastly increased self-consciousness, as an aspect of both the common methodology and the common theoretical orientation, with respect to the construction and utilization of typologies. Since they are used with great frequency in social inquiry it would appear to be methodologically imperative that we develop and proliferate a greater understanding of their multiple roles in that inquiry.

There are, of course, many unresolved problems involved in the disciplined construction and utilization of typologies. On the other hand, there have been a number of scholarly efforts that have helped erode some of the mystique of typological procedure. A brief description of selected problematic features of typification follows.

Typologists have fallen heir to a very old controversy, namely that of nominalism versus realism. The question as to whether forms or configurations exist ontologically (as the realist tradition holds), or whether the form or configuration is merely an abstraction characteristic of the nomenclature (as held by the nominalist position), has persistently been reflected in the argument as to whether types are real or merely convenient fictions. Are types *just* constructs or are they dictated to observation by some natural arrangement of the phenomena themselves? The literature regarding the "ideal type" has contributed heavily to this controversy which, by and large, has been a spurious and fruitless one for the social sciences. The question of

22. See McKinney, *passim,* for extensive citations of sociological literature cast in typological form.

whether types are real is obviously a metaphysical one and may be of some relevance to philosophers, but it has little to do with the methodology of the social sciences. The reality of *anything* can be questioned in the same sense that the reality of types is questioned, if one wants merely to play the metaphysical game. He who is to behave as a scientist, however, has to assume that there is a certain order in the social world because the logical prerequisite of any induction or empirical generalization he makes is the recognition of the validity of the principle of uniformity, which holds that there have been and will be regularities or uniformities in phenomena because of a lasting order of things in the universe. As Znaniecki has indicated, "sociologists must postulate that some kind of objective order exists among all social phenomena." [23] According to John Stuart Mill, "The unity implied in reality is . . . a unity of order . . . order within a system." [24] This assumption constitutes the latent structure behind any specific induction. Hence, Weber, for example, fully aware of that order, could not really have presumed it to be a function of his methodological approach (such as the ideal type) or a function of the empirical sciences' bringing order into the empirical world, where it already exists. Our earlier discussion of the general process of typification and existential types indicates that the sociologist is presented a preconceived and prestructured social order by actors constructing and utilizing their own typifications. These typifications as they exist in social activity constitute a given for the sociologist and are representative of the structure within which he perceives his problems to lie. The order which the sociologist is committed to "capturing" is already there, the order which he is committed to "supplying" is one of further specification, reduction, and statement of relationship. The sociologist, just like man generally, wishes to establish intellectual control over his sphere of experience. Intellectual control over the vast content of social existence can only be asserted, however, if it is reduced in symbolic form. Science, including sociology, is just that special mode of comprehension which attempts to reduce and simplify big and great reality down to, and for, us. As we have said, the sociologists' concepts are generalizations and all generalization implies abstraction and reduction. One aspect of this is described as the process of typification and the construction of typologies. In effect, types are as "real" as sociologists make them. The pertinent questions to be raised are methodological rather than metaphysical. It is clear that types have been used very differently in different disciplines, and moreover, very differently within the discipline of sociology. The previously developed typology of types indicates that types vary considerably in their structure and function within the process of inquiry. The bases and ingredients of this

23. Florian Znaniecki, *Cultural Sciences* (Urbana: University of Illinois Press, 1952), p. 392.
24. Cited in Peter Coffey, *The Science of Logic* (New York: Peter Smith, 1938), p. 106.

construction vary and hence they vary in the ways in which they purport to represent social phenomena. For the sociologist, questions as to how and from what specific types were constructed, for what purpose, and with what applicability, are the relevant questions.

With regard to the further development of typological procedure it is essential that one take note of the development of ethnomethodology, particularly in the work of Garfinkel and associates. Obviously a methodology drawn from several sources, it nevertheless stands in a clear and salient relationship to the phenomenological approach of Schutz. It is concerned with a social system's folk classifications, its particular ways of classifying its material and social universe. The intent is to discover how members of a system perceive, delineate, define, and classify, and how they actually perform these activities. It represents an attempt to discover what meanings actors attach to their own acts. The challenge is not merely to describe social phenomena or events from an observer's perspective, but to get inside the events to see what kind of conceptual equipment or theories the actors themselves are utilizing as they organize the phenomena in their daily lives. As Psathas puts it: "The ethnomethodologist seeks to discover the 'folk methods' that persons use in daily life in society. In studying, for example, the way that jurors recognize the 'correctness' of a verdict, he focuses on the jurors' methodology, how *they* approach a verdict, what *they* define and decide as relevant, what *they* use as criteria in that assessment, etc." [25] Schutz's view that "the social scientist's task is the reconstruction of the way in which men in daily life interpret their own world" is subscribed to as a basic tenet by ethnomethodologists.[26] The extraction of the folk methods or modes of thought from social action results in what we have called existential typologies. As noted by Tiryakian, these existential typologies are becoming "treated in their own right as important revealers of the fundamental foci of social structure and social organization." [27] Nevertheless, as indicated previously, the social scientist cannot settle for these existential types; he must, in turn, treat them as data in the construction of types which in effect typify the typifications.

Shifting the focus again, it is important to point out an area of great typological potential, one that has long been promising as a major feature of the development of sociology as a science and yet is admittedly an area of almost complete failure to date: social morphology. Although many people have suggested the need of societal classifications, or classifications of social systems, perhaps the strongest case was presented by Durkheim at the turn of the century.[28] The viewpoint was again eloquently expressed by Radcliffe-

25. George Psathas, "Ethnomethodology and Ethnoscience," paper presented at the annual meetings of the American Sociological Association, August, 1967, p. 7.
26. Maurice Natanson in "Introduction" to Schutz, *Collected Papers,* p. 46.
27. Tiryakian, "Typological Classification."
28. Emile Durkheim and Marcel Mauss, *Primitive Classification,* trans. and ed. Rodney Needham (London: Cohen and West, 1963). First published in 1903.

Brown [29] in the thirties and more recently by Tiryakian.[30] Durkheim felt that sociology sorely needed a social morphology and that the primary task of this branch would be to develop a systematic classification of social types or social species and relate them to social structure. The very same Durkheim who strongly disapproved speculative typologies was the first (antedating Weber) to give strong theoretical support to the typological approach by his trenchant advocacy of the comparative method and by his conceptualization of individual social phenomena as reproductions of a corresponding "social model." Although Durkheim himself made some types famous (consider his types of society characterized by *solidarité mécanique* and *solidarité organique,* and his types of suicide), what is really relevant is his extreme emphasis on the comparative method. At a time in history when experimentation of any sort was nonexistent in sociology, Durkheim concluded that since ". . . social phenomena evidently escape the control of the experimenter, the comparative method is the *only* one suited to sociology." [31] It was this strong commitment to the notion of comparative research that led Durkheim to see the necessity of a rigorously elaborated social morphology. He states that ". . . to explain a social institution belonging to a given species one will compare its different forms, not only among people of that species . . . in order that the manner in which it grew progressively more complex may then be followed, step by step." [32] This, of course, is still an unrealized program, in large part due to the still lacking social morphology.

The recent rapid growth of interest and activity in macro- and global sociology, cross-cultural research, comparative study of social institutions and systems, and socioeconomic development places a renewed emphasis on the view expressed by Durkheim so long ago. An elaborate and rigorous typology of social systems, for instance, would greatly facilitate comparative research and lessen the chances of adapting too simplistic a view of social change and its conditions. The intrinsic relation between typologizing and comparative study has long been recognized. Znaniecki, for instance, states that ". . . the only kind of comparative generalization about cultural data that has been made and can be made is typological." [33] It is to be noted here that although most of the historical efforts in social morphology have been at the societal level, the flexibility of typological procedure permits the construction of types at all levels, from micro to macro. On the other hand, the largely *ad hoc* construction of types has clearly not established anything approaching the social morphology that has so long been advocated.

29. A. R. Radcliffe-Brown, *A Natural Science of Society* (Glencoe: Free Press, 1957), esp. pp. 32-39.
30. Tiryakian, "Typological Classification."
31. Emile Durkheim, *The Rules of Sociological Method,* trans. S. A. Solovay and J. H. Mueller (Glencoe: Free Press, 1950), p. 125. First published in 1895.
32. Ibid., p. 138.
33. Znaniecki, p. 179.

One of the more persistent problems in typologizing has been the lack of specification of the operations performed in the construction of the types. This has undoubtedly contributed to the ambiguities surrounding the relationship of the types to the phenomena they purport to represent. The fact that types represent phenomena in widely varied ways is evident, even in the light of our simple typology of types. All too few sociologists have attempted to explain how they arrive at the types they have used for a variety of purposes. Some of these attempts have been noteworthy, and there is little question that it is in the work of Paul Lazarsfeld and his students that one finds the most consistent and significant effort to date with respect to the general problem of relating types to subordinate indicators of phenomena. Starting in 1937 with his critique of Hempel and Oppenheim's *Der Typusbegriff im Lichte der Neuen Logik,* which dealt with the logical problems of typification in psychology, down to the present, his work on qualitative analysis has manifested a consistent concern with the operations and consequences of typification.[34] This has been an aspect of the broader concern with the issue of relations between concept formation and empirical social research generally.

The notion of property-space, as developed by Lazarsfeld over many years, not only is a remarkable symbolic device for "seeing" types, but also furnishes the framework within which their empirical applicability and validity can be tested. Since any type is a composite of properties (attributes, traits, criteria, characteristics) one can easily visualize it in property-space terms. Warnecke and Back recently summarized the Lazarsfeld methodology with respect to typologies as follows.

1. *Type construction* which includes the development of a "scientific perception" of the regularities, uniformities or relationships which "ought" to obtain in terms of prior research and the theoretical framework which exists for the field under study. . . .

2. *Substruction* is the second step. The process of substruction is in essence the logical evaluation of the typology. It is the definition of the property-space from which the typology may be empirically produced.

a. Property-space may be defined as a swarm of empirically definable measures or properties which are developed to measure the dimensions of the typological construction. The most familiar example might be a 9 x 80 space defined by the IBM card.

34. See P. F. Lazarsfeld, "Some Remarks on Typological Procedure"; P. F. Lazarsfeld and A. H. Barton, "Qualitative Measurement in the Social Sciences"; A. H. Barton, "The Concept of Property Space in Social Research"; P. F. Lazarsfeld, "Philosophy of Science and Empirical Social Research," in Ernest Nagel, Patrick Suppes, and Alfred Tarski, eds., *Logic, Methodology and Philosophy of Science* (Stanford: Stanford University Press, 1962), pp. 463-473; P. F. Lazarsfeld, "A Conceptual Introduction to Latent Structure Analysis," *Mathematical Thinking in the Social Sciences* (Glencoe: Free Press, 1954), pp. 349-387; and P. F. Lazarsfeld, "Latent Structure Analysis" in Sigmund Koch, ed., *Psychology: A Study of a Science,* vol. 3 (New York: McGraw, 1959), pp. 476-543.

b. This step then implies the construction of indices and other operational definitions of the elements in the typological construct.

3. *Data collection* is the third logical step in this procedure. At this stage the groups which are to be compared should be defined and the measures should be applied to them.

4. The *reduction of the property-space* to a set of empirical representations of the initially constructed typology then follows. It is this step in which discriminant analysis is believed to be most helpful. It is at this phase of the analysis that the methodological issues concerning the reality of the types as discrete entities and their relationship to some underlying continuum may best be specified. Particularly with respect to comparative analysis, discriminant analysis is especially adapted to deal with these issues.

5. The final stage of this procedure is the *comparison* of the constructions developed in the initial state with the empirical approximations which emerge from the analysis.[35]

This is an orderly process which retains the configurational character of the types. Although the initial constructions may well be modified in the process, those constructions one is left with at the end may be thought of as possessing a validity in their abstract representation of phenomena. In their recent study of role conflict, Warnecke and Back attempted to demonstrate the potential use of discriminant analysis for empirically evaluating and explicating comparative typological data. In summarizing their study, they state that ". . . it appears that discriminant analysis is a way of reducing the property-spaces produced through the process of substructing typological constructions. It is useful as a technique for clarifying, elaborating, and refining configurational data for use in comparative analysis of types. Moreover, it is possible through the use of this technique to establish the reality of types as discrete entities. Finally, the dimensionality of types, which distinguishes them from points on a single continuum, becomes, through this process, a matter for empirical determination rather than an implicit assumption. Through this process additional information regarding the relationship among complex systemic patterns may be obtained." [36] Although it is too early to tell how utilitarian the technique of multiple discriminant analysis will be in refining typological analysis, it is evident that the family of multivariate technique constitutes a potentially valuable resource for such refinement. The translation of types, usually somewhat impressionistically constructed initially into variate language and then back into types again through the filter of data, is what we have termed the full *cognitive loop*. Historically, this loop has rarely been completed since we have either left the types in their initial formulation, or let the variates stand outside of a construction in any configurational sense of phenomena.

35. R. B. Warnecke and K. W. Back, "Multiple Discriminant Analysis and the Constructed Typology: An Attempt at Quantifying Typologies for Comparative Analysis" (in press).
36. Ibid.

One final problem area to be explored is the relation of types to socio-logical theory. Again it is necessary to point out that types vary widely in their function, depending on their structure and the purposes for which they were constructed. They can be used for classificatory or descriptive pur-poses, as heuristic devices, and as methodological conveniences. It is also important to note, however, that types function as theory. This capability is built into them, since as composites they are given a structure with func-tional consequences, and hence types are *systems*. Systems exist, they are really "there" in the phenomenal world. Systems of *a* man, *a* family, *a* bu-reau, *a* university, *a* society are there to be discovered, but man, family, bureau, university, and society exist in the abstract as typified forms of the intellectual construct *social system*. In their abstract character they repre-sent, in varied ways and in varying approximation, the phenomena of rele-vance to them as types. In short, types represent phenomena in both a classificatory sense (a relation of similarity contrasting them with all other phenomena) and in systemic sense (structural-functional relations main-tained in the social process). A clear distinction between the properties of class and of system is essential here.[37]

Class	*System*
Relations of similarity	Relations of interconnectedness
Relations simple	Relations complex
Without form	Characteristic form
No quality of integration: coordinated by similarity	Integrated-coordinated by interdependence
Members may be moved about without violence to them or to class	Units may not be moved about without violence to them or to system
No cohesion between members of a class	Units cohere and thereby isolate the system from the rest of the universe
No functional relationship between members	Functional consistency
An aggregate	A genuine whole, having a structure
The sum of its parts	Organic unity: not the sum of its constituent units

Relations of both class and system are there in the phenomena, they are equally real. Classes and systems as they are perceived and constructed by the social scientist, however, are differentially abstract. They represent dif-ferent ways of perceiving order in the phenomena. The ubiquitous types perform the very significant function of linking these two fundamentally

37. Adapted from Radcliffe-Brown, p. 22.

different modes of cognitively ordering phenomena. It is from class that we draw our indicators (properties, attributes, criteria) from which we construct types as systems theoretically representative of the phenomena defined as falling within the scope of the type. It is from system that we substruct our indicators to investigate the nature and representativeness of this scope. Moreover, it is in this process of traveling the cognitive loop that we develop the ability to specify statements about bureau rather than *a* bureau, about family rather than *a* family, and so forth. The type is gradually transformed from an initial impressionistic, very hypothetical formulation, an uninterpreted theoretical system, into an interpreted theoretical system with defined *probable* relations to phenomena. In practice, types or typologies are a sort of poor man's system which have the potential for conversion into theoretically interpreted systems with specified domains of relevance. Such conversion requires the movement through an orderly process of inquiry, such as the one specified above by Lazarsfeld. Since this is not likely to happen with any degree of frequency, given our propensity to construct and utilize types in the most impressionistic ways for a wide variety of purposes, it is pertinent to suggest what appears to be the primary danger in typologizing. Historically, it has been repeatedly suggested that this danger lies in the reification of the types by the scholars who created or adapted them. Disagreement with that view is hereby registered, since, as we have indicated, types can be as real as any other conceptual scheme. The view here is that the primary danger lies in the early "freezing" of typologies and the premature reliance on any particular type or set of types as *explanatory* devices without having exposed the typology to the test of the "goodness of fit" as expressed in our description of the cognitive loop. It must be reiterated that the structure of the type as it has been constructed consists in a hypothetical relationship between a set of attributes or properties. The type is really a hypothetical or model course of action, process, structure, system, or object. When using the type as an explanatory scheme, one is really saying, in a probabilistic sense, that this is the *expected* behavior of the sect, the bureau, the profession, the feudal system, or whatever the type might be. It is the reliability requirement of this type of predictive statement that must give us pause with respect to imputing explanation to typologies which have not traversed the cognitive loop.

Another aspect of this treatment of types as systems makes it relevant to comment on their relation to the most general level of conceptual development in sociology. The generally *ad hoc* construction of types for very pragmatic purposes has led many people to assume that types are antisystematic, indeed, antitheoretical. Parsons, for example, has commented on the extreme difficulty of constructing a general conceptual system with a utilization of typologies. Ironically, the most general formulation of Parsons, encompassing a complex of disciplines, not just sociology, is essentially a framework of typifications. As noted by Tiryakian, "The 'theory of action'

developed by Talcott Parsons and associates not only owes much to Weber for its inspiration but is also essentially a complex theory of types of social actions and social structures (which transcends a narrow sociological focus); it may be seen, in terms of the present context, as an elaborate typological classification of interrelated systems of action."[38] As a high-risk interpretation it may well be that Parsons originally thought of this system as a "categorical system," but when the categories began to make "empirical sense" to him, they underwent a transformation into typifications.

Within the context of action theory, the notion of the social system probably is the most powerful ordering construct in sociology. Our familiar distinction must be made between the social system as an intellectual construct, model, or type of system, and social systems as "going concerns," as phenomena. All systems of real life, such as a particular society, community, corporation, or family, are open systems. They are interacting with their environment, which includes other social systems, in many and varied ways. Empirically we recognize that these interactive foci or relational clusters which we view as social systems are always involved with, and interlinked with, other social systems. Their autonomy and isolation are always relative rather than absolute, and *de facto* they are always, to varying degrees and in widely varied ways, a part of a more extensive network of social relationships within which they are nested. For purpose of analysis, however, it is necessary to assume that in the application of the intellectual construct of social system to particular real life systems, the operation of the system is affected only by specifiable conditions previously established in the environment and by relations among the elements of the system obtaining at the time of the analysis. The domain of relevance of the construct social system is, on the one hand, broad enough to encompass all relational clusters conceivable as social systems despite variations in type, and, on the other hand, always so delimited that it never completely or perfectly represents the complexities, actualities, and uniqueness of any social system as an active going concern. There is nothing unusual about this, since it is in the nature of all constructs and analyses. However, consistent failure to recognize this has resulted in the imputation of certain difficulties to sociological analysis—particularly with reference to the problem of conceptualizing and explaining social change—that are not inherent in sociological analysis but, on the contrary, are reflective of the stage of development of that analysis.

Our ability to utilize the construct of social system, particularly in comparative work, is contingent upon our ability to distinguish similarities and differences between and within *types* of systems. This requires a specification of the application of the intellectual construct to empirical phenomena. It is in this sense that we maintain that types and typologies function as theory.

38. Tiryakian, "Typological Classification," p. 183.

Selected Substantive Sociological Problems

Sociology is a pluralistic, highly diversified and largely uncodified discipline. In its major development it is primarily a product of the twentieth century although it has roots that go a very long way back in the history of social philosophy. At the present time sociology has developed to a point where certain key theoretical conflicts have emerged and require solution for future expansion and proper development of the field. There is reason to believe that research efforts to solve these conflicts will not only have a profound impact on our knowledge of social behavior, but will also make a significant contribution to the solution of a variety of social problems.

This prognosis is, of course, dependent upon a great many factors. The contemporary "sociological explosion" constituted by a rapid increase in trained manpower, numerous methodological developments, sharply increased technical capability, greatly accelerated theoretical exploration, and greatly expanded and extended views of the range and type of sociological problems, not only is strikingly visible in the traditional strongholds of sociology, but is also noteworthy in the non-Western sectors of the world. In magnitude and scope the problems under investigation range from the anonymity of macro- and global sociology to the highly personalized "view from within" of phenomenological sociology, from large-scale comparative study on the international scene to the most elegantly controlled "little" experiment in the social psychology laboratory. One can prophesy with a high degree of confidence that this approach in magnitude and scope, previously unknown, will require a great increase in typologizing—in the cognitive structuring of the observational field. A primary function of types is to identify, simplify, and order data so that they may be described in terms which make them comparable. They function in this way at any level of abstraction, and hence can be utilized with respect to problems varying from a limited to a very broad scope. Indeed, a primary role of the constructed type would seem to be that of a "sensitizing device." In effect, a type constitutes a reduction from the complex to the simple; hence the careful construction and use of types, as an intermediate procedure, can potentially make many large-scale problems accessible to more refined methodology and technique. The following areas of general theoretical concern, conflict, vitality, and promise are cited as areas in which typologizing would be particularly helpful in the years ahead.

At the most general level of theoretical concern, one finds the issue of the capability of modern structural-functionalism or systems analysis to deal adequately with problems of social change. In the eyes of many sociologists, social change constitutes the most significant of all social phenomena, and any general theoretical perspective that has a limited capability of dealing with or indeed predicting sectors of change is looked upon as being less

than adequate. To many sociologists it is evident that social systems analysis is among the sectors of sociology in a state of readiness for imminent rapid development in theoretical specification and empirical application. The social system as a theoretical construct is applicable to human relationships at levels varying from those of two persons up to and including society itself. Further explication of the nature of social systems provides us with an increasingly reliable context within which to make functional interpretations of research in many diverse and limited areas of social behavior. Such interpretations enable us to "make sense" of or "fit together" many seemingly discrete bits of knowledge about social behavior. As a consequence, a greater depth of understanding of the structure and function of American society as well as of societies in general is obtained. Such advance in knowledge is crucially related to the potential for success of any planning for, initiation of, and implementation of change in society. Continued doubt of this capability in the field, however, by its very existence, is at once stimulating an expanded attack upon problems of social change and further explicating the theoretical construct of the social system.

Sociology has not developed evenly around the world; at this moment in time it has achieved its highest stage of technical development in the United States. It has long been recognized, however, that if the discipline is to realize its full potential, it will have to internationalize its activities and inquiry. If it is to develop the capability of expressing theories and propositions about society, and about societal life generally, then it has to conduct inquiry in societies in all sectors of the world. It is inevitable that when one frees his curiosity from the particularities of nation or area, he will see many situations in other parts of the world comparable in certain respects to those local interests. As a consequence, there will be a search for similarities and differences, for the general and recurrent in contrast to the merely particular and localized. The concern with that which is common to man under diverse circumstances constitutes the "seed bed" of the social sciences. The study of social institutions began and continues to lead the social sciences to emphasize a comparative point of view. The study of social, political, and economic systems as systems has similarly emphasized those components of man's behavior which are persistent through time and space. Comparative study may be defined as that approach which is concerned with the systematic and explicit comparison of social phenomena in two or more societies. Cross-societal (cross-cultural or cross-national) comparison is the essential ingredient. Intrasocietal comparisons may or may not be made concurrently with these cross-societal comparisons. Clearly it is intrasocietal comparisons which will continue to draw the main effort of sociologists and other social scientists in all societies. Nevertheless, comparative study is a broadly inclusive field and is rapidly drawing increased research effort. It contains a great variety of methodological strategies varying from holistic, descriptive analyses to studies which rigorously test theoretically

derived, or at least theoretically relevant, propositions and hypotheses. In brief, comparative sociology has the very difficult task of progressively specifying which theories and propositions hold for societies generally, which for only certain classes or types of society, and which for only individual societies. There is increasing recognition that pursuit of inquiry with this explicitly comparative aim is essential if sociology is to realize its potential as a science of society.

Another issue of concern in the field is whether or not sociology has been ahistorical. This raises the question of whether or not the most typical approach of sociology to social phenomena can really have any validity if it persists in largely ignoring the temporal dimension, the chronology of development of the social institutions or systems with which it is concerned. In brief, it has been suggested that the tendency of sociologists to look at things as they are at a moment in time has limited their ability to understand them other than superficially. This criticism and concern has resulted in the emergence in sociology of an interest in and an increased capability of reworking historical materials. The utilization of a behavioral or sociologistic perspective in contrast to the usual idiographic perspective of historians promises to shed new light on the import and contemporary meaning of historical events. Understanding of present behavioral modes and the structure and function of modern social institutions and systems is deepened and enriched through the addition of the historical dimension. For instance, the utilization of analysis of historical data greatly enhances our understanding of family structure and the behavior of children in contemporary society.

Sociology has had a long-term interest in the study of formal organization. Traditionally, the study of such organizations as business firms, labor unions, farm cooperatives, military units, and so forth, has been approached either by developing abstract theories of complex organization, typically relating to variant forms of bureaucracy, or by case studies of single organizations. The hiatus between the two approaches has been based upon the assumption that large bureaucracies are so complex that it is impossible empirically to investigate more than one or two at a time. Recently however, and in part due to the developing computer technology, it has been possible to initiate a different approach, namely, a systematic comparative study of samples of many organizations at a time. These studies explicitly confine themselves to the formal characteristics of organization such as size, the relative proportion of administrative personnel, the shape of the hierarchical pyramid, the written rules or codes, and the degree of professional training on the staff. This comparative approach continues to be the subject of criticism because it ignores informal relations, unofficial practices, personal experiences of the membership, their morale, their attitudes, and so on. In response to this internal criticism, one may say that the core of organizational theory consists of an understanding of the relations among the basic formal characteristics of organization. Advances in such a theory require

systematic, quantitative comparison of organizations. The issue as it has been traditionally posed is in no sense resolved; on the other hand, it has effectively stimulated a whole new approach to the study of organization. In brief, one can suggest that the two opposing approaches—that is, formulating a theory of complex organization on the one hand, and case study of the informal processes that go on within a specific organization, on the other hand are not really competitive but are mutually complementary approaches to the same phenomenon. The addition of the capability of dealing with multiple organizations, based upon our ability to manage samples of organizations rather than merely samples of individuals, means that we are now in a position to specify more adequately the varying characteristics of formal organizations as they function within diverse settings. The obvious centrality of organizational life in modern societies suggests that it is of great importance that we better understand the nature of organizations and the relations of individuals to them.

Clearly, one of the great problems facing the world, and in varying degrees its member nations, is the problem of population control. There is an evident public concern with the serious implications for the future of present rates of population growth. This, of course, leads to a concern for delineating the necessary conditions for vastly reduced birth rates. In the field of social demography, at present, there are at least three different levels of optimism, each with some supportive research evidence. The most optimistic researchers assume that if a cheap, efficacious, and easily administered contraceptive is devised, and knowledge of it widely diffused, birth rates will fall to acceptable and manageable levels. Many researchers take the less optimistic view that until a group obtains middle-class urban status and aspirations, its birth rate will not decline substantially. And finally, opening up an even more pessimistic view, data from the most industrially advanced urban societies suggest that even under those relatively ideal conditions, families will choose to have enough children to produce a population explosion. Obviously, the inconclusive situation in which we now find ourselves strongly implies that continued research toward the specification of those conditions and factors conducive to population reduction is of the utmost importance, not merely nationally but internationally.

Closely related to population problems generally are those of age structure and distribution. The emphasis on youth and the development of a discernible "youth culture" in American, as well as in other societies, appears to have grown stronger with general shifts in the age structure, including dramatic increases in the number of aged people. The consequences for society of having rapidly increasing numbers of older people while the predominant value orientation favors youth and things youthful needs extensive examination. Paradoxically, the increased propensity of youth to revolt against adult authority and values takes place in an epoch in which the young seem to be more advantaged and rewarded than ever before. At the

same time, the achievement of a long life for a larger number of people is often accompanied by lessened social rewards and reduced gratifications. The phenomenon of intergenerational relationships needs serious study against the backdrop of the changing age structure in society. One must hasten to point out that this is not merely an American phenomenon but is occurring in varying degrees in many parts of the world.

Another one of the traditional areas of interest in sociology has been that of urban life and the process of urbanization. As a consequence, American sociology has accumulated a considerable body of theoretical and substantive knowledge on the ecology of the city and the problems of urban living. Today virtually everyone recognizes that one of the great problems facing American society is the restructuring of its cities. The problems of urban housing, residential segregation, outmoded transportation systems, inadequate educational facilities, environmental pollution, and the inadequacies of social control, to mention only a few, have obviously reached crisis proportions. These problems are receiving a great deal of public and political attention. The current situation, despite our long urban sociological tradition, demands new approaches and intensified research efforts if workable solutions to urban problems are to be found in the foreseeable future. This will obviously require the efforts of people in many disciplines, but it is essential that additional sociological knowledge of urbanization and urban life be provided if urban conditions are to be ameliorated.

Recently an area of inquiry, which for want of a better name is called economic sociology, has developed out of the realization that economic growth is dependent upon a broad range of social factors operative in a nation. The economy is nested in a whole complex of social institutions which are either in restraint of, or are conducive to, economic development. Clearly, the acceleration of economic development takes place not in a vacuum but within the context of broader social change. The focus of sociological interest is on the significance of the wide range of social institutions that are prerequisite to or essential concomitants of economic development in a society. One problem of interest is the relation between political and economic institutions and the indirect as well as the direct influences of each on the other. For instance, stable political authority is known to be an important prerequisite for economic development. Another prerequisite is the stimulating or retarding effect on economic growth of a wide variety of social conditions, such as a society's family structure, its fertility patterns, its type and level of school systems, its social status and class divisions, and the belief and value orientations of its people. Advancing knowledge in this field has much potential significance for increasing our ability to recognize what has to be done in order to raise the standard of living in underdeveloped countries and to improve economic conditions generally. Economic sociology has barely begun to realize its potential, but it promises much for the future.

Another sociological issue that seems to have provided a very great stimulus to current research concerns the processes whereby an individual learns to play social roles, the process of socialization. The importance of the family in the development of a child into a functioning adult has been a long-time concern of sociologists as well as psychologists. Recent research has raised considerable doubt about the effects of early infant discipline on later personality, and has suggested instead the critical importance of early cognitive perceptual experience on later social learning, and hence on later social capability. There is a clear and evident need for further research on these disparate conclusions, especially on the extent to which early deprivation can be overcome or modified by later remedial programs. Studies of periods beyond the earliest childhood are needed to determine the lasting effects of early school and adolescent experiences on later behavior. Are there really critical periods for the establishment of particular attitudes, values, and personal skills? Moreover, what are the carry-over qualities of these attitudes, values, and skills? What are the limits within which re-socialization can operate in adolescence, adulthood, and in the advanced years?

Another subfield of inquiry where a live issue has been very stimulating is that of deviant behavior. In the area of deviant behavior there exist two opposing viewpoints which involve the relative importance of the social definition of deviance as the crucial factor in the development of behavior running counter to that which is considered to be normal. Some sociologists assert that delinquency, drug addiction, alcoholism, and other forms of deviant behavior have causes that are largely contained within the individual, and basically stem from early patterns of socialization and interaction within the family. Others take the view that the differential recognition and processing of potential deviants plays a significant role in creating and maintaining deviant behavior. It is suggested that the social process of defining (or labeling) the deviant creates, or at least heavily contributes to, the phenomenon. This leads one to suggest that further developments in the study of deviant behavior will require extensive, long-range observation and analysis of social organizations, in addition to the observation of isolated individuals in their social settings. The relation of deviant to normal behavior is not a fixed or static thing, and the social mechanisms that operate to constrain deviant behavior have to be developed out of a broader understanding of the factors conducive to deviance from the social norms.

These are just a few of the sectors of sociology which have recently experienced heightened interest and increased research activity. Many other sectors could be mentioned. For example, one should take note of the great activity centered around the simulation of social processes; the study of the transfer of ideas and modes of organization between highly developed and underdeveloped countries; the study of political behavior, particularly including the distribution of power and the factors involved in differential

political participation; the study of the critical social conditions and situations prerequisite for scientific and artistic creativity; exploration of the factors underlying the acceptance or rejection and diffusion of innovation; investigation of the influence of legal institutions on social behavior; concern with problems of manpower, adaptability of the labor force, the changing occupational structure; the study of communication systems varying from those concerned with the mass level all the way down to those operative at the level of an intimate face-to-face relationship; study of group formation and the dynamics of small groups in particular; and examination of family structure and its changes especially with respect to alterations in social stratification. These are additional sectors of vital inquiry in the field of sociology.

By and large, the discipline continues to develop in an uncoordinated and highly fragmented fashion. It remains a "little science" and in all likelihood will, for many years to come. The discipline is still heavily based upon the interests and motivations of the individual investigator or scholar, although there has been some tendency for collective or team research and the development of research organizations to facilitate larger-scale inquiry into social phenomena. As the internationalizing of sociology is accelerated, one may make the optimistic assumption that the discipline will, in the relatively near future, make increasingly significant contributions to our knowledge about social man, and hence, at least indirectly, make some contributions to the solution of his practical problems. The scope and magnitude of the sociological enterprise has become quite impressive; indeed, it is rather overwhelming to many of us who joined the discipline in a simpler, more parochial state of its development. It is hypothesized here that this rapid expansion in very diverse areas of sociological inquiry will require a considerable increase in typologizing. Typologies can, as a form of intermediate symbolism, aid significantly in helping us to know more precisely what mechanisms or structural relations are being postulated with respect to a problem area in furnishing the cognitive maps so essential for the delineation of increasingly specific objects and relations.

In Sum

An analysis of the process of typification has been made, starting from the premise that it is a natural aspect of the social process. Typification, as a central feature of cognition, is the development of a selective and persistent attitude of an actor toward his environment. Typification is a process in conduct which organizes the field of action so that social interaction can proceed on an orderly basis. In the socialization process, by taking over the typifications that people habitually assume under given conditions, the structure of society is preserved in the individual. This takes place within

a differentiated society, implying that there are distinguishable subsystems of action maintained and altered by different typifications.

These typifications as they exist in societal activity constitute a given in the form of existential types for the sociologist and are representative of the structure within which he perceives his problems to lie. The order which the sociologist is committed to "capturing" is one of specification, reduction, and relationship. One aspect of this capturing of order is described as the process of typification. Within the realm of sociological inquiry this process is manifest in the construction of types and typologies. Typologies must be understood as representative of a pragmatic research methodology and as being subordinate to the aim of research, which is the establishment of uniformities of explanatory value.

We may legitimately ask whether, by advocating the typological approach, we join some dwindling group of obsolescent scholars and favor some antiquated method. It is true that typology, in its existential sense, is as old as society and, in its constructed sense, as old as scientific reflection on society. On the other hand, it is also true that all the abuses, past and present, of type construction could not eliminate the typological approach from sociological investigation. Moreover, to quote Weber, ". . . there are sciences to which eternal youth is granted, and the historical disciplines are among them—all those to which the eternally onward flowing stream of culture perpetually brings new problems. At the very heart of their task lies not only the transiency of *all* . . . types, *but* also at the same time the inevitability of *new* ones." [39] Furthermore, we can cite the great increase of sociological activity and the vastly expanded range of sociological problems being investigated as evidence of the continuing need of typologizing. Types and typologies are demonstrably useful as composite theoretical-methodological devices; the fundamental question is, therefore, how we can make them more useful within the expanding realm of sociological inquiry. The "working answer" has to lie in the more sophisticated methodological explication and theoretical construction of the future.

39. Max Weber, *The Methodology of the Social Sciences,* trans. and ed. E. A. Shils and H. A. Finch (Glencoe: Free Press, 1949), p. 104.

10.

The Formalization of Sociological Theory

Hubert M. Blalock, Jr.

Hubert M. Blalock, Jr., was born in Baltimore, Maryland, in 1926 and was educated at Dartmouth College, Brown University, and the University of North Carolina (Ph.D.). He has taught at the University of Michigan and Yale University and is presently professor of sociology at the University of North Carolina at Chapel Hill. His principal interests are in theory construction, general methodology, applied statistics, and race relations. He is the author of Social Statistics, Causal Inferences in Nonexperimental Research, Toward a Theory of Minority-Group Relations, *and* Theory Construction: From Verbal to Mathematical Formulations.

I am grateful to the National Science Foundation for partial support of this research and to Ann B. Blalock, Charles E. Bowerman, M. Richard Cramer, Amos H. Hawley, and Alan C. Kerckhoff for their helpful criticisms of the original manuscript.

$\mathcal{T}$he main thesis of this chapter is that the formalization of existing verbal theory in sociology is highly desirable for a number of important reasons. Formalization, which involves stating the theory in deductive form, requires the careful specification of variables. It also forces one to make explicit the numerous assumptions that are necessary in deriving testable propositions and in appraising internal consistency. It makes one more fully aware of the limitations of the theory and the necessity of choosing among alternative assumptions at each decision point. Constructive criticism is thereby facilitated, and one can modify the theory by changing the propositions and assumptions a few at a time until it is made sufficiently complex to provide a more adequate understanding of the real world. Furthermore, formalization of the assumptions necessary for *testing* the theory may provide a better understanding of methodological problems encountered in relating theory and research.

Sociologists are of course very familiar with this theme, since it has been championed by numerous scholars, not only by those identified with mathematical model building, but also by men like Merton, Homans, and Zetterberg.[1] There is also a rather extensive technical literature on the

1. See Robert K. Merton, *Social Theory and Social Structure* (Glencoe: Free Press, 1957), chaps. 2 and 3; George C. Homans, "Contemporary Theory in Sociology," in R. E. L. Faris, ed., *Handbook of Modern Sociology* (Chicago: Rand, 1964), chap. 25; and Hans L. Zetterberg, *On Theory and Verification in Sociology* (Totowa, New Jersey: Bedminster Press, 1963).

subject.[2] My purpose here is to summarize nontechnically what I consider to be some of the most important features of the formalization process. In so doing I hope to communicate both the major advantages of formalization and some of the most difficult methodological problems that formalization may force us to face. It is my contention that these problems have always been with us but that they are most likely to be brought into the open when we take as our task the goal of making our assumptions as explicit as possible.

The reader who is facing some of these issues for the first time is likely to feel overwhelmed by the complexity of it all. This is as it should be. The construction of really testable theories is a highly difficult task, and it cannot realistically be undertaken without a serious study of methodology. In this chapter we intend to raise a number of questions, and to point out difficulties, without fully answering any of them. One of the reasons why simple answers cannot be given is that the resolutions to a given problem often involve rather technical points that are beyond the scope of this chapter. In many instances, while we may know something about the general strategy of attack that might be used, we do not presently possess either the detailed knowledge or the resources to resolve the difficulty. But certainly it is important to raise the questions in order to move in the right direction.

The major message I wish to convey, then, is that the issues are complex but that there is available an ample technical literature that is well worth mastering in spite of the effort that this will require. In emphasizing problems and methodological difficulties one always runs the risk of prematurely discouraging one's readers. Had I been aware of many of these complexities before I plunged into causal modeling, I might have given up the venture as hopeless. But I have come to see that there *are* ways of resolving each particular issue, though none is ever completely satisfactory. I have also become convinced that formalization, and the explicit statement of one's assumptions, is an absolutely necessary step that must be taken. At the same time it should be recognized that formalization, as a process, is always a matter of degree and that it will be manifestly impos-

2. While there is an extensive literature on formalization within the field of philosophy of science, I have found the most useful discussions to be centered in the applied multivariate analysis literature, particularly in econometrics. I have attempted to summarize much of this literature in H. M. Blalock, *Causal Inferences in Nonexperimental Research* (Chapel Hill: University of North Carolina Press, 1964), and in H. M. Blalock, *Theory Construction* (Englewood Cliffs: Prentice-Hall, 1969). The following are especially recommended: Carl F. Christ, *Econometric Models and Methods* (New York: Wiley, 1966); John Johnston, *Econometric Methods* (New York: McGraw, 1963); Franklin M. Fisher, *The Identification Problem in Econometrics* (New York: McGraw, 1966); William J. Baumol, *Economic Dynamics* (New York: Macmillan, 1959); Paul A. Samuelson, *Foundations of Economic Analysis* (Cambridge: Harvard University Press, 1947); Herbert A. Simon, *Models of Man* (New York: Wiley, 1957); and James S. Coleman, *Introduction to Mathematical Sociology* (Glencoe: Free Press, 1964).

sible to make *all* assumptions explicit. It would therefore be foolish to become immobilized at any given stage because of the fear that some portion of one's argument has been left vague or entirely implicit.

Most sociologists would undoubtedly agree with this general objective in principle, though perhaps some would argue that it is at present premature to become seriously engaged in the process of formalization. I suspect that behind the latter position there is the rather natural hesitation of sociologists and other social scientists to oversimplify reality by specifying a small number of variables and committing themselves on a few of the many possible assumptions that could be made in a given context. It does seem to be true that deductive systems should not be overly complex. As soon as one becomes involved with reasonably complex interrelationships among as many as eight or ten variables, he will begin to see just how complicated the testing process can be. Still, an adequate understanding of social reality will require many more variables than this, and the temptation is always to introduce additional complicating factors before the implications of a simpler theory are well understood. This tendency of sociologists to prefer the more complex but loosely knit verbal theories may very well be the greatest single barrier to formalization that exists in contemporary sociology.

Homans has forcefully argued that theories must contain propositions that interrelate variables.[3] Conceptual schemes and typologies, no matter how elaborate, do not constitute theories, though they may be useful starting points in the theory-building process. As such schemes become more and more complex, and as each scholar adds his own modifications and new definitions of concepts, the tendency is to forget the propositions altogether and to concentrate on the frameworks and perspectives. This seems to be one reason why "sociological theory" is sometimes identified with the history of social thought and with discussions of specific men, rather than the propositions they have stated. Once we have learned to focus more on the propositions and assumptions themselves, as contrasted with who said what, we will be more likely to produce cumulative results. Therefore in these pages I shall concentrate primarily on such propositions and assumptions, and not on a critique of existing sociological theory.

Also, sociologists who call themselves "theorists" have given far too little attention to the verification process, and in particular to the question of how the theory is to be tested and the parameters estimated. A fundamental point that will be emphasized in this essay is that one must pay a certain price for complexity, and in fact there will be many theories that are inherently untestable unless they are modified. This is not simply because the important variables cannot be measured. Even where all of them can be measured without error, there may be too many unknowns

3. Homans, "Contemporary Theory."

in the system. Formalization of the assumptions necessary in the testing process can help to make this fact explicit.

By a completely formalized theory I mean a deductive theory containing primitive or undefined concepts, derived concepts defined in terms of the primitive ones, axioms or assumptions, and derived theorems. There must also be certain rules for the derivation process. I assume that what constitutes a deductive theory is reasonably well understood on a practical level. An example of a deductive system would be Euclidean geometry. Our most formal languages in which deductive systems can be expressed are of course logic and mathematics. But we must also be concerned with less than fully developed deductive systems, and with the *process* of formalization. At this stage, ordinary verbal language can be used to good advantage, and certainly a very important part of the formalization process will involve taking existing theories and trying to make them as explicit as possible. This will consist of such simple devices as italicizing or numbering the propositions, defining the important variables, and searching for hidden assumptions that might be used to interrelate the explicit propositions. Other devices, such as attempting to diagram one's theory, should also be useful. Ultimately, the resulting verbal theory can then be translated into mathematical form.

I shall be concerned in this essay with causal assertions of the form "An increase in X will produce an increase in Y." Such assertions may be on any level of generality, ranging from highly abstract variables appropriate on the societal level to much more specific variables such as educational discrimination or marital satisfaction. This should be distinguished from Homans and Braithwaite's kind of "explanation," which refers to the process of subsuming particular phenomena under more general ones.[4]

Constructing and Elaborating the Model

Let us begin with a rather typical example that does not involve any highly abstract concepts or unusual methodological difficulties. Suppose that a social scientist wishes to study racial discrimination. After reviewing the relevant theory and the empirical studies most closely related to the topic of interest, he is likely to formulate a general causal argument in which certain assumptions are made about the most significant kinds of variables that must be considered. Many times this theory remains completely implicit. Or it may be stated as a simple assertion, for example, that discrimination is influenced by personality characteristics, specific prejudices toward the minority, various situational factors, and the behavior of the minority itself. One might also note that discrimination, in

4. Ibid. See also R. B. Braithwaite, *Scientific Explanation* (Cambridge: Cambridge University Press, 1953).

turn, will affect inequality rates and minority behavior, which will feed back and either reinforce or reduce the original level of prejudice. Perhaps this is as far as the very general theory will be taken.

A simple step beyond this kind of verbal theorizing is to draw a diagram in which each major kind of variable is blocked off from the others, thus making it easy to visualize the various combinations of variables whose interrelations will need to be studied. One possible schematic diagram is shown in Figure 1. In diagrams like this it is very tempting to draw

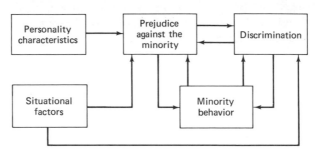

Figure 1. Major blocks or variables

arrows leading from each block to every other block. For example, it might be argued that prejudice directly affects minority behavior, which in turn affects prejudice. But as we shall see later, if one allows for the possibility that every variable affects every other variable, there will be too many unknowns in the system for empirical tests or for estimation of the parameters.[5] Though such a theory may represent reality more adequately than a simpler one, it may not imply any testable predictions; its utility would thus be destroyed.

According to convention, one can draw an arrow whenever there is thought to be a direct causal connection between two blocks of variables. For example, the linkage between prejudice and discrimination is taken as direct in the model of Figure 1, with the understanding that directness is always relative to the variables that have been included in the system.[6] It would always be possible to insert intervening links between any pair of variables taken to be directly related in this particular system. According to Figure 1, the relationship between general personality characteristics and discrimination is taken to be indirect; these characteristics are assumed to affect prejudice which in turn leads to discrimination.

Notice that in this model, two blocks of variables are shown to be exogenous, meaning that there is no feedback to either of these blocks.

5. The fact that there will be too many unknowns is of course not a good reason for ruling out reciprocal causation. But it does mean that some way must be found to reduce the number of unknowns relative to the number of pieces of empirical information. This question will be discussed in the next section.
6. I have discussed the problem of the directness of causal links and the mathematical representation of causal models in *Causal Inferences,* chaps. 1 and 2.

Neither general personality characteristics nor situational factors are affected by discrimination, minority behavior, or prejudice. These exogenous variables are the givens which cannot be explained by the theory in question. They can be considered the independent variables in the system, even though they may be empirically intercorrelated. Of course a different theory may see these same variables as endogenous, to be explained in terms of a different set of exogenous factors. It turns out that there must always be some exogenous variables in any testable theory. If all variables influence each other, there will be no place to start, so to speak. I will touch upon this rather technical question in the next section.

Certain of the variables in this system are what are sometimes referred to as "psychological" variables, whereas others are "sociological." This distinction is of course very much overworked. The social scientist who genuinely wishes to explain a phenomenon such as discrimination or educational desegregation should not be too concerned about such a distinction. More important, however, is the fact that certain of the variables pertain to individuals, whereas others deal with group properties. When these variables are fitted together in the same theory, one can automatically anticipate a number of conceptual problems, as well as measurement decisions relating to how the individuals are to be aggregated, or how the contextual variables or situational factors relate to individual behavior. This is a real theoretical problem that cannot be avoided; it will almost always come to the surface once a theory has been explicitly stated.[7]

Elaboration of the Model

A simple scheme such as that indicated in Figure 1 has the useful function of orienting the investigator and serving as a checklist, but it is obviously not specific enough to stand as an adequate theory. Each block will contain a number of particular variables, which must be explicitly identified and interrelated. Furthermore, the linkages between blocks must be specified more exactly. For example, the diagram indicates no feedback effects from *discrimination* to *situational factors,* which are taken as exogenous. But as soon as one begins to list specific situational factors such as political variables, the relative size of the minority, competition with the minority, environmental influences, and so forth, it may become apparent that over the long run some of these variables should be taken as dependent on discrimination. Over a three- or four-year period, a variable such as minority percentage may not be influenced to any noticeable degree by existing levels of discrimination. But over a longer period, when one ex-

7. Problems of aggregation do not seem to have been given adequate attention in the sociological literature. For an excellent summary statement of the problem see Coleman, *Mathematical Sociology,* chap. 2. For a review of the literature relating to so-called "ecological correlations" see O. D. Duncan, R. P. Cuzzort, and B. Duncan, *Statistical Geography* (Glencoe: Free Press, 1961). See also Peter M. Blau, "Structural Effects," *American Sociological Review,* 25 (April, 1960), 178-193.

plicitly allows for migration as one form of minority behavior, this factor may feed back to affect the relative size of the minority. If so, the original schematic diagram may have to be modified to allow for this feedback. This may require splitting up the original block of *situational factors,* so as to remove those that are not truly exogenous. The reasons why this may be necessary will be discussed in the next section.

One of the major failings of much sociological research is the inadequate attention given to interrelationships among variables taken to be independent. Although one may note that many such variables are intercorrelated, one might think that this fact can easily be handled through the use of multivariate controlling procedures. But the matter is not this simple. In the first place, high intercorrelations among independent variables may produce very large sampling errors that result in erroneous inferences.[8] Secondly, whenever two or more independent variables are highly correlated, one must always ask why this should be the case. At least one of them may be taken as dependent on some other variable, and this will necessitate working with simultaneous equations, rather than with a single equation and a single dependent variable. Simultaneous equation systems involve more complications than do single equations, and we shall see that there will be many equation systems that have no determinate solutions.

One way to begin the elaboration procedure is to attempt to specify the most important variables appearing in each of the separate blocks, and to indicate as well as one can just how they are expected to be interrelated. Let us focus on the two blocks *discrimination* and *minority behavior.* There are of course many types of discrimination, as well as certain ambiguities as to just what one means by the notion of discrimination. At this stage of the theory-building process, the need for conceptual clarification and careful measurement will inevitably come to the focus of attention. In the case of discrimination, one might find it useful to distinguish between (a) actual discriminatory behavior by individual members of the dominant group, (b) aggregate measures of discriminatory behavior, if these can be obtained, and (c) resultants of discrimination, such as educational or economic inequalities of various kinds. In fact, "discrimination" is often measured in terms of these resultants, although the exact nature of the linkage between aggregated discriminatory behavior and such inequalities may remain unspecified prior to formalization.

For the time being, let us set aside the problem of linking up discriminatory behavior with inequalities, as this will be considered later when we

---

8. This problem is discussed in the econometric literature under the heading of *multicollinearity.* In general, the higher the intercorrelations among the independent variables, relative to their correlations with the dependent variable, the greater the standard errors of partial slopes and correlations. See Johnston, *Econometric Methods,* pp. 201-207, and Christ, *Econometric Models,* pp. 387-390, and 478-480.

discuss measurement. Focusing on discriminatory behavior, we would obviously need to distinguish among various areas or kinds of discrimination, and how these may be causally interrelated. For illustrative purposes consider the following variables:

E = educational discrimination, or the withholding of equal access to training facilities (apart from segregation);

O = occupational discrimination, or the denial of jobs or promotions to minority-group members;

P = political discrimination, or the denial of the franchise to the minority;

R = residential exclusion, or the denial of access to certain residential areas to the minority; and

S = social exclusion, or the denial of access to voluntary organizations and informal cliques.

As soon as one begins to distinguish among variables such as these, a number of decisions must be made. First, oversimplifications will be inevitable. One must ignore many kinds of discriminatory behavior, some of which are difficult to distinguish because of their overlapping nature. Second, the very process of naming various kinds of discrimination makes one aware of measurement problems. For example, the term "segregation" has been avoided in the case of the variables *residential exclusion* and *social exclusion* because of the fact that segregation will later be taken as a measured indicator of exclusion. One may count the numbers of Negroes and whites in each census tract and construct various indices of residential segregation.[9] But this involves an indirect measure of the process of exclusion, since there will be factors other than exclusion (such as income differences or minority preferences) that also help to determine segregation rates. Similarly, educational inequality may be taken as an indicator of *educational discrimination,* provided a theoretical link can be postulated between the two phenomena.

Another important decision that must be made in any particular piece of research is whether to treat each of these variables as distinct, or whether to combine them into a single indicator for the entire block. On the theoretical level, it would seem advisable to attempt to specify how the variables within each block are causally related to each other. For example, one might postulate a model as in Figure 2 in which residential exclusion R is taken as a direct cause of educational discrimination E, which in turn affects occupational discrimination O as well as R. In this model, also, political discrimination P is taken as a cause of R and as both a direct

9. Even such a comparatively simple concept as that of residential segregation generated a considerable debate, once there were serious attempts to measure it. See O. D. Duncan and B. Duncan, "A Methodological Analysis of Segregation Indexes," *American Sociological Review,* 20 (April, 1955), 210-217.

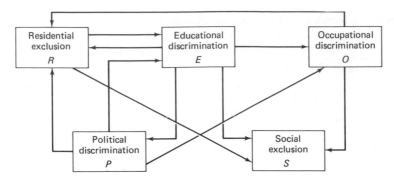

Figure 2. Discrimination variables

cause and a direct effect of educational discrimination. Occupational discrimination feeds back to affect R, and social exclusion S is taken as directly dependent on R, E, and O.

In the case of the block of variables *minority behavior*, we would likewise attempt to delineate a specific set of variables. Some of these minority reactions might be thought of as involving alternative paths (for example, apathy versus militancy), but others might be both conceptually distinct and causally interrelated. Suppose we designated the following variables:

W = degree of withdrawal from contacts with the dominant group;
A = amount of aggression against the dominant group;
V = degree to which there is block voting by the minority;
P_i = minority performance levels in various areas (for example, educational or occupational performance);
D_i = degree of minority deviance of various kinds (for example, crime rates, drug addiction, religious escapism).

We would again want to theorize about the causal connections among these variables. In some cases, a high level on one variable might produce a low level on another because of limitations of scarce resources; time (or money) spent doing one thing might reduce the amount of resources committed to another. In other instances, the linkage might even involve variables from other blocks. Thus, minority aggression might lead to punitive action on the part of the dominant group, which might result in political apathy and greater deviance of certain types. Suppose we construct a theoretical argument that could be diagrammed as in Figure 3.

Once the interrelationships among variables within each block have been specified as well as possible, attention can be focused on a reexamination of the relationships between blocks. Each time one is forced to make a decision as to whether or not to postulate a direct causal connection between a given pair of variables, either within or between blocks, he is apt to be made painfully aware of the inadequacies of his knowledge and of existing sociological theory. For example, whereas it may safely be assumed that, in general, discriminatory behavior affects minority behavior, it may be

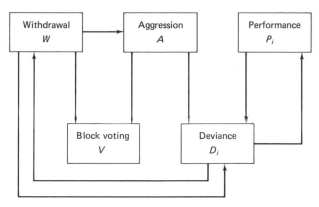

Figure 3. Minority behavior variables

much more difficult to specify exactly which of the variables in the discrimination block should be taken as direct causes of particular kinds of minority responses. Do we know enough to assume that residential exclusion helps to produce aggression, whereas educational discrimination does not? Lacking more definite knowledge, one may be tempted to draw in all possible arrows from each variable in the discrimination block to each variable in the minority behavior block. Perhaps this is an accurate assessment of reality. But, as we shall see, it may not lead to testable predictions.

Suppose, for the sake of illustration, that after careful thought it could be argued that minority behavior should not be expected to affect discrimination except through prejudice. Then one could erase the arrow leading directly from minority behavior to discrimination. This would mean that, whereas discrimination has a direct effect on minority behavior, the feedback from minority behavior to discrimination is more indirect. Perhaps this would suggest a longer time-lag in the latter case. If so, this assumption of a time-lag could be used in formulating a dynamic model that might be useful in resolving a problem created by too many unknowns in the system.[10] The major point is that an explicit formulation would help to suggest this and other kinds of specific modifications in the original theory.

The Identification Problem and Possible Resolutions

It has been suggested at several points that a theory may be inherently untestable because it contains too many unknowns.[11] This is completely apart from the question of whether each of the variables in the system can

10. Dynamic formulations will be discussed briefly below. I have attempted to deal with them more thoroughly and somewhat more technically in *Theory Construction*, chaps. 5 and 6. For still more technical discussions see Baumol, *Economic Dynamics*, Coleman, *Mathematical Sociology*, and Samuelson, *Economic Analysis*. For applications to social behavior, see Simon, *Models of Man*.
11. The literature on the identification problem is relatively technical. The most thorough discussion can be found in Fisher, *Identification Problem*. See also Christ, *Econometric Models*, chap. 8, and Blalock, *Theory Construction*, chap. 4.

be accurately measured and all disturbing influences controlled. Even with perfect measurement and no error term or unexplained variance, a theory may be untestable because it allows for too many loopholes. And if it is untestable, and therefore able to "account for" any set of data whatsoever, this means that one will be unable to use it to make specific predictions.

It can be shown that if one allows for the possibility that everything causes everything else, with unspecified parameters, then there will be an infinite number of sets of parameter values, all of which will be consistent with the same set of data. This implies that theorists can talk past one another, each arguing that a particular set of variables is "more important" than another, without there being any conceivable way of resolving the dispute by purely empirical means. Such a state of affairs is hardly desirable, but what may not be clearly recognized is that a certain price must be paid if the matter is to be resolved. An important advantage of mathematical formulations is that they can be used to tell us just how many unknowns there can be before an insoluble situation arises.

Let us consider the block of five discrimination variables, as interrelated in Figure 2. When we draw a direct arrow linking a given pair of variables, this indicates that the variable toward which an arrow is directed is to be taken as an unspecified function f_i of the variable from which the arrow originates.[12] Indirect relationships are handled by virtue of the fact that a separate equation must be written for each (endogenous) variable that has one or more arrows directed toward it. Thus, since there is no direct arrow from residential exclusion to occupational discrimination, the latter variable is not taken as an explicit function of the former. But since in this model, occupational discrimination is a function of educational discrimination, which in turn is caused by residential exclusion, we could say that occupational discrimination is an implicit function of residential exclusion. Substitutions could be made in the equation for occupational discrimination so that residential exclusion would appear in the equation.

Theoretically, however, we are interested in what are referred to as the structural equations that actually give the magnitudes of the *direct* effects of each of the variables on those other variables in the system with which it is causally connected. Once these have been specified, one can then answer all hypothetical questions about the direct and indirect changes in each variable that would be produced by a given change in any particular variable. Of course, this is an ideal that can seldom be realized in practice. But it may be possible to obtain approximate answers to this kind of ques-

12. If Y is an unspecified function of W and X, this can be represented symbolically as $Y = f(W,X)$. If there are several distinct functions, we can distinguish among them by representing them as f_1, f_2, . . . There will be only a very few general mathematical statements that can be made about such unspecified functions. Ordinarily we attempt to say something more definite about them. At the very least, one should specify the sign of the relationship and something about its shape (for example, that it is linear, or has an increasing slope).

tion, which basically deals with the evaluation of the relative importance of variables in an interrelated system.

It will be convenient to shift to a more standard notation in which the endogenous or mutually dependent variables are designated as X_i. The exogenous variables that are not to be explained by the theory are ordinarily designated as Z_i. Although the functions selected may be relatively complex, it will be necessary in this essay to deal only with the linear additive case, which can often be used as a reasonable approximation. Our notation will be as follows:

Residential exclusion $(R) = X_1 = f_1(E, O, P) = f_1(X_2, X_3, X_4)$
Educational discrimination $(E) = X_2 = f_2(R, P) = f_2(X_1, X_4)$
Occupational discrimination $(O) = X_3 = f_3(E, P) = f_3(X_2, X_4)$
Political discrimination $(P) = X_4 = f_4(E) = f_4(X_2)$
Social exclusion $(S) = X_5 = f_5(R, E, O) = f_5(X_1, X_2, X_3)$

In the case of linear additive relationships, assuming that all variables are measured in terms of deviations from their own means, these could be written as follows:

$$X_1 = b_{12}X_2 + b_{13}X_3 + b_{14}X_4 + e_1$$
$$X_2 = b_{21}X_1 + b_{24}X_4 + e_2$$
$$X_3 = b_{32}X_2 + b_{34}X_4 + e_3$$
$$X_4 = b_{42}X_2 + e_4$$
$$X_5 = b_{51}X_1 + b_{52}X_2 + b_{53}X_3 + e_5,$$

where the e_i are error terms to be discussed below, and where the b_{ij} are structural parameters indicating the direct change that would be produced in X_i by a unit change in X_j, with the other variables in the system held constant. For example, b_{12} gives the direct effect of educational discrimination X_2 on residential exclusion X_1, whereas b_{21} represents the direct effect of X_1 on X_2.[13]

Even if there were no error terms produced by variables left out of the theoretical system, there is no unique mathematical solution in this case. There are too many unknowns, and there will be an infinite number of sets of values for the b_{ij}, all of which are consistent with the same data. To put it another way, it will be possible to make a linear transformation of the system by multiplying each equation by an arbitrary constant and adding it to any of the remaining equations. The result will be a new set of equations, mathematically equivalent to the first, but having different sets of

13. These coefficients are not to be confused with ordinary least-squares regression estimators, which will generally be biased in simultaneous-equation systems. See Johnston, *Econometric Methods*, chaps. 9 and 10; and Christ, *Econometric Models*, chap. 9.

numerical values for the b_{ij}. In one set of equations b_{12} may be 12.0, whereas in another it may be zero or $-310,168$. This of course means that it will be impossible to assess the effects of any one variable on each of the others. This is referred to as the "identification problem." The values of the structural parameters, which provide us with a mathematical explanation of the empirical relationships, cannot be determined from the data alone.

The *necessary* condition for identifying the coefficients in any particular equation can be stated rather simply in the case of linear additive systems. One counts the number of endogenous variables in the theory. These will be all those variables that have an arrow directed toward them from any source. An equation must be written for each of these variables. Only under special conditions, such as one-way causation, can these equations be legitimately pulled apart and studied separately. The necessary condition states that if there are k endogenous variables, there must be $k - 1$ variables left out of any equation that is to be identified.[14] But in the case of any endogenous variable being explained by another, there will always be at least two variables in that equation, and therefore there cannot be more than $k - 2$ endogenous variables left out. For example, the equation for political discrimination contains only X_4 and X_2, but there are still only three variables left out, whereas identification requires that at least four be omitted. Clearly, there are not enough variables to go around.

One way out of the difficulty is to add more variables to the system in such a way that at least the proper number are left out of each equation. Since at least four ($k - 1$) variables must be left out of each equation, the first equation (which does not contain X_5) must be revised so that three additional variables do not appear in it. Furthermore, these must be variables that are major contributors to the remaining equations; they cannot be just any variable that the investigator thinks might be a cause of the other variables in the system. Most important, they must be either truly exogenous variables or lagged values of endogenous variables.[15] For if they are current endogenous variables, a separate equation must be written for each, and this will increase the value of $k - 1$, the number of variables that must be omitted.

This generally means that the more unknown coefficients one wishes to use in a given system of equations, the more selective or restrictive he must be in the use of exogenous variables. It will do no good to introduce exogenous variables thought to be direct causes of *all* of the endogenous vari-

14. More generally, there must be at least k-1 independent restrictions on the parameters in each equation that is to be identified. See Fisher, *Identification Problem*, chap. 2.

15. A lagged endogenous variable is simply the value of one of the endogenous variables at some previous point in time. Sometimes such a lagged value may be treated as though it were equivalent to a distinct exogenous variable. This approach will be discussed briefly below. For a more technical discussion, see Fisher, *Identification Problem*, pp. 168-175.

ables, since some must be left out of each equation. For example, if one had measures on a number of dimensions of prejudice or personality characteristics, but could not rule out the possibility that these factors directly affected each of the five types of discrimination, then it would be of no help to introduce them in order to identify the coefficients. Furthermore, according to the general schematic diagram of Figure 1, at least some of the discrimination variables may have feedback effects on prejudice, so that these prejudice variables would not be truly exogenous. Certain of the situational factors, however, might be selectively introduced so as to identify the discrimination equations. For example, variations in political systems might be expected to influence political discrimination directly, but not the remaining four kinds of discrimination.

If there is one-way causation among all of the variables in a theoretical system, then all of the equations can be identified, *provided* that it can be assumed that the error or disturbance term in each equation is uncorrelated with the disturbance terms in each of the other equations. This will mean that they will automatically also be uncorrelated with the independent variables that appear in their respective equations, thus satisfying the assumptions necessary for ordinary least squares. It can be shown, however, that this assumption cannot generally be met when there is reciprocal causation or feedback. Whenever there is one-way causation, the equation system is referred to as "recursive," and it will be possible to label the variables in such a way that a higher-numbered variable can never be a cause of a lower-numbered variable.[16] For example, in the case of four variables we would have:

$$X_1 = e_1$$
$$X_2 = b_{21}X_1 + e_2$$
$$X_3 = b_{31}X_1 + b_{32}X_2 + e_3$$
$$X_4 = b_{41}X_1 + b_{42}X_2 + b_{43}X_3 + e_4$$

Recursive systems have the important property that each equation can be analyzed separately from the rest. For example, the above equation for X_3 contains X_1 and X_2 but not X_4, and since X_4 also does not appear in the equations for X_1 and X_2, we can safely ignore it in analyzing the relationships among the remaining variables. Residential exclusion X_1 (in this model, but not in Figure 2) would be independent of the remaining forms of discrimination and could therefore be considered exogenous. Educational discrimination X_2 would depend only on residential exclusion. Occupational discrimination X_3 would depend on X_1 and X_2 but would not feed back to influence them; and political discrimination X_4 would be dependent on all

16. Recursive equations are associated with the work of Herman Wold. See especially Herman Wold and Lars Jureen, *Demand Analysis* (New York: Wiley, 1953); and R. H. Strotz and Herman Wold, "Recursive Versus Nonrecursive Systems," *Econometrica*, 28 (April, 1960), 417-427.

three of the other variables, though as a special case one might set b_{41} equal to zero, thereby ruling out a *direct* relationship with X_1. The above system is recursive, in the sense that it can be built up, one equation at a time, in this manner.

Block-Recursive Models

We have seen that it will be necessary to use at least some exogenous variables, to which there is no feedback, whenever there is reciprocal causation within or between theoretical blocks of variables. It will ordinarily be necessary to construct a compromise model between the one extreme that allows for reciprocal causation or feedback to every variable and the very simple model in which all variables are recursively related. It should be possible to reconstruct the blocks of variables in such a way that the *blocks* are recursively related, whereas feedback is permitted *within* each block. Such a system is termed "block recursive."

Referring to Figure 1 we see that, as the model was originally constructed, the block of variables *personality characteristics,* and the block *situational factors* are truly exogenous. These two blocks influence the remainder, but there is no feedback to them. However, feedback has been assumed among the remaining blocks. Therefore, the three original blocks dealing with prejudice, discrimination, and minority behavior might all be combined into a single larger block of endogenous variables. The three blocks in the new system would then be recursively related.

Whenever a large number of variables have been placed together in a single block within which there is feedback, the implication is that this entire system of variables must be studied simultaneously. In fact, the assumption that the real world can be adequately represented by a block-recursive model is always necessary in order to justify isolating a specific set of variables and studying their interrelationships by means of a finite number of simultaneous equations. Variables from other exogenous blocks may then be pulled in selectively to help resolve identification problems. Not all such variables need to be used, but the more complex the system of endogenous variables, the more exogenous variables one must find.

While a good deal more could be said about the technical aspects of this problem, one further point needs to be stressed in this connection. If the variables taken as exogenous turn out to be highly intercorrelated, then there is likely to be a substantial sampling error in the estimates of each individual effect, as indicated by the b_{ij}. One may therefore obtain a false sense of security on the basis of a single sample, and a second study may lead to very different conclusions about the relative magnitudes of the b_{ij}. Therefore it is essential to find exogenous variables that have two important characteristics: not only must they be important causes of some variables and not others, but they cannot be too highly intercorrelated.

Thus there may be considerable difficulties in testing a complicated theory which allows for feedback among numerous variables. It is relatively easy to state a complex verbal theory allowing for the possibility that each variable affects all the others. It is much more difficult to test it. A study of the conditions necessary for identification can at least show whether or not it is *mathematically* possible to test a theory or to estimate the parameters, even assuming no further complications due to measurement errors or variables left out of the system.

It should be emphasized that the identification problem and other related complexities are not produced as a result of formalization. They are present in verbal formulations as well, as evidenced by the number of unresolvable theoretical disputes that arise within the discipline. We have seen that their resolution requires that one make *a priori* untestable assumptions. It is disconcerting to realize that explicit formulations require such assumptions, but it should be recognized that there are always *implicit* assumptions that amount to the same thing. The simple phrase "other things being equal," which is often tacked onto a verbal theory, sometimes hides from view a number of major difficulties. Less obvious, perhaps, is the fact that it is easy to bypass the identification problem by assuming that one can study a series of dependent variables (such as each type of discrimination) without worrying about why the various independent variables are intercorrelated, or about possible feedback effects from the "dependent" variable to the so-called "independent" variables.

Dynamic Formulations

There is an alternative resolution to the identification problem that may turn out to be more appealing to sociologists, though it requires the collection of longitudinal data and a careful specification of a dynamic model in which assumptions are made about the relative length of delayed effects. One may treat time-lagged values of some of the endogenous variables as though they were exogenous. For example, suppose one argued that residential exclusion X_1 has an immediate effect on educational discrimination X_2, but that the impact of X_2 on X_1 is relatively delayed. Then the portions of the equation system connecting these particular variables might be written as $X_{1,t} = b_{12}X_{2,t-1}$ and $X_{2,t} = b_{21}X_{1,t}$, where the appropriate time lag would need to be specified. It can be shown that by using lagged endogenous variables as though they were truly exogenous, a nonrecursive system involving an identification problem can be made recursive, and the identification problem will thereby be resolved.[17]

One is required to specify rather clearly the appropriate lag periods, however. In the above example, if X_1 at time t were taken as a function of X_2

17. See Wold and Jureen, *Demand Analysis,* chap. 2; and Fisher, *Identification Problem,* pp. 168-175.

at time t or $t - 2$, as well as $t - 1$, additional unknown coefficients would have to be used, and the identification problem would be reintroduced. If one preferred to argue, as would seem reasonable in this illustration, that changes in both variables were occurring continuously rather than discretely, then the dynamic theory could be reformulated in terms of simultaneous differential equations.[18] But since estimates of the various parameters would need to be obtained at specific points in time, one would need to be concerned about the behavior of the error or disturbance terms through time. These will ordinarily be intercorrelated, and some rather difficult problems of estimation will thereby be introduced. Some of these will be discussed briefly in the next section under the heading of "autocorrelation."

There is a major advantage of such dynamic formulations that should be noted at this point. What distinguishes a dynamic from a static theory is not the fact that the former is a good theory and the latter a poor one, but that in a dynamic theory the time dimension enters into the formulation in an essential way. In the example we have been considering, it was explicitly assumed that there is a specified lag in the effect of X_2 on X_1, but not in the case of the effect of X_1 on X_2. A dynamic formulation such as this enables one to answer questions about the nature of the time path taken by the system, if it is disturbed from a stable equilibrium because of a change in some exogenous variable. But it also enables one to specify the conditions under which stability can be expected, as compared with those under which there may be an indefinite increase or decrease in the levels of each variable. A static formulation ordinarily *requires* the assumption that the system will tend to stabilize except for "random shocks." A dynamic formulation can handle the more general situation, of which stability is only a special case.

In the case of the discrimination variables in the model of Figure 2, one might wonder whether it could be possible to get continually increasing (or decreasing) levels of discrimination, since four of the discrimination variables feed back to influence each other. Rather than stabilizing, such a system might "explode" in the sense that values of each variable increased or decreased at accelerating rates. Myrdal pointed to this possibility in discussing what he termed a "principle of cumulation" in social change, through which a relatively minor change in one variable (say, prejudice) might set in motion progressively larger changes so that its ultimate impact was out of proportion to its original impetus.[19]

18. The use of differential equation systems is discussed in Baumol, *Economic Dynamics;* Coleman, *Mathematical Sociology;* Simon, *Models of Man;* and Blalock, *Theory Construction.* In brief, the "instantaneous" rate of change in Y (over a very brief period of time t), written as dy/dt, may be taken as a function of various factors, including the level of Y itself. Such a formulation permits one to solve for values of Y at any particular time and to trace out the time path that Y will follow.
19. Gunnar Myrdal, *An American Dilemma* (New York: Harper, 1944), appendix C.

Even where one is willing to assume that a system will ultimately stabilize, and where one is not particularly interested in describing or explaining what happens during the course of the equilibrating process, it may still be necessary to formulate a dynamic theory. It has been shown that if one is merely interested in determining how the equilibrium levels for each endogenous variable will shift with a given change in some exogenous variable, one must use the stability conditions implied by a dynamic model in order to determine these expected changes.[20]

For example, suppose the several discrimination variables, interrelated as in Figure 2, were in equilibrium at a specified level. One might want to know how a certain change in a governmental program might affect the new equilibrium positions of each of the discrimination variables. While common sense might in some cases indicate in a rough way what might be expected to happen, in any instance where the reciprocal causal relationships were at all complex, a dynamic formulation would be necessary to *deduce* from the theory the predicted consequences. A static or nontemporal version would not be sufficient.

Auxiliary Theories

Assumptions about disturbing influences affecting error terms, the exact forms of one's equations, and possible measurement errors are not commonly included in discussions of theory, but in a very real sense they are just as important in connection with the verification process as are the various propositions contained in the theory proper. In order to emphasize this fact, I have referred to these supplementary assumptions as constituting an auxiliary theory.[21]

A particular investigator or research team cannot possibly measure and analyze all of the variables that might be contained in a general theory. He must be selective in a number of important respects. Certain variables will be neglected altogether. Others not mentioned in the original theory may be introduced as control variables which are thought to disturb the predicted relationships. Distortions (such as the effects of experimental manipulations) will be introduced by the measurement process itself or perhaps by the research design. In many instances a choice must be made among a number of possible measures of a single variable. Where the theoretical concepts are highly abstract or not clearly defined, measurement may be very indirect, and various assumptions must be made, enabling one to link the unmeasured construct with its indicators.

20. See Baumol, *Economic Dynamics,* pp. 373-378; and Samuelson, *Economic Analysis,* chap. 9.
21. H. M. Blalock, "The Measurement Problem: A Gap Between the Languages of Theory and Research," in H. M. Blalock and Ann B. Blalock, eds., *Methodology in Social Research* (New York: McGraw, 1968), chap. 1.

These kinds of procedures and assumptions must also be made explicit. Otherwise, there will be slippage in the testing situation. If a theory is not supported by the data, it may nevertheless be retained by claiming that the measurement was poor, or that "other things" were not equal. If it appears to be supported, there will be numerous rival alternative explanations, including the possibility that relationships found were due to measurement artifacts or uncontrolled sources of spurious relationships. It is important to recognize that the testing process is always indirect and that a set of auxiliary assumptions will be required in order to link up the research results with the theoretical propositions. While this subject is much more complex than commonly realized, it is at least possible in this context to outline certain features of auxiliary theories.

Excluded Variables

First, there must inevitably be decisions about which variables can safely be ignored in one's empirical research. Here it is essential to have an explicit theory that involves many more variables than will ultimately be selected. Not only will this facilitate a division of labor among social scientists, but it will enable the investigator to make rational decisions based on explicit assumptions. Consider the various blocks of variables given in Figure 1. Suppose an investigator wishes to focus primarily on the discrimination block given in Figure 2. Which variables can he safely ignore? The theory of block-recursive systems justifies omitting from consideration any variables in blocks that are clearly dependent upon the block under investigation, provided there is no feedback from these omitted blocks to the one being studied. Figure 1 implies that there are two blocks, *minority behavior* and *prejudice,* that are dependent on discrimination, but arrows have also been drawn leading from both of these blocks to *discrimination.* Therefore, they cannot safely be ignored if one assumes the correctness of this model.

As already implied, these three blocks would have to be combined into a single block involving reciprocal causation in order for the system to be block recursive. At this point, the investigator might be willing to make further compromises with reality. For example, he might assume that the effects of minority behavior on discrimination are delayed, and that in short-run analyses they can be ignored.[22] He might then redraw the diagram, restricting the model to the short run, omitting the arrow from minority behavior to discrimination. This would justify omitting minority

---

22. More realistically, there would undoubtedly be a whole series of actions and reactions that would need to be summed. When one deals with interaction among individuals, this kind of problem can be handled much more simply than in situations where these actions and reactions must be aggregated over large numbers of individuals.

behavior variables from his study, though at the cost of assuming a more restrictive theory.

We have seen that it may be necessary to make use of exogenous variables to identify the coefficients in simultaneous-equation systems, but not *all* exogenous variables need to be used. The investigator might therefore select among a wide variety of personality characteristics and situational factors, using that combination of exogenous variables that would be most useful for his purposes. The model of Figure 1 implies that such a selective use of exogenous variables is justified. But if any of the personality characteristics or situational factors were assumed to be affected by discrimination, then these variables should be treated as endogenous.

Very few, if any, sociological studies have used interdependent equations and the appropriate analysis procedures. Instead, each "dependent" variable has been studied separately, with control variables introduced as though there were no question as to the legitimacy of this kind of analysis. But as econometricians have come to realize, these procedures lead to biased estimates. Just how serious these biases may be under different circumstances, however, is not well understood. The implication is that complex theories allowing for feedback will require complex analyses. If simple analysis techniques are used, there is always the implicit assumption that the underlying theory is also simple.

Variables that have been left out of the theoretical system, but which are thought to produce variation in any of the endogenous variables, enter into the auxiliary theory by contributing to the error terms in each equation. In order to test a theory, or to estimate any of the parameters, assumptions must *always* be made about the behavior of these error terms. Sometimes these assumptions are stated rather blindly, as for example by asserting that the errors are normally distributed with equal variances. But behind such assumptions about the empirical frequency distributions of the error terms, there is an implicit theory as to the behavior of the variables that are thought to produce these error terms. Such a theory should also be made explicit. For example, it may be assumed that no major cause of X_1 is also a direct cause of X_2. If this assumption does not seem plausible, then rather than rejecting it outright—which may very well make it impossible to derive any testable predictions at all—one must search for specific alternatives. If particular common causes of X_1 and X_2 can be located and measured, then they should be explicitly incorporated into the auxiliary theory. In effect, this is what one does in searching for sources of spurious relationships, but the point is much more general.[23] The auxiliary theory should contain explicit assumptions about all kinds of possible disturbing influences. Those

23. I am referring to those situations in which X_1 and X_2 are correlated due to common causes as involving "spurious" relationships. The implication is that if all common causes were controlled, the correlation between the two variables would disappear.

that have been measured can be explicitly controlled; those that have not must ideally be assumed to have known kinds of effects on the disturbance terms.

Assumptions about the behavior of variables that have been omitted from the original theory may be particularly difficult to justify on theoretical or *a priori* grounds. How can one make assumptions about variables that cannot even be named? For example, the use of simple least-squares procedures in a recursive system requires one to assume that the error term e_4 in an equation such as

$$X_4 = b_{41}X_1 + b_{42}X_2 + b_{43}X_3 + e_4$$

must be statistically unrelated to the independent variables X_1, X_2, and X_3 appearing in this equation. If we conceive of e_4 as a residual term affected by all other causes of X_4, then the aggregated effect of these unknown variables must be unrelated to X_1, X_2, and X_3. One might hope to substitute a more reasonable assumption than this. But what would it be? Certainly, one would not be in a position to specify what the correlations with X_1, X_2, and X_3 might be, and they cannot be estimated from the data without making additional *a priori* assumptions. It is important to realize that *some* assumptions must *always* be made about such error terms.

Making such assumptions explicit almost serves as a challenge to the critic to point to inadequacies in the model, and this is a highly desirable feature of formalized theories. Although some assumptions must always be made, we must remember that any particular theory can be modified, reformulated, and tested. If someone believes that the above equation involving only four variables is inadequate, he may look for additional variables to include. But his theory will also be incomplete, though it may be more adequate than the original formulation. Furthermore, once the additional variables have been incorporated and measured, the degree to which the model has been improved can be evaluated in terms of the data at hand. But if the critic merely notes that the assumptions are unrealistic, or that some important variables have been left out—without saying what these variables might be—then his criticism, while possibly being correct, is hardly constructive.

Autocorrelation

Another kind of assumption necessary in the testing process concerns the degree to which the observations or replications are really independent statistically. Whenever one is using time-series data, which will be necessary in testing dynamic models, this problem can be conceptualized in terms of

possible "autocorrelation" of the disturbance terms.[24] The use of lagged endogenous variables as though they were completely exogenous basically requires that disturbance factors affecting a variable at time 1 be uncorrelated with those at time 2. Obviously, the closer the intervals of observation, the less likely that this assumption will be met. This becomes a very serious problem whenever there are important variables affecting the error terms that change their values relatively slowly over the interval of observation.

Suppose, for example, that one wanted to infer the immediate or delayed effects of monthly changes in national employment levels on the *differential* between white and Negro employment levels. Certainly, factors such as the relative educational levels of whites and Negroes, the geographic dispersion of Negroes, and discriminatory policies of employers could be expected to influence this relationship. While each of these latter factors might also change over time, the rate of change in one or more of them might be such as to produce autocorrelated disturbance terms *unless* each variable could be measured and brought explicitly into the equation. Thus employer policies might gradually shift over a ten-year period from being highly discriminatory, through a stage of being nondiscriminatory, to being mildly discriminatory. If these policies could not be measured, the effect of this gradual change would be to produce cyclical disturbance terms in the monthly data relating general unemployment levels to the measure of inequality.

Although autocorrelation in time-series data is a well-known problem in the econometrics literature, relatively little attention has been given by sociologists to an analogous difficulty with spatially defined units. In brief, there may be mutual influence across boundaries, so that the disturbance terms for one unit (such as a county or nation) may be correlated with those for adjacent units. Again, the smaller the units, the more likely that the problem will be a serious one. In the anthropological literature the debate over diffusion versus independent invention has been difficult to resolve because of this problem. If one does not like the assumption that there are no common disturbance terms across adjacent units, he may be forced to modify his design or theoretical argument so as to identify and measure the major sources of disturbance or to select different units of analysis so as to make the assumption somewhat more realistic.[25]

24. For discussions of autocorrelations see Christ, *Econometric Models,* pp. 481-488; Johnston, *Econometric Methods,* pp. 187-192; and R. L. Anderson, "The Problem of Autocorrelation in Regression Analysis," *Journal of the American Statistical Association,* 49 (March, 1954), 113-129.
25. For example, one may select a *sample* of relatively small units (such as counties) that are not contiguous. Or one may make various tests for autocorrelation and modify one's design accordingly. In addition to the references given in footnote 24, the reader is referred to discussions of this problem in Raoul Naroll, "Some Thoughts on Comparative Method in Cultural Anthropology," in Blalock and Blalock, *Methodology,* chap. 7.

Specification Errors

In addition to faulty assumptions about the error terms, there may be various types of "specification errors" involving incorrect forms of relationships or postulated values of coefficients. Some such errors can be evaluated in terms of the data. Tests for linearity, for example, may suggest that alternative nonlinear models should have been used. A simple additive model may have to be replaced, say, by a multiplicative model if certain patterns of interaction or nonadditivity are found in the data.[26]

But there will be other kinds of specification errors that may be inherently untestable. We have noted that exogenous variables may be introduced selectively in order to identify the coefficients. In a system of interdependent equations, for example, if there are six exogenous variables Z_1, $Z_2, \ldots, Z_6$, it may be decided that Z_2 and Z_5 may be left out of the first equation. In effect, this amounts to *assuming* that the coefficients of these two exogenous variables are zero in this particular equation. It is the fact that *a priori* values of zero are assumed for some of these coefficients that reduces the number of unknowns to the point where the remainder can be estimated from the data. But if these assumptions are in fact wrong, and if others should have been substituted, then erroneous estimates will be obtained and there will be no way of knowing this fact. This again illustrates the important point that *some* untestable assumptions must always be made. In this case, we are concerned with assumptions about which variables do and do not appear in each equation.

Measurement Errors

Certainly one of the most difficult problems facing the social scientist is that of improving his measurement procedures. Perhaps this is the most crucial single obstacle inhibiting the advance of sociology as a discipline. But although measurement *techniques* have received considerable attention from sociologists, the *theoretical* problems of linking measured variables with underlying constructs have not been well studied. We have borrowed ideas from psychologists, and have taken over attitude measurement techniques and put them to good use. But we have not given careful thought to the general *theory* of measurement. Nor have we adequately considered the implications of various specific kinds of measurement errors.

Assumptions about measurement error, and about the relationship between a measured "indicator" and its underlying concept, must always be made in the testing process. Often these assumptions are implicit, as for

26. Illustrations of this kind of approach are given in H. M. Blalock, "Theory Building and the Statistical Concept of Interaction," *American Sociological Review,* 30 (June, 1965), 374-380.

example when one introduces a control variable as though measurement error in it were irrelevant or negligible. For example, one may dichotomize a control variable because of too few cases, or because it would create fewer tables, without realizing that such crude categorization may have introduced considerably more measurement error than even a trichotomy. Often data are reported using convenience to the reader as a more important consideration than measurement error. An advantage of formalization and stating one's assumptions explicitly is that it makes the shortcomings of one's theory and research painfully obvious. The explicit statement, "I am assuming *no* measurement errors whatsoever in any of my independent variables and only random error in my dependent variable," should challenge the reader to look for biasing effects of possible measurement errors.

But measurement errors will practically always be unknown, and therefore it is difficult to decide how to proceed. With repeated measurements —which are difficult in sociological research—one can assess reliability, but there will remain fundamental problems associated with the notion of validity. I have argued elsewhere that many of these problems can never be satisfactorily resolved without resorting to a series of inherently untestable assumptions about the causal connections between the underlying concept and indicator.[27] It may not always be possible to link concepts and indicators in a simple one-to-one fashion, and therefore in many instances it may be misleading to ask about the "validity" of an indicator. Often there must be a rather elaborate auxiliary theory connecting several unmeasured variables with several indicators. As a theory becomes more abstract, or more general in its implications, the linkage between measured and unmeasured variables may become increasingly complex, and the need for an explicit auxiliary theory correspondingly greater. The practice of merely telling the reader that the investigator has decided to use variables X, Y, and Z as indicators of a given concept should be clarified by explicitly stating the auxiliary theory relating all of these variables to the underlying concept.

Consider the example of discrimination. As already noted, the notion of discriminatory behavior by individuals is several steps removed from the usual measures of discrimination that can conveniently be obtained with limited resources. The latter ordinarily involve either physical segregation or inequalities of various kinds. It would be fortunate if one could take occupational inequalities as an indicator of occupational discrimination, educational inequalities as an indicator of educational discrimination, and residential segregation as an indicator of residential exclusion. But the real world is not this simple. In the first place, the various inequality measures are resultants of minority behavior as well as discriminatory practices. This means that a more complete theory would require connecting measures of

27. Blalock, "The Measurement Problem."

inequality with minority behavior variables as well as discriminatory behavior. Secondly, measured variables such as physical separation or income
inequalities might also be taken as functions of *other* discrimination variables besides the one they are intended to measure. One possible causal
model is exemplified in Figure 4. Obviously, there are numerous alternative

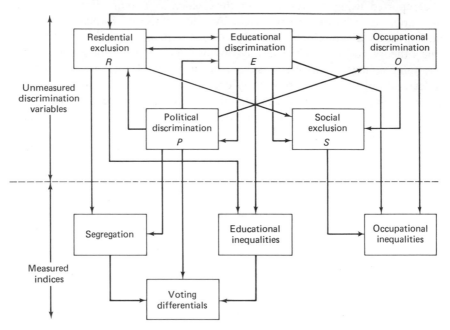

Figure 4. Discrimination variables combined with measured indices

possibilities. The fundamental problem that one encounters, once having
admitted this degree of complexity, is that since many of the variables in
the system are taken as unmeasured, the "testing" of the theory may become very indirect, and certain *a priori* assumptions must remain inherently
untestable.

It might seem as though this is too great a price to pay. But what are
the possible alternatives? If one merely links "occupational discrimination"
with "occupational inequalities," one is implicitly assuming that other variables in the system do *not* affect these particular inequalities except indirectly through occupational discrimination. The cost of greater simplicity
is therefore the sacrifice of realism. Of course, at some point a compromise
must be reached or the theory will become much too complex to be tested.
Formalization and attention given to the auxiliary theory make this kind of
decision process explicit.

Using the same example, it might be thought that simple standardization
procedures can be used to get one out of the difficulty. If factors other than
occupational discrimination affect occupational inequalities, why not intro-

duce controls for these variables? For instance, why not control for educational inequalities or differences in inherent abilities or motivation? But if these latter control variables are bound together in reciprocal causal relationships with occupational discrimination, the situation is not this simple. As already noted, the rationale for simple least squares breaks down, as does that for ordinary contingency methods of controlling. These questions are much too technical to be discussed in the present context. The essential point, which cannot be overemphasized, is that theoretical considerations cannot be divorced from measurement procedures as simply as one might wish. This kind of very difficult methodological problem deserves much more attention than it has thus far received in the sociological literature.

Even such a relatively simple phenomenon as purely random measurement error can lead to a number of important complications when it comes to testing a given theory and evaluating it in relation to competing alternatives. Since the attenuating effects of random measurement error in an independent variable are relative to the actual amount of variation in that variable, there may be differential attenuation of slopes which leads the investigator to infer statistical interactions or nonadditive relationships when, in fact, an additive model is more realistic. If one or more sources of spuriousness are inadequately measured, then when these are introduced as control variables, one may infer a direct causal relationship between two variables when it is actually spurious. Whenever one is attempting to disentangle the separate effects of independent variables that are highly intercorrelated, not only must he have a theory as to why they are correlated, but he must also have highly accurate measures of each of these variables. If one is measured more accurately than another, a slight difference in measurement accuracy (assuming purely random errors) may give rise to a major difference in the relative explanatory power of the variables. Slope estimates will also be highly inaccurate.

In summary, if a theorist is actually interested in formulating a rejectable theory capable of making specific predictions, then he must pay careful attention to a set of auxiliary assumptions that will need to be combined with the original theory. Since the general theory may have been stated in such a way that it is appropriate to a number of diverse empirical settings, different sets of auxiliary assumptions may be combined with a single general theory in order to make tests and predictions in a variety of contexts. But it is important to realize that in any particular context it will be a *combination* of the general theory and the auxiliary theory that must be tested. *Both* must be made explicit in order to derive testable propositions. If, for example, it is claimed that a given indicator takes on different "meanings" in different contexts, it will be necessary to make the causal connections between indicators and unmeasured concepts fully explicit. In the process the full range of untested assumptions will be brought into the open so that they may be challenged, one by one. This is the way scientifically constructed theories can become cumulative in nature.

Some Implications

When one sees the numerous assumptions that must be made in order to test a reasonably complex theory, the temptation is to become immobilized and to give up the effort to formalize the argument in detail. Or there may be a tendency to be overly perfectionistic about meeting certain of the assumptions at the expense of others. For example, if one does not have a legitimate interval-scale level of measurement, one may drop back to simple dichotomies, thereby increasing his measurement error. Or one may concentrate too exclusively on a small number of variables, neglecting others that may be operating to distort the relationships. Some variables may be ignored altogether because they are too difficult to measure. Of course it will be necessary to compromise at nearly every stage of the process, and one must always guard against the common tendency to construct highly complex theories that stand no chance of being tested and rejected.

The only rational way to balance these various considerations seems to be to formalize one's theory and assumptions at each stage, and then to select a reasonably plausible set of assumptions. To do so requires that the theorist-investigator be well aware of the methodological problems that he is confronting. Certainly these problems will not simply disappear. The inherent dilemma is that one must always settle for some set of specific assumptions in order to arrive at definite predictions capable of being rejected, though of course any *particular* set of theoretical assumptions may later be modified. This is a scientific fact of life that may prove difficult to live with for many sociologists, but it is a fact of life nevertheless.

The process of formalization should make us more fully aware of the magnitude of the task that lies ahead. Sociologists obviously know that the real world is complex, that our theories are highly imperfect, and that our research designs are never adequate. I am not convinced, however, that we have become fully aware of the implications of these facts in terms of the kinds of research we are doing and the ways we are organized to carry out this research.

Consider either cross-community or cross-cultural research. Such research is highly expensive and time-consuming, and individual investigators usually lack the resources to conduct comparable research in more than two or three communities. Therefore comparisons of different research findings are difficult to make, and there is little standardization of measurement procedures across such small-scale projects. Longitudinal studies suffer from the same defects. When sociologists are able to use secondary sources of data, such as census materials, they are usually required to construct very indirect indicators of the variables in which they are basically interested. The linkages between indicators and theoretical variables often remain unspecified and poorly understood, and they may in fact vary from one re-

search setting to the next. Under these circumstances comparative statements must be very approximate and crude.

Another difficulty is that few studies are adequately replicated or coordinated with each other so as to provide cumulative results. Ideally, it would be possible to block off sets of variables and work out a division of labor among investigators so that the pieces could be fitted together. For example, one investigator might study relationships within block 5, using blocks 2 and 3 as exogenous. A second might study block 3, using blocks 1 and 2 as exogenous. A third might interrelate blocks 3, 4, and 5. Provided that identical measures were used in each piece of research, and the same or nearly identical populations studied, it would be unnecessary for any one investigator to deal with all of the variables in the model. Unfortunately, such a high degree of integration of research has rarely been attempted by sociologists.

One obvious implication is that if we are really serious about testing complex theories, research must be conducted on a much more ambitious scale. At the very least, certain kinds of data will have to be collected by large research organizations in order to assure comparability across large units such as cities, regions, or nations, and also to assure continuity over time. While a few small-scale studies may be replicated perhaps five or ten years after the original period of data collection, there are many instances in which data will need to be collected at much more frequent and prolonged intervals. Since replication studies are both expensive and not highly regarded by the profession, institutional mechanisms will be needed in order to assure greater attention being given to such work. Large-scale research institutes would seem to be in a much better position to conduct replication studies than are lone scholars.

Existing data banks will need to be improved and information retrieval systems streamlined. But retrieval systems will not be sufficient if the quality of the original data is poor. Individual investigators wishing to use such data for secondary analyses obviously will not be acquainted with the details of the original data collection procedures, and they will therefore need to be given assessments of quality and enlightened guesses as to the extent of random and nonrandom measurement error. Detailed studies of measurement adequacy will have to be conducted by specialists who are intimately acquainted with the substantive area of concern, with the field research procedures, and with the more technical quantitative literature on measurement and statistics. The discipline of sociology will have to find ways of rewarding competent scholars for careful attention to such detailed work. Otherwise the users of secondary data sources will remain ignorant of possible sources of bias, lack of standardization, and the extent of even random measurement error.

There are certainly many fields of sociology in which much exploratory work still remains to be done. The individual investigator with rather

limited funds has the opportunity to do pioneering work that can generate new insights and lead to tentative hypotheses and theoretical reformulations. But it seems to me that many substantive areas of sociology have reached the point of diminishing returns with highly exploratory studies. In these areas we need massive quantities of data that have been carefully collected by standardized procedures so that meaningful quantitative comparisons can be made, both cross-sectionally and longitudinally.

Without such data we cannot hope to obtain adequate measures of our important variables. And without adequate measures we cannot carry out the kinds of detailed empirical studies that will be necessary to test, revise, and clarify our theories. Formalization of theories will help in this clarification process. But ultimately our ability to collect adequate data and to improve our measurement procedures will also determine the rate at which sociology matures as a scientific discipline.

11.

The Place of Empirical Social Research
in the Map of Contemporary Sociology

Paul F. Lazarsfeld

Paul F. Lazarsfeld was born in Vienna, Austria, in 1901. He received his Ph.D. from the University of Vienna and came to this country on a Rockefeller Foundation Fellowship in 1933. In 1940 he became professor of sociology and is now Quetelet Professor of social science at Columbia University. Mr. Lazarsfeld has contributed to many professional journals and symposia on social science research techniques. Among his publications are Radio and the Printed Page, The Academic Mind, *and* Latent Structure Analysis. *He is past president of the American Sociological Association and the American Association for Public Opinion Research, and a member of the National Academy of Education. He has honorary degrees from Yeshiva University and the University of Chicago.*

The German sociologist Tönnies once
proposed to divide sociology into three parts: social theory, applied sociology, and sociography. He understood social theory as essentially the
creation of conceptual distinctions. His own *Gesellschaft und Gemeinschaft*
and Parsons' *Pattern Variables* would be typical examples. By application
he meant the use of such distinctions in the analysis of social phenomena
as he himself discussed in the role of religion in *Gemeinschaft* and public
opinion in *Gesellschaft*. Parsons' analysis of the doctor–patient relation
in terms of the pattern variables would be another example. By sociography
he meant the detailed and systematic description of some contemporary
social situation.[1]

The author is the sociological member of a Unesco committee which prepares an
account of "The Main Trends of Research in the Sciences of Man." Some of the
most distinguished members of the committee are hardly acquainted with American
social research; the little they are aware of seems to have no relation to their conceptual interest. The present paper was originally written to bridge this gap. Some
of the content will be incorporated into the joint document the committee is preparing.
1. A similar threefold division of sociological work has been used by other authors.
Thus, Girod distinguishes general theory, concrete research studies, and what he calls
typological analysis of social systems. The latter is a special case of Tönnies'
application of theoretical ideas to broad social phenomena. Lévi-Strauss distinguishes
three phases of anthropological work: ethnography, ethnology, and social or cultural
anthropology. The first is descriptive, the second a first step toward theory, the third
systematic synthesis. This is Tönnies in reverse.

Two of these terms have undergone changes. By applied sociology we today mean work which is close to policy formation and practical decision. This leaves the second type of thinking without label, although it covers much of the work which the general public considers as characteristically sociological, such as talks about the role conflict of the working mother, the anomie of the city dweller, or the influence of reference groups on people's opinions.

The term "sociography" fell out of use because it came to connote a mechanical description instead of the systematic analysis of concrete data which it originally meant. It was tempting here to resume this colorful label to classify the kind of work which is characteristic of the majority of publications in American sociological journals. But in the end it seemed more advisable to stay with the term "empirical social research" (E.S.R.) which came into use when clearly inductive procedures were developed in opposition to the speculative bent of the larger sociological schools.[2]

Today it is generally acknowledged that the whole gamut of sociological work—from purely speculative conceptualizations to "mere" careful fact-finding—is needed. But the links between the different points in this spectrum are less known. This paper deals mainly with one of them: the contributions of E.S.R. to the clarification of basic intellectual procedures, which recur in every phase of sociological thinking. No formal definition will be attempted; as a matter of fact it would probably be impossible to give one. Rather, it is our purpose to discuss the logical nature of the procedures and to show their implication for all sociological analysis. In doing so, we will present a variety of substantive examples as illustrations of the kind of information that is accessible from sociographic findings. Before we proceed, however, one basic issue has to be briefly clarified, namely that of the relation between concepts and the kind of empirical data appearing in E.S.R.

The Flow from Concepts to Variates

By "variate" is understood any distinction by which people, groups, or any other objects of sociological interest can be classified. Thus, for example, sex is a variate because we can classify people as men and women. The rank given to candidates at the French *agrégation* is a variate because it makes possible an ordering of candidates. What is usually called a variable,

2. All through this text we shall use the abbreviation E.S.R., but from time to time we shall spell out the words "empirical social research" to remind the hastier readers what the initials mean.

such as the size or the age of a person, is a variate with special numerical properties.[3]

One of the main tasks of E.S.R. is to translate conceptual ideas into variates. Sometimes one is directly interested in particular variates by virtue of the problem at hand. Thus, if one studies income distribution, local currency is an obvious variate. The matter becomes more complex if one is concerned with the standard of living. The literature on the various standard of living indices will testify to the difficulties inherent in the translation of such a notion into a variate. The statement that white-collar and blue-collar workers with the same income have different standards of living cannot be made without carefully considered combinations from a variety of more elementary data. The same situation is true when the physical anthropologist talks of body types or the sociologist talks of cohesive or integrated collectives. The flow from concepts to variates generally proceeds in four steps.

1. Imagery. The thought and analysis which culminates in a classificatory instrument begins with a rather vague image or construct. The investigator might perceive disparate phenomena as having some underlying characteristic in common. Or he may have observed certain regularities and is trying to account for them. In any case, the concept, when first created, is some vaguely conceived entity that makes observed relations meaningful.

Suppose someone wants to "measure" the integration of communities. He might think of people who like each other, who cooperate in the improvement of their city, who live in peace, who would hate to live elsewhere. But the questions he must ask are subtle and involved. What accounts for degrees of integration? What consequences has it for the life of the citizenry? Whatever the starting point, the second step in variate formation will shortly be necessary.

2. Concept specification. This second step consists in dividing the imagery into components. The concept is specified by aspects, or dimensions, which are sometimes derived sociologically from the over-all concept, sometimes deduced from empirically observed correlations. The concept is shown to be a complex combination of phenomena, rather than a single direct observation.

In the case of integration of communities, for example, Landecker has expressed the following idea. The elementary units of a social group are norms and people. Integration then has to begin with two dimensions: the cultural, which requires that the prevailing norms not be too contradictory,

---

3. The logic and interrelation of different types of variates have been carefully studied by many writers. The terminology varies. They speak of scales, measurements, indices and so on, but it is always possible to separate the basic logical ideas from terminological variations. The term *variate* will be maintained here because it seems the most neutral.

and the personal, which refers to relations between people. The latter involves communicative discussion requiring the exchange of symbols, and a transaction dimension involving the exchange of goods and services. Finally, it is necessary that people obey the prevailing norms; thus we have a third dimension of integration, the normative. The next problem is to find concrete indicators for these dimensions.

3. Selection of indicators. How does one "think up" indicators? The problem is an old one. In *The Meaning of Truth,* William James writes, "Suppose, e.g., that we say a man is 'prudent.' Concretely, that means that he takes out insurance, hedges in betting, looks before he leaps. . . . As a constant habit in him . . . it is convenient to call him prudent in abstraction from any one of his acts . . ." [4] James proceeds from an image to a series of indicators suggested directly by common experience. Actually, one would not expect a prudent man always to hedge in betting, or to take out insurance on all possible risks; instead one would talk about the probability that he will perform a given act, as compared with a less prudent individual. And one would know that the appropriate indicators might vary considerably, depending on the social setting of the individual.

The dimensional analysis gives good leads in finding indicators for the integration idea. What conflicts of norms ("love thy neighbor but maximize profit") occur in *belles lettres,* in court decisions, in personal conflicts? How much communication is there between people, how much prejudice between groups? To what extent does everyone's daily life depend upon others; how often or how easily is the circulation of these services interrupted? How high is the crime rate? How generously do people contribute to public charity?

4. Formation of variates. Once the indicators have been selected for each dimension, one has to recombine them, because one cannot operate with all these dimensions and indicators separately. For some situations the analyst has to form an over-all index. If a professor has six students and only one fellowship to give, he must make an over-all rating of the six. At another time he may only be interested in how each of several achievement dimensions is related to an external variate.

Many indices for the evaluation of cities exist in the literature, some unidimensional, some multidimensional, and still others concerned only with some specific dimension. The final merits of such a variate often cannot be decided before a long period of use; they depend upon the value of the propositions to which it leads and how well these in turn combine into larger systems. Often one hears discussions to the effect that a certain variate does not "really" reflect the intended concepts. This often helps in the considering of more convincing dimensions or of additional indicators. But no absolute decision is possible. What is needed is a sharp clarifica-

4. William James, *The Meaning of Truth* (New York: Longmans, Green, 1932), pp. 149-150.

tion of the procedures involved. A larger number of mathematical models have been developed to this end, especially to clarify the fourth step, the combination of indicators.

Our summary gives, of course, an oversimplified version of the operations involved, and leaves many problems undiscussed. But it is sufficient to highlight the main points relevant for the present purpose. The following remarks are pertinent.

a. The operations involved apply to individuals as well as to collectives and to inanimate objects. Whether one compares temperaments of people or patterns of culture, the task is the same: to devise classificatory systems into which a concrete given object can be allocated.

b. These classifications are always intended or latent ones. Combinations of indicators are used in order to decide where an object is most likely to belong. The relation between manifest observations and latent classifications can best be demonstrated by its similarity to a medical diagnosis which uses a variety of tests to decide whether a patient has an infarction of the heart. Logicians have developed a general theory of disposition concepts of which the procedure under discussion here is a special case.

c. The relation between the manifest observation and the intended classification is a probabilistic one. An individual might maintain his basic position, but by chance shift on a specific indicator; or he might change his basic position, but by chance remain stable on a specific indicator. But if there are many indicators in an index, it is highly unlikely that a large number of them will all change in one direction by chance, when the individual under observation has not, in fact, changed his basic position.

d. A close connection exists between the logical problems of definition and the empirical problems of variate formation. It seems unnecessary to discuss these in more detail at this time.

Variate Language

The findings of empirical social research have one strong similarity with ordinary language. Just as we distinguish between words and sentences, we have in E.S.R. variates and the propositions into which they are combined. The "propositions" are necessarily all cross-tabulation between variates. This cross-tabulation can become quite complex if many variates are involved. Even if we deal with three variates only, a considerable diversity is provided by the use of contingent cross-tabulations, such as in the following sentence: "In upperclass strata, men and women are equally likely to vote; in lowerclass strata, men have a higher voting turnout than women." Obviously this statement comes about by sorting a sample of people first by status and then by cross-tabulation for the subsets *sex* and *voting turnout*.

One might suspect that such variate language becomes rather monotonous. But this is not the case, since the variates themselves can be of very different kinds. They might characterize collectives as well as individuals, could be taken at different time periods, will refer to behavior as well as to reports on subjective experiences. By combining the formalism of cross-tabulations with an appropriate classification of kinds of variates, one arrives at a typology of propositions in variate language which has far-reaching intellectual implications.

It is not possible here to develop this idea systematically. Rather, we shall give a number of characteristic examples to support the main thesis. Methodological paradigms abstracted from E.S.R. do provide the basic bricks from which the home of general sociology can be built—not from their content but from their form. The examples themselves are taken from a variety of research areas, which will add some substance to the statistics of the topic provided above. The reader will, we hope, think of similar cases in his own field of experience. Even those concerned with macro-sociological topics and necessarily thinking in a broader, and therefore less specific, language should recognize its basic affinity to what is here called variate language.

Intentionality

Occasionally one finds authors commenting that two traditions exist, a positivistic and an idealistic one. Positivists supposedly admit only observable behavior as objects of scientific study, excluding purposes and other "ideas." Whatever the philosophical meaning of such a controversy, it cannot be found in the praxis of E.S.R. There, the expressed intentions of people are legitimate variates. One is not concerned with free will, but studies the conditions under which intentions are more or less likely to be executed.

By way of example, a typical multivariate table based on interviews conducted toward the end of World War II with soldiers in the American army is presented below. Prior to discharge, these soldiers were asked whether they intended to return to their former employer. They could answer from four categories: (1) definitely yes, (2) probably, (3) possibly, (4) definitely not. The soldiers were also classified according to the number of years they had worked for their former employer previous to their service in the army. A few months after discharge, they were asked whether or not they had actually returned to their former position. Table 1 classifies the soldiers on these three variates: intention to return, length of previous employment, and actual return. It will be noted that one of these three expresses a subjective state and the other two are statements of past experience and present action.

TABLE 1

RATE OF ACTUAL RETURN TO PREVIOUS EMPLOYMENT

Duration of Previous Employment	*Rate of Return by Intention Expressed at Separation*			
	Definitely return	Probably return	Possibly return	Plan not to return
Less than 1 year	.76	.63	.41	.21
1 year to 2 years	.83	.72	.56	.23
2 years and over	.90	.77	.53	.29
Average Rate for Expressed Intention	(.85)	(.70)	(.49)	(.24)

One can look at the figures within each cell as the probability that a particular intention is executed under certain conditions. In reading the figures across the first row, one observes that the more definite the intention to return to work the higher is the probability this will occur in actuality. In looking down the columns, one can recognize the influence of past experience as expressed by the duration of previous employment. In the first column, for instance, we deal with all who definitely want to return to their former employer; the longer they had been with him, the higher the probability that this intention is carried out. (The probabilities rise from .76 to .90, a difference of 14 points.) In reading down the last column and comparing it with the other three, it is worth noting that a definite negative intention is least likely to be affected by personal history (the difference is only 8 points).

Process

A second example will illustrate the way in which the concept of *process* would be translated into multivariate language. In its most elementary form, a process consists of two variates which affect each other over a period of time. Thus, James Coleman presented high school students with the following question and statement on two different occasions, separated by an appropriate interval of time:

$x:$ Are you a member of the leading crowd in your class?
$y:$ If a fellow wants to be part of the leading crowd around here, he sometimes has to go against his principles.

A response of "yes" to the question (variate x) and a denial of the statement (variate y) are arbitrarily designated with a plus sign. Generally,

when a student claimed membership in the leading crowd he denied the need for sacrificing his principles, but if he felt excluded, he was more likely to have a negative image of the moral compromise involved. This can be observed by inspecting the totals in Table 2, where the replies of more than 3,000 students are summarized.

TABLE 2

RESPONSES MADE BY GIRLS TO QUESTION X AND STATEMENT Y

				May 1958				
				(1)	*(2)*	*(3)*	*(4)*	*Totals*
		x		+	+	−	−	
		y		+	−	+	−	
	(1)	+	+	484	93	107	32	716
October	(2)	+	−	112	110	30	46	298
1957	(3)	−	+	129	40	768	321	1258
	(4)	−	−	74	75	303	536	988
	Totals			799	318	1208	935	3260

x designates membership or exclusion from the "leading crowd." A + designates reported membership for this variate and a − designates reported exclusion.

y Designates responses to the statement about the compromise of principles in the "leading crowd." A + designates an attitude that there is no need to compromise principles, and a − designates the attitude that it is necessary to compromise one's principles.

Generally, as noted above, there is a positive association between membership in the élite and attitude toward it. The people who are dissonant [5] on the first survey with respect to these two variates can be located by reading across rows (2) and (3). If one looks at the underlined figures in these two rows, one can further locate those people who become consonant by the time of the second survey.

By looking at these four cells, it is possible to develop information about a process which would not have been feasible with a single cross-sectional survey. One can now ask which variate of the two in the process, membership or attitude, has the greater relative importance in accounting for the move from dissonance to consonance. Does belonging to the leading crowd make it probable that one will accept its norms, or does initial acceptance make one more eligible for membership? The pattern in the four underlined cells shows that membership affects attitude to a greater extent than the

5. Dissonant is used here in a purely formal sense to designate those people who are either members of the elite but have a negative attitude toward it, or those people who are not members but have a positive attitude.

reverse. The members with an initial negative image $(+ -)$ are much more likely to change their attitude $(+ +)$ than to drop their membership $(- -)$: 112 to 46. Those nonmembers with a positive attitude $(- +)$ are much more likely to develop a negative attitude $(- -)$ than to become members $(+ +)$: 129 to 321. (Statistically, a more complex computation would be needed, but this is irrelevant here.)

With little additional information, one could provide further insights into the dynamic process. As an illustration, suppose that on the first survey, those respondents who were nonmembers but had a positive attitude (third row) were asked, "Do you hope to join the leading crowd?" The additional information might show that aspirations may have been a source of dissonance. If success provided consonance in one direction and failure in another, this would add to the total understanding of the more critical role of membership variate.

The scheme presented in Table 2 has been applied in many studies where the mutual interaction of variates was at stake. Occupational choices and values, general party affiliation and position on political issues, exposure to advertised products, are typical examples.

Levels of Variate Formation

The third example is directed to the question of whether or not the idea of *structure* can be approximated in variate language. Before proceeding, we need to distinguish between variates which are characteristic of individuals and those which are characteristic of collectives; although it is poor English, it is expedient to speak of individual and collective variates.

For the present purpose, it is satisfactory to denote as *collective,* any combination of individuals which form a meaningful unit in the frame of a specific investigation, such as a small group assembled for the purpose of an experiment, or a large group, such as a city, a state, a nation. It is obvious that collectives as well as individuals can be elements of empirical propositions. For instance, Cantril has available from a number of countries the average caloric intake of the national diet as well as information from individuals about whether they would like to emigrate. There was a sharp negative correlation between the two variates, and the few exceptions could be reasonably explained in the light of historical data.[6] As another example, Kendall studied 150 hospitals for each of which she had the following kinds of information: (a) a table of organization describing the number of jobs available for interns who wanted to stay at the hospital a second year, and (b) a scale measuring the level of competitive-

6. The information on desire to emigrate comes from a survey of representative people in countries where information was also available on the average caloric intake. The worse the diet, the larger the proportion of people who wanted to emigrate.

ness among interns. The smaller the proportion of available jobs, the greater was the level of competitiveness. The objective structure was, as expected, reflected in the subjective attitude.

Such cross-sectional (synchronic) relations between collective variates become more and more available as the opportunity increases to assemble data from many collectives. It is more difficult to provide examples on the ~~different level where variates are~~ interrelated over at least two periods of time (diachronic). There is, however, an interesting and rare example based on historical material which comes from the American Civil War.

In the presidential election of 1860, which ended with the victory of Lincoln, the people who wanted to maintain slavery voted for a "radical" candidate, while those Southerners less radical on the slavery issue voted for other candidates. A few months after the election (at the beginning of the Civil War) a referendum was held in the same counties for the voters to declare themselves for or against seceding from the Union over the slavery issue. The referendum was experienced by the electorate as much more serious than the election, which reflected more conventional party lines. As a result many counties shifted their position. It was possible to explain many of these shifts by introducing a third variate: the number of slaves registered per capita of white population. The counties were classified into "high" and "low" slave-owning ones. (A middle group has been left out from the original study, to facilitate the present illustration.) Table 3

TABLE 3

Voting Shifts in Southern U.S. Counties

	High Slavery Counties				Low Slavery Counties		
	Referendum on Secession				*Referendum on Secession*		
	for	against			for	against	
vote in election	radical 82	18	100% (A)	vote in election	radical 50	50	100% (C)
	other 61	39	100% (B)		other 14	86	100% (D)

shows the shift from election to referendum for these two groups. The counties are divided into four groups. Groups *A* and *D* do not present any problem. Their party tradition as well as their economic structure put them consistently on the radical or the other side of the slavery issue. Consequently they shift little between the two events (18 and 14 percent respectively). The other two groups are in dissonance between their party tradition and their objective economic situation, and therefore exhibit sharp shifts. In group *C,* 50 percent vote differently in the referendum than in the

election. In group *B,* these switches amount even to two thirds of all counties involved.

This phenomenon of "cross pressures" is well known from the study of individual voters. In the present context, however, the elements of the table are *collectives* for which a process is described through variate language. The proportion of people choosing a particular occupational plan (Table 1) is similar to the proportion of counties choosing the secession policy, but with one important difference. In Table 1, the choice of each soldier was established when each expressed the strength of his intention to return to his former employer. In Table 3, the choice of the counties was established by an aggregation of party choices from the individual voters living within their confines.

At this point, certain distinctions concerning collective variates must be made. The most important one is that between aggregative and global variates. As the term indicates, a collective variate is aggregative if it is based on information about each member of the collective under study. In other cases our variate might be a product—material or symbolic—which has emanated from the collective without our knowing or caring which individual members have contributed to it or how they have done so. The distinction can best be understood if one visualizes two possible ways in which the wealth of cities might be measured. An aggregative variate might be the average income of the city derived from the individual incomes of households. A global characteristic might enumerate all the parks, theaters, and other resources which are used for leisure or purposes other than residence or business. What Durkheim has called "social facts" are generally global variates. For instance, when Durkheim characterizes countries by strict or lenient divorce laws, he uses a global variate derived from information unavailable by investigating some characteristic for each member of the population. On the other hand, the proportion of the population which is divorced is an aggregative variate of a collective as is the proportion of voters in a country. There are certain intermediate cases which must be classified somewhat arbitrarily. In the previous example, the number of slaves in each county should be considered a global characteristic because the figure is probably taken from files of the county government without reference to individual slave owners. This would also be true for the average caloric intake of a country's inhabitants.

The distinction between aggregative and global variates is important because the global variates are probably those that many sociologists have in mind when they speak of *structural characteristics.*

In addition, the meaning of structural characteristics can be derived from a further classification of the aggregate variates. Sociometrists, for instance, are likely to ask each member of a collective which other members are his friends. From this information he can construct a variate of the collective which indicates whether those friendship choices are distributed randomly

through it, or whether they cluster in smaller subsets. This would permit the classification of collectives by the degree to which primary groups are stratified within it. The degree of stratification is an aggregative variate because it is derived from information on each member. However, each piece of information includes information about other members. Many sociologists would experience such a variate of stratification as more structural than information on average income, for instance. Thus, the more careful the typological analysis of collective variates, the more precise do the various meanings of structural characteristics which appear in sociological discussions become. For the present purpose, the distinction between individual and collective variates is sufficient.

Contextual Propositions

The most important link between variate language and the idea of structure appears only when one moves to the analysis of propositions which relate variates. This kind of analysis leads to the notion of *contextual propositions*. The essential idea is that relations between two or more *individual* variates may change if they are observed in collectives with different aggregate or global characteristics. The following example will serve as an introduction.

In the United States, in the 1950's, Senator Joseph McCarthy made a number of attacks on college professors, accusing them of subversive activities. It was possible to classify colleges according to the number of such incidents which had occurred within the college. This enumeration of incidents is a typical global characteristic of a college. In a study of 77 colleges during the McCarthy period, a sample of *professors* were interviewed and classified on two individual variates: (a) how apprehensive they felt about the situation and (b) how intimidated they considered their colleagues.[7] The respondents were divided into those who were or were not apprehensive for themselves, and those who assumed that the majority of their colleagues were or were not intimidated. As expected, there was a strong association between the two variates. Those who were apprehensive for themselves were much more likely to perceive their colleagues as apprehensive. This relation can be explained in part by projection and in part by the fact that the actual situation would make anyone more apprehensive in the turbulent colleges. However, if the colleges are classified by the number of dangerous incidents which occurred, the frequency of experienced apprehension and imputed intimidation are quite different. The findings are summarized in the following table.

In colleges with few incidents, about 40 percent of the professors report personal apprehension, but only about half of these impute intimidation to

7. In this discussion, it is irrelevant to describe the way in which these two scales were constructed.

TABLE 4

EXPERIENCED APPREHENSION AND PERCEIVED INTIMIDATION

	Number of incidents on the campus			
	5 or less	6–10	10–15	16 or more
Professors personally apprehensive	40%	51%	54%	51%
Professors imputing intimidation to colleagues	23%	42%	50%	52%

their colleagues. When colleges are not locally under attack, not much discussion of the general issue is likely to occur. The faculty read about incidents elsewhere and are aware of the generally unpleasant atmosphere; however, they believe their colleagues insensitive to the professional values involved. As the two rows approach the turbulent colleges the pair of figures in each column indicates that imputed intimidation occurs as frequently as experienced apprehension. The former is even slightly more frequent than the latter in the most turbulent colleges where much talk about threats to academic freedom occurs, and each professor feels that he is calm relative to the hysteria which surrounds him.

In recent years, there have been a growing number of reports on such contextual propositions, complete with examples. For instance, scales have been developed to measure the inferiority feelings of young people, and the scores have been related to their religion. The prevailing religion of the neighborhood in which the respondent lived was ascertained. In this way it was known whether the young people lived in an environment where their own religious faith was or was not dominant. It was a consistent finding that for every religious group, living in a social context of predominantly shared religious affiliation had a reassuring effect.

In another study, the problem was to discover factors affecting the award of compensation by jurors in accident cases. The individual wealth of each juror was ascertained (an individual variate), as well as the average wealth of the county in which the case was tried (an aggregate variate). The wealthier the county, the larger the compensations awarded in accident cases. However, *within* counties, wealthier jurors made smaller awards, presumably because they were biased in favor of the insurance companies whose values represented the preservation of wealth. This interpretation points up the interplay between social norms and the frames of reference for individuals.

The importance of contextual propositions can best be seen if one takes into account the history of E.S.R. In the early 1930's, studies using a sample of the total population and statistically examining the answers of individuals

to various questions began to dominate American research. Some sociologists made the point that this was an atomistic view of social issues, and deplored the lack of consideration for the broader social context within which attitudes and behavior of people were formed. In answer to this criticism, attention began to be focused on the development of contextual propositions. The idea was that the researcher should study how one collective affected the attitudes of its members. The role of the context remained on the level of a case study even if statistical information was gathered within the context. Finally, contextual propositions were developed covering many collectives and applying a multi-level sampling procedure. First, organizations or other collectives are sampled; then individuals are sampled within them. Comparisons can thus be made between collectives. This, then, is one other meaning of the term *structure:* the influence of the varying broad contexts upon individual behavior patterns.

While recognition of the importance of the contextual proposition is recent, one can find examples from earlier periods. Durkheim, for instance, studied the relation between individual divorce and suicide as it differed between countries characterized by the collective variate of strict or lenient divorce laws. The future will certainly produce more complex patterns. It will no longer be sufficient to characterize a collective by only one variate. General techniques of organizational measurements are rapidly developing.

The development of comparative cross-national research should clearly be related to this discussion; but it is impossible to treat it here. As one brief example, however, we can call attention to Rokkan's comment that differences in child-rearing practices between countries might influence the development of economic entrepreneurship. Rokkan calls this a macroproposition and distinguishes it correctly from the corresponding microproposition: individuals who vary in the way they were reared might differ in their entrepreneurial spirit *within* a country. The elements of the macroproposition are countries, while of the microproposition they are people.

However, a corresponding *contextual* proposition would combine both collective and individual variates; it would further require at least one other individual variate—for instance, personal aggressiveness. An eligible theme might then read as follows: Does the relation between aggressiveness and the entrepreneurial spirit of *people* vary according to the *country* in which they grew up when these countries are classified by their modal child-rearing practices?

Relation to Qualitative Analysis

E.S.R. is not restricted to quantitative data. Sociologists overlap with anthropologists in the use of field observations, and with historians in the use of documents. But sociologists are especially selfconscious about the

methods of data collection. As a matter of fact, they have often provided instruments for the other social sciences. It is therefore not surprising that field observations, which are considered exclusively an art by anthropologists, have at least been classified systematically by sociologists.

At this juncture it is relevant to point out that definite transitions exist between multivariate analysis and the use of qualitative materials, as will be illustrated by two examples. The first example pertains to the forming of typologies, which is a crucial sector in qualitative work. It is sometimes possible and useful to take a proposed typology and translate it into a combination of variates. Thus, Erich Fromm has proposed that the relation of young people to their parents can be classified into four types: complete authority, simple authority, lack of authority, and rebellion. It so happened that questionnaires were available for a sampling of young people which provided information about the way they felt toward their parents.

The authority relationship in a family is classified by the way in which the parents exercise their authority and the way in which the children accept it. Through questionnaires, parental exercise of authority was rated as either strong, moderate, or weak; likewise, filial acceptance of authority was rated as high, medium, or low. Logically, this makes possible nine combinations. This scheme can be related to Fromm's four types which were, of course, originally conceived from very different qualitative considerations.

TABLE 5

VARIATE SPACE SUBSTRUCTED FOR A
TYPOLOGY OF FAMILY RELATIONSHIPS

		Filial acceptance		
		High	Medium	Low
Parental	Strong	1_I	2_I	3_IV
exercise	Moderate	4_II	5_II	6_IV
	Weak	7	8	9

TABLE 6

Fromm's Type		Variate Combinations	Exercise	Acceptance
I	Complete authority	1 and 2	Strong	High or medium
II	Simple authority	4 and 5	Moderate	High or medium
III	Lack of authority	8	Weak	Medium
IV	Rebellion	3 and 6	Strong or moderate	Low

Combinations 7 and 9 in Table 5 are not encompassed by Fromm's typology. Apparently it was assumed that neither very high nor very low acceptance was possible for an authority which was scarcely exercised. The substruction, however, may be useful as a source of discovery. It points to the logical possibility that there may be children who desire an authority which is not actually exercised by their parents—combination 7. These discovered combinations suggest further research.

The procedure just exemplified consists of substructing a multivariate space of an intuitively conceived typology. The advantage of such a substruction is twofold: it allows one to test the logical consistency of the typology, and it suggests empirical procedures by which the intuitive classification can be produced in a more objective manner.

The opposite procedure is known as deviant case analysis, our second example. One begins with some multivariate finding and attempts to go beyond it by using additional qualitative information. Once more a specific finding will best elucidate the idea. In the study of American university professors previously mentioned, the respondents were asked two questions: (1) should Communist professors be fired?, and (2) should students be permitted to form a Communist campus organization? The following table demonstrates that the respondents were likely to be anti-Communist with respect to both issues. But more than 300 respondents seem inconsistent.

TABLE 7

RELATIONSHIP BETWEEN TWO PERMISSIVE RESPONSES

Respondents Who Say Young Communist League	Respondents Who Say Communist Professors	
	Should be fired	Should not be fired
Should not be allowed	888	198
Should be allowed	145	598

Some accepted freedom of thought for professors but not for students, and others took the opposite but apparently equally inconsistent position. From qualitative remarks elicited from these two groups, the conclusion was reached that the respondents had different images of the role of professors and students respectively, and that this affected their responses. A respondent who felt that professors are dreamers but that students could easily become mobilized and then be out of control, was placed in the upper right cell of Table 7. Inversely, a respondent was placed in the lower left cell if he felt that youngsters are youngsters and would settle down once they are grown, whereas professors are very influential people who in a conservative society could use their position for subversive influences.

Obviously, in a future study one would introduce these attitudes as explicit variates and then test the conclusions which grew from the qualitative material. The basic structure of this deviant case analysis reappears in a more complex form when one scrutinizes macrosociological comparative analysis.

The procedures discussed here are by no means the only ones which link variate language to broader macrosociological thinking. But it should suffice to show how one can abstract from E.S.R. a number of basic methodological procedures which are relevant to the development of systematic social theory and to some of the perennial macrosociological issues.

12.

The Corpus of Knowledge as a Normative Order: Intellectual Critiques of the Social Order of Knowledge and the Commonsense Features of Bodies of Knowledge

Alan F. Blum

Alan F. Blum was born in 1935 and received his Ph.D. in 1964 from the University of Chicago. Mr. Blum spent the next two years as a U.S. Public Health post-doctoral fellow in the department of psychiatry at Harvard University. Following that, he served as an assistant professor in the department of sociology at Columbia University and is currently on the faculty of the department of sociology at New York University. Mr. Blum has published several papers on sociological theory and on the sociology of mental illness, and is currently preparing a monograph on The Process of Socialization.

Our intention in this paper is to examine several variants of one method which has been used historically by thinkers to characterize, criticize, and revise the authoritative bodies of knowledge of their disciplines.

While bodies of knowledge have been found deficient on a variety of grounds, one method of criticizing knowledge has been used persistently by a variety of thinkers. This method describes the producers of bodies of knowledge as commonsense actors; [1] such a description is essentially equivalent to faulting such knowledge as lacking objectivity. In this paper we shall inspect three different ways of accomplishing such a demonstration and examine some of the implications of this critical method.

To begin, we shall give general characterizations of the intellectual critiques developed by Descartes, Hobbes, and Marx, followed by fairly close discussions of each of their critiques. Our intention throughout is to demonstrate the ways in which these critiques play off a common theme: that the social organization of knowledge is describable not in terms of the "struc-

1. The notion of the commonsense character of bodies of knowledge was developed from my readings of the works of Alfred Schutz and Harold Garfinkel. I must particularly record my indebtedness to the tremendous corpus of published and unpublished writings of Garfinkel, which, while not being responsible for what follows, nevertheless provided me with a number of usable conceptions for organizing the materials.

tural" properties of events-in-the-world which the knowledge is intended to formulate, but rather as a product of the informal understandings negotiated among members of an organized intellectual collectivity. The social organization of knowledge, then, is viewed not as a product of the "factual," "real" character of the world, but rather, as an outcome of the commonsense theorizing that occurs in the process of organizing and applying some description of the world.

Depictions of Bodies of Knowledge as Problematic

Descartes' dissatisfaction with the corpus of knowledge which he confronted was preeminently occasioned by the "varied opinion" which seemed to him to characterize it.[2] Descartes presumed that the features of controversy and argumentation indicated the presence of varied and differing opinions as to the nature of things and thus reflected an absence of certain knowledge. If there were certain knowledge, opinion would not be varied, and there would be no controversy because there would be nothing over which to argue. Certainty indicates a body of knowledge warranted by indubitably clear standards which anyone can recognize as furnishing distinct and unambiguous knowledge. Throughout history, men have characterized bodies of knowledge in this way—and have found them deficient. Their position derives from the supposition that knowledge differs from belief as fact differs from opinion; knowledge is true and not really arguable.

In Hobbes we note a different and perhaps more complex confrontation with the normative order of knowledge.[3] It is recognized that Hobbes's depiction of the corpus of knowledge changed over time and that this was reflected in his changing preference for Plato rather than Aristotle as the preeminent philosopher of antiquity.

Essentially, Hobbes conceived of the corpus of knowledge as the body of norms and precepts laid down by classical philosophy. While in the earlier period he originally did not question the validity of these norms and precepts, he did ask himself whether the mere enumeration of precepts constitutes the most efficient format for organizing knowledge. Hobbes took as problematic the format for presenting knowledge and was thus led to reassign meaning to the corpus; he did not accept the meaning which classical philosophy had assigned to the corpus of political philosophy.

One variation of Hobbes's view is found in Machiavelli, who characterized the classic tradition of political philosophy as guided by speculation

2. For my discussion of Descartes, I used his *Discourse on Method,* trans. Arthur Wollaston (Baltimore: Penguin Books, 1960).
3. For my discussion of Hobbes, see Molesworth's edition of the English works, *The Elements of Law,* ed. Tönnies (Cambridge: The University Press, 1928), L. Strauss, *The Political Philosophy of Hobbes* (Chicago: University of Chicago Press, 1952).

and "ideals" rather than by empirical descriptions of political experience. In their respective ways, then, Hobbes and Machiavelli both depicted the traditional corpus of knowledge reflected in classical political thought as unrealistic, inapplicable, and conjectural. Their choice of such descriptions suggests that they had developed their own conceptions of the criteria which the corpus of political knowledge could be expected to fulfill. Such conceptions were based upon their notions of the uses for which political knowledge is designed.

The complexity of Marx's view stems from the fact that he depicted not one but many bodies of knowledge, and found them each problematic on quite different grounds.[4] One of his most important contributions was his argument that knowledge is not disinterested and that the construction of a corpus of knowledge is inextricably linked to the interests of those who produce it. Thus, a critique of knowledge is necessarily a critique of producers of knowledge. Moreover, he attempted to demonstrate that knowledge, in principle, cannot be disinterested and hence must be evaluated with reference to practical demonstrations of its efficacy.

Marx characterized at least three bodies of knowledge at various times— history, philosophy, and classical economics—and he tended to treat each of them as a separate corpus. Of all the problematic features which he located, the most important was this: all previous bodies of knowledge tended to generate their own self-justifying standards of evaluation which were so closely linked to the interests of the creators that any evaluation of the corpus must take these interests as a point of departure.

Moreover, Marx located the dominant feature of all bodies of knowledge in the fact that since this knowledge was constructed to serve the interests of its producers, while the producers did not share the interests of the objects of knowledge (that is, the masses), such knowledge was controlled by the interests of its creators and was necessarily a distortion of reality (under the premise that reality = the interests of the masses). Thus, Marx saw the corpus as biased and invalid. The strength of his indictment derived principally from the tactic of attributing deficiencies in the corpus not to the lack of certainty, but to the organized features of intellectual activity as an interest group.

In the case of each of these three thinkers, we may note that the depiction of a corpus of knowledge originates in his feelings that the corpus is, in

---

4. All of Marx's writings are useful for this discussion, but the following have the greatest relevance: K. Marx, *The Poverty of Philosophy* (New York: International Publishers, 1963); K. Marx and F. Engels, *The German Ideology* (New York: International Publishers, 1947); K. Marx, *A Contribution to the Critique of Political Economy* (Chicago: Charles Kerr, 1904); T. B. Bottomore and M. Rubel, eds., *Karl Marx: Selected Writings in Sociology and Social Philosophy* (New York: McGraw, 1964). We have also used H. Marcuse, *Reason and Revolution* (Boston: Beacon, 1960).

certain respects, deficient. Thus, his description of the corpus inevitably appears as a description of its inadequacy in some respect. This deficiency is used by the thinker to ascribe problematic status to the corpus, to criticize it in such ways as to make its problematic character explicit. We are dealing, then, with the common "signs" or cultural insignia of a deficient corpus of knowledge which thinkers "see" from within a tradition and which they accredit as legitimate evidence of the inadequate state of knowledge. Our point is that all of these "signs" are furnished by the thinker's recognition of the commonsense character of the corpus.

Revising of Bodies of Knowledge

Hobbes' Revision

Hobbes introduced a program for redefining the corpus of knowledge of political philosophy. Recall that his objection was to the inapplicability of the traditional corpus as reflected in the work of Aristotle. Hobbes did not appreciate the efficacy of the traditional corpus in providing men with knowledge that was useful for facilitating their attainment of political prudence. Hobbes sought to replace theory by the primacy of practice; he sought the justification of knowledge in its practical benefit to man.

What device did Hobbes use to reassert the primacy of practical political knowledge as the distinguishing feature of the corpus? What are the standard resources which a thinker has available for redefining a corpus of knowledge in order to adapt it to the requirements of practicality?

Note that Hobbes did not—in his early period—find the *content* of the corpus problematic. What he did find questionable was the way in which the corpus was organized. It was not organized in such a way that men would find believable; since knowledge must facilitate man's adaptation to the practical circumstances of his polity, it should be organized in a way that he could find usable. Hobbes's question now became: How does one redefine a corpus of knowledge so that men will find it usable?

In this respect, Hobbes decided that the most important characteristic of an adequate body of knowledge lies in the procedures which are provided for its determinate application. Since the only men of theoretic import were aristocrats, the question became one of redesigning the corpus of knowledge in such a way that the aristocracy would find it usable. According to Hobbes, such a corpus should not be organized around general precepts, but rather in terms of examples.[5]

Thus he urged that the corpus of knowledge be redefined in terms of examples rather than general precepts. He then searched for a format which

5. Think of academic political scientists who insist that the most adequate corpus of political knowledge is that which is intelligible to practicing politicians.

would suitably organize knowledge around a set of examples which would provide an educative influence. To this end he stated that history properly read and utilized would provide the substance of this new corpus of knowledge. Why history? Because it provides the empirical cases which are more compelling to men than general precepts are. Men could understand, believe, and find useful a corpus organized in such a way because such a body of knowledge provides them with more appropriate guidelines in particular cases than does an enumeration of norms and precepts. According to Hobbes, an adequate body of knowledge was one that a member could use as a set of instructions in particular instances. Examples are instructive in such cases, and history provides the empirical substance of such examples.[6] How may we then summarize the particular strategy introduced by Hobbes for his purposes of revising the traditional corpus of knowledge?

Beyond the obvious characterization of Hobbes' tactic as being organized around some version of an "applicability" criterion, we may note a much more powerful feature. Hobbes's proposal amounted to the assertion that a corpus of knowledge cannot be defined and warranted unless the objects of knowledge (societal members) are able to use such knowledge as normative orders in formulating routine courses of action. This means that producers of knowledge can be expected to meet criteria of adequacy only if they respect (and perhaps, share) the points of view of those societal members who will employ such knowledge. Thus, adequate bodies of knowledge are usable bodies of knowledge, and usable bodies of knowledge are those which both producers and consumers respect within the same community of meanings.

The defect of the traditional corpus of classical political philosophy was not to be found in the fact that it was insensitive to the problem of facilitating the political prudence of societal members, for it was aware of such a problem as the central task of political philosophy.[7] Rather, its defect sprang from the fact that the creators of knowledge did not understand the kinds of meanings which such members were likely to assign to knowledge, and thus could not properly execute this task. To put it another way, classical political philosophy's failure was a failure to respect the points of view of its subjects as political actors. Hobbes proposed that a satisfactory understanding of actors would indicate that they do not find knowledge in the form of general precepts usable and employable, while such would not be the case for knowledge organized in terms of empirical cases and instances.

6. Bear in mind that we are discussing Hobbes's critique and program of revision for only one point in his career; he subsequently found the *content* of the traditional corpus inadequate, and came to distrust history as providing the most adequate empirical grounds. Thus in the end he contested both the validity and the applicability of the traditional corpus, and saw the possibility of developing an applicable corpus of knowledge based upon the direct study of human nature (his theory of motives) rather than upon history.
7. For a compelling description of this "central task" see Leo Strauss, *What Is Political Philosophy?* (Glencoe: Free Press, 1959).

We find in Hobbes one of the great styles of challenging a corpus of knowledge: by accusing it of sterility, formalism, and abstractness, he indicted its creators for their failure adequately to respect the points of view of their subjects.

In retrospect, Hobbes' final position closely resembled the program of Machiavelli. The traditional corpus was rejected by both for roughly similar reasons; the new corpus was seen as needing to satisfy the criterion of usability by particular segments of the population, and the most effective way to attain usability was thought to be through the empirical study of human motivation.

Descartes' Revision

Perhaps the most famous philosophic strategy introduced for the purposes of revising a corpus of knowledge was Descartes' program of methodical doubt. Essentially, this program was organized around a systematic and selfconscious distrust of commonsense knowledge. It specified the in-principle suspension of commonsense knowledge for the purpose of "cleansing one's mind" in order to arrive at certainty. (Recall that his search for certainty derived from his recognition of the discontinuities within the corpus of knowledge.)

Descartes' program for such a reconstruction was this: by screening out all influences, one may arrive at a description of an indubitably clear state of affairs; then, given such a description, one proceeds by systematically unraveling all of the derivations which are concealed within this description.

The inconsistencies of the previous corpus were attributed to the fact that thinkers were responsive to sense data, and sense data were unreliable and deceptive. In other words, a corpus of knowledge based upon descriptions of sense data is problematic, since it rests upon spurious foundations.

Descartes proposed that the state of the world as it appeared to the thinker's senses be considered problematic, and offered instead a program based upon the discovery of simple, immediate, and certain truths by systematically distrusting what was known through the senses. We might summarize Descartes' program thus: suspend all knowledge, start with particular and certain instances, and derive systematically.

In part, Descartes' critique may be read as follows: since the corpus of knowledge is normatively stipulated (that is, since it serves intellectuals as a normative order), the act of doubting it can be seen as deviation. Descartes then proposed various justifications for his repudiation of the corpus of knowledge as a normative order. As methods for discovering new principles, he proposed intuition (immediate intellectual awareness) and deduction (correct inference from those facts known with certainty). He prescribed the following rules (1) avoid all prejudice and accept nothing as true which cannot be clearly recognized as such; (2) divide each problem into as many parts as possible; (3) develop an orderly connection of thinking, starting

with simple facts and gradually leading to more complex problems; and (4) make complete enumerations.

Descartes recommended that everything be distrusted unless it could be clearly recognized as true. He proposed the utilization of new criteria for warranting factual descriptions for, according to him, what was lacking was a procedure for collecting and systematizing thought in an orderly, efficient manner. He was doing nothing more than providing rules for disciplining thought.

Now, there are two interesting notions in this strategy of criticizing and revising a corpus of knowledge. In the first place, the corpus was indicted because it was generated by scholars who were not thinking efficiently. This is almost a pedagogical critique. But certain knowledge was possible if only the thinker would apply himself vigorously to specific rules. In following such rules, the thinker would be able to discover certain truth. Descartes' program, thus, was aimed at the psychological reconstruction of the mind of the thinker.

The second strategy was a variation on a recurrent theme in intellectual innovation: the reconstruction proceeds in terms of the rules furnished by an alternative or competing corpus of knowledge. One is not only encouraged to doubt, in order to free the mind from "clutter," but with a small nucleus of "certain" facts in hand which are collected as a residual effect of total doubt, one proceeds "constructively" in terms of specific rules. Whereas Hobbes used history as his alternative, Descartes used the model of inference and reasoning derived from mathematics and geometry.

The strategy of invoking an alternative corpus of knowledge to reconstruct a corpus which is quite different has been frequently utilized. In these cases the thinker generally proposes that the "new" corpus has demonstrated that it can resolve the same class of problems more effectively than the traditional corpus. Since Descartes conceived of the central problem of philosophy as establishing certain truth, he searched out other disciplines with the same concerns but with a different set of substantive problems. After all, he reasoned, certainty is certainty, and the methods productive of it in one domain should be useful in another.

Marx's Revision

We shall begin with Marx's indictment of the corpus of historical knowledge: ". . . we do not set out from what men say, imagine, conceive, nor from men as narrated, thought of, imagined, conceived, in order to arrive at men in the flesh. We set out from real, active men." [8]

8. *German Ideology*, p. 14.

Marx characterized the corpus of historical knowledge as deficient because historians had accepted the assertions of societal members and their theorizing as factually descriptive of the historical epoch. He accused historians of accepting and codifying such commonsense knowledge, and of treating it as "given" and factual, rather than as problematic.

Marx claimed that the basic fact of history—the relation of man to nature —could not be grasped by taking the theories of these men as givens; rather the actions of men in relating to nature should be studied directly, and empirically. Previous historians had developed an abstract conception of social organization based upon sets of ideas which members had asserted, with such ideas being used as the data of history. On the contrary though, it should not be the theories of societal members which are consulted, but the actual activities of such members.

> History does nothing; it "does not possess immense riches," it "does not fight battles." It is men, real living men who do all this, who possess things and fight battles. . . . History is nothing but the activities of men in pursuit of their ends . . .[9]

The corpus is problematic because the data upon which it is based are derivative and of peripheral relevance to the actual forces of change in society. The abstractions of historians were seen as commonsense descriptions which were inaccurate depictions of the "real" character of society. The immediate remedy to such abstract and misleading descriptions of society is the empirical observation of men as actors, relating to nature. Thinkers will manage to produce such descriptions, however, only when they are able to free themselves from the interests which control them.

The way to proceed is to anchor one's descriptions in "real" (that is, empirical) descriptions. A "real" description shows some aspect of man's relation to nature. Thus, we should begin with real premises and deduce our knowledge from them. The historical corpus of knowledge began with arbitrary premises.[10]

Marx found the historical corpus of knowledge and the philosophical corpus of knowledge deficient on two essential grounds: (1) they were abstract and disconnected from empirical description, and (2) they accepted commonsense conceptions of events as "given" without treating them as problematic, as mere commonsense descriptions whose formal character remained to be observed and explicated. Both bodies of knowledge, but particularly history, tended to conceal "real" factors, and to accept commonsense conceptions of members as factual. He also indicted these bodies of knowledge for their speculative character, since their descriptions did not

9. Bottomore and Rubel, *Karl Marx*, p. 63.
10. Note how both Marx and Descartes use a notion of the "real," "hard" starting points of inquiry.

afford practical demonstration of their warrant. His was one of the most articulate examples of discrediting a corpus of knowledge because of the difficulty in demonstrating its factual character.

It is instructive to compare Marx's critiques of history and philosophy with his indictment of the corpus of knowledge produced by the classical economists. Marx characterized this corpus as deficient not because it ignored real factors, but because it conceived of them inadequately: classical economics treated the totality of economic laws, relations, and institutions as a cluster of isolated, objective facts and called these facts by neutral, abstract names (such as commodity, value, ground rent). Such conceptualization deprived economic facts of their social meanings.

He proposed to translate these terms into factors "determinative of human existence," with labor serving as his medium of translation. Since he conceived of labor as the existential, or basic, activity of man, his conceptualization of the economy was specifically addressed to the problem of how the economy realizes man's basic nature.

In introducing the concept of labor, Marx was embarking upon a fundamental enterprise in reconceptualizing economics. He proposed that the abstract terminology of economics be translated into a terminology organized around man's nature and his potentialities. In this way, conceptualization became radical rather than abstract.[11]

To conceive of this enterprise in its proper perspective—as a grand tactic in reconceptualization—imagine a modern sociologist responding to behaviorist descriptions by contending that they do not assign appropriate sociological meaning to their terms; or, think of Durkheim attempting to reconceptualize a variable like "season of the year" or "time of day" by reassigning to it a sociological meaning. Marx was seeking to reconceptualize economics from the point of view of sociology; his polemic charged that every term must be conceived as an instance of social action and related to the typical mind of a typical actor. His particular medium, in this sense, was labor.

Thus, while his emphasis changed as he turned his attention to different bodies of knowledge, Marx's indictment was generally organized around his description of each corpus as inadequately conceptualized. The tactics he proposed for correcting such a state was designed to demonstrate how meaning should be reassigned to events from the perspective of one who is interested in "real" description. The device which Marx proposed for this purpose was the dialectic method.

The dialectic can be restated as a series of rules. Start with the premise that men are born to be free; to be rational decision-makers functioning in harmony with constraints that fit their potentialities. Then reflect upon the fact that, historically, men have never met this description, have never lived

11. In this sense, "radical" means "sociological."

in socially organized environments which have fulfilled this intrinsic potential. Following this, conceive of every act, activity, event, relationship, and object as mere factuality, as a datum which is not to be endorsed just because it is, but which, rather, because it is, is somehow imperfect. The mere existence of things in certain ways does not make them real except on a factual level. What is real is latent, concealed underneath mere factual appearance, for what is real is a potential essence which is attributed to man by virtue of his being human. Thus, one examines every fact in a spirit of negation, with a view to locating the contradiction. The world of mere factuality is a contradiction because it conceals the realization of what really is (or inhibits the development, expression, cultivation of rationality). Dialectic thought then begins with the premise that man is unfree, that man and nature exist in conditions of alienation or as other than they "really" are.

Thought and the objects of thought are judged in terms of a standard which the theorist ascribes intrinsically to the very nature of thought and objects. This standard is reason: thought and its objects both are judged in reference to this standard of rationality. The essence of thought is reason; this is the criterion used to assign the status of reality to thought and its objects. Rationality is real, that is, essences and purposes are real. The real, then, is not the existent or the factual, but lies "in the nature of things."

Marx's tactics for treating the social world as problematic can be characterized as follows: the comprehension of the world by commonsense thought and by scholars is often misleading and fails to reveal things "as they really are." Our task is to develop a tactic for transcending appearances in order to get at reality. Unlike Descartes, Marx did not propose the suspension of all knowledge, for he felt that the theorist using the dialectical method operates with a standard of reality that serves as a presupposition. To Marx, making the world problematic meant taking things as they appeared and then subverting them to expose their "real" character.

The use of the dialectic proceeds through the demonstration that a systematic examination of the actor's lot reveals him to be unfree, contrary to factual appearance. The actor generally does not know that he is unfree, but this is not important theoretically—one only grasps oneself in such a selfconscious way when one is free, and since men are unfree (creatures of a system into which they have no insight) they cannot attain such self-consciousness.

How does the sociologist demonstrate that despite factual appearances, men are not free? He can show that actors are controlled by stimuli and impulses which they cannot freely manipulate, and that such controls are generated by the organization of the system. He can also demonstrate that all actions assembled by members can be reinterpreted within some schema as contributing to the irrationality of the system by preventing actors from recognizing their potentialities. Thus, all social structures can be analyzed

in terms of the way in which they contribute to the perpetuation of the ignorance, or alienation, of the actors.

The Social Organization of Knowledge

We can better understand the methodology of criticism in these three cases if we see each of the critiques as directed to the question: How is this particular body of knowledge possible? What this amounts to is asking how the assembly of a corpus of knowledge can be described as a sociological event. Discussion of this question requires some attention to the social order problem. Each of these three thinkers was able (to a degree that most of us are not) to conceive of a body of knowledge as a socially organized set of activities; each of them tried to show how the organized features of the corpus were in some sense a function of the taken-for-granted and un-analyzed commonsense stipulations negotiated by the thinkers. These were the grounds which permitted each to accuse the corpus of lacking "ob-jectivity."

To find a corpus of knowledge problematic is equivalent to challenging the rules to which members of a collectivity subscribe. More than this, the challenge amounts to saying that the rules available for organizing the production of this particular corpus of knowledge are insufficient for re-producing such knowledge, and that therefore the producers *went outside of the rules* in various unspecified ways to settle the problem of adequate description. Descartes, Hobbes, and Marx do not assert that thinkers can do otherwise (for rules do have to be "interpreted" in ways for which the rules themselves do not apply), but they argue that thinkers avoid describing precisely how they do such interpretive work by imputing an artificial stabil-ity to events-in-the-world. Such imputations allow the thinker to avoid the problem of describing his methods and procedures for the production of such stability. Thus, Descartes, Hobbes, and Marx could each argue that behind every corpus's conception of a factual, stable, real world there lies an unanalyzed, socially organized set of methods for producing such con-ceptions.

Let us conceive of the tasks of these three critics as the description of traditions of knowledge in the following way. They were confronted with bodies of knowledge as empirical data which they judged to be inadequate, and on the basis of such judgments each presented a description of the course of action which he presumed to be the necessary conditions and causes of such bodies of knowledge. Thus each theorized about the develop-ment of knowledge, and presented a sociological description of intellectual activity as the organization of social actions.

A conception of intellectual activity as a course of social action pre-supposes a conception of inquiry as rule-guided. These three thinkers—like

all those who reflect on their intellectual traditions—conceived of the previous bodies of knowledge as the assembled products of the methodical treatments of intellectuals acting upon their symbolic environments. They differed, though, in their manner of depicting the rule-guided character of intellectual activity as a course of action.

Thus, the intellectuals as actors were depicted by Hobbes as dopes in the sense in which scholars, academics, and pedants are dopes: they were dopes who imposed their own theoretic models upon their subjects and who confused their own points of view with the points of view of these subjects. When their subjects failed to behave in ways congruent with the descriptions, they attributed this to the imperfections of the "real" world and to the irrationality of actors in this world.[12] Thus, the problem of previous learned men was the fact that they did not adapt their intellectual behavior to the contingencies of the concrete circumstances. They narcissistically manipulated their own theories while remaining indifferent to the necessity of consulting the world in which their subjects existed.

Descartes depicted his intellectual predecessors as dopes in another way, and in a manner quite distinct from Marx. We can note this distinction clearly in comparing the two.

To Descartes, the assembly of the preexisting corpus of knowledge was almost anomic; he had a laissez-faire vision of the process of generating knowledge. He depicted intellectuals as a collection of autonomous particles, each of whom followed his own path in sensing, experiencing, and producing knowledge. The body of knowledge thus appeared as a concerted effect produced by independent and autonomous intellectuals, and such a production had in common only the negative feature that it was produced through the independent exercise of commonsense theorizing. Intellectuals were seen as dopes in the sense that any man who does not formulate his activity in terms of a consensually shared normative order is a dope. Dopes are those actors whose behavior is governed exclusively by what Weber called usage, rather than by orientation to a normative order.[13]

Marx also saw intellectual activity as socially governed and socially controlled. Such activity could be accurately described as action oriented to a normative order; however, it was oriented to the order furnished by rational self-interest rather than by criteria of "truth." In this respect, Marx was one of the first thinkers to present a developed sociological description of intellectual activity as an organized interest group. Intellectuals appeared as dopes in Marx's indictment because they were chained to their theories and were not free to alter these theories. Such unfreedom was a necessary con-

12. See H. Garfinkel, "Studies of the Routine Grounds of Everyday Activities," *Social Problems,* 11 (Winter, 1964), 225-250, for a discussion of the "judgmental dope" which stimulated this conception.
13. M. Weber, *Theory of Social and Economic Organization* (Glencoe: Free Press, 1952).

sequence of their positions within the social organization of society. Thus, while the intellectual predecessors of Hobbes and Descartes were depicted as special kinds of intellectual dopes, Marx's predecessors were portrayed as dopes precisely because they were no different in character from the average normal members of society. To Marx, dopes were intellectuals whose theoretical activities were controlled by the same forces that controlled the thoughts of normal members of society.

In order to demonstrate the commonsense character of knowledge, one need only describe a producer of knowledge as an actor whose organized practices themselves become features of the knowledge he is producing.

Marx had no difficulty in conceiving of such producers as actors. The only way in which to characterize social theory as bourgeois is to depict social theorists as typical societal members who are controlled by the same forces and interests as any man in society. Such a depiction says in effect that the activity of theorizing can be reproduced simply by virtue of knowledge of the theorist's social position and interests in the world. The objectivity of such knowledge is at issue because members' theories and practices have more to do with assembling the completed description than does the so-called factual character of the world which the description is intended to display or mirror or depict. In this way Marx repudiated his predecessors, for they had failed to free themselves from their ordinary theories and to inspect the intrinsic features of events-in-the-world. To transcend their positions as ordinary societal members in order to consult the world empirically constituted an impossible feat for them because their culturally accredited practices of seeing, observing, and recording were inexorably tied to their interests.

Descartes proceeded somewhat differently but with much the same result. If there was a factual, stable, regular, and standard world "out there," a world which was discovered rather than created by investigative procedures, then all descriptions of this world should converge independently of the methods and procedures for accomplishing such descriptions. Descartes seized upon this classic notion of objectivity—that there are elements of experience which are invariant across all methods and procedures for finding and reporting them—as the standard by which he found previous knowledge deficient.

This deficiency was a consequence of the fact that different investigative procedures produced different factual worlds. Intellectuals failed to suspend their commonsense knowledge of the world sufficiently, and so their descriptions varied with their diverse ways of conceiving of the world which they tacitly utilized as culturally accredited investigative assumptions.

Both Marx and Descartes accused intellectuals of assembling treatments of their environments of cultural objects (ideas) whose methical and regular features were as much a function of their unanalyzed practices as of the stable character of these objects themselves.

Hobbes's critique was based upon different grounds, but it also resulted in a criticism of the objectivity of the preexisting corpus. Such knowledge failed to be objective because it was not empirical. By this, Hobbes meant that theorists did not consult events in the world before describing them, but rather, by first imposing their own descriptions upon the world, inspected events by measuring them with the yardstick of "reality" established by their descriptions.

Hobbes reasoned somewhat as follows: knowledge which men cannot use is not objective knowledge because if it is not usable it must not be relevant to them. Descriptions which are formulated in such ways as to be irrelevant to the actions of members are not reproducible because men do not act under their auspices.

Conclusion: The Social Order Problem of Sociology

Let us try to pull together the various important threads of this chapter. What is perhaps ostensibly an essay in this history of ideas is actually intended as a discussion of intellectual methodology and of the social organization of knowledge. We intend "social organization of knowledge" in this sense: that knowledge is organized and assembled methodically by actors acting under the auspices of some conception of an adequate corpus of knowledge as a maxim of conduct.

Scholars who have traditionally sought to discover "objective" knowledge have had to contend with the fact that the search for and discovery of such knowledge is socially organized. Philosophically, this has often constituted a dilemma. Sociologically, it is not so much a dilemma as an inescapable fact of inquiry. The implication is this: if objective knowledge is taken to mean knowledge of a reality independent of language, or presuppositionless knowledge, or knowledge of the world which is independent of the observer's procedures for finding and producing the knowledge, then there is no such thing as objective knowledge.

Hobbes, Descartes, and Marx each seized upon some feature of knowledge which reflected this lack of "pure" objectivity and used such a deficiency as grounds for their respective critiques. Yet it is interesting to note that each of these men, in producing his own corpus, could be held accountable and criticizable on similar grounds, for producing knowledge which could not stand the test of "pure" objectivity.

In point of fact, sociologists among others are able to produce accredited knowledge which they regard as "objective enough." The question then is, how do sociologists decide the status of knowledge as objective enough?

In order to begin to establish criteria for answering such a question, sociologists must come to grips with the issue of the interaction between their investigative procedures and their findings. This means that sociol-

ogists must begin to treat as problematic the unanalyzed features of their methods and procedures which become constitutive properties of the events-in-the-world as in themselves describable events-in-the-world.

In this sense, it is important to note that sociological investigation is essentially a topic of sociological inquiry. To put it more clearly, the methods and procedures of sociology are applicable to the empirical practices of sociology as an event-in-the-world.

The import of this is not often appreciated, for sociologists like to assume that their various gambits, such as standardization, hypothetico-deductive procedure, or scientific method serve to insulate them from potential describability with their own principles. On the contrary, it can be demonstrated quite easily that at every point within the course of sociological inquiry, the sociologist has to decide on the basis of his tact and his commonsense knowledge how to settle various matters which require resolution before the inquiry can be consummated.

It is not that sociologists fail to recognize this fact of life; rather, they treat it as irrelevant, as a problem to be either controlled or evaded. Yet when sociologists follow methodological canons as maxims of conduct, they invariably find it impossible to proceed unless they raise as problematic what the canons mean as describable practices.

When Homans instructs us in the proper ways of theorizing, when Merton gives us the rules for doing a functional analysis, when Lazarsfeld tells us how to "move from concepts to indicators," they rely upon our cooperation and willingness to make sense of what they are saying when such sensibility rests in every case upon unanalyzed and problematic features of an investigation which are waiting to be described. The fact that we can understand their counsel and make sense of their arguments, the fact that we often reproduce such counsel in our practices, means only that we share with them a common culture, a culture which is rarely described and analyzed. The challenge then is how to make this culture problematic and describable. One way to begin is to conceive of the sociologist as an actor whose descriptions of events-in-the-world stand as assembled products of his methods and procedures of describing as a socially organized activity. It is at this point that we can start to see the sociologist's relation to his corpus as an actor's relationship to maxims of conduct. We can begin to appreciate the ways in which the problematic relationship between knowing rules and following them operates in the case of sociological practice. In fact, it is through an examination of sociology as an event-in-the-world that we come to recognize the commonsense character of sociological description.

If sociology is an activity like any other, it is describable in the same ways as any other, and such description faces the problems encountered in all describing. Thus, describing the activity of sociology as a paradigmatic instance of sociological description, we can better understand the resources

available for a description when we apply them to our activity of describing. We illuminate a range of problems involved in description when we attempt to describe ourselves doing the activity of describing, and in so doing we teach ourselves how to describe.

We know that sociology is possible because it is done, it is *played* in Wittgenstein's sense. The production and circulation of sociological descriptions attests to the fact that sociology is done and that it constitutes an observable and reportable set of activities. We *do produce* such descriptions in regular, standard, and stable ways, and they are accredited by our colleagues as legitimate. The fact that sociology as an activity is assembled in regular, standard, and typical ways suggests that sociology is describable, and also serves to raise in another form the problem of social order: given the existence of a set of observable practices called sociology, how are they possible?

The prevailing conceptions of sociological description (most vigorously represented in this volume) fail to provide adequate solutions to the social order problem of sociology, which in turn suggests that because of their failure to account for the existence of sociology in a satisfactory way, they cannot be expected to account for other events of conduct.

One such solution is organized around a conception of sociological inquiry as completely circumscribed by rules. This conception is typically articulated in the authoritative canons of hypothetico-deductive theorizing and philosophy of science texts (Levy's paper is a good example in this volume). As a solution to the social order problem of sociology, this position implies that the existence of sociology as a set of activities in the world can be accounted for by the appeal to "common norms," "rules," and their "internalization." Levy's program for adequate theorizing, for example, consists of a set of rules which we are instructed to follow to produce the describable state of affairs which he strongly recommends—ideal, elegant, scientific theory. We contend that while such rules can be enumerated ad infinitum, the statement of them does not describe how they are done in such a way that an actor in the world can follow them as instructions so as to produce Levy's desirable state of affairs. The program is then not adequately descriptive; it is an elliptic and persuasive solution to the problem of social order.

The second solution differs in emphasis but derives from the same conception of sociological description. We could account for sociology in terms of the events which sociological descriptions depict. Thus, the methodically produced character of human activities is seen as controlling the existence of sociology as an activity.

It is because marriages, wars, and suicides are done regularly and methodically that the activity of describing them is possible. Under this view, we have the strongest possible argument for the "pure" scientific status of sociology. Thus, sociology exists because it describes an objective, pure,

and incorrigible "real" world; we can account for sociology by enumerating and "pointing to" the objects in the world to which sociological names and descriptions refer.

On the other hand, it is easy to see that the methodical character of marriage, war, and suicide is only seen, recognized, and made possible through the organized practices of sociology. These regularities do not exist "out there" in pristine form to which sociologists functionally respond, but rather, they acquire their character as regularities and their features as describable objects only through the grace of sociological imputation. Thus, it is not an objectively discernible, purely existing external world which accounts for sociology; it is the methods and procedures of sociology which create and sustain that world.

How then is sociology possible? How may we resolve the social order problem of sociology? How is this activity—doing sociology—achieved? Sociology exists because sociologists have managed to negotiate a set of practices for creating and acting upon external worlds. We shall have adequately described sociology and accounted for its existence when we have described these commonsense practices.

13.

On Formal Structures of Practical Actions

Harold Garfinkel & Harvey Sacks

Harold Garfinkel was born in 1917 in Newark, New Jersey, and was educated at the University of Newark, the University of North Carolina, and Harvard University. Mr. Garfinkel is professor of sociology at the University of California, Los Angeles, and is the author of Studies in Ethnomethodology.

Harvey Sacks was born in 1935. He was educated at Columbia, Yale University Law School, and the University of California, Berkeley (Ph.D.). He has taught at U.C.L.A., and U.C., Irvine, where he is currently associate professor of anthropology and sociology. He does research on conversation and has published several papers on this topic.

The work for this paper was supported in part by the Air Force Office of Scientific Research, grant Af-AFOSR 757-67. A version of this paper, "On 'Setting' in Conversation," was read at the annual meetings of the American Sociological Association in San Francisco, August 31, 1967, at the session on sociolinguistics, chaired by Dr. Joshua Fishman. Hubert L. Dreyfus, Elliot G. Mishler, Melvin Pollner, Emmanuel Schegloff, Edward A. Tiryakian, E. Lawrence Wieder, and Don H. Zimmerman commented on the paper. Particular thanks are due to David Sudnow and Joan Sacks for their generosity with editorial tasks. An exceptional undergraduate term paper, "Gloss Achievements of Enterprises" by Nancy McArthur, motivated many of the paper's reflections.

T he fact that natural language serves persons doing sociology—whether they are laymen or professionals—as circumstances, as topics, and as resources of their inquiries furnishes to the technology of their inquiries and to their practical sociological reasoning *its* circumstances, *its* topics, and *its* resources. That reflexivity is encountered by sociologists in the actual occasions of their inquiries as indexical properties of natural language. These properties are sometimes characterized by summarily observing that a description, for example, in the ways it may be a constituent part of the circumstances it describes, in endless ways and unavoidably, elaborates those circumstances and is elaborated by them. That reflexivity assures to natural language characteristic indexical properties such as the following: the definiteness of expressions resides in their consequences; definitions can be used to assure a definite collection of "considerations" without providing a boundary; the definiteness of a collection is assured by circumstantial possibilities of indefinite elaboration.[1]

Indexical features are not particular to laymen's accounts. They are familiar in the accounts of professionals as well. For example, the natural language formula, "The objective reality of social facts is sociology's fundamental principle," [2] is heard by professionals according to occasion as a

1. On pp. 348-349 the properties of indexical expressions are discussed at length.
2. Emile Durkheim, *The Rules of Sociological Method* (Chicago: University of Chicago Press, 1938).

338

definition of association members' activities, as their slogan, their task, aim, achievement, brag, sales pitch, justification, discovery, social phenomenon, or research constraint. Like any other indexical expression, the transient circumstances of its use assure it a definiteness of sense as definition or task or whatever, to someone who knows how to hear it.[3] Further, as Helmer and Rescher [4] showed, on no occasion is the formula assured a definiteness that exhibits structures other than those that are exhibited by pointed references. This is to say that when the definiteness of the expression is analyzed with prevailing methods of logic and linguistics it exhibits few or no structures that available methods can handle or make interesting. Sociology's methods of formal analysis are differently disappointed by these expressions. Their definiteness of sense is without structures that can be demonstrated in the *actual* expressions with the use of available mathematical methods, to specify a sense, definitely. In a search for rigor the ingenious practice is followed whereby such expressions are first transformed into ideal expressions. Structures are then analyzed as properties of the ideals, and the results are assigned to actual expressions as their properties, though with disclaimers of "appropriate scientific modesty."

The indexical properties of natural language assure to the technology of sociological inquiries, lay and professional, the following unavoidable and irremediable practice as their earmark: Wherever and by whomever practical sociological reasoning is done, it seeks to remedy the indexical properties of practical discourse; it does so in the interests of demonstrating the rational accountability of everyday activities; and it does so in order that its assessments be warranted by methodic observation and report of situated, socially organized particulars of everyday activities, which of course include particulars of natural language.

The remedial practices of practical sociological reasoning are aimed at accomplishing a thoroughgoing distinction between objective and indexical expressions with which to make possible the substitution of objective for indexical expressions. At present that distinction and substitutability provides professional sociology its infinite task.[5]

These motives and recommendations are easily observed in most of the papers in this volume, though they are perhaps liveliest in those of Blalock,

---

3. This property is elucidated in Don H. Zimmerman and Melvin Pollner, "The Everyday World as a Phenomenon," in Harold B. Pepinsky, ed., *Studies in Human Information Processing* (in press).

4. Olaf Helmer and Nicholas Rescher, *The Epistemology of the Inexact Sciences* (Santa Monica: RAND Corporation, October 13, 1958).

5. We mean by "infinite task" that the difference and substitutability motivate inquiries whose results are recognized and treated by members as grounds for further inferences and inquiries. It is with respect to the difference and substitutability as aims of inquiry that "infinite task" is understood by members to refer to the "open" character of sociological fact, to the "self-cleansing" body of social scientific knowledge, to the "present state of a problem," to cumulative results, to "progress" and the rest.

Douglas, Inkeles, Lazarsfeld, Levy, Moore, Parsons, and Spengler, who use them to locate needed tasks for sociological theorizing, to cite achievements, and to take note of available methods and results as professional stock-in-trade. The remedial program of practical sociological reasoning is specified in such characteristic practices of professional sociological inquiry as the elaboration and defense of unified sociological theory, model building, cost-benefit analysis, the use of natural metaphors to collect wider settings under the experience of a locally known setting, the use of laboratory arrangements as experimental schemes of inference, schematic reporting and statistical evaluations of frequency, reproducibility, or effectiveness of natural language practices and of various social arrangements that entail their use, and so on. For convenience, we shall collect such practices of professional sociology's practical technology with the term "constructive analysis."

Irreconcilable interests exist between constructive analysis and ethnomethodology in the phenomena of the rational accountability of everyday activities and its accompanying technology of practical sociological reasoning. Those differences have one of their foci in indexical expressions: in contrasting conceptions of the ties between objective and indexical expressions, and in contrasting conceptions of the relevance of indexicals to the tasks of clarifying the connections between routine and rationality in everyday activities. Extensive phenomena that constructive analysis has missed entirely are detailed in the ethnomethodological studies of Bittner, Churchill, Cicourel, Garfinkel, MacAndrew, Moerman, Pollner, Rose, Sacks, Schegloff, Sudnow, Wieder, and Zimmerman.[6] Their studies have

---

6. Egon Bittner, "Police Discretion in Emergency Apprehension of Mentally Ill Persons," *Social Problems,* 14 (Winter, 1967), 278-292; "The Police on Skid-row: A Study of Peace Keeping," *American Sociological Review,* 32 (October, 1967), 699-715. Lindsey Churchill, "Types of Formalization in Small-group Research," review article, *Sociometry,* vol. 26 (September, 1963); "The Economic Theory of Choice as a Method of Theorizing," paper delivered at the American Sociological Association meetings, August 31, 1964; "Notes on Everyday Quantitative Practices," in Harold Garfinkel and Harvey Sacks, eds., *Contributions to Ethnomethodology* (Bloomington: Indiana University Press, in press). Aaron Cicourel, *Method and Measurement in Sociology* (Glencoe: Free Press, 1964); *The Social Organization of Juvenile Justice* (New York: Wiley, 1968). Harold Garfinkel, *Studies in Ethnomethodology* (Englewood Cliffs: Prentice-Hall, 1967). Craig MacAndrew, "The Role of 'Knowledge at Hand' in the Practical Management of Institutionalized Idiots," in Garfinkel and Sacks, *Contributions;* with Robert Edgerton: *Time Out: A Social Theory of Drunken Comportment* (Chicago: Aldine, 1969). Michael Moerman, "Ethnic Identification in a Complex Civilization: Who Are the Lue?" *American Anthropologist,* 65 (1965), 1215-1230; "Kinship and Commerce in a Thai-Lue Village," *Ethnology,* 5 (1966), 360-364; "Reply to Naroll," *American Anthropologist,* 69 (1967), 512-513; "Being Lue: Uses and Abuses of Ethnic Identification," American Ethnological Society, *Proceedings of the 1967 Spring Meeting* (Seattle: University of Washington Press, 1968), 153-169. Zimmerman and Pollner, "The Everyday World." Edward Rose, "Small Languages," in Garfinkel and Sacks, *Contributions to Ethnomethodology; A Looking Glass Conversation in the Rare Languages of Sez and Pique,* Program on Cognitive Processes Report No. 102 (Boulder: Institute of Behavioral Science, University of Colorado, 1967); *Small Languages: The Making of Sez,* Bureau of Socio-

shown in demonstrable specifics (1) that the properties of indexical expressions are ordered properties,[7] and (2) *that* they are ordered properties is an ongoing, practical accomplishment of every actual occasion of commonplace speech and conduct. The results of their studies furnish an alternative to the repair of indexical expressions as a central task of general theory building in professional sociology.

The alternative task of general theory building is to describe that achievement in specifics in its organizational variety. The purposes of this paper are to locate that achievement as a phenomenon and to specify some of its features, to describe some structures in the practices which make up that achievement, and to take notice of the obviousness, enormous interest, and pervasiveness which that achievement has for members, be they lay or professional analysts of ordinary activities. We do so with the aim of recommending an alternative account of formal structures in practical actions to those accounts that make up the work and achievements of practical sociological reasoning wherever it occurs—among laymen, of course, but with overwhelming prevalence in contemporary professional sociology and other social sciences as well, and in all cases without serious competitors.

Members' Methods of Sociological Inquiry

Alfred Schutz made available for sociological study the practices of commonsense knowledge of social structures of everyday activities, practical circumstances, practical activities, and practical sociological reasoning.[8] It is his original achievement to have shown that these phenomena have characteristic properties of their own and that thereby they constitute a legit-

logical Research, Report No. 16, Part 1 (Boulder: Institute of Behavioral Science, University of Colorado, 1966). Harvey Sacks, *Social Aspects of Language: The Organization of Sequencing in Conversation* (Englewood Cliffs: Prentice-Hall, forthcoming, 1969). Emmanuel Schegloff, "Sequencing in Conversational Openings," *American Anthropologist* (in press); "The First Five Seconds," Ph.D. dissertation, Department of Sociology and Social Institutions, University of California, Berkeley, 1967. David Sudnow, *Passing On: The Social Organization of Dying* (Englewood Cliffs: Prentice-Hall, 1967); "Normal Crimes: Sociological Features of a Penal Code in a Public Defender's Office," *Social Problems,* 12 (Winter, 1965), 255-276. E. Lawrence Wieder, "Theories of Signs in Structural Semantics," in Garfinkel and Sacks, *Contributions.* Don H. Zimmerman, "Bureaucratic Fact Finding in a Public Assistance Agency," in Stanton Wheeler, ed., *The Dossier in American Society* (in press); "The Practicalities of Rule Use," in Garfinkel and Sacks, *Contributions;* "Paper Work and People Work: A Study of a Public Assistance Agency," Ph.D. dissertation, Department of Sociology, University of California, Los Angeles, 1966.
7. That is, socially organized in the sense in which this paper is talking of formal structures as accomplishments.
8. Alfred Schutz, *Collected Papers I: The Problem of Social Reality,* 1962; *Collected Papers II: Studies in Social Theory,* 1964; *Collected Papers III: Studies in Phenomenological Philosophy,* 1966 (The Hague: Martinus Nijhoff); *The Phenomenology of the Social World* (Chicago: Northwestern University Press, 1967).

imate area of inquiry in themselves. Schutz's writings furnished us with
endless directives in our studies of the circumstances and practices of practical sociological inquiry. The results of these studies are detailed in other
publications.[9] They furnish empirical justification for a research policy that
is distinctive to ethnomethodological studies. That policy provides that the
practices of sociological inquiry and theorizing, the topics for those practices, the findings from those practices, the circumstances of those practices,
the availability of those practices as research methodology, and the rest,
are through and through members' methods of sociological inquiry and
theorizing. Unavoidably and without hope of remedy the practices consist
of members' methods for assembling sets of alternatives, members' methods
for assembling, testing, and verifying the factual character of information,
members' methods for giving an account of circumstances of choice and
choices, members' methods for assessing, producing, recognizing, insuring,
and enforcing consistency, coherence, effectiveness, efficiency, planfulness,
and other rational properties of individual and concerted actions.

The notion of *member* is the heart of the matter. We do not use the term
to refer to a person. It refers instead to mastery of natural language, which
we understand in the following way.

We offer the observation that persons, because of the fact that they are
heard to be speaking a natural language, *somehow* are heard to be engaged
in the objective production and objective display of commonsense knowledge of everyday activities as observable and reportable phenomena. We
ask what it is about natural language that permits speakers and auditors to
hear, and in other ways to witness, the objective production and objective
display of commonsense knowledge, and of practical circumstances, practical actions, and practical sociological reasoning as well. What is it about
natural language that makes these phenomena observable-reportable, that
is, *account-able* phenomena? For speakers and auditors the practices of
natural language somehow exhibit these phenomena in the particulars of
speaking, and *that* these phenomena are exhibited is thereby itself made
exhibitable in further description, remark, questions, and in other ways for
the telling.

The interests of ethnomethodological research are directed to provide,
through detailed analyses, that account-able phenomena are through and
through practical accomplishments. We shall speak of "the work" of that
accomplishment in order to gain the emphasis for it of an ongoing course
of action. The work is done as assemblages of practices whereby speakers in
the situated particulars of speech mean something different from what they
can say in just so many words, that is, as "glossing practices." An understanding of glossing practices is critical to our arguments, and further discussion will be found in the appendix to this chapter.

9. See footnote 6.

I. A. Richards has provided a thematic example.[10] He suggests the use of question marks to bracket some spoken phrase or text. For example, ?empirical social research?, ?theoretical systems?, ?systems of sequences?, ?social psychological variables?, ?glossing practices? instruct a reader to proceed as follows. How a bracketed phrase is to be comprehended is at the outset specifically undecided. How it is to be comprehended is the task of a reading whereby some unknown procedure will be used to make the text comprehensible. Since nothing about the text or procedure needs to be decided for the while, we will wait for the while, for whatever the while. When and if we have read and talked about the text, we will review what might be made of it. Thus we can have used the text not as undefined terms but as a gloss over a lively context whose ways, as a sense assembly procedure, we found no need to specify.[11]

Richards' gloss consists of practices of talking with the use of particular texts in a fashion such that how their comprehended character will have worked out in the end remains unstated throughout, although the course of talk may be so directed as to compose a context which embeds the text and thereby provides the text's replicas with noticed, changing, but unremarked functional characters such as "a text in the beginning," "a text as an end result," "an intervening flow of conversation to link the two," and so on.[12]

Apparently speakers can, will, could, ought, and do proceed in the fashion for which Richards' gloss of a text is a thematic example, to accomplish recognizably sensible definiteness, clarity, identification, substitution, or relevance of the notational particulars of natural language. And apparently speakers can proceed by glossing, and do the immense work that they do with natural language, even though over the course of their talk it is not known and is never, not even "in the end," available for saying in so many words just what they are talking about. Emphatically, that does not mean that speakers do not know what they are talking about, *but instead they know what they are talking about in that way.*

Richards' gloss is merely one of these ways.[13] Glossing practices exist in empirical multitude. In endless but particular, analyzable ways, glossing practices *are* methods for producing observable-reportable understanding,

10. I. A. Richards, *Speculative Instruments* (Chicago: University of Chicago Press, 1955), pp. 17-56.
11. We mean that none was called for, and that in other glossing practices something else could be the case.
12. These remarks are adapted from suggestions that we took from Samuel Todes, "Comparative Phenomenology of Perception and Imagination: Part I: Perception," *The Journal of Existentialism,* 6 (Spring, 1966), 257-260.
13. This cannot be emphasized too strongly. Because we used the present perfect tense to report Richards' gloss there is the risk that our description may be read as though we were recommending that Richards' gloss defines *the* way that clear, definite speaking is done. Richards' gloss is only *one* way that clear, definite speaking is done. There are others, which consist of glossing practices different from Richards' gloss. Richards' gloss is used as a perspicuous example, not as a definition.

with, in, and of natural language. As a multitude of ways for exhibiting-*in*-speaking and exhibiting-*for*-the-telling that and how speaking is understood, glossing practices *are* "members," *are* "mastery of natural language," *are* "talking reasonably," *are* "plain speech," *are* "speaking English" (or French, or whatever), *are* "clear, consistent, cogent, rational speech."

We understand mastery of natural language to consist in this. In the particulars of his speech a speaker, in concert with others, is able to gloss those particulars and is thereby meaning something different than he can say in so many words; he is doing so over unknown contingencies in the actual occasions of interaction; and in so doing, the recognition *that* he is speaking and *how* he is speaking are specifically not matters for competent remarks. That is to say, the particulars of his speaking do not provide occasions for stories about his speaking that are worth telling, nor do they elicit questions that are worth asking, and so on.

The idea of "meaning differently than he can say in so many words" requires comment. It is not so much "differently than what he says" as that *whatever* he says provides the very materials to be used in *making out* what he says. However extensive or explicit what a speaker says may be, it does not by its extensiveness or its explicitness pose a task of deciding the correspondence between what he says and what he means that is resolved by citing his talk verbatim.[14] Instead, his talk itself, in that it becomes a part of the selfsame occasion of interaction, becomes another contingency of that

---

14. The following excerpt provides two structurally distinct examples. (1) Not only is the speaker making out from what was said, what was meant, by the person whose talk is being quoted by the speaker, but (2) the whole body of talk is introduced by the speaker as showing that its speaker knows what is meant by the talk of a just-prior speaker; that is, it is delivered with "I know what you mean" as its initial part.

T: I know just what you mean. We, we go through this thing every year. My father said, "No gifts." And we tried to analyze what—
B: Does no gifts mean no gifts or does it mean more gifts?
T: No, he, he gave us one reason why "no gifts." And I was questioning the reason. I didn't think it was his, a legitimate reason. I didn't think it was his real reason. He said, "Well, you know how the Christmas, all the stores, uh, well, make such a big killing over Christmas, killing, and Christmas is becoming commercialized, and therefore, I don't wanna be sucked into this thing. I'm not giving gifts this year."
J: "You spend your money and buy something you really want, and I'll spend my money and buy something I really want."
T: But we figured there must be something deeper, because if a guy is aware of, that Christmas is becoming very commercialized, uh, must he submit to this idea and reject it entirely, and end up giving no gifts, or is it because he really doesn't, he's not a person that likes to give anyway?
B: Yeah.
T: And this is just a phony excuse for not giving. And finally, I think we figured out it must be some kind of a, a combination, and he really isn't that stingy.

interaction.[15] It extends and elaborates indefinitely the circumstances it glosses and in this way contributes to its own accountably sensible character. The thing that is said assures to speaking's accountably sensible character its variable fortunes. In sum, the mastery of natural language is throughout and without relief an occasioned accomplishment.

Ethnomethodology's Interests in Formal Structures of Practical Actions

Ethnomethodology's interests, like those of constructive analysis, insistently focus on the formal structures of everyday activities. However, the two understand formal structures differently and in incompatible ways.

We call attention to the phenomenon that formal structures are available in the accounts of professional sociology where they are recognized by professionals and claimed by them as professional sociology's singular achievement. These accounts of formal structures are done via sociologists' mastery of natural language, and require that mastery as the *sine qua non* of adequate professional readership. This assures to professional sociologists' accounts of formal structures its character as a phenomenon for ethnomethodology's interest, not different from any other members' phenomenon where the mastery of natural language is similarly involved. Ethnomethodological studies of formal structures are directed to the study of such phenomena, seeking to describe members' accounts of formal structures wherever and by whomever they are done, while abstaining from all judgments of their adequacy, value, importance, necessity, practicality, success, or consequentiality. We refer to this procedural policy as "ethnomethodological indifference."

Ethnomethodological indifference cannot be viewed as a position which would claim that no matter how extensive a volume like Berelson's might become, problems yet could be found. Nor, in that regard, would it be the case that insofar as the predictive efficacy of professional sociology had an asymptotic form, one could count on a margin of error as a stable property within which research could proceed. Counting on the fact that given the statistical orientations of professional sociology one would always have unexplained variance is not our way of locating yet unexplained phenomena.

---

15. The developmental sense of *becomes* is intended; not its sense of a development in the past that is now finished. To emphasize "process" the sentence might be read as follows: "Instead, his talk itself, in that it is in becoming a part of the selfsame occasion of interaction is in becoming another contingency of that interaction." Similar remarks might be made about "another."

Our work does not stand then in any modifying, elaborating, contributing, detailing, subdividing, explicating, foundation-building relationship to professional sociological reasoning, nor is our "indifference" to those orders of tasks. Rather, our "indifference" is to the whole of practical sociological reasoning, and *that* reasoning involves for us, in whatever form of development, with whatever error or adequacy, in whatever forms, inseparably and unavoidably, the mastery of natural language. Professional sociological reasoning is in no way singled out as a phenomenon for our research attention. Persons doing ethnomethodological studies can "care" no more or less about professional sociological reasoning than they can "care" about the practices of legal reasoning, conversational reasoning, divinational reasoning, psychiatric reasoning, and the rest.

Given ethnomethodology's procedure of "indifference," by *formal structures* we understand everyday activities (a) in that they exhibit upon analysis the properties of uniformity, reproducibility, repetitiveness, standardization, typicality, and so on; (b) in that these properties are independent of particular production cohorts; (c) in that particular-cohort independence is a phenomenon for members' recognition; and (d) in that the phenomena (a), (b), and (c) are every particular cohort's practical, situated accomplishment.

The above development of formal structures contrasts with that which prevails in sociology and the social sciences in that the ethnomethodological procedure of "indifference" provides for the specifications (c) and (d) by studying everyday activities as practical ongoing achievements.

A further contrast between ethnomethodology's treatment of formal structures and that of constructive analysis is specified by the characteristic that it is as masters of natural language that constructive analysts recommend and understand that their accounts of formal structures provide aims and singular achievements of their technology of research and theory. It is as masters of natural language that constructive analysts understand the accomplishment of that recommendation to be constructive analysis' infinite task. Constructive analytic accounts of formal structures are thus practical achievements, through and through. Natural language provides to constructive analysis its topics, circumstances, resources, and results as natural language *formulations* of ordered particulars of members' talk and members' conduct, of territorial movements and distributions, of relationships of interaction, and the rest.

Ethnomethodologically, such practices whereby accounts of formal structures are done comprise the phenomena of practical sociological reasoning. Obviously those practices are not the monopoly of Association members. The remainder of this chapter takes that phenomenon under scrutiny, reviewing members' methods for producing and recognizing formal structures of everyday activities by examining members' practices of *formulating*.

The Phenomenon

In that inquiries are done that make use of or are about members' talk, an inquirer will invariably exhibit a concern to clarify that talk in the interests of the inquiry. So, for example, an interviewee's remark, "She didn't like it here so we moved, may provide a researcher occasion to do such things as give that utterance a name, tell who "she" is, where "here" is, whom the "we" covers. In the large literature in logic and linguistics such terms have been called indicators, egocentric particulars, indexical expressions, occasional expressions, indices, shifters, pronominals, and token reflexives. A list of such terms would start with "here, now, this, that, it, I, he, you, there, then, soon, today, tomorrow."

We begin with the observations about these phenomena that everyone regularly treats such utterances as occasions for reparative practices; that such practices are native not only to research but to all users of the natural language; that without knowing what a particular research dealt with one could list the terms that would need to be clarified, or translated, or replaced, or otherwise remedied, and that the terms could be located and their remedies proposed and demonstrated for all practical purposes, with or without research and with or without knowing how extensive are similar concerns of others. The large and ancient literature in logic and linguistics that bears on researchers' work is a minor tributary in the rush of that omniprevalent work.

We treat as fact that researchers—*any* researchers, lay or professional, naïve or wellversed in logic and linguistics—who start with a text, find themselves engaged in clarifying such terms that occur in it. What should be made of that sort of fact? What do we, in this article, want to make of that fact?

If, whenever housewives were let into a room, each one on her own went to some same spot and started to clean it, one might conclude that the spot surely needed cleaning. On the other hand, one might conclude that there is something about the spot and about the housewives that makes the encounter of one by the other an occasion for cleaning, in which case the fact of the cleaning, instead of being evidence of dirt, would be itself a phenomenon.

Indexical expressions have been studied and have been dealt with in identical fashion times without end, not only in naïveté, but more interestingly, in apparently required disregard of previous achievements. The academic literature furnishes evidence of how ancient is that reparative work. The *Dissoi Logii,* a fragment of text from approximately 300 B.C., gives attention to the sentence "I am an initiate" because it presents diffi-

culties.[16] The issue is that of the truth or falsity of a sentence when, if said by A it was true, but if said by B it was false; if said by A at one time it was true, but if said by A at another time it was false; if said by A from one status of A it was true, but if said by A from another it was false.

To the problems posed by sentences like this, programmatic solutions have long been available. One would begin by replacing "I" with a proper name, would add a date, would specify a status with respect to which the speaker was an initiate. A stupendous amount of work has been devoted to such phenomena.

That work is briefly characterized in the following section.

A Characterization of Indexical Expressions

An awareness of indexical expressions occurs not only in the earliest writing but in the work of major authors over the entire history of logic. Every major philosopher has commented on them. Consider for example Peirce and Wittgenstein, Peirce because he is usually cited to mark the beginning of the interest of modern logicians and linguists in indexicals, and Wittgenstein because when his later studies are read to see that he is examining philosopher's talk as indexical phenomena, and is describing these phenomena without thought of remedy, his studies will be found to consist of a sustained, extensive, and penetrating corpus of observations of indexical phenomena.[17]

We borrow from the remarks by logicians and linguists to characterize indexical expressions. Edmund Husserl spoke of expressions (i) whose sense cannot be decided by an auditor without his necessarily knowing or assuming something about the biography and purposes of the user of the expression, the circumstances of the utterance, the previous course of discourse, or the particular relationship of actual or potential interaction that exists between the user and the auditor.[18] (ii) Bertrand Russell pointed out that descriptions involving them apply on each occasion of use to only one thing, but to different things on different occasions.[19] (iii) Such expressions, he said, are used to make unequivocal statements that nevertheless seem to change in truth value. (iv) Nelson Goodman wrote that each of their utterances constitutes a word and refers to a certain person, time, or place

16. William Kneale and Martha Kneale, *The Development of Logic* (London: Oxford University Press, 1962), p. 16.
17. Charles S. Peirce, *Collected Papers, Vol. 2* (Cambridge: Harvard University Press, 1932), paras. 248, 265, 283, 305; Ludwig Wittgenstein, *Philosophical Investigations* (Oxford: Basil Blackwell, 1953).
18. Occasional expressions are discussed in Marvin Farber, *Foundation of Phenomenology* (Cambridge: Harvard University Press, 1943), pp. 237-238; and C. N. Mohanty, *Edmund Husserl's Theory of Meaning* (The Hague: Martinus Nijhoff, 1964), pp. 77-80.
19. Bertrand Russell, *Inquiry into Meaning and Truth* (London: Allen, 1940), chap. 7, pp. 102-109.

but names something not named by some replica of the word.[20] (v) Their denotation is relative to the user. (vi) Their use depends upon the relation of the use to the object with which the word is concerned. (vii) For a temporal indexical expression, time is relevant to what it names. (viii) Similarly, just what region a spatial indexical expression names depends upon the location of its utterance. (ix) Indexical expressions and statements containing them are not freely repeatable in a given discourse in that not all their replicas therein are also translations of them.[21]

In their explicit attempts to recover commonplace talk in its structural particulars, logicians and linguists encounter these expressions as obstinate nuisances.[22] The nuisances of indexicals are dramatic wherever inquiries are directed at achieving, for practical talk, the formulation and decidability of alternatives of sense, or fact, or methodic procedure, or agreement among "cultural colleagues." Features of indexical expressions have motivated among professionals endless methodological studies directed to their remedy. Indeed, the work by practitioners to rid the practices of *a* science, of *any* science, of these nuisances, because, and in the ways such work occurs in all sciences,[23] furnishes each science its distinctive character of preoccupation and productivity with methodological issues. Whatever the science, actual situations of practical investigative activities afford researchers endless occasions and motives for attempts to remedy indexical expressions. Thus methodological studies, wherever they occur, lay and professional, have been concerned, virtually without exception, with remedying indexical expressions while insistently holding as aims of their studies a programmatically relevant distinction between objective and indexical expressions, and a programmatically relevant substitutability of objective for indexical expressions. In these programmatic studies of the formal properties of natural languages and practical reasoning, the properties of indexicals, while furnishing investigators with motivating occasions for remedial actions, remain obstinately unavoidable and irremediable.

Such "methodological" concerns are not confined to the sciences. One finds ubiquitous concern among conversationalists with faults of natural

20. Nelson Goodman, *The Structure of Appearance* (Cambridge: Harvard University Press, 1951), pp. 290ff.
21. A review of indexical expressions is found in Yehoshua Bar-Hillel, "Indexical Expressions," *Mind*, 63 ns (1954), pp. 359-379.
22. Hubert L. Dreyfus, "Philosophical Issues in Artificial Intelligence," Publications in the Humanities, No. 80, Department of Humanities, Massachusetts Institute of Technology, Cambridge, Mass., 1967; Hubert L. Dreyfus, *Alchemy and Artificial Intelligence*, P-3244 (Santa Monica: RAND Corporation, December, 1965).
23. The reader is asked to read for "all sciences" any inquiries whatsoever that are directed to the detection and assessment of effectiveness of practical activities and to the production of members' accounts of that effectiveness. In addition to the academically taught sciences of the Western world, we include the "ethno" sciences that anthropologists have described, such as ethnomedicine and ethnobotany, as well as the enormous number of empirical disciplines that have their effectiveness in and as practical activities as their abiding phenomenon: Azande witchcraft, Yaqui shamanism, waterwitching, astrology, alchemy, operations research, and the rest.

language. Faults are seen by members to occur in the prevalence of demonstratives, pronouns, and tenses. Faults are assigned to members to usage by others about whom it is said that they have small vocabularies. Such concerns are accompanied by a prevalent recommendation that terms, utterances, and discourse may be clarified, and other shortcomings that consist in the properties of indexical expressions may be remedied by referring them to "their setting" (i.e., the familiar recommendations about the "decisive relevance of context").

More pointedly, we call particular attention to a conversational practice which has frank methodological intent. One finds conversationalists, in the course of a conversation, and as a recognized feature of that conversation, *formulating* their conversation. Formulating, in conversation, is discussed at length in the following sections.

Formulating a Conversation
as a Feature of that Conversation

Among conversationalists it is an immensely commonplace feature of conversations that a conversation exhibits *for its parties* its own familiar features of a "self-explicating colloquy." A member may treat some part of the conversation as an occasion to describe that conversation, to explain it, or characterize it, or explicate, or translate, or summarize, or furnish the gist of it, or take note of its accordance with rules, or remark on its departure from rules. That is to say, a member may use some part of the conversation as an occasion to *formulate* the conversation, as in the following colloquies.

A: Do you think the federal government can go in and try that man for murder?
B: No.
B: It's a matter of state.
A: [Now let me ask you this.]

B: You would not be critical at all.
A: Of Westmoreland.
B: Of the military,—of the—of this recent operation.
A: Of course I'd be critical.
B: [Well, you certainly don't show it!]

JH: Isn't it nice that there's such a crowd of you in the office?
SM: [You're asking us to leave, not telling us to leave, right?]

HG: I need some exhibits of persons evading questions. Will you do me a favor and evade some questions for me?
NW: [Oh, dear, I'm not very good at evading questions.]

(In fatigued excitement a psychiatric resident pauses in telling a supervising faculty member about his discovery of Harry Stack Sullivan's writings.) Faculty Member: [How long have you been feeling like this?]

Boston policeman to a motorist: [You asked me where Sparks Street is, didn't you? Well, I just told you.]

These excerpts illustrate the point that along with whatever else may be happening in conversation it may be a feature of the conversation for the conversationalists that they are doing something else; namely, what they are doing is saying-in-so-many-words-what-we-are-doing (or what we are talking about, or who is talking, or who we are, or where we are).

We shall speak of conversationalists' practices of saying-in-so-many-words-what-we-are-doing as *formulating*. We shall set off a text with brackets instead of hyphens to designate it as a formulation. In the preceding colloquies the formulating that one of the conversationalists is doing appears in brackets.

Two phenomena are of particular interest for us. (1) We offer as observations about practices of formulating that not only are they done, but they are also recognized by conversationalists as constituent features of the conversation in which they are done. We shall speak of this by saying *that* formulating is being done is, for conversationalists, "exhibited *in* the speaking." (2) We offer the further observation that formulating, as a witnessed feature of conversation, is available to conversationalists' report or comment. To have a way of speaking of this we shall say *that* formulating is done is "exhibitable *for* the telling."

Each of the colloquies provides an example of the first phenomenon. An example of the second phenomenon is found in the fact that we report these colloquies and call attention to the work of formulating being done in each. Brackets are used to designate the following features of formulating:

1. Above all, formulating is an account-able phenomenon. This is to say, (a) it is a phenomenon that members perform, and (b) it is observable by members. (c) In that members can do the phenomenon and observe it, it is reportable.[24] (d) The phenomenon is done and reportable by members

24. It is not only because members can *do* formulating and observe it that formulating is reportable. In that members are *doing* and *observing* formulating being done, it is reportable; or in that members do formulating and observe that it *was* done, it is reportable; or in that members when doing it observe it *will have been done,* it is reportable; in that members when doing it observe it *can have been done,* etc. The criterial consideration is not the availability of "tensed" verbs but the temporal structures of such enterprises. Temporal structures of formulating enterprises include of course the availability to members of time references in natural language.

The clumsiness of sentence structure may be something of a benefit if it earmarks the relevance and availability of the extensive, developed, and deep temporal "parameters" of members doing formulations as accountable enterprises. Particular attention is called to the work that David Sudnow is doing on the temporal parameters of accountable glances.

with texts such as those that are bracketed. (It is done as well with script, utterances, or graphics; that is, with circumstantially particular, notational displays. (e) The bracketed text is a phase of an interactional enterprise. Finally, (f) the text is meaning differently than the speaker can say in so many words.

2. All of the foregoing features are practical accomplishments over the exigencies of actual interaction.

3. The expression, [ ], is prefaced with "doing" in order to emphasize that accountable-conversation-as-a-practical-accomplishment consists only and entirely in and of its work. The prefix "doing" is also used to emphasize that this work of accountable conversation is members' work. That is to say, this work has essential ties to mastery of natural language.

Our illustrations have so far been chosen from laymen's work. The bracketing, and its effects, is relevant as well to the work of social scientists. If we place brackets on topicalized practices in the social sciences with which its practitioners speak of techniques of data collection, of research designs, of descriptive adequacy, of rules of evidence, and the like, we then ask what is the work for which these topics are its accountable texts. For example, linguists speak of "parsing a sentence with the use of phrase markers." By bracketing that text with gloss marks [parsing a sentence with the use of phrase markers], we understand that we are now addressed to the question: What is the work for which "parsing a sentence with the use of phrase markers" is that work's accountable text? The bracketing has similar relevance to the above case as it has to the case where we ask: What is the work for which [playing a game of chess according to the rules of chess] is that work's accountable text?

If we speak of work's accountable text as a proper gloss, we may ask: What is the work for which [speaking without interruption at a cocktail party] is its proper gloss? What is the work for which [the equilibrium size distribution of freely forming groups] is its proper gloss? The following diagram displays these relationships.

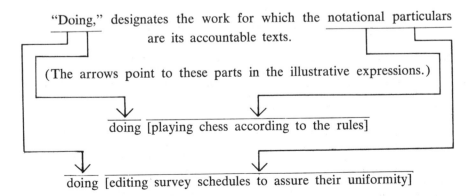

"Doing," designates the work for which the notational particulars are its accountable texts.

(The arrows point to these parts in the illustrative expressions.)

doing [playing chess according to the rules]

doing [editing survey schedules to assure their uniformity]

A final remark about brackets: their use reminds us that glossing practices are phases of interactional enterprises. Enterprises of intelligible, particular appearances of organized everyday activities are done unavoidably only and exclusively by competent speakers, who can do them only and entirely through the particulars of notational displays in natural language. Gloss enterprises are practical accomplishments. They are immensely varied phenomena, for they differ in ways dictated by a world of "social fact," albeit a world of social fact that is members' achievements. As practical achievements, gloss enterprises are as immensely varied as are organizational arrangements, for organizational arrangements are such achievements.

According to occasion, doing formulating may be members' undertakings, aims, rules, obligated behaviors, achievements, passing episodes, or standing circumstances. The work is not restricted to special circumstances. On the contrary, it occurs routinely, and on a massive scale. Members are particularly knowledgeable of, sensitive to, and skillful with this work, with doing it, assuring it, remedying it, and the like.

Doing Accountably Definite Talk

We used the analogy of housewives to characterize the prevalence of and insistence by members upon the work of doing formulations as remedies for the properties of indexical expressions. But, as we have noticed, in that formulations consist of glosses, and in that the properties that formulations exhibit as notational displays—properties that are used by speakers to accomplish rational speech—are properties of indexical expressions, the very resources of natural language assure that doing formulating is itself for members a routine source of complaints, faults, troubles, and recommended remedies, *essentially*. (See pp. 356-357.)

We take the critical phenomenon to consist in this: With ubiquitous prevalence and insistence members do formulations as remedies for problematic features that the properties of indexical expressions present to their attempts to satisfy the aims of distinguishing in actual occasions between objective and indexical expressions, and, in actual occasions, providing objective expressions as substitutes for indexicals. We observe that among members, remedial formulations are overwhelmingly advocated measures to accomplish proper subject matter, proper problems, proper methods, and warranted findings in studying formal structures of practical talk and practical reasoning. We observe that their advocacy of remedial formulations is accompanied by practices with which members are just as overwhelmingly knowledgeable and skilled, practices whereby speakers guarantee and are guaranteed that formulations are *not* the machinery whereby account-

ably sensible, clear, definite talk is done. Such practices are seen in the following phenomena.

1. There are innumerable conversational activities in doing which multitudes of names are available for naming them as conversational phenomena. People know the names, can mention the names, summarize with the names, and so on; and yet in the course of the activities the names are not much used. Indeed, a commonplace but little understood phenomenon consists of cases where in doing [saying in so many words what one is doing] the activity is recognizedly incongruous, or boring, or furnishes evidence of incompetence, of devious motivation, and so forth.

2. There is a tremendous topical coherence in ordinary conversations, and yet conversationalists' formulation of topics is a very special thing. It is rarely done. In any particular case it is not only probably but perhaps irremediably disputable, and though one gets talk that is topical, topical names are not inserted.

3. It occurs as a commonplace achievement in ordinary conversations—which for conversationalists furnishes commonplace evidence of conversational competence—that conversationalists title relevant texts, search for, remember, recognize, or offer relevant texts without those texts being topicalized, where success in so doing depends upon vagueness of topic, aim, rule of search, rule of relevance, and the rest, and where the work of storage and retrieval of relevant texts incorporates this vagueness as an essential feature in its design.

4. Another phenomenon was described in a previous study.[25] Students were asked to write what the parties to an ordinary conversation were overheard to have said, and then to write alongside what the parties actually were talking about. The students, having been set the task of saying in just so many words what the parties were actually talking about, immediately saw that the work of satisfying the task hopelessly elaborated the task's features. Somehow they saw immediately that the very task that had been set—"Tell me as if I don't know, what the parties were literally talking about"—was faulted, not in the sense that the author would not know, or could not or would not understand, or that there was not enough time or paper or stamina or vocabulary in English for a writer to tell it, but that

. . . I had required them to take on the impossible task of "repairing" the essential incompleteness of *any* set instructions no matter how carefully or elaborately written they might be. I had required them to formulate the method that the parties had used in speaking, as rules of procedure to follow in order to say what the parties said, rules that would withstand every exigency of situation, imagination, and development . . . [This was the task] that required them

25. Garfinkel, *Studies in Ethnomethodology,* pp. 29-30.

to write "more," that they found increasingly difficult and finally impossible, and that became elaborated in its features by the very procedures for doing it.

We take as the critical import of these phenomena that they furnish specifics for the observation that *for the member it is not in the work of doing formulations for conversation that the member is doing* [*the fact that our conversational activities are accountably rational*]. The two activities are neither identical nor interchangeable.

We notice also that doing formulating is "occasioned." By this we mean that cited times, places, and personnel whereby formulating is done—that concrete, definite, clear, determinate specifications of where? when? who? what? how many?—are unavoidably and without remedy done as accountable phenomena. Also, it is not only that members may use particular rules to provide for the occasioned character of a formulation, but the failure to use particular rules is usable by a member to find what it is that formulating is doing in a conversation, where the fact of formulating does not mean to those doing it that doing it is definitive of its work; but instead doing it can be found to be joking, or being obstinate, and the like.

In short, doing formulating for conversation itself exhibits for conversationalists an orientation to [the fact that our conversational activities are accountably rational]. Doing formulating is not the definitive means whereby the fact is itself done or established. The question of what one who is doing formulating is doing—which is a member's question—is not solved by members by consulting what the formulation proposes, but by engaging in practices that make up the *essentially* contexted character of the action of formulating. Even the briefest consideration of doing formulating in conversation returns us—naïve speaker or accomplished social scientist—to the phenomenon in conversation of doing [the fact that our conversational activities are accountably rational].

What are we proposing when we propose that the question of what one is doing who is doing formulating is solved by members by engaging in practices that make up the *essentially* contexted character of the action of formulating? What kind of work is it for which [the fact that our conversational activities are accountably rational] is its proper gloss?

Formal Structures in Accountably Rational Discourse: The "Machinery"

We learn to ask from the work of conversationalists: What kind of "machinery" makes up the practices of doing [accountably rational conversation]? Are there practices for doing and recognizing [the fact that our activities are accountably rational] without, for example, making a formulation of the setting that the practices are "contexted" in? What is the work

for which [the fact that our activities are accountably rational] is an accountable text? What is the work for which [definiteness, univocality, disambiguation, and uniqueness of conversational particulars is assured by conversationalists' competence with speech in context] is a proper gloss?

We ask such questions because we learn from the phenomena that are problematic for conversationalists that "time," "place," or "personnel," for example, with which conversationalists say in so many words who, or where, or when, or since when, or how long since, or how much more, or with whom, or what, are contexted phenomena. More accurately, they are *essentially* contexted phenomena.

By "contexted phenomena" we mean that there exist specific practices such that (1) they make up what a member is doing when he does and recognizes [the fact of relevant time, place, or personnel]; (2) they are done with or without formulating *which* now, or where, or with whom, or since when, or how much longer, and the like; (3) they make up members' work for which [practices of objective, clear, consistent, cogent—rational—language] is a proper gloss; and (4) they meet the first three criteria by satisfying the following constraints (to which we refer with the adjective *essential*).

1. They are cause for members' complaints; they are faulted; they are nuisances; troubles; proper grounds for corrective, that is, remedial, action.

2. They are without remedy in the sense that every measure that is taken to achieve a remedy preserves in specifics the features for which the remedy was sought.

3. They are unavoidable; they are inescapable; there is no hiding place from their use, no moratorium, no time out, no room in the world for relief.

4. Programmatic ideals characterized their workings.

5. These ideals are available as "plain spoken rules" to provide accounts of adequate description for all practical purposes, or adequate explanation, adequate identity, adequate characterization, adequate translation, adequate analysis and so forth.

6. Provision is made "in studies by practicing logicians" for each ideal's "poor relatives," as indexical expressions are the poor relatives of objective expressions; as commonsense knowledge is a poor relative of scientific knowledge; as natives' practices and natives' knowledge are poor relatives of professional practices and professional knowledge of natives' affairs, practices, and knowledge; as Calvin N. Mooers's descriptors are poor relatives of sets, categories, classes, or collections in formal logic; or, as formal structures in natural language are poor relatives of formal structures in invented languages. For "poor relatives" we understand "embarrassing but necessary nuisances," "lesser versions," "nonphenomena," "no causes for celebration," "ugly doubles" that are relied on by members to assure the claims of the relatives that went to college and came back

educated. Ideals are not the monopoly of academies, and neither are their poor relatives confined to the streets. Always in each others' company, they are available in immense varieties for they are as common as talk. Being theorized out of existence by members' ironic contrast between commonsense knowledge and scientific knowledge, they are also difficult to locate and report with the use of that contrast.

7. Members are unanimous in their recognition of the foregoing six characteristics of specific practices; they are also unanimous in their use of these characteristics to detect, sense, identify, locate, name—that is, to formulate—one or another "sense" of practical activities as an "invariant structure of appearances."

Speaking practices, insofar as they satisfy such constraints, are inescapably tied to particulars of talk, and thus speaking practices are inexorably exhibited and witnessed as ordered particulars of talk. Insofar as they satisfy such constraints, speaking practices also exhibit the features of "production cohort independence," or "invariant to in and out migrations of system personnel," or "invariant to transformations of context," or "universals." They exhibit features of invariance by providing members' methods with their accountable character as *unavoidably* used methods with which particulars are recovered, produced, identified, and recognized as connected particulars; as particulars in relationships of entailment, relevance, inference, allusion, reference, evidence; which is to say as collections of particulars, or classes, or sets, or families, or groups, or swarms.

Members use these constraints to detect various ways of doing [invariance] in members' practices. Because members do so, we shall use them in the same way, namely, as constraints that speaking practices must satisfy if we are to count those practices as members' resources for doing and recognizing [rational adequacy for practical purposes of natural language]. They provide characteristics of the practices with which members accomplish and recognize rational discourse in its indexical particulars, namely, "practical talk."

What are those practices? [26] We learn some if we ask about a *list* of indexical expressions how long the list might be. To answer this question we need a procedure that will get us a list of indexical terms. Such a procedure is easily available, for we notice that any "one" of the properties of indexical expressions cited on pp. 348-349, and any combination of them, may be read as a prescription with which to search an *actual* occasion of discourse, an *actual* utterance, or an *actual* text.

26. Because we are required to learn what these practices are by consulting members, we must require of the methods that we use to locate these practices, and of the practices that such methods locate that they satisfy the same constraints. The arguments to justify this assertion and to show that the method we use is adequate with respect to these requirements are detailed in Harold Garfinkel, "Practices and Structures of Practical Sociological Reasoning and Methods for their Elucidation," in *Contributions to Ethnomethodology.*

When this is done, we observe the following. Any actual occasion may be searched for indexical terms, and will furnish indexical terms. Whatever is the number of terms in an actual text, that text will furnish members.[27] An actual occasion with *no* text will furnish members. Any member of the list of indexical terms can be used as a prescription to locate replicas. Listing any replica of a member of the list is an adequate procedure for locating another member. Any procedure for finding *a* member is adequate for finding for *all* terms of a language that they are members, which includes "all"—which is to say that in finding for all terms of a language that they are members we are exploring and using the members' use of "all." "A one," "any one," and "all" lists of indexical terms exhibit the same properties as the particular members of "a one," "any one," and "all" lists. Any text without exception that is searched with the use of any one or combination of properties from a list of *properties* of indexical terms will furnish members to the list. Any text without exception that is searched with the use of one or combination of terms from a list of indexical terms will furnish members to the list. Any list of indexical terms can be indefinitely extended, as can any list of properties of indexical terms. Every procedure for finding more members and adding them to the list of properties exhibits the same properties as the members it finds. Every list of properties of indexical expressions can be extended indefinitely. Whatever holds above for "terms" holds equally for "expressions" and "utterances." Finally, the preceding properties remain invariant to such operations as search for, recognition of, collection, counting, forming sentences with, translating, identifying, or performing consistency proofs or computations upon list members.

Consequences

We have seen that and how members do [the fact that our activities are accountably rational]. We have seen that the work is done without having to do formulations; that the terms which have to be clarified are not to be replaced by formulations that would not do what they do; that they are organizable as a "machinery" for doing [accountably rational activities]; and that the abstract phenomenon of [accountable rationality] is available to natives, to ethnomethodologists, and to social scientists since the "machinery," because it is members' "machinery," in the way it is specifically used to do [accountably rational activities] is thereby part of the phenomenon as its production and recognition apparatus. We have given that some structure, and tried to exhibit both the obviousness of it, and its enormous interest and pervasiveness for members.

27. *Members* of the list has the conventional meaning of *items* of the list.

1. It seems that there is no room in the world definitively to propose formulations of activities, identifications, and contexts. Persons cannot be nonconsequentially, nonmethodically, nonalternatively involved in doing [saying in so many words what we are doing]. They cannot be engaged in nonconsequentially, nonmethodically, nonalternatively saying, for example, "This is after all a group therapy session," or "With respect to managerial roles, the size and complexity of organizations is increasing and hence the requirements necessary for their successful management also."

The fact that there is no room in the world for formulations as serious solutions to the problem of social order has to do with the prevailing recommendation in the social sciences that formulations can be done for practical purposes to accomplish empirical description, or to achieve the justification and test of hypotheses, and the rest. Formulations are recommended thereby as resources with which the social sciences may accomplish rigorous analyses of practical actions that are adequate for all practical purposes.

We are *not* saying that it is a specific trouble in the world that one cannot find out what somebody means—what any given person means in any next thing they say or meant in any last thing they said—by using a procedure of requesting a formulation for each piece of talk. But we *are* saying that insofar as formulations are recommended to be definitive of "meaningful talk," something is amiss because "meaningful talk" cannot have that sense. This is to say either that talk is not meaningful unless we construct a language which is subject to such procedures, or that *that* could not be what "meaningful talk" is, or "meaningful actions" either. We *are* saying that we ought not to suppose that in order for persons in the course of their conversations and other ordinary activities to behave in an orderly fashion, one set of things that has to be involved is that they are always able, say, to formulate their role relationships and systematically invoke their consequences. For if it is the case that there is no room in the world for that, then either orderly activity is impossible, or *that* requirement for orderly activity is in any actual case relevant, irrelevant, cogent, absurd, wrong, right, etc.—that requirement being formulatable in any actual case as any of these or others, separately or combined, for no more than for all practical purposes.

2. We took notice initially of the notion that formulating could save the difficulties with indexicals.[28] We saw that formulating could not do that and, furthermore, that indexicals would not need saving from difficulties. We have seen that the allegedly to-be-remedied features of terms are omnipervasive. And so one must entertain the fact that *none* of them needs saving.

3. Professional sociology's achievement is to have formulated rational

28. We take notice of how practices of practical sociological reasoning seek to remedy the indexical properties of talk: they seek essentially to do so.

accountability of social structures of practical activities as precepts of constructive analysis. The social structures of everyday activities, as we remarked before, are understood by the formulations of constructive analysis to consist of such properties as uniformity, social standardization, repetition, reproducibility, typicality, categorizability, reportability of ordinary conduct, of talk, of territorial distributions, of beliefs about one thing or another that are invariant to changes of production cohorts. The practical technology of constructive analytic theorizing is available, in apotheosis, in the work of Parsons, Lazarsfeld, and RAND techniques of systems analysis. We observe that its practitioners insist that the practices of constructive analysis are *members'* achievements. We learn from practitioners that, and how, adequate application of its precepts to demonstrations of formal structures in actual occasions demands members' competence. We observe, too, that particulars in procedures and results of constructive analysis furnish to members perspicuous exhibits of vaguely known "settings." [29] In every actual occasion of their use, particulars in procedures and particulars in results provide members with the combination of unavoidable, irremediable vagueness with equally unavoidable, irremediable relevance. From practitioners we understand that the combination of essential vagueness and relevance is available to members only, for members' production, evaluation, and recognition. In short, we learn from practitioners of constructive analysis that our findings about formulating are extendable to constructive analysis.

Formulating does not extend to constructive analysis as its gloss, nor is formulating a generalization of the experience of analysis. Least of all is formulating a generalization of the practices of professional sociologists. It is extendable in the ways that doing [constructive analysis] is what *members* do; like [saying specifically in so many words just what we are doing], or [saying what is meant and meaning what is said in a few well-chosen words], or [removing from cell titles the nuisances of indexical expressions], or [mapping the system of real numbers on collections of indexical expressions], or [abstracting methodological paradigms from the work of E.S.R.] or [thinking sequentially]. Because doing [constructive analysis] is what members do, what we observe about formulating is observed as well in the practices of professional sociologists doing [constructive analysis]. In that work we see *members* being careful to build context-free descriptions, relevant instructions, perspicuous anecdotes, cogent proverbs, precise definitions of ordinary activities, and context-free formalizations of natural language practices, and using members' competence with natural language practices to assure the doing and recognition of [adequate evidence], [objective description], [definite procedure], [clear, consistent, co-

29. We have borrowed from remarks made by Hubert L. Dreyfus about Wittgenstein and Merleau-Ponty during his informal seminar at Harvard University in March, 1968.

gent, relevant instructions], [computable conversations], and the rest. In that work we see professional sociologists' insistence on members' competence to assure these glosses as concerted accomplishments.

The machinery of professionals' gloss achievements is described only in barest part by the practices that were described in a preceding section as members' machinery for doing [rational talk for practical purposes]. How such glosses are done has not been elucidated beyond ethnographic remarks furnished by sociological practitioners, both lay and professional. What various kinds of enterprises, such as [objective sociological formulations], [definite instructions], and the like, are as conversational accomplishments is not known.

4. From an inspection of the work of constructive analysis we learn that rational accountability of everyday activities as practical accomplishments is accounted by members to consist of the practices of constructive analysis. From that work we learn, too, that such accounts are themselves warranted features of that practical accomplishment. From their practices we learn that formal structures in the practices of constructive analysis, which, in the sense described in an earlier section of this paper ("Ethnomethodology's Interest in Formal Structures of Practical Actions") *are formal structures in members' natural language practices,* are *not* available to the methods of constructive analysis. We are not proposing an "impossibility" argument in the sense of a logical proof, nor are we offering an in-principle account of constructive analysis. Nor are we recommending an attitude toward, a position on, or an approach to constructive analysis. Nor are we saying that formal structures are not available to constructive analysis because of trained incapacity, habitual preferences, vested interests, and the like. Most emphatically, we are not offering advice, praise, or criticism.

Instead, we are taking notice of that unavailability as a phenomenon. We offer the observation about that unavailability that it is invariant to the practices of constructive analysis. This is not to say that the phenomenon somehow defies the efforts of constructive analysis. The unavailability of formal structures is assured by the practices of constructive analysis for it *consists of* its practices. The unavailability of formal structures is an invariant feature of every actual occasion of constructive analysis, without exception, without time out, without relief or remedy, no actual occasion being excepted no matter how transient or enduring, the unavailability being reportable, assured, done, and recognized not only unanimously, but with required unanimity by whoever does sociology—or, equivalently, by whoever knows how to talk.

That formal structures in members' natural language practices are not available to the methods of constructive analysis establishes the study of practical sociological reasoning. Ethnomethodological studies have been using that unavailability to locate one or another "piece" of construc-

tive analysis and bring under scrutiny how its achievement is an accountable phenomenon for members. The availability of these studies establishes
the *de facto* existence of an alternative to the other prospects and perspectives in this volume, for although formal structures of constructive analysis
are not available to constructive analysis, they are not otherwise unavailable; they are available to ethnomethodology. That this is so is less interesting than the question of whether they are available to ethnomethodology
uniquely.

Appendix: Notes on Glossing

The following are examples of different methods for doing observable-
reportable understanding, i.e., account-able understanding. They were selected from a collection of reports of ordinary occasions in which persons
who, in the same ways that they recognize or understand each other as
knowing how to speak, are engaged in concertedly meaning differently than
they can say in just so many words.

The examples are intended to specify "glossing practices" as a topic.
The foregoing definition is used as a weak rule to serve our interests of
extending and organizing the collection: of search, detection, exclusion,
titling, and so on. Is it to be read as a weak rule for the time being? It
occurred to us, of course, that a more exact definition is an aim in collecting them. That aim is familiar to those who want their studies of natural
language to be taken seriously. Of course we, too, entertain such an aim;
but where glosses are concerned we do not entertain it too seriously because we learn when glosses are being studied, and from what we learn
about glossing practices, that such an aim is not interesting. It *is* interesting, rather, that that aim cannot be satisfied. We shall see this from some
of the examples. Further, *that* a weak definition is used to formulate as
a goal a strong definition aimed at by the use of a weak definition, and
for the accomplishment of which the weak definition is a resource, is
another hope that cannot be satisfied. Or better, it is a hope that is satisfied
in this way: One acquires a skill that counts as a recognized mastery of
natural language. And that, too, is interesting. Further features are provided by particular and definite ways that that aim cannot be satisfied,
and seem to add up to this: Definiteness of glossing practices is available
to study, irrespective of whether definitions are lacking, are weak, loose,
etc. We find that to be a repeating "logical" feature. We are fascinated by
it, and are seeking it out wherever we can.

Perhaps glossing practices can be person-specific. We are undecided. In
any case, the examples were selected to illustrate several differing ways in
which their production is organized as a concerted, practical accomplishment. For example, Richards' gloss consists of a method whereby yet-to-be-

comprehended texts are glossed over unknown ways of arriving at definite sense, where no account of a way of arriving at whatever definite sense the process comes to is called for by those doing it, or needs to be provided by them. Two variations on this thematic characteristic are provided in the case of mock-ups, and where definitions are used in first approximation to stronger ones.

Mock-ups It is possible to buy a plastic engine that will tell something about how auto engines work. The plastic engine preserves certain prop erties of the auto engine. For example, it will show how the pistons move with respect to the crankshaft; how they are timed to a firing sequence, and so on. As we shall see, it is interesting and relevant that to make the pistons work the user has to turn the flywheel with his finger.

Let us call that plastic engine an account of an observable state of affairs. We offer the following observations of that account's features. First, in the very way that it provides for an accurate representation of features in the actual situation, and in the very way it provides for an accurate representation of *some* relationships and *some* features in the observable situation, it also makes specifically and deliberately false provision for some of the *essential* features of that situation. Second, in making this deliberately false provision it provides that the deliberately false provisions must be there if the account is to be treated as an account of that situation. Third, by reason of this false provision, the account is said by the user of the account to "resemble" the situation he wants to use it to represent. Fourth, the knowledge of the ways in which the account— the plastic engine—makes false provision is for the user a controlling consideration in permitting it to be used as an account of the actual situation. Fifth, the mock-up—the plastic engine—in the entirety of its particular, actual features, whatever they are, and for whatever uses they might be used, is understood throughout by the user to have the status of a guide to practical actions in the actual situation, whatever it may consist of in an actual occasion, when the user must come to terms with an actual engine. Sixth, this intended use is exclusively the matter of the user's choice when deciding for himself the adequacy of the mock-up and the mock-up's correct use. Finally, its use is accompanied by the user's willingness, whenever he might encounter a feature in the actual situation that the mock-up falsely provides for, to pay full authority to the actual situation, and to let the mock-up stand without the necessary impulse of having to correct it.

A definition used in first approximation resembles Richards' gloss and mock-ups in that it furnishes still another way to accomplish recognized definiteness of talk without ever specifying how that definiteness is achieved.

Definitions used in first approximation occur in articles where an author at the beginning of an article may furnish a definition which he accompanies with the request that its looseness be forgiven for the time being, that (for whatever reasons) he will not define it more closely then and

there, but if the reader will permit its provisional character he will proceed with his arguments and at a later point provide a second definition which can then be substituted.

The following example of such a definition adds still another feature. It was chosen because it provides the reader an exhibit in which definiteness of talk is achieved, although how definiteness of talk is done is essentially unspecifiable.

Consider the following as a definition in first approximation of "glossing."

I want to speak about persons who know how to talk—speakers of a language—engaged in multitudinous practices of meaning differently than they can say in so many words over actual occasions of interaction. I want to collect their practices with the term *glossing*. I want to use this definition for the time being as a rule with which to locate relevant actual occasions that might be searched for exhibits, and with which exhibits might be compared, described, grouped, titled, captioned, and so on. A more exact definition will be treated as the aim of our inquiries. As we come, in the course of our collecting enterprise, to learn more about what I am using the term *glossing* to speak about, and as we are able to furnish the matter of our concern with greater definiteness, we shall rewrite the definition so as to formulate from the exhibits, and from the reflections that they motivate, their essential features and the essential connections between those features.

When, with the use of this definition, actual occasions are examined in the search for possible exhibits, the definition is used to an indefinitely specified depth of self-embeddedness. We notice, too, that no antinomies block or stifle its sense; nor are we confounded by the "depth" of its recursiveness.

Anthropological quotes. An anthropologist returns from the field with his notebooks to the company of professional colleagues. Having spent time in the field, he has the task of turning his texts into a professionally acceptable report. For example, Manning Nash [30] reminds graduate students in his seminars about the tandem features of criticism and field work. One day, each one in his turn will return from a strange society and will have to report his findings in coherent, declarative sentences. The anthropologist is going to have to write in detail what he learned from the natives to whom he is likely to have been a stranger in the critical sense that for months, and perhaps for his entire stay, their language was apt not to have been under his control. He need give no account of how his field notes were collected. Only rarely do anthropologists connect their notes and how they were collected, expanded, analyzed, revised, and otherwise used, with their field circumstances as constituent features of those

30. Personal communication.

circumstances. Even less frequently do they report how the notes were turned into a report intended to be read by co-professionals. Nevertheless, "the ways this is done" is treated by all—by writer and by colleagues—as contingently accountable over the occasions in which the "writing" is done and over the occasions in which the report is read and discussed. It is with respect to such circumstances of professional work that the use of anthropological quotes is an interesting and relevant glossing practice.

The procedure of reporting in anthropological quotes is as follows. The anthropologist proceeds to rewrite the texts as a report using a procedure that he calls "writing." A prevailing task that is done by writing is to propose an account of what his natives, in the language *they* talked, will be treated as actually and not supposedly having been talking about, given that the anthropologist cannot and will not say finally and in only so many words what they were really talking about. In this fashion he reports to colleagues that *they* talked in this way, definitely. So, for example, he cites the natives in their native terms and treats those terms with the device of a "glossary." That is to say, he recommends to colleagues that *he* will mean by *his* translations of natives' terms what the natives were really talking about, that he will treat the natives and their practices as final authority for, although what those might consist of beyond what he has written, he cannot say and says that he cannot. The writer means what the native really means, given that the writer elects to be cautious in specifying in just so many words "what the native really means." This further "what the native really means," which is incorporated into the report as the professional's paraphrase of native informants' reportage, is glossed over the report as it is available in an actual occasion through work of professionally unspecified methods of authorship and readership.

As far as professionals are concerned, practices of anthropological glossing provide anthropologists with practices and circumstances that distinguish them from other professionals. The professional association consists of the availability of competent readers and unexplicated circumstances over which that kind of writing gets glossed. Via association membership, definiteness of sense and facticity of the report are intimately tied to conversational settings, conversation devices, conversational "machinery" in which, and wherewith what is actually and not supposedly reported will have been "seen for the saying" to have been written in so many words.

Certifying an event that you did not bid for illustrates a practice whereby a definiteness is discovered within a conversational schedule, the point of interest being that definiteness is discovered by exploiting the differences between time ordering in the event's production and the accountable time ordering of the produced event. The practice is as follows. You are conversing with another person. The person laughs. You are momentarily surprised, for you had not meant to make a joke. In that you hear the person laugh, you smile so as to assign to the other person's laugh its feature that

his laugh detected your wit, but you conceal the fact that the other person, when he laughed, furnished you an opportunity to "claim a credit" you did not seek.

Rose's gloss. Professor Edward Rose, a colleague at the University of Colorado, reports a practice that makes deliberate use of the property that definiteness of circumstantial particulars *consists* of their consequences. He uses that property as follows, to find out definitely what he *has* been doing.

On a visit to a city he has never seen before, Rose is met at the airport by his host. They are driving home when Rose [looks] out the window—which is to say that Rose, after doing [looking ahead] then does [watching something go by] by turning his head to accord with the passage of the auto. Rose's problem is to get his partner to provide him with what he has been looking at. Doing the notable particulars [looking ahead] and [watching something go by] and their serial arrangement are the crux of the matter, and make up Rose's artfulness. Continuing to do [looking out the window] Rose remarks, "It certainly has changed." His host may say something like, "It was ten years before they rebuilt the block after the fire." Rose, by having said, "It certainly has changed," finds in the reply, and with the use of the reply, what he, Rose, was talking about in the first place. Picking that up he formulates further the concerted, sensible matter that the two parties are making happen as the recognizable, actual, plainly heard specifics in a course of conversation: "You don't say. What did it cost?"

14.

Deviance and Order in a Pluralistic Society

Jack D. Douglas

Jack D. Douglas was born in Miami, Florida, in 1937 and attended Harvard (B.A.) and Princeton (Ph.D.). He is now an associate professor of sociology at the University of California, San Diego. Most of his work has been in the areas of theory and methods, deviance, criminology, urban social problems, and the sociology of sciences (especially of the social sciences). His most important published work to date is The Social Meanings of Suicide.

*T*he field of deviance is today one of the most creative fields of sociology, perhaps being challenged in this respect only by the field of comparative studies of social change. It is a field which has not only experienced the intellectual ferment that increasingly characterizes most fields of sociological theory and methods, but one which can properly be said to have been undergoing a revolution in theory and methods. Like most political revolutions, this intellectual revolution has many ties with the past and is itself difficult to characterize in sharp outlines because of its rapidly changing, emergent forms and its intraparty struggles. I believe, however, that the most influential works in this field in recent years have been moving rapidly toward a set of fundamental theoretical and methodological propositions which, taken together, constitute a new theoretical perspective which is in sharp conflict with earlier sociological perspectives on deviance and on society in general.

My major purposes here are to show as clearly as possible what the theoretical propositions of this new perspective are, how they conflict with the earlier dominant perspective, that the new perspective is a more valid one, and finally, just how this new perspective challenges the presently dominant theoretical explanation of social order, that is, structural-functionalism.

The Structural-Functional Perspective

Morality and immorality (or values and their violation) have been the central concern of sociological theory and research since the emergence of sociology as an independent discipline in the nineteenth century. Most sociologists have either assumed or argued that human social actions must be explained in large part, if not entirely, in terms of shared values or the violation of those values. In fact, as I have previously argued,[1] the discipline of sociology and the present perspective embodied by structural-functionalism were largely created by the moral statisticians, public hygienists, medical statisticians, and many other groups of "proto-sociologists," going back as far as Süssmilch's work in the eighteenth century,[2] who were primarily concerned with understanding the various forms of immoral actions (or deviance) for reasons of science and as a means of ridding society of such "evils." The most important of these works in the nineteenth century, those by Guerry, Quetelet, Buckle, Esquirol, Parent-Duchatelet, Boismont, Masaryk, Oettingen, Wagner, Morselli, and Bertillon, led directly to the grand synthesis of the moral statistical works, Emile Durkheim's *Suicide*.[3]

Suicide proved to be a fateful synthesis; in time it became the paradigm for sociological theory and research on deviance, especially for that on suicide. While *Suicide* was harshly criticized for years by most European and American sociologists, by the 1930's it was explicitly cited by most sociologists as *the* model for theory and research on deviance. The immediate and continuing acclaim given Merton's essay on anomie and deviance, for example, was both cause and effect of this change in the status of *Suicide*.[4] In the 1930's the very influential social disorganization theory of deviance was merged with Durkheim's social disintegration theory of deviance. The traditional perspective on deviance is seen most clearly in this school of sociological thought, but until recently, almost all sociological works on deviance have at least implicitly assumed its theoretical perspective, even when their authors were not explicitly members of the school.

There are at least twelve fundamental theoretical propositions that con-

1. See Jack D. Douglas, *The Social Meanings of Suicide* (Princeton: Princeton University Press, 1967), pp. 3-33; "The Sociological Analysis of Social Meanings of Suicide," *Archives Européennes de Sociologie,* 7 (1966), 249-275; "Suicide: The Social Aspects," *International Encyclopedia of the Social Sciences* (New York: Macmillan, 1968).
2. Johann Peter Süssmilch, *Die Göttliche Ordnung in den Veränderungen des Menschlichen Geschlechts* (Berlin, 1761).
3. Trans. John A. Spaulding and George Simpson (Glencoe: Free Press, 1951).
4. Robert K. Merton, "Social Structure and Anomie," *American Sociological Review,* 3 (1938), 672-682.

stitute this earlier, traditionalized perspective on deviance.[5] Like many fundamental principles, they very often were assumed implicitly by these works, forming the unstated background which the readers, trained in the same tradition and sharing the same commonsense ideas about morality, could be expected to understand. Once they are pointed out, however, I believe it is easy to see that almost all of the works on deviance did make most of these assumptions, though space limitations prevent an analysis of such works here. A brief listing of the assumptions, to be followed by detailed, critical examinations of them in the context of the presentation of the new perspective, will help to keep our argument clear.

(1) The members of our society, including sociologists, normally know nonproblematically (or automatically) exactly what values (and other meanings) apply to any given situation and how they should be applied; that is, the moral meanings of actions are normally nonproblematic for members of the society and for sociologists.

(2) Because the moral (and immoral) meanings of actions are non-problematic, the subject matter of the sociology of deviance (namely immoral and related actions) is nonproblematic. This assumption, combined with the assumption of the stability of meanings (see below), justifies the acceptance of a conventionalized corpus of subject categories. Those subjects conventionally studied by students of deviance are "known" to constitute social "deviance" without any need for investigation.

(3) Because sociologists want to study deviant acts as *social* phenomena, they must study them statistically, and the ideal method of study is the statistical-hypothetical method by which one hypothesizes a general theory to be correct, derives specific hypotheses from this general theory, and tests the validity of these by statistical analyses of data.

(4) Official statistics on deviance and crime are adequately valid and reliable for sociological analyses of deviance.

(5) The sociologist must be primarily concerned with studying deviance from the perspective of official attempts to control it. Most importantly, deviance can be assumed to be caused almost entirely by factors independent of the official agencies, whereas the official agencies can be assumed to be a (functional) response by society intended to control deviance, thereby constraining forces which would be dysfunctional for society if left uncontrolled.

---

5. One could obviously cut the conceptual pie differently and come up with very different numbers of propositions. I have chosen that set of statements which seem to me to cover the traditional perspective most completely and briefly.

The critical discussions of these traditional propositions are combined under a smaller number of propositions constituting the new perspective. In this instance as well, the criteria have been those of completeness and brevity.

(6) There is a dominant set of values (or morals) in any society, such that the society can be treated as morally homogeneous.

(7) Where there are "apparent" or overt differences in values, these apparent differences are the result of reactions to the dominant social values, in terms of which the individual simply cannot succeed. That is, apparent differences are themselves the result of moral homogeneity (plus differences in opportunities).

(8) For all significant sociological purposes the dominant set of values can be assumed to be stable, to be the same over time.

(9) These dominant values do not conflict with each other or with other values and derivatives of values, such as laws, so that the values and laws will be congruent. Because of this, deviance and crime form a continuum in which crime is legally sanctioned deviance.

(10) There is a small, core set of these dominant values which are highly abstract and which are the direct causes of more specific, situated values.

(11) While other factors, including other meanings, may be important in explaining deviance, these core abstract values and their more specific, derivative values are the most important causes of deviance—and of all social actions. The *normative primacy* in the causation of deviance means that sociologists should be most concerned with explaining deviations from values in terms of values.

(12) To the extent that individual decisions and actions are relevant to explaining deviance, the individual can be assumed to know nonproblematically (see Assumption 1) that these actions are deviant and that they are associated with certain negative sanctions. In choosing or deciding to commit a deviant action he is, therefore, choosing to commit it as (or *qua*) a deviant action and is, thereby, choosing to be a deviant. In simplest terms, deviant acts are committed by deviant persons. Moreover, these deviant choices are normally believed to represent the "real selves"—the *substantial selves*—of deviants. Consequently, deviants are normally believed to be very different types of persons from nondeviants.

The traditional sociological perspective on deviance has, then, assumed that deviance takes place in a social world that is unproblematically meaningful, based on moral consensus, homogeneous, stable, closed, and deterministic. It has assumed that sociologists can best (or only) understand deviance in this social world by the use of statistical-hypothetical analyses of official rates of actions whose meanings to the members are known relatively unproblematically by sociologists. As most sociologists will readily recognize, these are also the general assumptions of the structural-functional perspective on society.

The simplest and clearest way to present the emerging perspective is in terms of its fundamental propositions or ideas, beginning with a considera-

tion of the sources of data. There is no one-to-one correspondence between these and the twelve basic assumptions of the structural-functional perspective. But, taken together, these fundamental propositions cover all of those basic assumptions and provide a sharp alternative perspective. The relations between the various assumptions and propositions will be clear from our discussion.

The Emerging Sociological Perspective on Deviance

In a very general way, the new perspective on deviance that can be seen emerging in recent works assumes that the meanings of deviant actions are very problematic and non-homogeneous; that they take place in a social world that is pluralistic, conflictful, open, and changing very rapidly; that deviance can be studied best (or only) by the use of information gotten through participant observation involving trust; that official information tells us primarily about official organizations, and then only guardedly; that deviance and official agencies of control are highly interdependent; and that deviance takes place in a world of uncertainty in which the meanings and consequences of our actions are always partly obscured, often realized only after the fact of our acts, and sometimes never known. This general perspective is best presented in terms of its fundamental propositions.

Official information on deviance and crime is highly unreliable, is the result of complex processes of practical activities, and is of value only for what it tells us about official agencies. The primary source of sociological information on deviance has been official statistics. Beginning in the seventeenth century, the use of official statistics to study moral phenomena has long enjoyed a traditional legitimacy that has made it largely impervious to critical, scientific examination.

This continued use of the official statistics has been primarily based upon the implicit assumption that the meaningful categorization by officials of such acts as suicide are relatively unproblematic. Official categorizations of suicide, for example, were considered to be "social facts" because, as Morselli said, "a corpse is a corpse." Had they made an empirical investigation of the nature of official categorizations of such things as suicide, sociologists would easily have found how very problematic the officials see these categorizations to be. For example, had Durkheim investigated official categorizations of suicide, he could easily have found that the various coroners, medical examiners, and doctors doing these categorizations use legal and commonsense definitions of suicide that include *intention* to die as the most crucial factor in defining suicide. He would have found them struggling with the very problematic meaning of intention, and developing rules of thumb to get the job done. He would have seen that they were using

the one definition of suicide (intentional death) which he himself had rejected as completely subjective. He should then have concluded that all of his statistical data on suicide were just as completely subjective, and rejected them.

The few studies that have been done of official categorization procedures rather consistently indicate (1) that the officials are concerned primarily with the practical problems of getting a job done, rather than with collecting scientific information; (2) that officials do their categorizing largely in terms of rules of thumb, rather than by scientific criteria; (3) that there are great variations in the formal and informal definitions of categories, organizational structures, and procedures followed among official organizations; (4) that there are great variations in the tendencies of different groups to report deviance to officials, in the official registration of members of different groups (class and race biases, for example), and in the disposition of cases from different groups; (5) that there tend to be great differences between the public (rhetorical) statements of official policy and actual (secret) practices in handling cases; and (6) that officials very often corrupt the statistics, using them for their own political purposes.[6]

All of these conclusions strongly indicate that official statistics are highly invalid and unreliable. In addition, there is every reason to expect that many of these variations are (systematic) biases, so there is no reasonable expectation that such "errors" will be randomized, as many sociologists like to believe. There are clearly class biases, racial biases, biases along the rural-urban dimension, age biases, sexual biases, and so on.

Participant-observer studies and descriptive case studies must provide the data for the sociology of deviance. Emile Durkheim wrote one book that was primarily concerned with the sociology of deviance—*Suicide*. Of all his many works, this was the only important one in which he made any significant use of statistical analyses. As I have tried to show before, *Suicide* used statistical analyses simply because this is what the hundreds of moral statisticians studying suicide, crime, and so forth, had done. Durkheim constructed a synthesis of their methods, data, and theory on suicide in an attempt both to explain suicide better and to establish sociology as an independent science and profession within the academic structure of French universities. To achieve this latter goal he tied the analyses of statistical rates to his "sociologistic" theory of society, arguing that only an analysis

6. The most important recent works on the nature of official information and statistics are J. I. Kitsuse and A. V. Cicourel, "A Note on the Official Use of Statistics," *Social Problems,* 11 (1963), 131-139; A. V. Cicourel, *The Social Organization of Juvenile Justice* (New York: Wiley, 1968); Kai T. Erikson, *Wayward Puritans* (New York: Wiley, 1966), pp. 163-181; Don Zimmerman, *Paper Work and People Work,* unpublished Ph.D. thesis, U.C.L.A., 1966; *Crime in a Free Society* (Washington: U.S. Govt. Printing Office, 1966); Robert Scott, *The Making of Blind Men* (New York: Russell Sage, 1969).

of rates depicts the operation of the society, as a whole, as a separate—
"social"—level of reality. The argument is a fallacious one, involving the
reification of an abstraction called "society." Durkheim himself was already
retrenching in *Suicide* itself, indicating roughly that he was talking of an
epistemologically (or analytically) distinct level, rather than an ontological
(or concrete) one. After all, it is metaphysical quibbling to demand that
"social" means something more special than "pertaining to interactions or
effects of interactions (such as shared meanings)." Durkheim's argument
that suicide rates must be the outcome of the operation of the society as a
whole because of their stability was equally unfounded, nothing more than
a matter of completely undemonstrable faith (or hope). Durkheim himself,
at least, was convinced enough of their irrelevance to his own studies to
devote himself exclusively to analyzing very unstatistical, ethnographic case
studies in all of his succeeding works.

Sociologists of deviance today are firmly committed to following Durkheim's example. But for several decades *Suicide* has stood as the great paradigm for studies of deviance, committing sociologists to uncritical analyses
of official statistical rates and later to the fully developed statistical-hypothetical method of research.

The use of the statistical-hypothetical method when applied to deviance
is no more justified than was Durkheim's argument. First, the statistical-
hypothetical method assumes that one already has good reason to suspect
he knows the general structure of reality and now needs only to test and
sharpen the general theory—for surely it would be senseless to put massive
effort into testing hypotheses derived from any theory other than one
strongly expected to be true. But this presupposes a solid base of empirical
evidence and low-level theory, which certainly has not existed in deviance,
as we shall see below in our analysis of official information. Second, the
valid use of the statistical-hypothetical method presupposes that one has
a representative sample, which presupposes knowledge of the structure or
members of a population. No one has such knowledge about any deviant
population, and it is unlikely that anyone will be able to get it, especially
given the problematic nature of the categories in terms of which any population must be conceptualized. Since member categories are both essentially
and situationally problematic (see below), and since we are primarily concerned with member categories, I believe that the very idea of a "real rate"
of deviant actions is a misconception of the nature of reality.[7] Third, theories
of deviance conceived in terms of the statistical-hypothetical model have
normally been untestable, or else the mathematical criteria of valid testing
have been so violated that almost any hypothesis can be supported by the
proper (or improper) juggling of factors. If we consider one of the best
examples of the structural-functional theory of deviance, Merton's theory

7. See Douglas, *Meanings of Suicide,* pp. 229-231.

of social structure, anomie, and deviance,[8] I believe we can easily see that it is untestable, though its supporters have quite overlooked this. Merton's theory predicts that a change in anomie will produce a change in the total rate of deviance, but that this change in deviance may occur in any of five different types of deviance. There is nothing in his formal theory that predicts that a given *type* of deviance will result from a given *type* of anomie. Those who have tested the theory have implicitly assumed that the theory predicts that relative poverty will lead to the use of illegitimate means to achieve success and that delinquency statistics are a representative test.[9] Actually, "ritualism" would be just as likely an outcome according to the formal theory. To test the theory, one would have to develop valid and reliable measures for all five types of deviance, and for anomie, and then to study a truly representative sample in order to see how changes in anomie affected relative rates of the five types of deviance. Moreover, some scales would have to be devised for *comparing* different degrees of the types of deviance (comparing oranges with watermelons). To my knowledge no one has tried this. What they have done is carefully select the supposed implications and the data and put the two together in commonsensically plausible manners. (For example, these researchers have never considered the obvious fact that the very poorest group, the old, have the very lowest rates of deviance.) The abuses of the criteria of statistical tests have been even more flagrant in the statistical-hypothetical studies of suicide, but I have dealt with these in great detail elsewhere.[10]

As sociologists of deviance have increasingly rejected official information on deviance, they have turned to various forms of participant-observation, using any combinations of participation and observation that seem to them to "work" for a given study. There have been very few systematic considerations of how one *should* do such studies. A few works which involve very complicated (and unusual) assumptions regarding the phenomenal experiences of the members, such as Matza's *Delinquency and Drift,* give only the slightest (footnote) indications of how they "know" such social meanings and how one might go about demonstrating them. On the other hand, a few very good treatments of these problems of methods by Dalton, Becker, Polsky, and Cavan [11] form the beginning of serious considerations of the problems.

The drive toward participant-observer, ethnographic, or ethnomethodological studies has been fired by a deep populist urge, a feeling that one

8. Merton, "Social Structure and Anomie."
9. One of the best of the many works falling in this category is Richard A. Cloward and Lloyd E. Ohlin, *Delinquency and Opportunity* (New York: Free Press, 1961).
10. Douglas, *Meanings of Suicide,* pp. 79-233.
11. Melville Dalton, *Men Who Manage* (New York: Wiley, 1955); Howard Becker, *Outsiders* (New York: Free Press, 1963); Ned Polsky, *Hustlers, Beats and Others* (Chicago: Aldine, 1967); Sherri Cavan, *Liquor License: An Ethnography of Bar Behavior* (Chicago: Aldine, 1966).

must return to the people to find inspiration and truth. But there has also been good reason behind the movement.

Once one has decided that member meanings are crucial for explaining social action and are also situationally problematic, it becomes vitally important to sweep away the ad hoc (official) structure of categories which functional sociologists have put between themselves and the phenomenal experiences of members. Sociologists must return to the fount of experience if they are to understand it. A whole new appreciation of "raw experience" and "reveling in the phenomena" has grown rapidly. Taken to the extreme, such a view merges sociology with art and common sense. While such a view could even be valuable as a corrective, few have succumbed wholly to the romantic allure of untrammeled nature. Most have, in fact, concentrated on developing technical and social ways of observing, recording, describing, and analyzing social communications and actions. Some have carried this radical empiricism to the extreme of trying to eliminate all member understanding gained through participation. However, this radical empiricism, this would-be total reliance on observation, seems as unacceptable as the opposite extreme of total reliance on participation. It fails to consider the ways in which unobservable and unspoken (taken-for-granted) contexts of communications determine their meanings; and this method winds up by bootlegging member understanding in the same way questionnaire studies have. Some combined use of hard empirical evidence (gotten through recordings, films, written descriptions) with member understandings gotten through participation, seems at present to be the only good strategy.

These sociologists have also become convinced that the *uncertainty principle* involved in any *obtrusive* investigations of human beings is extremely powerful. Because human action is so highly determined by the meanings of the immediate situation to the participants, and because human beings are so deeply concerned with controlling (presenting) the meanings of their selves to others in any immediate situation, it is almost inevitable that any attempt by outsiders to observe them will so change the meanings of the immediate situation for them that anything they say or do in that situation will primarily (or very largely) be presentational—an attempt to affect the outsider's image of them. When one is studying deviance, this *presentational effect* will be overwhelming, both because those observed have so much to lose by being revealed to the wrong people and because, as Becker and others have pointed out, they are so experienced at presenting "outsider information." [12] In our pluralistic, conflictful society, every man is his own public relations man; and every group, especially the very touchy deviant and official groups, is a public relations firm highly valuing the "put-on," "snow job," "run-around," secrecy, and so on for dealing with outsiders. The only way to get behind the screen of rhetoric is to establish trust

12. Becker, *Outsiders,* pp. 166-176. John Lofland has discussed "outsider information" in *Doomsday Cult* (Englewood Cliffs: Prentice-Hall, 1966), pp. 14-28.

and become taken-for-granted. Because deviants often want people they can trust to see them in their natural habitat so that they will communicate the "truth" about them to outsiders, Polsky is probably right in stressing how easily such studies can be done.[13] They are being done with great energy and imagination and they are providing some really reliable information which can be used to construct theories of deviance. In time it will be possible to make the methods more systematic and the information more representative.

The social meanings of deviance are essentially and situationally problematic, both to the members of society and to sociologists. Consequently, individuals must construct determinant (situated) moral meanings through their interactions with other individuals. The determination and analysis of social meanings seems deceptively easy. Being members of the society, we are accustomed to taking the social meanings as directly available to us, as given. This led sociologists to see the determination of social meanings as nonproblematic. The commonsense *assumption of member omniscience,* or the implicit assumption by each member that he knows the real meanings of any social event he observes, supported sociologists in this first assumption and kept them from seeing that in fact the social meanings are problematic for the members. As a consequence, sociologists concentrated their efforts on measuring the intensities and distributions of social meanings and analyzing the relations between various meanings (such as attitudes) through the use of questionnaires and other devices. Each of these devices implicitly assumed ultimately that the meanings were known unproblematically to the sociologists—and to the members.[14]

In spite of appearances, social meanings are actually very problematic for members of our society, and they should be taken as even more problematic by sociologists. In fact, I believe that the problem of creating objective, reliable means of determining and analyzing social meanings is *the* central problem of sociology and that we must solve this problem far better than we have thus far if we are ever to achieve valid theories of the sort to which most sociologists aspire.[15]

There are many obvious forms of evidence from everyday life that show the problematic nature of social meanings, especially of moral meanings. Arguments and disagreements are extremely common in everyday life. They range across the gamut of human discourse—arguments over sexual morality, arguments over the existence of God, arguments over whether a given death is an accident or a suicide, and so on interminably. Indeed, if there were not potential and actual disagreements over the meanings of

13. Polsky, *Hustlers,* pp. 117-149.
14. See A. V. Cicourel, *Method and Measurement in Sociology* (New York: The Free Press, 1964).
15. See Douglas, *Meanings of Suicide,* pp. 235-340.

things, if social meanings were obvious to all members, there would be little human discourse. America would be a land of blissful quiet, instead of the Babel of haggling disputants which it so obviously is. Perhaps John Dewey overlooked the expressive and playful element in thought and communication, but he was not far off in considering all thought to be the result of problems—problems of meaning.

The area of deviance is replete with arguments over the meanings of things to members and to sociologists. In one very important way, deviance can be looked at specifically as a generic term covering exactly those areas of social discourse in which the problems of social meanings are openly dealt with. Durkheim long ago argued that deviance serves the function of allowing society to make clear to all its members just what the norms and boundaries of society are, and Erikson has recently applied this idea very effectively to analyzing deviance among the American Puritans.[16] This argument assumes that the meanings are not really unclear or uncertain, but, rather, that they simply must be used so that they can be dramatized and reinforced. Actually, I think the dramatization, the conflict, the anxiety, and—in critical community combats such as the ones studied by Erikson —the confusion, can all best be explained as being due to the problematic nature of the meanings. As Cohen and other jurists have argued, "the law is always uncertain until a decision is made" by the participants.[17] Through their struggles with the relevant "facts," "moral and legal questions," and so forth, the members of society must construct specific meanings for this situation which will be accepted by themselves and other members. By constructing a socially plausible or acceptable meaning for this specific situation, they are making the meanings of things a little less problematic, unless their construction is rejected. And the *ritualized* aspects of these encounters—the use of the magical paraphernalia and formulae of the society —was originally intended to gain acceptance for the constructed meaning; the relics of faith are to inspire trust, reverence, and obedient submission.[18] I believe this ritualized invocation of support is necessary simply because in fact it is never possible to eliminate all disagreements between or within individuals. The rituals hide the remaining problems in the meanings by mystification, and invoke our faith in the essential goodness and reasonableness of God's social world—trust in the things unseen, in the resolvability

16. Erikson, *Wayward Puritans.*
17. See, for example, Morris R. Cohen, *Reason and Law* (New York: Collier, 1961). The "interpretations" of the laws directed at officials such as police, and judicial interpretations of the laws of arrest and interrogation, are also very often extremely problematic to the officials. See the many obvious problems involved in such interpretations in *Police Power and Individual Freedom,* C. R. Sowle, ed. (Chicago: Aldine, 1962).
18. Men such as John Adams, who were very important in setting up the forms of American government, were very explicit about the reasons for using ritualistic paraphernalia. See Page Smith, *John Adams,* vol. 2 (Garden City: Doubleday, 1962).

of conflicts that have not otherwise been resolved. The proceedings supported in this way by the rituals provide us with *adequate meanings,* with *working meanings* we feel to be sufficient for attaining our intended goals in the given interaction.

The full extent of the problematic nature of social meanings has been largely obscured because adequate meaning is the criterion in everyday relations for accepting or rejecting a situation as understood or clear. We don't normally care exactly what someone means or how much he really agrees with us in his use of terms or rules. We care only that we understand well enough or have enough agreement on meanings to get the job at hand accomplished, whether this be enjoying each other's company or making an atom bomb. As a consequence, *members of the society rarely attend to problems of meanings until something goes wrong,* until the normally adequate, working relations no longer are working adequately for the participants. If this happens on a local level, we get arguments, sullenness, threats, expressions of dismay, refusals to talk to each other, identity crises, apologies, expressions of contrition, talking out the problems with friends, searching for the answers, praying for guidance, and so on. If a threat to or break in meaningful, working relations occurs on a more general community level, we get political arguments, public challenges, public threats, community identity crises, attempts to remake the local "system," public trials of all different types involving attempts by officials to publicly stigmatize the position they see as wrong, realignments of parties, and so on.

If sociologists in recent decades had been more concerned with the problems of theoretically and operationally defining their own terms for analyzing "values," they would quickly have learned that they themselves are in great disagreement and conflict over the meanings of the terms, and they might have seen that their problems are largely a result of the same problems in our society. It is very clear, for example, that philosophers in the western world have always had fundamental disagreements over the bases of morality [19] and that in the twentieth century the meanings of moral statements—and, thus, the specification of which statements are "moral" —has produced some of the greatest conflicts in modern linguistic philosophy. The works of Moore, Stevenson, Hare, Ziff, and Wellman show how important and basic this conflict has been.[20]

With very few exceptions, sociologists have chosen not to attend to the

19. For excellent historical reviews and analyses of such philosophical conflicts over the meanings of "morals" see W. E. H. Lecky, *History of European Morals from Augustus to Charlemagne* (New York: Braziller, 1955), and Crane Brinton, *A History of Western Morals* (New York: Harcourt, 1959).
20. G. E. Moore, *Principia Ethica* (Cambridge: Cambridge University Press, 1962); C. L. Stevenson, *Ethics and Language* (New Haven: Yale University Press, 1944); R. M. Hare, *The Language of Morals* (New York: Oxford University Press, 1964); Paul Ziff, *Semantic Analysis* (Ithaca: Cornell University Press, 1960); C. Wellman, *The Language of Ethics* (Cambridge: Harvard University Press, 1961).

problems of defining and operationalizing morals, values, norms, rules, and so on. Some have chosen to accept Kluckhohn's definition, but Kluckhohn's analysis of hundreds of definitions of values by social scientists actually showed how little agreement and how much conflict there was over the meanings of the term.[21] Most sociologists, even those whose entire structural-functional theories must ultimately rest in good part on the adequate definitions of these terms, have failed to see the question, taken the answer to be obvious, or briefly defined values as being statements involving "should or ought." The problem with this one definition is that it simply cannot work. First, why are these words supposed to communicate the essential social meanings any better than myriads of other words such as moral, immoral, right, wrong, good, bad, appropriate, upright, justifiable, fair, lousy, and so on? "Should" and "ought" are not synonymous with these other terms. They are no less complicated by the meaning of instrumental value, since it is very good usage today to say such things as "you ought to (or should) use a bigger drill for that job," and few sociologists would consider this a value (moral) statement. Most importantly of all, even if these terms were used only for moral (or value) purposes, they would still fail completely as adequate operationalizations of value judgments for the simple reason that *most moral judgments made in our society are understood—not stated—or else are stated indirectly,* even insinuated, and not stated pontifically in the manner sociologists seem to envision. Most moral meanings, like most meanings in general, are background meanings; they are not stated because they do not have to be. They are stated primarily when the adequate, working meanings have failed—when the meanings are seen as problematic by the members themselves. We make the statements as clarifications. We sometimes state them for purposes of instructing children, but even here some of the most important are communicated indirectly or in silence. In our society today, I believe, it is even considered "immoral" by most groups to make a strong moral statement. To do so marks one as a prig, moralist, square, or busybody. *We have to insinuate or communicate indirectly our moral feelings if we are going to be socially effective, very often by nonverbal communications, such as a look of disgust.*

The conclusion is obvious: the proffered sociological definitions would in no way allow a nonmember to know a moral judgment when he ran into one. The sociologists are implicitly assuming that one will make use of his member understanding to know what the values of our society are and are

---

21. See Kluckhohn et al., "Values and Value-Orientations in the Theory of Action: An Exploration in Definition and Classification," in *Toward a General Theory of Action,* ed. Talcott Parsons and Edward A. Shils (Cambridge: Harvard University Press, 1954), pp. 388-433.

not, when they are being made and when they are not.[22] But this approach is also unacceptable, because it overlooks the problematic nature of moral meanings within our society.

When social moral meanings, especially as found in moral arguments, are investigated today, I believe it is clear that members find them to be quite problematic, both situationally and in the abstract. Moral meanings are generally *situationally problematic* for members because (1) the meanings of the 'realities' involved are problematic or that the morals are problematic; (2) there are disagreements and conflicts between participants which they must weigh in reaching their own decisions; (3) the relations between morals and situations are problematic; or (4) some combinations of these.

But moral meanings are not simply situationally problematic. They may also be, and increasingly are, *essentially problematic*. That is, the meanings of the symbolic categories are problematic considered even in the abstract, independently of the situations in which they are used. Moral categories that are essentially problematic are normally given adequate meaning for purposes of interaction only by being used in specific situations in which the situations and background understandings indicate for members what sense of the category is to be attended to at the time.

Moral meanings are essentially problematic in two general ways. First, they are *reflexively problematic,* that is, they are essentially problematic when related to establishing blame or fault for what has already happened. This is primarily so because establishing intention (or *mens rea*) in some way is normally a necessary part of establishing moral blame, and intention is one of the most essentially problematic categories of human experience, as Durkheim and the positivists well realized, banning it from consideration for just this reason (its complete "subjectivity"). *Intention* is basic to our conceptions of legal blame and to our conceptions of moral blame in everyday life. It is highly essentially problematic in both spheres. Second, moral meanings are often *proscriptively (or futuristically) problematic*. That is, moral judgments concerning actions yet to be taken are often essentially problematic, primarily because the meanings of the morals and the relations between them are often essentially problematic today.

These problems of moral meanings seem more likely to occur (1) the more meaningfully complex a society is (there are more encounters with individuals and situations that do not agree with or fit old moral meanings); (2) the more one encounters meaningful conflicts with other individuals and

---

22. The only alternative, and one frequently chosen by structural-functionalists, is to use obtrusive, elicited statements of morals. But this is also fundamentally inadequate because this method becomes a primary determinant of the responses (see below). The results of such a method must themselves be checked against member understandings.

groups; (3) the more social change (new situations and relations) the individuals and groups are subject to both within groups and between groups (for example, in international relations); (4) the more moral provocateurial (or challenging) and moral entrepreneurial (or organizing to produce results) activity the individuals and groups encounter—the more freedom of moral speech and action there is; and (5) the more open (or flexible) to new moral meanings, the more accepting of changes in moral meanings, the individuals and groups are.

Clearly, these can only be general guiding (or heuristic) principles, since we know so little about moral phenomena. But I believe it is reasonably clear that American society has for some time been characterized by a high degree of each of these factors and each of the components of meaningful problems, both between and, increasing more slowly, within individuals, between and within groups. Sociologists concerned with deviance have increasingly been doing work relevant to all of these heuristic principles and the resulting types of problems, though not within such a general theoretical framework. But certain factors have received special attention. Lindesmith, Sutherland, Gusfield, Becker, Timberlake, and others have been especially concerned with what Becker has so felicitously called *moral entrepreneurial activity* (factor [4]).[23] This has given rise to a great deal of new, imaginative work. Garfinkel, Lemert, Scheff, Cavan, Polsky, and others have begun some very exciting thought and research on the associated *moral provocateurial activity*.[24] One of the most striking things about the American social scene today is the great freedom given to (and demanded by) *moral provocateurs,* people who specifically articulate and challenge our taken-for-granted moral meanings, and who often make lucrative careers out of doing so. Their activities are most apparent today in the realm of nudity. "Unretouched" nudity has rapidly become a part of public entertainment, and the mass circulation magazines have published many articles supportive of the "permissive" society. Having the freedom from negative consequences and many incentives to do so, they have challenged the belief in a stereotyped middle-class morality, and they and their publics have learned how problematic moral meanings are in fact in our society.

The most general (partial) effects of the increasingly problematic nature

23. A. Lindesmith, *Opiate Addiction* (Bloomington: Indiana University Press, 1947); E. H. Sutherland, "The Diffusion of Sexual Psychopath Laws," *American Journal of Sociology,* 56 (1950), 142-148; J. R. Gusfield, "Social Structure and Moral Reform," *American Journal of Sociology,* 61 (1955), 221-232; Becker, *Outsiders,* pp. 147-163; James H. Timberlake, *Prohibition and the Progressive Movement* (Cambridge: Harvard University Press, 1963).
24. Harold Garfinkel, "The Routine Grounds . . ." in *Ethnomethodology* (Englewood Cliffs: Prentice-Hall, 1967); E. M. Lemert, "Paranoia and the Dynamics of Exclusion," *Sociometry,* 25 (1962), 2-20; Thomas J. Scheff, *Being Mentally Ill* (Chicago: Aldine, 1965); Cavan, *Liquor License;* Polsky, *Hustlers.*

of moral meanings (of deviance) in our society have been (1) to lead men of common sense to recognize this fact; (2) to destroy the plausibility to members of the assumption of a set of (stereotyped) absolute morals that supposedly dominate our society; (3) to make any group more willing to assert its own moral position against any opposition, thereby making moral argument all the more pervasive, though in indirect form; and (4) to produce a demoralizing of deviant categories themselves—that is, categories of deviance have less emphasis on moral meaning and more emphasis on other meanings (for example, "outsiders" emphasizes "separateness" instead of moral meanings, as "outcasts" would). Each of these probably then acts to make the moral meanings even more problematic.

Deviance must be defined substantively in terms of social meanings and actions. As the meanings of social phenomena change, the phenomena included in the field of deviance must change. In the beginning the field of deviance was specifically concerned with the study of "immorality," with violations of social morals, values, norms, mores, rules (or whatever term was used to refer to moral phenomena). For the most part, this is still the main jurisdiction of the field, but the corpus of subjects and the interpretation of the meanings of "moral" are changing and the focus is less and less sharp.

Once moral meanings are seen as problematic for members, the corpus of a field concerned with moral meanings becomes problematic. The corpus becomes a matter not for conventional definition, but rather for empirical determination. We are beginning to face up to the question of just what subjects belong in such a field.

Hopefully, the field will increasingly be defined loosely in terms of the fundamental problems involved in studying moral meanings and social actions, rather than in terms of an ad hoc, fragmented subject matter. The field should be increasingly concerned with determining the nature of moral statements and their effects on actions—the analysis of the language of morality, participant-observer methods of getting at taken-for-granted values, and so on. In this case the subject matter of the field will be theoretically defined; and these theoretical problems will be investigated wherever they are found.

Obviously, such an approach means that the field will overlap more with so-called general sociology. But it is clear that specialization is still being maintained by studying those phenomena that involve high degrees of moral argument, with various methods used by participants to stigmatize their opponents by gaining public acceptance of imputations of relatively extreme categories of immorality to them.

At the same time, the relative de-moralizing of social arguments means that students of deviance must be increasingly concerned with other, more

cognitive and affective dimensions of social meanings. Besides the moral–immoral dimension, the field is increasingly concerned with such dimensions of meaning as normal–abnormal, ordinary–strange, sane–insane, insider–outsider, friend–enemy, and so on. Part of the de-moralizing of social discourse consists specifically in recasting (including rhetorical masking) moral discourse in nonmoral (more acceptable, cooler) terms. The spatial metaphor of insider–outsider, analogous to citizen–outcast, yet very toned-down and "unmoralistic," is one of the more powerful of these, and was very fittingly adopted by Becker to present his view of the new perspective on deviance in *Outsiders*. Each of these categories includes some "moral" meaning, but each of them is different as well; and their use in discourse (or arguments) that would at one time have been seen as "moral" is a strong indication that the phenomenal experience behind such conversations is itself changing very rapidly. We are using different words (rather than "morals," or "values") because we have different meanings to communicate. The field of deviance, itself denoted by a term communicating this concern with a broader spectrum of meanings, will increasingly have to be concerned with analyzing these other, related phenomena.

Actions are determined primarily by the construction of situated meanings in which abstract meanings and moral meanings usually play minor but variable roles. As a consequence, moral meanings usually play minor roles in determining (what is socially categorized as) deviance and its consequences. It should be apparent from the argument so far that abstract moral meanings, such as equality, virtue, or honor, are of minor significance in determining actions in our society. In such a pluralistic society (see below) the meanings of any moral statements are quite problematic; and the more abstract the statements, the more problematic the meanings. In a simple society, a statement such as "be loyal" has relatively determinate meaning for specific actions in specific situations. In a pluralistic society, in which one has such complex and conflicting moral commitments, its meaning for specific action is extremely problematic. Loyal to whom, when, how, to what degree—and what do "loyal" actions look like? Abstract moral statements (and statements of all kinds) are too situationally problematic to serve as very good guides to action.

The situational problems of meaning can be decreased, though probably never eliminated entirely, only by making the meanings more situated, that is, by providing more information about both the relevant situations and the relevant acts. This is done partly by making the statements themselves more situational—"be loyal to friends when they need help"—and even more by the development of constituent rules or understood deep meanings which implicitly specify for the members with vast social experience just how such morals are to be interpreted for a vast number of different types

of situations.[25] (The members experience these situational specifications of relevant meanings as *"feelings* of appropriateness," "it just *seems* right somehow," and so on, just as they have the same sense about the appropriate use of language without being able to articulate any abstract rules for it.) As Harold Garfinkel has argued, sociologists and other outsiders often see social actions as involving moral conflict because they assume the actors are (or *should* be) attending to certain abstract morals in a "rational" way, whereas there are generally understood, situated meanings or commonsense criteria of rationality specifying the appropriate processes of inference, all of which lead the members to see no conflict at all. However, it is also most important to note that most of us live highly compartmentalized moral lives. We have *situated* moral and other meanings for many different types of situations, and feel relatively little need to relate the situations to each other via abstract meanings. We generally leave such abstract thought, such philosophizing, to our moral entrepreneurs and prophets, though every man is subject to rare periods of philosophical contemplation during which he is bothered or humored by the many moral conflicts in his own life.

Because of the essential and situational problems of meaning (*even* perceptual meaning) that any individual faces in almost any situation of everyday life, each individual must construct for himself (and relevant others) the past, present, and future determinant (or specific) meanings relating actions to external situations.[26] Arriving at *determinant meanings* is always problematic, but the degree to which they are problematic and the degrees to which the different components of meaning are problematic vary greatly. Some sequences of actions and their meanings are highly ritualized (such as public invocations of godly and founding-father morals), most are patterned to some extent, and some are specifically seen as situations demanding creativity or as being meaningless. Future meanings of actions—or anticipated consequences, real expectations—are almost always seen as more problematic than past or present meanings.

In our pluralistic society and complex, conflictful world, the members have come to recognize that meanings are so problematic that they have created a vast array of experts whose specific purpose is to determine the real meanings of things and make the best scientific decisions. The members have also developed a high evaluation simply of the capacity to arrive at determinant meanings and then act in accord with them; "decisiveness" is a major virtue in our society and indecision, quibbling, softheadedness make

25. For a discussion of "constituent rules" see Harold Garfinkel, "A Conception of and Experiments with, 'Trust' as a Condition of Stable Concerted Actions," in *Motivation and Social Interaction,* ed. O. J. Harvey (New York: Ronald Press, 1963), p. 187-239.
26. I have previously tried to show how individuals go about constructing the meanings of suicidal phenomena, in *Meanings of Suicide,* pp. 235-340.

people anxious. (The ideal executive and political leader makes rapid—but not hasty—decisions with stony courage—but not foolhardiness—and carries them out unflinchingly—but not obstinately.)

The abstract meanings are, of course, sometimes used by individuals in constructing their determinant meanings in specific situations, but I suspect that the highly abstract meanings, such as equality, or equal treatment before the law, are largely used for rhetorical purposes on public occasions when accommodation and social integration are the basic goal. In most workaday situations, we use far more situated meanings in constructing our determinant meanings.

In most of these construction processes, as I have argued before, even situated moral meanings play only one part, and part of that is rhetorical. For example, sociologists following Durkheim might well expect that suicides are essentially moral (or immoral) phenomena. But when the various communications of suicides and others involved are investigated, one finds that the moral meanings involved are not even given much consideration. Moral meanings are considered primarily in the cases where individuals want to place the blame for their suicides on significant others (revenge suicides). Whereas Durkheim believed that the moral prohibitions against suicide were strong in all Western groups, the analysis of suicide notes shows that individuals are able to construct plausible excuses *and* justifications for their actions out of the institutionalized religious morals. There is a great deal of freedom in individual constructive effort in these matters; and moral meanings play only one part, and rarely a dominant part in these actions.

The same seems to be true of many other forms of action generally considered to be immoral by many members of our society. Even such violations of laws as black marketing, chiseling, price fixing, traffic violations, and many other forms of individual and organizational activity are judged in terms of situated meanings that lead a high percentage of the members of our society to see them as either legitimate or as having very little to do with morality.

One of the chief implications of the crucial importance of situated meanings in determining actions, and of the general disjunction between abstract and situated meanings, is that social meanings must be studied in the situations of everyday life. It is simply impossible to infer the situated meanings from abstract meanings, and vice versa. They operate as two largely independent realms of thought. In addition, any obtrusive attempt to measure the meanings of importance in causing actions which does not faithfully reproduce the meaningful situation for the member, both by specifying the explicit and taken-for-granted meanings of the situation, will not be able to elicit the meanings that actual situations elicit. In such situations the members will either (most likely) respond in terms of abstract meanings or will provide ad hoc definitions of the situation. In both cases

the measured meanings will differ from actual situated meanings with the consequence that the measured meaning (given by responses to question-naire items, for example) will not be predictive of the actions. I believe it is the failure of sociologists to do this that has led to the almost total lack of demonstrated relationship between measured attitudes and actual behavior, a failing meticulously documented by Irwin Deutscher.[27] More-over, since it seems unlikely that sociologists will ever be able to repro-duce faithfully the meaningful structure within which the determinant constructions of meanings take place, there is further strong reason to study social action in its natural setting, as everyday life, by means of participant observation.

However, no matter how extensively and meticulously we study every-day life, I doubt that we shall be able to eliminate the gap that exists be-tween the individually constructed determinant meanings and actions and the vastly greater gap between intended consequences and actual conse-quences.

Just as it is a grave mistake to see each social actor as a little John von Neumann—or even von Neumann the social actor as von Neumann the gamester—so is it a grave mistake to see social actors as meaning-ma-chines cranking out well-articulated sets of meaningful symbols. While I have often written in this paper as though meaning is to be interpreted simply as symbolic thought, this is not because these are the only meanings of importance in causing social actions. I have concentrated on symbolic, verbally communicated meanings primarily because these are the most accessible to objective observation and because I believe that they are in fact the most important in causing actions, and that man is a conscious, commonsensically rational, purposeful actor. But it seems clear in terms of our own individual experiences that there are certainly times when the emotional meanings of things control our actions, even at times in spite of ourselves. There are times when feelings of guilt overwhelm us, quite contrary to our expectations and our more symbolic understandings of our-selves.

There is also a general gap between our determinant meanings, espe-cially our conscious intentions, and our actions. Living in a problematic world, we are quite aware of the many slips and accidents that intervene between what we intend to do and what we actually do. Even more, we know that there are greater gaps between the intended consequences and the actual consequences of the actions we do commit. Commonsensically we know that these two overlapping realms of unintended accidents (with-out negligence) and intended accidents (with negligence) cover a wide range of events in our lives. Accidents and chance events occur all the time and are often determinants of life and death. The law, being *ulti-*

27. "Attitudes and Actions," *Social Problems,* 13 (1966), 235-254.

mately derived from commonsense moral meanings, has made such considerations basic to legal procedures. But the social sciences have largely assumed a completely deterministic relation between the meaning states of actors and the consequences. For this reason, sociologists have implicitly assumed that deviant actions are unproblematically the result of choices to commit deviant actions and that, therefore, actions categorized as deviant can be assumed to be committed by deviants, which in turn means that these people are categorically different from nondeviants.

While the first part of this assumption is in conflict with the commonsense meanings of evidence and guilt, the latter part is largely based on commonsense ideas about the stigmatized individual. Unlike most commonsense categories of persons (barber, tipper, stroller), the categories of deviance, especially those imputed by official organizations (*official stigmas*), communicate the meanings of the *substantial self* rather than just the *situated selves.*[28] These stigmatizing categories tell what the person really, essentially, is, independently of situations in which he acts. They tell what his "soul" or "heart" is like, and they say that this substantial self is immoral and cannot be trusted. Categories of situated selves tell only about the person in the given situation (a barber may be a saint or a Bluebeard, but the category says only that he cuts hair for a living). It is for this reason that a "deviant," especially an officially categorized one (criminal, psychotic, destitute), finds it so terribly hard to escape the category by any means other than achieving a new social identity: the category sticks across situations and time, because at heart he is still the same man and an untrustworthy man who may even be simulating goodness to deceive you. The acceptance of this substantial-self theory of deviance is the basis of the *biographical (record) approach to deviance* taken by officials: "once a deviant, always a deviant." (There are, of course, differences between categories in their degrees of substantiality, with criminal, traitor, whore, and homosexual being highly substantial; and there are very difficult processes of reintegration or *status-upgrading*. But these are not our direct concern here.) A situated self, on the other hand, can easily be changed.

In a simple society such a view probably worked reasonably well in isolating and thus controlling deviance. With largely unproblematic, stable, and nonconflictful meanings, individuals could generally see which actions were deviant and what the consequences of committing them were. However, in a pluralistic society with very problematic, conflictful, and changing moral meanings, this view has a completely different effect. In a pluralistic society, individuals far more often do not know that certain actions are considered immoral or illegal by certain groups, do not share such

28. See Douglas, *Meanings of Suicide,* pp. 279-283. Becker and Matza have previously criticized sociologists' acceptance of the idea that deviants are very different kinds of people. (See Becker, *Outsiders.*)

meanings, do not realize the consequences, or have very unrealistic ideas of what the consequences are. In such a society it is *normal* to get committed to many individuals, groups, patterns of actions, and outcomes of actions without having any very clear ideas about their "actual" natures. Academics sign petitions by unknown organizations, and lonely girls go on dates with strangers. In a pluralistic society there are many kinds of seducers and seductions that the most innocent often have the hardest time seeing through. But all the innocence in the world is often not enough to save one from the consequences of categorization as a deviant. In a pluralistic society with rapidly changing morals, laws, interpretations, and discretionary actions, what looks very respectable one day—membership in leftist organizations, or marijuana use, for example—may be considered deviant tomorrow or in twenty years. Given the tremendous and organizationally "necessary" discretionary powers of officials, the same action may produce a "talking to" today and a three-year sentence tomorrow. Given the very low probabilities of apprehension in our probabilistic system of deterrence, given this general situation, and given the great differences in morals of different groups and the de-moralizing of meanings for individuals in our pluralistic society, committing acts that are deviant from some major interest group's standpoint is an inevitable part of life in our society. Consequently *all of us, except those who live alone in caves, run necessary risks of being publicly denounced as deviants.* More important, it is likely that the great majority of us commit many acts that *could* be officially categorized as illegal (felonies) or as insane and could get us officially stigmatized. Sometimes the highly improbable act of official "deterrence" occurs and we find ourselves categorized as criminals or insane. Such actions are generally casual, not a standard part of our lives. For example, the vast majority of children and adolescents in our society commit the *potential* crime of shoplifting at some time and it seems likely that they are joined in this by millions of adults, especially housewives. Such behavior is casual and intermittent for almost all individuals, though the aggregate shrinkage loss runs into the billions each year. Again, potential theft from employees is almost universal in American society, and is more a standard part of workers' lives. But only an extremely small part of these potential crimes becomes actual crimes (officially categorized as crime). Furthermore, studies of urban areas by psychiatrists make it apparent that a majority of us are potentially categorizable as insane or disturbed, needing only to be caught up in the net of psychiatric services to become actually categorized as such.

The vast majority of people in our society run these objective risks of official categorization as deviants in their everyday lives, so much so that these risks become taken for granted, not even thought about until the risk is immediate. (This universality of potential guilt makes it easy to arouse anger against the officials, though most people are afraid and

ambivalent about organized action against their policies.) In such situations, which probably include most forms of potential delinquency, there is little or no actual experience of risk-taking and the laws have no possible deterrent effect. But the pluralistic society even encourages the development of conscious, standardized risk-taking by individuals and organizations, especially when the risk is not of official stigmatization (as in price fixing) or when the officials are seen as enemies against whom one is playing a dangerous game to express resentment and show courage (as in many types of delinquency).

But the official machines do continue to run, processing their standard quota of stigmatized deviants, however low the probabilities of apprehension, however chancy the nature of the justice involved, however high the recidivism rates of the processees. One of the effects is to separate and alienate a cohort of criminals from the noncriminals, a group which will then be locked into the social category of criminal by the commonsense beliefs and official organizational policies.

Deviance and official control agencies are causally interdependent. Only a small part of the socially defined deviance in the world ever becomes the actual subject of concern of official organizations. But one of the striking facts about our society is that this part has been growing very rapidly. Little more than a hundred years ago there were relatively few officials concerned with controlling deviance. Police, parole and probation agents, juvenile detention officers, internal revenue agents, welfare investigators, anti-trust investigators, securities and exchange commissioners, official public health officers, school psychologists, family court psychiatrists, auditors—all of these and hundreds more were almost completely unknown. Today these are massive control organizations, their numbers and types rapidly proliferating, and it is very probable that the proportion of our manpower and resources committed to official control is also growing rapidly. Unfortunately, there has been very little attention given to the growth of official control organizations, so it is hard to explain this important change. However, it seems reasonable to expect that this rapid growth has been due primarily to (1) the increasingly problematic nature of social meanings, especially moral and legal meanings, as our society has become more pluralistic (complex and conflictful), (2) the growing importance of government both as the primary integrative factor in our society (see below) and as a provider of services, (3) the increasing tendencies for various power groups to try to control other (conflicting) groups through official rule-making, and (4) the increasing belief in the abilities of experts to control human actions "for their own good and the good of the community."

A growing proportion of deviance in the world is being processed by official organizations. It should not be shocking to sociologists to discover

that as these control activities have become more organized, the nature of the organizations has itself become an increasingly important determinant of the meanings, extents, and consequences of the behavior they are trying to control: deviance. Like other organizations, these have tried to have more control over the nature of their tasks, their own policymaking, their working conditions, and their futures. Especially as they have more and more assumed the social categories of (scientific) experts, they have come to have more power in all of these. They have increasingly become the experts who determine what the laws will be, as Sutherland, Becker, and others have tried to show. They have achieved wide discretion in handling cases, enforcing informal laws, and so on.

Of all of their powers, however, official organizations have one supreme power: they control the *(public) stigmatization processes*. While informal (private individual) imputations of deviance are important in our society, these imputations do not stigmatize as do official imputations of deviance. As Lemert pointed out some time ago, a man can be highly deviant and denounced by his neighbors for it without being much affected by it, but once he is subjected to one of the various kinds of official "ceremonies of degradation," or stigmatization, he finds that his whole social self is affected —he is a marked man.[29]

As has become increasingly clear, it is the first official charging (by arrest, by insanity hearing) of an individual by the official organization that successfully stigmatizes him, rather than the formal finding of guilt.[30] The exact nature and explanation of this crucial stigmatizing effect of official charging has not been investigated. But several factors seem most important. (1) Official charging makes one's "deviance" publicly available knowledge through the mass media, court hearings, and so on. (2) This means that anyone *might* know about the deviance and they *might* think very badly of one for it. (3) In our complex, pluralistic society individuals *must* make decisions about most other people on the basis of small bits of evidence because they are strangers. (4) People involved with the public (market) develop play-safe strategies for dealing with the complex, pluralistic society—they become largely concerned with avoiding trouble from conflicting interest groups. (5) The expert knowledge imputed to officials leads people to credit their accounts enough to distrust the charged, thereby making his accounts untrustworthy. (6) Once charged, a man has an official record, will be systematically surveyed, and "rousted" by officials.

If it is true that the actions of official organizations are of crucial importance in stigmatizing deviants, then we can expect that official action is the most important factor in producing (stable) "deviant careers," as

29. Lemert, "Paranoia."
30. See, for example, R. D. Schwartz and J. H. Skolnick, "Two Studies of Legal Stigma," in Howard Becker, ed., *The Other Side* (New York: Free Press, 1964), pp. 103-118.

Becker calls them.[31] Official stigmatization does more than anything else to change an individual's (substantial) social self and his own self-image, thereby leading to commitments to deviant patterns of action. Just as imprisonment seems to produce "prisonization"—making a man more criminal—so official charging goes a long way toward producing stigmatization that makes a man more deviant.

In a very real sense, whether intentionally or not, *the official agencies create a constantly growing body of stigmatized ex-citizens who can and are then used by the officials as the primary means of routinizing their organizational activities, of showing the public that they are working on important cases, and of proving that their work is effective.* Police work, especially, would be exceedingly difficult without the large, growing body of stigmatized "criminals." Those bearing the stigmata of official records provide the police with a permanent, ready-made group that can be legitimately, systematically surveyed, rousted, and processed at any time. They make a very large part of police work predictable, a necessity for a bureaucratic organization. When a crime occurs, the police can now go to their computers to get *the* prime suspects, show them to witnesses, investigate—fulfill their duty. Men in this situation find it hard to "go straight," just as Ray's addicts found it hard to "kick the habit" when no one was willing to believe they could.[32] Most of their subsequent arrests lead to no convictions ("too smart this time, but we'll get him next time"). Sometimes they are convicted for offenses most people would never be caught at because it takes careful surveillance and unusual unwillingness to handle it informally; often they plead guilty for consideration; and sometimes they act as patsies. The police get their results. The system works. And by working, it increases the probability that it will work next time.

American society is a rapidly changing, conflictful, morally pluralistic society; but the myths of the founding fathers and of middle-class morality hide these facts by producing a relatively homogeneous, stable public rhetoric. There is hardly an American alive who does not know the important difference between *public morality* and *private morality.* We even have public language, which is fit for respectable grandmothers, and private language, which is fit for barroom jibes, backroom arguments, raucous laughter, and intimate get-togethers. Most of us are capable of orchestrating our public and private vocabularies in complex ways across a broad scale —now prudishly disapproving, now intimating sinful thoughts and deeds with one word, now brutally accusing. The sum total of language used by the great majority of Americans is rich in such disparate vocabularies, as well as in clashing dialects (ethnic gutteral for wheeling-and-dealing,

31. Becker, *Outsiders,* pp. 25-40.
32. Marsh B. Ray, "The Cycle of Abstinence and Relapse Among Heroin Addicts," in *The Other Side,* pp. 163-177.

"standard" for education) and occasional rhetorics (Sunday maxims, Fourth of July ideals, sales pep talks.) It is a rich language full of harsh conflicts and well made for expressing a vast variety of human experience. It needs to be, for it is the symbolic tool of an immensely complex nation of peoples.

In the beginning, of course, (New England) American society was exceedingly simple. It was a largely monolithic, theocratic state in which everyone spoke one language, lived one way, worshiped one God in one way, and watched all his neighbors for the slightest deviation from the one true way.[33]

Within less than one hundred years, by the early eighteenth century, this pristine simplicity was rapidly disintegrating. In Massachusetts itself the old stock Puritans, men like Cotton Mather, began to feel themselves out of joint with the times. Rail as they would against the fleshpots and all evils of the flesh, their society was rapidly secularizing, turning from godly virtues to material values. In the eighteenth century they became increasingly interdependent with the aristocratic, slave-based enclaves of the tidewater, the Catholic enclaves, the Scotch-Irish lower-class enclaves, and the anarchic frontiersmen. After protracted conflict this enclave, colony-centered, sectionalist, pluralistic society was able to form a compromise-ridden federal government which was destined to be rent by continual secessionist conflicts, a terribly destructive civil war, uprisings, riots, anarchic terrorists, and vigilantes.

In 1820 there were approximately ten million United States citizens, the great majority of them English and Scottish Protestants. There were probably three million Negro slaves. By 1910, only ninety years later, twenty-eight million immigrants had been added to the earlier population. By 1930 another ten million were added. By today there have been over forty-four million immigrants, the great majority of them Catholic. There are now twenty-three million Negroes. Nearly 40 percent of the population is non-Protestant, with many more percentiles uncommitted.

At roughly the same time that this great tide of immigration was occurring, the United States was being transformed in almost every other way as well. It went from extremely rural and agricultural to extremely urban and industrial, from poor to rich, from one of the weakest to the most powerful, from one of the most isolated and neutral nations to the most internationally involved policeman, from an uneducated, inartistic society to the world center of education and art, from a society deeply suspicious of science to the devoted leader of the scientific and technological revolution, from a society of individual initiative and free enterprise to one of giant corporations, giant government agencies, graduated income taxes, government controls and long-run planning, from a society of anarchic, frontier freedoms

33. This is the America studied by Erikson in *Wayward Puritans*.

to one with vast, complicated, centralized organizations of social control and universal military obligations. In fact, almost all of these vast changes in our society have taken place within the last seventy-five years, most within the lifetime of the average adult, and almost all are continuing and accelerating today, while new forms of change are occurring at accelerating rates.

Few sociologists would deny these changes or doubt their significance for some purposes. Change has all too clearly become a central fact of our everyday lives. In fact, we have even come to value change (or innovation, creativity, newness) and planned investment for future (long-run) changes so greatly that we are rapidly developing a form of futuristic legitimacy, a justification of present acts in terms of what we hope they will do for tomorrow.

But this acceptance of change as a fact of life has only recently begun to affect most sociological theories or interpretations of American society. The dominant approach has been the structural-functional one, and this approach has normally assumed that a stable set of abstract, entirely or largely unconflictful and homogeneously shared values have remained intact and have continued to determine the general structure or basic patterns of social actions in this society.

While this approach may be of some value in analyzing relatively simple societies, it is almost inconceivable to me that such a huge, far-flung nation as this could undergo such extreme changes of every conceivable kind in its ways of life, its situations in the world, and its ways of dealing with the world while maintaining even a relatively homogeneous and stable set of abstract values that continue to determine how its members act in specific situations. If this should be so, it would undoubtedly be a scientific discovery of the first order, for it conflicts with so much of what we can observe to be the case in our everyday lives. On the surface of it, this is an immensely pluralistic society, with major interest groups struggling against other major interest groups for a huge number of extremely diverse and opposite moral positions.

Given all of the prima facie evidence in favor of the conclusion that our society is morally pluralistic, why would social theorists be so insistent on the opposite interpretation? Aside from the natural desire to simplify for reasons of science, which has already been rejected as being so overdone as to constitute falsification, the structural-functionalists have had some prima facie evidence on their side. The most obvious evidence supporting their assumptions is the existence of considerable order in our society, a reasonably stable form of government, some evidence of the existence of certain generally shared moral meanings, and the continued public appeal to the virtues of the founding fathers. I think all of these things clearly exist and are important, but I also think the structural-functionalists have misinterpreted their nature and significance by failing to also consider all of the prima facie evidence in favor of the pluralistic interpretation.

First, our society is not distintegrating, rotting at the core, or anything else quite so flamboyant and unusual in the history of nations. This is a dynamic, rapidly growing society capable of putting extremely well organized, massive efforts even into activities that arouse a great deal of violent dissent. Any valid theory of our society must take this integration, this degree of organization, into account and explain it, while at the same time accounting for the high degree of conflict (lack of integration) in our nnoioty.

Second, there is general consensus, or sharedness, of certain important meanings in our society, even a few moral meanings. There are, of course, the usual ten commandment types of meanings against incest, rape, treason, when perpetrated against the in-group, and there are the usual exceptions for such acts against enemy outsiders (such as "Commies"). But these are pretty nearly universal values and there is about as much disagreement about their specific interpretations (that is, their situated meanings) within our society as between our society and the Tikopia. Still, there are these abstract, shared values. More importantly, there are certain very generally shared, specific (situated) national meanings, both moral and otherwise. There are generally shared meanings of membership: the vast majority of us see ourselves as "Americans," citizens with rights and duties, different (and generally better) from members of other nations. In short, we have a reasonably stable, homogeneous social (national) identity, which is partly moral, though primarily cognitive. There are also generally shared moral meanings to which we are committed concerning our general form of federal government, though there is a great deal more conflict over the specific (situated) meanings of this, especially from the South and from radical political groups on the left and right.

Third, there are various abstract and specific (situated) moral meanings that are invoked on public occasions. While there is considerable variety and conflict over these (states rights speeches go well in Georgia, but not in New York; upper-class courtesy is somewhat different from lower-class courtesy), many of them have achieved considerable acceptance and commitment—courtesy, cleanliness, minding one's own business, and so on.

I believe the structural-functional approach involves three general mistakes in the interpretation of the significance of these shared meanings. First, it involves no consideration of the crucial distinction between public and private expressions of morality and actions. From the structural-functional standpoint the relative insignificance of differences and conflicts over moral meanings leads one to expect a fundamental similarity or congruence between public and private moral expressions and actions. But we have already referred to numerous ways in which this is not true in our society. As already noted, for example, the great majority of us have private languages that we do not use in public. We both hide our moral beliefs and adopt a moral relativism ("mind our own business") in most public

situations. (Moral relativism in public situations led Riesman to see an opinion "radar." He inferred from this that people are other-directed, whereas this is probably only so in public. In their own little social enclaves, Americans are still often moral dogmatists.)

Public morality in a pluralistic society does two things which are well understood commonsensically. It prevents our being continually involved in moral argument and it prevents physical violence. The importance of this is most easily seen in the case of moral entrepreneurs who try to enforce their morality (or public morality) on others, especially on their private actions. Such people are seen as surly, cranky, moralistic, prudish, mean, nasty, and brutish. They are shunned as quickly as those who can never escape the work morals, who can never "unbend." These are people who do not understand or cannot adopt the pluralistic nature of our (situated) moral meanings. These are people who do not share those commitments and understandings that make successful accommodation possible in a pluralistic society, which brings us to the second misinterpretations of structural-functionalism.

If members of a pluralistic society are going to work together successfully, they must be able to accommodate themselves to conflicting commitments and they probably must be able to withdraw to their own enclaves to express themselves freely to the like-minded. This latter condition (or "expressive function") of knowing and expressing the true self (one's self-image) is achieved in our society through a strong emphasis on privacy—private clubs, the sanctity of the home, the anonymity of the massive cities. Of far greater importance, accommodation is achieved largely through the development of specific commitments to moral meanings and understandings. It is very striking that some of our only highly shared moral commitments should be specifically in that area of our lives—public behavior—in which we come into contact with many thousands of strangers from every conceivable walk of life, that these commitments should be strongest and most widely shared among the executive middle-class groups who are specifically the people who must manage the moralities of strangers to achieve work goals; and that these groups specifically socialize their children to live by these morals for the express purpose of "getting along with people." As Dalton has so clearly seen, in a pluralistic society, acting in accord with such accommodative morals as courtesy, tolerance, keeping one's nose clean, decency, playing it cool, not being too assertive, is of utmost importance in achieving social status.[34] One of the common culture shocks in our society comes when adolescents raised in the private, homogeneous morality of the home first encounter the accommodative morality of the pluralistic world of work and political action. They see it as cynical (which it is), hypocritical (which it has to be), and damnable (which it is only to

34. Dalton, *Men Who Manage.*

those who are not committed to accommodative morals). This culture shock and the resulting alienation largely disappear once these adolescents get involved in the adult world, thereby being resocialized to *accommodative morals*. (Their cynicism and success may be greater because they understand the whole thing better.)

One of the most important accommodative values in our society today is that prohibiting a moralistic attitude toward workaday issues as public issues, which is one reason why those who have been thinking in terms of simple systems instead of pluralistic societies have seen our society as increasingly amoral and immoral. There are specific, widely shared moral commitments to de-moralizing public issues. There are very strong moral feelings against intruding moral issues into public issues. The "moral prude" is considered immoral in most public settings, except in so-called fundamentalist groups, which are themselves morally repugnant to most members of our society. (Fundamentalists, fire-eaters, preachers, are especially morally repugnant and are considered to be uncivilized, uneducated, boorish, hillbilly backwoodsmen. They are, of course, the closest thing we have to "original," founding-father Americans, since their hill-country society has remained largely outside of the many torrents of change.) The reason for this de-moralizing of public work and issues seems simple: in a pluralistic society with little moral agreement any public work which necessitates intergroup cooperation will be disrupted by bringing in moral meanings. The arguments over the moral issues make effective work almost impossible when such a Babel of morality is unleashed. Moral issues are, in fact, so disruptive of organized action in our society that we tend to talk of moral issues primarily in terms of facts and other practical (nonmoral) goals, so that the alchemy of our public debates transforms moral issues into factual, policy, practical issues for the experts and scientists. (Social scientists increasingly act as alchemists in these situations, secretly imposing their values on the rest of society. They are especially adept at this because their expert knowledge and their prestige as experts enable them to control and manipulate the "facts" to "prove" their positions are correct. For example, when the official statistics support their position, then they are facts. When they do not, the statistics are unreliable.) We have also developed various ways of denying moral issues and even of "suppressing the superego" for public purposes.

One of the most striking results of this whole accommodative process can be seen in national political decision-making. There seems to be an increasing tendency to tie almost all issues to a few ultimate goals, which can therefore be called *least-common-denominator goals*. The most important of these are economic progress (as measured by the GNP), national security (as measured by our position relative to the communist world), and public health (as measured by indexes of disease). These are goals which the great majority of people can agree on regardless of their moral positions.

Achieving each of these will help the greatest number achieve their myriad moral goals, since you have to be alive and well, and have the wherewithal to achieve almost any goals.[35] (Only those dedicated to Christian poverty, anti-medicine beliefs, communism, and so forth, dissent from these global goals.) The goals are even becoming the national moral goals both in domestic and foreign arguments, simply because they are such effective least-common-denominator moral positions.

Long before they had constructed these specific accommodative moral meanings to manage public encounters effectively in our pluralistic society, the members of American society had constructed an accommodative attitude toward the abstract moral meanings of pristine America (the founding fathers), and this accommodative attitude has fostered the commonsense and sociological acceptance of the *myth of the founding fathers* and the *myth of the dominant middle-class morality*. Structural-functionalists and other social analysts have generally assumed, at least implicitly, that each new immigrant group to America was successfully socialized by schools and other institutions to accept the values of the dominant Anglo-Saxon middle class whose own values had been transmitted by each generation since Revolutionary days or beyond. This is supposed to be the way in which the values are kept homogeneous and stable. However, as Lemert has argued, studies of culture-contact and acculturation show no support for such an assumption. Instead, they show that the subordinate groups develop accommodative values. This should be especially the case, rather than introjection of the superordinal group's values, when there has been a great deal of conflict between the groups, as has been true in the United States.

Accommodation to the abstract "conventional" morals, the founding-father morals, and various situated accommodative morals, especially those of not provoking moral feelings and showing tolerance, all help to maintain the myths of middle-class morality and founding-father morality. Since people do not challenge them, there is a strong tendency for each person who does disagree to suspect that he might be alone in disagreeing, that he might be the only "deviant" around. If he challenges them, he fears he will seem immoral. Moreover, and most importantly, as long as there exists a general public ignorance about the actual moral commitments of others, any public violator makes himself vulnerable to the moral attacks of his enemies, especially through the use of officials. Even if everyone agreed with him privately, they would fear that by helping him they too would look like deviants to everyone else. *Shared ignorance makes the public myths of morality immensely more powerful than the number committed to them would*. But then, there are various powerful groups committed to upholding the stereotyped conventional morality, both for pure and for cynical reasons.

35. John Kenneth Galbraith has seen much of this, but presented a different (complementary) explanation of it, in *The New Industrial State* (Boston: Houghton, 1967).

These act as moral enterpreneurs to mobilize the official action against vio-
lators of the mythical morality. In fact, each one of us is probably committed in some way to some parts of the conventional morality, making us
available for entrepreneurial organization as a veto interest group against
moral innovators and provocateurs. Since the conventional morality is
thought of as a package (monolithic) and is so treated by the official organizations historically committed to upholding it, this fragmentary support is
aggregated into general support through the support the different groups
give to law and order and the official organizations. Because of the great and
continuing difficulty in passing new laws in our society, partly because of
opposition from official organizations, there is a growing gap between laws
and morals; and official organizations are increasingly enforcing a traditional, conventional morality to which there is decreasing commitment. But
this enforcement helps to maintain the myth of moral consensus.

But it would be a mistake to see our fragmentary—or whole—support of
this conventional morality as generally moral in character. Today we are
probably more committed because of fears of consequences for us and for
social order in general. In large measure we sometimes present our objections, privately, in terms of morals because it is so much more powerful
rhetorically (though in public it could look "moralistic"). Many young
people, for example, probably prefer to think of their chastity as due to
"morals," rather than fears of consequences or lack of opportunities.

As is true of most myths, these *myths of moral consensus are the product
of anxiety and serve to reduce that anxiety*. The almost unbelievable changes
that we have been subject to in the last century and the complexity and
conflicts of meanings we are subject to in such a highly pluralistic society
threaten all sense of social identity and self-identity, which can give rise to
severe anxiety. The belief that all good Americans share the same moral
ideals, that these are self-evident, and that these moral ideals bind us in-
dissolubly across the ages to the revolutionary heroes gives us a deep sense
of identity and clarity of moral purpose that are so continually threatened
by our everyday lives. The anxious nightmares of chaos and conflict are
transformed by the social dream of a united people marching toward the
promised land. But the dream is a social reality and, as such, does in fact
help to ward off the chaos. The dream is increasingly challenged and rejected, being replaced by the accommodative and least-common-denominator values, but it is still very influential.

As noted before, there are moral provocateurs in our society who use
indirection, feeling out, and so on, to test or sound the actual moral feelings
of people. Men like Freud and Kinsey became experts in this. They
have had a tremendous effect on public morals by revealing the fact that
most people are involved in the same forms of deviance. Adolescent males,
for example, have been astounded (and relieved) to learn that almost everyone else is also masturbating. This moral sounding has gone a long way

toward destroying the myth of middle-class morality, but sociologists have been slow to look behind the front.

The unequal distribution of power and our shared morals concerning our form of government have been of crucial importance in constructing social order in American society. The third misinterpretation of structural-functionalists has been their view of the shared morals regarding the form of government as just some more shared morals. They have failed to see how absolutely crucial this is for constructing social order in a pluralistic society. Even a pluralistic society with a very strong, general commitment to situated accommodative morals cannot remain very well integrated for long. Various moral conflicts will eventually produce powerful coalitions of the major enclaves which will split the society apart through civil war, unless there is some other integrating force. In American society I believe we find these forces in (1) shared moral commitments to a few crucial principles of democratic government, commitments which we construct, transmit, and protect with religious fervor, (2) a conscious recognition of social order (or social organization) as something that is problematic and that must be solved by every possible rational means, which includes (3) the conscious, purposeful management of moral meanings and the construction of moral compromises in pursuit of the goal of constructing social order and getting things done, especially (4) the attainment of the three shared, materialistic (moral) goals of health, wealth, and security, and (5) the purposeful use of physical force to construct social order.

Americans, especially politicians, talk a great deal about the threat of moral decay, the destruction of the social structure, the threat to society, and so on. This type of statement is common fare to every Boston Commons orator, every housewife, every journalist, and certainly every politician. There are a great number of such commonsense ideas about relations between morals and social order. These are basic to the commonsense theories of man and society which help to determine the policies of politicians and other men.

These commonsense theories lead politicians to invoke, construct, manage, manipulate, and feign moral meanings for the specific purpose of constructing social order. *Americans of practical affairs, most especially political decision-makers, see social order as problematic. They purposefully set out to construct and maintain social order, and to do so they manage moral meanings with great care.* It is even likely that they often support the myths of moral consensus with the "cynical" purpose of using them to construct and maintain social order.

When combined with the reasonably strong moral consensus behind our present form of government and the systematic use of organized power, the political work to construct and maintain social order becomes the primary integrating force in our pluralistic society. Though the founding fathers had

a great number of moral conflicts, they were very practical social engineers setting out to construct a viable social order which would specifically allow and guarantee the freedoms of expression and action that have nurtured the ever-increasing pluralism in our society. Our government from the beginning to the present has been a *compromise or accommodative government,* supported almost as much by rational calculations of expected rewards (rational legitimacy) as by moral consensus about its forms, and working from one *moral and instrumental coalition* to another to meet specific (situated) issues as they arise. Only such an accommodative government could be accepted by a pluralistic set of colonial-state societies at that time and by such a highly pluralistic society as we have today. As Weber pointed out about the Italian city-states of the Renaissance, the existence of many conflicting groups largely equal in power was the primary determinant of democratic, representative forms of government.[36]

A society with the degree of monolithic consensus normally assumed by structural-functionalists would have no need or use for a government such as ours. It could want and get a theocratic, monolithic government or, possibly, little government at all, since the people could all reach the same decisions independently, as is done in some simple societies and as is supposed to be done in Quaker meetings. This was, in fact, precisely the form of government America had in the beginning when there was almost universal consensus. As the society became more pluralistic, it moved toward democratic forms, toward an accommodative, compromise method of governing. At the same time, some middle-range level of moral consensus, including rational legitimacy, was and is necessary for the present forms to work. Without this, the conflict of enclaves would be so great that government could work effectively only by the use of dictatorial power. American society is so tremendously pluralistic that there seems no possibility of a theocratic dictatorship, but this very pluralism leads people to feel that social order is continuously precarious, always being threatened, always decaying, and, therefore, always posing the threat of dictatorial control. The anxiety caused by this feeling of the imminent dissolution of social order leads people to nurture every morsel of moral consensus, to demand support of the forms of government, and to accept and perpetuate the myths of moral consensus.

One of the primary goals of sociological theory and research must be to surmount these anxieties, to study the ways in which these commonsense theories and myths of moral consensus and social entrepreneurs do construct social order, rather than accepting the myths and building our theories of morality and social order on them.

36. Max Weber, *The City* (New York: Collier, 1958).

15.

Sociological Theory in Relation
to Social Psychological Variables

Alex Inkeles

Alex Inkeles is professor of sociology at Harvard University and Director of Studies on Social and Cultural Aspects of Development at Harvard's Center for International Affairs. He combines an interest and expertise in the sociology of Soviet society as well as in the developing areas. Professor Inkeles was born in Brooklyn, New York, in 1920. He holds a B.A. and M.A. from Cornell University and a Ph.D. from Columbia University. As an outgrowth of an intensive program of interviewing refugees from the Soviet Union, Professor Inkeles published several studies: Public Opinion in Soviet Russia, Soviet Citizen, *and* Soviet Society. *He has spent a year at the Center for Advanced Study in the Behavioral Sciences at Palo Alto and is a member of the American Academy of Arts and Sciences and chairman of the section on social psychology of the American Sociological Association. Professor Inkeles is currently directing a six-nation study of the sociocultural aspects of economic development.*

It would not be at all difficult to assemble a set of fifty or one hundred recent articles in social psychology, chosen half from the psychological and half from the sociological journals, which would be so much alike that no one judging without knowledge of source or author could with any precision discriminate those written by professional sociologists from those written by psychologists. Several considerations follow from this simple fact. Clearly, the two disciplines cannot be defined in terms of what psychologists and sociologists respectively do, since they so often do the same thing. Recourse to the different history and development of the disciplines, while of intrinsic interest, must be treated as irrelevant to the appropriate formulation of their present nature. In any event, this approach is merely a variant on the theme of what psychologists and sociologists do. Reference to the wide range of problems dealt with by either psychology or sociology alone is not satisfactory either, since it fails to meet the problem of overlap with which we began.

Should we then have three disciplines, psychology, sociology, and social psychology? Perhaps; but before we add to the proliferating behavioral

These remarks are adapted from my paper "Sociology and Psychology," which appeared in vol. 6 of *Psychology: A Study of a Science,* ed. Sigmund Koch (New York: McGraw-Hill, 1963). In the present version, numerous examples, illustrations, and explications presented in the fuller account had to be omitted.

sciences we should have exhausted every other remedy. Furthermore, many of the problems not shared today may be shared tomorrow, depending on the accidents of academic and scientific history. Others which do not overlap or are peripheral to either discipline are such because of accidents of national academic history, and not on logical grounds. In England, for example, anthropology has a strong sociological flavor and is much more concerned with the study of social structure than it is in the United States. Indeed, as Kroeber points out, on the Continent "there is of course nothing corresponding to American anthropology; prehistory, ethnology and (physical) anthropology have different roots and affiliations, remain and mostly want to remain distinct." [1]

These considerations argue strongly in favor of some other way of defining the two disciplines. By far the simplest method is to define each in terms of one central, exclusive, and independent problem or focus of interest. For purposes of this discussion, I will treat psychology as the study of the individual as a *personality* system and sociology as the study of aggregates, large or small, of people constituting a *social* system. In selecting these definitions I am, of course, excluding from consideration a wide range of important theory and research customarily defined as part of psychology, such as psychoacoustics and comparable work on vision. There are various alternatives for conceptualizing the field of psychology, several of which are chiefly oriented toward biology and physiology. It is not my intention here to argue the relative merits of these approaches. My assigned task in this chapter is to consider the relations of sociology and psychology from the sociologist's perspective. From that point of view, it is mainly the psychology of the human personality which is of relevance and interest.

Insofar as psychology and sociology are defined primarily in terms of discrete analytic foci, many will find themselves assigned to a field quite other than the one in which they were trained and with which they identify professionally. Many psychologists concern themselves mainly with the efficiency of groups, which is a social system problem; while some trained as sociologists inquire into the personality traits that predispose one to suicide or crime, which is a personal system problem. In other words, I am classifying people according to what they do, but this principle has now been turned on its head. The discipline is not defined by what those accepting its label do. Instead, a discipline is defined in terms of a given problem or object of study and the relevant efforts to uncover the laws governing the particular phenomenon. The scholar or scientist is assigned to one or another discipline according to the problem on which he is in fact working. That many who think of themselves as sociologists will find them-

1. A. L. Kroeber, "History of Anthropological Thought," in W. L. Thomas, Jr., *Yearbook of Anthropology* (New York: Wenner Gren Foundation, 1955), p. 308.

selves psychologists by this definition, and vice versa, is of no importance. The purpose of this discussion is to achieve conceptual clarification, not to decide on membership criteria for professional societies.

The many analogues in the study of personality and society which follow from their sharing a conception of each as a system should not obscure the basic differences in the system referent. All such systems involve component elements or properties, and patterns of relation or interaction between these elements. Both social and personal systems may have patterns of development and distinctive histories. It may be important to consider the relations between the system studied and other systems of the same or a different type, and so on. These properties they share as systems do not make either the personal or the social system any less discrete. To achieve the purposes of either discipline, it may be necessary to consider certain aspects of the other, but the ultimate objects of study remain separate and distinct. Certain methods may also be held in common, and indeed certain situations might be studied by both disciplines, but in each case the data are integrated with different additional materials addressed to the solution of different problems. Psychology and sociology as here defined are similar not because person and society are "ultimately" the same object of study; the similarity lies only in the fact that both person and society are conceived of as systems of action.

The failure to recognize this distinction leads to the most serious confusion. Efforts to reduce one system to the other are sometimes justified as following from a principle of science which requires reducing more complex propositions to simpler and more "general" ones. Naïve generalization from this principle leads to absurdities. The engineering principles on which the construction of a house ultimately rests cannot be efficiently reduced to the atomic structure of the materials which compose it. This is not to say that the atomic structure is irrelevant. Indeed, knowledge of such properties of materials can have a marked effect on the kinds of structures attempted and built. Such knowledge would, however, be merely a datum available to those designing buildings rather than a principle governing their construction. Just so, knowledge of the cognitive mapping of which individuals are capable becomes a datum for the sociologist interested in the structure of opinion or the ideology dominant in the social system. Nevertheless, the pattern of cognitive mapping which characterizes individuals is not a principle of social structure. It may be a principle of personality structure, but it is only a relevant datum for the student of social structure.

It seems appropriate at this point to state the main argument of this discussion in broad outline. The study of social systems can often be much more incisive if one element in the analysis is a psychological theory, that is, a theory of the person as a system. This is true in at least three major respects. In the first instance, specification of the consequences of dif-

ferent institutional arrangements—that is, of the structural aspects of a social system—often depends on correct estimation of the given arrangements' meaning for, or effect on, the human personality. Since all institutional arrangements are ultimately mediated through individual human action, the consequences of *any* institutional arrangement will, at least in part, depend upon its effects on the human personality. To estimate the influence of one aspect of social structure on another one must, therefore, consider the role of the personality system as the main intervening variable. An adequate general theory of the personality as a system will, consequently, always be an important, and at times crucial, element in any analysis of a social system.

In the second instance, adequate assessment of the functioning of any social system, or of the maintenance and change of particular patterns within it, may in important degree depend on knowledge of the particular personality traits, needs, structures, and adjustments of the system. In this case it is not the general theory of personality which is critical, but rather the detailed knowledge about the distribution of particular qualities in the population. In the degree and quality of the fit between the modal personality patterns prevalent in the population and the role demands characteristic of the social system lies one of the keys to the system's functioning and one of the central points for the articulation of psychological and sociological theory.

As a third point, it seems evident that some of the more specialized psychological fields—most obviously the study of learning, but also of cognition and perception—have great potential relevance for our understanding of major social processes.

It will be noted that in each of the above points I only consider the significance of psychology for an understanding of sociological problems. To draw the conclusion that I believe sociology can be reduced to psychology would be incorrect. It would be equally wrong to assume that I do not believe sociological theory and research to be of great relevance for the solution of problems in which the personality system is the main focus of concern. This chapter, however, concerns itself exclusively with the ways in which psychology can be used as an aid in the solution of problems which are sociological in focus. It argues that sociological research has suffered from the failure to use psychological theory and established knowledge about personality as an element in sociological analysis. In reading this chapter, the psychologist cannot hope merely to stand by and enjoy it all. An equally important part of my argument is that psychology has been woefully inadequate in providing sociologists with general knowledge about human personality, with special knowledge about more important psychological processes such as cognition, with adequate conceptualization of the particular traits of personality and with techniques for measuring them adaptable to large-scale social research.

The Role of General Personality Theory

In the early part of the twentieth century, Freud provided us with the basic foundation for a reasonably adequate general theory of personality formation and functioning. Thanks to the group of neo-Freudians, notably Horney and Fromm, and to less easily classified men of talent, such as H. S. Sullivan and Erik Erikson, that theory has been extended and developed in a manner which greatly increases its importance and relevance for sociological analysis. All of these were, of course, from psychiatry and psychoanalysis, but academic psychology has not been entirely unrepresented among those contributing in important ways. In particular, Allport, Murray, and Lewin have made significant contributions.[2]

Many, perhaps most, of our theories of personality deal not with personality as a whole, but rather with some selected aspect or process. Freudian theory kept the whole personality more in view. In time Freud elaborated many of the elements necessary to an understanding of the total personality as a functioning system. Thus he specified the critical components of personality (id, ego, superego), the main modes of relationship between the parts, and the chief motive power in the system at large. He uncovered the main processes which characterize personality functioning, indicated the conditions under which it develops, and discriminated those influences which make for one or another "end state" or form of adjustment. Finally, he specified the conditions for the maintenance and dissolution of the personality system. In this sense this theory is relatively more complete than most, probably more so than any other.

Freud produced this general theory not out of a combination of existing elements, but largely by new creative insights. His theory therefore has a scope, a unity, and a coherence which is unmatched in psychology. Outstanding among those insights was his treatment of the role of unconscious motivation in behavior. One must also give great weight to his elaboration of the psychodynamic mechanisms, his calling attention to the crucial role of the early years, his insights into the role of the superego and values, his explorations into the meanings of symbols and symbolic behavior, and his elucidation of the importance and special character of various body zones.

Subsequent work has, of course, exposed major gaps in the system and has considerably altered the relative emphasis on one or another element. Freud's psychology, for example, was mainly concerned with the basic

2. Gordon Allport, *The Nature of Personality: Selected Papers* (Reading, Mass.: Addison-Wesley, 1950); Henry Murray, *Explorations in Personality* (New York: Oxford, 1938); Kurt Lewin, *A Dynamic Theory of Personality* (New York: McGraw-Hill, 1935), and *Resolving Social Conflicts: Selected Papers on Group Dynamics* (New York: Harper, 1948).

drives and their restraint. The theory of the ego, of the self-conception, was little developed. Despite substantial further work,[3] ego theory is still in its infancy. Freud gave prime emphasis to the early years of life and their formative influence and tended to neglect the importance of the experiences of the adolescent and adult in the networks of nonfamilial interpersonal relations. Although Sullivan, Horney, Fromm, and Lewin have all done much to remedy this condition, we still have great need for a fuller theoretical accounting of the functioning of the adult personality. Freud also left us substantially less than an adequate picture of the range and relative importance of human needs and motives. Henry Murray's work referred to above, and Erikson's [4] extremely perceptive discussion of typical ego problems, such as those involving trust, autonomy, and identity, have done much to give us a fuller picture of the range of human needs and their interrelations.

Considering that Freud's general theory of personality has had wide currency for at least a generation, it is striking that so little evidence can be found of its direct influence on modern sociological theory and research. In anthropology, by way of contrast, one of the main new currents, perhaps the most outstanding in modern times, has been the influence of Freudian theory in shaping the study of culture and personality.[5] Most sociologists probably accept Freud's as the foremost general theory of the human personality of our time, but this acceptance is limited to its application to the individual's psychic development and adjustment; that is, to his inner life. They do not accept it as the prime explanation of the social behavior of the individual—which they attribute more to his culture, his class, his historical time, or his immediate situation, including the network of interpersonal relations in which he is enmeshed.

Freud concentrated particularly on the more nearly ultimate causes of behavior lying in the nature of the human biological organism and on less immediate causes, such as experiences in the early life history of the individual. The sociologist has generally been concerned with the more proximate causes of behavior. Ultimate human motivation and distant causes have had less interest for him. Indeed, sociologists often feel that Freud dealt less with the causes than with the underlying *preconditions* of social behavior. The unconscious and irrational in behavior have seemed to them of less compelling interest than the more conscious, purposeful, and rationally goal-directed behavior. This has undoubtedly been important in the sociologists' apparent attachment to Cooley and Mead, whose prime

3. G. W. Allport, "The Ego in Contemporary Psychology," *Psychological Review,* 50 (1943), 451-478.
4. E. Erikson, *Childhood and Society* (New York: Norton, 1950).
5. C. Kluckhohn, "The Influence of Psychiatry on Anthropology in America During the Past One Hundred Years," in G. J. K. Hall, G. Zilboorg, and H. A. Bunker, *One Hundred Years of American Psychiatry* (New York: Columbia University Press, 1944), pp. 589-617.

concern was with the social self arising from a matrix of interpersonal relations, and to Sullivan, who stressed the interpersonal element in individual action and in psychodynamic adjustment.[6]

A second and undoubtedly important reason for the modest direct influence of Freud harks back to the old controversy between psychologism and sociologism with which Durkheim was so involved. To many sociologists, Freud and many Freudians seem to present merely a new variety of psychological reductionism which seeks to explain the most important human institutions as mere consequences of qualities or problems arising in individual psychology. Freud's general theory about the rise and maintenance of civilizations [7] and his more specific historical analyses, such as *Moses and Monotheism,*[8] as well as Kardiner's theories about religious and other "projective" institutional systems [9]—all would be cases in point. Levinson has made the same point with regard to the psychoanalytic treatment of political institutions as epiphenomena.[10]

But our objective here is not so much to explain the impact of Freud among sociologists as to discuss the relevance and use in sociology of a general theory of personality. It is necessary to state at the outset that just as there are large segments of traditional psychological work for which social forces are largely irrelevant, so for quite a large part of what is generally accepted as standard sociology a general theory of personality is probably not of crucial importance. This is true, for example, of the special applications of demographic or ecological analysis such as those of the great Chicago school of sociology. Their main concern was with the "social mapping" of the urban community, locating the distinctive patterning of its activities and defining the laws of growth and change of the city viewed as an agglomeration of specialized urban areas. Much the same thing can be said for many of the other social-mapping activities of the sociologist. For example, the student of stratification who takes his task to be delineation of the major strata in the stratification system and the distinctive rewards allocated to each stratum is not necessarily in need of a general personality theory to discover the objective facts about each stratum. Other subfields could be added to the list.

Nevertheless, there are several problems of substantial sociological in-

6. Charles Cooley, *Human Nature and the Social Order* (New York: Scribner, 1902); G. H. Mead, *Mind, Self, and Society,* ed. C. M. Morris (Chicago: University of Chicago Press, 1934); H. S. Sullivan, *Conceptions of Modern Psychiatry* (Washington: William Alanson White Psychiatric Foundation, 1945).
7. Sigmund Freud, *Civilization and Its Discontents,* trans. Joan Riviere (London: Hogarth, 1930).
8. Trans. Katherine Jones (New York: Knopf, 1939).
9. A. Kardiner, *The Individual and His Society* (New York: Columbia University Press, 1939); *The Psychological Frontiers of Society* (New York: Columbia University Press, 1945).
10. D. J. Levinson, "The Relevance of Personality for Political Participation," *Public Opinion Quarterly,* 22 (1958), 3-10.

terest which would seem to require—or would certainly yield more readily through—the use of an explicit and adequate theory of personality. Outstanding are those concerned with certain general rates. These are the end products of thousands or even millions of uncoordinated individual decisions or actions which yet produce those relatively distinctive stable rates, such as the suicide rate which attracted Durkheim's attention. Other similar rates would be that for homicide (and other crimes), that for mental illness, and, within limits, the marriage, divorce, and birth rates. Suicide, homicide, and mental illness are much the least ambiguous examples of the probable importance of personality in social processes since they are less likely to be patterned by some specific institutionalized requirement or arrangement. By contrast, for something like divorce, a law which makes it illegal will be well-nigh decisive. Making allowances for such factors, however, we can see all of these rates as presenting problems for sociological analysis. These problems promise to yield more easily to the sociologist who can effectively use a general theory of personality to deal with the individual who intervenes between the social condition and the resultant rate.

The problem is subject to several reformulations involving the same basic elements used in different arrangements, according to the focus of study. The elements are a rate of social action R, a state of society or a set of social conditions impinging on the individuals in the system S, and a general need or action propensity of the human personality P. Sociologists generally begin with the rate, which is called to their attention because it is a social problem. Their task is generally defined as that of discovering the appropriate causal state in society, which produced the given rate. They then formulate the relationship as a sociological $S–R$ proposition. Durkheim began with variations in the rate of suicide R, and sought to explain them through variations in the degree of integration of society S. In our reexamination of this problem, we introduce an element P, as a component of personality, asserting that suicide is most effectively conceived as an act of aggression against the self, and making the further assumption that such aggression is most likely to follow where the individual experiences an extreme sense of guilt, worthlessness, evil, or similar extreme negative self-evaluation.[11] The sequence then becomes $S–P–R$. This is similar to, but yet not identical with, Henry and Short's discussion of aggression as arising from frustration and expressed either against the self or some other, depending on the conditions of external restraint.[12] The sequence in that case would be the more complex $S–P \begin{smallmatrix} \nearrow D_1 - R_s \\ \searrow D_2 - R_h \end{smallmatrix}$.

The new element D represents the degree of restraint to which the indi-

---

11. The argument presented in extremely condensed form here is more fully elaborated in Inkeles, "Sociology and Psychology."
12. A. F. Henry and J. F. Short, *Suicide and Homicide* (Glencoe: Free Press, 1954)

vidual is subjected, with those under high restraint (D_1) producing suicide rate R_s and those under restraint D_2 producing homicide rate R_h.

Modal Personality Patterns

The second major point of articulation between sociology and psychology lies in the effects on any social system which follow from the distinctive or modal personality characteristics of the system's population or status incumbents. A number of problems lying at the center of sociological interest are greatly illuminated through consideration of the degree and kind of congruence between the role requirements typical of a given institution or social system and the personality patterns characteristic of those playing the roles the system provides. Since these terms and the relations they suggest are perhaps less familiar or obvious than those with which we have so far dealt, a brief elaboration is indicated.

The concept of the role is one of the central elements in sociological thinking.[13] Unfortunately, it has a multiplicity of meanings and uses—which would not be a serious difficulty except for the fact that the particular meaning intended is often left unspecified by those who use the term. Its most common use is to designate the set of rights and obligations which are granted to and placed upon the incumbent of a socially recognized status. The most obvious example is found where there is a specific chart of organization, as in the military or governmental bureaucracy, where each status is precisely specified and the required and permitted acts which constitute the role are also stated with some precision.

Confusion as to the meaning of role has arisen from several sources. In their analysis of societies, sociologists have often found clusters of behavior which seem to go together and to be of substantial importance, even though the society's members may not be aware of the pattern nor assign it to a recognized status. These roles are constructs of the sociologist rather than clearly formulated sets of expectations held by the society's members. Another source of confusion has involved the relation between the role as a society expects the status incumbent to play it and the actual behavior characteristic of status incumbents. These often seem to be only slightly related, and many sociologists prefer to treat the actual behavior rather than the expected behavior of status incumbents as the role. Still another use of the role concept treats it mainly in terms of the consequences or effects of the status incumbent's behavior on others. Thus, the role of the father may be described as one of providing a model of

13. See W. J. Goode, "Norm Commitment and Conformity to Role-Status Obligations," *American Journal of Sociology,* 66 (1960), 247-258; and T. R. Sarbin, "Role Theory," in G. Lindzey, *Handbook of Social Psychology* (Reading, Mass.: Addison-Wesley, 1954).

authority which is introjected by the child and which forms the unconscious basis or standard for all his subsequent relations with authority. In a further extension of this approach, the concept role loses all specific reference to a particular status in a network of statuses and becomes a general quality of the person. For example, one may say of X that in most groups his role is that of a peacemaker who tries to integrate opposing currents in the group.

In the following discussion, *role* will refer mainly to the set of generally expected or normative rights and obligations allowed to and demanded of a person generally felt to be the incumbent of a recognized status by others who participate in the same social system. When the term is used in another sense, that fact will be specifically indicated.

Every society makes some broad status distinctions in accord with the biological facts of sex and age. Further, each of the major institutional complexes in any society generates a list of status designations and their accompanying roles. The kinship system, for example, always yields an array of such terms ranging from the obvious mother–father–uncle–aunt–grandparent set to less universal terms such as those for cross cousins and clan or lineage mates. All the institutions concerned with religion, fraternal relations, economic activity, and political action generate such clusters of statuses.

Each status, then, is part of a cluster of statuses, and each role a set of actions importantly geared in with the sets of action making up other roles. Together, these sets constitute small interdependent systems of action. The term *institution* designates the subsystem which is the basic building block of sociological analysis. Institutions, like statuses, are generally but not always explicitly recognized and named by the societies in which they are found. The army or the war party, the clan, the household or family, the church or sect or cult, the nation, region, or village are generally named and known to all. They are the discernible membership units of the society, the "things" to which a person can and generally will belong in the course of his life and of which he will be a member.

Institutions are generally organized around the problems that all societies face, such as recruitment or socialization of the young, control of the use of force, the regulation of sex, maintenance of sustenance, and defense against external attack.[14] Societies will vary markedly, both in the degree to which their institutions have either broad and general or highly specialized functions and in the particular combination of system problems concentrated in any given institution. Although sociologists are often naïve in the assumptions they make about the "simplicity" of primitive societies, it seems that modern large-scale societies are distinguished by the elaboration of a very large number of discrete institutions, each organized around a

14. See D. F. Aberle et al., "The Functional Prerequisites of a Society," *Ethics,* 60 (1950), 100-111.

highly specific system need. In modern society, for example, the family is no longer a producing unit, provides little formal education, and has only rudimentary religious functions, having "lost" these responsibilities to the factory or shop, the school, the church, and so on.

The articulation of the individual's personality with the role demands of the social statuses he fills is of relevance to understanding three central problems of sociological analysis: the adequacy of role performance, the integration of the diverse institutions which make up a society, and the problem of change in social systems.

Personality and Role Performance

From the point of view of the individual, it is mainly his status *rights* that are important, since the gratifications which result from these are essential to the continued integration or maintenance of the person. From the point of view of the institution or social system, if we may so speak, the performance of the individual's assigned role *obligations* is the critical requirement laid on him, since others are dependent on that performance as one link in the network of such obligations. Sociologists have traditionally explained the fact that individuals do regularly perform their roles as being a logical consequence of the sanctions imposed on those who fail to meet the expectations laid on them and the rewards granted to those who do meet them. Role performance is thus typically understood by sociologists as largely dependent on factors outside the person. All that is posited inside is merely the simple desire to avoid punishment and to gain rewards.

Important as such drives may be, they are hardly sufficient to explain the complex phenomenon of differential role performance. Role performance obviously also depends on possession of the knowledge or skills a role requires and on the motivation to perform the role. In addition there may be "qualities" in the person which hinder or facilitate his role performance because they make it intrinsically rewarding or repugnant to him, quite apart from the formal system of sanctions. An obvious but extremely useful example which Roe calls to our attention involves a neurotic symptom such as claustrophobia.[15] Obviously a person with this characteristic cannot be employed as an elevator operator, coal miner, or underground telephone-cable repairman. Similarly, being somewhat phobic about dirt could in important degree facilitate role performance in a cleaning woman, and being somewhat compulsive might increase the pleasure a file clerk takes in his job.

Sociologists wish to explain the pattern of recruitment to statuses and subsequent performance in relevant roles as this affects the functioning of an institution or society. The measures of system functioning sociologists

15. Anne Roe, "Personality and Vocation," *Transactions of the New York Academy of Sciences,* 9, 2 (1947), 257-267.

use are generally efficiency measures of some sort—production in a factory, stability or happiness in a marriage, success in bringing up children in a family. Additional measures of side effects beyond those connected with the central purpose of an institution are often included in the evaluation of institutional functioning. For example, even if production is high in a factory, a high rate of labor turnover or a large number of wildcat strikes will be taken as evidence of institutional malfunctioning. To explain such institutional malfunctioning, the industrial sociologist will typically seek for certain institutional defects. He may look for an inadequate flow of communications up from the bottom which prevents grievances from coming to the attention of management, or he may suspect a tendency of management to shift workers without adequate consultation of their wishes and desires. Such situational factors may indeed be not merely important, but crucial, determinants of status incumbents' behavior and, consequently, of institutional functioning. I am not at all inclined to challenge the idea that the objective stimulus to social action requires serious sociological study.

In addition to such structural factors, however, institutional functioning may in important degree be influenced by the "qualities" of the persons who occupy the statuses in the institutional system. Furthermore, the quality of role performance is itself likely to be influenced by a prior process of differential recruitment to statuses on the basis of the personality of the candidates. We hold that the incumbents of statuses will often be found to reflect not random recruitment, but a highly selective process of assortment or assignment. To the degree that this is true, then, in order to predict the functioning of an institution of a small-scale or large-scale social system we need to know more than the system of statuses, the formal roles, the sanctions, and similar structural elements which characterize the system. We should also have knowledge of the personalities of those occupying the major statuses.

Although this proposition has great plausibility on the surface, it is extremely difficult to muster definitive evidence in support of it. Clearly the issues could best be investigated systematically in small groups in which it would be possible to vary both the social structure and the personality composition of the group. Although there are small-group studies which systematically vary elements of structure, such as the outstanding study of autocratic and democratic group atmospheres undertaken by Lewin and his associates,[16] and several which control the personality composition of the groups, there are very few in which simultaneous control of these variables is undertaken.

16. K. Lewin, R. Lippitt, and R. K. White, "Patterns of Aggressive Behavior in Experimentally Created 'Social Climates'," *Journal of Social Psychology*, 10 (1939), 271-279; and R. Lippitt, "An Experimental Study of Authoritarian and Democratic Atmospheres. Studies in Typological and Vector Psychology, I," *University of Iowa Studies in Child Welfare*, 16, 3 (1940), 44-195.

Until both personality and structural variables are simultaneously controlled and the *relative* impact of each on group effectiveness is tested, sociologists will probably remain somewhat skeptical of the meaning of the statistically significant, but not often absolutely large, differences which emerge when groups are assembled to represent different combinations of personality types. In addition, sociologists would stress that most groups in experimental research were "artificially" composed of carefully selected personality types. The sociologist evaluating the functioning of institutions might well feel that, in "real" groups and situations, the accidents of life history and factors other than personality which are responsible for recruitment will randomize personality distribution in the major social statuses sufficiently so that taking systematic account of the influence of personality composition is unnecessary.

Even if the personality composition of any group is randomly determined, random assortment would not in fact guarantee the *same* personality composition in the membership of all institutions of a given type. On the contrary, the very fact of randomness implies that the outcome would approximate a normal distribution. Consequently, some of the groups would by chance have a personality composition profoundly different from others, with possibly marked effects on the functioning of the institutions involved. Furthermore, there is no convincing evidence that randomness *does* consistently describe the assignment of personality types to major social statuses. On the contrary, there is a great deal of evidence to indicate that particular statuses often attract, or recruit preponderantly for, one or another personality characteristic, and that fact has a substantial effect on individual adjustment to roles and the general quality of institutional functioning. Relevant examples may be found in Swanson's research on newspaper staffs, Stern, Stein, and Bloom's study of college students, H. V. Dicks' investigation of Nazi prisoners of war, and Inkeles, Hanfmann, and Beier's study of Soviet refugees.[17] Such examples could be multiplied. They all indicate that occupational, political, and institutional groups may contain significantly large numbers, sometimes distinctive majorities, of a particular personality type. It may be that these types are mainly developed on the job through adult socialization, but this seems unlikely because so many of the reported differences involve depth components in the personality which are generally laid down in early life.

Whether based on recruitment or development on the job, such modal personality differences are relevant to the sociologist only if they can be

17. G. E. Swanson, "Agitation through the Press: A Study of the Personalities of Publicists," *Public Opinion Quarterly,* 20 (1956), 441-456; G. G. Stern, M. I. Stein, and B. S. Bloom, *Methods in Personality Assessment: Human Behavior in Complex Social Situations* (Glencoe: Free Press, 1956); H. V. Dicks, "German Personality Traits and Nazi Ideology," *Human Relations,* 3 (1950), 111-154; A. Inkeles, E. Hanfmann, and H. Beier, "Modal Personality and Adjustment to the Soviet Socio-political System," *Human Relations,* 11 (1958), 3-22.

shown to affect individual role performance, and consequently influence institutional functioning. Studies in which personality data and data on role performance are simultaneously reported are rare, but those available indicate marked effects of personality on role performance. Relevant studies are those by Gilbert and Levinson on staff personnel in mental hospitals, Rosen on academic performance of high school students, and Stern, Stein, and Bloom on the performance of college students.[18]

Personality and System Integration

When we deal with only one status, our problem is limited to the fit between a personality trait or set of traits and the restricted range of behavior which is distinctive for a particular role. When we consider a full-scale social system, however, the problem of the integration of diverse roles becomes prominent. Any social system which requires that individuals act in more than one role must somehow adjust to the fact that people are limited in their ability to combine in one integrated personality more than a certain number and range of psychic qualities or attributes. Societies can to some extent reduce the strains of integrating diverse-role requirements if they keep to a minimum the number of distinctive statuses. This is often the case with nonliterate societies; it is for this reason that we may speak of them as "simple" or relatively undifferentiated. Nevertheless, in any society each individual will have at least sex, age, and kinship roles, and may in addition have others of great importance, such as specialized occupational, religious, and political roles. The task of playing so many diverse roles can be made more manageable for the individual by structural arrangements which establish sets or congeries of statuses requiring similar or compatible qualities. This pattern is almost always adopted in the differentiation of the roles of men and women. It may also be used within a sex group to differentiate subgroups. Thus war, hunting, and political roles may largely be the province of one set of men, whereas art, religion, and learning may be equally restricted to another set. Such arrangements simplify but do not eliminate the basic problem; in fact, they also raise new problems. The integration of a society which particularly relies on such specialized role clusters will obviously require mechanisms rather different from those required where such segmentation is less prominent.

To understand the integration of full-scale social systems with and through the personalities occupying the major statuses requires study on a scale and with resources which so far have not been mustered anywhere.

18. Doris C. Gilbert and D. J. Levinson, "Role Performance, Ideology and Personality in Mental Hospital Aides," in M. Greenblatt, D. J. Levinson, and R. H. Williams, *The Patient and the Mental Hospital* (Glencoe: Free Press, 1957); B. C. Rosen, "The Achievement Syndrome: A Psychocultural Dimension of Social Stratification," *American Sociological Review*, 21 (1956), 203-211; Stern, Stein, and Bloom, *Personality Assessment.*

For many nations one can easily assemble all sorts of impressionistic lists of personality traits alleged to characterize the population. But there is not one national population, large or small, for which we have extensive and systematic information, based on adequate sampling, which would enable us to describe accurately the modal personality traits found within it. This situation is, happily, now being remedied. In 1953, Janowitz and Marvick presented data on the distribution of authoritarianism, based on a modified *F* scale, by age, sex, education, and occupation in the United States.[19] This was very likely the first time anyone published the results of a national sample used to assess the nationwide distribution of an important psychological characteristic. More recently, in connection with a national survey of adjustment, the Survey Research Center staff at Michigan used a modified TAT to measure the achievement, affiliation, and power motivations in the population of the United States.[20] The initial report on the findings of this investigation prepared by Gurin, Veroff, Atkinson, and Feld firmly establishes the feasibility of using survey methods to assess personality modes in large populations.[21]

We do have substantial data on a variety of small nonliterate societies, and some small but intensive studies of various segments of several modern large-scale societies. Although this material permits only the most tentative and exploratory hypotheses, it can be extremely important in suggesting a model of the studies we have yet to undertake. Of the many studies in personality in primitive societies, very few have achieved the clarity and precision attained by Spindler in maintaining a precise distinction between personality and the sociocultural system.[22] His chief concern was to discern and explain personality differences in several groups of Menomini who were differentiated in degree of acculturation. Nevertheless, his study also provides a rather striking example of apparent congruence between the typical role requirements of a sociolcultural system and the modal personality pattern of the society's members.

Insofar as the personality of the Soviet élite under Stalin was in fact markedly different from the patterns modal for the rank and file of Soviet industrial and agricultural workers, the Soviet case provides another important illustration of the earlier noted pattern of differential recruitment for occupations on grounds of personality for the integration of sets of specialized roles.[23] The presence of distinctive personality modes among

19. M. Janowitz and D. Marvick, "Authoritarianism and Political Behavior," *Public Opinion Quarterly,* 17 (1953), 185-201.
20. G. Gurin, J. Veroff, and S. Feld, *Americans View Their Mental Health* (New York: Basic Books, 1960).
21. G. Gurin, J. Veroff, J. W. Atkinson, and S. Feld, "The Use of Thematic Apperception to Assess Motivation in a Nationwide Interview Study," *Psychological Monographs,* vol. 74, no. 499 (1960).
22. G. D. Spindler, *Sociocultural and Psychological Processes in Menomini Acculturation* (Berkeley: University of California Press, 1955).
23. Inkeles, Hanfmann, and Beier, "Modal Personality."

the Soviet élite also points up the system integration problem posed by the existence of distinct modal personality patterns in different segments of national population. The qualities which facilitate a person's mobility or recruitment to élite status and which enhance his effective performance at that level may be the very traits most alien to the ordinary citizen. The same qualities may lead the élite to establish institutional arrangements not congruent with the modal personality patterns of the rank and file. This is by no means the only or necessary relation between élite modes and those of the rank and file. On the contrary, the German experience under Hitler suggests that the relation of the personality patterns of the élite to those of the rank and file may be one of similarity or complementarity. In either case, however, profound implications for the system's functioning follow from the degree and kind of congruence between the pattern of behavior of the élite and the modal personality patterns of the majority of the population.

It is a moot question whether the definition of a social system should include not merely its basic institutions and roles, which provide the framework for individual action, but also its cultural values and the particular set of personalities within it at any given time. In our opinion it is desirable not to include the component personalities in the definition of the social system, but merely to specify the statuses and roles and their interrelations. To estimate the quality of role performances, however, and to understand their coherence in institutional systems, it is important—indeed, one might say essential—to know the personality of the status incumbents. Just as a general theory of personality may be used as an intervening variable in specifying the behavioral consequences of any aspect of social structure, so the personality of the role incumbents may be treated as an intervening variable in specifying the quality of role performance. The "same" formal social system will produce different behavioral consequences, depending on the personalities in it, and the "same" roles will be performed differently, depending on the personalities of the status incumbents. This indicates the second major point of articulation between sociological problems and psychological facts. The student of social structure must have some means for assessing the special qualities and needs of the personalities acting in the social system if he is to maximize his estimate of role performance and general system functioning. For that assessment, he must rely on the personality psychologist.

Special Psychological Theories

In contrast to the general theories of personality and to the approaches for assessing personality modes, the special theories and findings of psychology such as those dealing with learning, cognition, or perception cannot at this

time be easily integrated with sociological theory and research. This is not surprising, since it was only in the period immediately after World War II that some of these special materials were even partially articulated with general personality theory itself. We hear, for example, of the "new look" in perception research,[24] only to discover that it is the readiness to relate certain aspects of perception theory to such personality factors as "need." We are still far from having systematically related variations in perceptual and cognitive patterns to factors in the individual's or group's sociocultural background. Further development which will permit these theories to contribute effectively to our understanding of the functioning of sociocultural systems lies some distance in the future. It may be instructive, however, to consider briefly a few pioneering efforts to study learning, cognition, and perception as they influence, and are influenced by, other aspects of personality and sociocultural forces.

Of the special branches of psychology, the theories of learning have perhaps the most direct relevance for the sociologist. Implicit in the idea that the members of a society share a system of action is the assumption that they have *learned* the appropriate responses to the cues given by others. The adults in a society are the end products of a long process of prior conditioning. They are thus equipped with a large repertory of standardized responses to meet the situations their sociocultural system will present. Societies experience a continuous turnover in personnel while maintaining relative stability in culture and social structure. The key to this continuity lies, in large measure, in the fact that successive generations learn their culture in all its complexity. They must also acquire a predisposition to accept, and an ability to act in accord with, the requirements of that part of the culture embedded in laws, art patterns, and a host of institutions. The key to this learning lies in the forms and content of childhood and later training. In other words, a necessary condition for sociocultural continuity is a system of socialization which ensures that each generation will learn the culture patterns sufficiently well to play all the appropriate social roles in much the same manner as did the preceding generation.

It is a moot point whether the study of this learning should be primarily the responsibility of the psychologist or is equally the province of the sociologist. In my opinion, the process is most appropriately studied by developmental and child psychologists, if they will accept the burden. Very few students of learning have shown much serious interest in this problem. Since the study of child training is one of the major points of articulation between psychology and sociocultural studies and is not amenable to a clearcut allocation of responsibility to either, we should perhaps encourage a pattern of collaboration between the psychologist of learning and the sociologist or anthropologist.

24. J. S. Bruner and D. Krech, eds., *Perception and Personality* (Durham: Duke University Press, 1950).

A full discussion of the sociologist's perspective on the study of child training is beyond my mandate and the scope of this chapter. It is not inappropriate to say, however, that contemporary learning theories seem inadequate to account for the process which transforms the infant into the fully socialized culture-bearing adult. Academic psychologists who study learning are mainly interested in the effects on learning of the time which elapses between stimulus and response, in the sequence of stimulus, conditioned and unconditioned response, in reinforcement and extinction, and in stimulus generalization. An understanding of these processes is essential to an understanding of human learning. But psychological students of learning have dealt with these problems at an extremely general level. They study learning as manifested in any species, rather than primarily in humans. Their desire to control what they regard as extraneous variables has led them to screen out elements of content and context which are not only most interesting and relevant for the sociologist, but which in his opinion are decisive for an understanding of the learning process, its success or failure, and its consequences. For these reasons the sociologist turns away from the student of learning and looks to the student of personality. Even in the case of the most intensive and explicit utilization of learning theories, in the study of socialization by Whiting and Child, it is apparent that traditional learning theories contribute substantially less to the analysis than does Freudian theory.[25] The blending of the two accomplished in that work may, however, provide a model for other efforts along the same line.

Learning theory may be very important in explaining how certain traits come to be prevalent in the adult members of a society. Once a given predisposition is established, however, the sociologist will be less concerned with its past development and more interested in understanding how the given trait affects the quality of role performance, or how certain role demands may affect the psychic adjustment of persons with the given trait. At the level at which most sociologists work, much that concerns contemporary students of learning seems to have little immediate relevance, even though its significance may be substantial in the study of behavior at more molecular levels.

To increase the relevance of learning theory and research for sociologists would require going far beyond what is traditionally defined as an appropriate concern of psychologists working in that realm. It does not seem likely, however, that the range of problems and the type of situation now covered in psychological research on learning can indefinitely remain so circumscribed. In time, psychologists who define themselves as specialists on learning must either broaden the area of their concern or allow others to share responsibility for, and legitimate entry into, the ranks of students of learning. Foremost among these new entrants into the ranks will be those who

25. J. W. Whiting and I. L. Child, *Child Training and Personality: A Crosscultural Study* (New Haven: Yale University Press, 1953).

study the early learning of the child in the socialization process. In addition, learning theory would be of great relevance for societal analysis if it would deal more systematically with the principles which account for *adult* learning and for the failure of individuals and cultures to learn new ways. However much one might be led to think so by the concentration of studies on *early* socialization, significant learning hardly ceases at the age of six. Social learning, often meaning unlearning and relearning, goes on all through life. Indeed, in modern large-scale societies, learning in early and late adolescence is extremely important in laying the bases for later social participation, and much of the process continues at the adult level as in socialization to a professional role. About such learning, however, there is little or nothing that I can find in the chapters on learning produced by most psychologists—indeed, there is not very much by students of personality. At least one major exception can be cited in the work of Miller and Dollard.[26]

Some Comments on Concepts and Methods

I have not specified in any detail what range of problems I consider sociological, perhaps thereby limiting the psychologist's opportunity to decide how his discipline might be related to sociology's needs or problems. This was not an oversight. As it is practiced, sociology is an extremely sprawling discipline which breaks down into a great welter of fairly discrete topics. Thus we have the sociology of the family, of industry, of the law, of religion, and of knowledge. Some study sociological factors in politics, others in economic behavior. Stratification and mobility, deviance and social control, invention, imitation, and change may be added to the list. To discuss each item of even this partial array is obviously far beyond what is possible here and would, in addition, be not only tedious but disconcerting. The central theme which ties sociology together as an intellectual discipline, I have suggested, is its concern with the development, integrated functioning, and change of social systems. The social system may be large or small, and it may have a self-sufficient system of action or not; in other words, it may be a society or merely a subsystem or group in a society. The articulation of psychology and sociology comes largely through the study of personality, both the general theory of personality structure and functioning and the assessment or measurement of discrete personality traits and syndromes.

So long as the personal system and the social system are kept clearly in mind as the distinctive foci of psychological and sociological research, the two disciplines seem to share few concepts or methods other than those common to all analyses of systems. Exception must, however, be made with

26. N. E. Miller and J. Dollard, *Social Learning and Imitation* (New Haven: Yale University Press, 1941).

regard to at least four foci of interest which seem to involve considerable overlap or sharing of concepts and methods: small-group research, choice patterns (sociometrics), attitude and opinion study, and the study of values and ideologies. The latter is indeed also of central importance in anthropology, and would undoubtedly qualify as one of the major "bridging" concepts in the behavioral sciences. It is characteristic of work done on these topics that it is extremely difficult to say whether the work was done by one whose professional identification is as a sociologist or a psychologist, at least if one judges only by the research design, the method of analyzing the findings, the concepts, and the general language used. Some people are dismayed by this, feeling it threatens the purity and distinctiveness of their discipline. Others are greatly heartened by the same fact. They see in it evidence that ultimately psychology and sociology "are the same thing," and the promise of a unified science of man which is yet to come. Both judgments seem to be overreactive.

Most recent studies of small groups follow a common pattern. They seek to find the "effects" on group processes of varying some aspect of the organization, setting, or composition of the group. The effects studied might be measures of the efficiency of the group, or more psychologically oriented measures, such as the members' satisfaction with their participation or their sense of solidarity. Such studies fall under the heading of "social system analysis," as that term has been used here. They are certainly not predominantly studies of personality and its adjustment. They deal with the elements of a system of action produced or shared by a group of people and trace adjustments of that system in response to internal or external stimuli. There is, of course, much small-group research which deals mainly with individual behavior and adjustment, although the setting for studying the individual is a small group. Such investigations are "personality studies" in the sense in which we have been using the term.

The professional identification of the researcher by no means permits accurate prediction as to which of these two types of study he may be doing. There is perhaps no reason why it should. What is regrettable is the assertion often made by one or another worker in the field that "only" psychological or "only" sociological factors are important in an understanding of group processes. This is all the more deplorable because often the disputants have only the most imprecise notion of what is a psychological as against a sociological factor, and they would not agree too well even if they could define these factors more precisely. The argument is perhaps futile. In any event, a decision as to whether or not a factor is psychological or sociological is much less important than the question as to whether or not it is systematically built into the research design.

Perhaps the best-known contemporary sociological student of small groups had until recently introduced absolutely no systematic controls in selecting the personalities of those who were joined together in his dis-

cussion groups. Consequently, Bales's [27] results presumably can be generalized only to groups in which the same methods of recruiting discussants are applied to the same or a matched population of college students. By the same token, the work of a personality-centered psychologist such as Schutz,[28] who systematically composes his group of individuals with certain personality traits, must be understood as applying only to groups working in a sociocultural structure comparable to that in which he organized his groups. The results cannot be generalized to apply to groups having the same personality composition but different social structures—to groups in size other than four, to those with appointed or elected leaders, to those governed by formal rules of procedures, to groups having responsibilities to a larger structure of organization going beyond the immediate discussion group, and so on.

Greater understanding of group processes, including changes in formal structure, efficiency, emotional tone, and solidarity, depends upon fuller control of variations in both structure and personality composition. Our ability to generalize the findings of research is also greatly enhanced by simultaneous control of both sets of variables. It probably matters little what the discipline of the researcher is, so long as he has adequate awareness of both types of variable and seeks to bring both systematically under control. It is the *articulation* of the study of personality with that of social structure, not their integration or reduction, that is required.

Much the same challenge is posed by sociometry and by the study of opinions and values. A person's choice of those he would most like to work or live with, the opinions he holds on world government, his beliefs about the trustworthiness of his fellow men, or the nature of good and evil are not basically different from any other behavioral datum. Each choice, opinion, or value can be related either to the personality or to the group and the social system of which it is a representative expression. Failure to recognize these different referents as analytically and concretely distinct entities leads to substantial confusion, since both psychologists and sociologists are in this case studying the same items of behavior.

Closer examination of most work in these areas will, however, reveal that there is almost always a personality or a social system referent. In sociometrics, for example, when the focus is on the girl who regularly makes many choices and rejects no one, or who rejects many and chooses many, we are clearly dealing with an attribute of the girl's personality. When we say of a set of such choice patterns that, compared to most groups

27. R. F. Bales, *Interaction Process Analysis: A Method for the Study of Small Groups* (Reading, Mass.: Addison-Wesley, 1950); and P. Hare, E. F. Borgatta, and R. F. Bales, eds., *Small Groups: Studies in Social Interaction* (New York: Knopf, 1955).
28. W. C. Schutz, "What Makes Groups Productive?" *Human Relations,* 8 (1955), 429-465.

of similar size, this one yields an unusually high number of reciprocated choices, we are dealing with an attribute of the group. A set of such attributes constitutes the *social system* in which the group participates, or the *culture* which it manifests.[29] There is no need to confuse the pattern characteristic of any person with that characteristic for the group. Within broad limits, either can change fundamentally without any basic change in the other. By the definitions used in this article, the first is a personality, the second a sociocultural, level of analysis. In this context it should be particularly noted that although the same *type* of data is used for both the psychological and sociological analysis, it is not strictly the same *body* of data which is used by each.

Much the same argument can be made with regard to opinions and values. Both psychologists and sociologists are and must be concerned with them if they are to understand personality and social system, respectively. To relate the values of a man to his typical pattern of perception is not the same as to relate the values in a society to its system of stratification. In any event, it is hardly the type of data which defines the problem. This is often a source of confusion for psychologists who venture into the use of group data. They assume that if values are a property of personality and therefore a focus of psychological concern, then the *structure* of values in a society is also primarily, or even exclusively, a psychological problem. It is an easy step to conclude that psychologists therefore have special competence to deal with the problem and can automatically carry over principles which hold for the integration of a person's values into the study of the integration of a culture's values. There is, of course, no reason why a psychologist should not study the structure of values in a society. But the laws which govern the coherence of a culture's values are not necessarily the same as those which govern the coherence of personal values. Much confusion and frustration can be avoided by keeping the two analytical referents distinct, at least until it can be demonstrated that systems of values in fact do obey the same laws of coherence, whether in *persons* or in *cultures*.

To suggest the value of maintaining the distinction between personality and social system is not to assert that it is in fact possible at all points to do so with clarity or precision. If a man chooses predominantly dependent or aggressive friends or workmates, we have no difficulty seeing this as definitely a manifestation of personality. If many other men manifest the same pattern, especially when the men also share a common social status, then this fact is an attribute of culture or social structure. It may be so without each individual manifestation of the "rate of choosing aggressive workmates" being any less an attribute of personality. In sociometric study, however, we must reckon not only with the choices made by a person, but

29. See Helen H. Jennings, *Leadership and Isolation,* 2nd ed. (New York: Longmans, 1950).

also with those received. Are the choices received by a person an attribute of his personality or an attribute of the group which bestows the choices? There are many advantages in conceptualizing "choices received" as an attribute of the person, but there are also obvious difficulties in making something which in itself includes no act of or by the person a part of his personality. In this case, therefore, it would seem mainly a matter of taste or convenience whether one would treat the problem as psychological or sociological.

A similar problem arises in the analysis of opinions and values. To relate a man's opinions to his needs, or his motives to his values, is clearly a problem in psychology. The relationship falls entirely within the personal system. But when we seek to relate a man's values or opinions to his social-class position, is the problem less one of personality? Part of the difficulty arises from the assumption that social class is principally an attribute of the person, a confusion to which sociologists have greatly contributed by publishing numerous studies purporting to weigh the influence of a man's values or education as against his "social class," as if this were always a discrete variable. How confusing it must be to discover that many other studies use education as *their* measures of social class. A man's social class can, of course, be a quality attributed to him and reacted to by others in the same way as they react to his color or his personality. The "social class" in most sociological studies, however, generally turns out, on closer examination, to be not an attribute of the person, but a set of objective situational factors within which the person must act or to which he reacts —for example, his occupational level or setting.

The *adjustment* of any person to his objective class situation is clearly a problem in psychology. If all or most of those who occupy a given class position adjust to their condition in a fairly standard way, however, the individual psychological fact becomes a social regularity. It seems none too obvious that the psychologist must bow out simply because the problem has assumed the proportions of a social regularity, since the regularity remains one of personal adjustment. It is only insofar as interest turns to the significance of this regularity for other aspects of the social system that the problem again becomes clearly sociological. But to assess the general pattern of personal adjustment to social-class situation, we must again have psychologically trained sociologists or sociologically trained psychologists or some working combination of representatives from both disciplines.

Articulating Sociology and Psychology

Difficulties between sociologists and psychologists involving overlap of interest, as in the study of sociometrics and in attitude and value research, represent only one type of tension between the disciplines. Perhaps equally important are those situations which arise from efforts to articulate the

disciplines, even when the sphere of action appropriate to each is perfectly clear. Tensions often develop when one discipline makes demands on or expresses need for the work of the other. For example, sociologists would like to have a large number of personality studies based on well-designed samples of different strata of the population. The design and conduct of such tests is largely the province of the personality psychologist. But, until very recently, personality psychologists have concentrated for the most part on studies of the individual, as in clinical testing in support of psychiatric diagnosis and counseling. The dimensions of personality important for an assessment of the individual's personal adjustment are often quite different from those significant for an assessment of performance in different social roles or occupational positions. In addition, the problems faced in scoring and interpreting tests performed for clinical study of the individual are quite different from those which arise when such tests are used with large samples. In the latter case, scoring must be valid and reliable, and objective and routinized as well. The probability that a sociologist will systematically use personality variables in his research is obviously slight if he must put each subject through a long and expensive process of clinical assessment which can be performed only by a highly specialized clinician and which, in any event, yields only rather imprecise clinical impressions of the personality of his subjects.

Many sociologists feel that personality psychologists have not been very responsive to this need. For their part, many psychologists may well complain that, however much they may wish to accommodate the sociologist, it is extremely difficult to design new tests or to use existing tests to measure qualities, attributes, or traits which the "client" sociologist cannot precisely specify or define. For it is a distressing fact, which psychologists often discover when they try to relate personality to role requirements, that the sociologist has not developed an adequate set of standard categories or dimensions for the analysis of role requirements. Furthermore, the sociologist is often hard put to specify the requirements of any role in a way that has clear psychological relevance. Consequently, it often happens that the psychologist's analysis of the personality of a status type seems to the sociologist to be greatly lacking in relevance to the social aspects of the role. In turn, the sociologist's description of the role requirements placed on a status incumbent can only with great difficulty be translated into the psychological qualities that might be relevant to role performance.

The problem does, however, yield to systematic analysis. Indeed, it yields with what seem extraordinarily promising results whenever the study design from the start holds to the demand that both the role description and the psychological test be designed with consideration for the final step of relating the two. Roe's studies of personality among scientists in different fields, although quite promising, suffered particularly from inadequate conceptualization of the role demands peculiar to the disciplines of biology,

physics, anthropology, and psychology.[30] By contrast, Swanson's study of the differences in personality between editorial writers and the sports and business staff on a college newspaper is a model of precision in separately specifying role demands and appropriate personality dimensions.[31] In his case, however, he was fortunate to have available an existing psychological test which measured precisely the variables of personality which his role analysis indicated to be relevant.

The extremely fine work by Stern, Stein, and Bloom in the study of divinity students, young physicists, and students at a liberal progressive college is particularly instructive here.[32] The analysis of role requirements was actually the first major step in their assessment program. Happily, their previous experience alerted them to the realization that a psychologist assessing the qualities required by a particular role often operates exclusively in terms of his own image of good and bad performance, without giving due consideration to "whether or not these determinants are free to operate in the actual job situation." They call this the "psychological fallacy in assessment research.[33] At the same time, they note, the sociological description of roles often seems to assume "a passive participant who becomes adapted" to any set of demands. Their own approach is based on the "psychologically functional analysis of the roles." By this they mean "the translation of the varieties of press . . . into statements of role-fulfillment in terms of the needs or personality characteristics which are required for most effective functioning. Thus, the same psychological terms are utilized to characterize the individual as well as the environment." [34] For example, a job might be described as requiring frequent friendly reciprocal reaction with others, obviously related to the strength of need affiliation. Another might put a premium on rough contact, even body contact, with materials or with other persons, which would make the strength of the personal tendency toward "harm avoidance" a critical dimension.

This method of "functional analysis of the role," especially when combined with testing procedures which are adapted to the requirements of large-scale testing, represents an important methodological advance. It should serve to bring personality study out of the limited confines of the clinic into broad usefulness in social science research. At the same time, it holds substantial promise of providing a set of general categories which may be used for the analysis of many different kinds of roles.

Even when role requirements are stated in terms of the personality qualities most adaptive for those in a given status, there is still the problem of assessing the presence or absence of the required traits in status incum-

30. Anne Roe, *The Psychology of Occupations* (New York: Wiley, 1956).
31. "Agitation through the Press."
32. *Personality Assessment.*
33. Ibid., p. 33.
34. Ibid., p. 55.

bents, in candidates for the position, and in the population at large. For purposes of sociological analysis, it is virtually indispensable that there be tests which permit rating personality on a series of fairly discrete variables by methods which require little in the way of special testing environments or conditions. The idea that any trait can be meaningfully measured or understood in isolation from the simultaneous measurement of virtually all other qualities of the person meets strong resistance in some psychological quarters. The consequence has been that we have made very slow progress in devising personality tests which can be simply administered and easily scored. Only a few clinically validated personality traits of sociological relevance, such as authoritarianism [35] and stereopathy,[36] can now be scored by simple paper-and-pencil tests. Methods of administration and scoring which are more complex, yet amenable to large-scale application, are available for need achievement, affiliation, and power.[37] But there is a long list of personality traits which, from a sociological viewpoint, it would be desirable to measure and which cannot now be treated in this way.

In debating with the clinical psychologist, the sociologist hears his critic decry the separation of the part from the whole and use of the routine test score in place of rich living analysis. The roles are strangely reversed in the sociologist's methodological disagreement with the experimental psychologist. Many sociologists decry the possibility of our learning anything meaningful about individual or social behavior in the context of most controlled experiments. They assume and assert that the individual's behavior in such settings is unnatural or unreal. For his part, the psychologist will often charge that the sociologist can never *really know* anything because too many of the relevant variables remain uncontrolled in all his studies.

Often the emotional quality of these arguments stands in the way of any increase in insight or understanding. These questions, in good part, concern matters of fact and can be answered only by the same tests we apply to other facts. Is their participation in a laboratory discussion group dealing with fraternity membership as "real" to participants as a discussion of someone's suitability as a member of their own fraternity would be? Is the "jury" deciding a case it heard on tape as involved as it would be if the case were actually on trial? Is a boy's achievement motive aroused to the same degree by a laboratory-test instruction and by competition for a crucial scholarship? None of these questions can be properly answered in absolute terms. Reality and involvement are variables which can be measured. Each laboratory setting and each experimenter differs in the capacity to affect these variables. Increased experience will undoubtedly

35. See T. W. Adorno, Else Frenkel-Brunswik, D. J. Levinson, and R. N. Sanford, *The Authoritarian Personality* (New York: Harper, 1950).
36. See Stern, Stein, and Bloom, *Personality Assessment*.
37. See D. C. McClelland et al., *The Achievement Motive* (New York: Appleton-Century-Crofts, 1953).

make for greater skill in eliciting involvement similar to that manifested outside the laboratory.

Many sociologists are too quick to reject experimentally controlled studies before having closely examined the comparability of the experimental with the original setting. Even "unreal" settings may permit important inferences with regard to "real" situations. Competitive feelings, for example, can be induced in group experiments. They can be as real as competitive feelings experienced in the classroom and may permit inferences with regard to other situations. At the same time, it must be recognized that the necessarily transitory and limited relationships developed in the laboratory can seldom match the significance for the individual of the great majority of the important roles which he plays in the social system. To deal with these, it seems indispensable to deal with them in nature. Considerable control over the relevant variables, however, is possible with smaller samples through careful matching on crucial variables, as in the Gluecks' delinquency study,[38] or through the method of controlled cross-tabulation with larger samples in the manner of most opinion surveys.

Insofar as the degree of personal involvement necessary for the problem and dimension under study can be developed in the laboratory, it is ridiculous for sociologists to do less than welcome this development for the greater control it affords. To the degree that matched samples permit control over the crucial variables, the psychologist should be equally impressed. It is foolish for either to make the deficiencies that he cannot help a matter of virtue—for the sociologist to claim precision for his findings when he cannot control the relevant variables, or for the psychologist to claim generality for his findings when he has been able to control only incidental variables at the price of wholly excluding from consideration the only factor which could give social meaning to his experiment.

We are on the verge of substantial progress in articulating sociology and personality psychology. We may anticipate, in the next two decades, the development of increased clinical understanding of many qualities of personality which are of maximum importance in the indvidual's social functioning. Increased knowledge of the child-rearing patterns which produce given traits and of the social environments which seem to induce the use of different child-rearing techniques may be expected. More character traits will become measurable through the development of simple, easily scored, yet valid and reliable psychological tests. As this goal is attained, the psychological mapping or census of major subgroups and total societal populations will become feasible and actual. When this is accomplished, the sociologist will be able—indeed, will be required—to build into his analyses not only such traditional sociological variables as the degree of social integration or cohesion, the freedom of communication, and the rigidity of

38. S. Glueck and E. Glueck, *Unravelling Juvenile Delinquency* (Cambridge: Harvard University Press, 1950).

stratification, but also a series of psychological variables. Along with the distribution of income or power, he will be able—and required—to consider the strength and distribution of needs for achievement, of tendencies toward projection, and of resentment of authority. Although this attainment will not mean the end of either sociology or psychology as separate disciplines, it will usher in an era of distinctively new approaches to and advances in the analysis of some of the traditionally most important and difficult problems of sociological research.

16.

Clio and Minerva

Charles Tilly

Charles Tilly was born near Chicago in 1929. He received most of his higher education, including the Ph.D., at Harvard University. After teaching and holding research appointments at the University of Delaware, Princeton University, Harvard University, the Massachusetts Institute of Technology, and the University of Toronto, Dr. Tilly is now professor of sociology and history at the University of Michigan. Most of his work concerns urbanization and political change; it includes studies of contemporary American cities and of western Europe since 1750. His best known book is The Vendée, *an analysis of rural resistance to the French Revolution.*

The discipline of sociology grew out of historical inquiry. Whatever their merits as historical craftsmen, Comte, Spencer, Weber, and most of their confreres were trying to make sense of long, broad changes in whole societies. Their European successors have generally maintained contact with their historical antecedents. The generations of North Americans who developed the standard analytic tools of contemporary sociology, on the other hand, plied their trade with scarcely a glance at history. Their aims and practices kept them outside of history; they were either ahistorical or metahistorical.

The increased pressures on North American sociologists to account for —and even to predict or prescribe—the changes occurring in Africa, Asia, and Latin America in our own age have, paradoxically, forced them to look again at the experiences of western countries over the last few hundred years. One version or another of the western experience provides the im-

Rainer Baum, Monica Boyd, Stephen Bunker, Daniel Collins, Louise Tilly, and Ian Weinberg gave me detailed and helpful critiques of an earlier draft of this paper; Edward Shorter helped me on a number of the technical questions. Colloquia at Northwestern University, the University of Rochester, the University of Pittsburgh, Reed College, and the University of Toronto heard and criticized portions of the argument. The Canada Council supported the research which lies behind the paper. All translations from texts cited in languages other than English are my own.

plicit models of how such processes as industrialization, urbanization, agricultural innovation, political centralization, or population growth operate. When the model breaks down in application to the present, it helps to go back and examine whether it really applied to the past.

Furthermore, social scientists who are attempting to generalize about such processes, or even to sum all of them up under a concept like modernization, find that they are theorizing about changes which take a long time to work out. But if they restrict themselves to the countries now experiencing the most vigorous industrial, urban, and demographic transformations, they have only a short span of change to observe. Again it is reasonable to try out long-run ideas on the long run of western history.

The sociological turn toward history produces a new variety of historical synthesis. Lipset's *First New Nation,* Bendix's *Nation-Building and Citizenship,* and Eisenstadt's *Modernization* exemplify the style of analysis I have in mind. These works differ from sweeping metahistorical analyses like Sorokin's *Dynamics* as well as from bold attempts at comparative history like Weber's *Wirtschaft und Gesellschaft.* The current historical syntheses start much more deliberately with the analogy between massive changes of the present and massive changes of the past.

They are also more directly aimed at reconstructing what happened in particular historical times and places—western countries in the periods during which bureaucratic nation-states, large-scale industries, and urban economies emerged. Yet they resemble the older sociological sweeps through history in schematizing far more extensively than most historians find comfortable or convincing, and in relying for data on secondary historical works rather than reanalyzing the primary sources.

Such sociological incursions into modern history are going on at the same time as many modern historians are edging toward sociological statements of their own problems. British historians of the seventeenth to nineteenth centuries, for example, have begun serious discussions and formal, quantitative investigations of social mobility, fertility change, and political participation. More important, they have begun to behave at times as if they were studying social mobility, fertility change, and political participation *as such,* instead of being primarily concerned with explaining the year 1640 or the man Cromwell. So they have broken out in sociological stigmata: explicit conceptualization (which historians have traditionally viewed as jargon), painstaking quantitative verification (commonly seen as needless apparatus), and deliberate, systematic comparison (frequently labeled as unhistorical analogy). They differ from almost all the sociologists working in history, however, in one essential way. Their raw materials are not the works of other historians, but the historian's primary sources: deeds, newspapers, letters, administrative reports, catechisms, memoirs, mercurials, maps, and monuments. Indeed, the abilities of Stone, Furet, or Benson to extract information from documents the systematic use of which

had been thought impractical or uninteresting have impressed their colleagues as much as any of their other accomplishments.[1]

The vigorous development of social scientific work in history and of historical work in the social sciences raises the main questions to which this chapter is devoted. How does the special character of historical material affect the application of social scientific theory to it? What changes in historical research does the arrival of social science induce? What changes in the practice of social science does the employment of historical materials bring about? I have neither the taste nor the wisdom to take up the huge hoary Hempelian questions of epistemology to which discussions of sociology and history often tend. In fact, I want to assume, rather than argue, two debatable principles: first, that there are regularities in history which are accessible to scientific analysis; second, that any social science which cannot provide an account of past instances of its own phenomena has failed.

Let me admit at once that in so doing I beg all the groanworthy questions traditional in discussions of history and social theory: whether history has laws, whether historiography requires a unique method, whether every set of generalizations about human beings is relative to a particular historical setting, and so on. My only excuse for this cowardice (aside from boredom with the questions and incompetence to resolve them) is that the issues I do wish to discuss have received little attention, have considerable importance, and may even shed light on the classical historiographical problems.

Years of wandering in the no-man's-land between history and sociology have filled me with notions of the wonders and dangers to be encountered there. In particular, there are some ideas of the ways historical records come into being, some impressions of what happens to social scientific specialties within history, and some notes on the way contact with real historical material affects the metahistorical and pseudohistorical theories sociologists fondly apply to large structural changes in societies.

One of the unreasoning prejudices both sociologists and historians commonly carry around with them is that data concerning the present are far better than data concerning the past. After all, you can't call Caesar and ask him! Given the predilection of historians for explanation in terms of the conscious intentions of limited numbers of actors, and the unreliability of inferences of conscious intentions from letters, memoirs, and the like, historians do have some reasons to envy contemporary psychiatrists and pollsters. And the heavy reliance of the last generation of sociologists on survey

---

1. See, for example, Lawrence Stone, *The Crisis of the Aristocracy* (Oxford: Clarendon Press, 1965), and *Social Change and Revolution in England, 1540–1640* (London: Longmans, 1965); François Furet, "Structures sociales parisiennes au XVIIIe siècle: l'apport d'une série fiscale," *Annales: Economies-Sociétés-Civilisations,* 16 (Sept.-Oct., 1961), 939-958; Lee Benson, *The Concept of Jacksonian Democracy: New York as a Test Case* (Princeton: Princeton University Press, 1961).

research did tie them to forms of analysis difficult to approximate outside the present. Yet the development of almost every new field within history involves the identification of data previously considered unavailable.

African history is a case in point. As Leonard Thompson says:

Until the mid-1950's African history was ignored by the historical profession in the United States even more completely than in Europe; and if an American historian had paused to consider why this was so, he would probably have anticipated Trevor-Roper's well-known verdict that the history of sub-Saharan Africa is undiscoverable (on the ground that it is not documented) and that, even if it were discoverable, it would be devoid of intellectual significance (on the ground that traditional African societies were barbarous and static).[2]

Since then, comparative linguistics, archeology, and the analysis of oral traditions have all begun to supplement the scanty written sources. The data are there, somewhere, for those who can frame their inquiries properly.

In recent years, prosopography—the collation of standard biographies of members of élite groups à la Namier, Syme, or Ho Ping-ti—has transformed the study of power and privilege in areas in which scholars had seemed condemned to the dissection and redissection of classical texts. For the earlier Chinese empire, dynastic histories provide numerous biographies of officials; from Ming times on, the candidate lists from imperial examinations identify not only the aspiring officials, but also those of his near kinsmen who also passed the examinations. The lists have been available for centuries. Only in the last twenty years have they been used systematically for the study of social mobility. We do not, of course, have every bit as much information about the Peiping of five hundred years ago as we might have *(Mao volente)* about the city today; the discrepancy is still smaller than common sense says it should be.

In some cases the information practically available to the student of a phenomenon is actually better for the past than for the present. Every modern historian has watched with fascination Clio's striptease: some version of the process whereby the French withholding of archives until the documents are fifty years old is gradually uncovering the years 1913, 1914, 1915, 1916, 1917, 1918 . . . and finally making well-documented histories of World War I possible. (No one should rush to his bookseller for the last word on the war. French doctoral theses take fifteen or twenty years to prepare.) Plausibly assuming the durability of French bureaucrats and their rules, we can expect the unveiling of World War II to take place in 1990, de Gaulle's 1958 coup to come into its own in 2008.

American students of ethnic and religious life who are working with the rich census materials of 1870 and 1880 have two large advantages over

2. "African History in the United States," *African Studies Bulletin,* 10 (April, 1967), 51.

their twentieth-century counterparts. The first is that they have access to the original, individual manuscript schedules rather than to summary data for cities, census tracts, and the like. The other is that the earlier census-takers collected more information about religion and national origin than their successors did. To be sure, the student of American ethnic and religious life in the 1960's has many alternatives to the census; attitudinal analysis like that of Gerhard Lenski would be hard to carry off for the year 1870.[3] Nonetheless, a great deal of contemporary analysis of racial, ethnic, and religious questions does rely on aggregate census data. Students of processes like occupational and residential mobility, which take a fair amount of time to work themselves out, are especially likely to discover that the historical materials fit their purposes better than current available data do.

Furthermore, the best cases to test a particular theory sometimes lie in the past. G. E. Swanson's remarkable pair of studies of the relations between theologies and social structures rely heavily on historical evidence rearranged into comparable cases, following standard experimental design. As Swanson describes the problem of finding evidence for the second study:

For anyone interested in understanding the meaning and origin of immanence, its very ubiquity is a problem. One can hope to find the sources only of those things that display some variation. Unless in some societies the doctrine applies to different things than it does in others, or unless this kind of belief is explicitly rejected in some societies, there is no effective method for judging what conditions might produce it. These facts lead us to consider afresh the origins and meaning of the Protestant Reformation because, alone among the world's major religious traditions, Protestantism—most dramatically Calvinist Protestantism—rejects all beliefs in immanence and particularly the Catholic belief in God's immanence in the visible church, the sacraments, and the soul transformed by sacramental grace.[4]

Swanson is stating one of the most pressing reasons sociologists have for turning to historical materials: to extend the number of observations or the range of observed variation of a phenomenon whose present manifestations are too few or too homogeneous. Sociological students of revolution, of language, and of kinship have commonly turned to history for their cases. But investigators of organizational structure, of urban spatial arrangements, or of educational institutions, who could equally well test their hypotheses on the past, have rarely ventured away from the present.

All things considered, it is surprising that sociologists work so little with primary historical materials. Their special concerns with large structures, big transformations, and formal organizations jibe rather badly with the conventional uses of survey research. Historical records, on the other hand,

3. *The Religious Factor,* rev. ed., (New York: Doubleday, 1963).
4. *Religion and Regime* (Ann Arbor: University of Michigan Press, 1967), pp. 7-8. See also his *The Birth of the Gods* (Ann Arbor: University of Michigan Press, 1960).

provide more information about large structures, big transformations, and formal organizations than about anything else. Indeed, the most worrisome thing about the historian's use of them to reconstruct the past is the heavy bias of the sources in that direction.

There are, to begin with the obvious, no written documents without writing; only peoples that have invented or adopted a form of writing leave them. And writing develops with the growth of administrative structures and of cities. The most important original scripts are the Egyptian, Sumerian, Hittite, Cretan, Mayan, and Chinese; the vast majority of the world's writing styles have descended from one or another of them. Each one's appearance came with the growth of cities and of complex organizations. When city life declined, as in the Crete of the fourteenth century B.C., writing declined as well.

Because trade, complex organization, and city life have so often grown together, it is difficult to estimate the independent importance of trade in the use of writing. Surely trade matters a great deal to its spread. The eastern Mediterranean trading port of Byblos, after about 2000 B.C., produced or disseminated a number of important innovations in writing, perhaps including the alphabet. The trading Phoenicians, who began their Mediterranean conquests from the vicinity of Byblos, spread their alphabet over much of the ancient world.

The origins of writing are in themselves an unsure sign of its function in later societies. The entire history of writing, however, is basically an urban history, confined to that fraction of humanity who have dealt with large-scale, far-ranging, impersonal organizations based in cities. The existence of such cities and such organizations has been the basic condition for the use of writing and, therefore, the basic condition for the production of written documents.

The earliest written documents that have survived are contracts, accounts, inventories, and primitive dictionaries; they were soon joined by rosters, treaties, diplomatic correspondence, chronicles, and boastful brief biographies, legal codes, liturgies, and magic spells. Most of these meet the needs of complex organizations: political, economic, and religious. Complex, formal organizations have continued to be the main producers of the written record.

Some kinds of activities, furthermore, have typically produced documents in volume. Over the centuries the most important have very likely been fiscal operations, trade, military action, religious administration, and the control of contracts (including treaties, deeds, and marriage agreements). Robert Adams describes the bias in the Mesopotamian cuneiform texts in this way:

Not merely the literary texts but also those of an economic or administrative character concentrate upon the activities of élite groups and undoubtedly fail to provide a balanced representation even of those. Insofar as the activities of

a general public can be perceived at all in such records, they are obviously activities that somehow were important in relation to state institutions; it follows that an accurate assessment of the real importance of such institutions in the lives of ordinary persons is extremely difficult or impossible. Further to obscure the tasks of reconstruction, there is no necessary relationship between the scale or importance of activities and the extent to which it was felt necessary to record them. Not a single account has come to light, for example, of the obviously large and thriving pottery industry that has provided for so large a proportion of the grist for all the mills of the archeologists. Or, again, there are virtually innumerable accounts of the receipt or disbursement of grain and animals, but administrative documents dealing with fresh, non-storable vegetables are noteworthy by their absence. What we have, in short, is highly fruitful and often tantalizingly detailed, but we must recognize also that it is highly selective. And, regrettably but not surprisingly, the small class of ancient scribes were not sufficiently detached from their social setting to have left us a description of the principles by which that selection was made.[5]

Literature and personal correspondence have only grown up around the edges of the great bureaucratic producers of documents, like moss on a tree trunk. Family affairs, crafts, lovemaking and entertainment, to name a few widespread activities, have left few traces in written documents—most commonly when they have come into contact with the state, the church, or some other massive organization. The last few centuries have, it is true, seen a great proliferation of personal documents (letters, memoirs, and the like) as literacy spread to most adults in western countries. But with increasing use of virtually traceless means of communication like the telephone, great stores of personal documents like those of Mme. de Sévigné or Boswell may already be things of the past.

In general, the purpose of the activity matters less for the production of documents than the kind of organization it entails. Fiscal operations, trade, military action, religious administration, and control of contracts frequently involve large, complex organizations. When these activities are pursued without complex organization, they do not produce documents in volume. Normally illiterate activities like fighting, gambling, sports, and sex begin producing documents aplenty when they start intertwining with big bureaucracies like professional leagues, criminal syndicates, and police departments.

Other features of the production of written records bend them even further toward large and complex organizations. Through the greater part of history, the majority of the few literate men—the only ones capable of producing written documents—have been functionaries of large organizations. They have done most of their writing in execution of their functions. The commander of a military outpost sending back a report to headquarters, the parish priest recording a birth, the merchant writing a bill of sale are all turning out routine documents of the most abundant variety.

5. *The Evolution of Urban Society* (Chicago: Aldine, 1966), pp. 32-33.

Furthermore, the usual routines for retention and storage of records discriminate not only against private papers and small organizations. Even within bureaucracies they eschew momentary jottings, rough drafts, interim reports, and preliminary computations in favor of finished and permanent copies, the most formal part of formal recording. Anyone who has ever prepared an official report as a member of a bureaucracy will realize that these documents in no sense represent all those produced by a complex organization.

Even archivists select. In 1879, the record-keeper of Russia's Department of Manufactures and Internal Commerce won himself the eventual hatred of twentieth-century economic historians by issuing the following recommendation to the department's director:

Although the reports on shops and factories for the previous year are the only source for historical research on the situation of production in Russia, it is hardly necessary for that purpose to examine the reports year by year, and therefore . . . to free space in the archives, may it please you to authorize leaving in the archives the reports for certain years and destroying the rest. . . . In the opinion of the editor of the departmental yearbook it would suffice to leave the reports for 1825, 1830, 1835, 1840, 1845, 1850, 1855, 1860, 1865, and the entire last ten years. [Archivist Orlov] [6]

Every working historian has his own favorite version of the Orlov story. Every working historian, indeed, has an acute practical sense of the organizational bias of his sources. Many of the finest fine points of the historian's craft are means of using or circumventing that bias. The odd thing is that the enormous lore of historians concerning the conditions of production and retention of documents has never been codified. It may take sociologists, eager to analyze so characteristic a feature of an organization as the pattern of its paperwork, to do the job of systematization.

The correlation of paperwork and complex organization (obviously no new discovery) promotes the emergence and spread of languages closely tied to organizational needs. Through all history, the world has bristled with dialects. One village, one tribe, one mountain valley has often understood only with difficulty the speech of the next village, tribe, or valley. The multifarious dialects rarely appear in written form. The written language, when it comes to the back country, is the instrument of organizations—churches, governments, trading outfits—of far more than local significance. The writing follows the language of the builders of these organizations. As the Capetians built a national monarchy, the dialect of the Ile de France became French. Babylonian, Greek, Latin, French, and English have all,

6. I. Meshalin, *Tekstil'naia promyshlennost' krest'ian Moskovskoy gubernii v XVIII i pervoy polovinie XIX veka* (Moscow: Izdatel'stvo Akademii Nauk SSSR, 1950), p. 14.

in their times, been international languages, never eradicating all other languages and dialects, but always following complex political, religious, and economic organizations to the ends of the known world.

We should not, however, picture this spread of an international administrative language as pure diffusion. Involvement in complex organization transforms and standardizes the language. Standard classical Latin, for example, emerged from a congeries of dialects through an organizational process. As one historian of the language puts it,

Finally, we shall be faced with another phenomenon of constant occurrence: the centralization of government in organized states, the domination of a certain class, the prestige enjoyed by its social habits, of which not the least important is its mode of speech, result in the growth and imposition of a standard language. In Latin this expression of class fastidiousness is summed up in the word *urbanitas*.[7]

Later, the Tuscan dialect changed as it became a national language. It did spread with the influence of Florence as a mercantile and literary capital; it did provide the basis for modern standard Italian; but its character changed in the process:

Tuscanization, if not complete, proceeded so rapidly that already in the Rome of the seventeenth century [Tuscan] could be treated as the base and the standard of measurement for the literary language; not because it was a purer Tuscan, but because a Tuscan had come into existence which was perhaps attentuated, but was of greater social value.[8]

The emergence of a standard language, in turn, encourages the proliferation of written records, facilitates the work of complex organizations, and makes possible the preachments of grammarians. Linguistic styles thus come to measure distance from the centers of power or prestige.

As the Latin *urbanitas* suggests, the standard, literary language which develops in this way commonly comes to distinguish not only the élite from the mass but also the city-dweller from the countryman. In western countries, "urbane" speech generally has this dual distinction. Speaking of classic Roman civilization, Pulgram remarks:

Quintilian describes urbanity of speech in this way: *"Urbanitas,* which I observe denotes language with a smack of the city in its words, accent, and idiom and further suggests a certain tincture of learning derived from associating with well-educated men; in a word, it represents the opposite of rusticity . . . . For my thinking urbanity involves the total absence of all that is incongruous, coarse,

7. L. R. Palmer, *The Latin Language* (London: Faber and Faber, 1954), p. 119.
8. Giacomo Devoto, *Profilo di storia linguistica Italiana,* 4th ed. (Florence: La Nuova Italia, 1964), p. 72.

unpolished, and exotic, whether in thought, language, voice, or gesture, and resides not so much in isolated sayings as in the whole complexion of our language,
just as for the Greeks Atticism means that elegance of taste which was peculiar
to Athens." In other words, urbanity is a term which refers, as in English, not
to language alone but rather to the attitude and behavior of the civilized gentle-
man and lady of the city. Of course, since this style of life bears the stamp of
approval of the educated people of Rome, it must be imitated and culti-
vated "As there is a particular accent peculiar to the Roman race and to our
city, involving no possibility of stumbling in pronunciation or in uncertainness
or objection, no note or flavor of provincialism, let us make this accent our
model, and learn to avoid not only the rustic roughness but also provincial
solecisms." [9]

Sic Cicero. In history complexity, urbanity, writing, and high-toned accents
have all kept company.

In each locality, the spread of complex political, religious, and economic
organizations creates élites, groups of individuals having simultaneous
places in the larger organizations and in local communities. Traders, priests,
and government agents are good examples. They speak and write the élite
language, which becomes the language appropriate for discussing affairs
going beyond the locality. Even after the élite language is generally known,
the local dialect remains the medium for discussion of farming, weather,
family matters, and parochial affairs. A century ago, the patois-speaking
peasants of Anjou called the act of speaking proper French *parler noblat,*
speaking the nobleman's language. In such a situation, the recording of
strictly local events is by the pens of the élite, and in translation.

Organization, in sum, produces documents. The more complex the
organization and the larger its scale, the more likely it is to leave written
records, and leave them in abundance. Conversely, the documents we have
the luck to come across from some distant place or time are much more
likely to be the products of the sprawling, intricate, lasting webs of social
relations than of the localized, simple, and temporary ones. No doubt this
has encouraged the writing of history in terms of states, and churches, and
international markets.

These biases tax the ingenuity of the investigator who comes to historical materials with questions about sexual relations, individual political
outlooks, or farming practices. He must search for the testimonies of
literate observers (with allowances for their élite perspectives), identify
those moments when the informal phenomenon and the formal organization come into contact, or both. The historiographic genius of Philippe
Ariès' explorations of family history shows up in his exploration of sources
which grew up around the edges of great stores of documents—memoirs,
written traces of colloquial language, epigraphy, iconography.[10] Rudolf

9. Ernest Pulgram, *The Tongues of Italy* (Cambridge: Harvard University Press,
1958), pp. 360-361.
10. *Centuries of Childhood* (New York: Knopf, 1962).

Braun, by contrast, constructs his rich portrayal of local life in the uplands of Zurich largely from the records left by contacts between the poor and the officials responsible for their welfare.[11] Finally, the sedulous recording of birth, deaths, and marriages by religious functionaries made European demographic history possible.

Fortunately for most inquiries, the questions with which sociologists have increasingly been turning to history, and to which the historians themselves have been turning, deal more directly with the very phenomena which produce written documents in abundance. Questions about urbanization, industrialization, and modernization are largely questions about the emergence of the organizational forms most inclined to leave records behind. It is a pity the sociologists have left the handling of the documents to the historians, who come at them with different, often blunter, questions.

The same two-way flow of men and ideas which has occurred between sociology and history has been passing between economics and history, political science and history, even occasionally between anthropology and history. (It is worth reflecting why psychology and history, despite frequent exhortations to unite, have made virtually no contact at all.) Again the outsiders have usually been content to let the historians find and analyze the primary sources, and the social scientific historians have set themselves off from their colleagues by their will and skill to quantify and compare.

All these incursions and excursions have placed three different groups of interpreters in the midst of modern western history. There are social scientists who have come into history through a concern with large contemporary social changes like urbanization. There are historians who have moved toward the social sciences through the attempt to account for changes going on in some particular time and place. There are also a great many historians who find the problems and procedures of the social sciences uninteresting, or even repugnant.

The interaction among these three groups working with historical materials affects the division of labor among scholars. It helps produce esoteric specialties within history, specialties like prosopography and industrial archeology. What differentiates these specialties from other historical esoterica is not so much their concrete subject matter as the theory and technique applied to the subject matter.

Some crossings of the line between the social sciences and conventional history have attracted a great deal of attention. Demographic history has emerged, in Europe at least, as a demanding, complex, exciting, and deeply important specialty. The quantitative study of social mobility, as illustrated by the current work of Lawrence Stone, is making great headway in history. And a breed of men working mainly out of economics have begun to call themselves "cliometricians"—champions of measurement in history.

11. *Industrialisierung und Volksleben* (Zurich: Rentsch, 1960), and *Sozialer und Kultureller Wandel in einem landlichen Industriegebiet* (Zurich: Rentsch, 1965).

The conventional hope in this sort of cross-disciplinary effort is that integration and synthesis will emerge. We all know the exhortations: E. H. Carr saying, "the more sociological history becomes, and the more historical sociology becomes, the better for both," [12] and S. D. Clark saying, "there is nothing in history any longer which would be considered beyond the search of sociological analysis." [13] But there are other possibilities than the disappearance of the dividing line. It could stand fast. Or it could move, ιι ̇ ιιιιιιιιιιιιι ιιιιιι ιιιιιιιι ιιιιι ιιιι problems which have traditionally belonged to historians.

The last alternative is worth thinking about. A while ago, a card-carrying cliometrician explained the whole thing to me very simply. History, he said, has no systematic theory worth mentioning, and therefore no decent ways of asking or answering questions. At least some of the social sciences do. Economists, he told me, are well on the way to taking over economic history, so much so that graduate students now being trained in the subject within history departments had better start looking for new outlets for their talents. The political scientists, in his view, were beginning to seize control of political history. That, he concluded, left only social history. Its conquest, he told me, was up to the sociologists. If this is true, we face the withering away of history.

That analysis came from an enthusiast, but it was not entirely dotty. There are some kinds of historical analysis which can only be practiced with extensive training outside the field as it is now constituted, which have strongly impressed both historians and nonhistorians, and which are likely to become the standard ways of dealing with questions once regarded as the special concerns of historians. In demographic history, the work of Louis Henry or Jacques Henripin will serve as an example; in political history, the work of Lee Benson or Duncan MacRae; in economic history, the work of Jan Marczewski or Robert Fogel.[14] Now that these scholars (some of whom are historians who acquired outside training) have shown the way, it is quite likely that their successors will come mainly from demography, political science, or economics and will pursue their work as demographers, political scientists, or economists.

12. *What Is History?* (New York: Knopf, 1963), p. 84.
13. "History and the Sociological Method," *Transactions of the Fifth World Congress of Sociology* (Louvain: International Sociological Association, 1964), p. 31.
14. The following writings are representative of the authors mentioned: Louis Henry, "Historical Demography," *Daedalus,* 97 (Spring, 1968), 385-396, and "The Population of France in the Eighteenth Century," in D. V. Glass and D. E. C. Eversley, eds., *Population in History* (Chicago: Aldine, 1965), pp. 434-456; Jacques Henripin, *La population canadienne au début du XVIIIe siècle* (Paris: Presses Universitaires de France; Institut National d'Etudes Démographiques, Travaux et Documents, Cahier 22, 1954); Lee Benson, *Jacksonian Democracy;* Duncan MacRae, Jr., *Parliament, Parties, and Society in France, 1946–1958* (New York: St. Martin's Press, 1967); Jan Marczewski, *Introduction à l'histoire quantitative* (Geneva: Droz, 1965); Robert Fogel, "The New Economic History: I. Its Findings and Methods," *The Economic History Review,* 19 (1966), 642-656.

One peculiarity of the interchanges between history and the social sciences reinforces the tendency of new specialties growing at the boundaries of history to fall away from historians. The kinds of analysis carried on in adjacent fields which are most like those already done by historians rarely have much influence on historical work. When they are relevant at all, analyses of a style very different from that ordinarily carried on by historians often have a very great impact on historical work.

At least that appears to be true of the relations between sociology and history. Sociologists like David Riesman, Leo Lowenthal, and Lewis Coser have written on historical themes in styles readily comprehensible to historians. Historians have occasionally taken up or challenged their arguments, but by and large their writings have had little effect on the ways historians actually do their work. In sociology, the four fields in which the most extensive development of formal models and mathematical analysis has occurred are probably small groups, demographic processes, social mobility, and individual political behavior. I know of no serious applications to historical work of theories, techniques, or findings from the study of small groups. But analyses of contemporary demographic processes, social mobility, and individual political behavior have stimulated more work in history and have produced greater changes in the character of historical work than anything else the sociologists have had to offer. Thus the fields of sociology stylistically most alien to history have had the greatest impact on history.

Whether sociologists practicing as sociologists will wrest these problems away from historians remains to be seen. What makes it possible is that the successful pursuit of these problems requires a technical training routinely available to sociologists but hard for the historians to acquire. I say "hard to acquire" not because of the intrinsic difficulty of the techniques or the essential incapacity of historians, but because the organization of the historical discipline itself stands in the way. Historians learn above all to become specialists in particular periods and places. Their attachment to a large public which demands interpretations of particular periods and places reinforces that way of dividing up history. So does the mode of documentation and explanation which consists of binding events tightly to their temporal and geographic settings. It takes so much effort to become a historian of Meiji Japan that there is little energy left for learning how to analyze intergenerational mobility tables. As a consequence, when specialists turn up materials from Meiji Japan which lend themselves to analysis via intergenerational mobility tables, it is quite possible that sociologists will seize that line of investigation as their own.

These possibilities, however, have stringent limits. The application of varieties of sociological theory and method to historical materials generally requires a fairly continuous and homogeneous body of data reporting numerous events which can be treated as equivalent to each other. In Amer-

ican political history, for example, the records of elections and of congressional roll calls have those attractive qualities. As a consequence, scholars have been able to apply statistical procedures from the social sciences to them; their work has upset cherished myths about American voters and legislators.

The study of civil violence will surely follow a different course. American riots and rebellions, while frequent enough, do not have the obvious comparability of votes. The documents which record them, while abundant enough, have none of the continuity and homogeneity of voting records In order to apply models of rebellion like those of Gurr, Feierabend, or Russett [15] to primary American historical materials, scholars will have to go through a long, strenuous effort at conceptualization, and at transformation of the existing data.

In the first sort of case, the outsider from whose discipline the ideas and procedures have come can often work with the historical materials as effectively as the trained historian. Indeed, a number of the significant contributions to the study of past American elections and legislatures have come from political scientists. In cases like the historical study of riot and rebellion, on the other hand, the piecing together of the sources and the establishment of criteria for comparison and classification ordinarily take considerable historical training. For that reason, we might most confidently expect new specialties involving the application of social scientific ideas and procedures to historical materials to fall away from the discipline of history and attach themselves to adjacent social sciences when the materials themselves are continuous, homogeneous, and obviously amenable to quantitative treatment.

A similar division of outcomes occurs when areas or periods differ in the character of materials they offer for social scientific analysis. The remarkable recent work on French and English demographic history using techniques developed by Louis Henry and his collaborators has capitalized on uniform series of parish registers recording births, deaths, and marriages in village after village during decade after decade. Henry's technique requires little historical knowledge and a good deal of demographic expertise. Furthermore, it produces results of great interest to contemporary demographers by providing a far finer account of the historical connections among changes in fertility, mortality, marriage patterns, family forms, and industrial activity than has ever been available heretofore. In England and France, men trained mainly in sociology and demography are doing much

15. Ted Gurr and Charles Ruttenberg, *The Conditions of Civil Violence: First Tests of a Causal Model* (Princeton: Center of International Studies, Princeton University, 1967); Ivo K. and Rosalind L. Feierabend, "Aggressive Behaviors within Polities, 1948–1962: A Cross-National Study," *Journal of Conflict Resolution,* 10 (September, 1966), 249-271; Bruce M. Russett, "Inequality and Instability: The Relation of Land Tenure to Politics," *World Politics,* 16 (April, 1964), 442-454.

of the important work on changes in fertility, mortality, and family patterns since the sixteenth century.

In Latin America, by contrast, the demographic record so far assembled is too fragmentary and disparate to attract many professional demographers. It takes great historical wit to puzzle together the odd pieces of information at hand concerning characteristics of the eighteenth-century urban population or even changes in GNP before 1900. In addition, the return to demographic theory from the fragile structure of conjecture, hypothesis, and fact is not very promising.

Latin American priests began keeping parish registers of births, deaths, and marriages on the European model during the sixteenth century. Nicolás Sánchez-Albornoz has found and analyzed a relatively continuous series of registers kept in an Argentine parish from early in the nineteenth century.[16] In working on that series, however, he came to recognize a severe limitation of the source.

Unlike the European case, the American rural church does not seem to have been the focus of a rural community, but rather the point of settlement of an outside cult among the rural masses. During the colonial period, even the period of independence, the parish was a kind of oasis. The church stood among a population largely of European origin in close contact with the curé, if there was one. However the parish was surrounded by a sort of no-man's-land, by genuine human deserts, whose inhabitants had only weak and intermittent ties to the curé. For that reason it is not surprising to see that the latter fulfilled his spiritual obligations through missions, except in the central settlement.

How did this situation affect the registers? Obviously the population regularly recorded in the book was the one living in the center where the church was located. The population of the marginal areas appeared as a function of proximity and of the curé's missionary zeal.[17]

Furthermore, says Sánchez-Albornoz, the priests often kept separate registers for people deemed Spanish, mixed, Black, and Indian. And the completeness of enumeration declined with the decline in the presumption of Spanish origin. In short, out at the fringes of the church's influence, the centralist bias which the production of documents displays in general extends even to those documents which in theory represent all souls equally.

If full collections of parish registers like the one used by Sánchez-Albornoz continue to be rare and those which turn up generally display the same biases as his, demographers will not rush to analyze the Latin Amer-

16. "La población de un valle calchaqui en el siglo XIX," *Desarollo Economico,* 19 (1964), 81-83, contains a description of the study itself.

17. "Les registres paroissiaux en Amérique latine." *Revue suisse d'histoire,* 17, 1 (1967), 66. Cf. Marvin Harris, *Town and Country in Brazil* (New York: Columbia University Press, 1956), pp. 26-28; and Gerardo and Alicia Reichel-Dolmatoff, *The People of Aritama* (Chicago: University of Chicago Press, 1961), pp. 21ff.

ican sources. We have reason to expect important parts of European demographic history to fall out of the hands of historians. No such outcome for Latin America is in view.

Another major consideration affects the likelihood that a historical subject will become the province of nonhistorians. That is the time-span of the theories imported from outside history. Paradoxically, theories dealing with short-run states or processes give the intellectual advantage to the practitioner from outside history who has had the opportunity to observe his phenomenon repeatedly in the contemporary world. Thus the theorist of voting can easily step into history to try out his already working models on past elections. But if the theory itself deals with long-run processes like modernization and economic growth, then its users will have to go to history for any test whatsoever of its validity. The present is too short.

In his controversial book on railroads in American economic growth, Robert Fogel attacks both sorts of problems.[18] When estimating the "social savings" due to the introduction of the railroads, he essentially converts classic statements about their effects into special cases of the theory of rent, the theory of transportation, and so on. He can easily move through these short-run theories to alternative statements contradicting the classic. In his confrontation with W. W. Rostow's theory of "takeoff," on the other hand, Fogel can use his economist's sense to find the numbers most embarrassing to Rostow's argument, but he cannot find an alternative formulation which lends itself to direct testing.

This contrast of short-run and long-run theories may seem to be a useless truism. Another glance at the question of civil violence will show that it is not. Theorists who emphasize the immediate structural conditions which promote or impede civil violence, as does Ted Gurr, do not need a long time-span. Although there may be certain points in long processes like urbanization in which these violence-inducing structural conditions are most widespread, presumably wherever they occur, violence will, too. Such theories can reasonably be tested over short spans of the present. If they work in the present, and then appear to account for outbursts of violence at various points in the past, the disciplines from which they come will tend to absorb the explanation of violence in both past and present.

But other theorists, like Barrington Moore,[19] see some major forms of collective violence as by-products of long and sweeping transformations of societies. Although there may be some structural conditions which characterize the crucial violent moments in those transformations, presumably their effectiveness in producing rebellion or violent protest depends on the ripening—or rotting—of the entire society. Such theories are almost inevitably historical or metahistorical. If they hold up while the short-run struc-

18. *Railroads in American Economic Growth* (Baltimore: Johns Hopkins University Press, 1964).
19. *The Social Origins of Dictatorship and Democracy* (Boston: Beacon Press, 1966).

tural theories fail, the explanation of civil violence will tend to remain a historical problem.

The next decade of contact between history and sociology should feature a number of theoretical confrontations of this sort. When the sociologists arose from their static slumber ten or twenty years ago, nothing could have been more natural than their reaching for evolutionary ideas, ideas tending toward unilinearity and irreversibility, in their attempts to account for large structural changes in societies. The apparently successful models the economists had to offer themselves emphasized "growth" and "development." More important, the view of society most sociologists had already adopted belonged to the tradition of Durkheim and Tönnies rather than, say, to the traditions of Spengler or Marx or Aristotle. Sociologists easily and reasonably turned to ideas of social change like those in *Gemeinschaft und Gesellschaft* or *The Division of Labor*.

What characterizes these ideas of social change? Foremost, the treatment of an advancing division of labor, of differentiation, as the primary process of change. Concomitantly, an emphasis on increases in the scale of social organization. Third, the analysis of changes in the character of personal relations as the consequences of differentiation and expanding scale. Fourth, the use of the "society" (often identified for practical purposes with the nation-state) as the principal unit of analysis. Fifth, the assertion that some sort of consensus holds the society together through the process of change, but that each new phase of change taxes the consensus—sometimes so greatly that the society breaks down. Sixth, a loosely linear view of social evolution, relying in one way or another on dichotomies like complex/single, developed/underdeveloped, modern/traditional. Finally, the assumption that except in the case of a general breakdown the processes of differentiation and increase in scale are irreversible. The recent works of Eisenstadt and Parsons best exemplify the fitting together of these neo-evolutionary ideas, but they pervade contemporary sociology.[20] In such a world, even so cautious a deviant as Bendix,[21] who dares to rely on ideas drawn mainly from Max Weber, stands out as odd.

Now, these evolutionary schemes have already drawn on history. Eisenstadt's *Political Systems of Empires,* Bellah's *Tokugawa Religion,* Smelser's *Social Change in the Industrial Revolution,* and Black's *Dynamics of Modernization* all apply neo-evolutionary perspectives to historical materials.[22] Nonetheless the real showdown between *current* evolutionary theories and

20. See S. N. Eisenstadt, *Modernization: Protest and Change* (Englewood Cliffs: Prentice-Hall, 1966); and Talcott Parsons, *Societies: Evolutionary and Comparative Perspectives* (Englewood Cliffs: Prentice-Hall, 1966).
21. Reinhard Bendix, *Nation-Building and Citizenship* (New York: Wiley, 1964).
22. S. N. Eisenstadt, *The Political Systems of Empires* (Glencoe: Free Press, 1963); Robert Bellah, *Tokugawa Religion* (Glencoe: Free Press, 1957); Neil J. Smelser, *Social Change in the Industrial Revolution* (Chicago: University of Chicago Press); and C. E. Black, *The Dynamics of Modernization* (New York: Harper, 1966).

historical work has not so much tested established hypotheses as it has identified uniformities and demonstrated the applicability of evolutionary concepts to interesting cases.

Smelser's study of the British cotton textile industry, for example, is illuminating and in many respects persuasive. It will nevertheless take a good deal more specification for his basic hypotheses to be amenable to comparative testing. It will take a good deal of systematic comparison before we know whether there was, indeed, a general tendency for pressure on the family structure of factory workers to produce symptoms of disturbance built around symbols of family life and for pressure on the organization of work itself to elicit different sorts of symptoms. Now that the gauntlet is down, historians seeking to make sense of industrialization and sociologists following the study of modernization into the past will surely pick it up.

In some ways the sociological theories will triumph; in others they will fail. It seems to me there is one major point at which the contact with history will be eminently salutary. That is in forcing sociologists to take account of *devolution* as well as evolution. History abounds with devolutionary processes; sociological theory does not. No doubt the main drift of the last sixty centuries has moved human societies toward differentiation, larger scale, more extensive creation, and freeing of resources. Yet from the fall of Babylon through the Dark Ages to the collapse of government in the Congo, the world has witnessed innumerable eddies going the other way. As S. D. Clark puts it:

Among the changes taking place in society can be discerned certainly changes in the direction of increasing structural differentiation. But so also can be discerned changes of the very opposite character. The fact that the model used excludes consideration of changes of this latter sort cannot be taken as sufficient answer to the charge that what is offered is a distorted picture of what is happening to society as it changes over time. Movements in the direction of increasing structural differentiation (and as well social integration) are intimately related to movements in the opposite direction and any theory of change must be able to account for the one type of movement as well as the other.[23]

What are these complementary processes sociologists will find in history? Since they have not yet found their theorist, current sociological concepts do not label them accurately. In the absence of a reasonable test for the survival of a society or even a reliable way of judging its adaptability, Parsons' appealing notion of devolution as a *reduction of adaptive capacity* is rather hard to apply. Parsons' analysis of changes in adaptive capacity, however, identifies several component evolutionary processes: differentiation, adaptive upgrading, integration, generalization, and specification.[24]

23. Clark, "History and the Sociological Method," p. 33.
24. Parsons, *Societies,* pp. 21-25.

I confess bewilderment in understanding and providing criteria for "adaptive upgrading" and "specification." But the other three processes have opposites which do operate on occasion: dedifferentiation, disintegration, and particularization. I shall take *dedifferentiation* to mean the fusing or disappearance of social units which were formerly structurally and functionally distinct. *Disintegration* will refer to a decline in the extent and/or complexity of coordination among a set of social units. And *particularization* will signify the strengthening of the attachment of resources to specific social units. Dedifferentiation, distintegration, and particularization are devolutionary processes.

Not that evolutionary theorists have completely ignored devolution. The standard theory allows for some major devolutionary cases: breakdowns, declines, and total transformations of societies. With his distinctions among "accommodable," "total," and "marginal" changes and his observation that they sometimes occur simultaneously, Eisenstadt leaves room for a considerable variety of devolutionary processes. His analysis of the historical bureaucratic polities emphasizes the coexistence, interdependence, and delicate balance of "traditional" and "free-floating" resources. Indeed, he points out that the very process which created "free-floating" resources also promoted their freezing or diminution.

As a result of developments like this, there was often a shrinkage of the available supply of free or flexible resources; a lowering of the general level of productivity; and/or the alienation of the economically and socially more active strata from the rulers and their policies and from the political institutions of the society. Such alienation was frequently intensified by the fact that many parts of these polities had often been incorporated through conquest. Thus, whatever passive loyalty may have been engendered at certain stages of their development, it was frequently undermined because of the various prescriptive policies of the rulers.[25]

Eisenstadt has tucked away the germ of a very interesting devolutionary scheme in his *Political Systems of Empires*. Still, his summary statement on the subject makes the devolutionary changes look like the backsliding of a mountain-climber rather than, let us say, the zigzag of a slalom racer.

The history of modern social systems is full of cases of unsuccessful adaptation, or of lack of adaptation of existing structures to new types of problems and organizations and of the lack of ability of these institutions to assimilate, to some extent, the various movements of protest inherent in the process of modernization.

The external manifestations of such blocking are usually some types of political "eruptions," i.e., of more or less violent outbreaks of political activities and development of symbols oriented against the existing system and its symbols.

25. Eisenstadt, *Political Systems of Empires,* p. 319.

The strength of such eruptions, as well as their repercussions on the stability of the regimes in which they take place, varies greatly from place to place. But the possibility of eruptions, of lack of absorption of change, is as inherent in the processes of modernization and the structure of modern society as are the tendencies to continual change.

Such eruptions may lead either to the transformation of the existing regime into a more flexible one, better adapted to deal with continually changing problems, or to breakdowns of modernization, to the development of regressive or deformed regimes with autocratic tendencies, as is the case of Fascism and Nazism; to outright attempts at deformation of modernity and of civil society and to outright demodernization.[26]

The theory stated in this passage has a measure of tautology in it. Nonetheless, it shows that the neo-evolutionary theory sociologists are now bringing to historical material has some capacity to deal with devolutionary processes—so long as they constitute changes in the direction of development of an entire society. Furthermore, in dealing with such reversals, the recent formulations have many advantages over the old portrayals of devolution as Decline and Fall.

The version of the evolutionary theory which emphasizes the progressive inclusion of wider and wider circles of the society in the activities of the central nexus (again Eisenstadt comes to mind, but so do Marshall, Lerner, Shils, and Kerr [27]) also has some implications for devolutionary processes. Frequently this inclusion means the atrophy of the smaller units in which the actors once participated. The growth of the nation-state in western Europe eroded the collective life of cities as it destroyed their autonomy and extended the role of citizen. From the point of view of the individual city, the process was devolutionary. The same sort of transformation affected provinces, principalities, and parishes. This could well be the general pattern: evolution to a larger scale, devolution at the smaller scale.

If this is the case, it probably means that the roles which have their chief significance at the smaller scale also shrivel with the expansion of scale, and persons who have their chief investments in those roles begin to lose their social identities. I have in mind the priest of a regional cult, the head of a clan, the bush trader, the lord of the manor, the local weaver. Their roles do not simply subdivide; they disappear. Here is a hidden form

26. Eisenstadt, *Modernization,* p. 40.
27. T. H. Marshall, *Citizenship and Social Class, and Other Essays* (Cambridge: Cambridge University Press, 1950); Daniel Lerner, "Comparative Analysis of Processes of Modernization," in Horace Miner, ed., *The City in Modern Africa* (New York: Praeger, 1967), pp. 21-38, and *The Passing of Traditional Society* (Glencoe: Free Press, 1958); E. A. Shils, "On the Comparative Study of the New States," in Clifford Geertz, ed., *Old Societies and New States* (New York: Free Press, 1963); Clark Kerr, "Changing Social Structures," in Wilbert E. Moore and Arnold S. Feldman, eds., *Labor Commitment and Social Change in Developing Areas* (New York: Social Science Research Council, 1960), pp. 348-359.

of dedifferentiation. Many bits of evidence from the modern history of western Europe suggest that these people (rather than the masses actually torn away from their old social settings by urbanization and industrialization) have an extraordinary propensity to mount backward-looking movements of protest. They are complaining about the devolutionary countercurrents of a larger evolutionary stream.

Let me stress a distinction. One phenomenon properly called devolutionary is the reversal (or its special case, the stagnation) of an entire society's development: a breakdown, decline, adaptive downgrading of the society as a whole. We have a long, rich tradition of theories of decline and fall. Sociologists have recently made some useful contributions to that tradition. Another form of devolution, however, is that reduction of the adaptive capacity of some element of a society which often occurs at the same time as other elements, or even the society as a whole, are acquiring enhanced adaptive capacities, or as a consequence of that change. It is not so clear that available theory gives us reliable clues to the interaction and simultaneous appearance of evolution and devolution within the same society. At best we can say that this side of the theory is ill developed, and likely to be challenged considerably by the contact with historical materials.

Very likely the lesson we have to learn parallels one of those bequeathed by Ravenstein to all subsequent students of migration: despite the illusion of continuous one-way movement from country to city, he pointed out, almost every stream of migration in one direction produces a substantial counterflow in exactly the opposite direction.[28] Hence the care with which analysts of migration distinguish between the net and the gross movements between two places. Perhaps we have to think of the net movement toward greater differentiation or freeing of resources as the product of very large changes in that direction countered to some extent by significant processes of dedifferentiation or freezing of resources. If this were the case, of course, the distinctions among reversals, breakdowns, and counterflows in the evolutionary process would become less important; they would all turn out to be special cases of the same general phenomenon.

The obvious advantage of taking these abstract questions to historical materials is that with such materials we can see devolutionary processes work themselves out over large spans of time and space and yet see them concretely, in all their variety. For there are a variety of well-documented historical cases of simultaneous, interdependent evolution and devolution. One example is the curious closing down, the dedifferentiation, of inland communities which Eric Wolf has shown to have occurred cyclically when the capitals of Mexico gained control over the subject territory. Here is his summary:

28. E. G. Ravenstein, "The Laws of Migration," *Journal of the Royal Statistical Society,* 48 (June, 1885), 167-235.

Each rearrangement produced a changed configuration in the relationship of community-oriented and nation-oriented groups. During the first period of post-Columbian Mexican history, political power was concentrated on the national level in the hands of royal officials. Royal officials and colonist entrepreneurs struggled with each other for control of the labor supply located in the Indian communities. In this struggle, the royal officials helped to organize the Indian peasantry into corporate communities which proved strongly resilient to outside change. During the second period, the colonist entreprenurs—and especially the owners of haciendas—threw off royal control and established autonomous local enclaves, centered on their enterprises. With the fusion of political and economic power in the hands of these intermediate power-holders, the national government was rendered impotent and the Indian peasant groups became satellites of the entrepreneurial complex. At the same time, their corporate communal organization was increasingly weakened by internal differentiation and the inroads of outsiders. During the third period, the entrepreneurial complexes standing between community and nation were swept away by the agrarian revolution and power again returned to a central government. Political means are once more applied to check the transformation of power-seekers from the local communities into independent entrepreneurs.[29]

Two features of this complicated set of changes call for attention. First, the differentiation of the Indian community was clearly a reversible process; the first phase after the conquest produced communities which were actually more homogeneous, more tightly bounded, and had more extensive collective controls over their members than their predecessors. Second, a presumably "modernizing" transformation—the growth of a national political authority and the involvement of the hinterland in an international market —promoted the appearance of a presumably "traditional" form of community.

Actually, the growth of a central political authority has often fortified the rural communities within its ambit. In Placide Rambaud's apothegm, "To bring itself into being, the state creates the commune." [30] The cash-hunger of the emerging sixteenth-century Piedmontese state, Rambaud points out, simultaneously drove the farmers of the high Alps into the market and reinforced the collective responsibility and control of the commune with respect to its members. Through the levying of land taxes in money (rather than kind) based on market value and productive capacity, which made the household's outside obligations proportional to an impersonal

29. "Aspects of Group Relations in a Complex Society: Mexico," *American Anthropologist,* vol. 58 (December, 1956), pp. 1073-1074. See also his "Types of Latin American Peasantry: A Preliminary Discussion," *American Anthropologist,* vol. 57 (June, 1955), pp. 452-471; and his "Closed Corporate Peasant Communities in Mesoamerica and Central Java," *Southwestern Journal of Anthropology,* vol. 13 (Spring, 1957), pp. 1-18.
30. *Economie et sociologie de la montagne* (Paris: Colin, 1962; Ecole Pratique des Hautes Etudes, VIe Section, Centre d'Etudes Economiques, Etudes et Mémoires, 50), p. 131.

evaluation of the land it happened to hold, the state actually reinforced the bonds between the household and its land.[31] In a sense, the land participated in the state, and the landholders participated insofar as they were attached to the land. (This arrangement later caused enormous difficulties throughout Europe, as the numbers of landless workers in rural areas swelled, and as what C. B. Macpherson calls the "political theory of possessive individualism" arose to urge the *person* as the relevant unit for participation in the state.) Over the short period of a century or two, the freeing of resources by the state (unquestionably an "evolutionary" process from a national perspective) produced both a diminution and a freezing of resources within the Alpine commune.

The processes going on in the Alps and in Mexico had quite a bit in common. Wolf sums up a major implication of his analysis as follows.

In dealing with present-day Latin America, it would seem advisable to beware of treating production for subsistence and production for the market as two progressive stages of development. Rather, we must allow for the cyclical alternation of the two kinds of production within the same community and realize that from the point of view of the community both kinds may be alternative responses to changes in conditions of the outside market. This means that a synchronic study of such a community is insufficient, because it cannot reveal how the community can adapt to such seemingly radical changes.[32]

In this case, the devolutionary and evolutionary changes actually depended on each other.

The same could be said for a second devolutionary process, which Clifford Geertz calls agricultural involution: that intensification of farming and population density in Indonesia which decreased the flexibility of the system and aggravated the lot of all concerned.[33] Others have considered the "dualism" of the Indonesian economy—its sharp division between complex, large-scale, capital-intensive enterprises and primitive, small-scale, labor-intensive subsistence farming—to result from an extremely incomplete penetration of modern modes of organization into a resistant traditional society. Geertz shows to what a large extent the growth of foreign-owned plantations *produced* ingrown, helpless peasant communities through such devices as the trading of access to small plots of land for seasoned labor in cane, rubber, or tobacco fields.

This part of the process has a good deal in common with the Mesoamerican hacienda operation analyzed by Wolf. Less obviously, its essential logic resembles that of the interaction between city and hinterland community in parts of contemporary Africa where circular labor migration pre-

31. Gabriel Ardant has documented the widespread and painful character of this combination of circumstances in his *Théorie sociologique de l'impôt* (2 vols.; Paris: SEVPEN, 1965).
32. Wolf, "Types of Latin American Peasantry," p. 463.
33. *Agricultural Involution* (Berkeley and Los Angeles: University of California Press, 1963).

vails.[34] Because most of the men withdraw their energy from the community but bring back enough cash to meet the demands for taxes and manufactured goods, the village recedes into subsistence agriculture. In fact, a whole class of exploitative relations (especially common in colonial situations) produce something like this pattern. In the Indonesian case, according to Geertz, the exploitative plantation helped form a new, dependent type of native community. The new community forms permitted rapid population increase in the labor-intensive rural sector, but inhibited increases in per capita productivity. In the longer run, the combination of swelling population and static agricultural productivity made the entire economy more vulnerable, and more immobile. The mode of colonization contributed to the dedifferentiation of rural communities, to the freezing of economic resources and, with the eventual collapse of the plantations themselves, to the disintegration of the entire society.[35]

A third devolutionary process is the "pastoralization" of much of the French countryside which François Crouzet points out occurred as scattered industrial production organized in the domestic system gave way to city-based factories.[36] Contrary to the simplest evolutionary assumptions, a great many French communities were decidedly more "rural"—in the sense of being more exclusively devoted to agriculture and less extensively involved in production for national and international markets—in 1850 than they had been in 1750. Over that century they actually dedifferentiated. To be sure, during the same period the industry of France as a whole became more complex; it evolved. But at the level of the rural community a process of devolution took place.

The French experience of pastoralization belongs in one of the great unwritten chapters of European history. The rise and fall of the domestic system of industrial production shaped the economic life of large sections of Europe over the three centuries before 1900.[37] It even supplied many of the

34. Elliot J. Berg, "The Economics of the Migrant Labor System," in Hilda Kuper, ed., *Urbanization and Migration in West Africa* (Berkeley and Los Angeles: University of California Press, 1965), pp. 160-181.

35. Cf. Nathan Keyfitz, "Political-Economic Aspects of Urbanization in South and Southeast Asia," in Philip M. Hauser and Leo F. Schnore, eds., *The Study of Urbanization* (New York: Wiley, 1965), pp. 265-309.

36. "Les conséquences économiques de la Révolution: à propos d'un inédit de Sir Francis d'Ivernois," *Annales historiques de la Revolution française*, 34 (April-June, 1962), 182-217.

37. There are good general surveys of the domestic system (especially its growth) in David S. Landes, "Technological Change and Development in Western Europe, 1750–1914," in H. J. Habakkuk and M. Postan, eds., *The Cambridge Economic History of Europe, Vol. 6: The Industrial Revolution and After: Incomes, Population and Technological Change* (Cambridge: Cambridge University Press, 1965), Part I, pp. 274-601, plus bibliography in Part II; Hermann Kellenbenz, "Les industries rurales en Occident de la fin du Moyen Age au XVIIIe siècle," *Annales: Economies-Sociétiés-Civilisations*, 18 (Sept.-Oct., 1963), 833-882; Josef Kulischer, *Allgemeine Wirtschaftsgeschichte des Mittelalters und der Neuzeit*, 2 vols. (Munich: Oldenbourg, 1965), vol. 2, pp. 113-137; and Werner Sombart and Rudolf Meerwartn, "Hausindustrie," in *Handwörterbuch der Staatswissenschaften* (Jena: Fischer, 1923), vol. 5, pp. 179-207.

preconditions for the technical and organizational changes we call the industrial revolution. From the sixteenth to the eighteenth centuries, some rural regions in almost every European country (but especially in England, France, the Low Countries, and Germany) moved into industrial production for national and international markets on an unprecedented scale. The production of woolen, silken, linen, and (later) cotton cloth predominated; but mining, metalworking, basketry, woodworking, papermaking, and glassmaking all had their regions. The central organizational principle behind this flourishing industry-without-factories was what the Germans call the *Verlagssystem*—the arrangement whereby an enterpreneur (clothier, *Verleger, fabricant*) acquires his own raw materials, arranges for individual men and women working in their own homes to finish the material, and then markets the product. The *fabricant* working in the linen industry of Cholet (France), for example, typically bought flax in one of the markets along the Loire, sent it out to different rural workers for spinning and for weaving at so much a piece, handed it over to other local craftsmen for fulling, bleaching, and dyeing, then sold the finished cloth at one of the regional markets, whence it left for one of the major French cities, to clothe the inhabitants, or for one of the Atlantic ports, to be traded in Africa or America. In the rural communities around Cholet, at the end of the eighteenth century, at least a quarter of the population was working mainly in this form of cottage industry.

In timing and geography, the spread of this sort of rural industry crudely anticipated the later spread of factory-based industrialization. In England and the Low Countries, cottage textile industry was already spreading in the fourteenth century, fast expanding in the fifteenth and sixteenth. In France, the seventeenth century produced the great spurt of expansion; in western Germany, the early eighteenth century; in eastern Europe and Russia it came toward the end of the eighteenth century.

Unlike the earlier expansion of intercity trade in luxury goods, the growth of cottage industry appears to have depended to an important extent on the development of strong states, national markets, and big cities. Joan Thirsk has suggested that, given a potential market for cheap cloth, cottage industry most regularly arose in areas which specialized in forms of agriculture, like dairying, which were difficult or costly for any particular farmer to expand and which left significant time for subsidiary occupations, especially where inheritance rules or demographic conditions produced a considerable population with insufficient land for survival.[38] Where it developed, cottage industry reorganized local life and absorbed large numbers of people; one plausible guess concerning the England of the early eigh-

---

38. "Industries in the Countryside," in F. J. Fisher, ed., *Essays in the Economic and Social History of Tudor and Stuart England in Honour of R. H. Tawney* (Cambridge: Cambridge University Press, 1961), pp. 70-88.

teenth century is that a full tenth of the population was somehow working in the woolen industry, most of which went on in the countryside.[39]

That was the heyday. In Europe as a whole, the eighteenth century brought the apogee of domestic textile production. Then the system gave way as city and factory-based spinning and weaving took over. However, the newer forms of organization grew out of the old. Long experience with cottage industry helped prepare a country for the later forms of industriali-ation. Rudolf Braun concludes that, writing the history of industry in the uplands beyond Zurich,

Industry rooted itself in men—was planted in their breasts. This fact was especially clear for the part of the population forced to resettle. As unseen baggage these men carried with them all the skill, experience, modes of behavior, life and thought they had learned in their industrial setting, and planted industry in their new communities.[40]

The continuity in personnel and style of life between rural textile production and the factory system, in fact, appear so great to Braun that he challenges the applicability of the abrupt term "industrial revolution" to the introduction of machine production and factory organization in the Zurich region.[41]

Yet for some regions, many communities, and millions of men and women the decline of cottage industry meant a thorough change of life. Almost every European area of rural textile production felt the keen competition of cheap, well-made British cottons before the middle of the nineteenth century; that competition shook even the rural producers of Moscow's hinterland.[42] In Lancashire, the fountainhead of Britain's competitive power, "In all but the highest quality goods, and in all districts except Bolton, the day of domestic weaving was coming to its close by the end of the first half of the nineteenth century, and in weaving, perhaps even more than spinning, the urbanization of the industry was almost complete." [43] This process left the sections distant from Manchester more purely agricultural than they had been for centuries.[44] This was the process of pastoralization, the underside of the textile industry's urbanization.

It is oddly difficult to learn what happened to the millions of rural workers, and their millions of children, as their livelihood withered. Four main paths were open to them in principle, if not always in practice: (1)

39. Phyllis Deane, *The First Industrial Revolution* (Cambridge: Cambridge University Press, 1967), p. 14.
40. *Industrialisierung und Volksleben*, p. 255.
41. *Sozialer und Kultureller Wandel*, esp. p. 16.
42. Meshalin, *Tekstil'naia;* Maurice Levy-Leboyer, *Les banques européennes et l'industrialisation internationale dans la première moitié du XIXe siècle* (Paris: Presses Universitaires de France, 1964), chaps. 1-8.
43. A. J. Taylor, "Concentration and Specialisation in the Lancashire Cotton Industry, 1825–1850," *The Economic History Review*, 2nd series, 1 (1949), 119.
44. T. W. Freeman, H. B. Rodgers, and R. H. Kinvig, *Lancashire, Cheshire, and the Isle of Man* (London: Nelson, 1967), chaps. 4, 5.

hang on to their craft in the face of diminishing income and employment, (2) turn to another form of craft or agriculture, (3) remain in the countryside but travel daily for work in an industrial center, or (4) migrate cityward with the industry. Over the long run the decline of rural industry incited an enormous migration to European cities, but the other three responses endured surprisingly long. Armengaud describes this for southwestern France:

It is true that the growth of urban textile activity was accompanied by a decline, or at least a stagnation, of rural industry throughout the arrondissement of Castres. Thus the use of carding and spinning machines started the concentration of spinning to the detriment of the rural population, which lost part of its traditional means of support. People saw in this fact, among others, one of the causes of the depopulation of the mountain areas. But here, too, the reversal was slow.[45]

Elsewhere, much of the population formerly involved in industry went into agriculture. In the region of Twente (Holland), during the eighteenth century, "Linen was being steadily ousted by the use of cotton. When, in addition, cereal prices began to rise again after 1750, it meant great poverty for the weavers. Then the process went into reverse and people left industry to return to the land.[46]

They did not always return to the land peacefully. Thompson's great portrait of English working-class radicalism and rebellion in the early nineteenth century gives pride of place to the dying class of handloom weavers.[47] Their German counterparts lashed out in the Revolution of 1848.[48] In France, the massive resistance to Louis Napoleon's coup of 1851 fed especially on the anger of rural artisans.[49] Throughout Europe, the rural worker's anguished sense of being squeezed out, of losing his identity, lent a curiously reactionary tone to the otherwise radical protests of early industrialization.

In the absence of close and systematic studies, the best account I can offer of the choice among the available responses to the urbanization of industry is simply a plausible working hypothesis: in the immediate vicinity of prospering industrial cities (as in the uplands of Zurich) the former centers of rural industry became either the loci of specialized auxiliary industries or

45. André Armengaud, *Les populations de l'Est-Aquitaine au debut de l'époque contemporaine* (Paris: Mouton, 1961), p. 240. Cf. Philippe Pinchemel, *Structures sociales et dépopulation rurale dans les campagnes picardes de 1836 à 1936* (Paris: Colin, 1957).
46. B. M. Slicher van Bath, *The Agrarian History of Western Europe, A.D. 500–1850* (London: Edward Arnold, 1963), p. 218.
47. E. P. Thompson, *The Making of the English Working Class* (London: Gollancz, 1963), esp. chap. 9.
48. Theodore S. Hamerow, *Restoration, Revolution, Reaction: Economics and Politics in Germany, 1815–1871* (Princeton: Princeton University Press, 1958).
49. Georges Duveau, *La vie ouvrière en France sous le Second Empire* (Paris: Gallimard, 1946), esp. p. 100.

suburbs from which workers commuted to their factories; further out, where the land was suitable (as in the development of intensive dairying in Rossendale under the impact of Manchester's growth), communities tended to turn to specialized cash-crop farming for the urban market; where the land was too poor and the cities too inaccessible (as in the slopes of the Alps and the Pyrenees), the workers tended to hang on in misery, to drift into subsistence agriculture, and eventually to emigrate.

The first outcome fits our classical evolutionary picture; further differentiation, integration, and generalization of resources through more intense involvement in the market. The second outcome (the shift to cash-crop agriculture) fits a bit less comfortably, since it clearly means a dedifferentiation of the rural community's occupational and class structures. But the third (reversion to subsistence, followed by eventual flight from the land) does not fit at all; this is the case to which Crouzet's term "pastoralization" best applies. In the west and south of France, at least, hundreds of communities which entered the Revolution of 1789 humming with industry and deeply involved in international markets left the Revolution of 1848 isolated, depressed, and chiefly engaged in what appeared to be "traditional" agriculture. In and among these communities, the economic changes of the early nineteenth century produced dedifferentiation, disintegration, and perhaps even particularization. The evolutionary growth of industry produced a devolutionary countercurrent through important parts of Europe.

That the first three examples to come to mind have to do with rural areas suggests the possibility that devolutionary processes occur especially on the edges of the great movements of centralization and control to which analysts of social change most commonly pay attention. That is probably true. Yet I should point out that Geertz's analysis deals with a set of changes—the changes creating a "dual society"—which scholars before him treated simply and wrongly as transitional phases in the movement from traditional to modern social structure. Furthermore, other devolutionary processes sometimes occur at the very center of things: counterrevolution, population decline, rigidification, political demobilization. We have no good sociological accounts of any of them.

That two of the best historical analyses of devolution should come from anthropologists (Wolf and Geertz) is also worth pondering. Why should the social science discipline most committed to the study of nonliterate peoples and the one most dependent on literate reporters converge? No doubt a style of research and training which emphasizes familiarity with the particular case brings the two disciplines together.[50] Very likely the anthro-

50. See Robert T. Anderson, "The Flirtation of Anthropology and History," *Research Studies,* 35 (December, 1967), 291-300; Charles J. Erasmus and Waldemar R. Smith, "Cultural Anthropology in the United States since 1900: A Quantitative Analysis," *Southwestern Journal of Anthropology,* 23 (Summer, 1967), 111-140; Conrad M. Arensberg, "Anthropology as History," in Karl Polanyi, Conrad M. Arensberg, and Harry W. Pearson, eds., *Trade and Market in the Early Empires* (Glencoe: Free Press, 1957), pp. 97-113.

pologist's willy-nilly concern with the experiences of the nonliterate and semiliterate populations at the margins of the great centralizing movements encourages him to notice devolution when it occurs. Surely the fortuitous assignment of much of the responsibility for analysis of the halting evolutionary processes of "prehistory" to anthropologists has increased that sensitivity.

There is one more factor. While ethnographic field work has often produced descriptions of communities or societies set in a timeless "anthropological present," it has also disciplined anthropologists to follow smaller social units continuously when they do consider change over time. Sociologists, political scientists, and economists have an itch to follow the action, to make leaps of scale when organization on a larger scale comes into existence. More precisely, they have a propensity to work mainly on the scale of the final stage of the process, producing pictures of the integration of outlying producers and consumers into a national market, for example, rather than the *creation* of a national market through the coalescence of local ones. For this reason, we have impressively few social scientific analyses of what Etzioni calls epigenesis: "units emerge through a process in which parts that carry out new functions are added to existing ones, until the entire unit is assembled." [51] Etzioni rightly contrasts this model of social change with a differentiation model. It looks as if analysts working back through time from the largest-scale phase of a massive change process tend to find differentiation models congenial, while those working forward from the smaller scale have a greater inclination to adopt epigenetic models. And the epigenetic model is somewhat more open to the possibility of simultaneous evolution and devolution. Anthropologists confronted with large-scale processes of change have a greater predisposition than most of their social scientific colleagues to follow the smaller units continuously, to work forward from the smaller scale, and therefore to observe devolutionary processes.

The world fixation on growth, expansion, development makes processes going in the opposite direction seem unworthy of sustained attention. Certainly a workable theory of economic development is more likely to find a quick and enthusiastic application than is an operable theory of economic decline. Yet the backward processes offer a more interesting challenge to our theories of social change than do the onward-and-upward transformations. Most importantly, they challenge the postulates of unidirectionality and irreversibility.

The cases we have reviewed suggest two major ways in which evolutionary transformations regularly produce devolutionary countertransformations. The first is straightforward *particularization,* the adaptation and attachment of general social forms or resources to specific contexts of time, place, and personnel. Members of organizations subvert and rework the

51. Amitai Etzioni, "The Epigenesis of Political Communities at the International Level," *American Journal of Sociology,* 68 (January, 1963), 409.

formal structure to meet their own goals. Closely related groups of speakers of international languages develop their own idioms. Kin groups fragmented by migration and social mobility reassert their control. Satraps seize local power.

It seems reasonable (if a trifle tautological) to say that the tendency to particularization increases as the value of generalized resources available to any specific social unit rises and as the incompatibility between the goals of the subunit and of the larger structure to which it belongs rises. In the absence of strong external controls, the effect of the creation and diffusion of a valuable resource or organizational form throughout a society may well be its seizure and adaptation—its particularization—by the society's subunits, leading to a strengthening of those subunits and a reduction of the adaptive capacity of the society as a whole.

The forcible mobilization of men, services, food, and goods in early empires, the constant struggle of emperors to keep their viceroys from diverting those resources and consolidating their rules, and the consequent tendency of the imperial structure to break into multiple kingdoms at the death of the emperor illustrate the problem and the process very well. If the resources grow faster than the controls, we may well expect the outcome of such a process to be a net devolution of the entire structure. But the important point is that both processes occur simultaneously, and depend on each other.

The second major way in which evolutionary transformations regularly produce devolutionary countertransformations we might call *shrinkage*. The standard model of functional differentiation itself implies that older units, such as families, commonly emerge from differentiation with simpler structures.[52] A general movement toward industrial specialization and integration, as we have seen, ordinarily makes some jobs and organizations redundant. Expansions of the scale of social organization, as in the emergence of nation-states and international markets, regularly produce some atrophy of the smaller units which are thus merged, subordinated, or bypassed. Shrinkage differs greatly from particularization, since it comes from a reduction of the resources available to particular social units. We might therefore imagine the net devolution of an entire society occurring either as the total resources available diminished or as resources were diverted from those units most crucial to the continuation of differentiation, integration, and generalization, either through some shift within the structure or through an expansion of scale which exceeded the structure's carrying capacity. While Jones attributes the decisive blow to the barbarians, his analysis of the weaknesses of the western Roman Empire which contributed to its collapse suggests that both forms of shrinkage were occurring.

---

52. Neil J. Smelser, "Mechanisms of Change and Adjustment to Change," in Bert F. Hoselitz and Wilbert E. Moore, eds., *Industrialization and Society* (Paris: UNESCO-Mouton, 1966), pp. 32-54.

The wars and plagues of the third century must have reduced the population and at the same time there was the increased demand for men by the army. The resulting shortage of agricultural manpower evidently tempted tenants to move in hopes of better conditions elsewhere, and attracted miners and other industrial workers to the land. In the second place the great inflation must have eaten away the profit margin of such classes as the *navicularii* who were paid in money. The increasing burden of levies in kind, which the collapse of the currency and the growth of the army entailed, must have made the life of the curial class which collected them much more onerous. At the same time the expansion of the administrative machine offered tempting avenues of escape to men of this class. . . .

The government reacted, as most governments do in times of crisis, to the simplest expedient—the use of its powers of coercion to compel the existing workers and property owners to go on performing their essential functions. That the system was from the beginning made hereditary was inevitable.[53]

In terms of differentiation, integration, and generalization, Jones's description implies a net devolution of the empire's structure. But again the main point is that both evolution and devolution occur simultaneously, and depend on each other.

If there is something to this formulation, it obviously calls for historical verification. For a better understanding of particularization, we need to examine systematically how a standard structure such as the Roman imperial organization changes as men install it in one social setting after another. We could use studies of the conditions under which nepotism, occupational inheritance, and absorption of wives and children into the orbit of the firm arise to counteract the functional differentiation of work from kinship. We ought to investigate what kinds of controls have kept military men in some nations to their technical roles, while in others the military have been able to seize and divert—to particularize—the power attached to their positions. Studies of these phenomena need not, of course, be historical. Historical material simply provides the advantages for this sort of inquiry which I inventoried earlier in this chapter: the access to the very cases on which our most common models of such social changes are based, the availability of a time span long enough for the process to work itself out, the observation of the phenomenon in a wide variety of settings.

Historical materials are also likely to make the analysis of shrinkage easier and more effective than cross-sectional contemporary studies could. Investigations of exactly how the inventory of occupational positions (or, for that matter, simply of occupational titles) in a labor force changes over considerable spans of time are curiously lacking. We all know that the net movement has produced a dizzy increase in the variety of positions in western countries since 1900; but how many disappeared, and how? Likewise,

53. A. H. M. Jones, *The Later Roman Empire,* 3 vols. (Oxford: Blackwell, 1964), vol. 2, pp. 1050-1051.

close analysis of changes in the structure of cities and city-states as they became incorporated into nation-states would provide important information concerning the devolutionary concomitants of increases in scale.[54] The feasibility of following smaller units of this sort continuously over long periods of time makes historical material peculiarly attractive for the study of shrinkage.

Yet we finally face a paradox. History abounds in devolutionary processes, yet the historical record itself conceals them. The very association of documentary production with centripetal movements slants the record to some extent against devolution. Just as the development of large-scale organization and central controls tends to accelerate the production of written records, particularization and shrinkage tend to choke it off. In addition, historians, like their sociological brethren, have themselves fixed their gazes on centralizing, differentiating, modernizing evolutionary changes when they could find them. Since they have so often taken their mandate to be the preparation of an account of how our contemporary world came into being, that is hardly surprising. That is one of the best reasons for insisting that sociologists cannot hope to work successfully with historical materials if they do it the easy way: by plucking the accounts the historians have prepared. The historians have too often ignored the facts of greatest sociological importance.

Still, the bias toward evolution rather than devolution in historical material, and even in historical writing, is slighter than that displayed in contemporary sociological theory and material. Two related phenomena reduce the evolutionary bias: first, the tendency of a record-producing routine, once established, to continue within the same unit over a substantial period of time and thus to permit the tracing of that particular unit's experience through changing social conditions; second, the tendency of the routines which produce documents to grind on, grind on after they have become relics. Sociologists can capitalize on these tendencies by taking one more cue from the historians: in the analysis of very large processes of change, make sure to follow continuously the experiences of the smaller units which at first stand alone, and later melt into the crowd.

I am not exhorting sociologists to desert their calling for history. We have already seen some ways in which history is being transformed by contact with the social sciences; a number of historical phenomena and materials are becoming the special concern of demographers, political scientists, and other nonhistorians. In any event, "historical material" is no less than the

54. Given the general evidence of devolution affecting whole classes and regions of Europe after 1550, the aggressive expansion of nation-states, the subjugation of communes and classes to the fiscal and military power of kings, and the furious civil strife of the time, I believe the much-debated "Seventeenth-Century Crisis" in Europe might profitably be examined as a devolutionary crisis. Many of the best statements on the subject are conveniently collected in Trevor Aston, ed., *Crisis in Europe* (London: Routledge, 1965); and Lawrence Stone, *Social Change*.

residue in the present world of all previous human behavior. In that sense, it already belongs to all the social sciences.

The residue, especially the part which is most comprehensible and accessible, is selective. It favors the activities and men involved in large-scale, complex organizations. The selectivity of historical materials, however, is no harder to contend with practically or theoretically than the selectivity of the procedures sociologists use to collect information about the contemporary world. In fact, as they again become concerned to account for large structural changes in societies, sociologists turn willy-nilly to historical material. The great danger there is that too few will push beyond the collation of published historical accounts to the systematic analysis of primary historical materials, and that sociologists will thereby compound the errors of the historians from whom they draw.

In the process, sociologists will find their conceptions of social change faulty, at least in some respects. The usual assumptions of unilinearity and irreversibility, in particular, will run afoul of the widespread historical evidence of devolutionary countermovements in times of evolutionary movement. Regardless of the theoretical revisions the encounter with history forces on sociologists, however, that encounter will open a vast space to sociologists who have worked, cramped, in the present. Their presence in the space of history will enrich and transform the writing of history itself.

17.

Complementary Approaches to Societal Analysis: The Economic versus the Sociological

Joseph J. Spengler

Joseph J. Spengler was born in Piqua, Ohio, in 1902 and was educated at Ohio State University (Ph.D.). Mr. Spengler, now James B. Duke Professor of Economics at Duke University, has published a number of essays on Southern economic and demographic problems and antebellum Southern economists. He has also published books and articles on the demography of France, economic development, population problems, and social and economic theory and its history. Mr. Spengler is coeditor of Population Theory and Policy *and* Essays in Economic Thought: Aristotle to Marshall. *He is a past president of the Population Association of America and of the American Economic Association.*

"The world rarely fits into the taxonomic classifications of pedagogues." [1]

"The economist, almost alone, takes man as he exists, and does not spend his effort in dreaming of man's perfectibility." [2]

"It is this purpose, of rendering familiar, when they have happened, the unprecedented events of life, which theory serves." [3]

The subject of this essay might be dealt with historically, perhaps with the assistance of both the sociology and the economics of knowledge. After all, many of the earlier sociologists (such as Pareto, E. A. Ross, Charles Cooley) had been economists before they turned to sociology. They did this, as a rule, in their search for what they believed to be more adequate explanations than they supposed economics to be capable of yielding. Indeed, as Parsons has shown, many economists, having found the concepts of orthodox economic theory inadequate to supply a "full theoretical explanation of a body of *concrete* facts, the facts of 'economic life' or of 'economic activities,'" sought to introduce additional elements to account for these facts. One possible outcome of this course of action might be an economics which was but a "branch of applied sociology" which was intended to explain "human conduct in general." [4]

This empiricist and essentially nontheoretical alternative was rejected by Parsons as incompatible with a theoretical science, either of economics or of sociology. The empiricist basis underlying this alternative needed rather to be abandoned altogether. One might instead, Parsons reasoned, limit eco-

1. P. A. Samuelson, *Foundations of Economic Analysis* (Cambridge: Harvard University Press, 1947), p. 320.
2. James Buchanan, "Economics and its Scientific Neighbors," in S. R. Krupp, ed., *The Structure of Economic Science* (Englewood Cliffs: Prentice-Hall, 1966), p. 175.
3. G. L. S. Shackle, *The Nature of Economic Thought* (Cambridge: Cambridge University Press, 1966), p. 3.
4. Talcott Parsons, "The Sociological Elements in Economic Thought. I. Historical," *Quarterly Journal of Economics,* 49 (May, 1935), 414-453, esp. 451-453; and *Structure of Social Action* (New York: McGraw, 1937), chaps. 1-4. Italics mine.

nomics "to the analytical abstraction of one of the fundamental factors in human action and its study for the purposes of the systematic formulation of theory in 'artificial' isolation from the rest"; one would then have to define sociology correspondingly.[5] This approach had indeed been that of Durkheim, Pareto, and Weber. From his analysis of their views Parsons inferred that, "if we look at human action from the 'subjective' point of view of the means–end relationship, economic theory occupies an intermediate position in the chain from ultimate means to ultimate ends." [6] Economic rationality emerges as the distinct concern of analytical, nonempiricist economics. Similarly, "common value integration," or "the role of ultimate common values" emerges as the concern of theoretical sociology. Distinct concerns assignable to politics and psychology also emerge.[7] It follows that a reasonably full explanation of collections of events is likely to require the cooperation of several social sciences. I touch upon their separate contributions in what follows.

A careful study of the scientific career of many an outstanding social scientist would reveal his confrontation by and response to difficulties of the sort earlier economists and sociologists faced. This is exemplified in the developing thought of Adolph Lowe, whose active career has been in a period marked by much greater intervention, usually in response to problems seemingly calling for collectivist action, than characterized the pre-1914 western world. Lowe describes how he gave up his early opinion that a universally applicable economic theory fitting all types of economic systems was possible. He continued for a time, however, to suppose that industrial market systems behaved regularly enough for their phenomena "to be formulated in laws of coexistence and succession." Even this view he subsequently found incompatible with experience—whence he developed what he calls "political economics." Of this economics "traditional economics is . . . a limiting case"; it holds only when "action directives and expectations of the micro-units *spontaneously* conform to those which are suitable to achieve one particular good, namely, the state of macro-equilibrium." This is seldom the case. In all other situations controls are necessary, and "political" rather than "traditional" economics is essential to concrete analysis and policy formation. The role of "political economics" is then to facilitate the bringing into existence of "the conditions—structural, behavioral, and motivational—which assure goal attainment." [8] This approach, while not

5. "Sociological Elements in Economic Thought. II. The Analytical Factor View," *Quarterly Journal of Economics,* 49 (Aug. 1935), 646-647.
6. Ibid., p. 662.
7. Ibid., pp. 662-666; *Structure of Social Action,* pp. 765-768, and chaps. 18-19, passim. See also my "Sociological Presuppositions in Economic Theory," *Southern Economic Journal,* 7 (Oct., 1940), 131-157, and "Generalists versus Specialists in Social Science: An Economist's View," *American Political Science Review,* 44 (June, 1950), 358-379.
8. Adolph Lowe, *On Economic Knowledge* (New York: Harper and Row, 1965), pp. xvii-xix, 311-322; also *Economics and Sociology* (London: Allen, 1935).

concerned with sociology as such, seems to involve the inclusion within the focus of economic inquiry of some elements which lie in the realm of sociology and politics. It does not permit as sharp a demarcation between economics and sociology, therefore, as does Parsons's approach described above.

Having described how several scholars have interpreted the relation of economics to sociology, I shall approach my assignment differently. It is to articulate economic and sociological theory. Doing this satisfactorily requires one to determine the respective capabilities of the two sciences. If these capabilities were known, it would be possible to indicate just where the one science might complement the other in the analysis of particular problems. Each social science, as Parsons showed, has developed "its own analytical pattern" and achieved "some explanatory processes." These "separate patterns are entirely autonomous, i.e., irreducible into each other," at least in the present state of social-science development. Whence, though the boundaries of a social science are subject to change, a single, monistic social science does not appear attainable.[9] Comtean dreams remain dreams.

Economics and sociology can, however, supplement one another. First, since any discipline can identify a range of possibilities, a supposed development or finding may be declared impossible if it lies outside the range of possibilities confirmed by a given science.[10] Second, while economics (sociology) may offer a more complete explanation of concrete phenomena than unaided sociology (economics), sociology (economics) may provide a supplementary explanation and thus enlarge the total explanation.[11] In general if $B = f (E_i, S_i, R_i)$ and empirical correspondents to these symbols are available, we can relate behavior B functionally to E_i, S_i, and R_i where these symbols denote subsets of economic, sociological, and residual determinants of behavior.

Since I am not able to assess the comparative capabilities of economics and sociology in general or with regard to specific problems, I shall proceed differently. I shall first deal generally with contrasts between economics and sociology and then compare them in a number of respects. This approach should provide some information regarding the comparative capabilities of the two sciences and perhaps illuminate the uses which each may make of modern theoretical, methodological, and instrumental findings (for example, communication theory, game theory, systems theory, simulation models, computers). The topical discussion is presented under the following headings. (1) Are the units of analysis comparable? (2) Is there a sociological

9. See W. Leontief, "Note on the Pluralistic Interpretation of History and the Problem of Interdisciplinary Cooperation," *Journal of Philosophy*, 45 (Nov. 4, 1948), 617-624, esp. 618-620.
10. Shackle observes that "in a world containing men there may or may not be laws determining what *will* happen, laws of necessity; but there are at any rate laws which effectively limit what is *possible*." *A Scheme of Economic Theory* (Cambridge: Cambridge University Press, 1965), p. 196.
11. Leontief, pp. 620-624.

distinction parallel to the distinction made in economics between micro- and macro-analysis? (3) Is the universe with which the economist deals at all isomorphous with the universe with which the sociologist deals? (4) Is there a parallel between the economist's and the sociologist's conceptions of statics and dynamics? (5) How does the concept of causation employed in sociology compare with that used in economics?

Economics and Sociology: Contrast

While economics and sociology resemble each other, they also differ significantly. In this section I shall point to sources of the contrast, aspects of which are treated in later sections. Margenau's analysis may be drawn upon to bring out the contrast. A theory, he states, embraces a complex of rational constructs or concepts (the *C*-field) and sensory elements or protocol experiences (the *P*-field). Protocols are given. Concepts, while associated with and corresponding to *P*-facts, are invented so that "reason" can "enter the scene." Sciences are either descriptive or explanatory, with the latter developing out of the former. When a science is descriptive it is essentially inductive, consisting almost entirely of correlations between *P*-facts and in but small measure of rudimentary theories amounting to slight excursions into the *C*-field. Rules exist for "passing from a given *P* to its counterpart in *C*." In time, enough counterparts in *C* to elements sensed in *P* may be constructed to support propositions sufficiently abstract and general to serve as sources whence lesser propositions, theorems, and laws may be deduced. Then what began as a descriptive science has become a deductive explanatory science consisting of interconnected concepts which can increasingly account for experience in the *P*-field. *C*-field constructs must find empirical verification through manifestation of predictive power in the *P*-field and, if necessary, meet supplementary criteria.[12]

Theory is thus an economic product which performs an economic role, though not always without producing noneconomic effects. "It is the object of science to replace, or *save,* experiences, by the production and anticipation of facts in thought." [13] Yet, even though an idea "originates in empirics" it can, as do mathematical ideas, begin "to live a peculiar life of its own." [14] It may then mislead researchers or become a brake on intellectual progress

12. Henry Margenau, "What Is a Theory?" in *Structure of Economic Science,* pp. 25-26.
13. Ernst Mach, "The Economy of Science," in James R. Newman, ed., *The World of Mathematics,* vol. 3 (New York: Simon and Schuster, 1956), p. 1787. Accumulated theory also serves instrumental needs, according to Nicholas Georgescu-Roegen. "Theory means a logical filing of *all* extant knowledge in some particular domain such that every known proposition be either contained in the logical foundation or deducible from it." *Analytical Economics* (Cambridge: Harvard University Press, 1966), p. 108.
14. John von Neumann, "The Mathematician," in *The World of Mathematics,* 4, 2063.

unless reinvigorated in empirics. A concept misleads when it is applied to a place or time period to which it is not applicable. Illustrative is the use of a modern concept of "frontier" to explain early American history.[15] A concept retards progress when it prevents the emergence or diffusion of needed new concepts. Illustrative is the reaction in 1913 to Niels Bohr's model of the hydrogen atom in which Bohr described the behavior of electrons going around the nucleus. "The proposal was so out of tune with the long-established laws of classical physics that even some very intelligent physicists said they would rather give up physics than admit such an arbitrary hypothesis. And yet with Bohr's model so many facts fell into place that one had to take it seriously." [16] Here we have illustrated Boulding's restatement of D'Arcy Thompson's principle, "Growth creates form, but form limits growth." Growth produces closure by sealing off "all the growing edges, the 'loose ends' of systems [of thought] that are their effective growing points." [17]

Neither economics nor sociology deals directly with the *P*-field. Each translates many elements in the portion of the *P*-field with which it is concerned into primitive constructs (such as family, tribe, group, price, supply, demand) and some into more abstract and general concepts. Economics approximates an explanatory science more closely than does sociology.

Somewhat in contrast to other social scientists, economists have begun to study and apply the full methodology of the scientific enterprise; have seen the need for careful, unambiguous, and reproducible rules of correspondence to effect the transition from *P* to *C;* and have come to recognize exact mathematical theories and their confirmation. . . . Crude facts . . . are translated into objective constructs by very specific operational definitions which make these protocol facts objective, meaningful, quantifiable, and subject to logic and mathematics. And the theories which are blossoming forth take on increasing refinement and predictive power.[18]

While economists make use of models which, while internally valid, may not fit any real-world situation, they also employ models which roughly fit and "explain" particular situations.[19]

15. J. T. Juricek, "American Usage of the Word 'Frontier' from Colonial Times to Frederick Jackson Turner," *Proceedings of the American Philosophical Society,* 110 (Feb. 18, 1966), 10-34.
16. O. R. Frisch, in a book review in *Scientific American,* 216 (June, 1967), 145.
17. K. E. Boulding, "Toward a General Theory of Growth," reprinted in J. J. Spengler and Otis Dudley Duncan, eds., *Population Theory and Policy* (Glencoe: Free Press, 1956), pp. 120-121. Compare also A. N. Whitehead on conservation and change. *Science and The Modern World* (New York: Macmillan, 1947), p. 289.
18. Margenau, pp. 37-38.
19. M. Bronfenbrenner, "A 'Middlebrow' Introduction to Economic Methodology," in *The Structure of Economic Science,* pp. 9-10. "A model is an abstraction, a map, an idealization, a dramatic heightening of supposed essentials . . . . Without a model, . . . we cannot even discern a fact or classify it." Shackle, *Nature of Economic Thought,* pp. 117-118.

The economist's *P*-field is smaller and less heterogeneous than that of the sociologist, though he could render it larger and more heterogeneous by departing from definitions which restrict economic subject matter to man's behavioral response to scarcity [20] and including subject matter less suited to economic analysis as practiced.[21] The economist seems to have a clearer notion regarding the attributes of economic phenomena than does the sociologist regarding "sociological" phenomena which still constitute a less well-defined residuum.[22] This is important in that one's models and theories and generalizations must fit the phenomena under analysis even though many of the statistical, mathematical, and other analytical techniques employed are common to each area of inquiry. The phenomena with which one concerns oneself determine also the degree to which one can file them, explain much by little (which has long been an objective of economic-hypothesis makers), and devise hypotheses which predict the consequences of action.[23] Multiplicity of detail can, of course, swamp thought and inquiry, progress in which turns on ideas which reflect and give meaning to details.[24]

Today both sociologist and economist are professionals, having become such within the past seventy-five to eighty-five years, especially with the revolutionary emergence since 1945 of so-called American social science. Each scientist accordingly is held to the standards of his profession, being carefully watched lest he depart from the ruling standards of scientific inquiry, verification, and dissemination. He lives under an "apparatus which makes violation of the principal tenets of scientific probity unprofitable." [25] The beneficial effect of this constraint may be somewhat diluted, however, in that so much of the demand for the services of economists (sociologists)

20. Bronfenbrenner's definition is representative. "Economics is the systematic study of social adjustment to, and management of, the scarcity of goods and resources" (p. 6). While economists differ widely respecting the content of economics, it usually includes rational, choosing behavior. See I. M. Kirzner, *The Economic Point of View* (Princeton: Van Nostrand, 1960).
21. K. E. Boulding, for example, suggests that economics is social science applied to economic problems while S. Schoeffler observes that economics is not "an autonomous, self-sufficient discipline" nor a "nomothetic empirical science," dealing as it does with an open system. See Boulding, *A Reconstruction of Economics* (New York: Wiley, 1950), p. viii; Schoeffler, *The Failures of Economics: A Diagnostic Study* (Cambridge: Harvard University Press, 1955), pp. 155-156, 158-161.
22. Even so, "our knowledge of the relevant facts of economic life is incomparably smaller than that commanded by physics at the time when mathematization of that subject was achieved." J. von Neumann and O. Morgenstern, *Theory of Games and Economic Behavior,* 3rd ed. (Princeton: Princeton University Press, 1953), p. 4.
23. For example, see Milton Friedman, *Essays in Positive Economics* (Chicago: University of Chicago Press, 1953), pp. 8-9, 11-15. Cf. L. J. Henderson, *Pareto's General Sociology* (Cambridge: Harvard University Press, 1935), p. 110-112. For an approach stressing limitations to economic predictability see G. L. S. Shackle, *Decision, Order and Time in Human Affairs* (London: Cambridge University Press, 1961).
24. Whitehead, p. 269.
25. Gordon Tullock, *The Organization of Inquiry* (Durham: Duke University Press, 1966), pp. 130-133.

comes from economists (sociologists) that they are relatively free of a variety of external market-oriented restraints and may, therefore, as has priestcraft in the past, engage in undertakings of little utility to the community at large so long as they are not offensive and retain financial support.[26] Economics probably enjoys some advantage over sociology inasmuch as economic ideas are less semantics-ridden and less likely to run counter to popular feelings and more likely to be considered applicable.[27] Each is at a disadvantage, however, compared with many natural sciences and hence less likely to progress as rapidly.

Both economics and sociology are at another disadvantage compared with both organic and inorganic science. An economic or sociological model is less isomorphic with its real referent than is a natural science model. Moreover, this referent may change through time since either the subsystems of a social system, or the social system, or their interrelations may change, whereas the referent of the physical science model tends to stay put. Furthermore, the effect of this tendency to change cannot be escaped, as in physical science, through reducing the components of a society or economy to immutable elements. Indeed, at least limited mutability is characteristic of all the elements with which the economist and the sociologist deal. Accordingly, while social theory can direct observation, observation of empirical change can bring about change in theory as well as in the concrete world to which it relates. Whence, argues Georgescu-Roegen, the principles of economics (and, we may add, of sociology) can be universally valid only in a formal sense, but not in a substantive sense, since their content is "determined by the institutional setting." [28] What is empirically relevant and valid in one setting or period may not be so in another.[29] In some measure, the changes taking place in economics after 1920 may have been in part a response to new settings, or to the view that there were new settings.[30]

Units of Analysis

The units of analysis of interest to the economist are few and, as a rule, relatively simple. So long as he is a micro-economist he deals with one form of human behavior, the behavior of individuals qua individuals, or as mem-

26. Ibid., p. 191. In contrast, the great English economist Alfred Marshall (1842-1924) wanted to be read by businessmen. See J. A. Schumpeter, *Ten Great Economists* (New York: Oxford University Press, 1951), p. 97.
27. Tullock, p. 179-191. Fritz Machlup, *Essays on Economic Semantics* (Englewood Cliffs: Prentice-Hall, 1963).
28. *Analytical Economics,* p. 109, also 113-114. It will be recalled that Thorstein Veblen often commented on neglect of institutional change by his economist contemporaries. See his *The Place of Science in Modern Civilization* (New York: Huebsch, 1919), passim; also the *Journal of Economic Issues,* vol. 1 (1967), devoted to evolutionary economics. Georgescu-Roegen illustrates his observation in his "Economic Theory and Agrarian Economics," pp. 359-397.
29. See Ibid., pp. 108-129.
30. Shackle, *Nature of Economic Thought,* pp. 13-14, 51-58, 64-67.

bers of small systems, who in effect are engaged in choosing among available alternatives. The alternatives open to such individuals are always numerous, since they consist not only of a variety of objects of choice but also of a variety of quantities of most objects of choice. If these objects are purchasable, how much (if any) a chooser will take of any one depends on its price, upon the prices at which other objects are available, and upon the purchasing power at his disposal. "We are constantly weighing apparently heterogeneous objects of desire against each other and selecting between them according to the terms on which we can secure them." [31] Given explicit choice, therefore, more will always be preferred to less. Hence it is easy for the economist to predict the outcome of choosing, at least roughly, if not with precision.

Who does the economic choosing? Individuals! They may choose for themselves or for systems including themselves; that is, for households, for small or large business firms or other organizations (such as trade unions), for agencies of the state. Choosing behavior may relate to inputs into productive undertakings or consumption, or to outputs of human effort or of goods and services. That which appears to be preferable will be chosen, given the governing time-horizon and the degree of uncertainty attaching to alternatives. Moreover, while the range of rational economic choice is subject to technological constraints and the operation of diminishing returns in one of its various guises, something like the optimization of choice is facilitated by the presence of a monetary medium of exchange and of markets tied together by an economic nexus.[32]

So long as the economist's emphasis is upon choosing behavior, his capacity for prediction is fairly high. Indeed, some economists, particularly Milton Friedman, judge an economic generalization or hypothesis (which should amount to an explanation of much by little) by its capacity to abstract what is crucial from the mass of circumstances "surrounding the phenomena to be explained [and] predict the consequences of changes in circumstances." [33] When the economist departs from prediction based upon micro-analysis of man's response to price and income changes, his predictive power greatly diminishes. Then he no longer has a tested theory of behavior on which to rest his predictions, and he may not have a specific objective to maximize.

In the field of macro-economics, for example, as noted later, relatively

31. Philip H. Wicksteed, *The Common Sense of Political Economy,* vol. 1 [1910] (London: Routledge, 1933), p. 13.
32. Wicksteed first pointed out that the marginal utility of any commodity could serve as the unit of utility, given that utilities were not interrelated, and suggested that the pain incurred in an hour of correcting examination papers might serve as the unit of utility. *The Alphabet of Economic Science* [1888] (New York: Kelly & Millman, 1955), p. 53.
33. *Essays in Positive Economics,* pp. 8-9, 14-15, 39. For critiques of Friedman's assertion that the realisticness of a model and its assumptions is not relevant, see Eugene Rotwein, "On 'The Methodology of Positive Economics'," *Quarterly Journal of Economics,* 73 (Nov. 1959), 554-573; also Bronfenbrenner, pp. 9-10, 14-18.

little predictive power is encountered.[34] Over longer time-periods, of course, even micro-economic models lose predictive power; conditions that remain relatively constant in the short run undergo change, and often in relatively nonpredictable ways. The present does not flow out of the past in a precisely predictable fashion, since the economic cosmos is not a machine.[35] Stochastic forces, too, may become operative and tend to mislead the analyst.[36]

The units employed in a social science, while always systems, are chosen in light of two conditions. What is that social science's sensory field like? What are the aims of the practitioners of the social science in question? Economists have always been concerned with the economic consequences of changes in circumstances, particularly of those in price and income. These changes function through motivational channels, though constrained by the framework in which economic behavers are situated.

The sociologist's aims have often been otherwise. It is true, of course, that the dependence of a mathematically formulated social process upon motivation is demonstrable.[37] It is also true that the economic theory of choice is considered applicable to noneconomic variables.[38] It may even be shown that uncritical analysis of choosing behavior produces incorrect results. Thus the Hawthorne data indicate that work performance depends upon financial reward, yet it was long associated with satisfactions.[39] It can be shown that often the group or system studied by the sociologist is engaging in choosing as well as in other behavior. When this is so, behavior usually can be found to be more predictable than is behavior gotten at through multivariate analysis and empirically generalized.[40] Of course, if behavior under analysis is subject to regularity (for known or unknown reasons), or under the control of a stochastic or some other equilibrating process, it may be predictable in the aggregate.[41]

The sociologist deals with choosing behavior even as does the economist. With respect to choosing behavior, however, the economist has several advantages over the sociologist. Economic goals are more precise, as a rule, than noneconomic goals. The system within which economic goals are

34. For example, see Schoeffler, chap. 6; also Shackle, *Scheme of Economic Theory,* pp. 184-189.
35. Shackle, *Nature of Economic Thought,* pp. 11-12.
36. William Feller, *An Introduction to Probability Theory and Its Applications,* vol. 1, 2nd ed. (New York: Wiley, 1960), pp. 67-68, 83-85.
37. Harrison White, "Uses of Mathematics in Sociology," in J. C. Charlesworth, ed., *Mathematics and The Social Sciences* (Philadelphia: American Academy of Political and Social Science, June, 1963), pp. 90-94.
38. E. V. Schneider and S. Krupp, "An Illustration of the Use of Analytical Theory in Sociology: The Application of the Economic Theory of Choice in Non-Economic Variables," *American Journal of Sociology,* 70 (May, 1965), 695-703.
39. Alex Carey, "The Hawthorne Study: A Radical Criticism," *American Sociological Review,* 32 (June, 1967), 403-416.
40. For example, see James S. Coleman, *Introduction to Mathematical Sociology* (Glencoe: Free Press, 1964), pp. 25-34, 52-53, 189-240.
41. Ibid., chaps. 11, 15.

sought is less open than that within which most noneconomic goals are sought. Of course, when noneconomic choice is ruled by habit, or when there is little change in the circumstances surrounding this choice, the sociologist is better able to forecast choice approximately. Economic goals, though ultimately specific, may initially appear in the guise of general-purpose purchasing power whose significance can be quite well perceived by those whose behavior is under analysis. Despite the disadvantages faced by a sociologist studying choosing behavior, the incorporation of choice into his analytical models increases their power.

Macro- vs. Micro-Approaches

Both economics and sociology deal with systems, with systems that may be analytically but not substantively isolated from more inclusive systems.[42] Even the most irreducible of the units with which these sciences may deal are systems—man, family, small group, and so forth. A macro-system, whether in economics or in sociology, is an assemblage of interacting systems; it may range in size and inclusiveness from one made up of two or more interacting minimal-unit systems to one including all *relevant* lesser systems which interact within an all-inclusive and enveloping societal system. In sociology the latter type would correspond to that which Pareto seems to have had in mind in his *Trattato di Sociologia;* in economics, merely a subsystem of a more inclusive social or societal system, it would correspond to the type Walras described [43] or to that implied by Quesnay, Adam Smith, or Ricardo.

What constitutes macro-economics or macro-sociology then turns on how large a system must be dealt with in order for its analysis to be describable as macro-economic. It is here taken for granted that the subsystems or components of a macro-system interact; otherwise the approach is oriented to one or more subsystems and not to the macro-system.[44] In the early history of both economics and sociology proto-macro-approaches were dominant, mainly because methods of analysis suited to lesser systems were slow to develop. Thus the approaches of the physiocrats, the classical economists, and the Marxists were essentially at a

42. See Georgescu-Roegen, pp. 101-107.
43. *Elements of Pure Economics* (London: Allen, 1954), trans. William Jaffe from the Edition Definitive of the *Eléments d'économie politique pure,* 4th ed. (Paris: R. Pechon et R. Durand-Auzias, 1926). The first edition was published in 1874. For a complete modern exposition, see R. E. Kuenne, *The Theory of General Economic Equilibrium* (Princeton: Princeton University Press, 1963).
44. For example, when a firm or industry is abstracted out of the economy, or when a model relates to a group as such instead of to a system of groups. On the latter distinction see Leo A. Goodman, "Mathematical Methods for the Study of Systems of Groups," *American Journal of Sociology,* 70 (Sept. 1964), 170-192.

macro-level, and so were those of Comte and most nineteenth-century sociologists, among them predecessors of the approach of Parsons and his "school." A micro-approach became ascendant in the later nineteenth century when incremental analysis and study of the behavior of firms and households and industries became important, mainly as a result of the work of Cournot, Von Thunen, and the marginalists. Having become ascendant, the micro-approach long remained so. General acceptance of Say's Law, together with the absence of heavy and persisting unemployment, kept attention away from systematic problems of the sort J. M. Keynes later dealt with.[45] Furthermore, while the Walrasian system made clear the interdependence of the components of an economy, and thus enabled analysts to see the economic system as a totality, it was not suitably aggregated to contribute nicely to policy formation,[46] and it did not yield substantive hypotheses as did Alfred Marshall's partial equilibrium theory and his small-system models of industries and firms.[47] Meanwhile, in sociology the macro-approach continued to be dominant though it failed to generate many productive hypotheses; models adapted to the effective analysis of elementary social systems were much slower to develop in sociology than in economics.

Today the macro-approach virtually enjoys parity with the micro-approach, though not on grounds suited to reasonably good prediction. In economics the popularity of macro-approaches is traceable to the advantages supposedly yielded by various input–output and related models (such as the Brookings–SSRC model) as well as by Keynesian and related models, all of which disaggregate the economy in considerable measure and seek to explain its workings. For example, input–output models enable one to see how a change is diffused through an economy, say an increase in wages or a shift from war to peace, given the parameters and the functional relations built into these models. Keynesian-type models seem to be able to "explain" unemployment, to suggest remedies, and to facilitate realization of certain goals.[48] Of perhaps greatest importance, since the equations

---

45. *General Theory of Employment, Interest and Money* (New York: Harcourt, Brace, 1936).

46. While Keynes proliferated micro-economic variables and brought "on the stage a crowd of individual earners, consumers, employers and so forth," he aggregated the "economic doings of the members of each of these classes" and treated "each aggregate as a single whole." Thus Keynes initiated *aggregative* or *macro-economics*. Shackle, *Scheme of Economic Theory*, p. 44.

47. See Milton Friedman, "Leon Walras and His System," *American Economic Review*, 45 (Dec. 1955), pp. 900-909. Shackle observes that Marshall's failure to supply "a universal principle of explanation able to cope with all economic phenomena" was corrected by the Paretian notion of general equilibrium founded upon Walras's work, but only imperfectly so since it did not include Keynes's concerns. *Nature of Economic Thought*, pp. 13-15, 50-52.

48. Keynesian macro-economics serves to inform the nation "how best to accomplish certain of its goals through budgetary policy." See J. S. Coleman, "Individual Interests and Collective Action," in Gordon Tullock, ed., *Papers on Non-Market Decision Making* (Charlottesville: University of Virginia Press, 1966), p. 58.

describing these models have counterparts in national income and other data, the models are adaptable to governmental manipulation even though realization of sought objectives is by no means assured.[49]

In sociology the macro-approach has continued ascendant both because useful small-system models comparable to economic models of firms and industries have not flourished and because functionalism usually assumes a macro-form. In consequence, sociology has tended to stress the self-maintenance of large societal systems and to move from the understanding of the whole to the understanding of the parts, whereas economics has tended to stress the behavior of lesser units and systems and to proceed from a study of interaction among small systems to an understanding of the whole economy and the development of capacity to manipulate the whole economy.

Functionalist theory focuses on the unity and directedness of a total system, while mechanistic theory tends to concentrate on the precise determination of relationships between parts of a system. Functionalist theory assumes a system to have a basic organizing principle of goals and self-regulating mechanisms. Mechanistic theory takes a system to be derived from relationships between the parts. Both types of theory, organizing their explanations in different ways, develop equilibrating systems.[50]

Macrofunctionalism, with its emphasis upon pattern variables and roles is best represented in the work of Parsons and his followers. Its equilibrative mechanisms are contrasted with those of economics below.[51]

While macro-analytical approaches have revealed aspects of economic and social behavior that micro-analytical approaches overlook, they suffer from a number of handicaps. By focusing excessively upon system-maintaining behavior and its significance for the behavior of subsystems, they exaggerate the role of structure and macro-system and, at least in sociology, neglect or underestimate the role and variability of behavior at subsystem and small-system levels. This tendency is intensified by the fact that macro-economics lacks a psychological underpinning comparable to that undergirding micro-economics. In Buchanan's words, macro-economics remains "a set of models for the workings of economic aggregates, models that have

49. Walter W. Heller, *New Dimensions of Political Economy* (New York: Norton, 1967); K. M. Carlson, "The Federal Budget and Economic Stabilization," *Review of Federal Reserve Bank of St. Louis,* 49 (February, 1967), 5-12, and "Estimates of the High Employment Budget: 1947–1967," ibid. (June, 1967), 6-14.
50. S. R. Krupp, "Equilibrium Theory in Economics and in Functional Analysis as Types of Explanation," in Don Martindale, ed., *Functionalism in the Social Sciences* (Philadelphia: American Academy of Political and Social Science, Feb. 1963), p. 65.
51. See Ian Whitaker, "The Nature and Value of Functionalism in Sociology," in *Functionalism in the Social Sciences,* pp. 127-143; Martindale, "Limits of and Alternatives to Functionalism in Sociology," in ibid., pp. 144-162. Micro-functionalism relates to small systems. See also Robert E. Dowse's critique of the use of functionalism in the political analysis of underdeveloped polities. "A Functionalist's Logic," *World Politics,* 18 (July, 1966), 607-622.

little predictive power." [52] The individual is responding, not to specific stimuli, but to the very general and conditional changes. He is responding to his interpretation both of changes in the actual and/or prospective general environment and of the prospective responses of other individuals to these changes. Similar defects characterize macro-sociology.[53] One does not find in sociological theory an effective bridge between its macro- and its micro-approaches. Moreover, sociological theory is lacking in capacity to come to empirical grips with the real worlds with which macro-sociological models are intended to be isomorphic.

R. K. Merton's middle-range theories have not provided a bridge at all comparable to that found in economics,[54] in part because, as we indicate in the following section, sociology has not developed a network of reciprocity to connect the components of the systems it studies. It is not surprising that Jules Henry inferred from an "inventory of scientific findings" [55] that "intellectual failure" was the most evaluative term to be applied to the "behavioral sciences." [56] Henry makes eleven points, each of which derives from the failure of behavioral science to concern itself with "human existence"; it lacks "an existential concept of man." Variables are misconceived, truism is not distinguished from discovery, causal sequence is confused, variables are misperceived, and platitude, tautology, and the delusion of precision are tolerated. Issues are avoided, too simple parallels are drawn, multiparaphrasis is indulged, and the law of homologous extrapolation is disregarded.[57]

The main strength of economics still lies at the micro- or subeconomic-system level. Its advantage over sociology in this respect may be associated with the greater age of economics, the greater homogeneity of its subject matter,[58] and its assuming form in an age when the Newtonian image was dominant. Even so, with the progress of specialization within the confines of both economics and sociology and the resulting emergence of subunits in each science, commonality of concern between a particular economic and a particular sociological subunit sometimes becomes manifest. In other words, the image some economists (sociologists) have of that portion of the world upon which they focus attention resembles closely that which some sociologists (economists) have of this same portion of the world.

52. "Economics and its Scientific Neighbors," p. 170.
53. For example, see Schneider and Krupp, pp. 695-697.
54. *Social Theory and Social Structure* (Glencoe: Free Press, 1957), passim.
55. Presented in Bernard Berelson and G. A. Schneider, *Human Behavior* (New York: Harcourt, 1964).
56. In a review of *Human Behavior* in *Scientific American,* 211 (July, 1964), 129.
57. Ibid., also pp. 129-134.
58. It is not incorrect to say that sociology initially concentrated on a variety of diverse and unappropriated subject matter. However, see L. L. Bernard and Jessie Bernard, *Origins of American Sociology: The Social Science Movement in the United States* (New York: Russell and Russell, 1965).

They can, therefore, supplement one another's work, provided that their concerns do intertwine.[59]

According to the classical mechanical view of nature (which replaced the Aristotelian view but later proved inapplicable to electrical and optical phenomena), "all phenomena can be explained by the action of forces representing either attraction or repulsion, depending only upon distance and acting between unchangeable particles."[60] This view was ascendant in the eighteenth and early nineteenth centuries and hence influenced the economist's image of that part of the world with which he dealt.[61] The economist's theory of equilibrium and equilibration and hence his view of statics and dynamics have, therefore, run in terms of mechanistic theory despite the failure of mechanical models to meet all the needs of the physicist.[62]

The emphasis on stable equilibrium, which has been basic to functionalist theory, is regarded mainly as a special case of equilibrium [in economics]. . . . Unstable and dynamic systems are explored. As a result, homeostatic mechanisms of self-regulation are merely special kinds of forces and are not basic to equilibrium. The equilibrating systems of economic theory, unlike those of the other social sciences, are more neutral with respect to goal-maintaining or integrating qualities of systems. In contrast, functional theory commonly predisposes analysis to those equilibrating forces which make for co-operation and harmony, and reduces the forces which move the system away from a stable equilibrium of high goal achievement.[63]

The economist conceives of every economic decision-maker as a maximizer. The consumer or household, it is assumed, endeavors to maximize the expected satisfaction to be derived from the expenditure of a given income, or income stream, with prices as they are. This is true whether the decision-maker is on relief or self-supporting, though in the latter case he must also determine how much or little of his time is to be devoted to work. Sensitivity to price and other changes tends to vary inversely with how much discretionary time and income are at the decision-maker's disposal. Each firm also endeavors to maximize something. Let us call this something net profits, or the present value of the return of the projected stream of gross returns over the projected stream of costs incurred to yield gross return. Given our assumption regarding maximizing, we can

59. K. E. Boulding, *The Image* (Ann Arbor: University of Michigan Press, 1956).
60. Albert Einstein and Leopold Infeld, *The Evolution of Physics* (New York: Simon and Schuster, 1938), p. 67.
61. See David Hamilton, *Newtonian Classicism and Darwinian Institutionalism* (Albuquerque: University of New Mexico Press, 1953), pp. 7-8, 28-35.
62. For example, Einstein and Infeld, chaps. 2-4.
63. Krupp, "Equilibrium Theory in Economics," pp. 65-66. Krupp develops his discussion on pp. 66ff. He draws somewhat upon Ernest Nagel, *The Structure of Science* (New York: Harcourt, 1961).

infer each maximizer to be behaving in a way that carries him to an equilibrium position, subject to price and income conditions and to the degree of competition characteristic of the economy. A general equilibrium would tend to result, given mutual compatibility of expectations [64] and the absence of possible sources of disequilibrium and indeterminacies.[65]

An optimal social order can be conceived of as a system in which the constraints imposed on individuals are just sufficient, and no more stringent than necessary, to admit a determinate solution to the simultaneous maximizing activities of its members. If there are too many constraints, there is a needless lack of freedom—the constraints could properly be called coercive; and if there are too few, there is necessarily a certain kind of disorder, or indeterminateness.[66]

The presence of incomplete information and uncertainty, together with consequent difficulties for the would-be maximizer, has given rise to two approaches which differ from one stressing maximization as such. It is impossible, in a world shot through with uncertainty, for a decision-maker to make, and then be guided by, a *unique* definition of rational behavior. In an uncertain world, therefore, "the goal of maximizing" should be replaced, it is said, "by the goal of satisficing, of finding a course of action that is 'good enough'." [67] For, given uncertainty, the adaptiveness of an organism's behavior falls short of the economist's rational ideal of optimizing. Yet, an individual's behavior-directing aspiration level may undergo change in the light of his capacity or incapacity to attain it until a satisfactory outcome develops.[68] Economic man thus gives place to administrative man who "satisfices" since he cannot maximize.[69] "A variety of solutions is therefore possible to organizational equilibrium," together with a variety of explanations.[70] When satisficing is stressed, as in organization theory, the focus of inquiry tends to be shifted. Thus "organization theory" deals with the firm "as a self-contained unit" whereas economic theory "relates the firm to the economy" [71] and seeks to "explain, predict, and legislate, in the broadest possible manner, a competitive economy." [72]

A second approach, biological in nature, and hence in keeping with the

64. F. A. Hayek, *Individualism and the Economic Order* (London: Routledge, 1949), chap. 2.
65. These are discussed by John S. Chipman, in "The Nature and Meaning of Equilibrium in Economic Theory," in *Functionalism in the Social Sciences,* pp. 35-64.
66. Ibid., p. 63.
67. H. A. Simon, *Models of Man* (New York: Wiley, 1957), pp. 204-205; see also pp. 170-175.
68. Ibid., pp. 253, 261.
69. H. A. Simon, *Administrative Behavior,* 2nd ed. (New York: Macmillan, 1958), pp. xxiv-xxvi.
70. Sherman Krupp, *Pattern in Organization Analysis: A Critical Examination* (Philadelphia: Chilton, 1961), pp. 111-113.
71. Ibid., p. 53.
72. Ibid., p. 11.

early use of biological models in economics,[73] has been put forward by
A. A. Alchian in order to get around the assumption "that firms attempt
to maximize profits in a world characterized by uncertainty about the future." [74] Although " 'profit maximization' is a *meaningless* guide to specifiable action" when foresight is uncertain, some firms realize profits and
survive whereas others do not and hence fail. It may be said, therefore,
that the methods of profitable firms make for survival whereas those of the
profitless firms do not. Whence it is in order to imitate and adapt the
methods of innovative and hence surviving, profitable firms. Survival becomes a test in the economic as in the biological world. "The economic
counterparts of genetic heredity, mutations, and natural selection are imitation, innovation, and positive profits." [75] The economic theorist who ana-
lyzes this selective process can, with present tools, "predict the more adaptable or viable types of economic interrelationships that will be induced
by environmental change even if individuals themselves are unable to
ascertain them." [76] This approach has been extended by Enke, who shows
that the economist predicts the characteristics of the firms which survive
intense, profit-eliminating competition. Among these characteristics is recourse to marginal analysis.[77]

Universe: Economic, Sociological

Perhaps the outstanding advantage enjoyed by the economic theorist over
the sociological theorist consists in this: the economist is dealing with an
all-encompassing system consisting of many interacting lesser systems,
whereas the sociologist is dealing with a discontinuous, Balkanized world
smelling here and there of a clinic. The units with whose behavior the
economist is concerned are bound together by the price system—or the
market, as common parlance has it [78]—to changes in which economic

73. E. T. Penrose, "Biological Analogies in the Theory of the Firm," *American
Economic Review,* 42 (Dec., 1952), 804-818. A. Marshall, writing in an age of small
firms, developed a "life cycle" theory of the firm, while C. R. Noyes, writing much
later, examined firm behavior in homeostatic terms. Ibid., pp. 804-809, 816-819. See
also my "Evolutionism in American Economics, 1800–1946," in Stow Persons, ed.,
Evolutionary Thought in America (New Haven: Yale University Press, 1950), pp.
202-266.
74. Penrose, p. 810.
75. Alchian, "Uncertainty, Evolution, and Economic Theory," *Journal of Political
Economy,* 58 (June, 1950), 211, 220.
76. Ibid., p. 220. Veblen's defense of evolutionary economics is not grounded upon
reasoning such as Alchian's. See Veblen's *The Place of Science,* chap. 3.
77. Stephen Enke, "On Maximizing Profits: A Distinction Between Chamberlin and
Robinson," *American Economic Review,* 41 (Sept. 1951), 566-578, esp. pp. 576-578.
See also my comment on marginalism in "Evolutionism," p. 252.
78. "The 'market' or market organization is not a *means* toward the accomplishment
of anything. It is, instead, the institutional embodiment of the voluntary exchange
processes that are entered into by individuals in their several capacities." J. M.
Buchanan, "What Should Economists Do?" *Southern Economic Journal,* 30 (Jan.
1964), 219.

behavioral units respond until they are satisfied and the system is in a kind of transitory equilibrium, though variously subject to the presence of constraints which help to define equilibrium at any point in time. The economist thus has his attention focused always upon bargaining and·the equilibrating process as well as upon the state of equilibrium toward which the economy apparently is being carried, even when external or other events are generating economic disturbance.[79] His belief in the usefulness of comparative statics is not, therefore, surprising.[80] The sociologist faces no such system. At best he may confront himself with a Parsons–Smelser or Levy type of system,[81] or with a Pareto type,[82] each of which is essentially a filing cabinet rather than a network of interrelated and interacting behavioral units. In sum, interrelatedness dominates the world of the economist whereas discontinuity and anarchy rule in much of that of the sociologist.[83]

This needs to be so. In fact, Pareto emphasized interrelatedness, though he insisted that the "social system" is "much more complicated" than an "economic system . . . made up of certain molecules set in motion by tastes and subject to ties (checks) in the form of obstacles to the acquisition of economic values." [84] A less complicated approach than Pareto's, though not one intended to serve all his purposes, is available. This approach focuses upon interaction systems of concern to economist, sociologist, social psychologist, political scientist, and others. It serves to connect

79. David McCord Wright, *Economics of Disturbance* (New York: Macmillan, 1947).
80. K. E. Boulding, "In Defense of Statics," *Quarterly Journal of Economics,* 69 (Nov. 1955), 485-502. See also P. A. Samuelson, *Foundations of Economic Analysis* (Cambridge: Harvard University Press, 1947), pp. 258, 311.
81. Talcott Parsons and Neil J. Smelser, *Economy and Society* (Glencoe: Free Press, 1956); also Talcott Parsons, *The Social System* (Glencoe: Free Press, 1951). Marion Levy's currently utilized system is developed and applied in *Modernization and the Structure of Society* (Princeton: Princeton University Press, 1966), vol. 2, pp. 503-570. Levy deals only with economic exchange.
82. "The form of a society is determined by all the elements acting upon it, and it, in turn, reacts upon them." The elements include both those external to a given society and those internal to it. They are not independent; "for the most part, they are interdependent. . . . If we intend to reason at all strictly, our first obligation is to fix upon the state in which we are choosing to consider the social system, which is constantly changing in form." V. Pareto, *The Mind and Society* (New York: Harcourt, Brace, 1935), paras. 2060, 2067.
83. "In the usual situation in economics, the universal validity of money makes the jointness of resource limitations obvious. . . . In sociological and political analysis, there is a greater tendency to separate different value areas and ignore their interrelations both on the value and on the resource sides." K. J. Arrow, "Utilities, Attitudes, Choices: A Review Note," *Econometrica,* 26 (January, 1958), 3. However, see Georg Karlsson, *Social Mechanisms* (Glencoe: Free Press, 1958). He not only tries to explain much by little in the realms of diffusion, choice, and interaction, but also to identify the mechanisms.
84. Para. 2079.

in each of these areas of concern facts of essentially the same kind, and it can lead to explanation by enabling relations among theoretical concepts to mirror corresponding relations among observables.[85] This approach would focus upon reciprocity, or, more specifically, the interaction underlying the network of reciprocity peculiar to one or more of the areas of behavior of concern to economists, sociologists, political scientists, and so forth.

Within each of these areas a relationship of reciprocity is to be found; and where this relationship is found one necessarily finds exchange, the means through which stable, reciprocal relationships are achieved and maintained. "Exchange is, after all, only a particular expression of this more general, and often more subtle, relationship [of reciprocity]." [86] The Golden Rule implies, "not that society is composed of a network of explicit bargains, but that it is held together by a pervasive bond of reciprocity." [87] Reciprocity, while voluntary in origin, imposes a moral and legal duty upon the parties involved in a *given* bargain or transaction.[88] Life in a free world may thus be viewed as an endless string of more or less specific bargains voluntarily entered into, temporally limited, and entailing rights and duties, most of which are essentially legal in character. Exchange resulting in reciprocity greatly expands man's freedom of combination and movement by minimizing obstacles to his transacting as well as by augmenting the range within which mutually acceptable bargains may be found.[89] The world of exchange and reciprocity is not, therefore, a world of "mutually exclusives" but one of "adjustment, of coordinated conflict, of mutual gains" [90]; it is one in which symbiosis rules, in which dissimilars associate for mutual benefit.[91] This approach is not wholly new,

---

85. R. Harré identifies two kinds of theory, "reticular" theories "which connect up sets of facts all of the same kind" and "explanatory" theories "which explain one set of facts by adducing another and different set of facts." *Matter and Method* (London: Macmillan, 1964), pp. 8-9, also 15, 18. R. W. Pfouts points out, however, that the reticular element in economic theory "is impermanent and variable." "Artistic Goals, Scientific Method and Economics," *Southern Economic Journal,* 33 (April, 1967), 466.
86. Lon L. Fuller, *The Morality of Law* (New Haven: Yale University Press, 1963), p. 19. See also Peter M. Blau, *Exchange and Power in Social Life* (New York: Wiley, 1964), pp. 25ff., 92-95, 314-315. In recent years, social scientists have been trying to apply to science the concept of a social system within which exchange of information takes place. See W. D. Garvey and B. C. Griffith, "Scientific Communication as a Social System," *Science,* 157 (Sept. 1, 1967), 1011-1016; Norman Kaplan, ed., *Science as a Social System* (Chicago: Rand McNally, 1966).
87. Fuller, p. 20.
88. Ibid., pp. 23-24.
89. On some of these matters, see ibid., pp. 23-24, 27.
90. Buchanan, "Economics and its Scientific Neighbors," p. 168, applied these words to the economist's world.
91. Buchanan, "What Should Economists Do?" pp. 217-218.

of course. It was stressed by some eighteenth-century writers [92] long after it had been assigned importance by Aristotle.[93]

The environment of concern to the economist is largely an exchange environment, one in which exchange is the main organizing agency, serving, by bringing about alterations in the terms on which individuals trade, to direct them into activities of which men want more and out of those of which men want less. Exchange may thus be viewed as a positive-sum game in that all parties to a transaction benefit even though price changes do tend to modify the distribution of incomes in the short run.[94]

Buchanan argues cogently that economists, as theorists, should concern themselves exclusively with how men attempt to "accomplish their own purposes, whatever they may be," through voluntary exchange that results in mutually satisfactory agreements regarding terms and volume of trade and gives rise to the "market" or "network of relationships that emerges or evolves out of this trading process." [95] The voluntary agreements arrived at may range, of course, from simple ones involving individuals to complex institutional arrangements adapted to the supply of public goods and the reconciliation of individual and collective interests and even to the voluntaristic exchange process underlying the contract theory of the state.[96] "Economics is the study of the whole system of exchange relationships. Politics is the study of the whole system of coercive or potentially coercive relationships." [97] The emerging field of non-market decision-making is focusing attention upon processes by which private and collective interests can be reconciled through exchange.

At issue here is the role of exchange and reciprocity in society, along with its study, and not the question of the degree to which sources of "organic solidarity" must buttress associations based upon "contractual relations." [98] This question was brought to the fore by the contractual approach of Spencer and the utilitarians and its neglect of undergirding

---

92. These "saw the division of labour as a principle originally pulling men together into society and also as the force carrying the society towards a high level of cultural, artistic, and intellectual achievement." M. L. Myers, "Division of Labour as a Principle of Social Cohesion," *Canadian Journal of Economics and Political Science,* 33 (Aug. 1967), 432.

93. See my "Hierarchy vs. Equality; Persisting Conflict," in *Kyklos* (April, 1968).

94. For example, see K. E. Boulding, *Conflict and Defense* (New York: Harper, 1962), chap. 10. On the "distributional" aspect of bargaining see T. C. Schelling, *The Strategy of Conflict* (Cambridge: Harvard University Press, 1960), chap. 2.

95. "What Should Economists Do?" p. 219.

96. Ibid., pp. 219-221.

97. Ibid., p. 220.

98. Parsons, *Structure of Social Action,* p. 311, also 101-102, 235-236. Auguste Comte recognized both the increasing importance of specialization and exchange and the significance of social bonds, thus noting oversights in the economist's treatment of division of labor as Durkheim did later. David Cohen, "Comte's Changing Sociology," *American Journal of Sociology,* 71 (Sept. 1965), 171-175.

elements.[99] "Exchange processes in a division of labour involve relations of contract"; and contracts, being social relationships, involve "non-contractual elements of contract" which "articulate precisely with traditional economic theory." [100]

Buchanan's emphasis upon the role of exchange has elements in common with the views of both nineteenth-century individualists and that of J. R. Commons and his followers. "The Science of Political Economy has therefore arisen out of conflicts of interests, and out of efforts to convert conflicts of interests into an idealistic harmony of interests." [101] Commons found in transaction the "ultimate unit of activity, which correlates law, economics, and ethics [and which must], contain in itself the three principles of *conflict, dependence,* and *order.*" This unit embraced the participants in a transaction as well as "the alienation and acquisition, between individuals, of the *rights* of future ownerships of physical things, as determined by the collective working rules of society." Bargaining is involved. "The *transfer of these rights* must therefore be negotiated between the parties concerned, according to the working rules of society, before labor can produce, or consumers can consume, or commodities be physically delivered to other persons." [102] Commons distinguishes three kinds of transactions: bargaining, managerial, and rationing.[103] The latter two, however, may be viewed as sequels to prior bargaining transactions.

Exchange, as was noted earlier, gives rise to reciprocity. Reciprocity is not, however, a homogenous good except insofar as it can be reduced to terms of a common psychological denominator. Economic reciprocity is the form most easily achieved, because both a price system and a monetary medium of exchange exist and facilitate the comparison of alternatives. Political reciprocity and sociological reciprocity are achieved through exchange even as is economic reciprocity, but without the assistance of a price system and a medium of exchange except insofar as money can contribute to solutions by enabling both parties to a bargain to translate that which is at issue into monetary terms. The development of sociological as of political exchange is handicapped in the absence of suitable institutional frameworks comparable to the market.

99. "What is omitted is the fact that these transactions are actually entered into in accordance with a body of binding rules which are not part of the *ad hoc* agreement of the parties. . . . The 'institution' of contract—the rules regulating relations of contract—has not been agreed to by the parties but exists prior to and independently by any such agreement." Parsons, *Structure of Social Action,* p. 311.
100. Parsons and Smelser, p. 184. "Economic theory is a special case of the general theory of social systems and hence of the general theory of action." Ibid., p. 306; also 307-308 on non-economic factors.
101. John Rogers Commons, *Institutional Economics* (New York: Macmillan, 1934), p. 109.
102. Ibid., p. 58. Italics mine.
103. Ibid., pp. 59-69.

Exchange takes place within political markets [104] as well as in economic markets, between agencies of the state, within agencies, and between groups in a society acting through representatives and spokesmen. There may or may not exist what Simon calls a "region of viability," within which lie the terms of trade of advantage to each trading party.[105] Outside this region lie terms which a stronger party may impose on a weaker party, though not with confidence that such imposition will be costless or sustainable. Political reciprocity does not result; the bargain, though enforceable, is unlikely to give rise to stability. Relevant in the present context, however, is the fact that political exchange and reciprocity have much in common with economic reciprocity. Most individuals are, or can be, members of groups through which agreement upon political objectives can be achieved and then given expression in larger and larger areas with the result that a kind of shadow political market may be brought into being.[106] If membership entails costs, however, and a group is large, the individual may be unwilling to support the group since he will benefit through its activities whether he supports it or not. The group, in short, is supplying a "public good" which he can enjoy as a free rider at no cost to himself.[107] There may, however, be other reasons why such a group exists and continues to function.[108]

Turning finally to sociological exchange.[109] Within nearly all groups one finds a heterogeneity of interests. If, as often happens, heterogeneity is excessive, it needs to be diminished through bargaining on the part of members with diverse interests. A stable outcome will result, however, only if the terms fall within a range comparable to what above we called a "region of viability." As in political exchange so also in sociological

104. James Madison seems to have had something like this in mind in No. 10 of *The Federalist,* written in 1787.
105. Simon, *Models of Man,* pp. 185-187. See also Schelling, chap. 2, on the actual process of hard bargaining; also Blau, chap. 5.
106. In reality, of course, the shaping of the "views" upon which members of a group supposedly "agree" is often dominated by a minority. Then the opinions of many count for much less than they would if they were dollars in a market place. Odd Ramsöy, *Social Groups As System and Subsystem* (Glencoe: Free Press, 1963), pp. 86-100, 180-201.
107. Mancur Olson, Jr., *The Logic of Collective Action* (Cambridge: Harvard University Press, 1965), chap. 1; also R. E. Wagner's review in Tullock, ed., *Papers on Non-Market Decision Making,* pp. 161-170.
108. Ibid., pp. 163-167.
109. A need for bargaining in small groups arises when one or more members are unable to coordinate their activities with those of other members. This need tends to increase with the size of a small group. As groups grow larger, therefore, "norms become increasingly important, both because consensus is so difficult to attain and (without norms) interferences in response sets are so likely to occur." See J. W. Thibaud and Harold H. Kelley, *The Social Psychology of Groups* (New York: Wiley, 1959), pp. 220-221, 254-255; also E. E. Jones and H. B. Gerard, *Foundations of Social Psychology* (New York: Wiley, 1967), pp. 644-645. "Bargaining is likely to occur when each person controls resources desired by the other and a range of agreements can be made that will benefit both persons more than no agreement" (ibid., p. 707).

exchange, the process of bargaining is rendered difficult by the heterogeneity of that which is exchanged and by the absence of a standard monetary unit in terms of which to express that which is exchanged and compare it to alternatives. Sociological exchange gives rise to reciprocity even as does political exchange. Analysis of each, therefore, resembles analysis of economic exchange.

Blau points out that there "are a number of similarities between social ～～～～～～ ～～～ ～～～～～～～ ～～～～～～ Individuals who do favors for others expect a return, at the very least in the form of expressions of gratitude and appreciation. . . . Individuals must be compensated for social rewards lest they cease to supply them, because they incur costs by doing so, notably the cost of alternatives foregone by devoting time to the association. The principle of the eventually diminishing marginal utility applies to social as well as to economic commodities. . . ." There are also dissimilarities. "Social exchange entails unspecified obligations. There is no contract, and there is no exact price. A person to whom others are indebted . . . cannot bargain with them over how much his favors are worth, and he has no recourse if they fail to reciprocate altogether, except, of course, that he can . . . discontinue to do favors for them. . . . Social exchange requires trust. . . . The gradual expansion of the exchange permits the partners to prove their trustworthiness to each other . . . The mutual trust between committed exchange partners encourages them to engage in a variety of transactions . . . and these diffuse transactions give the partnership some intrinsic significance. Only impersonal economic exchange remains exclusively focused on specific extrinsic benefits, whereas in social exchange the association itself invariably assumes a minimum of intrinsic significance." [110]

Consideration of the parallels between economic and social exchange focuses the attention of the analyst upon what may be called the *n*-problem, a problem recognized in economic theory but emphasized in game theory.[111] The behavior of the exchangers is a function of, *inter alia,* their number which conditions the expectations of each participant, their capacities for influencing the outcome, and the actual outcome. Concentration upon effects associated with variation in the size of *n* should contribute significantly to sociological knowledge and theory.

Statics and Dynamics

Several distinctions are essential to a discussion of statics and dynamics within a particular social science. First, the system of variables (such as

110. Blau, pp. 314-315.
111. For example, see J. C. C. McKinsey, *Introduction to the Theory of Games* (New York: McGraw, 1952), pp. 2-3.

quantities or prices) in whose determination the analyst is interested must be distinguished from the environment, or "matrix of conditions," within which the system is situated. Second, the specific variables to be treated as unknowns must be differentiated from the variables chosen to be treated as data. Which of the latter are so treated turns on the problem under consideration and the rapidity with which particular parameters change or processes move. One may, therefore, treat as data those variables in which changes proceed slowly, provided that the equilibrium process under consideration is relatively short-run in nature. Third, a distinction is necessary between the historical and causal. Within the framework of a system the relationships between the variables chosen to constitute it "are strictly those of mutual interdependence. . . . Once the conditions of equilibrium are imposed, all variables are simultaneously determined." Equilibrium itself, if attained, "displays certain properties." These enable us to deduce "certain properties of the resulting functions between our unknowns and parameters" and to study the "responses of our equilibrium unknowns to designated changes in parameters" or parts of the environment which are treated as explicit parameters.[112] Our equilibrium system may, of course, involve one variable or many variables, with *ceteris paribus* assumptions more numerous the smaller the number of variables and (hence) the larger the number of things taken as data.[113]

The task of comparative statics can be accomplished only if an initial equilibrium subject to external disturbance is succeeded by a new and different equilibrium, the system being convergent. This task, as Samuelson states, is to "show the determination of the equilibrium values of given variables (unknowns) under postulated conditions (functional relationships) with various data (parameters) specified." [114] Comparative statics may both illuminate the dynamic properties of a system and yet depend formally upon dynamics; then its equations describe "a special case of the general dynamic analysis." [115] This relation holds only for simpler types of dynamic systems, however.

Samuelson distinguishes four main categories for grouping the behavior of systems. (1) A system may be static and stationary; then the relevant variables behave in a constant or periodically repetitive fashion. (2) A system may be static and historical, as when, though statical, it is subject to irregular external disturbances or to a trend to which it adapts instantaneously. (3) A system is dynamic and causal (nonhistorical) if (a)

112. Samuelson, pp. 7, 9, 19-20, 330-331, also 21-23 on maximizing behavior.
113. Ibid., p. 8.
114. Ibid., p. 257.
115. Ibid., pp. 262, 284. Chaps. 9-10 deal with this dependence, with the "correspondence principle, enunciating the relationship between the stability conditions of dynamics and the evaluation of displacements in comparative statics" (p. 350). Don Patinkin shows that the "correspondence principle" fits only simpler types of dynamic systems. "Limitations of Samuelson's 'Correspondence Principle'," *Metroeconomica*, 4 (August, 1952), 37-43.

"its behavior over time is determined by functional equations in which 'variables at different points of time' are involved in an 'essential' way," and (b) its behavior "depends only upon its initial conditions *and the time which has elapsed.*" (4) A system is dynamic and historical (or incompletely causal) when it reacts to unexplained external data (such as technological change) "noninstantaneously or in a dynamic fashion." [116] To this list of categories Samuelson adds two more, (5) stochastical and nonhistorical and (6) stochastical and historical. Case (5) refers to instances in which the shocks to which a dynamical system is subject are regarded as random draws from a fixed universe. Case (6) refers to dynamical systems, "containing stochastical variables, and where either the structure of the system varies in an essential way with time, or where the universes characterizing the random variables change in an essential way with time.[117]

While the relevance of any one of these six categories may turn on how economics (or sociology) is bounded,[118] it is unlikely that a nonhistorical category will be sufficiently isomorphic with its empirical referent unless that referent is small.[119] The evolutionary nature of the economic process "precludes a grasping of its relevant aspects by a static scheme." [120] In the field of social science facts are less permanently connected by reticular theories than in that of natural science; in social science, therefore, explanatory theories have greater scope as well as greater capacity for discovering

---

116. As Leontief points out, "a small, hardly perceptible mistake in the description of the original base year position of an unstable dynamic system is bound to bring about a major error in the prediction, that is, explanation of its later states." The historian is well advised, therefore, to begin with the present or recent past and move backward, instead of conversely. "When Should History Be Written Backwards?" *Economic History Review,* 16 (August, 1963), 1-8, esp. 3-4. Hence he describes " 'comparativism' as a method of scientific inquiry" to be "greatly overrated" (p. 6).
117. Samuelson, pp. 314-317.
118. It may be noted here that, as H. A. Simon points out, "disciplinary boundaries remain rather effective barriers to the sharing of knowledge in areas that are certainly of common concern to economics and the behavior sciences, and areas to which all these disciplines have much to contribute. It is doubtful whether existing disciplines constitute a satisfactory frame of reference for the sciences of man." "Economics and Psychology," in Sigmund Koch, ed., *Psychology: A Study of a Science,* vol. 6 (New York: McGraw, 1963), p. 720. See also Samuelson, p. 316.
119. "To translate a problem into mathematical terms consists of defining at least a partial isomorphism between this problem and an adequate mathematical structure." Claude Flament, in his preface to his *Applications of Graph Theory to Group Structure* (Englewood Cliffs: Prentice-Hall, 1963). "The main object of sociology is . . . the building of theoretical models which approximate social reality as closely as possible." Karlsson, *Social Mechanisms,* p. 9.
120. Georgescu-Roegen, *Analytical Economics,* p. 107. "Evolutionary elements predominate in every concrete economic phenomenon of some significance . . . . If our scientific net lets these elements slip through it, we are left only with a shadow of the concrete phenomenon . . . . The sin of standard economics is the fallacy of misplaced concreteness, by which Whitehead understands 'neglecting the degree of abstraction when an actual entity is considered merely so far as it exemplifies certain [pre-selected] categories of thought' " (p. 106). See also chap. 11, on "economic theory and agrarian economics," and on "misplaced concreteness"; also Whitehead, pp. 75, 77, 85.

hidden mechanisms.[121] Prognostic power presupposes that "the future is a mere *interpretation or algebraic manipulation of the past*," that the "economic cosmos is in fact a machine," and that we "can discover enough about this machine" to have "a true, final grasp of its essential nature" and hence to be able to "calculate the future." [122] This presupposition is not met. In such a world "decision is illusory" whereas in the empirical world of creative decision, "a determinate future" is nonexistent.[123] Caprice and uncertainty are present and the future is shaped in part by men's imagination today of an unknown tomorrow.[124] "The conceptual entertainment of unrealized possibility becomes a major factor in human mentality" and hence a source of novelty and unpredictable change, observes Whitehead. "Science can never foretell the perpetual novelty of History." [125]

Static as well as dynamic sociological theory, while similar to economic theory, encounters much more difficult problems than the latter. The boundary-maintaining motivations and mechanisms animating lesser and greater social systems seem to be weaker than their economic counterparts and hence more susceptible to disorder of external or internal origin. Unpredictable change seems also to play a greater role than in economics where the effect of unpredictable change remains small at first, though growing through time, especially in larger systems. There is also less of a tradition of explaining much by little in sociology than in economics.[126]

Let us, with Davis, identify functionalism with sociological theory [127] and postulate that society is an essentially orderly and stable system consisting of interacting lesser systems which also tend to be orderly and stable. We may then further suppose that certain functions, or their equivalents, are essential to the operation and persistence of a society, though performable by any one of a number of combinations of systems or agencies.[128]

---

121. R. W. Pfouts, pp. 459-461, 465-466. See also Richard Stone's discussion of prediction in his *The Role of Measurement in Economics* (Cambridge: Cambridge University Press, 1951), pp. 27-37.
122. Shackle, *Nature of Economic Thought*, pp. 11-12, 13-14.
123. Ibid., pp. 74, 85, also 83-84, 104, 110, 118.
124. Shackle, *Scheme of Economic Theory*, pp. 186-187, also 5-6. When chance is introduced into the Walrasian model, stable equilibrium is no longer produced by the ordinary price mechanism. K. Borch, "Equilibrium in a Reinsurance Market," *Econometrica*, 30 (July, 1962), 424ff.
125. A. N. Whitehead, *Modes of Thought* (New York: Putnam, 1938), pp. 36, 80, 119, 142.
126. Karlsson, however, seems to be attempting to explain much by little in his *Social Mechanisms*.
127. Martindale has identified eleven more types. "Limits and Alternatives," 160-162.
128. On the postulates of functionalism see Kingsley Davis, "The Myth of Functional Analysis as a Special Method," reprinted in S. M. Lipset and N. J. Smelser, eds., *Sociology: The Progress of a Decade* (Englewood Cliffs: Prentice-Hall, 1961), pp. 52-54. See also Don Martindale, *The Nature and Types of Sociological Theory* (Boston: Houghton Mifflin, 1960), chaps. 17-19; Levy, passim. P. A. Sorokin touches upon the distribution of societal functions in *Social and Cultural Dynamics*, vol. 3 (New York: American Book, 1937), pp. 43-138.

We may therefore infer that some sort of equilibrium tends to come into existence at various levels,[129] though always subject to internal and external sources of change which may modify the distribution of functions among lesser systems and the conditions of equilibrium for the all-inclusive system itself. The analytical task then confronting the sociologist is more difficult than that confronting the economist because the boundaries of sociology are wider than those of economics, and the sociological analyst deals with nonrational as well as with rational behavior.[130] This task, of course, includes finding "the social mechanisms that make society work," perhaps even mechanisms analogous to those which impel irrational economic decision units to respond rationally to changes in opportunities.[131]

Two components of the functional approach are of use both to the sociologist and to the economist. First, the existence and persistence of a society implies that provision has been made for the continuing performance of specific tasks or their equivalents, the number and character of which vary with society and condition its complexity. Second, how these tasks are performed is not predetermined; they may be variously distributed among agencies or subsystems. It is probable, however, that within limits inferior distributions will give place to a superior one, though not necessarily to the optimal one. These tasks become the responsibility of individuals working within a variety of smaller systems or subsystems and subject to motivation from within such system or systems and not from the all-inclusive social or economic system which envelops the lesser systems.

Causation

What has been said in the preceding section tells us a great deal about "causation" in economics and sociology.[132] If we have defined and imposed conditions of equilibrium, we may speak of cause only in respect "to changes in external data or parameters" of our system of mutually interdependent variables, but not to the adjustment of variables to one another within the system. [133] These changes may be sufficiently great to modify the initial equilibrium. What produced these changes in the first place may,

129. "An equilibrating system relates structure (i.e., the relatively invariant properties of a system) to behavior variables and, through structural properties, relates behavior variables to one another." Krupp, *Pattern in Organization Analysis,* p. 39.
130. Davis, pp. 55-56.
131. Karlsson, *Social Mechanisms,* p. 9; also G. S. Becker, "Irrational Behavior and Economic Theory," *Journal of Political Economy,* 70 (Feb. 1962), 1-15.
132. R. M. MacIver's approach is more genetic, more historical, treating cause as a precipitant which gets a system out of an equilibrium situation. See *Social Causation* (New York: Ginn, 1942), chap. 6, also chaps. 9, 11.
133. Samuelson, pp. 9-10, 315n., 317-320. See also T. Parsons' "Cause and Effect in Sociology," in Daniel Lerner, ed., *Cause and Effect* (New York: Free Press, 1965), pp. 51-74.

however, be difficult if not impossible to identify with precision. The sources of social evolution seldom can be dealt with meaningfully, nor can the presence of a statistical association prove anything.[134] Yet, as Simon shows, when the relationship between two variables in a model is asymmetrical, the term *cause* "can perform a useful function and should be retained." [135]

Three factors account for the difficulties that beset the use of a principle of causality in social science. First, response to stimulus may be taking place within an essentially closed system. Second, since not all the conditions essential to the operation of the principle of causality are present, as a rule, one must be content in social science with noncausal explanation.[136] Third, as has already been suggested, a degree of indeterminacy characterizes the homosphere [137] as well as the sphere of nature.[138] At a minimum, as Feuer points out, "at every great historical crisis" the laws of the affected social system break down and "an interval of existential indeterminacy ensues." [139] Of greater importance is the presence of random statistical processes.

Stochastic processes can account for the emergence of cycles and the persistence of trends.[140] "It may be (and probably is) chasing a will-o'-the-wisp to suppose that social behavior is determined by principles of least something-or-other," writes M. G. Kendall in respect of Zipf's "principle of least effort," the economist's supposition of profit maximization, and the model-fitter's assumption that Nature minimizes his errors.[141] Various economic and demographic distributions are the product of Chance which not only "can mimic choice" but also acts "in a very inegalitarian way." [142]

134. See Samuelson, "Causality and Teleology in Economics," in *Cause and Effect*, pp. 103-104.
135. *Models of Man*, pp. 11-12, 50ff.
136. Abraham Kaplan, "Noncausal Explanation," in *Cause and Effect*, pp. 145-155. See also Parsons, in ibid., pp. 62-63; also Ernest Nagel, "Types of Causal Explanation in Science," in ibid., pp. 11-26, and *The Structure of Science* (New York: Harcourt, Brace, 1961), chap. 14. See also W. Tatarkiewicz, "Nomological and Typological Sciences," *Journal of Philosophy*, 57 (March 31, 1960), 234-240.
137. The term is Kenneth Boulding's. See B. F. Hoselitz, ed., *Economics and the Idea of Mankind* (New York: Columbia University Press, 1965).
138. On indeterminism in the physical world, see Nagel, *Structure of Science*, chap. 10; also pp. 464, 505-508, on indeterminism in social science.
139. Lewis S. Feuer, "Causality in the Social Sciences," in *Cause and Effect*, pp. 205-207.
140. For example, see Eugen Slutzky, "The Summation of Random Causes as the Source of Cyclic Processes," *Econometrica*, 5 (April, 1937), 105-146. "Most stochastic processes in physics, economics, and education are of this nature, and our findings should serve as a warning to those who are prone to discern secular trends and deviations from average norms." See Feller, p. 68, also pp. 83ff.
141. "Natural Law in the Social Sciences," *Journal of the Royal Statistical Society*, ser. A, vol. 124, part 1 (1961), pp. 1-16, esp. pp. 4-5.
142. Ibid., pp. 5-13. See also Jerzy Neyman and Elizabeth L. Scott, "Stochastic Models of Population Dynamics," *Science*, 130 (Aug. 7, 1959), pp. 303-308; Simon, "On a Class of Skew Distribution Functions," in *Models of Man*, chap. 9; Coleman, pp. 526-528.

Perhaps also the product of a stochastic process is Gunnar Myrdal's principle of cumulative causation.[143] Of interest is the degree to which stochastic processes operate in economic and noneconomic fields, respectively. Of interest also is the extent to which these processes may be controlled as well as the degree to which they may be reversed.

One type of cumulative causation identified by Myrdal and represented as unstable has been shown to eventuate in stable equilibrium. According to Myrdal, white prejudice made for reduction in the standards achievable by Negroes and this reduction in turn intensified white prejudice.[144] However, as Swann shows, these two types of response can be brought into equilibrium and this equilibrium probably can be made stable. The process here under analysis may correspond to various economic or social processes.[145]

Conclusion

Sociology and economics could be made quite parallel were they to eschew their excessive and uncritical concern with "welfare" in what by now has become an age of the sort which Nietzsche as well as Sumner anticipated. As sciences they share questions common to all sciences, namely, questions of fact, adequacy of constructs, and validity of hypotheses and theories. Similarly, they must decide upon the elements to be included in their systems of interacting variables, upon what are to be treated and measured as parameters, and upon what in enveloping matrices of conditions is to be disregarded. These are methodological issues.

Turning now to substantive issues we find both economics and sociology dealing with interaction, with the interaction of individuals or systems within a larger and more inclusive system and through diverse media of communication. There is little or no room, therefore, for the postulation of one-man Robinson Crusoe situations, though introspection may provide both the economist and the sociologist with information of use in his analytical undertakings. Interacting individuals live in an n-man system, with the value of n ranging from two to so large a magnitude that each individual can only adapt to relevant situations since his modifying any one of them is impossible or prohibitively costly. We thus have ranges of possible situations analogous to the economist's range of market situations stretching from monopoly to simple competition. The behavior of a unit (individual, small system) within the framework of a more inclusive system is thus a

---

143. *An American Dilemma,* vol. 1 (New York: Harper and Row, 1944), pp. 75-78, 1065-1070; see also his *Monetary Equilibrium* (London: William Hodge, 1939), pp. 24-28.
144. *American Dilemma,* p. 76.
145. On the equilibration of forces "causing" each other see T. W. Swann, "Circular Causation," *Economic Record,* 38 (Dec. 1962), 421-426.

function of the size of n and of expectations formed in view of the size of n. [146]

Sociological theory may be based upon the fact that society is a system of interacting subsystems even as is an economy. Its constructs should, of course, be isomorphic (as are economic constructs) with these interacting subsystems. Attention needs to be focused mainly upon the behavior of subsystems and of individuals acting and interacting within and between these subsystems. Then economic theory and sociological theory will parallel one another. Each in its application will need, moreover, to take into account the envelope within which it functions, culture and institutions in the case of sociology, and monetary, fiscal, and tax conditions and relevant institutions in the case of economics insofar as these conditions are determined by the polity and hence are not endogenous to the economic system. Sociological theory will accordingly have to identify—as economic theory has to identify—its interacting variables, its parameters (which are a function of time), pertinent constraints, and conditions which are deemed irrelevant. It may then focus attention upon parametrical change which, as we have seen, is not only important in itself but also useful to economists inasmuch as they often treat as parameters conditions (such as tastes) subject to change which sociological theory may be suited to explain. Attention may be focused also upon cyclical phenomena (for example, in institutions or in tastes) as well as upon social-worth phenomena. [147] Sociology can then contribute also to our understanding of ideological, ideational, and related kinds of change by which economies are modified and the body of economic theory may be modified. Joint undertakings by economists and sociologists may be facilitated through use of socioeconomic-system approaches. [148]

The emerging emphasis upon systems theory in sociology may transform the latter into a social science resembling economics more closely than does sociology at present. Systems theory views complex organizations as wholes much as economics views the collections of interrelated decision-makers with whom it deals. Information and communication play a fundamental role in both economics and systems, each of which focuses upon *relations* rather than upon entities. Dynamic economics concerns itself as does dynamic systems theory with the evolution and adaptation of the organiza-

---

146. This is well brought out in game theory as well as in price theory. See McKinsey, pp. 2-3.

147. These phenomena are less prominent, however, than growth phenomena in economies in which surpluses making for growth are almost automatically generated. See my "Social Evolution and the Theory of Economic Development," in H. R. Barringer, G. I. Blanksten, and R. W. Mack, eds., *Social Change in Developing Areas* (Cambridge: Schenkman, 1965), pp. 253-256.

148. For example, Guy H. Orcutt, et al., *Microanalysis of Socioeconomic Systems: A Simulation Study* (New York: Harper, 1961). See also Karlsson's map, p. 141; and Walter Buckley, *Sociology and Modern Systems Theory* (Englewood Cliffs: Prentice-Hall, 1967).

tions which it studies. Other parallels might be listed and described. Enough has been said, however, to show that emphasis upon a systems approach might serve, as could emphasis upon the universality of exchange, to increase the overlap between economics and sociology.

18.

Some Sociological Implications of Culture

T. O. Beidelman

T. O. Beidelman was born in Illinois in 1931 and was educated at the University of Illinois, University of California, University of Michigan, and University of Oxford (M.A., D.Phil.). When the paper included here was written, he was associate professor in the department of sociology and anthropology at Duke University; he is now in the department of anthropology at New York University. He has done extensive fieldwork in East Africa and has published over fifty papers on various aspects of African ethnography. His main theoretical interests relate to kinship studies, religion and ritual, and problems in local administration in colonial and newly independent states.

The aim of this essay is to discuss what seem to me to be some important aspects of current social anthropology which may be useful to sociologists. However, I make no claim toward familiarity with all of the trends in current research in anthropology which is now perhaps even more variegated than sociology. Furthermore, my own interests lead me to give priority to the study of the interplay between culture and society; that is, between ideology (as exhibited in cosmology and moral norms) and social action (as exhibited both in adherence to and divergence from such norms). Admittedly, this is only one of the many sectors of interest in current anthropology. Other topics would be the enormous new interest in problems of social change and their relation to the current affairs of newly independent nations, theories about the relation between socialization processes and social structure, the study of primate behavior in order to theorize about the evolution of human society, and the methodological and theoretical problems presented now that computerization has fostered ever wider and more complex comparative surveys of ethnographic data.

The connection between anthropology and sociology here in America has often been slight, with sociologists tending to borrow far more from

I should like to thank Dr. J. C. Crocker, Professor J. Middleton, and Dr. R. Needham for reading and commenting upon early drafts of this paper.

anthropologists than we from them. But British and French social anthropology, at least, descend from the same sources as classic sociology, especially from that developed by the interchange between British social scholars such as W. Robertson Smith, Maine, and Spencer on the one hand, and the founders of the French sociological tradition, such as Fustel de Coulanges, Durkheim, Hubert, and Mauss on the other. Considering this, one may still expect that sociology and social anthropology may find that they have far more in common than they suspect. Curiously, classic sociology failed to take root in Britain, though classic social anthropology flourished there; conversely, classic sociology developed enormously in America, even as social anthropology languished. Until recently, American anthropology was dominated by Boas and his students; a discussion of the reasons for this school's hostility to social anthropology and sociology would take us far beyond the limits of this paper. Unfortunately, such proselytization of social anthropology that did take place in America was mainly through visiting scholars who were far more psychologically than sociologically oriented in respect to their explanatory theories about social life. As a result, the types of exchange between sociologists and social anthropologists in America have often been distorted by misconceptions about each others' work, so that today many social anthropologists find that one of our greatest problems is that of correcting the misunderstandings held about the current nature of our field and research.[1] Some discussion of these misconceptions and the conditions under which they arose is required in order to clarify the main problem of this chapter. That problem centers around the present revival of interest in the notion of culture among social anthropologists and the value that this may hold for some sociologists, particularly those who have made some use of Parsonian schemes of categorizing culture and social structure as interdependent parts of a broader social system. Until the past ten or fifteen years, American anthropologists tended to distinguish themselves from their colleagues in Britain and France by their insistence on *culture* as the definitive focus of anthropological research, whereas their counterparts across the Atlantic tended to avoid that term, apparently in an attempt to emphasize that their interest lay in a fairly narrow concept of social structure rather than in a more complex field including almost the entire range of phenomena in human life. Today we find both these stereotypes considerably blurred: many American cultural anthropologists now call themselves social anthropologists while many social anthropologists now call themselves structural anthropologists or structuralists or even cultural anthropologists and are

---

1. It would perhaps be profitable for a student of the sociology of knowledge to try to explain the reasons for the time lag that exists between social anthropology and sociology regarding appreciation of interdisciplinary work. Although there are, of course, persons in each field well abreast of current research in the other, there appears to be a lag of ten to fifteen years in intercommunication between the fields, if we consider the ordinary members of the two disciplines.

using the term culture. Such shifts in labels may be merely signs of im-
mature chauvinism or of the fads that mar any discipline, but I should like
to believe that these indicate new and important reorientations in these
schools and an assumption of more common ground than before among the
various national branches in the discipline. For a number of reasons,
anthropology is today perhaps returning to less nationally parochial attitudes than were held during much of the period since the last world war.
Certainly scholars in the classic period of anthropology's growth, such men
as Tylor, Morgan, Frazer, Durkheim, and Mauss, were cosmopolitan in
their exchange of ideas and interest in one another's work.

The remainder of this chapter is divided into three parts. In the first I
discuss briefly some implications of past theories, the better to show the
current dilemmas faced by those anthropologists with sociological interests.
I especially emphasize the classical French sociological tradition and the
followers of Radcliffe-Brown and those of Malinowski.

I next go on to suggest how certain current anthropologists have opened
new and exciting directions which may solve some of the difficulties in-
herited from our intellectual past. The findings of some of these researchers
may be of value to sociologists. In the conclusion I suggest some reasons
why I think the work and attitudes of most sociologists and most anthropologists, regardless of their theoretical stripe, are and perhaps should remain rather different and how these differences complement one another.
Some of these differences cannot be resolved, and have led members of the
two disciplines to possess two very different types of academic personalities.
Social anthropology is not simply the sociology of non-Western or preliterate peoples. It is a form of comparative sociology, but of such a nature
that when done with the intensity required for excellence, it has a peculiar
and diffuse impact upon the practitioner quite unlike that of fieldwork by
the vast majority of social scientists who work within their own societies.

I

Certainly the main source of contemporary social anthropology is the
French school which is essentially the achievement of Durkheim, though in
some respects the work of Mauss represents its finest development and that
aspect with greatest relevance to this chaper. Yet Durkheim's view of
society has often been misrepresented, especially by anthropologists. For
example, despite his wide and flexible approach, Kroeber did not seem to
comprehend the sociological nature of Durkheim's theories but transposed
Durkheim's notions of moral symbols into the realm of cultural anthropology with little sociological significance.[2] Durkheim conceived of society

2. A. L. Kroeber, *The Nature of Culture* (Chicago: University of Chicago Press,
1952), p. 118.

as a moral community, and as such he saw social behavior as the reflection of norms and sentiments or lack thereof. He conceived of men as having no meaningful nature or worth outside society; his view of man was the converse of that held by Marx, who conceived of men as essentially good but corrupted and disrupted by the misworking of various social systems. Durkheim's basic view of man's relation to society (or culture) has exerted a profound effect upon all schools of social anthropology, directly in Britain and France, and indirectly through Radcliffe-Brown and the Chicago school in America.

In some respects, anthropological fieldwork, by its very nature, tends toward a model which emphasizes Durkheimian consistency. This is so for several reasons: the relatively small number of informants which are usually available for help to a fieldworker, the superficiality of observation due to limitations in time and language, and the very quality of the material which is often so alien that the fieldworker's first efforts are directed toward constructing a consistent model by which he may orient himself. Unfortunately, many fieldworkers exhaust their fieldtime when they have achieved only this preliminary step. The social anthropologist grasps the character of an alien society in the manner of a child being socialized. Yet this involves an added difficulty for the fieldworker who must also unlearn or transcend his own conceptual categories which represent his socialization into his own society. Much that the anthropologist first learns is through instruction both in language and later in ideal or proper behavior. Although this is not wholly true, it is true enough to lead the social anthropologist to have a preference, perhaps unconsciously, for normative models, and more particularly, for models derived far more from verbal behavior than from observed behavior. Indeed, this verbal behavior is of a peculiar and restricted sort since by the very nature of the questions usually asked his informants, a kind of abstracted and ideal normative position is often presented. (This is also often true of those sociologists who rely heavily on questionnaires.) This is not to imply that fieldworkers do not listen to conversations and attend social functions where they may observe less preformulated patterns of thought and behavior. However, even in these cases a fieldworker inevitably supplements such data with questions to informants. These features of most anthropological fieldwork may make Durkheimian models of ideal and normative systems especially attractive to European social anthropologists, but these same features of the anthropological method have had surprisingly similar effects in America, even where classic sociology has had little influence on anthropology. It is true that there is not usually the systematic concern with social relations and norms shown by British and French social anthropologists, but there is a concern with pattern or configuration of culture, and despite the conventional definitions of culture,[3] which spans the entire range of human be-

3. See, for example, ibid., pp. 104, 118-135.

havior, the cultural anthropologist tended to present his model also in terms of ideas and values, in patterns of culture.[4]

Until after the last world war, the main connection between European and American anthropological traditions was through Radcliffe-Brown and Malinowski, both of whom taught at American universities. Radcliffe-Brown's influence was more immediate and obvious but perhaps less beneficial and pervasive in the long run. His conception of social anthropology was an exceedingly narrow one in that his interest was centered mainly around social organization.[5] His model of society was more mechanistic and less subtle than Malinowski's in that he tended to envision a society essentially in terms of its social organization and that, in turn, in terms of the interdependent parts of a terminological and jural system which somehow enabled a people to conduct their affairs. Though he wrote of the need for a natural science of society, his own work was essentially anatomical or descriptive of kinship, rather than concerned with the complex levels of interdependence and possible causality between kin relations and other factors. A large part of his explanations about social action is simply armchair psychologizing about the kinds of affect or feelings which would be attached to certain roles or statuses in primary relations, such as a nuclear family, and then projecting these on to broader social catgories by a theory of extension. Radcliffe-Brown's use of terms such as structure and function has led many sociologists to hold him in high regard as a sociologically oriented anthropologist; sociologists, often unversed in understanding kinship analyses, credit him with far more of a sociological bent than he merits, for his explanations remain essentially psychological. If Radcliffe-Brown is significant, it is because he revitalized a waning interest in kinship and because he encouraged a return to first-hand rereading of many of the classics of sociology and anthropology. But unfortunately, subsequent research and reworking of Radcliffe-Brown's theories indicate that he was far

4. Some branches of American anthropology, mainly because of the influence of Boas and his disciples, spent their energies in a curious blend of goalless ethnography and diffusedly eclectic interests undisciplined by any clearcut sociological theory. This trend was founded in the name of more scientific concern with data, with facts. It was as though the facts would speak for themselves, would suggest their own theories, if only a sufficiently large number were gathered. Perhaps it was in despair at such an unsatisfactory prospect for research and analysis that so many of the practitioners of this craft, while zealously gathering their facts, also indulged in various forms of psychologizing, of humanistic philosophizing about the moral implications of primitive man to our modern world. For these reasons, American anthropologists have always held a seductive, albeit callow, attraction for the general intellectual public. In different ways, Malinowski and Frazer, and now Lévi-Strauss, have captured public fancy in Europe.

5. Of course, I am not referring to his *The Andaman Islanders,* which, despite its confusion between sociological and psychological explanations, and between manifest and latent functional explanations, is far subtler and more rewarding than his later work. Furthermore, at the close of his career, he did redirect much of his interest toward problems of religion and ideology.

Yet there is a second important aspect of the works of both Mauss and Lévi-Strauss. However unsuccessful these first efforts may be, both attempt to employ the comparative method. Though all useful generalization involves some comparative analysis, a commitment to this scholarly objective requires two other interrelated techniques which present considerable difficulty. One is the appreciation of a particular society as a complex and integrated whole in which any activity is fully meaningful only in terms of its significance within the entire matrix of related social behavior. The other is the wary understanding that any type of behavior which appears comparable to some behavior within another society may not, in fact, be comparable, because that observed by the analyst ignorant of a society's norms and values (the phenotype) is not actually closely related to the social meaning or cultural value (the genotype). Frazer's *The Golden Bough* is certainly the most famous example of this kind of use of data. The problem here, of course, is where one obtains the rules for defining the particular "truth" or "meaning" by which a conceptual genotype is fashioned. This may be in terms of the stated norms or purposes of a particular society or in terms of the latent functions or ends unknowingly achieved within a society. Both such methods may be legitimate, but they imply different estimations of the nature and purpose of social studies. Both present serious, perhaps insoluble problems. However, if a solution is to be found, it seems that only by an appreciation of the first set of factors will the analyst be able to extract comparable social phenomena.

Sociologists who have attempted to make use of anthropological material have tended to take reported phenomena at face value. This is also true of some anthropologists, the work of the Whitings and Murdock being particularly well known examples of this. Thus we find that Murdock, in his comparative studies of kinship organization, relies almost exclusively upon one set of relationships, the classification of cousins in formal terms of reference, as the criterion for his kinship types.[15] This seems triply ill-advised, for he extracts one facet from a complex system, he reduces an institution such as kinship to one level of analysis, namely, certain terms, and he examines social phenomena in terms of one institution, kinship, which may be significantly similar or different in terms only of more complex clusters of institutions. Thus, it may well be that from a broader perspective the sociological significance of certain agnatic systems of pastoralists having feuds may be such as to make them of one social type, regardless of their cousin terminology and other formal features; whereas by these same criteria they may be radically different from agnatic systems among sedentary, nonfeuding societies, some of which may have agnatic terminologies formally identical to pastoral folk. Similarly, one may find the term marriage used for the Nuer, where those rights to offspring and women that

15. G. P. Murdock, *Social Structure* (New York, Macmillan, 1949).

prevail are not necessarily dependent upon coresidence, sexual fidelity, or even the living presence of a husband; yet this same English term is utilized by comparativists for the institution that joins spouses in North India where coresidence, living spouses, and sexual fidelity are all considered essential. Clearly such definition depends greatly on what problems the analyst seeks to consider. In the case of the Whitings, one may consider an institution such as witchcraft or sorcery.[16] For some of their theories, the crucial factors may be the presence or absence of witchcraft or its prevalence or insignificance in social affairs. Yet one may well ask whether the *uhai* of Kaguru, the *tsav* of Tiv and the *mangu* of Azande are comparable at all. It may be that the only thing these three notions have indisputably in common is that they have all been translated by one English term. If they had more than this in common, one would have to defend the comparison by spelling out precisely how these three operate in their different societies. As for the measurements of the rate of occurrence of such practices, few anthropological monographs provide data which allow such assessment with any degree of reliability, and certainly this is also not true of most of the materials utilized in such comparative surveys.

Doubtless these comments may seem excessively negative to those unfamiliar with alien cultures. However, I am not suggesting that customs or practices may not or should not be compared. Rather, I suggest that we must be extremely careful to indicate what we are comparing. At present most comparativists have exhibited a disregard for such details of social facts and an impatient unwillingness to consult all of the relevant publications before punching an entry in their research cards.[17] Many of my social anthropological colleagues have criticized the American comparativists, in particular, for their failure to use all of the ethnographic sources and for their implicit claims that concomitance suggests causal relations. A far more serious criticism, it seems to me, lies in the question of whether they are not guilty of the "translation fallacy," of mistaking the ethnographer's use of a European term in describing an institution or custom as standing for more of a social similarity than might safely be warranted.

A consideration of these pitfalls is particularly pertinent in anthropology because the kind of social data with which we must deal are so alien to us. The very fact that most of us must write our accounts of alien cultures in a European language may well lend more of a notion of commonality or comparability than is justly due. It has been suggested that one way out of this problem would involve comparative studies of several different sub-

---

16. J. W. Whiting, "Sorcery, Sin and Superego," *Nebraska Symposium on Motivation,* vol. 7 (Lincoln: University of Nebraska Press, 1959), pp. 174-195. Beatrice Whiting, *Piaute Sorcery* (New York: Viking Fund Publication No. 15, 1950).
17. The HRAF files have been the source of a great deal of such careless scholarship. Their original purpose was to facilitate exploratory or preliminary research, but unfortunately they are now often used as the final and only source.

areas within one primitive society, where the variables may be more clearly appreciated and controlled. On another, broader level, comparative research might be undertaken within contiguous societies over a particular geographical and/or cultural area. In such a case, the cultural factors would be under somewhat better control by area specialists with a lifetime of familiarity with that area, rather than naïvely judged in a worldwide ꞏꞏꞏꞏꞏꞏꞏꞏꞏ. Unfortunately, such methods are time-consuming and require a patient scholarship which so far does not seem to have appealed to the majority of comparativists.[18] Implicit in all of my arguments is the problem of understanding a foreign language. It is here that we find one of the most crucial differences in the approaches of sociologists and social anthropologists.

Evans-Pritchard has stated that the most difficult and also most important aspect of social anthropology is translation.[19] By this he means far more than the mere obstacle of learning an alien language. Rather, he refers to the problem of perceiving the meaning of alien concepts for the social categories and processes which define a society. Let us take as an example one such concept held among the Nuer. The term marriage, as used by Evans-Pritchard in reference to the Nuer, obviously does not stand for the customs, rights, and obligations which we associate with marriage in our society. But this is only the beginning of the problem. For to understand Nuer marriage we must also understand the more basic Nuer notions which support and rationalize Nuer norms surrounding the various aspects of marital relations, such as notions of fertility, paternity, maternity, masculinity, femininity, descent, and physiology. As Evans-Pritchard has shown, these, in turn, involve complex association with Nuer concepts of time, death, spirit, and morality.

According to this point of view, then, a complete exegesis of an alien cosmology is required before one may even begin to fathom the norms and goals held by members of a society. (This may seem an obvious assertion, but it is in fact very rarely done.) Evans-Pritchard's work has concentrated upon expounding the systematic, normative aspects of ideological systems. He may be said to be the founder and master of this approach in contemporary social anthropology, even allowing for the considerable debt he owes to French scholars, primarily Lévy-Bruhl, but also Mauss, Durkheim, Hubert, and Hertz. However, despite its brilliance, and despite good intentions to the contrary, such work has not been very successful in relating ideological systems either to the details of norms or to the behavior of members of special and different social groups (especially as these involve conflict

18. One of the most curious aspects of current comparative research is that for the most part it is undertaken by persons who have failed to distinguish themselves by fieldwork.
19. E. E. Evans-Pritchard, *Theories of Primitive Religion* (Oxford: Clarendon Press, 1965), pp. 11-13.

and inconsistencies). It has been even less successful in demonstrating the possible social psychological or clinical psychological implications of the sentiments and symbols involved.

Nonetheless, this approach has provided useful and attractive models of the normative and ideological systems of alien societies and has shown, at least on the more formal level, how the cultural and social systems are interrelated. Implicit in such models were the notions of the existential quality of much of the ideological system involved; such analysts try to relate these ideologies to social relations, but this tends to be on a very superficial basis. Thus, their discussion usually presses the intellectual aspects of such ideological systems, but rarely any of the implications which these may have for questions concerning the psychological forces which support or reinforce certain attitudes, concepts, or values.

Now this aspect of classic European social anthropology is not very different from American cultural anthropology. In the past, some schools of American anthropology tended to stress a *sui generis* quality or pattern. Kroeber did so,[20] and later this was taken up by the ethnoscientists. Thus we find Lounsbury taking Leach to task for seeing the preliminary problems of understanding kinship categories in terms of social categories (both groups and related ideas and values). Instead, Lounsbury would explain these in terms of linguistic categories and processes and, in the spirit of Radcliffe-Brown, in terms of the psychological processes implicit in the theory of kinship extension from the primary relations of the nuclear family.[21] This is consistent with Kroeber and much of the American school which tried to see cultural patterns somehow both as manifestations of psychology and as the products of some historical processes.[22] Whatever the final verdict on the value of the ethnoscience school for anthropology and linguistics, it would seem to hold little immediate value to sociologists. At present, at least, it holds relatively little value for the mainstream of social anthropology since such researchers have shown little interest or facility in relating conceptual categories to social categories and norms. Furthermore, their rigid and artificial method of interview research tends to efface the flexible ambiguity so essential in the symbolic play which characterizes any kinship system, when this is seen as a language for ordering complex social relations.

At first glance the Kroeberians, and neo-Kroeberians such as Lounsbury, seem to be concerned with the interconnection between the individual and society or culture. But their interest is basically one of describing form and

20. Pp. 169-218.
21. F. Lounsbury, "Another View of the Trobriand Kinship Categories," *American Anthropologist*, 67, 5, Special Issue (October, 1965), 142-185.
22. C. Kluckhohn's celebrated but over-rated study, *Navaho Witchcraft* (Boston: Beacon Press, 1944), is a good example of this in that it attempts to explain a social institution mainly in terms of psychological mechanisms without first undertaking a proper sociological or cosmological analysis.

pattern (formal meaning); they make little of the intervening connections which link, say, the attributes of various categories of persons (such as men, women, elders, children, or novices). Furthermore, they show little or no interest in the psychological processes which may serve to connect social categories with individual motives and goals.

So far, my critical account of current and past work in social anthropology has centered upon two broad fronts. First, there is a tendency for analysis to describe societies in terms of normative models that are so homogeneous and mechanistic that they equip us poorly with means for describing the important differences which obtain within social relations in any society. At best, we may see such societies in terms of behavioral congruencies with and deviations from such systems of rules and values. We cannot get at the "reasons" for such deviations, or at the means by which such values and ideas reinforce and perpetuate such a social system. Yet these are, and have long been, at the center of much of sociological as well as anthropological theory. For example, these are the very guts of Durkheim's problem in *The Elementary Forms of the Religious Life*. There, despite his profound insights, Durkheim finally relies upon certain psychological notions derived from crowd theory and psychic needs not only to explain the final causes of periodicity in religious ceremonies, but also the effect of symbols and ceremonies. Second, there is a tendency, perhaps inevitable, for most social anthropologists to lean upon latent psychological or cognitive factors as explanations of social phenomena. Although this was strongly condemned by Durkheim, he himself could not elude such thinking.[23] This was the essence of Lévi-Strauss's apt, though somewhat harsh, criticism of Durkheim: "His theory of totemism starts with an urge *(besoin),* and ends with a recourse to sentiment *(sentiment)."* [24] Unfortunately, Lévi-Strauss's own solution to this quandary, at least in this study, makes less advance than it claims, for it simply ends with "certain modes of thought *(modes de reflexion)."* One would not quarrel with the affirmation that such systems of thought conform to certain principles of cognition which, on one level at least, make sense in and of themselves as arrangements of ideas. His concern over the process of ordering by which this is done and the nature of metaphors as the nexus between language, objects, and sensation are all insights of the first order, though hardly novel assertions. His originality lies far more in the areas to which he directs these insights. Unfortunately, Lévi-Strauss does not pursue this line of analysis into social psychological or clinical psychological channels, even though it would seem that this would be required, ultimately, if we were to understand the nature of these factors better.

Culture, then, for everyone from Durkheim and, in a sense, Kroeber, to

23. Emile Durkheim, *The Rules of Sociological Method* (Glencoe: Free Press, 1950), pp. xlvii-l.
24. C. Lévi-Strauss, *Totemism* (Boston: Beacon Press, 1963), pp. 70-71.

Lévi-Strauss has been above all else a moral phenomenon, one grounded in the imposition of existential systems of ideas upon a world of persons (and ultimately individuals) and objects. It is precisely at the points of interconnection and interdependence of these two levels that social anthropologists have experienced their deepest sense of intellectual bafflement and confusion. So long as these systems of ideas are seen in and of themselves, whether they are called symbolic categories, Kroeberian patterns, or norms and values, our models remain fairly neat. But they lack explanatory value when we try to ask more basic questions about how these are internalized or how they relate to men as individuals, as creatures with needs, feelings, and thoughts which somehow extend beyond these moral or social limits. It is here, then, that much of the best of current social anthropological research is now centered. That this research deals with various systems termed culture is due to the problem of trying to resolve or dissolve the existential and relativistic aspects of different cultural systems into more basic factors common to all societies, and hence to all men. In a sense, perhaps the problem cannot be answered by social anthropologists but must be taken up by psychologists and even physiologists. But if this is so, then it cannot be taken up without the mutual understanding and help among men of these varied disciplines working together.

Durkheim himself surely foresaw at least some of the problems which the study of symbolism and systems of ideas would create.

Is it not conceivable, for example, that contiguity and resemblance, logical contrasts and antagonisms, act in the same way, whatever may be the things they represent? Thus we arrive at the idea of the possibility of an entirely formal psychology which would be a sort of common ground for individual psychology and for sociology, and this perhaps explains the reluctance of certain scholars to distinguish too sharply between the two sciences.[25]

II

The works discussed above exhibit various facets of one basic problem. Analytical models of societies or cultures are constructed, by definition, in order to convey meaning to the analyst. Such meaning, in the social sciences, is not easily separated from some form of teleological construct. I am aware that, despite their everyday language, natural scientists do not construct their models or laws in simple terms of causality, but rather in terms of correlations.[26] But in social studies, the explanatory thrust of

25. Pp. l-li.
26. However, even here much of the prose of science smuggles in causal statements, even though these are not, strictly speaking, part of the formal structure of science. I suspect that this may be due in large part to the nature of verbal (as contrasted to mathematical) language, though I am assured that even mathematics cannot rid itself entirely of such use of verbal language in the exposition of proofs.

various models invariably relates to what may be called functions. In some instances these purposes or functions are defined in fairly formal terms, those of the normative set of rules in a society or in terms of various values and ideas consciously held by some members of that society. But in many other cases social phenomena are not readily explained in this manner and various psychological or even quasi-physiological processes are utilized. These are most often related to the problems of explaining the variation in systems of ideas and values and in explaining those forms of social inter action, such as religious behavior, where no pragmatic and discernible physical ends are achieved. Because men hold ideas and communicate through symbolic behavior, social scientists must eventually try to account for the form such behavior takes. Certain characteristics of idea systems appear *sui generis,* in that they cannot be entirely explained in terms of the social groups in which they are held, nor can they be explained simply in terms of general psychological processes, for they vary from society to society. Both of these explanatory factors may be useful in providing limited explanations, but none is fully satisfactory. Part of the problem lies in the limits set by the nature of the connection between symbols and the things for which they stand. Symbols do, of course, have a correspondence with the things they represent, but the represented things are more than what the symbols seem able to contain. This is probably because the analogies and metaphors by which language has developed are themselves limited by our own sensory equipment. Now these kinds of explanations which go beyond formal sociological causes are usually phrased in some form of latent functionalism. In the past this latency generally represented a quest for explanations outside the range of ordinary sociological causes and hence often disposed of problematical factors through psychologizing. This, in turn, implies some teleological model. I believe that some of the most provocative and far-reaching findings in current social anthropology center upon the kinds of explanations we can provide for the form and content of ideological or cosmological systems, for the sociological aspects of language.

The following are examples of some of the ways by which latent functions are utilized by sociologists and social anthropologists. In his discussion of functionalism, the sociologist Merton uses two interesting examples for his argument. These neatly illustrate the strengths and weaknesses of sociologists analyzing information from their own and alien cultures. In his consideration of the functions of the Hopi rain ceremony, Merton explains it as achieving a psychological state of social solidarity in the minds of the actors. That Merton relies upon unconsciously held notions as the real goals of a social group acting in some institutionalized manner may be because he can find no success in terms of the purported aim of the ceremonies—bringing rain—yet he is committed to believing that no institution can persist without some purposeful result. Had he some knowledge

of Hopi cosmology, I do not believe that he would have provided quite so simplistic a psychological cause which, after all, is little advanced over Durkheim's crowd theory.[27] In contrast, Merton's causal explanation of institutionalized corruption in American urban areas is much more sophisticated. Here he relies on more sociological factors—varied values and beliefs held by certain subgroups in our society. In this case, he is aware of the concepts held in his own culture and need not skirt social for psychological explanations.[28]

Social anthropologists often do little better than sociologists in explaining exotic institutions. For example, Radcliffe-Brown's explanations of joking behavior bypass the ideological motives.[29] This is not to deny any and all value to such explanations, but rather to suggest that we should first try to explain as much as possible by social notions relative to a particular culture before we embark on universal psychological processes as explanatory devices. It is clear that Radcliffe-Brown's steady reliance upon psychological factors derives from his lack of interest in cosmological or ideological factors.[30] But even a man with the analytical subtlety of Lévy-Bruhl utilized psychological factors to explain away certain problems resulting from his failure to appreciate fully the nature of alien conceptual categories. Because of this failure, Lévy-Bruhl tended to see certain alien systems of thought as displaying no concern for contradiction and inconsistency. This criticism was beautifully made by Rivers.[31]

Today there is a vigorous reinterest in recording and analyzing cosmological systems. If the preceding thirty years were the era of considerable strides in the study of the institutions of kinship and political affairs, then the present period is likely to be the era of the study of belief systems and symbolic behavior. It seems particularly useful to consider the work of four men as indicative of the major trends in such study: Leach, Middleton, Turner, and Lévi-Strauss. All of these writers have attempted, with varied success, to deal with certain problems across the conventional institutional categories usually assigned by analysts. All, to some degree, are deeply con-

---

27. R. Merton, *Social Theory and Social Structure* (Glencoe: Free Press, 1959), pp. 64-65. Gluckman provides a similar interpretation for Swazi royal ritual. See M. Gluckman, *Rituals of Rebellion in South-East Africa* (Manchester: Manchester University Press, 1954). I have provided an alternate analysis utilizing the formal cosmological system of the Swazi in "Swazi Royal Ritual," *Africa,* 36 (1966), 373-405. I am confident that a similar analysis could be provided for Hopi ceremonies.
28. Merton, pp. 73-81.
29. A. R. Radcliffe-Brown, *Structure and Function in Primitive Society* (Glencoe: Free Press, 1962), pp. 90-116.
30. Elsewhere I review Radcliffe-Brown's theories in more detail and try to show how joking relations may be analyzed without recourse to psychological hypotheses. See *"Utani:* Some Kaguru Notions of Death, Sexuality, and Affinity," *Southwestern Journal of Anthropology,* 22 (1966), 354-380.
31. W. H. R. Rivers, *Psychology and Ethnology,* ed. G. E. Smith (London: Kegan Paul, 1926), pp. 36-50.

cerned with the social implications of how conceptual systems are related to language.

In terms of success within a limited set of problems, Middleton's study of the Lugbara is the most rewarding of the works discussed below.[32] With matchless field data he charts the conflicts and coalitions within an extended kin group, showing how these are expressed in terms of religious ceremonies and the cosmological interpretation of events around which these ceremonies center. In supplementary essays he has outlined the general cosmological system of this society. This approach is probably the most readily understandable by sociologists: an idea system is shown affecting and being affected by social relations, but always within the broader terms of social norms. As it is presented, the ideological and normative systems form a rather consistent whole, and there is little indication regarding the kinds of intellectual processes at work determining or accounting for the effect generated by some of these ideas. In terms of the argument of this chapter, the study is a kind of baseline, a sociological starting point from which more difficult issues regarding ideology may be attacked.

Leach's work is far thinner in terms of data and methodology, but it takes the questions suggested by Middleton considerably further, both in terms of sociological complexity and in terms of their intellectual or psychological undertones. Unfortunately, Leach has little interest in theoretical consistency so that the posture assumed by him in a monograph or essay sometimes is reversed in one of his later publications. But Leach himself explicitly reminds us of this and seems to take some glee in playing the role of a theoretical Cheshire cat with only a grin remaining. Because of his manifold stands, I must cite three examples of Leach's work, two positive in their advancement of my argument, and one the exact antithesis.

In his study of political systems of highland Burma, Leach describes a complex culture of two social subsystems with highly contrasting values about equality versus hierarchy in authority and wealth.[33] The interest in his account lies not in his analysis of the two extremes in this culture but in the subcultures or subsocieties, the smaller communities in which groups and individuals, for various reasons, undertake actions driving their group toward that polar type they do not at present much resemble. At one level, the study is fascinating as an illustration of alternating, cyclical change within a system in which certain forms of social (ideological) feedback tend to prevent resolution into either polar type—at least in the case of a large part of that culture faced with certain economic, political, and demographic problems. But Leach's working cause is clearly ideological, despite his scholarly concern with various demographic, geographic, and historical

32. J. Middleton, *Lugbara Religion* (London: Oxford University Press [for International African Institute], 1960).
33. E. R. Leach, *Political Systems of Highland Burma* (Cambridge: Harvard University Press, 1954).

factors. What is even more interesting is his account of various groups within this system who are involved in symbolic (as well as physical) exchange of women, goods, and ceremonies. Here, he shows how such exchanges may sometimes be evaluated radically differently by the two participants. He has entered into the complex problem of asking to what degree values and ideology must be common to allow such exchange, yet to what extent and why important ideological differences persist and how these are significant in changing or dissolving the present interrelationship, the present social group. To put it another way, one may ask how ambitious persons belonging to a group stressing equality manage to strive for ascendancy and manipulate the system into more hierarchical lines. What this implies is the ability to work with two opposing systems at once and to dissociate (as does the subtlest sociologist) manifest norms and goals from the latent goals consistent with an actor's own individual motives. The very thinness of Leach's material allows him to present this with some apparent clarity, for the actual details, in terms of specific case histories and a rich catalogue of Rashomon-like differences in symbolic interpretations by the various actors would pose severe problems for presentation and analysis.

Leach's monograph has long been valued as one of the most provocative and illuminating studies in social anthropology, mainly by those who have, at least for operational purposes, assumed the primacy of ideology over other factors in the explanation of social relations. Consequently, Leach's study of Pul Eliya was a considerable disappointment in its emphasis upon causal factors of demography, economics, and the chance of human fertility and its variations in different kin groups.[34] It was as though the author of the Pul Eliya volume had attempted to disprove the author of the Burma study. Maine provides the best rejoinder to Leach, who seems to contend that a study of economic priorities or other forms of "expedient" or "pragmatic" behavior somehow is more basic and decisive causally than are the analyses of ideology and related normative values.

Nothing in law springs entirely from a sense of convenience. There are always certain ideas existing antecedently on which the sense of convenience works, and of which it can do no more than form some new combination; and to find these ideas in the present case is exactly the problem.[35]

But Leach has yet another side to his interest which is found in his various essays covering a no-man's-land vaguely between social anthropology, literary criticism, theology, and clinical psychology. These deal with a wide variety of topics such as the Garden of Eden, Trobriand shields, magical hair, the genealogy of King Solomon, English obscenity, and English trademarks. The factual data on which these essays are based are thin and often dubious, but the subtle insights and suggestions are of the highest

34. *Pul Eliya* (Cambridge: Cambridge University Press, 1961).
35. H. S. Maine, *Ancient Law* (London: Everyman, 1917), p. 137.

order. What they involve is an attempt to resolve the gaps between formal ideology (as expressed in such things as myth, decoration, or prohibited words and foods), social groups, and their related norms, and what he suggests are certain universal psychological problems.

What Leach does is point out (usually within one ideological system, but sometimes within several) certain themes or motifs which tend to appear within various contexts and in certain prescribed forms. At the first level of analysis, he is prepared to equate motifs which appear to be disparate but which are comparable if considered in terms of their functions or positions within an ideological structure. For example, the shaving of head-hair and the neglect of such hair by those in mourning or by those in certain religious states may be equated as both expressing a liminal, medial set of symbolic attributes, both divergent from normal body grooming and also from normal social statuses in certain societies. Given a series of such traits which he may isolate by such an operation, he then proceeds to relate these to the kinds of social groups and social situations in which they occur, and also to hypothesize regarding the kinds of psychic processes involved. For example, sufficient linguistic and ceremonial behavior are recorded, for some societies at least, to suggest that head-hair has certain ambiguous and liminal attributes often related to sexuality and even more often related to those other dubious zones of behavior involving food, body excretions, body set and gesture, and so forth. These form the tricky and difficult boundaries between the individual self and others. A fair example of Leach's method may be found in his essays on time [36] or on verbal abuse and animal categories and diet.[37] But an obvious problem in his approach (and one not solved by those with richer material) is the lack of really substantial psychological data for the societies discussed as well as an unclarity in exposing the methodology to be used. In this sense, Leach's essays, and those of his colleagues analyzing cosmological or symbolic systems, seem to resemble literary criticism or the analysis of history. There is no clearly discernible method by which such an analyst may isolate a significant motif. One can only say that somehow these are apprehended by analysts with a keen perception of what ceremonies or symbols are of greatest interest to members of a society. But since these same analysts admit that these factors are not always consciously appreciated—at least as systems—by those within a society, the formal interviews such as those conducted by ethnoscientists are not of much use in answering such problems.[38]

36. *Rethinking Anthropology* (London: Athlone Press, 1961), pp. 124-136.
37. "Some Anthropological Aspects of Language," in E. Lenneberg, *New Directions in the Study of Language* (Cambridge: M.I.T. Press, 1964), pp. 23-63.
38. For example, in "Hyena and Rabbit," *Africa*, 31 (1961), 61-74, a paper on the symbolism of one East African society, I try to show how the symbolic values expressed in a certain tale deal with ambiguous situations which are important yet repugnant to a society's values (here, the fact that any advance in male authority depends upon the death of certain kinswomen, even though it is formally maintained that such women are always the objects of positive affect by men).

The two most challenging lines of investigation in these problems are those developed by Turner and Lévi-Strauss. The former has developed his theory through intensive analysis of a particular culture, while Lévi-Strauss has developed his notions by a comparative approach in which fragments of any and all cultures are grist for his mill, to the extent that he at times plays rather fast and loose with the recorded data. Turner's approach is grounded in quasi-Freudian notions of latent explanations. Lévi-Strauss's approach is grounded in a very peculiar kind of neo-Kantian or quasi-Platonic set of notions about the ultimate processes of human thought inherent in the human mind. And yet the views of culture held by both Turner and Lévi-Strauss are fairly similar in many respects, especially in their inherent idealism.

Lévi-Strauss has a Job-like view of both men and culture. Men and the society they form stand in an ambiguous position between the natural, real world and the constructs of language and social norms. We may view this ambiguity both in terms of social persons and social groups composed of biological individuals and the clusters they sometimes form, and in terms of the complex and chaotic real world (nature) and the artificial ideological categories which language and symbols (culture) impose upon this. The "real" world cannot be entirely contained by language nor can the living individual be entirely confined and expressed within the rules and modifications of socially defined experience (such as prohibitions on sexuality, food, dress, linguistic rules for thought, or definitions of proper and improper occasions for emotions). Because of the inevitable discrepancy between the real world of nature and natural man on the one hand, and culture and social man on the other, Lévi-Strauss seems to see men as constantly struggling to resolve these differences. They cannot be resolved in the sphere of social relations nor in man's interaction with his physical surroundings, but they can be resolved in the transcendental sphere of myth and symbolic ritual.[39]

Such a view is almost poetic, and it has exerted considerable fascination upon a wide range of professionals and laymen. Indeed, Lévi-Strauss is perhaps the first anthropologist since Frazer and Malinowski to be cited extensively by the contemporary intellectual mainstream—though Margaret Mead may also be said to qualify for such popular success. Lévi-Strauss has been called the founder of structuralism.[40] Although structural

39. In this limited space I cannot do justice to the subtlety and complexity of Lévi-Strauss's views. His interpretation has altered considerably in the past decade, yet some of the clearest illustrations of this line of analysis are still found in the central chapters of *Tristes tropiques* (Paris: Plon, 1955), where he discusses the Caduveo, Bororo, and Nambikwara. See also his essay on models in *Structural Anthropology* (New York: Basic Books, 1963), chap. VIII.

40. One may acknowledge the brilliance of Lévi-Strauss's insights and panache of his style yet concede his enormous debt to Durkheim, Mauss, Hertz, Hubert, Lévy-Bruhl, Rivers, van Wouden, and even Kroeber. Unfortunately, many of his most vociferous admirers seem to have overestimated his originality as a result of their own unfamiliarity with the work of earlier anthropologists.

anthropology seems to hold somewhat different meanings for various people, the basic meaning seems to derive from a notion of form or pattern within which the specific content is of only secondary significance. Simply, this rests upon the elaborate construction of thought categories out of opposites which in turn are resolved or compounded by a third term or attribute which either contains the opposing categories or, more often, confounds them by being a blend of both. All of this might with some justice be termed a kind of Hegelian Anthropology. For example, the dichotomy between the wild and chaotic world (nature) and the ordered world of men (culture) may be expressed in one society (such as the Nuer) by means of twins (humans who are littered as animals) or (as among the Lele) by means of pangolins (animals which bear one young, which do not retreat from hunters, and which are scaled yet warm-blooded). In such cases, the creatures assigned such a liminal or medial categorization between important cosmological categories may also be assigned important ritual functions related to ceremony, myth, fertility rites, etc. The problem comes from the fact that there seem to be absolutely no *a priori* rules for determining what items will be singled out for attention within a particular society. Yet all societies have some such system of categorization. Lévi-Strauss has shown very little concern for the reasons why one set of items rather than another has been selected. He himself once compared his own interest to that of an architect who is ultimately less interested in the make and type of furniture enclosed within a room than in the volume, contours, and arrangement of clusters of furniture that it is possible to stack within the limitations of such a room. Neither is Lévi-Strauss keenly interested in the correlations of such categories with particular social units or statuses. But he is concerned with showing how such systems of categories do form total systems of ideas and values, and how these in turn may possibly be related to the kinds of ideal models held by the members of a society regarding how their society should appear and work. Unfortunately, he never makes explicit the connection between such ideas and experience; that is, between such values and the actual interaction between members of various social groups. Instead, he tends to rely upon some assumed, *a priori* set of features of the human mind itself which prelimit the form and nature of the process of categorization of experienced phenomena. Thus, ultimately, Lévi-Strauss's work leaves us with no recourse to causal explanations that will take us outside the study of form itself. This explains, of course, the elegance of his self-contained systems, but seems to destine such social anthropology to be merely a kind of artistic descriptive anatomy of language and some implicit but unclarified connection of this linguistic system to the social groups which form society. The connection itself is particularly difficult to make clear since it is already generally admitted that the system itself may be internally inconsistent (it may contain ambiguities or even contradictions, resolved by myth) and that it cannot ever be resolved with the totality of human

behavior or human perception of the external world. Without some recourse to psychology either in terms of a theory of motivation, or some theory of socialization, such structural expositions seem to lead nowhere, except to a kind of poetizing about the nature of the various intellectual systems of world societies. Of course, this is doing Lévi-Strauss something of an injustice, but this, in turn, is mainly because Lévi-Strauss himself smuggles in psychophysiological causal factors in his descriptive analyses. For example, he compares models of marriage and affinity with models of oral ingestion and cooking, and he assigns certain key symbolic referents such as those involving space, sexuality, and life/death to central positions in nearly all of his structural expositions. It is here that Lévi-Strauss's work touches that of Turner, even though Lévi-Strauss never cites his distinguished colleague.

Turner's work proceeds along very different lines from Lévi-Strauss's and, in my view, is considerably more reliable and convincing.[41] His research in cosmology and ritual has been published in a great many essays which are remarkable for their matchless ethnographic detail and subtlety; fortunately, most of these now appear in one volume.[42]

In contrast to Lévi-Strauss, Turner demonstrates his method and theory using data taken almost entirely from within one society, that of the Ndembu of Zambia. Turner's approach is ethnographically traditional in the sense that it depends upon the collection of an enormous mass of field data covering nearly all aspects of social life. This material was not collected through highly formalized interviews (such as those used by ethnoscientists) but rather appears to have developed out of the interests and behavior of those being studied, their own preoccupations and elaborations essentially determining the directions of emphasis in the study. Such a method of research has a great deal in common with informal psychiatric case work and is doubtless quite as difficult to teach and formulate. In this, Turner owes a considerable debt to Evans-Pritchard's earlier study of Zande belief.[43]

Turner records various motifs over a very wide range of social situations from myth and expressions in slang to ceremony and ritual. He proceeds to analyze the manifest meanings in terms of the various situations described by informants within the society he studied. He then goes on

41. Yet Lévi-Strauss seems gifted in his ability to see basic structural forms, even when detailed data are lacking to sustain such an interpretation. Thus, my friend Dr. J. C. Crocker assures me that, although there are many errors of detail, Lévi-Strauss's general model of Bororo society holds despite the shortness of his fieldstay with such an exceedingly complex society. However, Dr. R. Needham has called it to my attention that a society such as the Bororo is "very positively structured." In this sense, its basic model is perhaps more readily apprehended than that of a less formalized system—the Nuer, Shoshone, or Eskimo, for example—might be.
42. Victor Turner, *The Forest of Symbols* (Ithaca: Cornell University Press, 1967).
43. E. E. Evans-Pritchard, *Witchcraft, Oracles, and Magic Among the Azande* (Oxford: Clarendon Press, 1937).

to extrapolate latent meanings in terms of the various other situations in which these motifs occur. There is no clear and explicit set of clues by which these meanings may be gained. His exposition is like a law brief or like the essays of a literary critic trying to interpret the significance of terms within the sense of meaning conveyed by the general system of ideas and attitudes current at a particular literary period. Turner's assumption, which seems justified, is that these more subtle meanings are implied by the general nature of ideas and attitudes of the society considered. Even here there is no clear set of rules, no methodology, for analysis. One can only "prove" one's contention in terms of its consistency within a massive body of recorded data, a web of systematic motifs. Elsewhere, I have tried to summarize Turner's explanatory theory.

His argument runs something like this: basic cultural values or ideologies are existential, and yet ritual behaviour seems to suggest that individuals do not maintain such beliefs simply because these are part of a cognitive system shared by the members of a society. Some features of such ideologies, especially those involving moral notions, tend to be expressed emotionally through certain psycho-physiological terms, e.g., body states and sensations. These bodily experiences have had important bearing on each individual's interpretation of his surroundings, even before speech, and they appear to have provided important metaphorical means by which many word concepts developed. According to this neo-Freudian approach, for example, feelings of oral gratification, satiety, body states related to bodily emissions, temperature, body surface contacts, lightness and darkness, bodily spatial orientation, etc., begin to be associated with various human interrelations. These individual relations, in turn, form the core from which certain social relations are built up and made meaningful in each child's thought. The ideology of any particular social group may represent, in large part, an abstract elaboration based upon these more primitive sets of psycho-physiological associations. Because these most basic psycho-physiological associations are often preverbal, they possess an immediacy inviolate to the onslaughts of verbal, rational argument and it is this intractable aspect of such sense-oriented attributes that provides some of the impetus of symbols and the resilience of many religious and political ideologies which make prominent use of such symbols. In short, the particular configuration of any symbolic value system is a social or cultural problem; but the efficacy of such symbols must be studied by psycho-linguists, social psychologists, and similar specialists. It presents an important though uncharted field for interdisciplinary research, provided that each expert remains acutely aware of the limits of his own field and his own capabilities.[44]

At this point, then, the arguments of social anthropologists or sociologists break down and we must call in the help of colleagues in related fields to assist us in our causal analysis. According to such a model, the "raw individual" is seduced or socialized into a culture through his sensory

44. Beidelman, "Swazi Royal Ritual," pp. 402-403.

apparatus and related psycho-physiological needs, through the combination of his sensory apparatus and the symbolic cues which members of his society attach to various acts of nurturing. In Turner's system, there is still enormous emphasis upon the symbolic system of ideas, but the motivational and effective impetus behind such symbols is in part "explained" in terms of the social conditioning of socialization. Whatever the faults of such a means of analysis, this allows some way out from the closed symbolic analysis presented by Lévi-Strauss and Kroeber and to that extent may be more useful as an analytical tool. To me it appears to present avenues of analysis which may explain those aspects of symbolic affect and social altruism which are so central to Durkheim's consideration of the symbolic aspects of social morality.

Unfortunately, the intermediary zone of symbolic content remains existential and problematic and there seems to be no simple method which we may introduce to enable specialists alien to a particular culture to decode its relative language of significance. In this intermedial zone of interpretation, the hunches or "feel" which the social anthropologist develops may still provide the surest and only means of ordering such material and assigning some ranking of significance and importance to the wide range of cues and symbols utilized within a society. In this sense, we are little better off than we were with Lévi-Strauss's nebulous patterns or models. Nevertheless, it is possible that these interpretations can be sustained, not only through the detailed comparison of great masses of data related to language and symbolism, but also "from the back door" of social psychological or clinical tests and interviews of subjects from particular cultures. However, the intensive and detailed analyses of subjects within alien societies is a field of research almost untouched by psychologists at present, and until such work is commenced (with the cooperation, at least in the beginning, of the social anthropologists) we must rely upon the social anthropologists for our models of idea systems.

If the interpretations of Turner and Lévi-Strauss are correct, then we have new means for mapping out the cognitive systems of different societies and may thereby seek to measure the ways by which these relate to the actual psycho-social behavior of those who hold such beliefs. Without such insights, we can only continue to introspect, often without justification, into the meaning that social acts hold for the actors within a culture.

III

While these are some of the new and important uses which sociologists may find for current social anthropological theory and research, it remains clear that despite their overlap in interests, the two disciplines are quite different.

Two aspects of anthropology may well make it of unusual value to its sister social studies. One is the fieldwork experience. Those who stress this are sometimes dismissed as romantics, especially by those who note that many who have contributed most to our discipline never conducted fieldwork. After all, Durkheim, Mauss, Hertz, Hubert, and Lévy-Bruhl remained far removed from the societies they studied; even such men as Lévi-Strauss and Morgan were far from having the long residence and intensive experience considered essential by most contemporary researchers nor are their more brilliant insights explicitly drawn from their field experience. One can only claim that among the latter, the field encounter did have profound effects upon their perspectives. However, men such as Evans-Pritchard, Malinowski, Turner, Campbell, Middleton, and others present uniquely rich ethnography and a feel for a culture which seems to spring directly from the field situation. What I stress here is the constructive alienation which all good anthropologists occasionally endure—or, if you prefer, a double or triple perspective earned by socialization into several societies other than one's own. This multi-perspective is very rare among sociologists, but not uncommon among anthropologists.

Secondly, many social anthropologists have bemoaned the amorphous and heterogenous quality of the field termed anthropology. With respect to teaching and training of students this creates monstrous problems for students and faculty, yet, for all its bad sides, it does hold certain important advantages: only anthropology remains a field of such institutionalized eclecticism. The patchwork quality is formed by borrowing not only from biology, psychology, geology, and geography, but from demography, history, philosophy, linguistics, economics, political science, art, literary analysis, and technology. This allows a freshness of approach, an originality and flexibility often lacking in more clearly defined and limited fields. Lévi-Strauss has stressed the quality of the *bricoleur* [45] in culture; the same quality would seem essential to the skilled anthropologist. Our competence for sophisticated statement is, of course, lowered by spreading ourselves so widely, and the potential for naïve blunders is great, but so, too, is the uninhibited insight, the potential for new exciting syntheses of several disciplines. I realize that this same eclecticism has sometimes led anthropologists to play the roles of court jesters in the academic community, but these are exceptions,

---

45. This term is very difficult to translate. Perhaps the best way to explain it is by comparing the *bricoleur* to the inventive adolescent who builds a machine or house out of disparate pieces of junk, or to the soldier in combat who builds some needed gadget out of a myriad collection of parts taken from other machines, from debris and junk whose original functions are greatly different from the uses to which they are now successfully fitted. For Lévi-Strauss, then, the materials of culture may be disparate, even wild or unpredictable, but the forms in which these are put together are significant and limited. The same may be said for the anthropologist who tries to generalize from his own field experience and his reading of accounts of the field experience of others.

and the occasions where great insights and wide scholarship are combined more than compensate for this. At such points, anthropologists, more than any other social scholars, approach the imposing ideals set by Mauss's definition of the topic in terms of the study of "total social phenomena."

I began writing this essay with the assumption that in large part good social anthropologists resemble good sociologists and that members of each field may profitably instruct the others. This is surely true, but in the course of my review of the work of my colleagues, I sensed a wide gap between the attitudes and preconceptions held by the majority in each discipline. Nor do I believe that it is entirely good for differences to be effaced.

It may be argued that were, say, a social anthropologist to reside among and study the Nuer of the southern Sudan for thirty years, eventually writing much of his material in the Nuer language and directing many of his interests toward those problems of concern to the Nuer themselves, we might justly speak of a Nuer sociology. But the very nature of our comparative problems and our own social selves makes such an ethnic sociology highly unlikely. The alien and necessarily superficial quality of our coverage allows a broad view of a society such as the Nuer and enables us to interrelate a wide range of social institutions and physical and historical factors, but it precludes any kind of highly sophisticated techniques in probing the details of that society. Furthermore, this same alien or exotic quality of the material forces us, however much we strain against it, to interpret such data from our own perspectives within western European society. That we do not do so entirely is to the lasting credit of social anthropology; but to that extent, too, our work contains within it a kind of agonized incertitude and nagging ambiguity which are difficult for the honest ethnographer to deny. Of course, these same doubts exist even on the part of sociologists and psychologists who cannot get inside their informants or see clearly and surely behind their questionnaires; but their familiarity with the language and institutions of their own society does to some extent stack the deck for them. By such implicit assumptions about the nature of their own language and culture, the work of sociologists and psychologists gains in detail and volume but loses in perspective and also often in subtlety and originality. In the case of the social anthropologist, his involuntary alienation is matched by a corresponding willful act of trying to translate, to understand, that of which he is not a part. He must try (and, to some extent, he succeeds) to think, see, and evaluate as a Nuer; yet he fails, according to the highest standards, and he knows he fails, even though he may entertain glimmerings of some part of success and insight. And at the same time that this effort is going on, his perspectives of his own society are subtly altered. In the end, his appreciation (yet also his self doubts) of his understanding of both the alien society and his own is vastly increased. In this sense, the social anthropologist himself becomes an illustration of a fascinating cultural puzzle: that of men standing within and without the objects they must

understand. In this respect, it may not be unduly dramatic to suggest that the greatest of social anthropologists, those from whom we learn most, appear as the most alienated and therefore perhaps the freest but most troubled of the social scientists.

Index